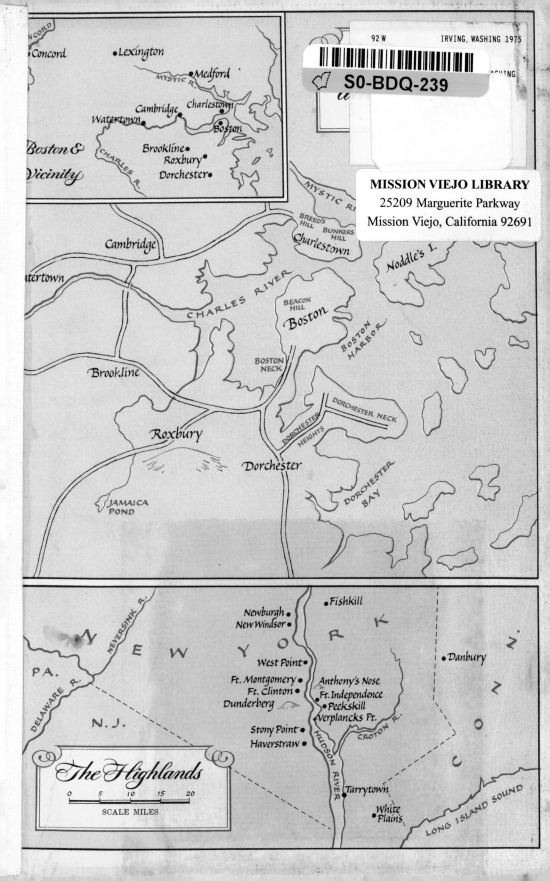

Boston & Vicinity

Concord
Lexington
MYSTIC R.
Medford
Cambridge   Charlestown
Watertown
Boston
Brookline
Roxbury
Dorchester

CHARLES R.

MYSTIC RIVER

BREED'S HILL
BUNKERS HILL
Charlestown

Cambridge

Watertown

Noddle's I.

CHARLES RIVER

BEACON HILL
Boston

BOSTON HARBOR

Brookline

BOSTON NECK

DORCHESTER NECK

Roxbury

DORCHESTER HEIGHTS

Dorchester

JAMAICA POND

DORCHESTER BAY

The Highlands

N E W   Y O R K

NEVERSINK R.

Fishkill
Newburgh
New Windsor

PA.

West Point
Ft. Montgomery
Ft. Clinton
Dunderberg

Anthony's Nose
Ft. Independence
Peekskill
Verplancks Pt.

Danbury

C O N N.

DELAWARE R.

N. J.

Stony Point
Haverstraw

HUDSON RIVER

CROTON R.

Tarrytown

White Plains

LONG ISLAND SOUND

0   5   10   15   20
SCALE MILES

Life of George Washington

G. Stuart.

H.B. Hall.

From the Original Picture in the Boston Athenæum.

taken from life in 1795

ENGRAVED FOR IRVING'S LIFE OF WASHINGTON.

G.P. Putnam & Cᵒ N.York.

LIFE

OF

GEORGE WASHINGTON

BY

WASHINGTON IRVING

EDITED AND ABRIDGED
by Jess Stein

WITH AN INTRODUCTION
by Richard B. Morris

SLEEPY HOLLOW RESTORATIONS
Tarrytown, New York
1975

In the preparation of this volume, the text of the original edition of 1855–59 has been retained as exactly as possible. A small number of changes in language, spelling, and punctuation have been introduced for the sake of greater clarity for the modern reader. Part titles were supplied by the editor.

The illustrations were selected and reproduced from steel engravings included in the separate volume *Illustrations to Irving's Life of Washington*, published in New York in 1859

The editor gratefully acknowledges advice and assistance from the several Editors and Research Consultants of SLEEPY HOLLOW RESTORATIONS, as well as from Mrs. Regina Beth Wilson, Mrs. Nettie Weinberg, and especially (as always) his wife, Dorothy Gerner Stein.

First Printing

Copyright © 1975 by Sleepy Hollow Restorations, Inc.
All rights reserved.

For information, address the publisher:
Sleepy Hollow Restorations, Inc.
Tarrytown, New York 10591

Library of Congress Catalog Card Number: 74-7845
ISBN, cloth 0-912882-18-2

Manufactured in the United States of America

Designed by Ray Freiman

Library of Congress Cataloging in Publication Data
Irving, Washington, 1783–1859.
Life of George Washington.
An Abridgment of the 1855–59 ed.
Includes index.
1. Washington, George, Pres. U. S., 1732–1799.
I. Stein, Jess M. II. Title.
E312.I77 1975   973.4′1′0924 [B]   74-7845
ISBN 0-912882-18-2

Contents

Contents

Illustrations

·◦⊰ vii ⊱◦·

Illustrations

Introduction

BY RICHARD B. MORRIS

It seemed inevitable that one day Washington Irving would devote his literary talents to a life of George Washington. Named after the General, blessed, according to family account, by Washington when the President-elect was in New York City for his inauguration, Irving in childhood, youth, and manhood reflected the formative traditions of the new nation which made Washington its central and most charismatic figure. For years the challenge and obligation lay heavily upon the writer, but in fact the actual writing was begun by Irving in his declining years and completed in the agonies of failing health, only a few months before he died. For essaying a monumental undertaking at the age of sixty-six and completing it ten years later, Irving challenged comparison with the latter-day achievements of a Parkman, a Bancroft, or a Verdi.

Irving did not write this biography in the narrow sense in which the term is generally construed. It would be more correct to entitle his five-volume work "George Washington and the World He Lived In." His account, expertly condensed in the present single-volume edition, relates the epochal events in which Washington was the central figure. Except for the early years of Washington's life, Irving felt a compulsion to tell the whole story and to introduce all the leading actors rather than to keep the focus on the General. Its shortcomings notwithstanding, the *Life* for better than a generation was treasured by readers as the most up-to-date treatment of Washington.

That the author of *Knickerbocker's History of New York* and the creator of Rip Van Winkle and Ichabod Crane should turn his hand from creative writing to serious historical work would have seemed less idiosyncratic then, perhaps, than today. In Irving's time the line between the man of letters and the professional historian was not yet sharply delineated. None of Irving's predecessors as Washington biographers was a trained historian. John Marshall was a lawyer and towering jurist. The Washington that emerged from his multi-volume treatment is seen from the point of view of Federalist party politics. Mason Weems was a parson and book peddler, whose inaccurate, careless, and stylized life of the General combined hagiography and myth-making. Jared Sparks, most serious of the early students of George Washington and the one Irving leaned upon most heavily, was especially concerned about creating or perpetuating the image of a figure from out of the heroic age, one whose life would inspire lesser mortals to nobler personal achievement. Having such lofty objectives in mind, Sparks had no hesitancy in tinkering with the sources, in excising or altering Washington's language to fit the character created by a worshipful America. The reader was impoverished by his prissiness, the scholar at times misled by his editorial liberties. Even George Bancroft, the first of America's professional historians, had been a preacher, poet, and schoolteacher before turning historian, achieving distinction, too, as statesman and diplomat.

Hence, it was almost expected that a man of letters would try his hand at historical writing. Irving's talents as a biographer had already been tested in his biography of Columbus, widely acclaimed in his day, and his less highly regarded life of Mahomet. As an historian, he had demonstrated his talents in the writing of *The Conquest of Granada*, a work distinguished for its sympathies with the Moorish side of the struggle in Spain.

Introduction

Irving had researched his biography of Washington over the better part of a lifetime. He had used to advantage his travels both abroad and in the United States to gather material on the General. He had visited Sulgrave Manor and researched Washington's ancestry in England. He had gone to Mount Vernon and explored many of the battle sites of the American Revolution. He had ploughed through Peter Force's *American Archives*, a multivolume documentary record of the American Revolution, which, unfortunately, was prematurely terminated by lack of government funding some years before Irving had completed the first volume of his *Life* of the General. Irving drew upon other sources as well, upon George Parke Custis' *Memoir* of Martha Washington, upon Dr. James Thacher's extensive and illuminating military journal of the Revolution, on a variety of orderly books and diaries, including Washington's own, and, most of all, on Jared Sparks' twelve-volume edition of Washington's *Writings*, volumes which appeared between 1834 and 1839, supplemented by that editor's *Correspondence of the American Revolution*, a collection of letters from prominent men to Washington, which Sparks published in 1853. Today we would consider Irving a pioneer "oral historian", as he drew upon the unpublished recollections of many of those who knew the General at first hand, and upon testimony sometimes one generation removed. All in all, for its time, Irving found that the sources were considerable and the gleanings richly rewarding.

What gave Irving's *Life* special distinction was not alone his broad coverage of the events in which Washington was either centrally or peripherally involved, but the human interest touches that as a literary artist he brought to the biography. If Washington is presented as a man with few blemishes and a sterling character, he emerges from Irving's pen not as a marble statue but a human being, whose life is told in simple prose but with descriptive power and enriched by a fund of anecdotal material quite unusual in biographical writing of that day.

If Irving's style seems ornate, he himself by way of conclusion asserted that he had "avoided rhetorical amplification and embellishments, and all gratuitous assumptions, and have sought, by simple and truthful details, to give his character an opportunity of developing itself, and of manifesting those fixed principles and that noble consistency which reigned all throughout his civil and military career." Despite his disavowals, Irving often presented his prose in deeply purple cast, appropriate to an author who approached the great actors with veneration. Thus, in describing the famous Virginians who attended the First Continental Congress, he observed: "Washington, in the meridian of his days, mature in wisdom, comprehensive in mind, sagacious in foresight. Such were the apostles of liberty, repairing in their august pilgrimage to Philadelphia from all parts of the land, to lay the foundations of a mighty empire. Well may we say of that eventful period, 'There were giants in those days.' " If Irving thought his prose lacked "amplification and embellishments," then fortunate are we in being spared some of the rhetorical effusions of his less disciplined contemporaries!

Readers of today might well be prepared to accept Irving's sentimental and occasionally even naive biographical treatment because it is so often redeemed by the powerfully descriptive passages in which his volumes abound and a wealth of anecdotal material capturing both the man and the times. Few can read Irving's account of the conspiracy against Washington plotted at Corbie's tavern without gaining insight into the dangers posed by internal subversion to the Revolutionary movement. The battles of Long Island and Manhattan take on added color in the account of Scammel's blunder in mistakenly ordering Mifflin's troops to leave their lines, thereby jeopardizing that withdrawal of the American troops from Brooklyn so skillfully concealed from the enemy. The lively exchange between the General and Mifflin has the ring of verisimilitude. Irving records Washington's legendary exclamation of dismay on seeing the militia abandoning the breastworks below Turtle Bay. "Are these the men with whom I am to defend America!"

Irving recreates other memorable moments from the testimony of participants. Who can forget Washington's dramatic confrontation with his mutinous officers at Newburgh, and Major Shaw's comment that the General's natural and unaffected oratory "forced its way to the heart, and you might see sensibility moisten in every eye." Irving captures Washingtonian humor and even gives us examples of a laughing Washington, a rarely observed specimen, it would seem. The etiquette at Washington's Presidential court, so tedious an affair to the first Chief Executive, prompted that dignitary to confess ruefully that he was unable "to make bows to the taste of poor Colonel B——." The literary artist of Sunnyside skillfully depicts that characteristic vanity and pomposity that John Hancock demonstrated in welcoming President Washington to Massachusetts, while the touching deathbed scene, as depicted by Tobias Lear, carries a ring of authenticity.

Simple and moving though Irving's biographical treatment of Washington may be, and always warm and sympathetic to its hero, the *Life* lacks critical judgment and penetration. The portrait of Washington that we are given is that of a paragon with few blemishes. In fact, the General was a highly complex man, whose blunders, whether minimized or overlooked by his biographer, make him more intensely human for the very reason that they show him to be fallible. Here was a man whose drive and vaunting ambition underscored a deeply-felt insecurity. That he was ultimately able to curb his irascible moods and avaricious propensities constitutes a triumph of character over self-interest, of self-control over ill temper, of national purpose over parochial concerns.

There is, indeed, another side to Washington's youth which Irving did not capture. Washington's father died when he was eleven years old. Nine years later he lost his older half-brother Lawrence whom he idolized. These losses were irreparable ones to young Washington, who had little or no rapport with his mother, Mary Ball Washington. That imperious, self-centered, and possessive matron commanded Washington's dutiful attention throughout his life, but hardly his affection. A fast-growing and restless adolescent could not be expected to stay tied to his mother's apron strings. George's early career, his stint at surveying and his long involvement in military service, gave him a sense of independence from smothering home influences, an independence that he desperately needed. His was a minor rebellion which was part of an identity crisis.

Washington's military career in the service of Virginia on the eve of and during the French and Indian War tested his qualities of leadership, courage, and military judgment. As regards the last, he appears more fallible than Irving was prepared to concede. He underestimated the enemy and pursued a reckless course which involved two great powers in direct confrontation. His abiding concern about rank and his penchant for high-level quarrels made him seem more a liability than an asset to Virginia's Governor Dinwiddie. Irving's narrative of Braddock's campaign is masterly. Due justice is paid Washington for his heroics under fire and his almost miraculous emergence from that disaster with his reputation greatly enhanced. What Irving does not choose to detail is Washington's subsequent stretch of service on the frontier, a period which proved the most galling and frustrating of Washington's entire career. Indeed, Irving seems quite myopic in his account of Washington's controversy with Brigadier John Forbes over the choice of a road to Fort Duquesne. It is almost incomprehensible that so experienced a surveyor and explorer as Washington should have stood out so adamantly for the old Braddock Road, involving as it did the perilous crossing of both the Youghiogheny and the Monongahela, and that he should behave so emotionally when his choice was passed over in favor of the more advantageous road which passed entirely through Pennsylvania. It seems incomprehensible, unless one remembers that Washington was a member of a Virginia land company with claims to the West, a company which stood to gain much by opening up the Old Braddock Road.

Today we know a good deal more than in Irving's time about western land speculation on the eve of the Revolution. Hence, Washington's own speculative operations in the West, which revealed an acquisitive, even an avaricious streak and an inclination to circumvent technicalities to secure title to choice locations in bounty lands promised the Virginia Regiment, command more attention than a century ago. Washington never lost that immense curiosity and enthusiasm for the West. Perhaps the first to speak of the "American Empire," Washington was preoccupied at various moments in his active career with both Western lands and interior navigation. Envisioning a great future for the West, Washington, both as a Virginian and an American with a continental outlook had a deep attachment for that region and its problems.

Introduction

Irving's *Life* pays due obeisance to Washington's whirlwind courtship of Martha Dandridge Custis. Like his successors, Irving is unable to identify the "low Land Beauty," with whom George had an early flirtation, nor does he mention Betsy Fauntleroy who twice rejected Washington. Irving does tell us how the military hero set tongues wagging when on a visit to New York he squired Mary Eliza Philipse, the sensuous beauty and heiress of a great estate, who was one day to be on the Tory side.

What Irving does not seem to realize was that at the very time when Washington was paying court to Mary Eliza he was head-over-heels in love with Sally, the wife of his good friend and neighbor George William Fairfax. Without identifying her, Irving refers to a "Sally" as "a female confidant" of George, but she was something more than that. Irving probably had not heard of Washington's revealing letter to Sally Fairfax, written not long after his engagement to Martha Custis. That letter, which turned up a century ago, only to disappear and then surface again in 1958, suggests that when Martha and George took the nuptial vows, the latter was madly in love with another woman. The available evidence suggests that George managed to keep his feelings toward his neighbor's wife under some checkrein, and that the tantalizing Sally provided her husband with no overt ground for suspicion. Loyal to the King, the Fairfaxes left Virginia before the Revolution began, but despite their political differences Washington never forgot either of his neighbors. Years after the death of her husband Sally received a note from ex-President Washington, written near the close of his own life, in which he confessed that none of the great events of his career, "nor all of them together, have been able to eradicate from my mind the recollection of those happy moments, the happiest [of] my life, which I have enjoyed in your company."

Irving makes a special point of stressing Washington's fondness for children and his devotion to his step-children, "Patsy" and "Jackie" Custis. What he suggests but does not spell out is how deeply Washington yearned for children and grandchildren of his own, and how concerned he was about his childless state. That condition must so frequently have been brought home to him as he assumed the father image fixed upon him by his countrymen. Irving was probably not aware of the draft of a presidential inaugural address that Washington had prepared and then discarded. Therein one finds a personal revelation seemingly extraordinary to discover in a state paper. "It will be recollected," Washington observed in that draft, "that the Divine Providence hath not seen fit that my blood should be transmitted or my name perpetuated by the endearing, though sometimes seducing, channel of immediate offspring. I have no child for whom I could wish to make a provision—no family to build in greatness upon my country's ruins." Do not concern yourselves unduly, my countrymen, Washington seems to be implying. There is no prospect that a childless president will set up a royal dynasty!

It is clear from the evidence set forth in Irving's *Life* that Washington was an early convert to the cause of radical protest. What is not clear is the reason why the Virginia planter elite, men of the standing of Washington and his neighbor George Mason, should espouse the Whig cause. New England's radicalism Irving attributes to that region's innate republicanism and to the fact that its commercial and maritime interests were adversely affected by British tax measures. On the other hand, the Virginia planters, as he views them, were aroused "on all points of honorable pride" owing to their "quick and generous spirit." To assume, as Irving implies, that Virginians acted from a sense of honor and noble principles while New Englanders responded to self-interest, is to oversimplify motivations while failing to give due weight to the grievances shared by Virginians generally, as well as those which were very special to Washington.

For more than a century Virginians had found the Navigation Laws discriminatory, compelling tobacco planters to ship their product to England rather than to markets closer to their consumers on the European continent. More recently they felt the constraints of the act of Parliament forbidding paper money emissions in Virginia. They were also concerned about recent imperial regulations restraining western land speculation and settlement. As for Washington, his years of military service had exposed him to the systematic discrimination against colonials practiced in the British army. His efforts to secure a regular army commission had been consistently flouted despite his exceptional experience and proven ability. As a producer of farm staples and an importer of British goods Washington had suffered a series of grievances which he found implicit in the empire's trade and navigation policies. His correspondence is replete with complaints against having to pay higher freight rates than other shippers and excessive insurance premiums. He reveals that his tobacco cargo was damaged in transport, and that the prices his factor obtained for his tobacco in England came pretty consistently below prevailing market prices in Virginia. In turn, the farm equipment he ordered from England often arrived poorly packed, defective, broken, or damaged, cloth came moth-eaten, suits ruined, and cargoes reached him too late to be used. He charged British businessmen with palming off on colonials inferior goods for which they upped the prices as much as twenty per cent above prices current in England. It is against this background of distrust and resentment of Britain and British businessmen that we can appreciate why Washington so enthusiastically supported nonimportation and why, with George Mason, he co-authored the notable Fairfax Resolves, that major state paper asserting the principle of government by the consent of the governed to be "the most important and valuable part of the British Constitution," denying Parliament's right to tax the colonies, and calling upon the colonies to unite in measures to redress grievances.

If Washington had shown extraordinary qualities of leadership as a youth, qualities which may have stamped him as a young man in a hurry, those very qualities were to serve his nation extraordinarily well during the Revolutionary War. Washington managed to bridle his aggressiveness, to subordinate his self-interest to a cause larger than self, and to build a reputation for character and integrity that a host of critics then and since have been unable to destroy. As a war leader he displayed the saving grace of a healthy humility which he lacked as a youth, and demonstrated that humility by his readiness to abide by the judgment of a Council of War and in his deference to the judgment of Congress.

Throughout his life, however, Washington remained hypersensitive to criticism, demanding a degree of loyalty from his subordinate officers which few, if any, military men since his day have been able to command. Irving, who champions Washington at all times everywhere, gives greater credence to the existence of a formal cabal against Washington than the evidence now supports. True, Washington did have his critics. Dissatisfied by his Fabian tactics marked by retreat and defeat, his opponents in Congress and in the army compared him unfavorably with Horatio Gates, the victor at Saratoga. The fact is that the so-called "Conway Cabal" represented no real "plot" against Washington, that his opponents did not co-ordinate their moves to displace him, and that any serious effort to unseat him collapsed the instant of exposure.

That same sensitivity to criticism was manifest by Washington as President, albeit the abuse which was heaped upon him was largely undeserved. As Washington made clear in his "Farewell Address," with its warning against parties and factions, the first President was not prepared for the party system which emerged during his administration, an event which must have come as a surprise to most of the other framers of the Constitution, which made no provision for so significant a development.

Those who accused the President of monarchist leanings, of being pro-British, and even of corruption were very wide of the mark. Admittedly, Washington's latter days in the office of the Presidency did not find him in full command of his best executive talents, but on the whole his administration was an extraordinary one and he himself served with distinction. Washington's willingness to renounce a well-deserved privacy and accept the Presidency served to allay suspicions of the central government which the federal Constitution had stirred up among the anti-Federalists. His administration demonstrated that the Constitution was a viable instrument of government. In his two terms as President Washington fixed the powers and traditions of his great office, was responsible for the evolution of the cabinet system, saw that the taxing power was wielded audaciously and effectively along Hamiltonian economic principles, and created a national debt to strengthen the national authority and stimulate the economy. During those years, too, American credit was fixed at home and abroad on a firm foundation, American territory cleared of British and Spanish interlopers, and the frontiers stabilized against Indian threats.

Introduction

Washington Irving chose to devote considerably more attention to the equally controversial record of Washington's administration in the field of foreign affairs, which he defends as any good Federalist would. However unpopular Washington's policy toward foreign powers might have seemed at one time or another to the opposing faction, the President prudently steered a course of neutrality. Its objective, and that of the successor administration of John Adams, was survival. Measured by that objective, it was a stunning success.

Irving prudently avoids attribution of authorship between Washington, Madison, and Hamilton of various portions of the President's "Farewell Address." The evidence now available supports his contention that "the address breathes his spirit throughout, is in perfect accordance with his words and actions, and 'in an honest, unaffected simple garb,' embodies the system of policy on which he had acted throughout his administrations." In the two drafts Hamilton prepared he faithfully followed Washington's scheme of organization and the President's principal ideas, while rephrasing them in a masterly way. Washington preferred Hamilton's first, or original draft, but the final state paper was very much Washington's own. His rephrasing was felicitous and often less wordy, but at times there is a subtle but important change of concept. Hamilton's draft speaks of trusting to "occasional alliances;" Washington's final address of "temporary alliances." Nowhere, it should be remembered, did Washington use the phrase "entangling alliances," later found in Jefferson's First Inaugural.

For some reason Washington Irving found the domestic accomplishments of Washington's administration less challenging than the involvements on the diplomatic front. We are given tantalizingly few details about the Whisky Insurrection, that uprising of a handful of Westerners against Hamilton's excise tax. Neither the grounds of Western protest nor Hamilton's own view that the enforcement of the tax was a test of the authority of the federal government is brought out. Yet, while the confrontation was Hamilton's idea, it was Washington's decision to use armed force to suppress the insurrection, thereby establishing at one stroke two principles for which the Confederation had been unable to secure recognition—the idea of the supremacy of the law and the federal government's power to levy and collect taxes. As a fiction writer with a keen eye for dramatic incident, Irving failed to dramatize the fact that the military operations against the "Whisky Boys" was the only occasion in American history when a President, who under the Constitution is commander-in-chief of the armed forces, actually took the field with his troops, although neither he nor any of his men saw any fighting. The "Whisky Boys" vanished in the face of the army's advance, and Washington pardoned two of the leaders found guilty of high treason.

What Irving also missed was the anticlimactic aspect of the Whisky Rebellion, signalling as it did the beginning of the decline in popularity of the Federalist party. The eloquent Fisher Ames, a strong Federalist himself, was led to observe that "a regular government, by overcoming an unsuccessful insurrection, becomes stronger; but elective rulers can scarcely ever employ the physical force of a democracy without turning the moral force, or the power of public opinion, against the government."

It was remarked early in this Introduction that Irving's multivolume *Life* was really about Washington and his times. It was a deep-felt tribute not only to a foremost Founding Father but to the American people who, against enormous odds, achieved independence, built a nation, and framed a constitutional structure which made it viable. Hence, it is especially fitting at a time when this nation is commemorating the Bicentennial anniversary of its creation that we bear in mind Irving's memorable tribute to the American Revolution itself. Nowhere can there be found a more elevating testimonial to the "moral grandeur" of that event:

We have endeavored to keep in view the prevailing poverty of resources, the scandalous neglects, the squalid miseries of all kinds, with which its champions had to contend in their expeditions through trackless wildernesses, or thinly peopled regions; beneath scorching suns or inclement skies; their wintry marches to be traced by bloody footprints on snow and ice; their desolate wintry encampments, rendered still more desolate by nakedness and famine. It was in the patience and fortitude with which these ills were sustained by a half-disciplined yeomanry, voluntary exiles from their homes, destitute of all the "pomp and circumstance" of war to excite them, and animated solely by their patriotism, that we read the noblest and most affecting characteristics of that great struggle for human rights. They do wrong to its moral grandeur, who seek by commonplace exaggeration, to give a melodramatic effect and false glare to its military operations, and to place its greatest triumphs in the conflicts of the field. Lafayette showed a true sense of the nature of the struggle, when Napoleon, accustomed to effect ambitious purposes by hundreds of thousands of troops, and tens of thousands of slain, sneered at the scanty armies of the American Revolution and its "boasted allies." "Sire," was the admirable and comprehensive reply, "it was the grandest of causes won by skirmishes of sentinels and outposts."

No man exemplified that "moral grandeur" better than the personage who looms so large in Irving's pages as an indispensable symbol of selfless patriotism and integrity. In this volume we see Washington quickening the Patriot cause in Virginia on the eve of crisis, taking command of a rabble in arms at Cambridge, outwitted but undismayed at Long Island, delivering lightning blows at Trenton and Princeton, standing fast through the ordeals of Valley Forge and Morristown, overriding his enemies in Congress and the army, and in the end by the sheer power of determination and force of personality, keeping an army in being until the day of deliverance at Yorktown. Then, leaving a well-deserved retirement, we see him reluctantly assuming the arduous tasks of the Presidency in answering his country's call once again.

What makes Washington so especially relevant to our own time, when events have made us keenly conscious of the limitations on executive power imposed by the Constitution, is the example that Washington himself set of subordinating self to the national interest when he voluntarily yielded power both as military commander at the conclusion of the American Revolution and as President at the end of his second term. That peaceful transition of power which distinguishes the American Revolution from so many others to follow was largely fixed by its extraordinary leader. For reminding us of George Washington's central role in the great theater of events, of his unique qualities of leadership, and of his continued identification in the public mind with the great principles for which the Revolutionary War was fought, readers will be eternally indebted to Washington Irving.

Charles Martin del

F. Halpin sculp.

New York
Jan 1851

Washington Irving

Sunnyside Dec. 15th 1851.

PART I

(CHAPTERS 1–6)

The Early Years
[1732–1763]

⎯⎯⎯⎯⎯⎯⎯⎯⎯⎯⎯

The Washington family is of an ancient English stock, the genealogy of which has been traced up to the century succeeding the Conquest. At that time it was in possession of landed estates and manorial privileges in the county of Durham, such as were enjoyed only by those, or their descendants, who had come over from Normandy with the Conqueror or fought under his standard.

Among the knights who held estates was William de Hertburn, the progenitor of the Washingtons. His Norman name of William would seem to point out his national descent. The surname of De Hertburn was taken from a village which he held in knight's fee. The first actual mention we find of the family is in a record of all the lands appertaining to the diocese in 1183. In this it is stated that William de Hertburn had exchanged his village of Hertburn for the manor and village of Wessyngton, likewise in the diocese. The family changed its surname with its estate and thenceforward assumed that of De Wessyngton.

By 1500 the primitive stock of the De Wessyngtons had separated into divers branches, holding estates in various parts of England, some distinguishing themselves in the learned professions, others receiving knighthood for public services. By degrees the *de* disappeared from before the family surname, which also varied from Wessynton to Wassington, Wasshington and, finally, to Washington.

The branch of the family to which our Washington belongs sprang from Laurence Washington, Esquire, of Gray's Inn, who was mayor of Northampton and who, on the dissolution of the priories by Henry VIII, received a grant of the manor of Sulgrave, in North-amptonshire, with other lands in the vicinity. Sulgrave remained in the family until 1620 and was commonly called "Washington's manor."

We have little note of the Sulgrave branch of the family after the death of Charles I and the exile of his successor. England, during the protectorate, became an uncomfortable residence to adherents to the house of Stuart. Many sought refuge in other lands. This may have been the case with two brothers, John and Andrew Washington, great-grandsons of the grantee of Sulgrave. John emig-rated with his brother to Virginia in 1657 and purchased lands in Westmoreland County, on the northern neck, between the Potomac and Rappahannock rivers. John married Anne Pope, of the same county and took up his residence on Bridges Creek, near where it falls into the Potomac. He became an extensive planter and, in time, a magistrate and member of the House of Burgesses. We find him, as Colonel Washington, leading the Virginia forces in co-operation with those of Maryland against a band of Seneca In-dians who were ravaging the settlements along the Potomac. In honor of his public services and private virtues, the parish in which he resided bears the name of Washington.

The estate continued in the family. His grandson Augustine, the father of our Washington, was born there in 1694. He was twice married; first (1715) to Jane Butler, by whom he had four children, of whom only two, Lawrence and Augustine, survived the years of childhood; she died November 24th, 1728. In 1730, he married Mary Ball, a young and beautiful girl. By her he had four sons, George, Samuel, John Augustine, and Charles, and two daughters, Elizabeth and Mildred.

George, the eldest, was born on the 22d of Feb. (11th, O.S.),

1732, in the homestead of Bridges Creek. This house commanded a view over many miles of the Potomac and the opposite shore of Maryland. It had probably been purchased with the property and was one of the primitive farm-houses of Virginia. Not a vestige of it remains.

Not long after the birth of George, his father removed to an estate in Stafford County opposite Fredericksburg. The house, which stood on a rising ground overlooking a meadow which bordered the Rappahannock, was the home of George's boyhood. The site is only to be traced by fragments of bricks, china, and earthenware.

The means of instruction in Virginia were limited and it was the custom among the wealthy planters to send their sons to England to complete their education. This was done by Augustine Washington with his eldest son Lawrence, then about fifteen years of age. George was yet in early childhood; he received the rudiments of education in the best establishment for the purpose that the neighborhood afforded. The instruction must have been of the simplest kind, reading, writing, and ciphering, but George had the benefit of mental and moral culture at home from an excellent father. Augustine Washington impressed his child with maxims of religion and virtue and imbued him with a spirit of justice and generosity and, above all, a scrupulous love of truth.

When George was seven or eight years old Lawrence returned from England, a well-educated and accomplished youth. Lawrence looked with a protecting eye upon the boy, whose intelligence and rectitude won his regard, while George looked up to his manly and cultivated brother as a model in mind and manners.

Lawrence had something of the old military spirit of the family and circumstance soon called it into action. Spanish depredations on British commerce had recently provoked reprisals. Troops were embarked in England for a campaign in the West Indies; a regiment was to be raised in the colonies and sent to join them at Jamaica. Lawrence, now twenty-two years of age, obtained a captain's commission in the newly raised regiment and embarked with it for the West Indies in 1740. He served in the joint expeditions of Admiral

Vernon and General Wentworth and acquired the friendship and confidence of both officers.

Lawrence returned home in the autumn of 1742, the campaigns in the West Indies being ended. He formed an attachment to Anne, the daughter of William Fairfax, and they became engaged. Their nuptials were delayed by the sudden death of his father on the 12th of April, 1743. George had been absent from home on a visit during his father's illness and just returned in time to receive a parting look of affection.

Augustine Washington left large possessions to his children: to Lawrence, the estate on the Potomac with other real property; to Augustine, the second son by the first marriage, the estate in Westmoreland. The children by the second marriage were well provided for, and George, when of age, was to have the house and lands on the Rappahannock.

In July the marriage of Lawrence with Miss Fairfax took place. He settled himself on his estate on the Potomac, to which he gave the name of Mount Vernon in honor of the admiral. Augustine took up his abode at the homestead on Bridges Creek and married Anne Aylett of Westmoreland County.

George, now eleven years of age, and the other children of the second marriage, had been left under the guardianship of their mother, to whom was intrusted the proceeds of their property until each should come of age. She proved herself worthy of the trust. Endowed with plain, direct good sense, thorough conscientiousness, and prompt decision, she governed her family strictly, but kindly, exacting deference while she inspired affection. George inherited from her a high temper and a spirit of command, but her early precepts and example taught him to restrain and govern that temper and to square his conduct on the exact principles of equity and justice.

George was sent to reside with Augustine at Bridges Creek and enjoy the benefit of a superior school in that neighborhood. His education, however, was plain and practical. He never attempted the learned languages nor manifested any inclination for rhetoric or belles-lettres. His object, or the object of his friends, seems to have been confined to fitting him for ordinary business. He was a self-

Residence of the Washington Family *

disciplinarian in physical as well as mental matters and practiced all kinds of athletic exercises. His frame even in infancy had been large and powerful, and he now excelled most of his playmates in contests of agility and strength. In horsemanship he already excelled and was able to manage the most fiery steed. Above all, his inherent probity and the principles of justice on which he regulated all his conduct were appreciated by his schoolmates; he was referred to as an umpire in their disputes and his decisions were never reversed.

The attachment of Lawrence to his brother George seems to have acquired additional strength and tenderness on their father's death; he took a truly paternal interest and had him as frequently as possible a guest at Mount Vernon. Lawrence had deservedly become a popular and leading personage in the country. He was a member of the House of Burgesses and adjutant-general of the district with the rank of major. A frequent sojourn with him brought George into familiar association with the family of Lawrence's father-in-law, William Fairfax, who resided at Belvoir, a few miles below Mount Vernon.

William Fairfax, a man of liberal education, had seen much of the world and his mind had been enriched by varied and adventurous experience. For some years past he had resided in Virginia to manage the immense landed estates of his cousin, Lord Fairfax, and lived at Belvoir in the style of an English country gentleman, surrounded by an intelligent and cultivated family of sons and daughters. An intimacy with a family like this, in which the frankness and simplicity of rural and colonial life were united with European refinement, could not but have a beneficial effect in moulding the character and manners of a somewhat homebred school-boy.

George continued his studies, devoting himself especially to mathematics, accomplishing himself in those branches calculated to fit him either for civil or military service. Among these, one of the most important was land surveying. In this he schooled himself thoroughly, using the highest processes of the art. He took a final leave of school in the autumn of 1747, and went to reside with Lawrence at Mount Vernon. Here he continued his mathematical studies and his practice in surveying. Though by no means of a poetical temperament, the waste pages of his journal betray several attempts to pour forth his amorous sorrows in verse.

Being a favorite of Sir William Fairfax, he was now an occasional resident at Belvoir. Among the persons residing there was Thomas Lord Fairfax, nearly 60 years of age, cousin of William Fairfax, of whose immense landed property the latter was the agent. He made a voyage to Virginia about 1739 to visit his vast estates there. He was so delighted by the climate, the forest scenery, the abundance of game, and the frank, cordial character of the Virginians that he returned with the resolution of taking up his abode there for the remainder of his days.

Another resident of Belvoir at this time was George William Fairfax, about twenty-two years of age, eldest son of the proprietor. Educated in England, since his return he had married and brought his bride and her sister to his father's house.

The merits of Washington were known and appreciated by the Fairfax family. Though not quite sixteen years of age, he no longer seemed a boy nor was he treated as such. Tall, athletic, and manly for his years, his early self-training and code of conduct gave a gravity and decision to his conduct; his frankness and modesty inspired cordial regard, and his melancholy may have produced a softness in his manner calculated to win favor in ladies' eyes.

Whatever may have been the soothing effect of the female society at Belvoir, Washington found a more effectual remedy for his love melancholy in the company of Lord Fairfax. His lordship was a staunch fox-hunter and kept horses and hounds in the English style. He found Washington as bold as himself in the saddle and as eager to follow the hounds. He forthwith took him into peculiar favor, made him his hunting companion, and it was probably under the tuition of this hard-riding old nobleman that the youth imbibed that fondness for the chase for which he was afterwards remarked.

Their fox-hunting was attended with more important results. His lordship's possessions beyond the Blue Ridge had never been regularly settled nor surveyed. Lawless intruders—squatters as they were called—were planting themselves along the finest streams and in the richest valleys and virtually taking possession of the country. It was the anxious desire of Lord Fairfax to have these lands examined, surveyed, and portioned out into lots, preparatory to ejecting these interlopers or bringing them to reasonable terms. In Washington, notwithstanding his youth, he beheld one fit for the task. The proposition had only to be offered to be eagerly accepted. It was the very kind of occupation for which he had been diligently training himself, and in a few days he was ready for his first expedition into the wilderness.

In March, 1748, just after his sixteenth year, Washington set out on horseback on this surveying expedition, in company with George William Fairfax. Their route lay by Ashley's Gap, a pass through the Blue Ridge, that beautiful line of mountains which, as yet, almost formed the western frontier of inhabited Virginia. They entered the great valley of Virginia, where it is about twenty-five miles wide, a temperate region admirably adapted to cultivation. The Blue Ridge bounds it on one side, the North Mountain, a ridge of the Alleganies, on the other; while through it flows that river named by the Indians the Shenandoah—"daughter of the stars."

Washington's surveys commenced in the lower part of the valley, some distance above the junction of the Shenandoah with the Potomac, and extended for many miles along the former river. Here and there partial clearings had been made by squatters and hardy pioneers and their rude husbandry had produced abundant crops of grain, hemp, and tobacco.

Proceeding down the valley to the banks of the Potomac, Washington and his companions procured a canoe, on which they crossed to the Maryland side, swimming their horses. A weary day's ride of 40 miles up the left side of the river brought them opposite the south branch of the Potomac, where they put up for the night. From this encampment they proceeded to Patterson's Creek, where they recrossed the river in a canoe, swimming their horses. More than two weeks were passed by them in the wild mountainous regions of Frederick County and about the south branch of the Potomac, surveying lands and laying out lots, camped out the greater part of the time and subsisting on wild turkeys and other game.

Having completed his surveys, he set forth homeward and on the 12th of April found himself once more at Mount Vernon. The manner in which he acquitted himself in this arduous expedition and his accounts of the country surveyed gave great satisfaction to Lord Fairfax, who shortly afterwards moved across the Blue Ridge, and took up his residence there. He projected a spacious manor-house, giving to the place the name of Greenway Court.

It was probably through the influence of Lord Fairfax that Washington received the appointment of public surveyor. For three years he continued in this occupation, which proved extremely profitable from the vast extent of country to be surveyed and the very limited number of public surveyors. It made him acquainted with the country, the nature of the soil in various parts, and the value of localities, all which proved advantageous to him in his purchases in after years.

While thus employed for months at a time surveying the lands beyond the Blue Ridge, he was often a guest of Greenway Court. Here Washington had full opportunity of indulging his fondness for field sports and accompanying his lordship in the chase. The conversation of Lord Fairfax was full of instruction to an inexperienced youth, from his cultivated talents, his literary taste, and his past association with the best society of Europe and its most distinguished authors.

Three or four years were thus passed by Washington, the greater part beyond the Blue Ridge, but occasionally with his brother Lawrence at Mount Vernon. His rugged and toilsome expeditions in the mountains inured him to hardships, while his association with his cultivated brother and the Fairfax family had a happy effect in toning up his mind and manners.

(CHAPTER 2)

During the time of Washington's surveying campaigns among the mountains, a grand colonizing scheme had been set on foot, destined to enlist him in hardy enterprises and in some degree to shape the course of his future fortunes.

The Early Years (1732–1763)

The treaty of peace concluded at Aix-la-Chapelle, which had put an end to the general war of Europe, had left undefined the boundaries between the British and French possessions in America. Immense regions were still claimed by both nations, and each was eager to forestall the other by getting possession of them and strengthening its claim by occupancy.

The most desirable of these regions lay west of the Allegany Mountains, extending from the lakes to the Ohio, embracing the valley of that river and its tributary streams—an immense territory possessing a salubrious climate, fertile soil, fine hunting and fishing grounds, and facilities by lakes and rivers for a vast internal commerce. The French claimed most of this country by the right of discovery, while the English claimed it by the right of a treaty made with Indians.

To gain a foothold in this region became the wish of some of the most enterprising men of Virginia and Maryland, among whom were Lawrence and Augustine Washington. With these views they projected a scheme in connection with John Hanbury, a wealthy London merchant, to obtain a grant of land from the British government for forming settlements or colonies beyond the Alleganies. Government readily countenanced a scheme by which French encroachments might be forestalled and prompt possession secured of the great Ohio valley. An association was accordingly chartered in 1749 by the name of "the Ohio Company," and 500,000 acres were granted to it west of the Alleganies, between the Monongahela and Kanawha rivers, though part of the land might be taken up north of the Ohio, should it be deemed expedient. The company were to pay no quitrent for ten years, but they were to select two fifths of their lands immediately, to settle 100 families upon them within seven years, to build a fort at their own expense, and maintain a sufficient garrison for defence against Indians.

Mr. Thomas Lee, president of the council of Virginia, took the lead in the concerns of the company at the outset. On his death, Lawrence Washington had the chief management. The company proceeded to make preparations for their colonizing scheme. Goods were imported from England suited to the Indian trade or for presents to the chiefs.

Before the company had received its charter, the French were in the field. Early in 1749, the Governor of Canada despatched Celeron de Bienville at the head of 300 men to the banks of the Ohio to make peace, as he said, between the tribes embroiled with each other during the late war and to renew French possession of the country. He distributed presents among the Indians, made speeches reminding them of former friendship, and warned them not to trade with the English. He nailed leaden plates to trees and buried others in the earth at the confluence of the Ohio and its tributaries bearing inscriptions that all lands on both sides of the rivers to their sources appertained, as in foregone times, to the crown of France. The Indians surmised their purport. "They mean to steal our country from us," murmured they, and determined to seek protection from the English.

Governor Hamilton of Pennsylvania knew the value of Indian friendship and suggested the Assembly clinch it with presents as soon as possible. An envoy accordingly was sent off early in October who was supposed to have great influence among the western tribes. This was George Croghan, a veteran trader who had been frequently to the Ohio country and made himself popular among the Indians by dispensing presents with a lavish hand. He was accompanied by Andrew Montour, a Canadian of half Indian descent, who was to act as interpreter. They were provided with a small present for the emergency, but were to convoke a meeting of all the tribes at Logstown, on the Ohio, early in the ensuing spring, to receive an ample present which would be provided by the Assembly.

It was some time later in the same autumn that the Ohio company brought their plans into operation and despatched an agent to explore the lands upon the Ohio and its branches as low as the Great Falls, take note of their fitness for cultivation, of the passes of the mountains, the courses of the rivers, and the strength and disposition of the native tribes. The man chosen for the purpose was Christopher Gist, a hardy pioneer, experienced in woodcraft and Indian life. He set out on the 31st of October, crossed the ridges of the Allegany, and arrived at Logstown, an important Indian village below the site of the present city of Pittsburg. Here usually resided Tanacharisson, a Seneca chief, being head sachem of the mixed tribes who had migrated to the Ohio and its branches. He was generally surnamed the half-king, being subordinate to the Iroquois confederacy. The chief was absent at this time, as were most of his people, it being the hunting season. Gist took his departure from Logstown, struck into the interior of Ohio, and overtook George Croghan at Muskingum, a town of Wyandots and Mingoes.

Gist was well received by the people of Muskingum. A council of the nation was held, in which Gist invited them to visit Virginia, where a large present of goods awaited them sent by their father, the great king, over the water to his Ohio children. The invitation was graciously received but no answer could be given until a grand council of the western tribes had been held at Logstown in the ensuing spring.

Piqua, where Gist and Croghan had arrived, was the principal town of the Miamis, the most powerful confederacy of the West, combining four tribes and extending its influence even beyond the Mississippi. A king or sachem of one of the tribes presided over the whole. The head chief at present was the king of the Piankeshas. At this town Croghan formed a treaty of alliance in the name of the Governor of Pennsylvania with two of the Miami tribes. And Gist was promised by the king of the Piankeshas that the chiefs of the various tribes would attend the meeting at Logstown to make a treaty with Virginia. When Gist returned to the Shawnee town, near the mouth of the Scioto, and reported to his Indian friends the alliance formed with the Miami confederacy, there was great feasting and speech-making and firing of guns. He had now happily accomplished the chief object of his mission.

It was a great object with the French to prevent this treaty, and to spirit up the Ohio Indians against the English. This they hoped to effect through Captain Joncaire, a veteran diplomatist of the wilderness. He appeared at Logstown accompanied by another Frenchman and forty Iroquois warriors. He found an assemblage of the western tribes, feasting and rejoicing, for Croghan and Montour were there and had been distributing presents on behalf of the Governor of Pennsylvania.

Joncaire made an animated speech to the chiefs in their own tongue. His eloquence was of no avail; a chief rose indignantly, shook his finger in his face, and, stamping on the ground, "this is our land," said he. "The English are our brothers. We will trade with them and not with you."

In the mean time, in the face of French protests and menaces, Gist, under sanction of the Virginia Legislature, proceeded to survey the lands within the grant of the Ohio company lying south of the Ohio river as far down as the Kanawha. An old Delaware sachem, meeting him while thus employed, propounded a somewhat puzzling question. "The French," said he, "claim all the land on one side of the Ohio, the English claim all the land on the other side— now where does the Indians' land lie?" Between their "fathers," the French, and their "brothers," the English, they were in a fair way of being most lovingly shared out of the whole country.

The French now prepared for hostile contingencies. They launched an armed vessel of unusual size on Lake Ontario, fortified their trading house at Niagara, strengthened their outposts, and advanced others on the upper waters of the Ohio. A stir of warlike preparation was likewise to be observed among the British colonies. It was evident that the claims to the disputed territories, if pushed home, could only be settled by the sword.

In Virginia, especially, the war spirit was manifest. The province was divided into military districts, each having an adjutant-general, with the rank of major, whose duty was to attend to the organization and equipment of the militia. Such an appointment was sought by Lawrence Washington for his brother George. It was readily obtained though he was yet but nineteen years of age. He set about preparing himself with his usual method and assiduity for his new duties.

Virginia had among its population some relics of the late Spanish war. Among these was Adjutant Muse, a Westmoreland volunteer, who had served with Lawrence in the West Indies. He undertook to instruct George in the art of war, lent him treatises on military tactics, put him through the manual exercise, and gave him some idea of evolutions in the field. Another of Lawrence's comrades was Jacob Van Braam, a Dutchman by birth, who had been in the British army, but was now out of service. He recruited his slender purse by giving the Virginian youth lessons in the sword exercise.

Under the instructions of these veterans Mount Vernon, from being a quiet rural retreat, was transformed into a school of arms, as Washington practised the manual exercise with Muse or took lessons on the broadsword from Van Braam.

His martial studies were interrupted for a time by the critical state of his brother's health. The constitution of Lawrence had always been delicate; there were now pulmonary symptoms of a threatening nature. By advice of his physicians he determined to pass a winter in the West Indies, taking with him George as a companion. They accordingly sailed for Barbadoes on the 28th of September, 1751. The physician there gave a favorable report of Lawrence's case and held out hopes of a cure.

The brothers had scarcely been a fortnight at the island when George was taken down by a severe attack of small-pox. Skillful medical treatment restored him to health in about three weeks, but his face always remained slightly marked.

The residence at Barbadoes failed to have the anticipated effect on the health of Lawrence and he determined to seek the climate of Bermuda in the spring. He felt the absence from his wife, and it was arranged that George should return to Virginia and bring her to that island. Lawrence remained through the winter at Barbadoes. Some of the worst symptoms of his disorder had disappeared, but nervous restlessness and desire of change had taken hold of him and early in March he hastened to Bermuda. He had come too soon. The keen air of early spring brought on an aggravated return of his worst symptoms. He was now afflicted with painful indecision and his letters perplexed his family. At one time he talked of remaining a year at Bermuda, and wrote to his wife to come with George and rejoin him there; in the very next letter, written in a moment of despondency, he talks of "hurrying home to his grave!"

The last was no empty foreboding. He did indeed hasten back and just reached Mount Vernon in time to die under his own roof, surrounded by his family and friends. His death took place on the 26th July, 1752, when but thirty-four years of age. Lawrence left a wife and an infant daughter to inherit his ample estates. In case his daughter should die without issue, the estate of Mount Vernon and other lands specified in his will were to be enjoyed by her mother during her lifetime and, at her death, to be inherited by his brother George.

The meeting of the Ohio tribes, Delawares, Shawnees, and Mingoes to form a treaty of alliance with Virginia took place at Logstown at the appointed time. The chiefs of the Six Nations declined to attend. At Logstown, Colonel Fry and two other commissioners from Virginia concluded a treaty with the tribes above named by which the latter engaged not to molest any English settlers south of the Ohio.

The Ohio tribes, greatly incensed at the aggressions of the French, who were erecting posts within their territories, sent deputations to remonstrate but without effect. The chief of the western tribes returned, wounded at heart, both by the language and the haughty manner of the French commandant. He saw the ruin impending over his race but looked with hope and trust to the English as the power least disposed to wrong the red man.

But French influence was successful in other quarters. Some of the Indians who had been friendly to the English showed signs of alienation. There were reports that the French were ascending the Mississippi from Louisiana. France, it was said, intended to connect Louisiana and Canada by a chain of military posts and hem the English within the Allegany Mountains. The Ohio Company complained loudly to the Lieutenant-governor of Virginia, Robert Dinwiddie, of the hostile conduct of the French and their Indian allies.

A commissioner, Captain William Trent, was sent to expostulate with the French commander on the Ohio for his aggressions on the territory of his Britannic majesty; he bore presents also of guns, powder, shot, and clothing for the friendly Indians. Trent was not a man of the true spirit for a mission to the frontier. The whole aspect of affairs was so threatening on the frontier that Trent lost heart and returned home without accomplishing his errand.

Dinwiddie now looked round for a person more fitted to fulfil a mission which required physical strength and moral energy, a courage to cope with savages, and a sagacity to negotiate with white men.

Washington was pointed out as possessed of those requisites. His woodland experience fitted him for an expedition through the wilderness, and his great discretion and self-command for negotiation with wily commanders and fickle savages. He was accordingly chosen for the expedition.

By his letter of instructions he was directed to hold a communication with sachems of the mixed tribes friendly to the English, inform them of the purport of his errand, and request an escort to the head-quarters of the French commander. To that commander he was to deliver his credentials and the letter of Dinwiddie and demand an answer in the name of his Britannic majesty, but not to wait for it beyond a week. On receiving it, he was to request a sufficient escort to protect him on his return.

He was, moreover, to acquaint himself with the numbers and force of the French stationed on the Ohio and in its vicinity, their capability of being reinforced from Canada, the forts they had erected, where situated, how garrisoned, the object of their advancing into those parts, and how they were likely to be supported. Washington set off from Williamsburg on the 30th of October, 1753, the very day on which he received his credentials. At Fredericksburg he engaged Jacob Van Braam to accompany him as interpreter.

Washington met with Gist, the intrepid pioneer who had explored the Ohio in the employ of the company, whom he engaged to accompany him in the expedition. He secured the services also of John Davidson as Indian interpreter and of four frontiersmen, two of whom were Indian traders. With this little band and Van Braam, he set forth on the 15th of November, through a wild country rendered almost impassable by recent storms of rain and snow. They arrived at Logstown after sunset on the 24th of November.

On the following day, Washington met with the Indian chiefs there. The nearest and levellest way, they told him, was now impassable, lying through large and miry savannas; they would have, therefore, to go by Venango and it would take five or six days of good travelling to reach the nearest French fort.

After several days of delay and further consultations in the council-house, the chiefs determined that but three of their number should accompany the mission, as a greater number might awaken the suspicions of the French. Accordingly, on the 30th of November, Washington set out for the French post.

Although the distance to Venango, by the route taken, was not above 70 miles, yet such was the inclemency of the weather and the difficulty of travelling that Washington and his party did not arrive there until the 4th of December. On the 7th of December, Washington recommenced his journey.

After four days of weary travel through snow and rain and mire and swamp, the party reached the fort. It was situated on a kind of island on the west fork of French Creek, about 15 miles south of Lake Erie, and consisted of four houses, forming a hollow square, defended by bastions made of palisades twelve feet high, picketed, and pierced for cannon and small arms. When Washington presented himself at the gate, he was met by the officer second in command and conducted in due military form to Chevalier Legardeur de St. Pierre.

Having announced his errand through Van Braam, Washington offered his credentials and the letter of Governor Dinwiddie and was disposed to proceed at once to business with the prompt frankness of a young man unhackneyed in diplomacy. In this letter, Dinwiddie complained of the intrusion of French forces into the Ohio country, erecting forts and making settlements in the western parts of Virginia, so known to be the property of the crown of Great Britain. He inquired by whose authority and instructions the French Commander-general had made this invasion, intimating that his own action would be regulated by the answer he should receive. At the same time he required of the commandant his peaceable departure.

The two following days were consumed in councils of the chevalier and his officers over the letter and the necessary reply. Washington occupied himself in the mean time in observing and taking notes of the plan, dimensions, and strength of the fort and of everything about it. He gave orders to his people, also, to take an exact account of the canoes in readiness, and others in the process of construction, for the conveyance of troops down the river in the ensuing spring.

The Early Years (1732–1763)

On the evening of the 14th, the Chevalier de St. Pierre delivered to Washington his sealed reply to the letter of Governor Dinwiddie. The purport of previous conversations with the chevalier and the whole complexion of affairs on the frontier left no doubt of the nature of that reply.

The business of his mission being accomplished, Washington prepared on the 15th to return by water to Venango. It was rough and laborious navigation. French Creek was swollen and turbulent and full of floating ice. The frail canoes were several times in danger of being staved to pieces against rocks. It was not until the 22d that they reached Venango.

On the 25th of December, Washington and his little party set out by land from Venango homeward. They had a long winter's journey before them through a wilderness beset with dangers and difficulties. The packhorses, laden with tents, baggage, and provisions, were completely jaded; it was feared they would give out. Washington gave up his saddle-horse to aid in transporting the baggage and requested his companions to do the same. None but the drivers remained in the saddle.

The cold increased. There was deep snow that froze as it fell. The horses grew less and less capable of travelling. For three days they toiled on slowly and wearily. Washington was impatient to accomplish his journey, and make his report to the governor; he determined, therefore, to hasten some distance in advance of the party and then strike for the fork of the Ohio by the nearest course directly through the woods. He accordingly put the cavalcade under the command of Van Braam. Then disencumbering himself of all superflous clothing, strapping his pack on his shoulders, and taking gun in hand, he left the horses to flounder on and struck manfully ahead, accompanied only by Gist, who had equipped himself in like manner.

On the 2d of January, after much hardship and peril, they arrived at the residence of Gist, on the Monongahela. Here they separated and Washington, having purchased a horse, continued his homeward course. Having crossed the Blue Ridge and stopped one day at Belvoir to rest, he reached Williamsburg on the 16th of

January, where he delivered to Dinwiddie the letter of the French commandant and made him a full report of the events of his mission.

The prudence, sagacity, resolution, firmness, and self-devotion manifested by Washington throughout; his tact and self-possession in treating with fickle savages and crafty white men; the soldier's eye with which he had noticed every thing that would bear upon military operations; and the hardihood with which he had acquitted himself during a wintry tramp through the wilderness, through constant storms of rain and snow—all pointed him out, not merely to the governor but to the public at large, as one eminently fitted, not-withstanding his youth, for important trusts involving civil as well as military duties. From that moment he was the rising hope of Virginia.

The reply of the Chevalier de St. Pierre was such as might have been expected from that courteous but wary commander. He should transmit, he said, the letter of Dinwiddie to his general, the Marquis du Quesne, "to whom," observed he, "it better belongs than to me to set forth the evidence and reality of the rights of the king, my master, upon the land situated along the river Ohio, and to contest the pretensions of the king of Great Britain thereto." The letter was considered evasive and only intended to gain time. The information given by Washington convinced Dinwiddie and his council that the French were preparing to descend the Ohio in the spring and take military possession of the country.

Captain Trent was despatched to the frontier, commissioned to raise a company of 100 men, march with all speed to the fork of the Ohio and finish the fort commenced there by the Ohio Company. He was enjoined to act only on the defensive but to capture or destroy whoever should oppose the construction of the works or disturb their settlements. Washington was empowered to raise a like force at Alexandria, to procure and forward munitions and supplies for the fort at the fork, and ultimately to have command of both companies.

Governor Dinwiddie in the mean time called upon the governors of the other provinces to make common cause against the foe; he endeavored, also, to effect alliances with the Indian tribes of the south, the Catawbas and Cherokees, by way of counterbalancing the

Chippewas and Ottawas, who were devoted to the French. The colonies, however, felt as yet too much like isolated territories; the spirit of union was wanting.

Dinwiddie convened the House of Burgesses to devise measures for the public security. When Dinwiddie propounded his scheme of operations on the Ohio, some of the burgesses demurred to any grant for military purposes which might be construed into an act of hostility. To meet this scruple, it was suggested that the grant might be made for the purpose of encouraging and protecting all settlers on the waters of the Mississippi. And under this specious plea, 10,000 pounds were grudgingly voted.

Ways and means being provided, Dinwiddie augmented the number of troops to be enlisted to 300, divided into six companies. The command of the whole, as before, was offered to Washington, but he shrank from it as a charge too great for his inexperience. It was given, therefore, to Colonel Joshua Fry and Washington was made second in command with the rank of lieutenant-colonel.

The recruiting, at first, went on slowly. Governor Dinwiddie, sensible of this, proclaimed a bounty of 200,000 acres on the Ohio River, to be divided among the officers and soldiers in this expedition, 1000 to be laid off contiguous to the fort for the use of the garrison. This was a tempting bait to the sons of farmers, who readily enlisted in the hope of having a farm of their own in this land of promise. It was a more difficult matter to get officers than soldiers. Washington found himself left, almost alone, to manage self-willed, undisciplined recruits. Happily he had with him, in the rank of lieutenant, Van Braam, his old "master of fence" and travelling interpreter. In his emergency he forthwith nominated him captain and wrote to the governor to confirm the appointment.

On the 2d of April, Washington set off from Alexandria for the new fort at the fork of the Ohio. He had but two companies with him, amounting to about 150 men; the remainder of the regiment was to follow under Colonel Fry with the artillery, which was to be conveyed up the Potomac. While on the march he was joined by a detachment under Captain Adam Stephens.

Slenderly fitted out, Washington and his little force made their way toilfully across the mountains, having to prepare the roads as

they went for the transportation of the cannon. They cheered themselves with the thoughts that this hard work would cease when they
should arrive at the company's trading-post and storehouse at Wills'
Creek, where Captain Trent was to have packhorses in readiness.
Before arriving there, they were startled by a rumor that Trent and
his men had been captured by the French. With regard to Trent, the
news proved to be false, for they found him at Wills' Creek on the
20th of April. With regard to his men there was still an uncertainty.
He had recently left them busily at work on the fort under the
command of his lieutenant. Washington was eager to press forward
but Trent, inefficient as usual, had failed to provide packhorses. It
was necessary to send to Winchester, forty miles distant, for baggage waggons and await their arrival. All uncertainty as to the fate of
the men, however, was brought to a close by their arrival, on the
25th, conducted by an ensign. Captain Contrecoeur, an alert
French officer, bringing about 1,000 men in batteaux and canoes
down the river from Venango, had suddenly made his appearance
before the fort, which was not half completed. He summoned the
fort to surrender, allowing one hour for a written reply. All that the
ensign in command could obtain was permission to depart with his
men, taking with them their working tools.

Regarding the conduct of the French an overt act of war,
Washington found himself thrown with a handful of raw recruits in
the midst of a wilderness with an enemy at hand greatly superior in
number, discipline, artillery, munitions of war, and within reach of
constant supplies and reinforcements. He had also received accounts of another party ascending the Ohio and of Chippewas and
Ottawas marching to join the hostile camp. Still it would not do to
fall back nor show signs of apprehension. His Indian allies in such
case might desert him. The soldiery, too, might grow restless and
dissatisfied. In this dilemma he called a council of war, in which it
was determined to proceed to the Ohio Company store-houses at
the mouth of Redstone Creek, fortify themselves there, and wait for
reinforcements. Here they might watch the enemy and get notice of
any movement in time for defence, or retreat; and, should they be
reinforced sufficiently to enable them to attack the fort, they could
easily drop down the river with their artillery.

Washington detached 60 men in advance to make a road, and at the same time wrote to Dinwiddie for mortars and grenadoes and cannon of heavy metal.

Aware that the Assembly of Pennsylvania was in session and that the Maryland Assembly would meet in a few days, he wrote to the governors of those provinces, acquainting them with the hostile acts of the French and endeavoring to rouse them to co-operation in the common cause. The youthful commander had here a foretaste of the perils and perplexities which awaited him from enemies in the field and lax friends in legislative councils in the grander operations of his future years.

On the 29th of April, Washington set out for Wills' Creek, at the head of 160 men. He soon overtook those sent in advance to work the road; they had made but little progress. It was a difficult task to break a road through the wilderness sufficient for the artillery coming on with Colonel Fry's division. All hands were now set to work, but with all their labor they could not accomplish more than four miles a day. On the 9th of May they were not further than 20 miles from Wills' Creek, at Little Meadows.

Every day came gloomy accounts from the Ohio brought chiefly by traders, who were retreating to more settled parts of the country. Some exaggerated the number of the French, as if strongly reinforced. All represented them as diligently constructing a fort. Among the flying reports and alarms, Washington was gratified to learn that the half king was on his way with 50 warriors.

After infinite toil through swamps and forests and over rugged mountains, the detachment arrived at the Youghiogeny River, where they were detained some days constructing a bridge to cross it. While the bridge was in the course of construction, Washington was told on the 23d that the French were crossing the ford of the Youghiogeny about 18 miles distant. He now hastened to take a position in the Great Meadows, where he caused the bushes to be cleared away, made an intrenchment, and prepared what he termed "a charming field for an encounter."

On the 25th, Washington detached 75 men in pursuit of La Force, a French commissary, and his prowling band which had been at Gist's place the day before in the latter's absence. About nine o'clock at night came an Indian messenger from the half-king, who was encamped about six miles off. The chief had seen tracks of two Frenchmen and was convinced their whole body must be in ambush near by. Washington considered this the force which had been hovering about him for several days and determined to forestall their hostile designs. Leaving a guard with the baggage and ammunition, he set out with 40 men to join his Indian ally.

The chieftain received the youthful commander with great demonstrations of friendship and engaged to go with him against the lurking enemy. He conducted Washington to the tracks he had discovered. Upon these he put two of his Indians, who traced them to a low bottom, surrounded by rocks and trees, where the French were encamped, having built a few cabins for shelter from the rain.

A plan was now concerted to come upon them by surprise, Washington on the right and the half-king on the left. Washington was the first upon the ground. As he advanced at the head of his men, the French caught sight of him and ran to their arms. A sharp firing instantly took place and was kept up on both sides for about fifteen minutes. The French at length gave way and ran, but were soon overtaken and captured. The Indians would have massacred the prisoners had not Washington prevented them. The prisoners, including La Force, were sent on the following day under a strong escort to Dinwiddie, then at Winchester.

The situation of Washington was now extremely perilous. Contrecoeur, the French commander, it was said, had nearly 1,000 men with him at the fort, beside Indian allies, and reinforcements were on the way to join him.

The half-king was full of fight. He summoned all his allies to take up arms and join him at Redstone Creek. He went off for his home, promising to send down the river for all the Mingoes and Shawnees and to be back at the camp on the 30th with thirty or forty warriors.

"I shall expect every hour to be attacked," writes Washington to Dinwiddie on the 29th, "and by unequal numbers, which I must withstand, . . . for I fear . . . that we shall lose the Indians if we suffer ourselves to be driven back. . . . I doubt not if you hear I am beaten, but you will hear at the same time that we have done our duty in fighting as long as there is a shadow of hope." The fact is that Washington was in a high state of military excitement. He was a young soldier; he had been for the first time in action and been successful.

News came of the death of Colonel Fry at Wills' Creek, and command of the regiment devolved on Washington. Finding a blank major's commission among Fry's papers, he gave it to Stephens, who had conducted himself with spirit.

The palisaded fort was now completed and named Fort Necessity, from the pinching famine that had prevailed during its construction. The scanty force in camp was augmented to 300 by the arrival of the men who had been under Fry. With them came the surgeon of the regiment, Dr. James Craik, destined to become a faithful and confidential friend of Washington for the remainder of his life.

A letter from Dinwiddie announced that Captain Mackay would soon arrive with an independent company of 100 men from South Carolina. The title of independent company had a sound ominous of trouble. Troops of the kind raised in the colonies under direction of the governors were paid by the crown and the officers had king's commissions; such, doubtless, had Captain Mackay. "I should have been particularly obliged," writes Washington to Dinwiddie, "if you had declared whether he was under my command or independent of it. I hope he will have more sense than to insist upon any unreasonable distinction because he and his officers have commissions from his majesty. . . . We have the same spirit to serve our gracious king as they have and are as ready and willing to sacrifice our lives for our country's good."

On the 9th arrived Washington's early instructor in military tactics, Adjutant Muse, recently appointed a major in the regiment. Fifty or sixty horses were forthwith sent to Wills' Creek to bring on further supplies and Gist was urged to hasten forward the artillery.

On the 10th there was agitation in the camp. Scouts hurried in with word that 90 Frenchmen were approaching. Washington ordered out 150 of his best men, put himself at their head, leaving Major Muse with the rest to man the fort. It was another effervescence of his youthful military ardor, doomed to disappointment. The report had been either exaggerated or misunderstood. The 90 Frenchmen in military array dwindled down into 9 French deserters. According to their account, the fort at the fork was completed and named Duquesne in honor of the Governor of Canada. It was proof against all attack excepting with bombs on the land side. The garrison did not exceed 500, but 200 more were hourly expected and 900 in the course of a fortnight.

On the same day Captain Mackay arrived with his independent company of South Carolinians. The captain, holding a commission direct from the king, could not bring himself to acknowledge a provincial officer as his superior. He encamped separately, kept separate guards, and would not agree that Washington should assign any rallying place for his men in case of alarm. Washington conducted himself with circumspection, avoiding every thing that might call up a question of command, but he urged the governor by letter to prescribe their relative rank and authority.

On the 11th of June, Washington resumed the laborious march for Redstone Creek. Leaving Mackay and his independent company as a guard at Fort Necessity, Washington and his Virginia troops toiled forward through the narrow defiles of the mountains, working on the road as they went.

At Gist's establishment, about 13 miles from Fort Necessity, Washington received intelligence that reinforcements had arrived at Fort Duquesne and a large force would be detached against him. Coming to a halt, he began to throw up intrenchments, calling in two foraging parties and sending word to Mackay to join him with all speed. The captain and his company arrived in the evening, the foraging parties the next morning. A council of war was held in which the idea of awaiting the enemy at this place was unanimously abandoned. A rapid and toilsome retreat ensued. On the 1st of July they reached the Great Meadows. Here the Virginians, exhausted by fatigue, hunger, and vexation, declared they would carry the baggage and drag the swivels no further. Contrary to his original intentions, therefore, Washington determined to halt here for the present and fortify, sending off expresses to hasten supplies and reinforcements from Wills' Creek, where he had reason to believe that two companies from New York were by this time arrived.

The retreat to the Great Meadows had not been in the least too precipitate. Captain de Villiers had sallied forth from Fort Duquesne at the head of 500 French and several hundred Indians. Arriving at Gist's plantation, he surrounded the works which Washington had hastily thrown up there and fired into them. Finding them deserted, he concluded that it was too late to pursue them. He was on the point of returning to Fort Duquesne, when a deserter arrived who gave word that Washington had come to a halt in the Great Meadows, where his troops were in a starving condition. De Villiers then pushed forward for the Great Meadows.

In the mean time Washington had exerted himself to enlarge and strengthen Fort Necessity. The fort was about 100 feet square, protected by trenches and palisades. It stood on the margin of a small stream, nearly in the centre of the Great Meadows, which is a grassy plain surrounded by wooded hills of a moderate height, at that place about 250 yards wide.

At this critical juncture he was deserted by his Indian allies. They were disheartened at the scanty preparations for defence against a superior force and offended at being subjected to military command.

Early in the morning of the 3d, a sentinel came in bleeding, having been fired upon. Scouts brought word shortly afterwards that the French were in force about four miles off. Washington drew up his men outside of the works to await the attack. About 11 o'clock, there was a firing of musketry from among trees on rising ground but so distant as to do no harm; suspecting this to be a stratagem to draw his men into the woods, he ordered them to keep quiet and refrain from firing until the foe should draw near.

The firing was kept up, but still under cover. He now fell back with his men into the trenches, ordering them to fire whenever they could get sight of an enemy. In this way there was skirmishing throughout the day, the French and Indians advancing as near as the covert of the wood would permit, but never into open sight. In the mean while the rain fell in torents; the harrassed troops were half drowned in their trenches and many of their muskets were rendered unfit for use.

About eight at night the French requested a parley. Washington hesitated. It might be a stratagem to gain admittance for a spy into the fort. The request was repeated. Unfortunately, because the only one who could speak French correctly was disabled, Washington had to send Jacob Van Braam. The captain returned twice with separate terms, in which the garrison was required to surrender; both were rejected. He returned a third time, with articles of capitulation written in French. The captain rendered the capitulation in mongrel English while Washington and his officers stood listening, endeavoring to disentangle the meaning.

The main articles, as Washington and his officers understood them, were that they should be allowed to return to the settlements without molestation from French or Indians; that they should march out of the fort with the honors of war, drums beating and colors flying, and with all their effects and military stores excepting the artillery, which should be destroyed; that they should be allowed to deposit their effects in some secret place and leave a guard to protect them until they could send horses to bring them away; that they should give their word of honor not to attempt any buildings or improvements on the lands of his most Christian majesty, for the space of a year; that the prisoners taken in the skirmish of Jumonville should be restored and, until their delivery, Van Braam and Major Stobo should remain with the French as hostages.

The next morning, accordingly, Washington and his men marched out of their fortress with the honors of war, bearing with them their regimental colors. Scarcely had they begun their march, however, when, in defiance of the terms of capitulation, they were beset by a large body of Indians, allies of the French, who began plundering the baggage and committing other irregularities. Seeing that the French did not or could not prevent them and that all the baggage which could not be transported on the shoulders of his troops would fall into the hands of these savages, Washington ordered it to be destroyed as well as the artillery, gunpowder, and other military stores.

In the following days' march, the troops seemed jaded and disheartened; they were encumbered and delayed by the wounded; provisions were scanty. Washington, however, encouraged them by his own steadfast and cheerful demeanor, sharing all their toils and privations, and conducted them in safety to Wills' Creek, where they found ample provisions in the military magazines. Leaving them here to recover their strength, he proceeded with Mackay to Williamsburg, to make his military report to the governor.

A copy of the capitulation was laid before the Virginia House of Burgesses with explanations. Notwithstanding the unfortunate result of the campaign, Washington and his officers received a vote of thanks for their bravery and gallant defence of their country. From the vote of thanks, Washington's unfortunate blundering interpreter, Jacob Van Braam, was excepted, accused of treachery in purposely misrepresenting the articles of capitulation.

Early in August Washington rejoined his regiment, which had arrived at Alexandria by the way of Winchester. Dinwiddie urged him to recruit it to the former number of 300 men and join Colonel Innes at Wills' Creek, where that officer, stationed with Mackay's independent company of South Carolinians and two independent companies from New York, had been employed in erecting a work to serve as a frontier post and rallying point, which work received the name of Fort Cumberland in honor of the Duke of Cumberland, captain-general of the British army.

Dinwiddie was sorely perplexed about this time by contradictions and cross-purposes both in military and civil affairs. The governor found the House of Burgesses unmanageable. His demands for military supplies were resisted on what he considered presumptuous pretexts or granted sparingly under mortifying restrictions.

In October the House of Burgesses made a grant of 20,000 pounds for the public service, and 10,000 more were sent out from England, beside a supply of fire-arms. The governor now applied himself to military matters with renewed spirit; he increased the actual force to ten companies and, as there had been difficulties among the different kinds of troops with regard to precedence, he reduced them all to independent companies so that there would be no officer in a Virginia regiment above the rank of captain.

This shrewd measure, upon which Dinwiddie prided himself, immediately drove Washington out of the service, considering it derogatory to accept a lower commission than that under which his conduct had gained him a vote of thanks from the Legislature.

Even had Washington hesitated to take this step, it would have been forced upon him by a further regulation of government in the ensuing winter, settling the rank of officers of his majesty's forces when joined or serving with the provincial forces in North America, "which directed that all such as were commissioned by the king, or by his general commander-in-chief in North America, should take rank of all officers commissioned by the governors of the respective provinces. And further, that the general and field officers of the provincial troops should have no rank when serving with the general and field officers commissioned by the crown; but that all captains and other inferior officers of the royal troops should take rank over provincial officers of the same grade, having older commissions." These regulations would have been spurned by Washington as insulting to the character and conduct of his high-minded brethren of the colonies. This open disparagement of colonial honor and understanding contributed to wean from England the affection of her American subjects and prepared the way for their ultimate assertion of independence.

(CHAPTER 3)

Having resigned his commission and disengaged himself from public affairs, Washington took up his abode at Mount Vernon and prepared to engage in those agricultural pursuits for which, even in his youthful days, he had as keen a relish as for the profession of arms. Scarcely had he entered upon his rural occupations, however, when the service of his country once more called him to the field.

The disastrous affair at the Great Meadows and the other acts of French hostility on the Ohio had roused the attention of the British ministry. Their ambassador at Paris was instructed to complain of those violations of the peace. The court of Versailles amused him with general assurances of amity and strict adherence to treaties. In the mean time, however, French ships were fitted out and troops embarked to carry out the schemes of the government in America.

The British government now prepared for military operations in America, none of them professedly aggressive but rather to resist and counteract aggressions. A plan of campaign was devised for 1755 having four objects:

1. To eject the French from the lands which they held unjustly in the province of Nova Scotia.

2. To dislodge them from a fortress which they had erected at Crown Point, on Lake Champlain, within what was claimed as British territory.

3. To dispossess them of the fort which they had constructed at Niagara, between Lake Ontario and Lake Erie.

4. To drive them from the frontiers of Pennsylvania and Virginia and recover the valley of the Ohio.

The Duke of Cumberland, captain-general of the British army, had the organization of this campaign; through his patronage Major-general Edward Braddock was intrusted with the execution of it, being appointed generalissimo of all forces in the colonies. Braddock was a veteran in service, who had been upwards of 40 years in the guards, that school of exact discipline and technical punctilio. Cumberland, who held a commission in the guards, may have considered Braddock fitted by his skill and preciseness as a tactician for a command in a new country, inexperienced in military science, to bring its raw levies into order and to settle those questions of rank and etiquette apt to arise where regular and provincial troops are to act together.

Braddock was to lead in person the grand enterprise of the campaign, that destined for the frontiers of Virginia and Pennsylvania; it was the enterprise in which Washington became enlisted and, therefore, claims our especial attention.

Prior to the arrival of Braddock, came out from England Lieutenant-colonel Sir John St. Clair, deputy quartermaster-general, eager to make himself acquainted with the field of operations. He made a tour of inspection, in company with Governor Sharpe of Maryland and appears to have been dismayed at sight of the impracticable wilderness, the region of Washington's campaign. From Fort Cumberland, he wrote in February to Governor Morris of Pennsylvania to have the road cut or repaired toward the head of the river Youghiogeny and another opened from Philadelphia for the transportation of supplies.

Unfortunately the Governor of Pennsylvania had no money at his command, and was obliged, for expenses, to apply to his Assembly, "a set of men," writes he, "quite unacquainted with every kind of military service, and exceedingly unwilling to part with money on any terms." By dint of exertions, he procured the appointment of commissioners to explore the country and survey and lay out the roads required. At the head of the commission was George Croghan, the Indian trader who enjoyed the patronage of the Pennsylvania government.

When St. Clair had finished his tour of inspection, he repaired to Virginia to meet General Braddock, who had landed at Hampton and proceeded to Williamsburg to consult with Dinwiddie. Shortly afterwards he was joined by Commodore Keppel, whose squadron of two ships of war and several transports had anchored in Chesapeake. On board of these ships were two prime regiments of about 500 men each, together with a train of artillery and the necessary munitions of war. The regiments were to be augmented to 700 men each by men selected by St. Clair from Virginia companies recently raised. Alexandria was fixed upon as the place where the troops should disembark and encamp. The ships were accordingly ordered up to that place and the levies directed to repair thither.

The plan of the campaign included the use of Indian allies. Dinwiddie had already sent Gist, Washington's guide in 1753, to engage the Cherokees and Catawbas, who he had no doubt would take up the hatchet for the English, and he gave Braddock reason to expect at least 400 Indians to join him at Fort Cumberland.

General Braddock apprehended difficulty in procuring waggons and horses sufficient to attend him in his march. St. Clair, in the course of his tour of inspection, had met with two Dutch settlers at the foot of the Blue Ridge who engaged to furnish 200 waggons and 1500 carrying horses, to be at Fort Cumberland early in May.

Governor Sharpe was to furnish above 100 waggons for the transportation of stores on the Maryland side of the Potomac.

"Every thing," writes one of the general's aides-de-camp, "seemed to promise so far the greatest success. The transports were all arrived safe and the men in health. Provisions, Indians, carriages, and horses were already provided; at least were to be esteemed so, considering the authorities on which they were promised to the general."

Trusting to these arrangements, Braddock proceeded to Alexandria. The troops had all been disembarked before his arrival and the Virginia levies, selected by St. Clair to join the regiments of regulars, were arrived. There were beside two companies of carpenters, six of rangers and one troop of light horse. The levies, having been clothed, were ordered to march immediately for Winchester, to be armed, and the general gave them in charge of an ensign "to make them as like soldiers as possible." The light horse were retained by the general as his escort and body guard.

The din and stir of warlike preparation disturbed the quiet of Mount Vernon. Washington looked down from his rural retreat upon the ships of war and transports as they passed up the Potomac, the array of arms gleaming along their decks. Occasionally he mounted his horse and rode to Alexandria; it was like a garrisoned town, teeming with troops and resounding with the drum and fife. A brilliant campaign was about to open under the auspices of an experienced general with all the means and appurtenances of European warfare. All his thoughts of rural life were put to flight. The military part of his character was again in the ascendant; his great desire was to join the expedition as a volunteer.

It was reported to Braddock. The latter was apprised by Dinwiddie and others of Washington's personal merits, his knowledge of the country, and his experience in frontier service. The consequence was a letter written by the general's order, inviting Washington to join his staff. A volunteer situation on the staff of General Braddock offered no emolument nor command; still he did not hesitate a moment to accept the invitation.

His mother heard with concern of another projected expedition into the wilderness. Hurrying to Mount Vernon, she entreated him

not again to expose himself to the hardships and perils of these
frontier campaigns. However much a mother's pride may have been
gratified by his early advancement and renown, she had rejoiced on
his return to the safer walks of peaceful life. She was not dazzled by
military glory. The passion for arms which mingled with the more
sober elements of Washington's character would seem to have been
inherited from his father's side of the house. His mother had once
prevented him from entering the navy, when a gallant frigate was at
hand, anchored in the waters of the Potomac; with all his deference
for her, he could not resist the appeal to his martial sympathies,
which called him to the head-quarters of General Braddock.

His arrival was hailed by Captains Orme and Morris, the general's aides-de-camp, who at once received him into frank companionship, and a cordial intimacy commenced between them that
continued throughout the campaign. He experienced a courteous
reception from the general, who expressed in flattering terms the
impression he had received of his merits.

There were at that time four governors, beside Dinwiddie, assembled at Alexandria at Braddock's request to concert a plan of military operations: Governor Shirley of Massachusetts; Lieutenant-
governor Delancey of New York; Lieutenant-governor Sharpe of
Maryland; Lieutenant-governor Morris of Pennsylvania. A grand
council was held on the 14th of April, composed of Braddock,
Keppel, and the governors, at which the general's commission was
read, as were his instructions from the king relating to a common
fund to be established by the several colonies toward defraying the
expenses of the campaign. The governors informed Braddock that
they had applied to their respective Assemblies for the establishment of such a fund, but in vain, and gave it as their unanimous
opinion that such a fund could never be established in the colonies
without the aid of Parliament.

Niagara and Crown Point were to be attacked about the same
time with Fort Duquesne, the former by Governor Shirley, with his
own and Sir William Pepperell's regiments, and some New York
companies; the latter by Colonel William Johnson, sole manager
and director of Indian affairs. The end of June was fixed upon as the
time when the attacks upon Forts Duquesne, Niagara, and Crown

Point should be carried into execution. The expulsion of the French from the lands wrongfully held by them in Nova Scotia was assigned to Colonel Lawrence, Lieutenant-governor of that province.

Braddock would have set out for Fredericktown, in Maryland, but few waggons or teams had yet come to remove the artillery. Washington had looked with wonder and dismay at the huge paraphernalia of war to be transported across the mountains. His predictions excited a sarcastic smile in Braddock, as betraying the limited notions of a young provincial officer, little acquainted with the march of armies.

In the mean while, St. Clair, who had returned to the frontier, was storming at the camp at Fort Cumberland. The road required of the Pennsylvania government had not been commenced. Sir John "stormed like a lion rampant," declaring that the want of the road and provisions promised by Pennsylvania had retarded the expedition and might cost them their lives from the fresh numbers of French that might be poured into the country.

The explosive wrath of Sir John shook the souls of the commissioners and they wrote to Governor Morris, urging that people be set at work upon the road and that flour be sent without delay to the mouth of Canococheague River. In reply, Mr. Richard Peters, Governor Morris's secretary, wrote in his name: "Get a number of hands immediately and further the work by all possible methods. Your expenses will be paid at the next sitting of Assembly."

An additional commission was intrusted to George Croghan. Governor Morris requested him to convene at Aughquick, in Pennsylvania, as many warriors as possible of the tribes of the Ohio, distribute wampum belts sent for the purpose, and engage them to meet Braddock when on the march and render him all the assistance in their power. Croghan also secured the services of a band of hunters, resolute men, well acquainted with the country and inured to hardships. They were under the command of Captain Jack, one of the most remarkable characters of Pennsylvania, a complete hero of the wilderness. He had been for many years a captive among the Indians, and, having learnt their ways, had formed this association for the protection of the settlements, receiving a commission of captain from the Governor of Pennsylvania.

Braddock set out from Alexandria on the 20th of April. Washington remained behind a few days to arrange his affairs, and then rejoined him at Fredericktown, in Maryland, where, on the 10th of May, he was proclaimed one of the general's aides-de-camp. The troubles of Braddock had already commenced. The Virginian contractors failed to fulfil their engagements; of all the transportation promised, but 15 waggons and 100 draft-horses arrived. There was equal disappointment in provisions both as to quantity and quality.

Fortunately, while the general was venting his spleen against army contractors, Benjamin Franklin arrived at Fredericktown. That eminent man had been for many years member of the Pennsylvania Assembly and was now postmaster-general for America. The Assembly understood that Braddock was incensed against them, supposing them adverse to the service of the war. They had procured Franklin to wait upon him, not as if sent by them, but as if he came in his capacity of postmaster-general, to arrange for the sure and speedy transmission of despatches between the commander-in-chief and the governors of the provinces. He was well received, and became a daily guest at the general's table.

As the whole delay of the army was caused by the want of conveyances, Franklin observed one day to the general that in Pennsylvania almost every farmer had his waggon. "Then, sir," replied Braddock, "you can probably procure them for me and I beg you will." Franklin consented. An instrument in writing was drawn up, empowering him to contract for 150 waggons with four horses to each waggon, and 1500 saddle or packhorses to be at Wills' Creek on or before the 20th of May, and he promptly departed for Lancaster to execute the commission.

After his departure, Braddock, attended by his staff and his guard of light horse, set off for Wills' Creek by the way of Winchester. He arrived at Fort Cumberland, amid a thundering salute of seventeen guns.

By the 19th of May, the forces were assembled at Fort Cumberland: two royal regiments, originally 1000 strong, now increased to 1400 by men chosen from the Maryland and Virginia levies; two provincial companies of carpenters, thirty men each, with subalterns and captains; a company of guides, composed of a captain, two aids, and ten men; the troop of Virginia light horse commanded by Captain Stewart; the detachment of thirty sailors with their officers; and the remnants of two independent companies from New York, one of which was commanded by Captain Horatio Gates.

At Fort Cumberland, Washington had an opportunity of seeing a force encamped according to the plan approved of by the council of war and military tactics enforced with all the precision of a martinet. Braddock's camp, in a word, gave Washington an opportunity of seeing military routine in its strictest forms.

Braddock was completely chagrined and disappointed about the Indians. The Cherokees and Catawbas, whom Dinwiddie had given him reason to expect in such numbers, never arrived.

During the halt of the troops at Wills' Creek, Washington had been sent to Williamsburg to bring on 4000 pounds for the military chest. He returned after a fortnight's absence and found the general out of all patience at the delays and disappointments in regard to horses, waggons, and forage. He accused the army contractors of want of faith, honor, and honesty and, in moments of passion, extended the stigma to the whole country. This stung the patriotic sensibility of Washington and the proud and passionate commander was surprised by a well-merited rebuke from his aide-de-camp.

The same pertinacity was maintained with respect to the Indians. The sachems, whom Croghan had brought to the camp for a grand council, considered themselves treated with slight in never being consulted in war matters. Croghan had offered the services of the 50 warriors he had engaged as scouts and outguards, but his offers had been rejected. Either from disgust or from being dismissed, almost all of the warriors disappeared from the camp.

Seeing the general's impatience at the non-arrival of conveyances, Washington again represented to him the difficulties in attempting to traverse the mountains with such a train of wheel-carriages; he recommended, from his own experience, the substitution, as much as possible, of packhorses. Braddock, however, was not to be swayed in his military operations by so green a counsellor. At length the general was relieved by the arrival of the horses and waggons which Franklin had undertaken to procure.

On the 10th of June, Braddock set off from Fort Cumberland with his aides-de-camp, others of his staff, and his body guard of light horse. Sir Peter Halket, with his brigade, had marched three days previously, and a detachment of 600 men, under Colonel Chapman, had been employed ten days in opening a road.

The march over the mountains proved, as Washington foretold, a "tremendous undertaking." It was with difficulty the heavily laden waggons could be dragged up the steep and rugged roads, often extending for three or four miles in a straggling line, with the soldiers so dispersed in guarding them that an attack would have thrown the whole in confusion. What outraged Washington was the great number of horses and waggons required by the officers for the transportation of their baggage, camp equipage, and articles of artificial necessity.

By the time the advanced corps had struggled over two mountains, through the intervening forest, and reached (16 June) the Little Meadows, Braddock had become aware of the difference between campaigning in a new country or on the old battle-grounds of Europe. He now, of his own accord, turned to Washington for advice. Thus called on, Washington gave his counsel with becoming modesty but with his accustomed clearness. There was an opportunity to strike an effective blow at Fort Duquesne but it might be lost by delay. The garrison, according to credible reports, was weak; large reinforcements and supplies would be detained by the drought, which rendered the river by which they must come low and unnavigable. He advised the general to divide his forces, leave one part to come on with the stores and baggage and cumbrous appurtenances of an army, and throw himself in the advance with the other part, composed of his choicest troops, lightened of every thing superfluous that might impede a rapid march.

His advice was adopted. Twelve hundred selected men, furnished with ten field-pieces, were to form the first division, their provisions and other necessaries to be carried on packhorses. The second division, with all the stores, munitions, and heavy baggage, was to be brought on by Colonel Dunbar.

The officers of the advance were still so encumbered with what they considered indispensable necessaries that out of 212 horses appropriated to their use not more than 12 could be spared by them for public service.

During the halt at the Little Meadows, Captain Jack and his band of forest rangers made their appearance in the camp, equipped with rifle, knife, hunting-shirts, leggings and moccasins looking like Indians as they issued from the woods. The captain asked an interview with the general. Braddock received him in his tent in his usual stiff and stately manner. The "Black Rifle" spoke of himself and his followers as men—inured to hardships and accustomed to deal with Indians—who preferred stealth and stratagem to open warfare. He requested his company should be employed as a reconnoitering party. Braddock, who had a sovereign contempt for the chivalry of the woods, replied that he had experienced troops on whom he could completely rely for all purposes.

Captain Jack withdrew, indignant at so haughty a reception, and informed his leathern-clad followers of his rebuff. They forthwith shouldered their rifles, turned their backs upon the camp, and departed for the usual scenes of their exploits, where men knew their value.

On the 19th of June Braddock's first division set out with less than 30 carriages, including those that transported ammunition for the artillery, all strongly horsed. Washington was disappointed in his anticipations of a rapid march. The general, though he had adopted his advice in the main, could not carry it out in detail. "I found," said Washington, "that instead of pushing on with vigor, . . . they were halting to level every mole hill and to erect bridges over every brook, by which means we were four days in getting twelve miles."

For several days Washington had suffered from fever, accompanied by intense headache, and his illness increased in violence to such a degree that he was unable to ride and had to be conveyed for a part of the time in a covered waggon. He was still unable to bear the jolting of the waggon but it needed an interposition of Braddock to bring him to a halt at the great crossings of the Youghiogeny. Here the general assigned him a guard, provided him with necessaries, and requested him to remain under care of Dr. Craik until the arrival of Dunbar's detachment, which was two days' march in the rear, giving him his word of honor that he should, at all events, be enabled to rejoin the main division before it reached the French fort.

Braddock, in the course of the first day (June 24), came to a deserted Indian camp; judging from the number of wigwams, there must have been about 170 warriors. The next day's march passed by the Great Meadows and Fort Necessity; several Indians were seen hovering in the woods and the light horse and Indian allies were sent out to surround them but did not succeed. The camp for the night was about two miles beyond Fort Necessity.

The following day (26th) there was a laborious march of but four miles owing to the difficulties of the road. The evening halt was at another deserted Indian camp, which the Indians and French, who were hovering about the army, had just left. A party was sent out with guides to follow their tracks and fall on them in the night but again without success.

On the 4th of July they encamped at Thicketty Run. The general now supposed himself to be within 30 miles of Fort Duquesne. He prevailed upon two Indians to scout in the direction of the fort and bring him intelligence; shortly after their departure, Christopher Gist, the resolute pioneer who acted as guide to the general, likewise set off as a scout.

The Indians returned on the 6th. They had been close to Fort Duquesne. There were no additional works there; there were few men to be seen, and few tracks of any; none of the passes between the camp and fort were occupied. Gist returned soon after them. His account corroborated theirs, but he had seen smoke in a valley between the camp and the fort, made probably by some scouting party. He had intended to prowl about the fort at night but had been discovered and narrowly escaped with his life.

We return now to Washington in his sick encampment at the banks of the Youghiogheny, where he was left repining at the departure of the troops without him. He now considered himself sufficiently recovered to rejoin the troops and his only anxiety was that he be able to do it in time for the great blow. He was rejoiced, therefore, on the 3d of July, by the arrival of an advanced party of 100 men convoying provisions. Still too weak to mount his horse, he set off with the escort in a covered waggon and, after a most fatiguing journey, reached Braddock's camp on the 8th of July. It was on the east side of the Monongahela, about 15 miles from Fort Duquesne.

Washington was just in time, for the attack upon Fort Duquesne was to be made on the following day. The fort stood on the same side of the Monongahela with the camp, but the narrow pass between them of about two miles, with the river on the left and a very high mountain on the right, was impassable for carriages. The route determined on was to cross the Monongahela by a ford opposite the camp, proceed along the west bank of the river for five miles, recross by another ford to the eastern side, and push on to the fort. The river at these fords was shallow and the banks were not steep.

According to the plan of arrangement, Gage, with the advance, was to cross the river before daybreak, march to the second ford, and, recrossing there, take post to secure the passage of the main force. The advance was to be composed of two companies of grenadiers, 160 infantry, the independent company of Gates, and two six-pounders.

Washington, who had already seen enough of regular troops to doubt their infallibility and who knew the dangerous nature of the ground they were to traverse, ventured to suggest that the Virginia rangers, being accustomed to the country and to Indian warfare, might be thrown in the advance. The proposition drew an angry reply from the general, indignant, very probably, that a young provincial officer should presume to school a veteran like himself.

Early next morning (July 9th), before daylight, Gage crossed with the advance. He was followed at some distance by St. Clair with a working party of 250 men to make roads for the artillery and baggage. They had with them their waggons of tools and two six-pounders.

By sunrise the main body turned out in full uniform. The officers were perfectly equipped. All looked as if arrayed for a fête rather than a battle. As it was supposed the enemy would be on the watch for the crossing of the troops, it had been agreed that they should do it in the greatest order, bayonets fixed, colors flying, and drums and fifes beating and playing. They accordingly made a gallant appearance as they forded the Monongahela and wound along its banks and through the open forests, gleaming and glittering in morning sunshine and stepping buoyantly to the Grenadier's march.

About noon they reached the second ford. Gage was on the opposite side of the Monongahela, posted according to orders; the second crossing took place, drums beating, fifes playing, and colors flying. When all had passed, there was again a halt until the general arranged the order of march.

First went the advance, under Gage, preceded by the engineers and guides and six light horsemen. Then, St. Clair and the working party with their waggons and the two six-pounders; on each side were thrown out four flanking parties. Then, at some distance, the general was to follow with the main body, the artillery and baggage preceded and flanked by light horse and squads of infantry; the Virginian and other provincial troops were to form the rear guard.

The ground before them was level until about half a mile from the river, where a rising ground, covered with long grass, low bushes, and scattered trees, sloped gently up to a range of hills. The whole country, generally speaking, was a forest with no clear opening but the road, which was about 12 feet wide and flanked by two ravines, concealed by trees and thickets.

Had Braddock been schooled in the warfare of the woods or had he adopted the suggestions of Washington, he would have thrown out Indian scouts or Virginia rangers in the advance and on the flanks, but, as has been sarcastically observed, he suffered his troops to march forward "as if in a review in St. James's Park."

It was now near two o'clock. The advanced party and the working party had crossed the plain and were ascending the rising ground. Braddock was about to follow with the main body and had given the word to march, when he heard quick and heavy firing in front. Washington, who was with the general, surmised that the evil he had apprehended had come to pass. For want of scouting parties ahead the advance parties were suddenly and warmly attacked.

Braddock ordered Lieutenant-colonel Burton to hasten to their assistance with the vanguard of the main body, 800 strong. The residue of 400 were halted and posted to protect the artillery and baggage.

The firing continued, with fearful yelling. There was a terrible uproar. By the general's orders an aide-de-camp spurred forward to bring him an account of the attack. Without waiting for his return the general himself, finding the turmoil increase, moved forward.

The van of the advance had indeed been taken by surprise. It was composed of two companies of carpenters or pioneers to cut the road and two flank companies of grenadiers to protect them. Suddenly the engineer who preceded them to mark out the road gave the alarm, "French and Indians!" There was sharp firing on both sides at first. Several of the enemy fell, among them their leader, but a murderous fire broke out from among trees and a ravine on the right and the woods resounded with unearthly whoops and yellings. The Indian rifle was at work. Most of the grenadiers and many of the pioneers were shot down. The survivors were driven in on the advance.

Gage ordered his men to fix bayonets and form in order of battle. They were more dismayed by the yells than by the rifles of the unseen savages, whose whereabouts were only known by their demoniac cries and the puffs of smoke from their rifles. All orders were unheeded; in their fright the soldiers shot at random, killing some of their own as they came running in. In a short time most of the officers and many of the men of the advance were killed or wounded. Gage himself received a wound. The advance fell back in dismay upon St. Clair's corps, which was equally dismayed. Burton had come up with the reinforcement and was forming his men to face the rising ground on the right, when both of the advanced detachments fell back upon him and all now was confusion.

By this time the general was upon the ground. He tried to rally the men. The colors were advanced in different places to separate the men of the two regiments. The general ordered the officers to form the men into small divisions and advance with them, but the soldiers could not be prevailed upon either by threats or entreaties. The Virginia troops, accustomed to the Indian mode of fighting, scattered themselves and took post behind trees, where they could pick off the lurking foe. In this way they, in some degree, protected the regulars. Washington advised Braddock to adopt the same plan with the regulars, but he persisted in forming them into platoons; consequently they were cut down from behind logs and trees as fast as they could advance.

Washington beheld with admiration those who, in the vain hope of inspiriting the men to drive off the enemy from the flanks and regain the cannon, would dash forward singly or in groups. They were invariably shot down, for the Indians aimed at every one on horseback or who appeared to have command.

Some were killed by random shot of their own men, who fired with affrighted rapidity but without aim. Soldiers in the front ranks were killed by those in the rear. Between friend and foe, the slaughter of the officers was terrible.

Throughout this disastrous day, Washington distinguished himself by his courage and presence of mind. His brother aids, Orme and Morris, were wounded early in the action and the whole duty of carrying the orders of the general devolved on him. His danger was imminent and incessant. He was in every part of the field, a conspicuous mark for the murderous rifle. Two horses were shot under him. Four bullets passed through his coat. His escape without a wound was almost miraculous. At one time he was sent to the main body to bring the artillery into action. All there was likewise in confusion; the men who should have served the guns were paralyzed. In his ardor, Washington sprang from his horse, wheeled and pointed a brass field-piece with his own hand and directed an effective discharge into the woods, but neither his efforts nor example were of avail. The men could not be kept to the guns.

Braddock still remained in the centre of the field in the desperate hope of retrieving the fortunes of the day. The Virginia rangers, who had been most efficient in covering his position, were nearly all killed or wounded. Many of his officers had been slain within his sight and still he kept his ground, vainly endeavoring to check the flight of his men or at least to effect their retreat in good order. At length a bullet passed through his right arm and lodged itself in his

Original in Possession of G.W.P. Custis Esq.

G. Washington

1772. Æt. 40.

NEW YORK. G.P. PUTNAM. & Cº

lungs. He fell from his horse but was caught by Captain Stewart of the Virginia guards, who, with the assistance of another American and a servant, placed him in a tumbril. It was with much difficulty they got him out of the field—in his despair he desired to be left there.

The rout now became complete. Baggage, stores, artillery, every thing was abandoned. The waggoners took each a horse out of his team and fled. The officers were swept off with the men in this headlong flight. It was rendered more precipitate by the shouts and yells of the savages, numbers of whom rushed forth and pursued the fugitives to the river side. Fortunately, the victors gave up the pursuit in their eagerness to collect the spoil.

The shattered army continued its flight after it had crossed the Monongahela, a wretched wreck of the brilliant little force that had recently gleamed along its banks, confident of victory. About 100 men were brought to a halt about a quarter of a mile from the ford of the river. Braddock still had a faint hope of being able to keep possession of the ground until reinforced. Most of the men were stationed in a very advantageous spot about 200 yards from the road and Burton posted out small parties and sentinels. Before an hour had elapsed most of the men had stolen off. Deserted, Braddock and his officers continued their retreat; he would have mounted his horse but was unable and had to be carried by soldiers. Orme and Morris were placed on litters borne by horses. They were subsequently joined by Gage with 80 men whom he had rallied.

Washington, in the mean time, notwithstanding his weak state, was sent to Dunbar's camp 40 miles distant with orders for him to hurry forward provisions, hospital stores, and waggons for the wounded under the escort of two grenadier companies. It was a hard and a melancholy ride throughout the night and the following day. The tidings of the defeat preceded him, borne by the waggoners who had fled from the field of battle. They had arrived, haggard, at Dunbar's camp at midday; panic fell upon the camp. Many of the soldiers, waggoners and attendants, took to flight, but most of them were forced back by the sentinels.

Washington arrived at the camp in the evening and found the agitation still prevailing. The orders which he brought were executed during the night and he was in the saddle early in the morning accompanying the convoy of supplies. At Gist's plantation, about 13 miles off, he met Gage and his scanty force escorting Braddock and his wounded officers. Stewart and a sad remnant of the Virginia light horse still accompanied the general as his guard. There was a halt of one day at Dunbar's camp for the repose and relief of the wounded. On the 13th they resumed their melancholy march and that night reached the Great Meadows.

The proud spirit of Braddock was broken by his defeat. He died on the night of the 13th, at the Great Meadows. The chaplain having been wounded, Washington read the funeral service. All was done in sadness, without parade so as not to attract the attention of lurking savages who might discover and outrage his grave.

Reproach spared him not, even when in his grave. The failure of the expedition was attributed to his obstinacy, technical pedantry, and military conceit. He had been warned to be on his guard against ambush and surprise but without avail.

Still, whatever may have been his faults and errors, he expiated them by the hardest lot that can befall a brave soldier, ambitious of renown—an unhonored grave in a strange land, a memory clouded by misfortune, and a name for ever coupled with defeat.

The obsequies of the unfortunate Braddock being finished, the escort continued its retreat with the sick and wounded. On the 17th, the sad cavalcade reached the Fort Cumberland and were relieved from the incessant apprehension of pursuit. Dunbar arrived shortly afterward with the remainder of the army.

The true reason why the enemy did not pursue the retreating army was not known until some time afterwards and added to the disgrace of the defeat. They were not the main force of the French but a mere detachment of 855 regulars, Canadians, and Indians, that had sallied forth to form an ambush and give check to the enemy. Such was the scanty force which the imagination of the panic-stricken army had magnified into a great host and from which they had fled in breathless terror, abandoning the whole frontier.

The affair of Braddock remains a memorable event in American history and has been characterized as "the farthest flight ever made." It struck a fatal blow to the deference for British prowess. "This whole transaction," observes Franklin, "gave us the first suspicion that our exalted ideas of the prowess of British regular troops had not been well founded."

(CHAPTER 4)

Washington arrived at Mount Vernon on the 26th of July, still in feeble condition from his long illness. The martial spirit still burned within him. His connection with the army ceased at the death of Braddock, but his military duties continued as adjutant-general of the northern division of the province. He immediately issued orders for the county lieutenants to hold the militia in readiness because of the present defenceless state of the frontier. Tidings of the rout and retreat of the army had spread consternation throughout the country. Immediate incursions were apprehended and volunteer companies began to form to march across the mountains to the scene of danger.

On the 4th of August, Dinwiddie convened the Assembly to devise measures for the public safety. Danger had quickened the slow patriotism of the burgesses; supplies and funds were promptly voted and orders issued for raising a regiment of 1000 men.

Washington's friends urged him to present himself at Williamsburg as a candidate for the command. With mingled modesty and pride, Washington declined to be a solicitor. The only terms, he said, on which he would accept command were a certainty as to rank and emoluments, a right to appoint his field officers, and the supply of a sufficient military chest.

While this was in agitation, he received letters from his mother imploring him not to risk himself in these frontier wars. His answer was characteristic, blending the filial deference with which he was accustomed from childhood to treat her with a calm patriotism of the Roman stamp. If "the command is pressed upon me by the general voice of the country and offered upon such terms as cannot be objected against, it would reflect dishonor on me to refuse it; and that, I am sure, must, and ought, to give you greater uneasiness, than my going in an honorable command. . . . At present I have no proposals made to me, nor have I any advice of such an intention, except from private hands."

On the very day this letter was despatched (Aug. 14), he received his appointment to the command on the terms specified in his letters to his friends. His commission nominated him commander-in-chief of all the forces raised, or to be raised in the colony. The officers next in command under him were Lieutenant-colonel Adam Stephens and Major Andrew Lewis.

It is worthy of note that the early popularity of Washington was not the result of brilliant achievements; on the contrary, it rose among trials and reverses and may almost be said to have been the fruit of defeats. The sterling, enduring, but undazzling qualities of Washington were early discerned though only heralded by misfortunes; the admirable manner in which he conducted himself under misfortune and the sagacity and practical wisdom he had displayed on all occasions were universally acknowledged.

Having held a conference with Dinwiddie at Williamsburg and received his instructions, Washington repaired on the 14th of September to Winchester, where he fixed his head-quarters. Washington now informed himself of the fate of the other enterprises included in this year's plan of military operations.

The defeat of Braddock paralyzed the expedition against Niagara. Many of Shirley's troops, assembled at Albany, struck with the consternation caused throughout the country, deserted. It was the end of August before Shirley was in force at Oswego. Time was lost in building boats for the lake; storms and head winds ensued; then sickness. Deferring completion of the enterprise until the following year, Shirley returned to Albany with the main part of his forces, leaving about 700 men at Oswego.

To Johnson had been confided the expedition against Crown Point, on Lake Champlain. Preparations were made for it in Albany, whence the troops were to march and the artillery, ammunition, and stores to be conveyed up the Hudson to the carrying-place, between that river and Lake George. At the carrying-place a fort was commenced, subsequently called Fort Edward. Part of the troops remained to complete and garrison it; the main force proceeded under Johnson to Lake George, the plan being to descend that lake to Ticonderoga. Johnson encamped at the south end of the lake having with him about 6000 troops of New York and New England and a host of Mohawk warriors loyally devoted to him.

It so happened that a French force of 3000 men, under the Baron de Dieskau, had recently arrived at Montreal. The baron sent forward 700 of his troops when news arrived of the army gathering on Lake George for the attack on Crown Point, perhaps for an inroad into Canada. The baron took post at Crown Point for its defence. Beside his regular troops, he had with him 800 Canadians, and 700 Indians of different tribes.

On the 7th of September, Indian scouts brought word to Johnson that they had discovered three roads made through the forests toward Fort Edward. About midnight came other scouts, reporting the French within four miles of the carrying-place. In the morning, Colonel Williams was detached with 1000 men and 200 Indians to intercept the enemy. Within two hours after their departure a heavy fire of musketry told of a warm encounter. The firing grew nearer and nearer. In a short time fugitives made their appearance, flying in confusion. Consternation seized upon the camp, especially when the French emerged from the forest in battle array, led by Dieskau. The camp might have been carried by assault, but the Canadians and Indians held back. The baron was left with his regulars (200 grenadiers) in front of the camp. The camp, having recovered from its panic, opened a fire of musketry. The engagement became general. The action slackened on the part of the French until, after a long contest, they gave way. Johnson's men and Indians leaped over the breastwork and a medley fight ensued that ended in the slaughter, rout, or capture of the enemy.

Johnson did not follow up the victory, alleging that it was first necessary to build a fort at his encampment to keep up communication with Albany and that, by the time this was completed, it would be too late to advance against Crown Point. He accordingly erected a stockaded fort, which received the name of William Henry, and, having garrisoned it, returned to Albany.

Experience had convinced Washington of the inefficiency of the militia laws and he set about effecting a reformation. Through his efforts an act was passed in the Virginia Legislature giving prompt operation to courts-martial; punishing insubordination, mutiny and desertion with adequate severity; strengthening the authority of a commander to enable him to enforce discipline and to avail himself in emergency of the means and services of individuals.

This being effected, he proceeded to fill up his companies and to enforce this newly-defined authority within his camp. His men were instructed, not merely in regular tactics, but in all the strategy of Indian warfare—a knowledge indispensable in the wars of the wilderness. Stockaded forts were constructed as places of refuge and defence in exposed neighborhoods. A shorter and better road was opened between Winchester and Cumberland for the transmission of reinforcements and supplies.

His exertions, however, were impeded by one of those questions of precedence arising from the difference between crown and provincial commissions. Maryland raised a small militia force and stationed Captain Dagworthy, with a company of 30 men at Fort Cumberland, which stood within that province. Dagworthy had served in Canada in the preceding war and had received a king's commission. He now refused to obey the orders of any officer however high his rank, who merely held his commission from a governor.

Washington intimated that, if the commander-in-chief of the forces of Virginia must yield precedence to a Maryland captain of 30 men, he should have to resign his commission. It was determined to refer the matter to Major-general Shirley, who had succeeded Braddock in general command of the colonies. For this purpose Washington was to go to Boston, obtain a decision from Shirley of the point in dispute and a general regulation by which these difficulties could be prevented in future.

The mission to Shirley was successful as to the question of rank.

Engraved by H.B.Hall.

MISS MARY PHILIPSE.

From the original picture in the possession of Frederic Philipse Esq.

NEW YORK. G.P.PUTNAM & CO.

A written order from the commander-in-chief determined that Dagworthy was entitled to the rank of a provincial captain only and must give precedence to Colonel Washington as a provincial field officer. The latter was disappointed, however, in the hope of getting himself and his officers put upon the regular establishment, with commissions from the king, and had to remain subjected to questions of rank when serving with regular troops.

From Shirley he learnt that the main objects of the ensuing campaign would be the reduction of Fort Niagara, so as to cut off the communication between Canada and Louisiana; the capture of Ticonderoga and Crown Point, as a measure of safety for New York; the besieging of Fort Duquesne and the menacing of Quebec by a body of troops which were to advance by the Kennebec River.

The official career of Shirley was drawing to a close. He was recalled to England and was to be superseded by General Abercrombie, who was coming with two regiments. General command in America, however, was to be held by the Earl of Loudoun, who was invested with powers almost equal to those of a viceroy, being placed above all the colonial governors. Beside his general command, the Earl of Loudoun was to be governor of Virginia and colonel of a royal American regiment of four battalions, to be raised in the colonies but furnished with officers who had seen foreign service. The campaign would open on his arrival early in the spring.

Washington remained ten days in Boston, after which he returned to New York. Tradition gives very different motives from those of business for his sojourns in the latter city. He found there an early friend and school-mate, Beverly Robinson, who was living happily with a young and wealthy bride, having married one of the nieces and heiresses of Adolphus Philipse, a rich landholder whose manor-house is still to be seen on the banks of the Hudson. At the house of Robinson, Washington met Mary Philipse, sister and co-heiress of Mrs. Robinson, a young lady whose personal attractions rivalled her reputed wealth. A life passed for the most part in the wilderness and on the frontier, far from female society, had made him more sensible, in the present brief interval of gay and social life, to the attractions of an elegant woman brought up in the polite circle of New York. That he was an open admirer of Miss Philipse is an historical fact; that he sought her hand but was refused is traditional and not very probable. He may have been diffident in urging his suit with a lady accustomed to the homage of society and surrounded by admirers. The most probable version is, that he was called away by his duties before he had made sufficient siege of the lady's heart to warrant a summons to surrender.

In the latter part of March we find him at Williamsburg, attending the opening of the Legislature of Virginia, eager to promote measures for the protection of the frontier and the capture of Fort Duquesne. While thus engaged, he received a letter from a friend in New York, warning him to hasten back to that city before it was too late, as Captain Morris, his fellow aide-de-camp under Braddock, was laying close siege to Miss Philipse. Sterner alarms, however, summoned him in another direction. Expresses from Winchester brought word that the French had made another sortie from Fort Duquesne, accompanied by savages, and were spreading terror and desolation through the country. In this moment of exigency all softer claims were forgotten. Washington repaired in all haste to his post at Winchester and Morris was left to urge his suit unrivalled and carry off the prize.

Report had not exaggerated the troubles of the frontier. It was marauded by merciless bands of savages, led in some instances by Frenchmen. Travellers were murdered, farm-houses burnt down, and families butchered. The marauders had crossed the mountains and penetrated the valley of the Shenandoah; several persons had fallen beneath the tomahawk in the neighborhood of Winchester.

Washington, on his arrival at Winchester, found the inhabitants in great dismay. He resolved immediately to organize a force, partly of troops from Fort Cumberland, partly of militia from Winchester and its vicinity; to put himself at its head and "scour the woods and suspected places in all the mountains and valleys of this part of the frontier, in quest of the Indians and their more cruel associates."

He accordingly despatched an express to Fort Cumberland with orders for a detachment from the garrison; "but how," said he, "are men to be raised at Winchester, since orders are no longer regarded in the county?"

Lord Fairfax and other militia officers advised that each captain call a private muster of his men and read them an appeal to their patriotism and fears and a summons to assemble on the 15th of April to enroll themselves for the projected mountain foray.

This measure was adopted, but, when the day of enrolment arrived, not more that 15 men appeared upon the ground. In the mean time the express returned with sad accounts from Fort Cumberland. No troops could be furnished from that quarter. The garrison was scarcely strong enough for self-defence, having sent out detachments in different directions.

An attack on Winchester was apprehended, and the terrors of the people rose to agony. They now turned to Washington as their main hope. The youthful commander looked round on the suppliant crowd with a countenance beaming with pity and a heart wrung with anguish. A letter to Dinwiddie shows the conflict of his feelings. "I am too little acquainted with pathetic language to attempt a description of these people's distresses. But what can I do? I see their situation; I know their danger and participate their sufferings without having it in my power to give them further relief than uncertain promises."

The letter drew from the governor an instant order for a militia force from the upper counties to his assistance, but the Virginia newspapers, in descanting on the frontier troubles, threw discredit on the army and its officers and attached blame to its commander. Stung to the quick by this injustice, Washington publicly declared that nothing but the imminent danger of the times prevented him from instantly resigning a command from which he could never reap either honor or benefit. His sensitiveness called forth strong letters from his friends, assuring him of the high sense entertained at the seat of government and elsewhere of his merits and services.

The Legislature, too, began at length to act, but timidly and inefficiently. The measure of relief voted by the Assembly was an additional appropriation of 20,000 pounds and an increase of the provincial force to 1500 men. With this, it was proposed to erect and garrison a chain of frontier forts, extending through the ranges of the Allegany Mountains, from the Potomac to the borders of North Carolina, a distance of about 400 miles.

Washington, in letters to the governor and to the speaker of the House of Burgesses, urged the impolicy of such a plan with their actual force and means. It was evident, observed he, that to garrison properly such a line of forts would require at least 2000 men. And even then, a line of such extent might be broken through at one end before the other end could yield assistance. Then must be taken into consideration the immense cost of building so many forts and the constant expense of supplies and transportation.

His idea of a defensive plan was to build a strong fort at Winchester, the central point, where all the main roads met of a wide range of scattered settlements whence reinforcements and supplies could most readily be forwarded. Beside this, he would have three or four large fortresses at convenient distances upon the frontier, with powerful garrisons, so as to be able to throw out strong scouting parties to range the country.

These suggestions, as well as others concerned with the discipline and control of the militia, were repeatedly urged upon Dinwiddie with very little effect. The plan of a frontier line of 23 forts was persisted in. Fort Cumberland was pertinaciously kept up at a great and useless expense of men and money, and the militia laws remained lax and inefficient. It was decreed, however, that the great central fort at Winchester recommended by Washington should be erected.

About the beginning of May, scouts brought word that the tracks of the marauding savages tended toward Fort Duquesne, as if on the return. In a little while it was ascertained that they had recrossed the Allegany Mountain to the Ohio and the state of alarm was over.

The repeated inroads of the savages called for an effectual and permanent check. The beautiful valley of the Shenandoah was fast becoming a deserted and a silent place. Her people, for the most part, had fled to the older settlements south of the mountains and the Blue Ridge was likely soon to become virtually the frontier line of the province.

Throughout the summer of 1756 Washington exerted himself diligently in carrying out measures determined upon for frontier security. The fortress at Winchester was commenced; it received the name of Fort Loudoun in honor of the commander-in-chief whose arrival in Virginia was hopefully anticipated. As to the sites of the frontier posts, they were decided upon by Washington and his officers after consultations; parties were sent out to work on them and men recruited and militia drafted to garrison them. Washington visited occasionally such as were in progress and near at hand.

In the autumn, he made a tour of inspection along the whole line, accompanied by his friend, Captain Hugh Mercer. This tour furnished repeated proofs of the inefficiency of the militia system. The garrisons were weak for want of men, but more so from indolence and irregularity. None were in a posture of defence; few but might be surprised with the greatest ease.

Washington had repeatedly urged the abandonment of Fort Cumberland as a place of frontier deposit, being within the bounds of another province and out of the track of Indian incursion, so that often the alarm would not reach there until after the mischief had been effected. Governor Dinwiddie, taking offence at some of Washington's comments on the military affairs of the frontier, made the stand of a self-willed and obstinate man in the case of Fort Cumberland. He represented it in such light to Lord Loudoun as to draw from his lordship an order that it should be kept up.

Dinwiddie went so far as to order that the garrisons should be withdrawn from the stockades and small frontier forts, and most of the troops from Winchester, to strengthen Fort Cumberland, which was now to become head-quarters—thus weakening the most important places to concentrate a force where it was not wanted and would be out of the way in most cases of alarm. By these meddlesome moves, all previous arrangements were reversed, every thing was thrown into confusion, and enormous losses and expenses were incurred.

While these events were occurring on the Virginia frontier, military affairs went on tardily at the north. The campaign against Canada, which was to have opened early in the year, hung fire. The armament coming out for the purpose, under Lord Loudoun, was delayed through the want of energy and union in the British cabinet. Abercrombie, who was to be next in command to his lordship, set sail for New York with two regiments but did not reach Albany, the head-quarters of military operation, until the 25th of June. He billeted his soldiers upon the town, much to the disgust of the inhabitants, and talked of ditching and stockading it.

On the 12th of July, came word that the forts Ontario and Oswego were menaced by the French. Imperfectly constructed and insufficiently garrisoned, they contained a great amount of stores and protected vessels on Lake Ontario.

Major-general Webb was ordered by Abercrombie to hold himself in readiness to march with one regiment to the relief of these forts but received no further orders. Every thing awaited the arrival at Albany of Loudoun, which at length took place, on the 29th of July. There were now at least 10,000 troops at Albany, yet relief to Oswego was still delayed. After much debate, it was agreed that Webb should march to the relief of Oswego. He left Albany on the 12th of August, but had scarce reached the carrying-place when he received news that Oswego was reduced and its garrison captured. While the British commanders had debated, Field-marshal the Marquis De Montcalm, newly arrived from France, had acted. He was a different kind of soldier from Abercrombie or Loudoun. Quick in thought, quick in speech, quicker still in action, he moved with a celerity and secrecy that completely baffled his slow and pondering antagonists. Crown Point and Ticonderoga were visited and steps taken to strengthen their works. Then hastening to Montreal, he put himself at the head of a force that ascended the St. Lawrence to Lake Ontario; he blocked the mouth of the Oswego by his vessels, landed his guns, and besieged the two forts; he drove the garrison out of one into the other and compelled the garrisons to surrender. His blow achieved, Montcalm returned in triumph to Montreal.

The season was now too far advanced for Loudoun to enter upon any great military enterprise; he postponed, therefore, the great Northern campaign until the following year, returned to New York, and went into comfortable winter quarters.

Circumstances had led Washington to think that Loudoun "had received impressions to his prejudice by false representations of facts" and that a wrong idea prevailed at head-quarters respecting the state of military affairs in Virginia. He was anxious, therefore, for an opportunity of placing all these matters in a proper light; understanding that there was to be a meeting in Philadelphia in March between Loudoun and the southern governors, he wrote to Dinwiddie for permission to attend it.

"I cannot conceive," writes Dinwiddie in reply, "what service you can be of in going there, as the plan concerted will, in course, be communicated to you and the other officers. However, as you seem so earnest to go, I now give you leave."

About a month before the time of the meeting, Washington addressed a letter to his lordship, explanatory of affairs in the quarter he commanded. In this he set forth the defects in the militia laws of Virginia, the errors in its system of defence, and the inevitable confusion which had thence resulted. The manner in which Washington was received by Loudoun in Philadelphia, showed him that his letter had produced the desired effect and that his character and conduct were justly appreciated. During his sojourn in Philadelphia he was frequently consulted on points of frontier service and his advice was generally adopted. His representations with respect to Fort Cumberland had the desired effect in counteracting the intermeddling of Dinwiddie. The Virginia troops and stores were ordered to be removed to Fort Loudoun, at Winchester, which once more became head-quarters, while Fort Cumberland was left to be occupied by a Maryland garrison.

The great plan of operations at the north was again doomed to failure. The reduction of Crown Point, on Lake Champlain, which had long been meditated, was laid aside and the capture of Louisburg substituted as of far greater importance. This was a place of great consequence, situated on the isle of Cape Breton and strongly fortified. It commanded the fisheries of Newfoundland, overawed New England, and was a main bulwark to Acadia.

In the course of July, Loudoun set sail for Halifax with about 6000 men to join with Admiral Holbourne, who had just arrived at that port with ships of the the line and a fleet of transports, having on board 6000 men. With this united force Loudoun anticipated the capture of Louisburg.

Scarce had the tidings of his lordship's departure reached Canada than Montcalm took the field. Fort William Henry, on the southern shore of Lake George, was his object; it commanded the lake and was an important protection to the British frontier. A brave officer, Colonel Monro, with about 500 men, formed the garrison; more than three times that number of militia were intrenched near by. Montcalm, with nearly 8000 men, advanced up the lake on the 1st of August in a fleet of boats with swarms of Indian canoes in the advance. A summons to surrender was answered by a brave defiance. For five days its commander kept up a defence, trusting to receive assistance from Webb, who was at Fort Edward, about 15 miles distant, with upwards of 5000 men. Instead, Webb sent him a letter advising him to capitulate. The obstinate old soldier, however, persisted in his defence, until most of his cannon were burst and his ammunition expended. At length, he hung out a flag of truce and obtained honorable terms. Montcalm demolished the fort; having completed his destruction of the British defences on this frontier, he returned in triumph to Canada.

Loudoun, in the mean time, formed his junction with Holbourne at Halifax and the troops were embarked with all diligence. The French were again too quick for them. Admiral De Bois de la Mothe had arrived at Louisburg, with a large naval and land force; the place was well fortified, supplied, and garrisoned. Loudoun, aware of the probability of defeat and the disgrace and ruin it would bring upon British arms in America, wisely, though ingloriously, returned to New York.

During these unfortunate operations to the north, Washington was stationed at Winchester, shorn of part of his force by the detachment to South Carolina, and left with 700 men to defend a frontier 350 miles in extent. The capture of Oswego by Montcalm had produced a disastrous effect. The whole country of the five nations was abandoned to the French. The frontiers of Pennsylvania, Maryland, and Virginia were harassed by repeated inroads of French and Indians. The year wore away on Washington's part in defending a wide frontier with an insufficient and badly organized force. The vexations he experienced were heightened by continual misunderstandings with Dinwiddie, who was evidently actuated by the petty pique of a narrow and illiberal mind, impatient of contradiction even when in error. He took advantage of his official station to gratify his petulance in a variety of ways; it may excite a smile at present to find Washington charged by this small-minded man with looseness in his way of writing to him, with remissness in his duty towards him, and even with impertinence in the able representations he felt compelled to make of mismanagement in military affairs.

The multiplied vexations which Washington experienced from Dinwiddie preyed upon his spirits and contributed, with his incessant toils and anxieties, to undermine his health. For some time he struggled with repeated attacks of dysentery and fever, but continued in the exercise of his duties. Only the increased violence of his malady and the urgent advice of Dr. Craik induced him to relinquish his post towards the end of the year and retire to Mount Vernon.

The administration of Dinwiddie was now at an end. He set sail for England in January, 1758, very little regretted, excepting by his hangers-on. He was a sordid, narrow-minded, arrogant man, prone to meddle with matters of which he was profoundly ignorant and absurdly unwilling to have his ignorance enlightened.

(C H A P T E R 5)

For several months, Washington was afflicted by his malady, accompanied by symptoms indicative, as he thought, of a decline. A gradual improvement in his health, however, encouraged him to continue in what really was his favorite career and at the beginning of April he was again in command at Fort Loudoun.

The general aspect of affairs was more animating. Under the administration of William Pitt, who had control of the British cabinet, an effort was made to retrieve the disgraces of the late American campaign and to carry on the war with greater vigor. The instructions for a common fund were discontinued; there was no more talk of taxation by Parliament. Lord Loudoun, from whom so much had been anticipated, had been relieved from a command in which he had attempted much and done so little. On the return of his lordship to England, general command in America devolved on Abercrombie and the forces were divided into three bodies: one, under Major-general Amherst, was to operate in the north with the fleet under Boscawen for the reduction of Louisburg and the island of Cape Breton; another, under Abercrombie himself, was to proceed against Ticonderoga and Crown Point; the third, under Brigadier-general Forbes, who had charge of the middle and southern colonies, was to undertake the reduction of Fort Duquesne. The colonial troops were to be supplied, like the regulars, with arms, ammunition, tents, and provisions at the expense of government but clothed and paid by the colonies. The provincial officers, appointed by the governors and of no higher rank than colonel, were to be equal in command when united in service with those who held direct from the king. By these wise provisions of Pitt, a fertile cause of dissension was removed. It was with the greatest satisfaction Washington saw his favorite measure at last adopted, the reduction of Fort Duquesne; and he resolved to continue in the service until that object was accomplished.

Washington still was commander-in-chief of the Virginia troops, now augmented by an act of the Assembly to two regiments of 1000 men each, one led by himself and the other by Colonel Byrd, the whole to make a part of the army of Forbes in the expedition against Fort Duquesne.

Before we narrate the expedition against Fort Duquesne we will briefly notice the conduct of the two other expeditions, first that against Louisburg and the Island of Cape Breton.

Amherst, who conducted this expedition, embarked with about 12,000 men in the fleet of Admiral Boscawen and set sail about the end of May from Halifax. Along with him went Brigadier-general James Wolfe, an officer young in years, destined to gain an almost romantic celebrity.

On the 2d of June, the fleet arrived at the Bay of Gabarus, seven miles west of Louisburg. The latter place was garrisoned by 2500 regulars and 300 militia, subsequently reinforced by 400 Canadians and Indians. In the harbor were six ships of the line, and five frigates, three of which were sunk across the mouth. For several days the troops were prevented from landing by boisterous weather and a heavy surf.

On the 8th of June, preparations for landing were made before daybreak. The surf still ran high; the enemy opened a fire of cannon and musketry from their batteries, but Wolfe pushed forward, stormed the enemy's breastworks and batteries and drove them from the shore. The other two divisions also effected a landing after severe conflict; artillery and stores were brought on shore and Louisburg was formally invested.

The weather continued boisterous; the heavy cannon and the munitions necessary for a siege were landed with difficulty. Amherst made his approaches slowly, securing his camp by redoubts and epaulements. The Chevalier Drucour, who commanded at Louisburg, prepared for a desperate defence.

The brave Drucour kept up the defence until all his ships were either taken or destroyed, 40 out of 52 pieces of cannon dismounted, and his works mere heaps of ruins. Threatened with a general assault by sea and land, he determined to abide it rather than submit to humiliation. The prayers and petitions of the inhabitants, however, overcame his obstinacy. The place was surrendered and he and his garrison became prisoners of war.

The second expedition was against the French forts on Lakes George and Champlain. At the beginning of July, Abercrombie was encamped at Lake George with about 7000 regulars and about 9000 provincials. Major Israel Putnam of Connecticut had been detached with a scouting party to reconnoitre the neighborhood. After his return and report, Abercrombie prepared to proceed against Ticonderoga.

On the 5th of July, the forces, embarked in a flotilla of whale boats, batteaux, and rafts, proceeded down the lake with banners and pennons fluttering in the summer breeze, arms glittering in the sunshine, and martial music echoing along the wood-clad mountains. The next day they landed on the western shore at the entrance of the strait leading to Lake Champlain. Here they were formed into three columns and pushed forward.

Lord Howe urged on with the van of the centre column until they came upon a detachment of the retreating foe. A severe conflict ensued but Lord Howe, who gallantly led the van, was killed at the onset. The enemy were routed. Abercrombie fell back to the landing-place. The next day he sent out a strong detachment to secure a saw-mill which the enemy had abandoned. This done, he followed on the same evening with the main forces and took post at the mill, within two miles of the fort.

Montcalm was strongly posted behind deep intrenchments and breastworks 8 feet high, and with felled trees in front of his lines, presenting a horrid barrier with their jagged boughs pointing outward. Abercrombie was deceived as to the strength of the French works. Against the opinion of his most judicious officers, he gave orders to storm the works. Repeated assaults were made, and as often repelled, with dreadful havoc. After four hours of desperate and fruitless fighting, Abercrombie gave up the ill-judged attempt and withdrew once more to the landing-place. Abercrombie had still nearly four times the number of the enemy and all the means of carrying on a siege but the failure of this rash assault seems completely to have dismayed him. The next day he re-embarked all his troops and returned across that lake.

While the general was planning fortifications on Lake George, Colonel Bradstreet obtained permission to carry into effect an expedition which he had for some time meditated: to reduce Fort Frontenac, the stronghold of the French on the north side of the entrance of Lake Ontario, commanding the mouth of the St. Lawrence. Bradstreet, pushing his way along the valley of the Mohawk, arrived at Oswego, where he embarked and crossed Lake Ontario, landing within a mile of Frontenac, at the head of 3000 men. The fort, though a place of importance, was garrisoned by merely 110 men and a few Indians. These either fled or surrendered. In the fort was an immense amount of stores. In the harbor were nine armed vessels, the whole of the enemy's shipping on the lake. Two of these Bradstreet freighted with spoils of the fort; the others he destroyed.

Then, having dismantled the fortifications and laid waste every thing he could not carry away, he returned with his troops to the army on Lake George.

Operations went on slowly in that part of the campaign in which Washington was engaged—the expedition against Fort Duquesne. Forbes, who was commander-in-chief, was detained at Philadelphia by those delays and cross-purposes incident to military affairs in a new country. Colonel Bouquet, who was to command the advanced division, took his station with a corps of regulars at Raystown in the centre of Pennsylvania. There slowly assembled troops from various parts: 3000 Pennsylvanians, 1250 South Carolinians, and a few hundred men from elsewhere.

Washington, in the mean time, gathered together his scattered regiment at Winchester and diligently disciplined his recruits. He had two Virginia regiments under him, amounting, when complete, to about 1900 men. Seven hundred Indian warriors, also, came into his camp, lured by the prospect of a successful campaign. The force thus assembling was in want of arms, tents, field-equipage, and almost every requisite. Washington was ordered by Sir John St. Clair to repair to Williamsburg and lay the case before the council.

It proved an eventful journey, though not in a military point of view. In crossing a ferry of the Pamunkey, he fell in company with a Mr. Chamberlayne, who lived in the neighborhood and who, in the spirit of Virginian hospitality, claimed him as a guest.

Among the guests at Chamberlayne's was a young and blooming widow, Martha Custis, daughter of John Dandridge, both patrician names in the province. Her husband, John Parke Custis, had been dead three years, leaving her with two young children and a large fortune. She was extremely well shaped, with an agreeable countenance, dark hazel eyes and hair, and those frank, engaging manners so captivating in Southern women. With all his gravity and reserve, he was quickly susceptible to female charms; they may have had a greater effect upon him in fleeting moments snatched from the cares and perplexities of frontier warfare. At any rate, his heart appears to have been taken by surprise.

The dinner seemed all too short. For once Washington loitered in the path of duty, and it was not until the next morning that he was again in the saddle, spurring for Williamsburg. Happily, the residence of Mrs. Custis, was at no great distance from that city so that he had opportunities of visiting her in the intervals of business. His time for courtship, however, was brief. Military duties called him back to Winchester, but he feared some enterprising rival might supplant him during his absence, as in the case of Miss Philipse at New York. He improved, therefore, his brief opportunity to the utmost. Before they separated, they had mutually plighted their faith and the marriage was to take place as soon as the campaign against Fort Duquesne was at an end.

On arriving at Winchester, he found his troops restless and discontented from prolonged inaction, the inhabitants impatient of the burdens imposed on them and of the disturbances of an idle camp, while the Indians had deserted outright. It was a great relief, therefore, when he received orders to repair to Fort Cumberland. He arrived there on the 2d of July, and proceeded to open a road between that post and headquarters, at Raystown, thirty miles distant.

His troops were scantily supplied with regimental clothing. The weather was oppressively warm. He now conceived the idea of equipping them in the light Indian hunting garb and even of adopting it himself. Two companies were accordingly equipped in this style and sent under the command of Major Lewis to head-quarters. The experiment was successful. Such was probably the origin of the American rifle dress, afterwards so much worn in warfare.

The army was now annoyed by scouting parties of Indians hovering about the neighborhood. Washington sent out counter-parties of Cherokees. Bouquet required that each party be accompanied by an officer and a number of white men. Washington complied with the order though he considered them an encumbrance rather than an advantage. With all his efforts he was never able fully to make the officers of the regular army appreciate the importance of Indian allies in these campaigns in the wilderness.

On the other hand, he earnestly discountenanced a proposition of Bouquet to make an irruption into the enemy's country with a strong party of regulars. Such a detachment, he observed, could not be sent without a train of supplies, which would discover it to the enemy; the enterprise would terminate in a miscarriage if not in the destruction of the party.

As Washington intended to retire from military life at the close of this campaign, he proposed himself to the electors of Frederick County as their representative in the House of Burgesses. The election was coming on at Winchester; Bouquet gave him leave of absence, but he declined to absent himself from his post for the promotion of his political interests. There were three competitors in the field, yet he was elected by a large majority.

On the 21st of July arrived tidings of the brilliant success of the campaign conducted by Amherst and Boscawen, who had reduced Louisburg and gained possession of the Island of Cape Breton. This intelligence increased Washington's impatience at the delays of the expedition with which he was connected. Perhaps a desire for distinction in the eyes of the lady of his choice may have been at the bottom of this impatience, for he kept up a constant correspondence with her throughout the campaign.

Understanding that the commander-in-chief had some thoughts of throwing a body of light troops in the advance, he wrote to Bouquet, earnestly soliciting his influence to have himself and his Virginia regiment included in the detachment.

He learned to his surprise, however, that the road to which his men were accustomed and which had been worked by Braddock's troops was not to be taken in the present expedition, but a new one opened from Raystown to Fort Duquesne, on the track generally taken by northern traders. He instantly commenced remonstrances on the subject, representing that Braddock's road only needed partial repairs and that an army could reach Fort Duquesne by that route in 34 days, whereas opening a new road across mountains, swamps, and through a densely wooded country would detain them so late that the season would be over before they could reach the scene of action. His representations were of no avail. This route, therefore, to the great regret of Washington, was adopted, and men were thrown in the advance from Raystown to work upon it.

The first of September found Washington still encamped at Fort Cumberland, his troops sickly and dispirited, and the expedition dwindling down into a tedious operation of road-making. At length, in September, he received orders from Forbes to join him with his troops at Raystown. That commander, who always treated Washington's opinions with the greatest deference, adopted a plan drawn out by Washington for the march of the army and an order of battle which furnishes proof of his skill in frontier warfare.

It was now the middle of September; yet the great body of men engaged in opening the new military road, after incredible toil, had not advanced above 45 miles, to Loyal Hannan. Bouquet, who commanded the division of nearly 2000 men sent forward to open this road, halted at Loyal Hannan to establish a military post and deposit.

He was 50 miles from Fort Duquesne and was tempted to adopt the measure so strongly discountenanced by Washington of sending a party on a foray into the enemy's country. He accordingly detached Major Grant with 800 picked men with instructions merely to reconnoitre the country in the neighborhood of Fort Duquesne and ascertain the strength and position of the enemy. Grant conducted the enterprise with foolhardiness. He ordered the reveille to be beaten in the morning in several places; then, he marshalled his regulars in battle array and sent an engineer, with a covering party, to take a plan of the works in full view of the garrison.

Not a gun was fired by the fort; the silence increased the arrogance and blind security of the British commander. At length, there was a sudden sally of the garrison and an attack on the flanks by Indians in ambush. A scene now occurred similar to that at the defeat of Braddock. The British officers marshalled their men according to European tactics, but the destructive fire and horrid yells of the Indians soon produced panic and confusion. Grant surrendered himself and the whole detachment, put to the rout with dreadful carnage, came back in fragments to Loyal Hannan.

As a mark of the high opinion now entertained of provincial troops for frontier service, Washington was given command of a division, partly of his own men, to keep in the advance of the main body, clear the roads, throw out scouting parties, and repel Indian attacks.

It was the 5th of November before the whole army assembled at Loyal Hannan. Winter was now at hand and 50 miles of wilderness were yet to be traversed by a road not yet formed before they could reach Fort Duquesne. In a council of war it was determined to be impracticable to advance further with the army that season. Three prisoners, however, who were brought in, gave such an account of the weak state of the garrison at Fort Duquesne that it was determined to push forward. The march was accordingly resumed, without tents or baggage, and with only a light train of artillery.

Washington still kept the advance. At length the army arrived in sight of Fort Duquesne, advancing with great precaution and expecting a vigorous defence; but that formidable fortress, the terror and scourge of the frontier, fell without a blow. The recent successes of the English forces in Canada had left the garrison without hope of reinforcements and supplies. The whole force did not exceed 500 men and the provisions were nearly exhausted. The commander waited only until the English army was within one day's march when he embarked his troops in batteaux, blew up his magazines, set fire to the fort, and retreated down the Ohio by the light of the flames. On the 25th of November, Washington marched in and planted the British flag on the smoking ruins.

The fortress was now put in a defensible state and garrisoned by 200 men from Washington's regiment. The name was changed to Fort Pitt, in honor of the illustrious British minister; it has since been modified into Pittsburg.

The reduction of Fort Duquesne terminated, as Washington had foreseen, the troubles and dangers of the southern frontier. French domination of the Ohio was at an end; the Indians paid homage to the conquering power and a treaty of peace was concluded with all the tribes between the Ohio and the lakes.

With this campaign ended, for the present, the military career of Washington. His object was attained: the restoration of security to his native province. Having abandoned all hope of attaining rank in the regular army and his health being much impaired, he gave up his commission at the close of the year and retired from service.

His marriage with Mrs. Custis took place shortly after his return. It was celebrated on the 6th of January, 1759, at the White House, the residence of the bride, in the good hospitable style of Virginia amid a joyous assemblage of relatives and friends.

Before following Washington into retirement, we think it proper to notice the events which closed the great struggle between England and France for empire in America.

Abercrombie had been superseded as commander-in-chief by Amherst, who had gained great favor by the reduction of Louisburg. According to the plan of operations for 1759, General Wolfe was to ascend the St. Lawrence in a fleet of ships of war with 8000 men and lay siege to Quebec. Amherst, in the mean time, was to advance by Lake George against Ticonderoga and Crown Point, reduce those forts, cross Lake Champlain, push on to the St. Lawrence, and co-operate with Wolfe.

A third expedition, under Brigadier-general Prideaux, was to attack Fort Niagara, which controlled the whole country of the Six Nations and commanded the navigation of the great lakes. Having reduced this fort, he was to traverse Lake Ontario, descend the St. Lawrence, capture Montreal, and join forces with Amherst.

Prideaux embarked at Oswego on the first of July with a large body of troops, regulars and provincials, accompanied by Sir William Johnson and his Indian braves of the Mohawk. Landing within a few miles of Fort Niagara, he advanced and proceeded to invest it. The garrison, 600 strong, made a resolute defence. On the 20th of July, Prideaux was killed and Amherst sent Brigadier-general Gage to take command.

In the mean time, the siege had been conducted by Sir William Johnson with courage and sagacity. Informed by his scouts that 1200 regular troops, with a number of Indian auxiliaries, were hastening to the rescue, he detached a force of grenadiers and light infantry, with some of his Mohawk warriors, to intercept them. They came in sight of each other on the road between Niagara Falls and the fort. After a sharp conflict, the French were broken, routed, and pursued through the woods with great carnage. The next day the garrison surrendered.

We now proceed to notice the expedition against Ticonderoga and Crown Point. In July, Amherst embarked with 12,000 men at the upper part of Lake George and proceeded down it; on the 22d, the army debarked at the lower part of the lake and advanced toward Ticonderoga.

Montcalm was absent for the protection of Quebec. The garrison did not exceed 400 men and Bourlamarque, who commanded, recognized that a defence against such overwhelming force would have been madness. Dismantling the fortifications, he abandoned them, as he did those at Crown Point, and retreated down the lake to make a stand at the Isle Aux Noix for the protection of Montreal.

Instead of following him up, Amherst proceeded to repair the works at Ticonderoga and erect a new fort at Crown Point, though neither were in danger of being attacked. His delay enabled the enemy to rally their forces at Isle Aux Noix, while it deprived Wolfe of that co-operation most essential to the success of the campaign.

Wolfe, with 8000 men, ascended the St. Lawrence in the fleet in June. The troops debarked on the Isle of Orleans, a little below Quebec, and encamped in its fertile fields. Quebec, the citadel of Canada, was strong by nature. It was built round the point of a rocky promontory and flanked by precipices. The St. Lawrence swept by it on the right and the St. Charles flowed on the left.

Montcalm commanded the post. His troops, more numerous than the assailants, were drawn out along the northern shore below the city, from the St. Charles to the Falls of Montmorency, and their position was secured by deep intrenchments.

After much resistance, Wolfe established batteries at the west point of the Isle of Orleans and at Point Levi on the south bank of the St. Lawrence, within cannon range of the city. From Point Levi, bombshells and red-hot shot were discharged; many houses were set on fire in the upper town and the lower town was reduced to rubbish; the main fort, however, remained unharmed.

Anxious for a decisive action, Wolfe, on the 9th of July, crossed over to the north bank of the St. Lawrence and encamped below the Montmorency.

Wolfe made a reconnoitering expedition up the river; he passed Quebec and noted the rugged cliffs that rose almost from the water's edge. Above them, he was told, was level ground, called the Plains of Abraham, by which the upper town might be approached on its weakest side. But how was that plain to be attained, when the cliffs were inaccessible and every practicable place fortified?

He returned to Montmorency resolved to attack Montcalm in his camp, however difficult to be approached. As usual in complicated orders, part were misunderstood or neglected and confusion was the consequence. The weather became stormy; at a later hour retreat would be impossible. Wolfe, therefore, gave up the attack and withdrew across the river, having lost about 400 men as a result of the premature attack by his impetuous grenadiers and their precipitate retreat after being mowed down by sheeted fire. Mean while, news came of the capture of Fort Niagara, Ticonderoga, and Crown Point, and that Amherst was preparing to attack the Isle Aux Noix. Wolfe, of a sensitive nature, had been deeply mortified by the severe check sustained at the Falls of Montmorency, fancying himself disgraced and the successes of his fellow-commanders increased his self-upbraiding. He called a council of war, in which the whole plan of operations was altered. It was determined to convey troops above the town, and endeavor to make a diversion in that direction or draw Montcalm into the open field. He was unremitting in his exertions, seeking to wipe out the fancied disgrace incurred at the Falls of Montmorency.

The descent was made in flat-bottomed boats, past midnight, on the 13th of September. They dropped down silently with the swift current. The landing took place in a cove near Cape Diamond. He had marked it in reconnoitering and saw that a cragged path straggled up from it to the Heights of Abraham, which might be climbed, though with difficulty, and that it appeared to be slightly guarded at top. Wolfe was among the first that ascended the steep and narrow path. Colonel Howe, at the same time, with the light infantry and Highlanders scrambled up the woody precipices, putting to flight a sergeant's guard posted at the summit. Wolfe, by the break of day, found himself in possession of the fateful Plains of Abraham.

Montcalm was thunderstruck when word was brought to him in his camp that the English were on the heights threatening the weakest part of the town. He hastened across the river St. Charles and ascended the heights, which slope up gradually from its banks.

Montcalm led his disciplined troops to a close conflict with small arms, the Indians to support them from thickets and corn-fields. The French advanced gallantly, firing rapidly but with little effect. The English reserved their fire until their assailants were within 40 yards and then delivered it in deadly volleys. Wolfe, who was in front of the line, was wounded by a ball in the wrist. He bound his handkerchief round the wound and led on the grenadiers, with fixed bayonets, to charge the foe, who began to waver. Another ball struck him in the breast. He felt the wound to be mortal and feared his fall might dishearten the troops. He was borne off to the rear and he was asked if he would have a surgeon. "It is needless," he replied; "it is all over with me." He desired those about him to lay him down. "They run! they run!" cried one of the attendants. "Who run?" demanded Wolfe, like one aroused from sleep. "The enemy, sir; they give way every where." The spirit of the expiring hero flashed up. "Now, God be praised, I will die in peace!" said he, and expired, soothed by the idea that victory would obliterate the imagined disgrace at Montmorency.

The gallant Montcalm had received his death-wound near St. John's Gate while endeavoring to rally his flying troops and had been borne into the town. The English had obtained a complete victory and had a strong position on the Plains of Abraham, which they hastened to fortify with redoubts and artillery drawn up the heights.

Montcalm, when told by his surgeon that he could not survive above a few hours, replied, "So much the better. I shall not live to see the surrender of Quebec." He expired early in the morning, dying like a brave soldier and a devout Catholic. Never did two worthier foes mingle their life-blood on the battle-field than Wolfe and Montcalm. On the 17th of September, Quebec capitulated and was taken possession of by the British, who hastened to put it in a complete posture of defence.

Had Amherst followed up his success at Ticonderoga the pre-ceding summer, the year's campaign would have ended, as had been projected, in the subjugation of Canada. His cautious delay gave De Levi, the successor of Montcalm, time to rally, concentrate the scattered French forces, and struggle for the salvation of the province.

In the following spring, as soon as the river St. Lawrence opened, De Levi approached Quebec and landed at Point au Tremble, 12 miles off. After a sharp battle in which he drove the English back into the town, De Levi prepared to besiege Quebec, when a British fleet arrived in the river. The whole scene was now reversed. The besieging army retreated in the night, leaving provisions, implements, and artillery behind them.

A last stand for the preservation of the colony was now made by the French at Montreal, where De Vaudreuil fixed his headquarters, fortified himself, and called in all possible aid, Canadian and Indian. Vaudreuil, however, found himself threatened by an army of nearly 10,000 men and a host of Indians. To withstand a siege in an almost open town against such superior force was out of the question; capitulation accordingly took place on the 8th of September, including the surrender not merely of Montreal, but of all Canada. Thus ended the contest between France and England for dominion in America.

(CHAPTER 6)

For three months after his marriage, Washington resided with his bride at her estate. During his sojourn there, he repaired to Williamsburg to take his seat in the House of Burgesses. In his civil life he was to be distinguished by the same judgment, devotion, courage, and magnanimity exhibited in his military career. He attended the House frequently during the remainder of the session, after which he conducted his bride to Mount Vernon.

Mr. Custis, the first husband of Mrs. Washington, had left large landed property and considerable money. One third fell to his widow in her own right; two thirds were inherited equally by her two children. By a decree of the General Court, Washington was intrusted with the care of the property inherited by the children, a trust which he discharged in the most faithful and judicious manner, becoming more like a parent than a mere guardian to them. In a letter from Mount Vernon, he writes: "I am now, I believe, fixed in this seat, with an agreeable partner for life, and I hope to find more happiness in retirement than I ever experienced in the wide and bustling world."

Mount Vernon was his harbor of repose. No impulse of ambition tempted him thence; nothing but the call of his country. The place was endeared to him by the remembrance of his brother Lawrence and of the happy days he had passed here in boyhood.

The mansion was beautifully situated on a swelling height, crowned with wood and commanding a magnificent view up and down the Potomac. The grounds immediately about it were laid out somewhat in the English taste. The estate was apportioned into separate farms, devoted to different kinds of culture. Much, however, was still covered with wild woods, seamed with deep dells and runs of water and indented with inlets, haunts of deer and lurking-places of foxes.

These were, as yet, the aristocratical days of Virginia. The estates were large and continued in the same families by entails. Many of the wealthy planters were connected with old families in England. The young men, especially the elder sons, were often sent to finish their education there and on their return brought out the tastes and habits of the mother country. The governors of Virginia were from the higher ranks of society and maintained a corresponding state. The "established," or Episcopal Church, predominated throughout the "ancient dominion." A style of living prevailed among the opulent Virginian families in those days that has long since faded away. The houses were spacious, commodious, and fitted to cope with the open-hearted hospitality of the owners. Nothing was more common than to see handsome services of plate, elegant equipages, and superb carriage horses—all imported from England.

Washington was an early riser, often before daybreak in the winter when the nights were long. On such occasions he lit his own fire and wrote or read by candle-light. He breakfasted at seven in summer, at eight in winter. Two small cups of tea and three or four cakes of Indian meal (hoe-cakes) formed his frugal repast. After breakfast, he mounted his horse and visited those parts of the estate where work was going on, seeing to every thing with his own eyes and often aiding with his own hand.

Dinner was served at two o'clock. He ate heartily but was no epicure. His beverage was small beer or cider and two glasses of old Madeira. He took tea, of which he was very fond, early in the evening and retired for the night about nine o'clock.

If confined to the house by bad weather, he took that occasion to arrange his papers, post up his accounts, or write letters, passing part of the time in reading, occasionally reading aloud to the family.

Washington delighted in the chase. He was a bold rider and an admirable horseman, though he never claimed the merit of being an accomplished fox-hunter. In the height of the season, however, he would be out with the fox-hounds two or three times a week, accompanied by his guests at Mount Vernon and the gentlemen of the neighborhood. On such occasions there would be a hunting dinner at one or other of those establishments, at which convivial repasts Washington is said to have enjoyed himself with unwonted hilarity.

The waters of the Potomac also afforded occasional amusement in fishing and shooting. The fishing was sometimes on a grand scale, when the herrings came up the river in shoals and the Negroes of Mount Vernon were marshalled forth to draw the seine, which was generally done with great success. Canvas-back ducks abounded at the proper season and the shooting of them was one of Washington's favorite recreations.

Occasionally he and Mrs. Washington would visit Annapolis, at that time the seat of government of Maryland, and partake of the gayeties which prevailed during the session of the legislature. The society was always polite and fashionable and more exclusive than in these republican days, being, in a manner, the outposts of the English aristocracy.

During the session of the Legislature, dinners and balls abounded and there were occasional attempts at theatricals. The latter was an amusement for which Washington always had a relish though he never had an opportunity of gratifying it effectually. Neither was he disinclined to mingle in the dance and we remember to have heard venerable ladies, who had been belles in his day, pride themselves on having had him for a partner, though, they added, he was apt to be a ceremonious and grave one.

In this round of rural occupation, rural amusements, and social intercourse, Washington passed several tranquil years, the halcyon season of his life. His marriage was unblessed with children, but those of Mrs. Washington experienced from him parental care and affection, and the formation of their minds and manners was one of the dearest objects of his attention. His domestic concerns and social enjoyments, however, were not permitted to interfere with his public duties. As judge of the county court and member of the House of Burgesses, he had numerous calls upon his time and was often drawn from home, for whatever trust he undertook, he was sure to fulfil with scrupulous exactness.

About this time we find him engaged, with other men of enterprise, in a project to drain the great Dismal Swamp and render it capable of cultivation. This vast morass was 30 miles long and 10 miles wide. With his usual zeal and hardihood he explored it on horseback and on foot. In the centre of the morass he came to a great piece of water, called Drummond's Pond but more poetically celebrated as the Lake of the Dismal Swamp. It was more elevated than any other part of the swamp and capable of feeding canals by which the whole might be traversed.

In the ensuing session of the Virginia Legislature, the association in behalf of which he had acted, was chartered under the name of the Dismal Swamp Company. To his observations and forecast may be traced the subsequent improvement and prosperity of that once desolate region.

Tidings of peace gladdened the colonies in the spring of 1763. The definitive treaty between England and France had been signed and, it was trusted there would be an end to those ravages that had desolated the interior of the country.

The month of May proved the fallacy of such hopes. In that month the insurrection of the Indian tribes broke out, which, from the name of the chief who was its prime mover, is called Pontiac's war. The Delawares and Shawnees and other tribes of the Ohio, among whom Washington had mingled, had now taken up the hatchet against the English. At a concerted time, an attack was made upon all the posts from Detroit to Fort Pitt. The frontiers of Pennsylvania, Maryland, and Virginia were laid waste, hamlets and farm-houses were wrapped in flames and their inhabitants massacred. A considerable time elapsed before the frontier was restored to tolerable tranquillity.

Fortunately, Washington's retirement from the army prevented his being entangled in this savage war; his active spirit had been diverted at this time in the enterprise for draining the great Dismal Swamp.

PART II

(CHAPTERS 7–9)

The Gathering Crisis
[1763–1774]

——————·•◦•·——————

The recent war of Great Britain for dominion in America, though crowned with success, had engendered a progeny of discontents in her colonies. Whatever might be the natural affection of the colonies for the mother country, it had never been properly reciprocated. British navigation laws had shut their ports against foreign vessels; obliged them to export their productions only to countries belonging to the British crown; to import European goods solely from England and in English ships; and had subjected the trade between the colonies to duties. All manufactures in the colonies that might interfere with those of the mother country had been either totally prohibited or subjected to intolerable restraints.

The acts of Parliament, imposing these prohibitions and restrictions, had produced discontent and opposition in the colonies, especially those of New England. The interests of these last were chiefly commercial and among them the republican spirit predominated. The Pilgrims, who had sought the wilds of America for the indulgence of freedom of opinion, had brought with them the spirit of independence and self-government. Other colonies, formed under other circumstances, might be disposed to acquiesce in monarchial exactions, but the republican spirit in New England, watching over "natural and chartered rights," had gradually an effect on the other colonies.

There was nothing to which the sensibilities of the colonies were more alive than any attempt of the mother country to draw revenue from them by taxation. From the earliest period of their existence, they had maintained the principle that they could only be taxed by a Legislature in which they were represented.

In 1760, there was an attempt in Boston to collect duties on foreign sugar and molasses imported into the colonies. Writs of assistance were applied for by the custom-house officers, authorizing them to break open ships, stores, and private dwellings in quest of articles that had paid no duty, and to call the assistance of others in the discharge of their odious task. The merchants opposed execution of the writ on constitutional grounds. The question was argued in court, where James Otis spoke so eloquently in vindication of American rights that all his hearers went away ready to take arms against writs of assistance. "Then and there," says John Adams, "was the first scene of opposition to the arbitrary claims of Great Britain. Then and there American Independence was born."

In 1764, George Grenville, now prime minister, raised the eventful question of "whether they had a right to tax America." It was decided in the affirmative. Next followed a resolution declaring it proper to charge certain stamp duties in the colonies and plantations but no immediate step was taken to carry it into effect. In the mean time, Parliament perpetuated certain duties on sugar and molasses, now reduced to discourage smuggling and thereby render them more productive. Duties, also, were imposed on other articles of foreign produce or manufacture imported into the colonies. To reconcile the latter to these impositions, it was stated that the revenue thus raised was to be appropriated to their protection; in other words, to support a standing army to be quartered upon them.

The New Englanders were first to take the field against the taxation. They denounced it as a violation of their rights as freemen; of their chartered rights, by which they were to tax themselves for their support and defence; of their rights as British subjects, who ought not to be taxed but by themselves or their representatives. They sent petitions and remonstrances to the king, the lords, and the commons, in which they were seconded by New York and Virginia. Grenville was warned of the spirit of resistance he might provoke. All was in vain. In March, 1765, the act was passed, according to which all instruments in writing were to be executed on stamped paper purchased from the agents of the British government. What was more, offences against the act could be tried in any court, however distant from the place where the offence had been committed, thus interfering with that most inestimable right, a trial by jury.

It was an ominous sign that the first burst of opposition to this act should take place in Virginia. That colony had grown up in loyal attachment to king, church, and constitution, was aristocratical in its tastes and habits, and had been remarked above all the other colonies for its sympathies with the mother country. But the Virginians, readily aroused on all points of honorable pride, resented the stamp act as an outrage on their rights.

Washington occupied his seat in the House of Burgesses, when, on the 29th of May, the stamp act became a subject of discussion. Among the Burgesses sat Patrick Henry, a young lawyer, who introduced his celebrated resolutions declaring that the General Assembly of Virginia had the exclusive right and power to lay taxes and impositions upon the inhabitants and that whoever maintained the contrary should be deemed an enemy to the colony. Henry went into an able discussion of colonial rights and an exposition of the manner in which they had been assailed. He wound up by one of those daring flights of declamation for which he was remarkable: "Caesar had his Brutus; Charles his Cromwell; and George the Third—('Treason! treason!' resounded from the neighborhood of the Chair)—may profit by their examples," added Henry. "Sir, if this be treason, make the most of it!"

The resolutions were modified but their spirit was retained. The Lieutenant-governor, startled by this patriotic outbreak, dissolved the Assembly and issued writs for a new election, but the clarion had sounded.

Washington returned to Mount Vernon full of anxious thoughts inspired by the political events of the day and the legislative scene he witnessed. He fully participated in the popular feeling and, while he had a presentiment of an arduous struggle, his patriotic mind was revolving means of coping with it.

From his quiet abode at Mount Vernon, he seemed to hear the voice of Patrick Henry echoing throughout the land, rousing one legislative body after another to follow the example of Virginia. At the instigation of the General Court or Assembly of Massachusetts, a Congress was held in New York in October of delegates from Massachusetts, Rhode Island, Connecticut, New York, New Jersey, Pennsylvania, Delaware, Maryland, and South Carolina. In this they denounced the acts of Parliament imposing taxes on them without their consent as violations of their rights and liberties as natural born subjects of Great Britain. They prepared an address to the king and a petition to both Houses of Parliament praying for redress. Similar petitions were forwarded to England by the colonies not represented in the Congress.

The very preparations for enforcing the stamp act called forth popular tumults in various places. In Boston the stamp officer thought himself happy to be hanged merely in effigy and next day publicly renounced the perilous office.

The 1st of November, the day when the act was to go into operation, was ushered in with portentous solemnities. There was great tolling of bells and burning of effigies in the New England colonies. Many shops were shut, funeral knells resounded from the steeples, and the promoters of the act suffered martyrdom in effigy.

No stamped paper was to be seen; all had been either destroyed or concealed. Transactions which required stamps were suspended or were executed by private compact. The courts of justice were closed until at length some conducted their business without stamps. Union was becoming the watch-word. The merchants of New York, Philadelphia, Boston, and such other colonies as had ventured to oppose the stamp act agreed to import no more British manufactures after the 1st of January unless it should be repealed. So passed away the year 1765.

The dismissal of Mr. Grenville from the cabinet gave a temporary change to public affairs. The stamp act was repealed on the 18th of March, 1766 to the great joy of the friends of both countries, and to no one more than to Washington. In one of his letters he observes: "Had the Parliament of Great Britain resolved upon enforcing it, the consequences, I conceive, would have been more direful than is generally apprehended, both to the mother country and her colonies."

Still, there was a fatal clause in the repeal, which declared that the king, with the consent of Parliament, had power and authority to make laws and statutes of sufficient force and validity to "bind the colonies and people of America in all cases whatsoever."

As the people of America were contending for principles, not mere pecuniary interests, this reserved power of the crown and Parliament left the dispute still open. Further aliment for public discontent was furnished by other acts of Parliament. One imposed duties on glass, pasteboard, white and red lead, painters' colors, and tea, the duties to be collected on the arrival of the articles in the colonies. Another empowered naval officers to enforce the acts of trade and navigation. Another wounded to the quick the pride and sensibilities of New York. The mutiny act had recently been extended to America, with an additional clause requiring provincial Assemblies to provide troops sent out with quarters, fire, beds, candles, and other necessaries at the expense of the colonies. The Governor and Assembly of New York refused to comply with this requisition as to stationary forces, insisting that it applied only to troops on a march. An act of Parliament now suspended the powers of the Governor and Assembly until they should comply.

Boston continued to be the focus of what the ministerialists termed sedition. The General Court of Massachusetts drew up a circular calling on the other colonial Legislatures to join with them in suitable efforts to obtain redress. In the ensuing session, Governor Sir Francis Bernard called upon them to rescind the resolution on which the circular was founded; they refused to comply and the General Court was dissolved. The governors of other colonies required of their Legislatures an assurance that they would not reply to the Massachusetts circular; these Legislatures likewise refused compliance and were dissolved. All this added to the growing excitement.

Nothing, however, produced a more powerful effect throughout the country than certain military demonstrations at Boston. In consequence of repeated collisions between the people of that place and the commissioners of customs, two regiments arrived from Halifax with seven armed vessels. It was resolved in a town meeting that the king had no right to send troops thither without the consent of the Assembly and that Great Britain had broken the original compact. The selectmen accordingly refused to find quarters for the soldiers. Some of the troops, therefore, were encamped on the Common; others were quartered in the state-house and in Faneuil Hall, to the great indignation of the public.

Washington was too true a patriot not to sympathize in the struggle for colonial rights which now agitated the whole country and we find him gradually carried more and more into the current of political affairs.

A letter written on the 5th of April, 1769, to his friend, George Mason, shows the stand he was disposed to take. In the previous year the merchants and traders of Boston, Salem, Connecticut, and New York had agreed to suspend the importation of all articles subject to taxation. Similar resolutions had recently been adopted by the merchants of Philadelphia. Washington's letter is emphatic in support of the measure. "At a time," writes he, "when our lordly masters in Great Britain will be satisfied with nothing less than the deprivation of American freedom, it seems highly necessary that something should be done to avert the stroke, and maintain the liberty which we have derived from our ancestors. . . . That no man should scruple, or hesitate a moment in defence of so valuable a blessing, is clearly my opinion; yet arms should be the last resource—the *dernier ressort*."

Mason, in his reply, concurred with him in opinion. "Our all is at stake," said he, "and the little conveniences and comforts of life, when set in competition with our liberty, ought to be rejected, not with reluctance, but with pleasure. . . . I am thoroughly convinced, that, justice and harmony happily restored, it is not the interest of these colonies to refuse British manufactures. Our supplying our mother country with gross materials and taking her manufactures in return is the true chain of connection between us. These are the bands which, if not broken by oppression, must long hold us together by maintaining a constant reciprocation of interests."

The above quotation shows the spirit which actuated Washington and the friends of his confidence; there was no thought of alienation from the mother country but only a determination to be placed on an equality of rights and privileges with her other children.

The result of the correspondence between Washington and Mason was a plan of association, the members of which were to pledge themselves not to import or use any articles of British merchandise or manufacture subject to duty. This paper Washington was to submit to the House of Burgesses at the approaching session in May.

The Legislature of Virginia opened on this occasion with a brilliant pageant. While military force was arrayed to overawe the republican Puritans of the east, it was thought to dazzle the aristocratical descendants of the Cavaliers by regal splendor. Lord Botetourt, who had recently come out as governor of the province, had a wrong idea of the Americans. They had been represented to him as factious, immoral, and prone to sedition, but vain, luxurious, and easily captivated by parade and splendor. The latter foibles were aimed at in his appointment and fitting out. His opening of the session was in the style of the royal opening of Parliament. He proceeded in due parade from his dwelling to the capital in his state coach drawn by six milk-white horses. Having delivered his speech according to royal form, he returned home with the same pomp and circumstance.

The time had gone by, however, for such display to have the anticipated effect. The Virginian legislators penetrated the intention of this pompous ceremonial. Sterner matters occupied their thoughts; they had come prepared to battle for their rights. Spirited resolutions were passed, denouncing the recent act of Parliament imposing taxes, the power to do which, on the inhabitants of this colony, "was legally and constitutionally vested in the House of

Burgesses, with consent of the council and of the king or of his governor, for the time being." Copies of these resolutions were forwarded to the Legislatures of the other colonies with a request for their concurrence.

Other proceedings of the Burgesses showed their sympathy with their fellow-patriots of New England. A joint address of Parliament had recently been made to the king, assuring him of their support in the execution of the laws in Massachusetts and beseeching him that all persons charged with treason, or misprision of treason, committed within that colony might be sent to Great Britain for trial. As Massachusetts had no General Assembly, having been dissolved by government, the Legislature of Virginia took up the cause. An address to the king was resolved on, stating that all trials for treason, misprision of treason, or any crime whatever committed by any person residing in a colony ought to be before his majesty's courts within said colony; and beseeching the king to avert from his loyal subjects those dangers and miseries which would ensue from carrying beyond sea any person residing in America suspected of any crime whatever, thereby depriving them of the privilege of being tried by a jury from the vicinage as well as the liberty of producing witnesses on such trial.

Lord Botetourt was astonished and dismayed when he heard of these proceedings. Repairing to the capitol on the following day, he summoned the speaker and members to the council chamber and addressed them: "Mr. Speaker and gentlemen of the House of Burgesses, I have heard of your resolves and augur ill of their effects. You have made it my duty to dissolve you and you are dissolved accordingly."

The Burgesses adjourned to a private house. Peyton Randolph, their late speaker, was elected moderator. Washington now brought forward the articles of association concerted between him and Mason. They formed the groundwork of an instrument signed by all present, pledging themselves neither to import nor use any goods, merchandise, or manufactures taxed by Parliament to raise a revenue in America. This instrument was sent throughout the country for signature and the scheme of non-importation, hitherto confined to a few northern colonies, was soon universally adopted.

The Gathering Crisis (1763–1774)

The ferment in Virginia was gradually allayed by the conciliatory conduct of Lord Botetourt. His semi-royal equipage and state were laid aside. He examined into public grievances, became a strenuous advocate for the repeal of taxes, and, authorized by his despatches from the ministry, assured the public that such repeal would speedily take place. His assurance was received with implicit faith and for a while Virginia was quieted.

In the mean time, the non-importation associations, being generally observed throughout the colonies, produced the effect on British commerce which Washington had anticipated and Parliament was incessantly importuned by petitions from British merchants, imploring its intervention to save them from ruin.

(CHAPTER 8)

Early in 1770, an important change took place in the British cabinet: the reins of government passed into the hands of Lord North. He was a man of limited capacity, subservient to the king's narrow colonial policy. His administration commenced with an error. In March, an act was passed revoking all the duties laid in 1767, excepting that on tea. This single tax was continued "to maintain the parliamentary right of taxation"—the very right which was the object of the contest. In vain the opposition urged that this single exception, while it would produce no revenue, would keep alive the whole cause of contention; that, so long as a single external duty was enforced, the colonies would consider their rights invaded and would remain unappeased. North was not to be convinced, or rather, he knew the royal will was inflexible and he complied with its behests.

On the very day in which this bill was passed in Parliament, a sinister occurrence took place in Boston. Some young men insulted the military; the latter resented it; the young men, after a scuffle, were put to flight and pursued. The alarm bells rang and a mob assembled; the custom-house was threatened; the troops, in protecting it, were assailed with clubs and stones and obliged to use their fire-arms before the tumult could be quelled. Four of the populace were killed and several wounded. The troops were now removed from the town, which remained in the highest state of exasperation, and this occurrence received the opprobrious, somewhat extravagant name of "the Boston massacre."

The colonists resumed consumption of those articles on which duties had been repealed, but continued, on principle, the disuse of tea, excepting such as had been smuggled in. New England was particularly earnest in the matter; many of the inhabitants made a covenant to drink no more of the forbidden beverage until the duty should be repealed.

In Virginia the public discontents, allayed by Lord Botetourt's assurances, on the strength of letters received from the ministry, that the grievances would be speedily redressed, now broke out with more violence than ever. His lordship also felt deeply wounded by the disingenuousness of the ministers and wrote home demanding his discharge. Before it arrived, an attack of bilious fever, acting upon a delicate frame enfeebled by chagrin, laid him in his grave. He left behind him a name endeared to the Virginians by his amiable manners, his liberal patronage of the arts, and, above all, by his zealous intercession for their rights.

In the midst of these popular turmoils Washington was induced to make another expedition to the Ohio. He was one of the Virginia Board of Commissioners, appointed at the close of the late war to settle the military accounts of the colony. Among the claims before the board were those of officers and soldiers who had engaged to serve under the proclamation of Dinwiddie, holding forth a bounty of 200,000 acres of land to be apportioned among them according to rank. Washington became the champion of those claims and an opportunity now presented itself for their liquidation. The Six Nations, by a treaty in 1768, had ceded to the British crown all the lands possessed by them south of the Ohio. Land offices would soon be opened for the sale of them. Squatters and speculators were already preparing to set up their marks on the choicest spots and establish pre-emption rights. Washington determined at once to visit the lands thus ceded, affix his mark on such tracts as he should select and apply for a grant from government in behalf of the "soldiers' claim."

Washington had for a companion in this expedition his friend and neighbor, Dr. Craik, and they set out on the 5th of October with three Negro attendants, two belonging to Washington and one to the doctor. The whole party was mounted and there was a led horse for the baggage. After twelve days' travelling they arrived at Fort Pitt. It was garrisoned by two companies of royal Irish; a hamlet of 20 log-houses, inhabited by Indian traders, had sprung up around the fort and was called "the town." At one of the houses, they took up their quarters; during their brief sojourn, they were entertained with great hospitality at the fort.

Here at dinner Washington met his old acquaintance, George Croghan, who had figured in so many capacities and experienced so many vicissitudes on the frontier. On the day following the repast at the fort, Washington visited Croghan at his abode on the Allegany River, where he found several chiefs of the Six Nations assembled. They had come to welcome him to their country and requested him to inform the governor of their desire to live in peace and harmony with the white men. Washington made a suitable reply, assuring the chiefs that nothing was more desired by the people of Virginia than to live with them on terms of the strictest friendship.

At Pittsburg the travellers left their horses, and embarked in a large canoe, to make a voyage down the Ohio as far as the Great Kanawha. Several days of voyaging brought them to an Indian hunting camp near the mouth of the Muskingum. Here it was necessary to make a ceremonious visit, for the chief of the hunting party was Kiashuta, a Seneca sachem, the head of the river tribes. As Washington approached the chieftain, he recognized him for one of the Indians who had accompanied him on his mission to the French in 1753 and Kiashuta retained a perfect recollection of the youthful ambassador. Kiashuta was eager to express his own desire for peace and friendship with Virginia and fair dealings with her traders, all which Washington promised to report faithfully to the governor. It was not until a late hour in the morning that he was enabled to pursue his voyage.

At the mouth of the Great Kanawha, the voyagers encamped for a day or two to examine the lands in the neighborhood and Washington set up his mark upon such as he intended to claim on behalf of the soldiers' grant.

Here Washington was visited by an old sachem, who made known that he was one of the warriors in the service of the French who wrought such havoc in Braddock's army. He declared that he and his young men had singled out Washington riding about the field of battle and had fired at him repeatedly but without success, whence they had concluded that he was under the protection of the Great Spirit, had a charmed life, and could not be slain in battle.

At the Great Kanawha Washington's expedition down the Ohio terminated, having visited all the points he wished to examine. His return to Fort Pitt, and thence homeward, affords no incident worthy of note.

The discontents of Virginia were irritated anew under Botetourt's successor, the Earl of Dunmore. When appointed to Virginia, he lingered for several months at his former post in New York. In the mean time, he sent his military secretary to attend to the despatch of business until his arrival, awarding to him a salary and fees to be paid by the colony. The pride of the Virginians was piqued at his lingering at New York. Their pride was still more piqued on his arrival by haughtiness on his part.

The first measure of the Assembly, at its opening, was to demand by what right he had awarded a salary and fees to his secretary without consulting it and to question whether it was authorized by the crown. His lordship had the good policy to rescind the unauthorized act and in so doing mitigated the ire of the Assembly, but he lost no time in proroguing a body which appeared to be too independent and disposed to be untractable. He continued to prorogue it from time to time, seeking in the interim to conciliate the Virginians. At length, he was compelled by circumstances to convene it on the 1st of March, 1773.

Washington was among the patriotic members who eagerly availed themselves of this opportunity to legislate upon the general affairs of the colonies. One of their most important measures was the appointment of a committee of eleven persons, "whose business it should be to obtain the most clear and authentic intelligence of all such acts and resolutions of the British Parliament, or proceedings of administration, as may relate to or affect the British colonies, and to maintain with their sister colonies a correspondence and communication."

The plan thus proposed by their "noble, patriotic sister colony of Virginia," was promptly adopted by the people of Massachusetts and soon met with general concurrence. These corresponding committees became the executive power of the patriot party, producing the happiest concert of design and action throughout the colonies.

Notwithstanding the part taken by Washington in the popular movement, very friendly relations existed between him and Lord Dunmore. The latter appreciated his character and sought to avail himself of his experience in the affairs of the province.

We have spoken of Washington's paternal conduct towards the two children of Mrs. Washington. The daughter, Miss Custis, had long been an object of extreme solicitude. She was of a fragile constitution and for some time past had been in very declining health. Early in the present summer, symptoms indicated a rapid change for the worse. Washington was absent from home at the time. On his return to Mount Vernon, he found her in the last stage of consumption. He is said to have evinced the deepest affliction, kneeling by her bedside and pouring out earnest prayers for her recovery. She expired on the 19th of June, in the seventeenth year of her age. This, of course, put an end to Washington's intention of accompanying Lord Dunmore to the frontier; he remained at home to console Mrs. Washington in her affliction, furnishing his lordship, however, with travelling hints and directions and recommending proper guides.

Previous to the death of Miss Custis, her mother, despairing of her recovery, had centered her hopes in her son, John Parke Custis. He was lively, susceptible and impulsive; and he had an indulgent mother, ever ready to plead in his behalf against wholesome discipline. He had been placed under the instruction of an Episcopal clergyman at Annapolis, but his education had not been such as

Washington would have enforced had he the absolute authority of a father.

The sallying impulses of the youth had taken a new direction. He was engaged to the object of his passion and on the high road to matrimony. Washington opposed premature marriage and correspondence ensued between him and the young lady's father, Benedict Calvert. The match was a satisfactory one to all parties, but it was agreed it was expedient for the youth to pass a year or two previously at college. Washington placed him under the care of the president of King's (now Columbia) College to pursue his studies in that institution. All this occurred before the death of his sister. Within a year after that melancholy event, he became impatient for a union with the object of his choice. His mother, now more indulgent than ever, yielded her consent and Washington no longer made opposition. The marriage was celebrated on the 3d of February, 1774, before the bridegroom was twenty-one years of age.

The general covenant throughout the colonies against the use of taxed tea had operated disastrously against the interest of the East India Company and produced an immense accumulation in their warehouses. To remedy this, North brought in a bill (1773) by which the company were allowed to export their teas from England to any part whatever without paying export duty. This, by enabling them to offer their teas at a low price in the colonies, would, he supposed, tempt the Americans to purchase large quantities. Confiding in the wisdom of this policy, the company freighted several ships with tea to various parts of the colonies. This brought matters to a crisis. From New York and Philadelphia the ships were sent back, unladen, to London. In Charleston the tea was unloaded and stored, where it perished. In Boston some small parcels of tea were brought on shore but the sale of them was prohibited. The captains of the ships would have made sail back for England but they could not obtain the consent of the consignees, a clearance at the customhouse, or a passport from the governor to clear the fort. It was evident the tea was to be forced upon the people of Boston and the principle of taxation established. To settle the matter completely, a number of inhabitants, disguised as Indians, boarded the ships in the night (18th December), broke open all the chests of tea, and emptied the contents into the sea. This was no rash and intemperate proceeding of a mob but the well-considered act of sober respectable citizens. The whole was done calmly, after which the actors dispersed without tumult and returned quietly to their homes.

The general opposition of the colonies to taxation had given great annoyance to government, but this individual act concentrated all its wrath upon Boston. A bill was forthwith passed in Parliament by which all lading and unlading of goods, wares, and merchandise were to cease in that town and harbor on the 4th of June. Another law altered the charter of the province, decreeing that all counsellors, judges, and magistrates should be appointed by the crown and hold office during the royal pleasure. This was followed by a third, intended for the suppression of riots, providing that any person indicted for murder or other capital offence committed in aiding the magistracy might be sent by the governor to some other colony or to Great Britain for trial.

All things were going on smoothly in Virginia when a letter, received through the corresponding committee, brought intelligence of the vindictive measure of Parliament, by which the port of Boston was to be closed. The letter was read in the House of Burgesses and produced a general burst of indignation. All other business was thrown aside and a resolution was adopted setting apart the 1st of June as a day of fasting, prayer, and humiliation. On the following morning, the royal governor dissolved the House of Burgesses.

The Assembly, though dissolved, was not dispersed. The members adjourned to the Raleigh tavern and passed resolutions denouncing the Boston port bill as a dangerous attempt to destroy the constitutional liberty and rights of all North America; recommending their countrymen to desist from the use, not merely of tea, but of all East Indian commodities; pronouncing an attack on one of the colonies, to enforce arbitrary taxes, an attack on all; and ordering the committee of correspondence to communicate with the other corresponding committees on the expediency of appointing deputies from the several colonies of British America to meet annually in General Congress to deliberate on such measures as their united interests might require.

The recommendation of a General Congress met with prompt and general concurrence throughout the colonies and the fifth of September was fixed upon for the meeting of the first Congress, to be held at Philadelphia.

On the 29th of May, letters arrived from Boston giving the proceedings of a town meeting, recommending a league be formed throughout the colonies suspending all trade with Great Britain. Twenty-five members of the late House of Burgesses, including Washington, who were still in Williamsburg held a meeting on the following day, at which it was determined to issue a printed circular calling a meeting of all members of the late House of Burgesses on the 1st of August to consider a general league.

In the mean time the Boston port bill had been carried into effect. On the 1st of June, the harbor of Boston was closed and all business ceased. The two other acts altering the charter of Massachusetts were to be enforced. No public meetings, except the annual town meetings in March and May, were to be held without permission of the governor.

At the suggestion of the Massachusetts Assembly, a paper was circulated through the province by the committee of correspondence, the subscribers to which bound themselves to break off all intercourse with Great Britain from the 1st of August until the colony should be restored to the enjoyment of its chartered rights and to renounce all dealings with those who refuse to enter into this compact.

The very title of league and covenant had an ominous sound and startled General Thomas Gage, who had recently been appointed to the military command of Massachusetts. He issued a proclamation denouncing it as illegal and traitorous. Furthermore, he encamped a force of infantry and artillery on Boston Common. An alarm spread through the adjacent country. "Boston is to be blockaded! Boston is to be reduced to obedience by force or famine!" Affairs were coming to a crisis. It was predicted that the new acts of Parliament would bring on "a most important and decisive trial."

The Gathering Crisis (1763–1774)

Shortly after Washington's return to Mount Vernon in June, he presided at a meeting of the inhabitants of Fairfax County, wherein, after the recent acts of Parliament had been discussed, a committee was appointed to draw up resolutions expressive of the sentiments of the meeting and to report the same at a general meeting of the county to be held in the court-house on the 18th of July.

The committee met, with Washington as chairman, and the resolutions insisted on the right of self-government and the principle that taxation and representation were inseparable. The various acts of Parliament, it was stated, were all part of a premeditated design to introduce arbitrary government into the colonies. The sudden and repeated dissolutions of Assemblies whenever they presumed to examine the illegality of ministerial mandates or deliberated on the violated rights of their constituents, it was resolved, were intended to dissolve the compact by which their ancestors bound themselves and their posterity to the British crown. The resolutions, furthermore, recommended union and co-operation among the colonies, solemn covenants with respect to non-importation and non-intercourse, and renunciation of all dealings with any colony, town, or province that should refuse to agree to the plan adopted by the General Congress. They also recommended a dutiful petition and remonstrance from the Congress to the king, asserting their constitutional rights and privileges, declaring their attachment to his person, family and government, and beseeching him not to reduce his faithful subjects to desperation and to reflect that from our sovereign there can be but one appeal. The resolutions were adopted and Washington was chosen to represent the county at the General Convention of the province to be held at Williamsburg.

On the 1st of August, the Convention assembled and, roused to an unusual pitch of enthusiasm, Washington declared that he was ready to raise 1000 men, subsist them at his own expense, and march at their head to the relief of Boston.

The Convention was six days in session. Resolutions of protest were adopted and Peyton Randolph, Richard Henry Lee, George Washington, Patrick Henry, Richard Bland, Benjamin Harrison, and Edmund Pendleton were appointed delegates to represent the people of Virginia in the General Congress.

Gage, from the time of taking command at Boston, had been perplexed how to manage its inhabitants. Had they been hot-headed, his task would have been comparatively easy, but it was the cool, shrewd common sense by which all their movements were regulated that confounded him. It would not do to disperse the assemblages by force of arms, for the people who composed them, like the covenanters of yore, if prone to argue, were as ready to fight. So the meetings continued to be held. Faneuil Hall was at times unable to hold them and they swarmed from that revolutionary hive into old South Church. The liberty tree became a rallying place for any popular movement.

(CHAPTER 9)

When the time approached for the meeting at Philadelphia, Washington was joined by Patrick Henry and Edmund Pendleton and they performed the journey together on horseback. Henry was then in the youthful vigor of his bounding genius, ardent, acute, eloquent. Pendleton, schooled in public life, was a veteran in council, with native force of intellect. Washington, in the meridian of his days, was mature in wisdom, comprehensive in mind, sagacious in foresight. Such were the apostles of liberty repairing to Philadelphia from all parts of the land to lay the foundations of a mighty empire.

Congress assembled on the 5th of September in Carpenter's Hall. There were 51 delegates, representing all the colonies excepting Georgia. The most eminent men of the colonies were now for the first time brought together; they were known to each other by fame but were, personally, strangers. "It is such an assembly," writes John Adams, who was present, "as never before came together on a sudden, in any part of the world. Here are fortunes, abilities, learning, eloquence, acuteness, equal to any I ever met with in my life. Here is a diversity of religions, educations, manners, interests, such as it would seem impossible to unite in one plan of conduct."

After some debate, it was determined that each colony should have but one vote, whatever the number of its delegates. The deliberations of the House were to be with closed doors and nothing but the resolves promulgated, unless by order of the majority. To give proper dignity and solemnity to the proceedings of the House, each morning the session was opened by prayer.

In the course of the day, a rumor reached Philadelphia that Boston had been cannonaded by the British. It produced a strong sensation; the effect was visible in every countenance. They were one political family, sympathizing with the weal and woe of each individual member. The rumor proved erroneous, but it quickened the spirit of union so vitally important in that assemblage.

Owing to closed doors and the want of reporters, no record exists of the discussions and speeches in the first Congress. Tradition informs us that a long and deep silence followed the organization of that august body, the members individually reluctant to open a business so fearfully momentous, when Patrick Henry arose. He faltered at first, but, as he launched forth into a recital of colonial wrongs, he poured forth one of those eloquent appeals which had so often shaken the House of Burgesses and gained him the fame of being the greatest orator of Virginia. He was followed by Richard Henry Lee, who charmed the House with a different kind of eloquence, chaste and classical, contrasting in its cultivated graces with the grand effusions of Henry.

The first public measure of Congress was a resolution declaratory of their feelings with regard to the recent acts of Parliament violating the rights of the people of Massachusetts and of their determination to combine in resisting any attempt to carry those acts into execution.

A committee of two from each province reported a series of resolutions, which were adopted and promulgated by Congress, as a "declaration of colonial rights." In this were enumerated their natural rights to the enjoyment of life, liberty, and property and their rights as British subjects. Among the latter was participation in legislative councils. This they could not exercise through representatives in Parliament; they claimed, therefore, the power of legislating in their provincial Assemblies, consenting to such acts of Parliament as might be essential to the regulation of trade but excluding all taxation for raising revenue in America.

The common law of England was claimed as a birthright, including the right of trial by a jury of the vicinage, of holding public meetings to consider grievances, and of petitioning the king. The benefits of all such statutes as existed at the time of the colonization were likewise claimed, together with the immunities and privileges granted by royal charters or secured by provincial laws.

The maintenance of a standing army in any colony in time of peace without the consent of its Legislature was pronounced contrary to law. The exercise of the legislative power in the colonies by a council appointed during pleasure by the crown was declared to be unconstitutional and destructive to the freedom of American legislation.

Then followed a specification of the acts of Parliament infringing and violating these rights. These were: the sugar act, the stamp act, the two acts for quartering troops, the tea act, the act suspending the New York Legislature, the two acts for the trial in Great Britain of offences committed in America, the Boston port bill, the act for regulating the government of Massachusetts, and the Quebec act. "To these grievous acts and measures," it was added, "Americans cannot submit, but in hopes their fellow-subjects in Great Britain will, on a revision of them, restore us to that state in which both countries found happiness and prosperity, we have, for the present, only resolved to pursue the following peaceable measures: 1st. To enter into a non-importation, non-consumption, and non-exportation agreement or association. 2d. To prepare an address to the people of Great Britain and a memorial to the inhabitants of British America. 3d. To prepare a loyal address to his majesty."

The above-mentioned association was accordingly formed and committees were to be appointed in every county, city, and town, to maintain it vigilantly and strictly. The Congress remained in session fifty-one days.

How thoroughly and zealously Washington participated in the feelings which actuated Congress in this memorable session may be gathered from his correspondence with a friend enlisted in the royal cause: "None of them will ever submit to the loss of their valuable rights and privileges, which are essential to the happiness of every free state and, without which, life, liberty, and property are rendered totally insecure." In concluding, he writes with respect to independence: "I am well satisfied that no such thing is desired by any thinking man in all North America; on the contrary, that it is the ardent wish of the warmest advocates for liberty that peace and tranquillity, upon constitutional grounds, may be restored and the horrors of civil discord prevented."

On the breaking up of Congress, Washington hastened back to Mount Vernon, where his presence was more than usually important to the happiness of Mrs. Washington from the loneliness caused by the recent death of her daughter and the absence of her son. The cheerfulness of the neighborhood had been diminished of late by the departure of George William Fairfax for England to take possession of estates which had devolved to him. His estate of Belvoir, so closely allied with Mount Vernon by family ties and hospitality, through some accident, took fire and was burnt to the ground. It was never rebuilt. The course of political events prevented Fairfax, who was a royalist, though a liberal one, from returning and the intercommunion in Mount Vernon and Belvoir was at an end for ever.

PART III

(CHAPTERS 10–16)

The Resort to Arms
[1774–1775]

The rumor of the cannonading of Boston, at the opening of Congress, had been caused by measures of Governor Gage. The public mind in Boston and its vicinity had been rendered sensitive by the encamping of artillery upon the Common and Welsh Fusiliers on Fort Hill and by the planting of four large field-pieces on Boston Neck, the only entrance to the town by land. The country people were arming themselves and depositing arms and ammunition where they would be at hand in case of emergency. Gage, on the other hand, issued orders that munitions of war in all public magazines be brought to Boston. One of these magazines was the arsenal in the north-west part of Charlestown. Two companies of the king's troops passed silently in boats up Mystic River in the night, took possession of gunpowder there and conveyed it to Castle Williams. Intelligence of this sacking of the arsenal flew through the neighborhood. In the morning thousands of patriots assembled at Cambridge, weapon in hand, and were with difficulty prevented from marching upon Boston to compel a restitution of the powder. In the confusion, rumors spread that Boston was to be attacked, that ships were cannonading the town and soldiers shooting down the inhabitants. The whole country was forthwith in arms.

To guard against any irruption from the country, Gage encamped the 59th regiment on Boston Neck and employed the soldiers in intrenching and fortifying it. In the mean time the belligerent feelings of the inhabitants were encouraged by learning how the rumor of their being cannonaded had been received in the General Congress and by assurances that the cause of Boston would be made the common cause of America.

Gage, before this popular agitation, had issued writs for a general election to be held at Salem in October; seeing the irritated state of the public mind, he now countermanded the same by proclamation. The people, disregarding the countermand, carried the election and 90 members thus elected met at the appointed time. They waited a whole day for the governor to attend, administer the oaths, and open the session; but, as he did not make his appearance, they voted themselves a provincial Congress and chose for president of it John Hancock—a man of great wealth, popular, of ardent patriotism, and eminent from his social position.

This body adjourned to Concord, quietly assumed supreme authority, and issued a remonstrance to the governor, virtually calling him to account for his operations in fortifying Boston Neck and collecting warlike stores about him, thereby menacing the lives and property of the Bostonians.

Gage, overlooking the irregularity of its organization, entered into explanations with the Assembly but failed to give satisfaction. He found his situation more and more critical. Boston was the only place in Massachusetts that now contained British forces and it had become the refuge of all those devoted to the British government. The town itself, almost insulated by nature and surrounded by a hostile country, was like a place besieged.

The provincial Congress conducted its affairs with the order and system so formidable to Gage. Having adopted a plan for organizing the militia, it had nominated general officers, Artemas Ward and Seth Pomeroy. Executive powers were vested in a committee of safety. This was to determine when the services of the militia were necessary: to call them forth, to nominate their officers to the Congress, to commission them, and direct the operations of the army. Another committee was appointed to furnish supplies to the forces when called out. The militia went on arming and disciplining itself in every direction. They engaged to assemble in arms at the shortest notice for the common defence, subject to the orders of the committee of safety.

This semi-belligerent state of affairs in Massachusetts produced a general restlessness throughout the land. Military measures, hitherto confined to New England, extended to the middle and southern provinces and the roll of the drum resounded through the villages.

Virginia was among the first to buckle on its armor. It had long been a custom among its inhabitants to form companies, equipped at their own expense, having their own peculiar uniform and electing their own officers, though holding themselves subject to militia law. They had hitherto been self-disciplined, but now they continually resorted to Washington for instruction and advice, considering him the highest authority on military affairs. He was frequently called from home to review independent companies, all of which were anxious to put themselves under his command.

Mount Vernon again assumed a military tone as in former days, when he took his first lessons there in the art of war. Two occasional and important guests at Mount Vernon, in this momentous crisis, where General Charles Lee and Major Horatio Gates. Both were Englishmen by birth, who had spent most of their years in military service. Lee, after serving in the British and Polish armies, came to America in 1773 and took an active part in the colonial agitations. Gates, who had served under Cornwallis, Braddock, and Monckton, discontent with his prospects of advancement in the army or in the government, emigrated to Virginia in 1772, purchased an estate beyond the Blue Ridge, espoused the popular cause, and renewed his old campaigning acquaintance with Washington. Lee, who was an old friend and former associate of Gates in arms, had been induced by him likewise to purchase an estate in Berkeley County, having a moderate competency, a claim to land on the Ohio, and the half-pay of a British colonel.

To Washington the visits of these gentlemen were extremely welcome at this juncture, from their military knowledge and experience, especially as much of it had been acquired in America in the same kind of warfare, if not the very same campaigns, in which he himself had mingled. Both were interested in the popular cause. Lee was full of plans for the organization and disciplining of the militia and occasionally accompanied Washington on provincial reviews. He was subsequently very efficient in promoting and superintending the Maryland militia. It is doubtful whether the visits of Lee were interesting to Mrs. Washington. He was eccentric, almost rude, and slovenly in person and attire. What was still more annoying in a well regulated mansion, he was always followed by a legion of dogs, which took their seats by him when at table.

In March the second Virginia Convention was held at Richmond. Washington attended as delegate from Fairfax County. In this assembly, Patrick Henry, with his usual ardor and eloquence, advocated measures for a militia force to provide defence of the colony. Washington joined him in the conviction and was one of a committee that reported a plan for carrying those measures into effect. He was not an impulsive man to raise the battle cry but the executive man to marshal the troops into the field and carry on the war.

His brother, John Augustine, was raising and disciplining an independent company; Washington offered to accept command of it. He did the same with respect to an independent company at Richmond. "It is my full intention, if needful," writes he to his brother, "to devote my life and fortune to the cause."

While the spirit of revolt was daily gaining strength and determination in America, a strange infatuation reigned in the British councils. While the wisdom and eloquence of Chatham were exerted in vain in behalf of American rights, an empty braggadocio—Colonel Grant, whose foolhardy bravado at Fort Duquesne had brought slaughter and defeat upon his troops— elevated to Parliament, was able to influence their votes by gross misrepresentations of the Americans and their cause. The counsels of the arrogant and scornful prevailed; further measures of a stringent nature were adopted, coercive of some of the middle and southern colonies, but ruinous to the trade and fisheries of New England.

At length the bolt, so long suspended, fell! The troops at Boston had been augmented to about 4000 men. Alarmed by the energetic measures of the whigs, Gage resolved to deal the latter a crippling blow. This was to surprise and destroy their military stores at Concord in the night of the 18th of April.

Preparations were made with great secrecy, but the measures had not been shrouded in all the secrecy he imagined. Dr. Joseph Warren, one of the committee of safety, had observed the preparatory disposition of the boats and troops and surmised some sinister intention. He sent notice of these movements to John Hancock and Samuel Adams, both at that time sojourning with a friend at Lexington. A design on the magazine at Concord was suspected; the committee of safety ordered that the cannon collected there should be secreted and part of the stores removed.

On the night of the 18th, Dr. Warren sent two messengers by different routes to give the alarm that the king's troops were sallying forth. About the same time a lantern was hung out of an upper window of the north church, in the direction of Charlestown, a preconcerted signal to the patriots of that place, who instantly despatched swift messengers to rouse the country.

In the mean time, Colonel Smith, on his nocturnal march from Lechmere Point, had proceeded but a few miles when alarm guns and village bells showed that news of his approach was travelling before him and the people were rising. He sent back to Gage for reinforcement while Major Pitcairn was detached with six companies to press forward and secure the bridges at Concord.

Within a mile and a half of Lexington, however, a horseman was too quick on the spur for Pitcairn and, galloping to the village, gave the alarm that the redcoats were coming. By the time Pitcairn entered the village, about 80 of the yeomanry, in military array, were mustered on the green near the church.

Pitcairn halted his men within a short distance of the church and ordered them to prime and load. They then advanced at double quick time. The major, riding forward, ordered the rebels, as he termed them, to disperse. The orders were disregarded. A scene of confusion ensued, with firing on both sides; which party commenced it has been a matter of dispute. The firing of the Americans was without much effect; that of the British was more fatal. Eight of the patriots were killed, ten wounded, and the whole put to flight. The victors formed on the common, fired a volley, and gave three cheers for one of the most inglorious triumphs ever achieved by British arms.

Smith soon arrived with the residue of the detachment, and they all marched on towards Concord. The alarm had reached that place the preceding night. The militia and minute men seized their arms and repaired to the parade ground near the church. Here they were joined by armed yeomanry from Lincoln and elsewhere. Exertions were now made to remove and conceal the military stores. Part of the militia marched down the Lexington road to meet them but returned, reporting their force to be three times that of the Americans. The whole of the militia now retired to an eminence a mile from the centre of town and formed themselves into two battalions.

About seven o'clock, the British entered in two divisions by different roads. Concord is traversed by a river having two bridges, the north and the south. The grenadiers and light infantry took post in the centre of town, while strong parties of light troops were detached to secure the bridges and destroy the military stores. Two hours were expended in destruction without much success, so much of the stores having been removed or concealed. During all this time the yeomanry from neighboring towns were hurrying in with such weapons as were at hand, until the gathering there numbered about 450.

About ten o'clock, a body of 300 undertook to dislodge the British from the north bridge. As they approached, the latter fired upon them. The patriots returned the fire with spirit and effect. The British retreated to the main body, the Americans pursuing them across the bridge.

By this time all the military stores which could be found had been destroyed; Smith, therefore, made preparations for a retreat and, about noon, he commenced his march for Boston. As the British began their retreat, the Americans began the work of retaliation. Along the open road, the former were harassed incessantly by rustic marksmen, who took aim from behind trees or over stone fences. Where the road passed through woods, the British found themselves between two fires, dealt by unseen foes, the minute men having posted themselves on each side among the bushes. The retreat grew more and more disastrous; some were shot down, some gave out through exhaustion; the rest hurried on without stopping to aid the fatigued or wounded. Before reaching Lexington, Smith received a severe wound in the leg and the situation of the retreating troops was becoming extremely critical, when, about two o'clock, they were met by Lord Percy, with a brigade of 1000 men and two field-pieces. His lordship had been detached from Boston by Gage, in compliance with Smith's call for reinforcement. Opening his brigade to the right and left, he received the retreating troops into a hollow square, where, exhausted, they threw themselves on the ground to rest. His lordship showed no disposition to advance upon the assailants but contented himself with keeping them at bay with his field-pieces, which opened a vigorous fire from an eminence.

Hitherto the Provincials, being hasty levies, had acted from individual impulse, without much concert, but now General Heath was upon the ground. He was one of those authorized to take command when the minute men should be called out. Dr. Warren, also, arrived on horseback, having spurred from Boston on receiving news of the skirmishing. In the subsequent part of the day, he was one of the most active men in the field. His presence, like that of Heath, regulated the infuriated ardor of the militia and brought it into system.

Percy, having allowed the troops a short interval for refreshment, continued the retreat toward Boston. As soon as he got under march, the assault by the yeomanry was recommenced in flank and rear. The British soldiery, irritated in turn, acted as if in an enemy's country. Houses and shops were burnt down, private dwellings along the road were plundered, and their inhabitants maltreated. There was occasional sharp skirmishing, but in general a dogged pursuit in which the retreating troops were galled at every step. Percy's ammunition was failing as he approached Charlestown. The Provincials pressed upon him in rear; others were advancing from Roxbury, Dorchester, and Milton; Colonel Pickering, with the Essex militia, 700 strong, was at hand; there was danger of being intercepted in the retreat to Charlestown. The field-pieces were again brought into play to check the ardor of the pursuit, but they were no longer objects of terror. The pursuit terminated a little after sunset, at Charlestown Common, where Heath brought the minute men to a halt. Within half an hour more, a powerful body of men from Marblehead and Salem came up to join the chase.

The British loss was 73 killed, 174 wounded, and 26 missing. Among the slain were 18 officers. The loss of the Americans was 49 killed, 39 wounded, and 5 missing. This was the first blood shed in the revolutionary struggle, a mere drop in amount but a deluge in its effects, rending the colonies for ever from the mother country.

The cry from the field of Lexington went through the land. None felt the appeal more than the old soldiers of the French war. It roused John Stark of New Hampshire—a veteran in Indian warfare, a campaigner under Abercrombie and Amherst. Within ten minutes after receiving the alarm, he was spurring towards the seacoast, stirring up volunteers of the Massachusetts borders to assemble forthwith at Bedford.

Equally alert was his old comrade in frontier exploits, Colonel Israel Putnam. A man on horseback, with a drum, passed through his neighborhood in Connecticut, proclaiming British violence at Lexington. Putnam was, in an instant, on horseback, in his working garb, urging with all speed to the camp. Such was the spirit aroused throughout the country.

The news reached Virginia at a critical moment. Lord Dunmore, obeying a general order by the ministry to all provincial governors, had seized the military munitions of the province. The cry went forth that subjugation of the colonies was to be attempted. All Virginia was in combustion. There was a general cry to arms. Washington was looked to, from various quarters, to take command. His old comrade in arms, Hugh Mercer, was marching to Williamsburg at the head of a body of resolute men, 700 strong, and nothing but a timely concession of Dunmore with respect to some powder he had seized prevented his being beset in his palace.

Washington was at Mount Vernon preparing to set out for Philadelphia as a delegate to the second Congress when he received tidings of the affair at Lexington. Bryan Fairfax and Major Horatio

Gates were his guests at the time. They all regarded the event as decisive in its consequences. The worthy and gentle-spirited Fairfax deplored it deeply, arraying his dearest friends against the government to which he was loyally attached. Gates, on the contrary, viewed it with the eye of a soldier and a place-hunter. This event promised to open a new avenue to importance and command and he determined to enter upon it.

Washington's feelings were of a mingled nature. They may be gathered from a letter to George William Fairfax, then in England, in which the yearnings of the patriot give affecting solemnity to the resolve of the soldier: "Unhappy it is to reflect that a brother's sword has been sheathed in a brother's breast and that the once happy and peaceful plains of America are to be either drenched with blood or inhabited by slaves. Sad alternative! But can a virtuous man hesitate in his choice?"

The march of the Revolution went on with accelerated speed. Thirty thousand men had been deemed necessary for the defence of the country. The provincial Congress of Massachusetts resolved to raise 13,600 as its quota. Circular letters were issued by the committee of safety, urging the towns to enlist troops with all speed and calling for military aid from the other New England provinces.

Their appeals were promptly answered. Bodies of militia and parties of volunteers from New Hampshire, Rhode Island, and Connecticut hastened to join the minute men of Massachusetts in forming a camp in the neighborhood of Boston. With the troops of Connecticut came Israel Putnam. The command of the camp was given to General Artemas Ward, who had recently been made, by the provincial Congress of Massachusetts, commander-in-chief of its forces.

The Resort to Arms (1774–1775)

(CHAPTER 11)

As war was considered inevitable, some bold spirits in Connecticut conceived a project for the outset. This was the surprisal of the old forts of Ticonderoga and Crown Point. Their situation on Lake Champlain gave them command of the main route to Canada; possession of them would be all-important in case of hostilities. They were feebly garrisoned and abundantly furnished with artillery and military stores, so much needed by the patriot army.

This scheme was set on foot by the provincial Legislature of Connecticut, not openly sanctioned, but secretly favored. Sixteen men were enlisted in Connecticut, a greater number in Massachusetts, but the greatest accession of force was from the "New Hampshire Grants." This was a region forming the present State of Vermont. It had long been a disputed territory, claimed by New York and New Hampshire. George II had decided in favor of New York, but the Governor of New Hampshire had made grants of townships in it, whence it had acquired its name. The settlers on those grants resisted the attempts of New York to eject them and formed an association called "The Green Mountain Boys." Ethan Allen was at their head, a native of Connecticut but brought up among the Green Mountains. He and his lieutenants were outlawed by the Legislature of New York and rewards offered for their apprehension.

The present crisis changed things as if by magic. Boundary feuds were forgotten and Ethan Allen at once volunteered with his Green Mountain Boys to serve in the popular cause. Thus reinforced, the party, now 270 strong, pushed forward to Castleton, within a few miles of the head of Lake Champlain. Here a council of war was held on the 2d of May and Ethan Allen was placed at the head of the expedition. Detachments were sent off to seize all the boats they could find and bring them to Shoreham, opposite Ticonderoga, whither Allen prepared to proceed with the main body.

At this juncture, another adventurous spirit arrived at Castleton. Benedict Arnold, too, had conceived the project of surprising Ticonderoga and Crown Point and he had proposed the scheme to the Massachusetts committee of safety. It met with their approbation; they gave him a colonel's commission, authorized him to raise a force in Western Massachusetts, and furnished him with money and means. Arnold had enlisted but a few officers and men when he heard of the expedition from Connecticut; leaving his few recruits to follow, he reached Castleton just after the council of war. Producing the colonel's commission from the Massachusetts committee of safety, he aspired to the supreme command. His claims were disregarded by the Green Mountain Boys; they would follow no leader but Ethan Allen. As they formed the majority of the party, Arnold acquiesced to serve as a volunteer with the rank but not the command of colonel.

The party arrived opposite Ticonderoga on the night of the 9th of May. The detachment sent in quest of boats had failed to arrive. There were a few boats at hand; the night wore away; and but 83 men with Allen and Arnold had crossed. Should they wait for the residue, day would dawn, the garrison awake, and their enterprise might fail. Allen announced his intention to make a dash at the fort without waiting for more force.

They mounted the hill briskly but in silence. A sentry was struck down by Allen and begged for quarter. It was granted on condition of his leading the way to the quarters of the commandant, Captain Delaplace, who was yet in bed. Being arrived there, Allen thundered at the door and demanded a surrender of the fort. By this time his followers had formed into two lines on the parade-ground and given three hearty cheers. The commandant appeared at his door half-dressed. The garrison, like the commander, had been startled from sleep and made prisoners as they rushed forth in their confusion. A surrender accordingly took place. A great supply of military and naval stores, so important in the present crisis, was found in the fortress.

Colonel Seth Warner, who had brought over the residue of the party from Shoreham, was now sent with a detachment against

Crown Point, which surrendered on the 12th of May without firing a gun. Here were taken upward of 100 cannon.

Arnold now insisted on his right to command Ticonderoga but his claims had again to yield to the superior popularity of Ethan Allen, to whom the Connecticut committee gave an instrument in writing investing him with command of the fortress. Arnold's chagrin was appeased by a new project. The detachment originally sent to seize upon boats at Skenesborough arrived with a schooner and several batteaux. It was immediately concerted to cruise down the lake and surprise St. John's, on the Sorel River, the frontier post of Canada. Arnold, who had been a seaman in his youth, took command of the armed schooner, while Allen and his Green Mountain Boys embarked in the batteaux.

Arnold outsailed the other craft and, arriving at St. John's, surprised and made prisoners of a sergeant and 12 men, captured a king's sloop of 70 tons with 2 brass six-pounders and 7 men, took 4 batteaux, destroyed several others, and then, learning that troops were on the way from Montreal and Chamblee, swept up the lake with his prizes, prisoners, and valuable stores, and returned to Ticonderoga.

Thus a partisan band, had, by daring exploits, won for the patriots command of Lakes George and Champlain and thrown open the great highway to Canada.

The second General Congress assembled at Philadelphia on the 10th of May. John Hancock was elected president after Peyton Randolph was obliged to return to his place as speaker of the Virginia Assembly.

A lingering feeling of attachment to the mother country was manifested in the proceedings of this remarkable body. Many of those most active in vindicating colonial rights, Washington among the number, still indulged the hope of an eventual reconciliation. A second "humble and dutiful" petition to the king was moved but met with strong opposition. When it was carried, Congress, in face of it, went on to assume the powers of a sovereign authority. A federal union was formed, leaving to each colony the right of regulating its internal affairs according to its own individual constitution, but vesting in Congress the power of making peace or war, of entering into treaties and alliances, of regulating general commerce—in a word, of legislating on all such matters as regarded the whole community.

The executive power was vested in a council of twelve, chosen by Congress from among its own members and to hold office for a limited time. Such colonies as had not sent delegates to Congress might become members of the confederacy by agreeing to its conditions. Georgia, which had hitherto hesitated, soon joined the league.

Congress lost no time in exercising their federated powers. They ordered the enlistment of troops, the construction of forts in various parts of the colonies, the provision of arms, ammunition and military stores. To defray the expense of these and other measures avowedly of self-defence, they authorized the emission of notes to the amount of $3,000,000 bearing the inscription of "The United Colonies," the faith of the confederacy being pledged for their redemption.

The public sense of Washington's military talents and experience, was evinced in his being chairman of all the committees for military affairs. Most of the rules and regulations for the army and the measures for defence were devised by him.

The situation of the New England army, actually besieging Boston, became an early and absorbing consideration. It was without munitions of war, without arms, clothing, or pay—in fact, without legislative countenance or encouragement. Unless sanctioned and assisted by Congress there was danger of its dissolution. The disposition to uphold the army was general but who should be commander-in-chief? Hancock himself had an ambition to be appointed commander-in-chief, but his entire want of experience in actual service, though an excellent militia officer, were decisive objections to him. General Charles Lee's active interest in the cause was well known and the public had an almost extravagant idea of his military qualifications. He was of foreign birth, however, and it was deemed improper to confide the supreme command to any but a native-born American. The opinion evidently inclined in favor of Washington; yet it was promoted by no clique of partisans or admirers. It is scarcely necessary to add that Washington made no step in advance to clutch the impending honor.

Adams, in his diary, claims the credit of bringing the members of Congress to a decision. Rising in his place one day, he moved that Congress adopt the army at Cambridge and appoint a general. He proposed Washington, "a gentleman, whose skill and experience as an officer, whose independent fortune, great talents, and excellent universal character, would command the approbation of all America, and unite the cordial exertions of all the colonies better than any other person in the Union."

Several delegates opposed the appointment of Washington because the army were all from New England and had a general of their own, Artemas Ward, under whose command they had proved themselves able to imprison the British army in Boston. The subject was postponed until the 15th of June, when the army was regularly adopted by Congress. In this stage of the business, Johnson of Maryland rose and nominated Washington for commander-in-chief. The election, by ballot, was unanimous. It was formally announced to him by the president on the following day, when he had taken his seat in Congress. Rising in his place, he briefly expressed his high and grateful sense of the honor conferred on him and his sincere devotion to the cause.

Four major-generals were to be appointed. General Ward was elected the second in command and Lee the third. The other two major-generals were Philip Schuyler of New York and Israel Putnam of Connecticut. Eight brigadier-generals were appointed: Seth Pomeroy, Richard Montgomery, David Wooster, William Heath, Joseph Spencer, John Thomas, John Sullivan, and Nathaniel Green. At Washington's request, Major Horatio Gates, then absent at his estate in Virginia, was appointed adjutant-general, with the rank of brigadier.

In this momentous change which called him immediately to the camp, Washington's thoughts recurred to Mount Vernon, so dear to his heart, whence he was to be again exiled. His chief concern, however, was the distress it might cause to his wife. His letter to her is written in manly tenderness: "I assure you . . . that, so far from seeking this appointment, I have used every endeavor in my power to avoid it, not only from my unwillingness to part with you and the family, but from a consciousness of its being a trust too great for my capacity. . . . But as it has been a kind of destiny that has thrown me upon this service, I shall hope that my undertaking it is designed to answer some good purpose. . . . I shall feel no pain from the toil or danger of the campaign; my unhappiness will flow from the uneasiness I know you will feel from being left alone. I therefore beg that you will summon your whole fortitude and pass your time as agreeably as possible. Nothing will give me so much sincere satisfaction as to hear this, and to hear it from your own pen."

On the 20th of June, he received his commission from the president of Congress. The following day was fixed upon for his departure for the army. He reviewed previously, at the request of their officers, several militia companies of horse and foot. Every one was anxious to see the new commander and rarely has the public *beau ideal* of a commander been so fully answered. He was in the vigor of his days, stately in person, noble in demeanor, dignified in deportment. As he sat his horse, with manly grace, his military presence delighted every eye and wherever he went the air rang with acclamations.

(CHAPTER 12)

While Congress had been deliberating on the adoption of the army and the nomination of a commander-in-chief, events had been drawing to a crisis in Boston. The provincial troops which blockaded the town prevented supplies by land and the neighboring country refused to furnish them by water; Boston began to experience the privations of a besieged city.

On the 25th of May arrived ships of war and transports from England, bringing large reinforcements under Generals Howe, Burgoyne, and Henry Clinton, commanders of high reputation. Inspirited by these reinforcements, Gage determined to take the field. He issued a proclamation (12th June) putting the province under martial law, threatening to treat as rebels and traitors all malcontents who continue under arms, together with their abettors; but offering pardon to all who return to their allegiance. From this proffered amnesty, however, John Hancock and Samuel Adams were especially excepted. This proclamation only served to put the patriots on the alert against such measures as might be expected to follow.

The besieging force, daily augmented by recruits and volunteers, now amounted to 15,000 men at various points. Its character and organization were peculiar. About 10,000 belonged to Massachusetts under the command of Ward, whose head-quarters were at Cambridge. Another body of troops, under Stark, came from New Hampshire. Rhode Island furnished a third, under the command of Nathaniel Greene. A fourth was from Connecticut, under Putnam.

These bodies of troops, being from different colonies, were independent of each other and had their several commanders. Those from New Hampshire were instructed to obey Ward as commander-in-chief; with the rest, it was a voluntary act in consideration of his being military chief of Massachusetts, the province which, as allies, they came to defend.

The troops knew but little of military discipline. Many had served in frontier campaigns against the French and in "bush fighting" with the Indians, but none were acquainted with the discipline of European armies. There was a regiment of artillery, partly organized by Colonel Richard Gridley, furnished with nine field-pieces. The greater part of the troops were without military dress; most of them had seized their rifles and fowling-pieces and turned out in their working clothes and homespun country garbs. Such was the army spread over ten or twelve miles, keeping watch upon Boston, garrisoned with more than 10,000 British troops, disciplined and experienced in the wars of Europe.

Ward had stationed himself at Cambridge, with the main body of about 9000 men and four companies of artillery. Lieutenant-general Thomas, second in command, was posted with 5000 Massachusetts, Connecticut, and Rhode Island troops and three or four companies of artillery at Roxbury and Dorchester, forming the right wing of the army; while the left, composed in great measure of New Hampshire troops, stretched through Medford to Chelsea. Both parties panted for action, the British through impatience of their humiliating position, the Provincials through enthusiasm in their cause.

We have already mentioned the peninsula of Charlestown (from a village of the same name), opposite the north side of Boston. The project was conceived in the besieging camp to seize the heights in rear of the village, which overlook the town and shipping. A council of war was held upon the subject. Putnam was one of the most strenuous in favor of the measure. Some of the more wary and judicious, among whom were Ward and Warren, doubted the expediency of intrenching themselves on those heights, maintaining so exposed a post, scantily furnished with ordnance and ammunition.

Putnam made light of the danger. He was confident of the bravery of the militia if intrenched, having seen it in the French war. He was seconded by General Pomeroy, a leader of like stamp and a veteran of the French war. The daring counsels were sanctioned by one whose opinion in this vicinity possessed peculiar weight. This was Colonel William Prescott, who commanded a regiment of minute men. He, too, had seen service in the French war and his opinion, probably, settled the question; it was determined to seize and fortify Bunker's Hill and Dorchester Heights.

Secret intelligence hurried forward the project. Gage, it was said, intended to take possession of Dorchester Heights on the night of the 18th of June. The heights on Charlestown Neck had some time before been reconnoitered by Gridley and other engineers. It was determined to seize and fortify these heights on the night of the 16th of June.

A little before sunset the troops, about 1200 in all, assembled in front of Ward's quarters. Prescott had been chosen by Ward to conduct the enterprise. His orders were to fortify Bunker's Hill and defend the works until relieved. Gridley was to accompany him and plan the fortifications. It was understood that reinforcements and refreshments would be sent in the morning. The detachment left Cambridge about 9 o'clock. At Charlestown Neck they were joined by Major Brooks of Bridges' regiment and Putnam. Charlestown

FORTIFYING BREED'S HILL IN THE NIGHT JUNE 16. 1775.

Vol.I.p.467

(From the original drawing in the possession of the publishers)

Entered according to act of Congress AD.1856 by G.P.Putnam & Co. in the Clerks office of the District court of the Southern District of New York.

Neck is a narrow isthmus, connecting the peninsula with the main land, having the Mystic River on the north and a large embayment of Charles River on the south side. It was necessary to proceed with utmost caution for they were coming on ground over which the British kept jealous watch. They had erected a battery at Boston on Copp's Hill, opposite Charlestown. Five of their vessels of war were stationed so as to bear upon the peninsula from different directions and the guns of one of them swept the isthmus. Prescott conducted the detachment undiscovered and up the ascent of Bunker's Hill. This commences at the Neck and slopes up for 300 yards to its summit, which is 112 feet high. It then declines toward the south and is connected by a ridge with Breed's Hill, about 70 feet high. The crests of the two hills are about 700 yards apart.

On attaining the heights, a question rose which of the two they should fortify. Bunker's Hill was specified in the orders given to Prescott by Ward but Breed's Hill was nearer to Boston and had a better command of the town and shipping. Bunker's Hill, being on the upper part of the peninsula, was itself commanded by the same ship which raked the Neck. Putnam was for commencing at Breed's Hill, while a minor work might be thrown up at Bunker's Hill as a protection in the rear and a rallying point in case of being driven out of the main work. Others concurred with this opinion, yet there was a hesitation in deviating from the letter of their orders. At length Breed's Hill was determined on. Gridley marked out the lines for the fortifications; the men stacked their guns, threw off their packs, seized their trenching tools, and set to work with great spirit. By morning a strong redoubt was thrown up as a main work, flanked on the left by a breastwork extending down the crest of Breed's Hill to a marshy ground called the Slough. To support the right of the redoubt, some troops were thrown into the village of Charlestown at the southern foot of the hill.

At dawn the Americans were espied by the sailors on the ships of war and the alarm was given. The captain of the Lively, the nearest ship, opened fire upon the hill. The other ships and a floating battery followed his example. Their shot did no mischief to the works. To inspire confidence, Prescott walked leisurely about, inspecting the works and talking cheerfully with the men.

The cannonading roused the town of Boston. Gage could scarcely believe his eyes when he beheld on the opposite hill a fortification full of men which had sprung up in the night. He called a council of war. The Americans might cannonade Boston from this new fortification; it was unanimously resolved to dislodge them. How was this to be done? A majority of the council advised that a force be landed on Charlestown Neck under the protection of their batteries to attack the Americans in rear and cut off their retreat. Gage objected that it would place his troops between two armies: one at Cambridge, superior in numbers, the other on the heights, strongly fortified. He was for landing in front of the works and pushing directly up the hill, confident that raw militia would never stand their ground against the assault of veteran troops.

The military din and bustle in Boston soon apprised the Americans on their rudely fortified height of an impending attack. They were ill fitted to withstand it, being jaded by the night's labor, hungry and thirsty, and oppressed by the heat of the weather. Prescott sent repeated messages to Ward, asking reinforcements and provisions; Putnam seconded the request in person. Ward hesitated, but at length, he issued orders for Stark and Reed, then at Medford, to march to the relief of Prescott with their New Hampshire regiments.

In the mean while, the Americans on Breed's Hill were sustaining the fire from the ships and from the battery on Copp's Hill. They continued strengthening their position anxiously for the anticipated reinforcements and supplies.

About this time Putnam, who had been to head-quarters, arrived at the redoubt on horseback. Some words passed between him and Prescott with regard to the intrenching tools, which have been variously reported. In any case, a large part of the tools were ultimately carried to Bunker's Hill and a breastwork commenced. The importance of such a work was afterwards made apparent.

About noon the Americans descried 28 barges crossing from Boston. They contained a large detachment of grenadiers, rangers, and light infantry, commanded by Major-general Howe. They made a splendid and formidable appearance with their scarlet uniforms, the sun flashing upon muskets and bayonets. A heavy fire covered their advance but no attempt was made to oppose them and they landed about 1 o'clock at Moulton's Point, to the north of Breed's Hill.

Here Howe made a pause. On reconnoitering the works from this point, the Americans appeared to be much more strongly posted than he had imagined. He descried troops also hastening to their assistance. Howe immediately sent to Gage for more forces, and, while awaiting their arrival, refreshments were served out to the troops, and tantalizing it was to the hungry and thirsty provincials to see invaders preparing themselves by a hearty meal for the coming encounter. Their only consolation was to take advantage of the delay to strengthen their position. The breastwork on the left of the redoubt extended to the Slough but, beyond this, the ridge of the hill and the slope toward Mystic River were undefended, leaving a pass by which the enemy might turn the left flank of the position and seize upon Bunker's Hill. Putnam ordered Captain Knowlton to cover this pass with the Connecticut troops under his command. A novel kind of rampart was suggested by the rustic general. About 600 feet in the rear of the redoubt and about 100 feet to the left of the breastwork was a post-and-rail fence, set in a low foot-wall of stone and extending down to Mystic River. The posts and rails of another fence were hastily pulled up and set a few feet behind this, and the intermediate space was filled up with hay from the adjacent meadows. This double fence proved an important protection to the redoubt although there still remained an unprotected interval of about 700 feet.

While Knowlton and his men were putting up this fence, Putnam proceeded with other troops to throw up the work on Bunker's Hill, despatching his son, Captain Putnam, to hurry up the remainder of his men from Cambridge. By this time Stark made his appearance with the New Hampshire troops, 500 strong. Putnam detained some of Stark's men to aid in throwing up the works on Bunker's Hill and directed him to reinforce Knowlton with the rest. About 2 o'clock, Warren arrived on the heights, ready to engage in their perilous defence, although he had opposed the scheme of their occupation. He had recently been elected a major-general but had not received his commission. Putnam offered him the command at the fence; he declined it and merely asked where he could be of most service. Putnam pointed to the redoubt. Warren was cheered by the troops as he entered the redoubt. Colonel Prescott tendered him the command, but he again declined. Such were the noble spirits assembled on these perilous heights.

The British now prepared for a general assault. An easy victory was anticipated; the main thought was how to make it most effectual. The left wing, commanded by Pigot, was to mount the hill and force the redoubt, while Howe, with the right wing, was to push on between the fort and Mystic River, turn the left flank of the Americans and cut off their retreat.

Pigot, accordingly, advanced up the hill under cover of a fire from field-pieces and howitzers. The Americans within the works, obedient to command, retained their fire until the enemy were within thirty or forty paces, when they opened upon them with a tremendous volley. Being all marksmen, accustomed to take deliberate aim, the slaughter was immense, especially fatal to officers. The assailants fell back in confusion, but, rallied on by their officers, advanced within pistol shot. Another volley, more effective than the first, made them again recoil. To add to their confusion, they were galled by a flanking fire from the Provincials posted in Charlestown. Shocked at the carnage and seeing the confusion of his troops, Pigot was urged to retreat.

In the mean while, Howe, with the left wing, advanced along Mystic River, toward the fence where Stark, Reed and Knowlton were stationed, thinking to carry this slight breastwork with ease and so get in the rear of the fortress. His artillery proved of little avail, being stopped by swampy ground, while his columns suffered from two or three field-pieces with which Putnam had fortified the fence. Howe's men kept up a fire of musketry as they advanced, but the Americans had received orders not to fire until the enemy should be within thirty paces. When the British arrived within the stated distance, a sheeted fire opened upon them from rifles, muskets, and fowling-pieces, all levelled with deadly aim. The carnage was horrible. The British were thrown into confusion and fell back; some even retreated to the boats.

There was a general pause on the part of the British. The American officers availed themselves of it to prepare for another attack, which must soon be made. Prescott mingled among his men in the redoubt, praised them for their steadfastness and their good conduct in reserving their fire until the command, and exhorted them to do the same in the next attack. Putnam rode about Bunker's Hill and its skirts to rally and bring on reinforcements which had been checked or scattered in crossing Charlestown Neck by the raking fire from the ships and batteries. Before many could be brought to the scene of action the British had commenced their second attack. They again ascended the hill to storm the redoubt; their advance was covered as before by artillery. Charlestown, which had annoyed them on their first attack by a flanking fire, was in flames by shells from Copp's Hill and from the ships.

The American troops stood undismayed amidst a scene where it was bursting upon them with all its horrors. Reserving their fire, as before, until the enemy was close at hand, they again poured forth volleys with the fatal aim of sharpshooters. The British continued to advance, but the incessant stream of fire staggered them. The havoc was deadly; whole ranks were mowed down; the troops again gave way and retreated down the hill.

The British soldiery in Boston gazed with astonishment and incredulity at the resolute stand of raw militia, whom they had been taught to despise, and at the havoc made among their own veteran troops. Clinton, who had watched from Copp's Hill, embarking in a boat, hurried over with reinforcements.

A third attack was now determined on, though some of Howe's officers declared it would be downright butchery. A different plan was adopted. Instead of advancing in front of the redoubt, it was to be taken in flank on the left, where the open space between the breastwork and fortified fence presented a weak point. It having been accidentally discovered that the ammunition of the Americans was nearly expended, preparations were made to carry the works at the point of the bayonet.

Howe, with the main body, made a feint of attacking the fortified fence; while part of his force was thus engaged, the rest brought some of the field-pieces to enfilade the breastwork on the left of the redoubt. A raking fire soon drove the Americans out of this exposed place into the enclosure. The troops were now led on to assail the works. The Americans again reserved their fire until their assailants were close at hand and then made a murderous volley by which several officers were laid low; Howe himself was wounded in the foot. The British soldiery rushed on with fixed bayonet. Clinton and Pigot had reached the southern and eastern sides of the redoubt and it was now assailed on three sides at once. Prescott ordered those who had no bayonets to retire to the back part of the redoubt and fire on the enemy as they showed themselves on the parapet. The Americans, however, had fired their last round, their ammunition was exhausted, and now succeeded a desperate and deadly struggle, hand to hand, with bayonets, stones, and the stocks of their muskets. At length, as the British continued to pour in, Prescott gave the order to retreat. His men had to cut their way through two divisions of the enemy who were in rear of the redoubt and they received a destructive volley from those who had formed on the captured works. By that volley fell the patriot Warren, who had distinguished himself throughout the action.

While the Americans were thus slowly dislodged from the redoubt, Stark, Reed and Knowlton maintained their ground at the fortified fence, which had been nobly defended throughout the action. The resistance at this work was kept up after the troops in the redoubt had given way and until Prescott had left the hill, thus defeating Howe's design of cutting off the retreat of the main body. Having effected their purpose, the brave associates at the fence abandoned their outpost, retiring slowly and disputing the ground inch by inch.

The main retreat was across Bunker's Hill, where Putnam had endeavored to throw up a breastwork. The veteran's only thought was to rally them at the unfinished works. Pomeroy seconded him in his efforts to stay the torrent. It was impossible, however, to bring the troops to a stand. They continued on down the hill to the Neck and across it to Cambridge, exposed to a raking fire from the ships and batteries. The British, too exhausted to pursue them, contented themselves with taking possession of Bunker's Hill, were reinforced from Boston, and threw up additional works during the night.

The Resort to Arms (1774–1775)

It was one of the most momentous conflicts in our revolutionary history. It was the first regular battle between the British and the Americans, most eventful in its consequences. The former had gained the ground for which they contended, but, if a victory, it was more disastrous and humiliating than a defeat. They had ridiculed their enemy, yet their best troops, led by experienced officers, had repeatedly been repulsed by that enemy from works thrown up in a single night. To the latter this defeat, if defeat it might be called, had the effect of a triumph. It gave them confidence in themselves and consequence in the eyes of their enemies. They had proved that they could measure weapons with the disciplined soldiers of Europe.

(CHAPTER 13)

In a preceding chapter we left Washington preparing to depart from Philadelphia for the army before Boston. He set out on horseback on the 21st of June, having for military companions Major-generals Lee and Schuyler, accompanied for a distance by several private friends and an escort of a "gentleman troop" of Philadelphia.

General Schuyler, eminently calculated to sympathize with Washington in all his patriotic views and feelings, became one of his most faithful coadjutors. Sprung from one of the earliest and most respectable Dutch families which colonized New York, all his interests and affections were identified with the country. He was one of those soldiers who had acquired experience in that American school of arms, the French war. Since the close of the French war he had served his country in various civil stations and been one of the most zealous and eloquent vindicators of colonial rights. As a delegate to Congress, he had served with Washington on the committee to prepare rules and regulations for the army, where the latter had witnessed his judgment, activity, practical science, and sincere devotion to the cause.

They had scarcely proceeded twenty miles from Philadelphia when they were met by a courier, spurring with all speed, bearing despatches from the army to Congress, communicating tidings of the battle of Bunker's Hill. Washington eagerly inquired particulars—above all, how acted the militia? When told that they stood their ground bravely, sustained the enemy's fire, reserved their own until at close quarters, and then delivered it with deadly effect, it seemed as if a weight were lifted from his heart. "The liberties of the country are safe!" exclaimed he.

The journey may be said to have been a continual council of war between Washington and the two generals. One of the most frequent subjects of conversation was the province of New York. Its power and position rendered it the great link of the confederacy; what measures were necessary for its defence and most calculated to secure its adherence to the cause? A lingering attachment to the crown, kept up by the influence of British merchants and military and civil functionaries in royal pay, had rendered it slow in coming into the colonial compact; it was only on the contemptuous dismissal of their statement of grievances, unheard, that its people had thrown off their allegiance, as much in sorrow as in anger.

The population of New York was more varied in its elements than that of almost any other of the provinces. The New Yorkers were of a mixed origin, and stamped with the peculiarities of their respective ancestors. The descendants of the old Dutch and Huguenot families, the earliest settlers, were still among the best of the population. They inherited the love of liberty of their forefathers and were those who stood foremost in the present struggle for popular rights. Such were the Jays, Bensons, Beekmans, Hoffmans, Van Hornes, Roosevelts, Duyckinks, Pintards, Yateses, and others whose names figure in the patriotic documents of the day. A great proportion of the more modern families were English and Scotch; among these were many loyal adherents to the crown. Then there was a mixture of the whole, produced by the intermarriages of upwards of a century, which partook of every shade of character and sentiment.

There was a power, too, of a formidable kind within the interior of the province, which was an object of much solicitude. This was the

"Johnson Family." We have had occasion to speak of Sir William Johnson, his majesty's general agent for Indian affairs, his great wealth, and his almost sovereign sway over the Six Nations. In the recent difficulties between the crown and colonies, Sir William had naturally been in favor of the government which had enriched and honored him but he viewed with deep concern the acts of Parliament which were goading the colonists to armed resistance. In the height of his solicitude, he received despatches ordering him, in case of hostilities, to enlist the Indians in the cause of government. To the agitation produced by these orders many have attributed a stroke of apoplexy, of which he died on the 11th of July, 1774, about a year before the time of which we are treating.

His son and heir, Sir John Johnson, and his sons-in-law, Colonel Guy Johnson and Colonel Claus, felt none of the reluctance of Sir William to use harsh measures in support of royalty. They lived in a feudal style in stone mansions capable of defence, situated on the Mohawk River and in its vicinity; they had many Scottish Highlanders for tenants and among their adherents were violent men, such as the Butlers of Tryon County and Brant, the Mohawk sachem. They had recently gone about with armed retainers, breaking up patriotic assemblages and it was known they could at any time bring a force of warriors in the field. Recent accounts stated that Sir John was fortifying the old family hall at Johnstown and had 150 Highlanders quartered in it, armed and ready to obey his orders. Colonel Guy Johnson was the most active and zealous of the family. He fortified his stone mansion on the Mohawk and assembled there a part of his militia regiment and other adherents to the number of 500. He held a great Indian council there, in which the chiefs of the Six Nations avowed their determination to stand by and defend every branch of the Johnson family.

Tryon, the governor of New York, was at present in England, having been called home by the ministry to give an account of the affairs of the province and to receive instructions for its management. He was a zealous opponent of all colonial movements and his talents and address gave him great influence over an important part of the community. Should he and the Johnsons co-operate—the one controlling the bay and harbor of New York and the waters of the

Hudson by means of ships and land forces; the others overrunning the valley of the Mohawk and the regions beyond Albany with savage hordes—this great central province might be wrested from the confederacy and all intercourse broken off between the eastern and southern colonies.

All these circumstances and considerations rendered the command of New York a post of especial importance and determined Washington to confide it to Schuyler. He was peculiarly fitted for it by his military talents, his intimate knowledge of the province and its concerns, especially what related to the upper parts of it, and his experience in Indian affairs.

At New York, Washington had learned all the details of the battle of Bunker's Hill; they quickened his impatience to arrive at the camp. He departed, therefore, on the 26th, accompanied by Lee.

In the mean time the provincial Congress of Massachusetts, then in session at Watertown, had made arrangements for the expected arrival of Washington. The Congress sent a deputation which met Washington at Springfield, on the frontiers of the province, and provided escorts and accommodations for him along the road. Thus attended from town to town and escorted by volunteer companies and cavalcades of gentlemen, he arrived at Watertown on the 2d of July, where he was greeted by Congress with a congratulatory address, in which, however, was frankly stated the undisciplined state of the army he was summoned to command. An address of cordial welcome was likewise made to Lee.

The ceremony over, Washington was again in the saddle and, escorted by a troop of light horse and a cavalcade of citizens, proceeded to the head-quarters provided for him at Cambridge. As he entered the camp, the shouts of the multitude and the thundering of artillery gave note to the enemy beleaguered in Boston of his arrival. His personal appearance, notwithstanding the dust of travel, was calculated to captivate the public eye. As he rode through the camp amidst a throng of officers, he was the admiration of the soldiery and of a throng collected from the surrounding country. The fair sex were still more enthusiastic in their admiration, if we may judge from the following passage of a letter written by the wife of John

Adams to her husband: "Dignity, ease and complacency, the gentleman and the soldier, look agreeably blended in him. Modesty marks every line and feature of his face."

With Washington, modest at all times, there was nothing to call forth emotions of self-glorification. The honors with which he was received, the acclamations of the public, the cheerings of the army only told him how much was expected from him. And when he looked round upon the raw and rustic levies he was to command, scattered in rough encampments above hill and dale, beleaguering a city garrisoned by veteran troops, with ships of war anchored about its harbor, and strong outposts guarding it, he felt the awful responsibility of his situation and the complicated and stupendous task before him. He spoke of it, however, not despondingly nor boastfully, but with that solemn resolution and that hopeful reliance on Supreme Goodness which belonged to his magnanimous nature.

On the 3d of July, the morning after his arrival at Cambridge, Washington took formal command of the army. Accompanied by Lee, on whose military judgment he had great reliance, Washington visited the different posts and rode to the heights commanding views over Boston and its environs, anxious to make himself acquainted with the strength and relative position of both armies.

In visiting the posts, Washington halted for a time at Prospect Hill, which commanded a wide view over Boston and the surrounding country. Here Putnam had taken his position after the battle of Bunker's Hill, fortifying himself with works he deemed impregnable; here he was able to point out the main features of the region before them.

Bunker's Hill was but a mile distant to the west; the main force under Howe was intrenching itself about half a mile beyond the place of the recent battle. At the base of the hill lay Charlestown in ashes.

Howe's sentries extended 150 yards beyond the isthmus over which the Americans retreated. Three floating batteries in Mystic River commanded this isthmus and a twenty-gun ship was anchored between the peninsula and Boston.

Gage still had his head-quarters in the town but there were few troops there besides Burgoyne's light-horse. A large force, however, was intrenched south of the town on the neck leading to Roxbury, the only entrance to Boston by land.

The American troops were irregularly distributed in a semicircle eight or nine miles in extent, the left resting on Winter Hill, the most northern post, and the right extending on the south to Roxbury and Dorchester Neck.

Washington reconnoitred the British posts from various points of view. Every thing about them was in admirable order. The American camp, on the contrary, disappointed him. He had expected to find about 20,000 men under arms; there were not much more than 14,000. He had expected to find some degree of system and discipline, whereas all were raw militia. He had expected to find works scientifically constructed, whereas what he saw was very imperfect. There was abundant evidence of aptness at trenching and throwing up rough defences, but the rudely-constructed works were far too extensive for the troops at hand to man them.

Within this attenuated semicircle, the British forces lay concentrated and, having command of the water, might suddenly bring their strength to bear upon some weak point and sever the American camp.

When we consider the scanty, ill-conditioned force stretched out to beleaguer a town and harbor defended by ships and garrisoned by strongly posted veterans, we are at a loss whether to attribute its hazardous position to ignorance or to that daring self-confidence which at times in our military history has snatched success in defiance of scientific rule.

In riding through the camp, Washington observed that 9000 of the troops belonged to Massachusetts, the rest from other provinces. They were encamped in separate bodies, each with its own regulations and officers of its own appointment. All, said Washington, were strongly imbued with the spirit of insubordination, which they mistook for independence.

One of the encampments, however, was in striking contrast with the rest. Here were tents and marquees pitched in the English style, soldiers well drilled and well equipped; every thing had an air of discipline and subordination. It was a body of Rhode Island troops which had been raised, drilled, and brought to the camp by Brigadier-general Nathaniel Greene of that province.

Greene made a soldier-like address to Washington, welcoming him to the camp. He stepped at once into the confidence of the commander-in-chief and became one of his most attached, faithful, and efficient coadjutors throughout the war.

Having taken his survey, Washington wrote to the President of Congress, representing its deficiencies and, among other things, urging the appointment of a commissary-general, a quarter-master-general, a commissary of musters, and a commissary of artillery. Above all things, he requested a supply of money as soon as possible. "I find myself already much embarrassed for want of a military chest." Speaking of the ragged condition of the army, he advises that hunting-shirts should be provided. "I know nothing in a speculative view more trivial, yet which, if put in practice, would have a happier tendency to unite the men and abolish those provincial distinctions that lead to jealousy and dissatisfaction."

The justice and impartiality of Washington were called into exercise as soon as he entered upon his command in allaying discontents among his general officers caused by appointments and promotions by the Continental Congress. General Spencer was so offended that Putnam should be promoted over his head that he left the army, but was subsequently induced to return. General Thomas felt aggrieved by being outranked by Pomeroy; the latter, declining to serve, he found himself senior brigadier and was appeased. The sterling merits of Putnam soon made every one acquiesce in his promotion. There was a generosity and buoyancy about the brave old man that made him a favorite throughout the army, especially with the younger officers.

The Congress of Massachusetts manifested considerate liberality with respect to head-quarters. A committee was charged to procure a steward, housekeeper, and two or three women cooks. Every day a number of his officers dined with Washington. He would occasionally have members of Congress and other functionaries at his board. Though social, however, he was not convivial in his habits. He received his guests with courtesy, but his mind and time were too much occupied to permit him the genial indulgence of the table. His own diet was extremely simple. Sometimes nothing but baked apples or berries with cream and milk. He would retire early from the board, leaving one of his officers to take his place.

Colonel Mifflin was the first person who officiated as aide-de-camp. He was a Philadelphia gentleman of high respectability, who had accompanied him from that city and received his appointment shortly after their arrival at Cambridge. The second aide-de-camp was John Trumbull, son of the Governor of Connecticut. Trumbull, young and unaccustomed to society, soon found himself unequal to the elegant duties of his situation and gladly exchanged it for that of major of brigade.

The member of Washington's family most deserving of mention was his secretary, Joseph Reed. With this gentleman he had formed an intimacy in the course of his visits to Philadelphia to attend the sessions of the Continental Congress. Reed, who had gained a high reputation at the Philadelphia bar, had been highly instrumental in rousing the Philadelphians to co-operate with the patriots of Boston. A sympathy of views and feelings had attached him to Washington and induced him to accompany him to the camp. Washington's friendship towards him was frank and cordial, the confidence he reposed in him full and implicit. Reed, in fact, became the intimate companion of his thoughts, his bosom counsellor.

The arrival of Gates in camp was heartily welcomed by the commander-in-chief, who had received a letter from that officer gratefully acknowledging his friendly influence in procuring him the appointment of adjutant-general. Washington may have promised himself much cordial co-operation from him, but of that kind of friendship there was no further manifestation. Gates was certainly of great service at this juncture, when the whole army had to be organized, but from the familiar intimacy of Washington he gradually estranged himself. A contemporary has accounted for this by alleging that he was chagrined at not having received the appointment of major-general, to which he considered himself well fitted by his military experience and which he thought Washington might have obtained for him had he used his influence with Congress.

The Resort to Arms (1774–1775)

The hazardous position of the army from the great extent and weakness of its lines was what most pressed on the attention of Washington; and he summoned a council of war. In this it was urged that to abandon the line of works would be dispiriting to the troops and would expose a wide extent of country to maraud and ravage. Beside, no safer position presented itself on which to fall back. This being generally admitted, it was determined to hold on to the works and defend them as long as possible, and, in the mean time, to augment the army to at least 20,000 men. Washington now hastened to improve the defences of the camp, strengthen the weak parts of the line, and throw up additional works round the main forts.

The army was distributed by Washington into three grand divisions. One, forming the right wing, was stationed on the heights of Roxbury, commanded by Ward, who had under him Spencer and Thomas. Another, forming the left wing under Lee, having with him Sullivan and Greene, was stationed on Winter and Prospect Hills. The centre, under Putnam and Heath, was stationed at Cambridge.

At Washington's recommendation, Joseph Trumbull, the eldest son of the governor, received the appointment of commissary-general of the continental army. He had already officiated with talent in that capacity in the Connecticut militia.

Nothing excited more gaze and wonder than the arrival of several rifle companies, 1400 men in all, from Pennsylvania, Maryland and Virginia, stalwart fellows Washington had known in his early campaigns—stark hunters and bush fighters, many of them six feet high and of vigorous frame, dressed in fringed frocks or rifle shirts and round hats. Their displays of sharp shooting were soon among the marvels of the camp. One of these companies was commanded by Captain Daniel Morgan, a native of New Jersey, whose first experience in war had been to accompany Braddock's army. He had since carried arms on the frontier and obtained a command. He and his riflemen in coming to camp had marched 600 miles in three weeks. They will be found of signal efficiency in the sharpest conflicts of the revolutionary war.

While all his forces were required for the investment of Boston, Washington was importuned by the Legislature of Massachusetts and the Governor of Connecticut to detach troops for points of the sea-coast where depredations by armed vessels were apprehended. Washington referred to his instructions and consulted with his general officers and such members of the Continental Congress as happened to be in camp before he replied to these requests; he then respectfully declined compliance.

In his reply to the General Assembly of Massachusetts, he stated "It has been debated in Congress and settled that the militia . . . of each province is to be applied for defence against those small and particular depredations. . . . This will appear the more proper when it is considered that every . . . part of our sea-coast . . . would have an equal claim upon this army."

His reply to the Governor of Connecticut was to the same effect. "I wish I could extend protection to all, but the numerous detachments necessary to remedy the evil would amount to a dissolution of the army or make the most important operations of the campaign depend upon the piratical expeditions of two or three men-of-war and transports."

His refusal to grant the detachments gave much dissatisfaction in some quarters until sanctioned and enforced by the Continental Congress. All at length saw the wisdom of his decision. It was a vital question, involving the whole character and fortune of the war, and he met it with determination befitting a commander-in-chief.

The great object of Washington, at present, was to force the enemy to come out of Boston and try a decisive action. His lines had for some time cut off all communication of the town with the country. Fresh provisions and vegetables were consequently growing more and more scarce and sickness began to prevail. "I have done and shall do every thing in my power to distress them," writes he to his brother John Augustine. "The transports have all arrived, and their whole reinforcement is landed, so that I see no reason why they should not, if they ever attempt it, come boldly out and put the matter to issue at once."

At this critical juncture, when Washington was pressing the siege, and endeavoring to provoke a general action, a startling fact came to light; the whole amount of powder in the camp would not furnish more than nine cartridges to a man!

The Resort to Arms (1774–1775)

A gross error had been made by the committee of supplies when Washington, on taking command, had required a return of the ammunition. They had returned the whole amount of powder collected by the province, upwards of 300 barrels, without stating what had been expended. The blunder was detected on an order being issued for a new supply of cartridges. It was found there were but 32 barrels of powder in store. Washington instantly despatched letters and expresses to Rhode Island, the Jerseys, Ticonderoga and elsewhere, urging immediate supplies of powder and lead, no quantity, however small, to be considered beneath notice.

Day after day elapsed without the arrival of any supplies, for the munitions of war were not readily procured. It seemed hardly possible that the matter could be kept concealed from the enemy. In this critical state, the American camp remained for a fortnight, the anxious commander incessantly apprehending an attack. At length a partial supply from the Jerseys put an end to this imminent risk. It is thought that intelligence of this deficiency of ammunition on the part of the besiegers must have been conveyed to the British commander, but that the bold face with which the Americans continued to maintain their position made him discredit it.

A correspondence took place between Washington and General Gage, intended to put the hostile services on a proper footing. A strong disposition had been manifested among the British officers to regard those engaged in the patriot cause as malefactors, outlawed from the courtesies of chivalric warfare. Washington was determined to have a full understanding on this point. He took an early opportunity to let Gage know that he claimed to be the commander of a legitimate force, engaged in a legitimate cause, and that both himself and his army were to be treated on a footing of perfect equality.

"I understand," writes Washington to Gage, "that the officers engaged in the cause of liberty and their country, who by the fortune of war have fallen into your hands, have been thrown indiscriminately into a common jail, appropriated to felons; that no consideration has been had for those of the most respectable rank, when languishing with wounds and sickness, and that some have been amputated in this unworthy situation. . . . My duty now makes it necessary to apprise you that, for the future, I shall regulate all my conduct towards those gentlemen who are, or may be, in our possession, exactly by the rule you shall observe towards those of ours, now in your custody."

Washington thus set forth the principles on which hostilities on his part would be conducted. It was planting, with the pen, that standard which was to be maintained by the sword.

(CHAPTER 14)

We must interrupt our narrative of the siege of Boston to give an account of events in other quarters requiring the care of Washington as commander-in-chief.

The Johnsons were said to be stirring up the Indians in western New York to hostility and preparing to join the British forces in Canada, so that, while the patriots were battling for their rights along the seaboard, they were menaced by a powerful combination in rear. Since the exploits of Ethan Allen and Benedict Arnold at Ticonderoga and on Lake Champlain, great rivalry had arisen between these leaders. Allen claimed command at Ticonderoga on the authority of the committee from the Connecticut Assembly, which had originated the enterprise. Arnold claimed it on the strength of his instructions from the Massachusetts committee of safety.

The public bodies themselves seemed perplexed what to do with the prize so bravely seized upon by these bold men. The New York committee and the Massachusetts General Assembly turned for decision to the Continental Congress. The Continental Congress at length legitimated the exploit, and, as it were, accepted the captured fortress. As it was situated within New York, custody was committed to that province, aided if necessary by the New England colonies, on whom it was authorized to call for assistance. New York forthwith invited Connecticut to place forces in these captured posts until relieved by New York troops. The Governor of Connecticut

soon gave notice that 1000 men under Colonel Hinman were marching to Ticonderoga and Crown Point.

It had been the idea of the Continental Congress to have those
posts dismantled and the cannon and stores removed to the south
end of Lake George, where a strong post was to be established. Both
Allen and Arnold exclaimed against such a measure, vaunting the
importance of those forts for an expedition into Canada. In his letter
to the Continental Congress urging an invasion of Canada, Arnold
said 2000 men, he was certain, would be sufficient to get possession
of the province. "I beg leave to add that if no person appears who will
undertake to carry the plan into execution, I will undertake, and,
with the smiles of Heaven, answer for the success, provided I am
supplied with men, &c., to carry it into execution without loss of
time. . . . In order to give satisfaction to the different colonies, I
propose that Colonel Hinman's regiment, now on their march from
Connecticut to Ticonderoga, should form part of the army; say 1000
men; 500 men to be sent from New York, 500 of General Arnold's
regiment, including the seamen and marines on board the vessels
(no *Green Mountain* Boys)."

Within a few days after the date of this letter, Hinman with the
Connecticut troops arrived. The greater part of the Green Mountain
Boys now returned home, their term of enlistment having expired.
Ethan Allen and his brother in arms, Seth Warner, repaired to
Congress to get authority to raise a new regiment. It was recommended to the New York convention that, should it meet the
approbation of Schuyler, a fresh corps of Green Mountain Boys be
employed under such officers as the Green Mountain Boys should
choose. A regiment of Green Mountain Boys, 500 strong, was
decreed and Schuyler notified the people of the New Hampshire
Grants of the resolve.

As to Arnold, difficulties instantly took place between him and
Hinman. Arnold refused to give up command of either post, claiming, on the strength of his instructions from the committee of safety
of Massachusetts, a right to command of all posts and fortresses at
the south end of Lake Champlain and Lake George. This threw
every thing into confusion.

At this juncture arrived a committee of three members of the

Congress of Massachusetts, sent to inquire into the manner in which he had executed instructions, complaints having been made of his arrogant and undue assumption of command. Arnold was thunderstruck at being subjected to inquiry. He requested a sight of the committee's instructions. They were to acquaint themselves with his spirit, capacity, and conduct. Should they think proper, they might order him to return to Massachusetts. While at Ticonderoga, he and his men were to be under command of the principal officer from Connecticut.

Arnold was furious. He swore he would be second in command to no one, disbanded his men, and threw up his commission. Quite a scene ensued. His men became turbulent; some refused to serve under any other leader; others clamored for their pay, which was in arrears. At length the storm was allayed and Arnold set off for Cambridge to settle his accounts with the committee of safety.

The project of an invasion of Canada had at first met with no favor, the Continental Congress having formally resolved to make no hostile attempts upon that province. Intelligence subsequently received induced it to change its plans. Carleton was said to be strengthening the fortifications at St. Johns and preparing to launch vessels on the lake wherewith to retake the captured posts. Powerful reinforcements were coming from England and elsewhere. Guy Johnson was holding councils with the Cayugas and Senecas and stirring up the Six Nations to hostility. On the other hand, now was the time to strike a blow to paralyze all hostility from this quarter; now, while Carleton's regular force was weak and before the arrival of additional troops. Influenced by these considerations, Congress determined to extend the revolution into Canada but it was an enterprise too important to be entrusted to any but discreet hands. Schuyler, then in New York, was accordingly ordered on the 27th of June, to proceed to Ticonderoga and, "should he find it practicable, and not disagreeable to the Canadians, immediately to take possession of St. Johns and Montreal, and pursue such other measures in Canada as might have a tendency to promote the peace and security of these provinces."

Schuyler arrived at Ticonderoga on the 18th of July. Hinman was in temporary command of Ticonderoga, if that could be called a command where none seemed to obey. The garrison was about 1200 strong, the greater part Connecticut men brought by himself. Schuyler, on taking command, despatched a confidential agent into Canada, Major John Brown, an American who resided on the Sorel River and was popular among the Canadians. He was to collect information as to the British forces and fortifications, and to ascertain how an invasion and an attack on St. Johns would be considered by the people of the province. In the mean time, Schuyler set to work to build boats and prepare for the enterprise, should it ultimately be ordered by Congress.

Schuyler had calculated on being joined by the regiment of Green Mountain Boys which Allen and Warner had undertaken to raise. Unfortunately, a quarrel had arisen between those brothers in arms, which filled the Green Mountains with discord and party feud. The election of officers took place on the 27th of July. Allen was entirely passed by and Warner nominated as Lieutenant-colonel of the regiment. Allen's patriotism and love of adventure were not quelled; he forthwith repaired to Ticonderoga to offer himself as a volunteer. Schuyler, at first, hesitated to accept his services. He feared there would be a difficulty in keeping him within due bounds, but was at length persuaded by his officers to retain him as a pioneer on the Canadian frontier.

Schuyler was on the alert with respect to the expedition against Canada. From Brown and other sources he had learnt that there were but about 700 king's troops in that province; 300 of them at St. Johns, about 50 at Quebec, the remainder at Montreal, Chamblee, and the upper posts. Guy Johnson was at Montreal with 300 men, mostly his tenants, and with a number of Indians. Two batteries had been finished at St. Johns, mounting nine guns each; other works were intrenched and picketed. Two large row galleys were on the stocks and would soon be finished. Now was the time, according to his informants, to carry Canada. The Canadians, disaffected to British rule, would join the Americans and so would many of the Indians. "I am prepared," writes he to Washington, "to move against the enemy, unless your Excellency and Congress should direct otherwise. In the course of a few days I expect to receive the ultimate determination."

While awaiting orders on this head, he repaired to Albany, to hold a conference and negotiate a treaty with the Caughnawagas and the warriors of the Six Nations, whom, as one of the commissioners of Indian affairs, he had invited to meet him at that place. General Richard Montgomery was to remain in command at Ticonderoga during his absence and to urge forward the military preparations.

While these things were occurring at Ticonderoga, several Indian chiefs made their appearance in the camp at Cambridge as ambassadors from their respective tribes to talk about the impending invasion of Canada. One was chief of the Caughnawaga tribe, whose residence was on the banks of the St. Lawrence, six miles above Montreal. Others were from St. Francis, about forty-five leagues above Quebec.

Washington, accustomed to deal with the red warriors of the wilderness, received them with great ceremonial. A council fire was held. The sachems all offered to take up the hatchet for the Americans, should the latter invade Canada. The offer was embarrassing. Congress had publicly resolved to seek nothing but neutrality from the Indian nations, unless the British should make an offensive alliance with them. The chief of the St. Francis tribe declared that Governor Carleton had endeavored to persuade him to take up the hatchet against the Americans. Washington wished to be certain of the conduct of the enemy before he gave a reply to these Indian overtures. He wrote by express, therefore, to Schuyler, requesting him to ascertain the intentions of the British governor with respect to the tribes.

By the same express he communicated a plan which had occupied his thoughts for several days. As the contemplated movement of Schuyler would probably cause all the British force in Canada to be concentrated in the neighborhood of Montreal and St. Johns, he proposed to send off an expedition of about 1200 men to penetrate to Quebec by the way of the Kennebec River.

The express found Schuyler in Albany, where he had been attending the conference with the Six Nations. He had just received intelligence which convinced him of the propriety of an expedition into Canada, had sent word to Montgomery to get every thing ready for it, and was on the point of departing for Ticonderoga to carry it into effect. In reply to Washington, he declared his conviction, from accounts which he had received, that Carleton and his agents were exciting the Indian tribes to hostility and expressed himself delighted with Washington's project of sending off an expedition to Quebec.

Schuyler hastened back to Ticonderoga. Before he reached there, Montgomery had received intelligence that Carleton had completed his armed vessels at St. Johns and was about to send them into Lake Champlain by the Sorel River. No time, therefore, was to be lost in getting possession of the Isle aux Noix, which commanded the entrance to that river. Montgomery hastened to embark with about 1000 men, as many as the boats now ready could hold, taking with him two pieces of artillery; with this force he set off down the lake. A letter to Schuyler explained the cause of his sudden departure and entreated him to follow on in a whale-boat, leaving the residue of the artillery to come on as soon as conveyances could be procured.

Schuyler arrived at Ticonderoga on the night of the 30th of August, too ill of a bilious fever to push on in a whale-boat. He caused a bed to be prepared for him in a covered bateau and, ill as he was, continued forward on the following day. On the 4th of September he overtook Montgomery at the Isle la Motte, where he had been detained by contrary weather, and, assuming command of the little army, kept on the same day to the Isle aux Noix, about twelve miles south of St. Johns.

The siege of Boston had been kept up for several weeks without any remarkable occurrence. The British remained within their lines, diligently strengthening them; the besiegers, having received further supplies of ammunition, were growing impatient of inactivity. Towards the latter part of August there were rumors from Boston that the enemy were preparing for a sortie. Washington, resolved to provoke it, detached 1400 men to seize at night upon a height within musket shot of the enemy's line on Charlestown Neck, presuming that the latter would sally forth on the following day to dispute possession and thus be drawn into a general battle. The task was executed with silence and celerity, but the challenge was not accepted. The British opened a heavy cannonade from Bunker's Hill, but kept within their works. The evident unwillingness of the latter to come forth was perplexing. "Unless the ministerial troops in Boston are waiting for reinforcements," writes Washington, "I cannot devise what they are staying there for, nor why, as they affect to despise the Americans, they do not come forth and put an end to the contest at once."

Washington rode about the commanding points, considering how he might strike a decisive blow that would put an end to the murmuring inactivity of the army and relieve the country from the consuming expense of maintaining it. The result was a letter to the major and brigadier-generals, summoning them to a council of war to know whether, in their judgment, a successful attack might not be made upon the troops at Boston by means of boats, in co-operation with an attempt upon their lines at Roxbury. The council, composed of Ward, Lee, Putnam, Thomas, Heath, Sullivan, Spencer and Greene, unanimously pronounced the suggested attempt inexpedient, at least for the present.

As it was evident the enemy did not intend to come out but were strengthening their defences and preparing for winter, Washington turned his attention to the expedition to Canada by way of the Kennebec River.

A detachment of about 1100 men was soon encamped on Cambridge Common. There were ten companies of New England infantry, some from Rhode Island, three rifle companies from Pennsylvania and Virginia, one of them Morgan's famous company, and a number of volunteers, among whom was Aaron Burr (then just commencing his brilliant but ultimately unfortunate career). The proposed expedition required a hardy, skilful and intrepid leader. Such a one was at hand: Benedict Arnold was at Cambridge, settling his accounts with the Massachusetts committee of safety. Washington considered him the very man for the present enterprise. He had shown aptness for military service, whether on land or water, and he was acquainted with Canada, especially with Quebec. Washington intrusted him with command of the expedition, giving him the commission of lieutenant-colonel in the continental army.

The Resort to Arms (1774–1775)

Washington, beside a general letter of instructions, addressed one to him individually, full of cautious and considerate advice. "I charge you . . . and the officers and soldiers under your command . . . that you consider yourselves as marching, not through the country of an enemy, but of our friends and brethren; . . . that you check, by every motive of duty and fear of punishment, every attempt to plunder or insult the inhabitants of Canada. . . . I also give in charge to you to avoid all disrespect to the religion of the country and its ceremonies. . . . While we are contending for our own liberty, we should be very cautious not to violate the rights of conscience in others."

Arnold was, moreover, furnished with handbills for distribution in Canada, setting forth the friendly objects of the present expedition, as well as of that under Schuyler, and calling on the Canadians to furnish necessaries and accommodations for which they were assured ample compensation.

On the 13th of September, Arnold struck his tents and set out in high spirits. More fortunate than his rival, Ethan Allen, he had attained the object of his ambition, command of an expedition into Canada. Washington enjoined upon him to push forward as rapidly as possible, expecting the expedition would reach Quebec about the middle of October.

In the interim came letters from Schuyler, giving particulars of the main expedition. We last left the general and his little army at the Isle aux Noix, near the Sorel River, the outlet of the lake. Thence, on the 5th of September, he sent Allen and Brown to reconnoitre the country between that river and the St. Lawrence, to distribute friendly addresses among the people and ascertain their feelings. This done, and having landed his baggage and provisions, the general proceeded along the Sorel River the next day with his boats, until within two miles of St. Johns, when a cannonade was opened from the fort. Half a mile further, he landed his troops in a swamp, where they had a sharp skirmish with tories and Indians, whom they beat off. Night coming on, they cast up a small intrenchment and encamped.

In the night the camp was visited secretly by a person who informed Schuyler of the state of the fort. The works were completed and furnished with cannon. A vessel pierced for sixteen guns was launched and would be ready to sail in three or four days. It was not probable that any Canadians would join the army, being disposed to remain neutral. In a council of war in the morning, it was determined that they had neither men nor artillery sufficient to undertake a siege. They returned, therefore, to the Isle aux Noix, cast up fortifications, threw a boom across the channel of the river to prevent passage of the enemy's vessel into the lake, and awaited the arrival of artillery and reinforcements from Ticonderoga.

In the course of a few days the reinforcements arrived, and with them a small train of artillery. Allen also returned from his reconnoitring expedition, of which he made a most encouraging report. The Canadian captains of militia were ready, he said, to join the Americans whenever they should appear with sufficient force. He had held talks, too, with the Indians and found them well disposed. He was convinced that an attack on St. Johns and an inroad into the province would meet with hearty co-operation.

Preparations were now made for the investment of St. Johns by land and water. Brown, who had already acted as a scout, was sent with 100 Americans and about 30 Canadians towards Chamblee to make friends in that quarter and to join the army as soon as it should arrive at St. Johns. To quiet the restless Allen, who had no command in the army, he was sent with an escort of 30 men to La Prairie to recruit among the people whom he had recently visited.

For some time past, Schuyler had been struggling with a complication of maladies, still hoping to be able to move with the army. When every thing was nearly ready, he was attacked by a severe access of his disorder, which compelled him to surrender conduct of the expedition to Montgomery. Since he could be of no further use in this quarter, he caused his bed to be placed on board a covered bateau and set off for Ticonderoga to hasten forward reinforcements and supplies.

On the 16th of September, the day after Schuyler's departure for Ticonderoga, Montgomery proceeded to carry out the plans which had been concerted between them. Landing on the 17th at the place where they had formerly encamped, within a mile and a half of the fort, he detached a force of 500 men to take a position at the junction of two roads leading to Montreal and Chamblee so as to intercept relief from those points. He now proceeded to invest St. Johns. The siege went on slowly, until the arrival of an artillery company under Captain Lamb, who immediately bedded a thirteen-inch mortar and commenced a fire of shot and shells upon the fort. The distance, however, was too great and the positions of the batteries were ill chosen.

A flourishing letter was received by the general from Allen, giving hope of further reinforcement. "I am now," writes he," . . . four leagues from Sorel to the south. I have 250 Canadians under arms. . . . I shall join you in about three days with 500 or more Canadian volunteers."

Allen was on his way toward St. Johns, when, between Longueil and La Prairie, he met Brown with his party of Americans and Canadians. Brown assured him that the garrison at Montreal did not exceed 30 men and might easily be surprised. Allen's partisan spirit was instantly excited. A plan was agreed upon. Allen was to return to Longueil, nearly opposite Montreal, and cross the St. Lawrence in canoes in the night so as to land a little below the town. Brown, with 200 men, was to cross above, and Montreal was to be attacked simultaneously at opposite points.

All this was put in action without the knowledge of Montgomery; Allen was again the partisan leader, acting from individual impulse. His late letter to Montgomery would seem to have partaken of fanfaronade, for his whole force was 30 Americans, and 80 Canadians. He crossed the river on the night of the 24th of September, and guards were stationed on the roads to prevent any one passing and giving the alarm in Montreal. Day dawned but there was no signal of Brown having performed his part of the scheme. Allen would gladly have recrossed the river, but it was too late. An alarm had been given to the town and he soon found himself encountered by about 40 regular soldiers and a hasty levy of Canadians and Indians. A smart action ensued; most of Allen's Canadian recruits fled, a number of Americans were slain, and he at length surrendered to the British officer.

The reckless dash at Montreal was viewed with concern and severely censured by Washington. Partisan exploit had unfitted

Allen for regular warfare. Still his name will ever be a favorite one with his countrymen, for he was among the hardy pioneers of our Revolution whose untutored valor gave the first triumphs.

"My anxiety," writes Washington to Schuyler, "extends itself to poor Arnold, whose fate depends upon the issue of your campaign. . . . I look upon the interests and salvation of our bleeding country in a great degree as depending upon your success."

While he was still full of solicitude about the fate of Arnold, he received a despatch from the latter, dated October 13th, from the great portage between the Kennebec and Dead River.

The toils of the expedition up the Kennebec River had indeed been excessive. Part of the men of each division managed the boats; part marched along the banks. Those on board had to labor against swift currents, to unload at rapids, transport the cargoes, and sometimes the boats themselves, for some distance on their shoulders, and then reload. Several times their boats were upset, to the loss or damage of arms, ammunition, and provisions. Those on land had to scramble over rocks and precipices, to struggle through swamps and fenny streams, or cut their way through tangled thickets. Their progress was but from four to ten miles a day.

By the time they arrived at the place whence the letter was written, fatigue, swamp fevers and desertion had reduced their numbers to about 950 effective men. Arnold, however, wrote in good heart. "The last division," said he, "is just arrived; three divisions are over the first carrying-place, and as the men are in high spirits, I make no doubt of reaching the river Chaudiere in eight or ten days, the greatest difficulty being, I hope, already past."

(CHAPTER 15)

While the two expeditions were threatening Canada from different quarters, the war was going on along the seaboard. The British in Boston, cut off from supplies by land, fitted out small armed vessels to seek them along the coast of New England. The inhabitants drove their cattle into the interior or boldly resisted the aggressors. Parties landing to forage were often repulsed by hasty levies of the yeomanry. Scenes of ravage and violence occured.

To check these maraudings and to capture the enemy transports laden with supplies, the provinces of Massachusetts, Rhode Island and Connecticut fitted out two armed vessels each, at their own expense, without seeking the sanction of Congress. Washington, also, on his own responsibility, ordered several to be equipped for like purpose, to be manned by hardy mariners and commanded by able sea captains actually serving in the army. One of these vessels was despatched as soon as ready to cruise between Cape Ann and Cape Cod. Two others were sent to the St. Lawrence to intercept two unarmed brigantines which had sailed from England for Quebec with ammunition and military stores.

Among the New England seaports which had become obnoxious to punishment by resistance to nautical exactions was Falmouth (now Portland), Maine. On the evening of the 11th of October, Lieutenant Mowat of the royal navy appeared before it with several armed vessels and sent a letter on shore apprising the inhabitants that he was come to execute a just punishment on them for their "premeditated attacks on the legal prerogatives of the best of sovereigns." Two hours were given them, "to remove the human species out of the town," at the period of which, a red pendant at the main-topgallant masthead would be the signal for destruction.

The letter brought a deputation of three persons on board. The lieutenant informed them that he had orders to set fire to all the seaport towns between Boston and Halifax. With much difficulty, the committee obtained a respite until nine o'clock the next morning and the inhabitants employed the interval in removing their families and effects. About half past nine the red pendant was run up to the masthead and within five minutes several houses were in flames. In one day, 139 dwelling houses and 228 stores are said to have been burnt. Vessels in the harbor were destroyed or carried away as prizes.

The conflagration of Falmouth was as a bale fire throughout the country. "The desolation and misery," writes Washington, "which ministerial vengeance had planned, in contempt of every principle of humanity, and so lately brought on the town of Falmouth, I know not how sufficiently to commiserate, nor can my compassion for the general suffering be conceived beyond the true measure of my feelings."

Sullivan was sent to Portsmouth, where there was a fortification of some strength, to give the inhabitants advice and assistance in warding off the menaced blow. Newport, also, was put on the alert and recommended to fortify itself. Under the feeling roused by these reports, the General Court of Massachusetts passed an act encouraging the fitting out of armed vessels to defend the sea coast of America and erecting a court to try and condemn all vessels that should be found infesting the same. This act, granting letters of marque and reprisal, anticipated any measure of the kind on the part of the General Government and was pronounced by John Adams, "one of the most important documents in history."

General Gage sailed for England on the 10th of October. The battle of Bunker's Hill had withered his laurels as a commander. Still he was not absolutely superseded, but called home, as it was considerately said, "to give his majesty exact information of every thing, and suggest such matters as his knowledge and experience of the service might enable him to furnish." During his absence Major-general Howe would act as commander-in-chief of the colonies on the Atlantic Ocean and Major-general Carleton of the British forces in Canada and on the frontiers. Gage never returned to America.

On the 15th of October a committee from Congress arrived in camp to hold a conference with Washington and with delegates from the governments of Connecticut, Rhode Island, Massachusetts and New Hampshire on the new organization of the army. The committee consisted of Benjamin Franklin, Thomas Lynch of Carolina, and Colonel Harrison of Virginia. Washington was president of the board of conference and Mr. Joseph Reed secretary.

The committee brought an intimation from Congress that an attack upon Boston was much desired, if practicable. Washington called a council of war of his generals on the subject; they were unanimously of the opinion that an attack would not be prudent at present.

Another question arose. An attack upon the British forces in Boston might require a bombardment; Washington inquired how far it might be pushed to the destruction of houses and property. They decided the question must be referred to Congress.

The board of conference was repeatedly in session for three or four days. The report of the committee produced a resolution of Congress that a new army of 22,272 men and officers should be formed, recruited as much as possible from the troops actually in service. Unfortunately the term for which they were to be enlisted was to be but for one year, a precedent which became a recurring cause of embarrassment throughout the war.

Reed, after the close of the conference, signified his intention to return to Philadelphia, where his private concerns required his presence. His fluent pen had been of great assistance to Washington in his multifarious correspondence and his judicious counsels and cordial sympathies had been appreciated by the commander-in-chief. Reed's place was temporarily supplied by Robert Harrison of Maryland and subsequently by Colonel Mifflin; neither, however, attained to the affectionate confidence reposed in their predecessor.

The measures which Howe adopted after taking command in Boston rejoiced the royalists, seeming to justify their anticipations. He proceeded to strengthen the works on Bunker's Hill and Boston Neck and to throw up redoubts on eminences within the town. The patriot inhabitants were shocked by the desecration of the Old South Church, where, pulpit and pews removed, the floor was covered with earth and the sacred edifice was converted into a riding school for Burgoyne's light dragoons. The North Church was entirely demolished and used for fuel.

About the last of October Howe issued three proclamations. The first forbade all persons to leave Boston without his permission under pain of execution; the second forbade any one, so permitted, to take with him more than five pounds sterling under pain of forfeiting all the money found upon his person and being subject to fine and imprisonment; the third called upon the inhabitants to arm themselves for the preservation of order within the town, to be commanded by officers of his appointment.

The season was fast approaching when the bay between the camp and Boston would be frozen over and military operations might be conducted upon the ice. General Howe, if reinforced, would then very probably endeavor to relieve himself from the confinement in which the troops had been all summer. Washington felt the necessity, therefore, of guarding the camps wherever they were most assailable and of throwing up batteries for the purpose. He had been embarrassed throughout the siege by the want of artillery and ordnance stores, but never more so than at the present moment. In this juncture, Henry Knox stepped forward and offered to proceed to the frontier forts on Champlain in quest of a supply. Knox was one of the patriots who had fought on Bunker's Hill, since when he had aided in planning the defences of the camp before Boston. The talent displayed by him as an artillerist had recently induced Washington to recommend him to Congress for the command of the regiment of artillery but Congress had not yet acted on that recommendation. In the mean time Washington availed himself of the offered services of Knox. He was instructed to examine into the state of the artillery in camp and take an account of the cannon, mortars, shells, lead and ammunition that were wanting. He was then to hasten to New York, procure and forward all that could be had there; and thence proceed to the head-quarters of Schuyler, who was requested by letter to aid him in obtaining what further supplies of the kind were wanting from the forts at Ticonderoga, Crown Point, St. Johns, and even Quebec, should it be in the hands of the Americans. Knox set off on his errand with alacrity, and shortly afterwards the commission of colonel was forwarded to him by Congress.

The re-enlistment of troops actually in service was now attempted, and proved a fruitful source of perplexity. In a letter to the President of Congress, Washington observes that half of the officers of the rank of captain were inclined to retire. Of those disposed to remain, the officers of one colony were unwilling to mix in the same regiment with those of another. The difficulties were greater, if possible, with the soldiers than with the officers. They would not enlist unless they knew their colonel, lieutenant-colonel and captain; so that it was necessary to appoint the officers first.

Twenty days later he again writes to the President of Congress: "I am sorry to be necessitated to mention to you the egregious want of public spirit which prevails here. Instead of pressing to be engaged in the cause of their country, which I vainly flattered myself would be the case, I find we are likely to be deserted in a most critical time."

(CHAPTER 16)

Despatches from Schuyler dated October 26th gave Washington another chapter of the Canada expedition. Chamblee, an inferior fort, within five miles of St. Johns, had been taken by Brown and Livingston at the head of 50 Americans and 300 Canadians. Montgomery now pressed the siege of St. Johns with vigor. The garrison, cut off from supplies, were suffering from want of provisions, but the commander, Major Preston, held out, hoping speedy relief from Carleton, who was assembling troops for that purpose at Montreal.

Carleton calculated greatly on the co-operation of Colonel Maclean, a veteran Scot who had enlisted 300 of his countrymen at Quebec and was to land at the mouth of the Sorel where it empties into the St. Lawrence, proceed along the former river to St. Johns to join Carleton, who would repair thither by the way of Longueil.

In the mean time Montgomery received accounts from various quarters that Allen and his men, captured in the ill-advised attack upon Montreal, were treated with cruel and unnecessary severity, being loaded with irons, and that even the colonel himself was subjected to this "shocking indignity." Montgomery addressed a letter to Carleton, strong and decided in its purport but written in the spirit of a courteous and high-minded gentleman, ending with an expression of that sad feeling which gallant officers must often have experienced in this revolutionary conflict on being brought into collision with former brothers in arms.

While waiting for a reply, Montgomery pressed the siege of St. Johns, though thwarted continually by the want of subordination and discipline among his troops, hasty levies from various colonies, who, said he, "carry the spirit of freedom into the field, and think for themselves." He had advanced his lines and played from his batteries on two sides of the fort for some hours when tidings brought by four prisoners caused him to cease his fire.

Carleton, on the 31st of September, had embarked his force at Montreal in 34 boats to cross the St. Lawrence, land at Longueil, and push on for St. Johns. As the boats approached Longueil, a terrible fire of artillery and musketry opened upon them and threw them into confusion. It was from Warner's detachment of Green Mountain Boys and New Yorkers. Some of the boats were disabled, some were driven on shore on an island; Carleton retreated with the rest to Montreal.

Aware that the garrison held out in expectation of the relief thus intercepted, Montgomery ceased his fire and sent a flag by one of the Canadian prisoners with a letter to Preston inviting a surrender to spare the effusion of blood. The gallant major was obliged to capitulate. His garrison consisted of 500 regulars and 100 Canadians. Montgomery sent his prisoners to Ticonderoga and prepared to proceed to Montreal, requesting Schuyler to forward all the men he could possibly spare.

Maclean's troops, who were to have co-operated with Carleton, met with no better fortune than that commander. Maclean landed at the mouth of the Sorel and was in full march for St. Johns when he was encountered by Brown and Livingston with their party, fresh from the capture of Chamblee and reinforced by a number of Green Mountain Boys. These pressed him back to the mouth of the Sorel, where, hearing of the repulse of Carleton and being deserted by his Canadian recruits, he embarked the residue of his troops and set off down the St. Lawrence to Quebec. The Americans now took post at the mouth of the Sorel, where they erected batteries so as to command the St. Lawrence and prevent the descent of any armed vessels from Montreal.

"Not a word of Arnold yet," said Montgomery, in his last despatch. "I have sent two expresses to him lately, one by an Indian who promised to return with expedition. The instant I have any news of him, I will acquaint you by express." We will anticipate his express, by giving the reader the purport of letters received by Washington direct from Arnold himself.

The transportation of troops and effects across the carrying-place between the Kennebec and Dead Rivers, had been a work of severe toil but performed with admirable spirit. Launching their boats on the sluggish waters of the Dead River, they navigated it to the foot of snow-crowned mountains. Here, while encamped to repose themselves, heavy rains set in, and they came near being swept away by sudden torrents from the mountains. Several of their boats were overturned, much of their provisions were lost, the sick list increased, and the good spirits which had hitherto sustained them began to give way. They were on scanty allowance, with a prospect of harder times, for there were still twelve or fifteen days of wilderness before them, where no supplies were to be had. Arnold kept on with unflinching spirit until he arrived at the ridge which divides the streams of New England and Canada. Here, at Lake Megantic, the source of the Chaudiere, Arnold shared out the scanty provisions which remained, while he, with a light foraging party, would push rapidly ahead to procure and send back supplies.

He accordingly embarked with his little party in five bateaux and a birch canoe on the swift current of the Chaudiere. It was little better than a mountain torrent, full of rocks and rapids. Three of their boats were dashed to pieces, the cargoes lost, and the crews saved with difficulty. At length they reached Sertigan, the first French settlement, where they were cordially received. Here Arnold bought provisions, which he sent back by the Canadians and Indians to his troops.

Arnold halted for a short time in the hospitable valley of the Chaudiere, to give his troops repose, and he was joined by about 40 Norridgewock Indians. On the 9th of November, the little army emerged at Point Levi, on the St. Lawrence, opposite to Quebec.

Leaving Arnold in full sight of Quebec, which must have appeared like a land of promise, we turn to narrate the events of the upper expedition into Canada.

Montgomery appeared before Montreal on the 12th of November. Carleton had embarked with his little garrison and several of the civil officers on board of a flotilla of small vessels, and made sail in the night, carrying away with him the powder and other important stores. The town capitulated, of course, and Montgomery took quiet possession. His urbanity and kindness soon won the good will of the inhabitants and made the Canadians sensible that he really came to secure their rights, not to molest them.

His great immediate object was the capture of Carleton, which might decide the fate of Canada. The flotilla in which the general was embarked had made repeated attempts to escape down the St. Lawrence, but had as often been driven back by the batteries thrown up by the Americans at the mouth of the Sorel. It now lay anchored about fifteen miles above that river; Montgomery prepared to attack it with bateaux and light artillery so as to force it down upon the batteries.

Carleton saw his imminent peril. Disguising himself as a Canadian voyager, he set off on a dark night accompanied by six peasants, in a boat with muffled oars, slipped quietly past all the batteries and guard-boats, and effected his escape to Three Rivers, where he embarked in a vessel for Quebec. After his departure the flotilla surrendered, and all on board were made prisoners of war.

Montgomery now placed garrisons in Montreal, St. Johns, and Chamblee and made final preparations for descending the St. Lawrence and co-operating with Arnold against Quebec. To his deep chagrin, he found but a handful of his troops disposed to accompany him. Nothing but a sense of public duty had induced Montgomery to engage in the service; wearied by the continual vexations which beset it, he avowed, in a letter to Schuyler, his determination to retire as soon as the intended expedition against Quebec was finished.

The troops which had given Montgomery so much annoyance and refused to continue with him in Canada, soon began to arrive at Ticonderoga. This home-sickness in rustic soldiers after a rough campaign was natural enough and seems only to have provoked the testy and subacid humor of Schuyler; but other instances of conduct roused his indignation to such public rebuke that it rankled in the breasts of those whose conduct had merited it and insured to Schuyler that persevering hostility with which mean minds revenge the exposure of their meanness.

The tidings of the capture of Montreal had given Washington the liveliest satisfaction. He now looked forward to equal success in the expedition against Quebec. In a letter to Schuyler, he passed a high eulogium on Arnold. "I am convinced that he will do every thing that prudence and valor shall suggest . . . reducing Quebec to our possession. Should he not be able to accomplish so desirable a work with the forces he has, I flatter myself that it will be effected when General Montgomery joins him, and our conquest of Canada will be complete."

Certain passages of Schuyler's letters, however, gave him deep concern, wherein that general complained of the embarrassments and annoyances he had experienced from the insubordination of the army. He was determined to retire; of this resolution he had advised Congress. In communicating to the President of Congress the complaints of Montgomery and his intention to retire, "my sentiments," said Schuyler, "exactly coincide with his. I shall, with him, do every thing in my power to put a finishing stroke to the campaign, and make the best arrangement in my power, in order to insure success to the next. This done, I must beg leave to retire."

Congress, however, was too well aware of his value readily to dispense with his services. His letter produced a prompt resolution expressive of their high sense of his attention and perseverance, "which merited the thanks of the United Colonies."

What, however, produced a greater effect upon Schuyler than any encomium or entreaty on the part of Congress were the expostulations of Washington, inspired by strong friendship and kindred sympathies. "I am exceedingly sorry," writes the latter, "to find you so much embarrassed by the disregard of discipline, confusion, and want of order among the troops as to have occasioned you to mention to Congress an inclination to retire. I know that your complaints are too well founded, but would willingly hope that nothing will induce you to quit the service." And in another letter he appeals to his patriotism. "I am sorry that you and General Montgomery incline to quit the service. Let me ask you, sir, when is the time for brave men to exert themselves in the cause of liberty and their country, if this is not? . . . Let me, therefore, conjure you and Mr. Montgomery to lay aside such thoughts—as thoughts injurious to yourselves and extremely so to your country which calls aloud for gentlemen of your ability."

This noble appeal went straight to the heart of Schuyler, and brought out a magnanimous reply. "I do not hesitate," writes he, "to answer my dear general's question in the affirmative by declaring that now or never is the time for every virtuous American to exert himself in the cause of liberty and his country; and that it is become a duty cheerfully to sacrifice the sweets of domestic felicity to attain the honest and glorious end America has in view."

The forming even of the skeleton of an army under the new regulations had been a work of infinite difficulty; to fill it up was still more difficult. The first burst of revolutionary zeal had passed away; enthusiasm had been chilled by the inaction and monotony of a long encampment. The troops had suffered privations of every kind, want of fuel, clothing, provisions. They looked forward with dismay to the rigors of winter and longed for their homes and family firesides.

Apprehending that some would go home when their enlistment expired, Washington summoned the general officers at headquarters and invited a delegation of the General Court to be present to adopt measures for the defence and support of the lines. The result of their deliberations was an order that 3000 of the minute men and militia of Massachusetts and 2000 from New Hampshire should be at Cambridge by the 10th of December to relieve the Connecticut regiments and supply the deficiency that would be caused by their departure and by the absence of others on furlough.

With this arrangement the Connecticut troops were made acquainted, and, as the time of most of them would not be out before the 10th, they were ordered to remain in camp until relieved. On the 1st of December, many of the men resolved to go home immediately. Efforts were made to prevent them, but in vain. The homeward-bound warriors seem to have run the gauntlet along the road, for their conduct on quitting the army drew upon them such indignation that they could hardly get anything to eat on their journey and when they arrived at home they met with such a reception (to the credit of the Connecticut women be it recorded) that many were soon disposed to return again to the camp.

On the very day after the departure homeward of these troops, a long, lumbering train of waggons, laden with ordnance and military stores and decorated with flags, came wheeling into the camp escorted by continental troops and country militia. They were part of the cargo of a large brigantine captured and sent in to Cape Ann. Beside the ordnance captured, there were 2000 stand of arms, 100,000 flints, 30,000 round shot, and 32 tons of musket balls.

It was indeed a cheering incident. Among the ordnance was a huge brass mortar weighing near 3000 pounds. The mortar was fixed in a bed, old Putnam mounted it, dashed on it a bottle of rum, and gave it the name of "Congress."

With Washington, this transient gleam of nautical success was soon overshadowed by the conduct of the cruisers he had sent to the St. Lawrence. Failing to intercept the brigantines, the objects of their cruise, they landed on the island of St. Johns, plundered the house of the governor and several private dwellings, and brought off three of the principal inhabitants prisoners, one of whom, Mr. Callbeck, was president of the council and acted as governor. These gentlemen made a memorial to Washington of this scandalous maraud. He instantly ordered the restoration of the effects which had been pillaged.

Shortly after the foregoing occurrence, information was received of the indignities which had been heaped upon Allen, when captured at Montreal by Prescott, who, himself, was now a prisoner in the hands of the Americans. It touched Washington on a point on which he was most sensitive and tenacious, the treatment of American officers when captured; he wrote to General Howe in protest and stated "that whatever treatment Colonel Allen receives, whatever fate he undergoes, such exactly shall be the treatment and fate of Brigadier Prescott, now in our hands. The law of retaliation is not only justifiable in the eyes of God and man, but absolutely a duty, which, in our present circumstances, we owe to our relations, friends and fellow-citizens."

Howe replied that his command did not extend to Canada. "But trusting Major-general Carleton's conduct will never incur censure upon any occasion, I am to conclude in the instance of your inquiry that he has not forfeited his past pretensions to decency and humanity."

The measure of retaliation mentioned in Washington's letter to Howe was actually meted out by Congress on the arrival of Prescott in Philadelphia. He was ordered into close confinement in the jail, though not put in irons. He was subsequently released from confinement on account of ill health and was treated by some Philadelphia families with unmerited hospitality.

At the time of the foregoing correspondence with Howe, Washington was earnestly occupied preparing works for the bombardment of Boston, should that measure be resolved upon by Congress. Putnam in the preceding month had taken possession in the night of Cobble Hill without molestation from the enemy, though a commanding eminence; in two days he had constructed a work which, from its strength, was named Putnam's impregnable fortress.

He was now engaged on another work on Lechmere Point, to be connected with the works at Cobble Hill by a bridge thrown across Willis's Creek and a covered way. Lechmere Point is immediately opposite the north part of Boston, and the Scarborough ship-of-war was anchored near it. Putnam availed himself of a dark and foggy day (Dec. 17) to commence operations in the morning on a hill at the Point. "The mist," says a contemporary account, "was so great as to prevent the enemy from discovering what he was about until near twelve o'clock, when it cleared up. . . . The Scarborough, anchored off the Point, poured in a broadside. The enemy from Boston threw shells. The garrison at Cobble Hill returned fire. Our men were obliged to decamp from the Point but the work was resumed by the brave old general at night."

On the next morning, a cannonade from Cobble Hill obliged the Scarborough to weigh anchor and drop down below the ferry. Heath was detached with a party of men to carry on the work which

MAJ. GEN. ISRAEL PUTNAM.

Printed by W. Pate.

Israel Putnam

NEW YORK. G. P. PUTNAM & CO.

The Resort to Arms (1774–1775)

Putnam had commenced. It was to consist of two redoubts, on one of which was to be a mortar battery. There was, as yet, a deficiency of ordnance, but the prize mortar was to be mounted which Putnam had recently christened.

For several days the labor at the works was continued; the two redoubts were thrown up, and a covered way was constructed leading down to the bridge. All this was done notwithstanding the continual fire of the enemy. Putnam anticipated great effects from this work, especially from his grand mortar. Shells there were in abundance for a bombardment; the only thing wanting was a supply of powder. One of the officers, writing of the unusual mildness of the winter, observes: "Every thing thaws here except old Put. He is still as hard as ever, crying out for powder—powder—powder. Ye gods, give us powder!"

Amid the various concerns of the war and the multiplied perplexities of the camp, the thoughts of Washington continually reverted to his home on the Potomac.

According to recent accounts, Mount Vernon had been considered in danger. It was feared that the abode of the "rebel commander-in-chief" would be marked out for hostility and that the enemy might lay it waste. Washington's brother, John Augustine, had entreated Mrs. Washington to leave it. The people of Loudoun had advised her to seek refuge beyond the Blue Ridge and had offered to send a guard to escort her. She had declined the offer, not considering herself in danger. Washington agreed in deeming it in no present danger of molestation by the enemy. Still he felt for the loneliness of Mrs. Washington's situation, heightened as it must be by anxiety on his own account. On taking command of the army, he had held out a prospect to her that he would rejoin her at home in the autumn; there was now a probability of his being detained before Boston all winter. He wrote to her, therefore, in November inviting her to join him at the camp.

Mrs. Washington came on with her own carriage and horses, accompanied by her son and his wife. Her arrival at Cambridge was a glad event in the army. It would appear that dinner invitations to headquarters, were becoming matters of pride and solicitude. The presence of Mrs. Washington soon relieved the general from this kind of perplexity. She presided at head-quarters with mingled dignity and affability.

We again turn from the siege of Boston to the invasion of Canada, which at that time shared the anxious thoughts of Washington. His last accounts of the movements of Arnold, left him at Point Levi, opposite to Quebec. It was his intention to cross the river immediately. Had he done so, he might have carried the town by a coup de main. However, he was brought to a stand; not a boat was to be found there. Letters which he had despatched previously by two Indians to Schuyler and Montgomery had been carried by his faithless messengers to Caramhe, the lieutenant-governor, who, thus apprised of the impending danger, had caused all the boats of Point Levi to be either removed or destroyed.

Arnold was not a man to be disheartened by difficulties. With great exertions he procured about 40 birch canoes from the Canadians and Indians, but stormy winds arose and for some days the river was too boisterous for such frail craft. In the mean time the garrison at Quebec was gaining strength. Recruits arrived from Nova Scotia. The veteran Maclean, too, arrived down the river with his corps. The Lizard frigate, the Hornet sloop-of-war, and two armed schooners were stationed in the river, and guard boats patrolled at night. The prospect of a sucessful attack upon the place was growing desperate.

On the 13th of November, Arnold received intelligence that Montgomery had captured St. Johns. He was instantly roused to emulation. He determined to cross the river that very night. In the evening he embarked with the first division, principally riflemen. By four o'clock in the morning, a large part of his force had crossed and landed about a mile and a half above Cape Diamond, at Wolfe's Cove.

Just then a guard boat, belonging to the Lizard, came slowly along shore and discovered them. The boat instantly pulled for the frigate, giving vociferous alarm. Without waiting the arrival of the residue of his men, Arnold led those who had landed to the foot of the cragged defile, once scaled by the intrepid Wolfe, and scrambled up it in all haste. By daylight he had planted his daring flag on the far-famed Heights of Abraham.

Here the main difficulty stared him in the face. A strong line of walls and bastions traversed the promontory from one of its precipitous sides to the other, enclosing the upper and lower towns. On the right the great bastion of Cape Diamond crowned the rocky height of that name. On the left was the bastion of La Potasse, close by the gate of St. Johns opening upon the barracks.

A council of war was now held. Arnold was for dashing forward at once and storming the gate of St. Johns. Had they done so, they might have been successful. The gate was open and unguarded. Through some blunder, a message from the commander of the Lizard to the lieutenant-governor had not yet been delivered and no alarm had reached the fortress.

The formidable aspect of the place, however, awed Arnold's associates in council. While the council of war deliberated, the favorable moment passed away. The lieutenant-governor received the tardy message and hastily assembled the merchants, officers of militia, and captains of merchant vessels. All promised to stand by him. The din of arms now resounded through the streets. The walls looking upon the heights were soon manned by the military.

Arnold paraded his men within a hundred yards of the walls, hoping to excite a revolt in the place or to provoke the scanty garrison to a sally, but the taunting bravado failed to produce a sortie. A large cannon on the ramparts was brought to bear on them and a few shots obliged the Americans to retire and encamp.

In the evening Arnold sent a flag, demanding in the name of the United Colonies the surrender of the place. Some of the disaffected and the faint-hearted were inclined to open the gates, but were held in check by Maclean.

Several days elapsed. The inhabitants gradually recovered from their alarm and armed themselves to defend their property. The sailors and marines proved a valuable addition to the garrison, which now really meditated a sortie.

Arnold received information of all this from friends within the walls; he heard about the same time of the capture of Montreal and that General Carleton, having escaped from that place, was on his way down to Quebec. He thought at present, therefore, to draw off on the 19th to Point aux Trembles, twenty miles above Quebec, there to await the arrival of Montgomery with troops and artillery. As his little army wended its way along the bank of the river, a vessel passed below which had just touched at Point aux Trembles. On board of it was Carleton, hurrying on to Quebec.

The Widening Breach
[1775–1776]

In the month of December a vessel had been captured, bearing supplies from Dunmore to the army at Boston. A letter on board, from his lordship to Howe, invited him to transfer the war to the southern colonies or to send reinforcements there, intimating his plan of proclaiming liberty to indentured servants, Negroes, and others appertaining to rebels, inviting them to join his majesty's troops. "If this man is not crushed before spring," writes Washington, "he will become the most formidable enemy America has."

General Lee took the occasion to set forth his own system of policy, which was particularly rigid wherever men in authority and tories were concerned. "I propose the following measures:" he said, "To seize every governor, government man, placeman, tory and enemy to liberty on the continent; to confiscate their estates or at least lay them under heavy contributions for the public. Their persons should be secured in some of the interior towns as hostages for the treatment of those of our party whom the fortune of war shall throw into their hands." Lee soon had an opportunity of carrying it partly into operation. It was reported that a naval armament was coming from Boston against Rhode Island and in this emergency, the governor wrote to Washington, requesting military aid and an officer to put the island in a state of defence.

Lee undertook the task with alacrity. He set out for Rhode Island with his guard and a party of riflemen, and at Providence was joined by the cadet company of that place and a number of minute men. At Newport, he summoned before him a number of persons who had supplied the enemy and obliged them to take an oath of his own devising, by which they swore they would not furnish the king's troops and navy with provisions and refreshments, that they would denounce all traitors before the public authority, and that they would take arms in defence of American liberty whenever required by authority. Those who refused to take the oath were put under guard and sent to Providence. Having laid out works and given directions for fortifications, Lee returned to camp after ten days. Some of his proceedings were considered too high-handed by Congress, Washington approved of his measures.

December had been a month of severe trial to Washington, during which he saw his army dropping away piecemeal before his eyes. Homeward every face was turned as soon as the term of enlistment was at an end. Washington made repeated and animated appeals to their patriotism; they were almost unheeded. Can we wonder at it? They were for the most part yeomanry, unused to military restraint, suffering all the hardships of a starveling camp almost within sight of the smoke of their own firesides.

Greene, throughout this trying month, was continually by Washington's side. His letters expressing the same apprehensions, occasionally in the same language of the commander-in-chief, show how completely he was in his councils. Still he was buoyant and cheerful, endeavoring to keep his men in good humor. He wore the same cheery aspect to the commander-in-chief; he partook of his own hopeful spirit. It was this loyalty, this buoyancy, this thorough patriotism which won for him the entire confidence of Washington.

The thirty-first of December arrived, the crisis of the army, for with that month expired the last of the old terms of enlistment. "We never have been so weak," writes Greene, "as we shall be to-morrow, when we dismiss the old troops." On this day Washington received cheering intelligence from Canada. A junction had taken place, a month previously, between Arnold and Montgomery at Point aux Trembles. They were about 2000 strong and were making preparation for attacking Quebec. It was thought that the French would give up Quebec if they could get the same conditions granted to Montreal. Thus the year closed upon Washington with a ray of light from Canada, while all was doubt around him.

On the following morning (January 1st, 1776), his army did not amount to 10,000 men, composed of half-filled regiments. The detachments of militia which replaced the disbanding troops remained but for brief periods, so that the lines were often feebly manned and might easily have been forced.

In the midst of his discouragements, Washington received letters from Knox showing the spirit with which he was executing his quest of cannon and ordnance stores. He had struggled manfully and successfully with all kinds of difficulties in getting them from Ticonderoga to the head of Lake George. "Three days ago," writes he, on the 17th of December, "it was very uncertain whether we could get them over until next spring; but now, please God, they shall go. I have made forty-two exceedingly strong sleds and have provided eighty yoke of oxen to drag them as far as Springfield, where I shall get fresh cattle to take them to camp."

Early in the month of January there was a great stir of preparation in Boston harbor. A fleet of transports were taking in supplies and making arrangements for the embarkation of troops. Bomb-ketches and flat-bottomed boats were getting ready for sea, as were two sloops-of-war, which were to convey the armament. Its destination was kept secret, but was confidently surmised by Washington.

In the preceding October, a letter had been laid before Congress, written by some person in London of high credibility, revealing a plan of operations sent to the commanders in Boston. The following is the purport: Possession was to be gained of New York and Albany through the assistance of Governor Tryon, on whose influence with the tories much reliance was placed. These cities were to be strongly garrisoned. All who did not join the king's forces were to be declared rebels. The Hudson River and the East

River were to be commanded by small men-of-war and cutters, stationed so as to cut off all communication by water between New York and the provinces to the north and between New York and Albany, and to prevent, also, all communication between the city of New York and the provinces to the south. "By these means," said the letter, "the administration and their friends fancy they shall . . . retake . . . Crown Point and Ticonderoga and open . . . a safe intercourse . . . between Quebec, Albany and New York; and thereby offer the fairest opportunity . . . to make continual irruptions into New Hampshire, Massachusetts and Connecticut, and so distract and divide the Provincial forces as to render it easy for the British army at Boston to defeat them, break the spirits of the Massachusetts people, . . . and compel an absolute subjection to Great Britain."

This information had already excited solicitude respecting the Hudson and led to measures for its protection. It was now surmised that the expedition preparing to sail from Boston, conducted by Clinton, might seize upon New York. How was the apprehended blow to be parried? General Lee, who was just returned from his energetic visit to Rhode Island, offered his advice and services in the matter. In a letter to Washington, he urged him to act at once on his own responsibility without awaiting the sanction of Congress.

"New York must be secured," writes he," . . . I would propose that you should detach me into Connecticut, and lend your name for collecting a body of volunteers. I am assured that I shall find no difficulty in assembling a sufficient number for the purposes wanted. This body, in conjunction . . . with the Jersey regiment under the command of Lord Stirling, . . . will effect the security of New York and the expulsion or suppression of that dangerous banditti of tories who have appeared on Long Island."

Washington, while he approved of Lee's suggestions, was cautious in exercising the extraordinary powers so recently vested in him. John Adams was in the vicinity of the camp and he asked his opinion of the plan and whether it "might not be regarded as beyond his line." Adams, resolute of spirit, thought the enterprise might easily be accomplished by the friends of liberty in New York, in connection with the Connecticut people. That it was within the limits of Washington's command, he considered perfectly clear, he being "vested with full power and authority to act as he should think for the good and welfare of the service."

Thus fortified, as it were, by congressional sanction, through one of its most important members, Washington gave Lee authority to carry out his plans. He was to raise volunteers in Connecticut; march at their head to New York; call in military aid from New Jersey; put the city and the posts on the Hudson in a posture of security against surprise; disarm all persons on Long Island and elsewhere inimical to the views of Congress or secure them in some other manner if necessary; and seize upon all medicines, shirts, and blankets and send them on for the use of the American army. Lee departed on his mission on the 8th of January.

The people of New York were thrown into a panic on hearing that Lee was in Connecticut on his way to take military possession of the city. They apprehended his appearance there would provoke an attack from the ships in the harbor. The committee of safety, through Pierre Van Cortlandt, their chairman, addressed a letter to Lee inquiring into the motives of his coming with an army to New York and stating the incapacity of the city to act against the ships of war in port from deficiency in powder and want of military works.

Lee, in reply, dated Jan. 23d, disclaimed all intention of commencing actual hostilities against the men-of-war in the harbor, his instructions from the commander-in-chief being solely to prevent the enemy from taking post in the city or on Long Island. Some subordinate purposes were likewise to be executed, more properly communicated by word of mouth than by writing. In compliance with the wishes of the committee, he promised to carry into the town just troops enough to secure it against designs of the enemy, leaving his main force in Connecticut. "I give you my word," added he, "that no active service is proposed. . . . If the ships of war are quiet, I shall be quiet; but . . . if they make a pretext of my presence to fire on the town, the first house set on flames by their guns shall be the funeral pile of some of their best friends."

The threat about a "funeral pile," coming from a soldier of his mettle, did not soothe the hysterical feelings of the committee of safety. How he conducted himself on his arrival in the city, we shall relate in a future chapter.

(CHAPTER 18)

From amid surrounding perplexities, Washington still turned a hopeful eye to Canada. He expected daily to receive tidings that Montgomery and Arnold were within the walls of Quebec.

On the 18th of January came despatches to him from General Schuyler, containing withering tidings. Montgomery, on the day after his arrival at Point aux Trembles, set off for Quebec and arrived before it on the 5th. The works, from their great extent, appeared to him incapable of being defended by the actual garrison. His own force did not exceed 900 effective men, 300 of whom he had brought with him; the rest he found with Arnold. The latter he pronounced an exceeding fine corps, inured to fatigue and well accustomed to cannon shot.

On the day of his arrival, he sent a flag with a summons to surrender. It was fired upon and obliged to retire. Montgomery wrote an indignant letter to Carleton, reiterating the demand and warning him against the consequences of an assault. It too was rejected, and Montgomery now prepared for an attack. The ground was frozen to a great depth and covered with snow; a breastwork was thrown up, 400 yards from the walls, opposite the gate of St. Louis, which is nearly in the centre. It was formed of gabions, ranged side by side and filled with snow, over which water was thrown until thoroughly frozen. Here Lamb mounted five light field-pieces and a howitzer. Several mortars were placed in St. Roque, which extends on the left of the promontory below the heights, nearly on a level with the river.

Captain Lamb opened a well-sustained and well-directed fire upon the walls, but his field-pieces were too light to be effective. For five days and nights, the garrison was kept on the alert by the fire of this battery. The object of Montgomery was to harrass the town and increase the dissatisfaction of the inhabitants. It was all in vain; whatever might have been the disposition of the inhabitants, they were completely under the control of the military.

On the evening of the fifth day, Montgomery paid a visit to the ice battery. The heavy artillery from the walls had repaid its ineffectual fire with ample usury. The general saw the insufficiency of the battery and, on retiring, gave Lamb permission to leave it whenever he thought proper. The veteran waited until after dark, when, securing all the guns, he abandoned the ruined redoubt.

Nearly three weeks had been consumed in these futile operations. The army, ill-clothed and ill-provided, was becoming impatient of the rigors of a Canadian winter. Montgomery, sadly conscious of the insufficiency of his means, still could not endure the thoughts of retiring from before the place without striking a blow. He determined, therefore, to attempt to carry the place by escalade. It was a hazardous, desperate project, but he calculated upon the devotion and daring spirit of his men, upon the discontent among the Canadians, and upon the incompetency of the garrison.

The ladders were provided for the escalade, and Montgomery waited with impatience for a favorable night to put it in execution. Livingston was to make a false attack on the gate of St. Johns and set fire to it; Brown, with another detachment, was to menace the bastion of Cape Diamond. Arnold, with 350 of the hardy fellows who had followed him through the wilderness, strengthened by Captain Lamb and 40 of his company, was to assault the suburbs and batteries of St. Roque. Montgomery was to pass below the bastion of Cape Diamond, defile along the river, carry the defences at Drummond's Wharf, and enter the lower town on one side while Arnold forced his way into it on the other. These movements were all to be made at the same time, on the discharge of signal rockets.

On the 31st of December, at two o'clock in the morning, the troops repaired to their several destinations under cover of a violent snow-storm. By some mistake the signal rockets were let off before the lower divisions had time to get to their fighting ground. They were descried by one of Maclean's officers, who gave the alarm.

Livingston, also, failed to make the false attack on the gate of St. Johns to cause a diversion favorable to Arnold's attack on the suburb below.

The feint by Brown on the bastion of Cape Diamond was successful and concealed the march of General Montgomery. The gallant commander descended from the heights to Wolfe's Cove and led his division along the St. Lawrence round the beetling promontory of Cape Diamond. The narrow approach to the lower town was traversed by a picket, defended by militia and beyond it was a second defence, a kind of block-house, forming a battery of small pieces. The aim of Montgomery was to come upon these barriers by surprise.

The troops made their way painfully, in extended and straggling files, along the narrow foot-way and over the slippery piles of ice. Montgomery threw himself far in advance and made a dash at the first barrier. The Canadians stationed there, taken by surprise, threw down their muskets and fled from the picket to the block-house but seemed to have carried the panic with them for the battery remained silent.

Montgomery felt for a moment as if the surprise had been complete. He again dashed forward but, when within 40 paces of the battery, a discharge of grape-shot from a single cannon made deadly havoc. Montgomery and McPherson, one of his aides, were killed on the spot. Captain Cheeseman, who was leading his New Yorkers, received a canister shot through the body and fell back a corpse. This fearful slaughter and the death of their general threw every thing in confusion. The officer next in lineal rank to the general was far in the rear; in this emergency Colonel Campbell, quarter-master-general, took command, but, instead of rallying the men to effect the junction with Arnold, ordered a retreat and abandoned the half-won field.

While all this was occurring on the side of Cape Diamond, Arnold led his division against the opposite side of the lower town. Like Montgomery, he took the advance at the head of a forlorn hope of 25 men. Lamb and his artillery company came next, with a field-piece mounted on a sledge. Then came a company with ladders and scaling implements, followed by Morgan and his riflemen. In the rear of all these came the main body. A battery on a wharf commanded the pass by which they had to advance. This was to be attacked with the field-piece and then scaled with ladders by the forlorn hope while Captain Morgan with his riflemen was to pass round the wharf on the ice.

The false attack by Livingston not having taken place, there was nothing to call off the attention of the enemy in this quarter. The troops, as they straggled through the snow, were sadly galled by a flanking fire from walls and pickets. The field-piece at length became so deeply embedded in a snow-drift that it could not be moved. Lamb and his artillery company were brought to a halt. The company with the scaling ladders would have halted also, having been told to keep in the rear of the artillery, but they were urged on by Morgan with a thundering oath, who pushed on after them with his riflemen, the artillery company opening to let them pass.

They arrived in the advance, just as Arnold, leading on his forlorn hope to attack the barrier, was disabled by a severe wound in the right leg and had to be borne from the field. Morgan instantly took command. Just then Lamb came up with his company, armed with muskets and bayonets, having received orders to abandon the field-piece and support the advance. The battery which commanded the defile mounted two pieces of cannon. There was a discharge of grape-shot when the assailants were close, but, before there could be a second discharge, the battery was carried by assault.

The day was just dawning as Morgan led on to attack the second barrier and his men had to advance under a fire from the town walls. The second barrier reached, they applied their scaling ladders to storm it. The defence was brave and obstinate, but the defenders were at length driven from their guns and the battery was gained. At the last moment one of the gunners ran back to give one more shot. Lamb snapped a fusee at him, but it missed fire. The cannon was discharged and a grape-shot wounded Lamb in the head; he was borne off senseless to a neighboring shed.

The two barriers being now taken, the way on this side into the lower town seemed open. Morgan prepared to enter it with the victorious vanguard, first stationing some provincials at Palace Gate, which opened down into the defile from the upper town. By this time, however, the death of Montgomery and retreat of Campbell had enabled the enemy to turn all their attention in this direction. A large detachment sent by General Carleton sallied out of Palace Gate after Morgan had passed it and completely cut off the advanced party. The main body, informed of the death of Montgomery and giving up the game as lost, retreated to the camp.

Morgan and his men were now hemmed in on all sides and obliged to take refuge in a stone house from the fire which assailed them. From the windows of this house they kept up a desperate defence until cannon were brought to bear upon it. Then, hearing of the death of Montgomery and seeing that there was no prospect of relief, Morgan and his gallant followers were compelled to surrender.

The wrecks of the little army abandoned their camp and retreated about three miles from the town, where they hastily fortified themselves, apprehending a pursuit by the garrison. Carleton, however, contented himself with having secured the safety of the place and remained cautiously passive. The remains of the gallant Montgomery received a soldier's grave, within the fortifications of Quebec.

Arnold, disabled, had been assisted back to the camp, dragging one foot after the other for nearly a mile in great agony and exposed continually to the musketry from the walls. He took temporary command of the shattered army until General Wooster should arrive from Montreal, to whom he sent an express, urging him to bring on succor. He put his troops into such a situation as to keep them still formidable. With a mere handful of men, he maintained a blockade of the strong fortress from which he had just been repulsed.

Happy for him had he fallen at this moment. Happy for him had he found a patriot's grave beneath the rock-built walls of Quebec. His country would have been spared the single traitorous blot that dims the bright page of its revolutionary history.

Schuyler's letter to Washington, announcing the recent events, was written with manly feeling. "I wish," said he, "I had no occasion to send my dear general this melancholy account. My amiable friend, the gallant Montgomery, is no more; the brave Arnold is wounded; and we have met with a severe check in an unsuccessful attempt on Quebec. May Heaven be graciously pleased that the misfortune may terminate here! I tremble for our people in Canada."

Schuyler, who was in Albany, urged an immediate reinforcement of 3000 men for the army in Canada. Washington had not a man to spare from the army before Boston. He applied, therefore, on his own responsibility to Massachusetts, New Hampshire and Connecticut for three regiments, which were granted. His measure received the approbation of Congress and further reinforcements were ordered from the same quarters.

Solicitude was awakened about the interior of the province of New York. Arms and ammunition were said to be concealed in Tryon County and numbers of the tories in that neighborhood preparing for hostilities. Sir John Johnson had fortified Johnson Hall, gathered about him his Scotch Highland tenants and Indian allies, and it was rumored he intended to carry fire and sword along the valley of the Mohawk. Schuyler received orders from Congress, to take measures for securing the military stores, disarming the disaffected, and apprehending their chiefs. He hastened from Albany at the head of a body of soldiers, was joined by Colonel Herkimer with the militia of Tryon County, and appeared before Sir John's stronghold, near Johnstown, on the 19th of January. Thus beleagured, Sir John, after much negotiation, capitulated. He was to surrender all weapons of war and military stores in his possession, and to give his parole not to take arms against America.

The recent reverses in Canada had, in fact, heightened the solicitude of Washington about the province of New York, the central and all important link in the confederacy. He feared it might prove a brittle one. We have already mentioned the adverse influences in operation there: a large number of friends to the crown among the official and commercial classes; rank tories in the city and about the neighboring country, particularly on Long and Staten Islands; king's ships at anchor in the bay and harbor, while Governor Tryon, on board of one of the ships, carried on intrigues with those disaffected to the popular cause. Disaffection to the cause was said to be rife in the province and Washington looked to Lee for effective measures to suppress it.

Lee arrived at New York on the 4th of February. By a singular coincidence, on the very same day Sir Henry Clinton, with the squadron which had sailed so mysteriously from Boston, looked into the harbor. "Though it was Sabbath," says a letter writer of the day, "it threw the whole city into such a convulsion as it never knew before. . . . All that day and all night, were there carts going and boats loading, and women and children crying, and distressed voices heard in the roads in the dead of night."

Clinton sent for the mayor and expressed much surprise and concern at the distress caused by his arrival, which was merely, he said, on a short visit to his friend Tryon and to see how matters stood. He desired that the inhabitants be informed of the purport of his visit and that he would go away as soon as possible. For this time, the inhabitants of New York were let off for their fears. Clinton, after a brief visit, continued his mysterious cruise, openly avowing his destination to be North Carolina—which nobody believed, simply because he avowed it.

The necessity of conferring with committees at every step was a hard restraint upon a man of Lee's ardent and impatient temper, yet at the outset he bore it better than might have been expected.

"The Congress committees, a certain number of the committee of safety, and your humble servant," writes he to Washington, "have had two conferences. The result is such as will agreeably surprise you. It is . . . agreed . . . that to fortify the town against shipping is impracticable, but we are to fortify lodgements on some command-ing part of the city for 2000 men. We are to erect enclosed batteries on both sides of the water near Hell Gate, . . . securing the town against piracies through the Sound . . . our communication with Long Island, now become a more important point than ever, as it is determined to form a strong fortified camp of 3000 men on the Island, immediately opposite to New York. The pass in the High-lands is to be made as respectable as possible and guarded by a battalion."

The pass in the Highlands alluded to is that defile of the

Hudson, where, for 15 miles, it wends its deep channel between stern, forest-clad mountains and rocky promontories. Two forts commanding narrow parts of the river at its bends had been commenced in the preceding autumn, but they were insufficient for the security of that important pass and were to be extended and strengthened.

Washington charged Lee in his instructions to keep a stern eye upon the tories, who were active in New York. In the exercise of his military functions, Lee set Tryon and the captain of the Asia at defiance. "They had threatened perdition to the town," writes he to Washington, "if the cannon were removed from the batteries and wharves, but . . . we . . . conveyed them to a place of safety in the middle of the day and no cannonade ensued."

He now proceeded with his plan of defences. A strong redoubt, capable of holding 300 men, was commenced at Horen's Hook, commanding the pass at Hell Gate, so as to block up from the enemy's ships the passage between the mainland and Long Island. A regiment was stationed on the island, making fascines and preparing other materials for constructing the works for an intrenched camp, which Lee hoped would render it impossible for the enemy to get a footing there. "What to do with this city," writes he, "I own puzzles me. It is so encircled with deep navigable water that whoever commands the sea must command the town." Batteries were to be erected on an eminence behind Trinity Church to keep the enemy's ships at so great a distance as not to injure the town.

King's Bridge, at the upper end of Manhattan, linking it with the mainland, was pronounced by Lee "a most important pass, without which the city could have no communication with Connecticut." It was, therefore, to be made as strong as possible. Heavy cannon were to be sent up to the forts in the Highlands, which were to be enlarged and strengthened.

In the midst of his schemes, Lee received orders from Congress to the command in Canada, vacant by the death of Montgomery. He bewailed the defenceless condition of the city; the Continental Congress, as he said, not having, as yet, taken the least step for its security. "The instant I leave it," said he, ". . . the men-of-war and

Mr. Tryon will return to their old station at the wharves, and the first regiments who arrive from England will take quiet possession of the town and Long Island."

(CHAPTER 19)

The siege of Boston continued through the winter. The British remained within their works, leaving the beleaguering army slowly to augment its forces. Congress was anxious for some successful blow that might revive popular enthusiasm. Washington shared this anxiety and had repeatedly, in councils of war, suggested an attack upon the town but had found a majority opposed to it. He had hoped some opportunity would present, when, the harbor being frozen, the troops might approach the town upon the ice. The winter, however, proved a mild one and the bay continued open. Putnam, in the mean time, having completed the new works at Lechmere Point and being desirous of keeping up the spirit of his men, resolved to treat them to an exploit. Accordingly, from his "impregnable fortress" of Cobble Hill, he detached a party of about 200 under Major Knowlton to surprise and capture a British guard stationed at Charlestown. It was a daring enterprise, executed with spirit. As Charlestown Neck was completely protected, Knowlton led his men across the mill-dam, round the base of the hill, and immediately below the fort. He set fire to the guard-house and some buildings in its vicinity, made several prisoners and retired without loss although thundered upon by the cannon of the fort.

The condition of the besieged town was daily becoming more and more distressing. There was a lack of fuel, too, as well as food. The smallpox broke out and it was necessary to inoculate the army. Several houses were broken open and plundered; others were demolished by the soldiery for fuel. General Howe resorted to the sternest measures to put a stop to these excesses.

Washington still adhered to his opinion in favor of an attempt upon the town, but his field-officers assembled in council (Feb 16th) objected that there was not force nor arms and ammunition sufficient in camp for such an attempt. Washington acquiesced in the decision, it being almost unanimous; yet he felt the irksomeness of his situation.

At length the camp was rejoiced by the arrival of Knox, with his long train of sledges drawn by oxen, bringing more than 50 cannon, mortars, and howitzers, beside supplies of lead and flints. The zeal and perseverance he had displayed in his wintry expedition across frozen lakes and snowy wastes and the intelligence with which he had fulfilled his instructions won him the entire confidence of Washington.

Further ammunition being received from the royal arsenal at New York and other quarters and a reinforcement of ten regiments of militia, Washington no longer met with opposition to his warlike measures. Lechmere Point, which Putnam had fortified, was immediately to be supplied with mortars and heavy cannon so as to command Boston on the north; Dorchester Heights, on the south of the town, were forthwith to be taken possession of. Their possession would enable him to push his works to Nook's Hill and other points opposite Boston, whence a cannonade and bombardment must drive the enemy from the city.

The council of Massachusetts, at his request, ordered the militia of the towns contiguous to Dorchester and Roxbury to hold themselves in readiness to repair to the lines at these places with arms, ammunition and accoutrements on receiving a preconcerted signal.

Washington felt painfully aware how much depended upon the success of this attempt. There was a cloud of gloom and distrust lowering upon the public mind. Danger threatened on the north and on the south. Montgomery had fallen before the walls of Quebec. The army in Canada was shattered. Tryon and the tories were plotting mischief in New York. Dunmore was harassing the lower part of Virginia, and Clinton and his fleet were prowling along the coast on a secret errand of mischief.

In the general plan it was concerted that, should the enemy detach a large force to dislodge our men from Dorchester Heights, an attack upon the opposite side of the town should forthwith be made by Putnam. For this purpose he was to have 4000 picked men in readiness in two divisions under Sullivan and Greene. At a signal from Roxbury, they were to embark in boats near the mouth of Charles River, cross under cover of the fire of three floating batteries, land in two places in Boston, secure its strong posts, force the gates and works at the Neck, and let in the Roxbury troops.

The evening of Monday, the 4th of March, was fixed upon for the occupation of Dorchester Heights. During the two preceding nights the enemy's batteries were cannonaded and bombarded from opposite points to occupy their attention and prevent their noticing the preparations. They replied with spirit and the incessant roar of artillery covered completely the rumbling of waggons and ordnance.

On Monday evening, as soon as the firing commenced, the detachment under Thomas set out from the lines of Roxbury and Dorchester. Everything was conducted as quietly as possible. A covering party of 800 men preceded the carts with the intrenching tools; then came Thomas with the working party, 1200 strong, followed by 300 waggons laden with fascines, gabions, and hay screwed into bundles. Fortunately, although the moon was shining in its full lustre, the flash and roar of cannonry and the bursting of bombshells high in the air so engaged the attention of the enemy that the detachment reached the heights about eight o'clock without being perceived. The covering party then divided, one half proceeded to the point nearest Boston, the other to the one nearest to Castle Williams. The working party commenced to fortify under the directions of Gridley, the veteran engineer who had planned the works on Bunker's Hill. It was severe labor, for the earth was frozen deep, but the men worked with more than their usual spirit, for the eye of the commander-in-chief was upon them. Though not called there by his duties, Washington could not be absent from this eventful operation.

The labors of the night were carried on by the Americans with activity and address. When a relief party arrived at four o'clock in the morning, two forts were in sufficient forwardness to furnish protection against small-arms and grape-shot, and such use was made of the fascines and bundles of screwed hay that at dawn a formidable-looking fortress frowned along the height.

Howe gazed at the mushroom fortress with astonishment as it loomed indistinctly but grandly through a morning fog. "The rebels," exclaimed he, "have done more work in one night than my whole army would have done in one month."

Washington had watched with intense anxiety the effect of the revelation at daybreak. "When the enemy first discovered our works in the morning," writes he, "they seemed to be in great confusion and, from their movements, to intend an attack." A tremendous cannonade was commenced from the forts in Boston and the shipping in the harbor.

Thomas was reinforced with 2000 men. Putnam stood ready to make a descent upon the north side of the town with his 4000 picked men as soon as the heights on the south should be assailed. As Washington rode about the heights, he reminded the troops that it was the 5th of March, the anniversary of the Boston massacre, and called on them to revenge the slaughter of their brethren.

Howe, in the mean time, was perplexed between his pride and the hazards of his position. In his letters to the ministry, he had hoped the Americans would attack him. Apparently they were about to fulfil his hopes, and with formidable advantages of position. He must dislodge them from Dorchester Heights or evacuate Boston. The latter was an alternative too mortifying to be readily adopted. He resolved on an attack but it was to be a night one.

In the evening the British began to move. Lord Percy was to lead the attack. Twenty-five hundred men were embarked in transports which were to convey them to the rendezvous at Castle Williams. A violent storm set in from the east. The transports could not reach their place of destination. The men-of-war could not cover and support them. The attack was consequently postponed until the following day. That day was equally unpropitious. The storm continued with torrents of rain. The attack was again postponed. In the mean time the Americans went on strengthening their works; by the time the storm subsided, Howe deemed them too strong to be easily carried. The attempt, therefore, was relinquished altogether.

What was to be done? The shells thrown from the heights into the town proved it was no longer tenable. The fleet was equally exposed. Admiral Shuldham, the successor to Graves, assured Howe that if the Americans maintained possession of the heights, his ships could not remain in the harbor. It was determined, therefore, to evacuate the place as soon as possible. But now came on a humiliating perplexity. The troops, in embarking, would be exposed to a destructive fire. How was this to be prevented? General Howe's pride would not suffer him to make capitulations; he endeavored to work on the fears of the Bostonians by hinting that if his troops were molested while embarking, he might be obliged to cover their retreat by setting fire to the town.

The hint had its effect. A paper was concocted and signed by several "select men" of Boston, stating that their fears of the destruction of the place had been quieted by Howe's declaration that it should remain uninjured provided his troops were unmolested while embarking; the select men, therefore, begged "some assurance that so dreadful a calamity might not be brought on."

This paper was sent from Boston, on the evening of the 8th, with a flag of truce, which bore it to the American lines at Roxbury. There it was received by Colonel Learned and carried by him to head-quarters. Washington consulted with such general officers as he could immediately assemble. The paper was not addressed to him nor to any one else. It was not authenticated by the signature of General Howe. It was deemed proper, therefore, that Washington should give no answer to the paper, but that Learned should signify in a letter his having laid it before the commander-in-chief and the reasons for not answering it. With this uncompromising letter, the flag returned to Boston. The Americans suspended their fire but continued to fortify their positions.

Daily preparations were now made by the enemy for departure. For some days embarkation of the troops was delayed by adverse winds. Washington feared the movements there might be a feint. Determined to bring things to a crisis, he detached a force to Nooks Hill, an eminence at Dorchester, on the 16th, which threw up a breastwork in the night regardless of the cannonading of the enemy. This commanded Boston Neck and the south part of the town.

A deserter brought a false report to the British that a general assault was intended. The embarkation began with hurry and confusion at four o'clock in the morning. The harbor of Boston soon presented a striking and tumultuous scene. There were 78 ships and transports casting loose for sea, and about 12,000 soldiers, sailors, and refugees hurrying to embark, many with their families and personal effects.

While this tumultuous embarkation was going on, the Americans looked on from their batteries on Dorchester Heights without firing a shot. At an early hour of the morning, the troops stationed at Cambridge and Roxbury had paraded, and several regiments under Putnam had embarked in boats and dropped down Charles River to Sewall's Point to watch the movements of the enemy by land and water. About nine o'clock a large body of troops was seen marching down Bunker's Hill, while boats full of soldiers were putting off for the shipping. Two scouts were sent from the camp to reconnoitre. The works appeared still to be occupied, for sentries were posted about them with shouldered muskets. Observing them to be motionless, the scouts discovered them to be mere effigies. Pushing on, they found the works deserted and gave signal of the fact, whereupon a detachment was sent from the camp to take possession.

Part of Putnam's troops were sent back to Cambridge and part were ordered forward to occupy Boston. General Ward, too, with 500 men, made his way from Roxbury across the neck. The gates were unbarred and thrown open and the Americans entered in triumph, drums beating and colors flying. By ten o'clock the enemy were all embarked and under way. Putnam had taken command of the city, occupied the important points, and the flag of thirteen stripes, the standard of the Union, floated above all the forts. On the following day, Washington himself entered the town, where he was joyfully welcomed.

Notwithstanding the haste with which the British army was embarked, the fleet lingered for some days in Nantucket road. Apprehensive that the enemy, now that their forces were collected in one body, might attempt by some blow to retrieve their late disgrace, Washington hastily threw up works on Fort Hill, which commanded the harbor. The fleet at length disappeared entirely from the coast and the deliverance of Boston was assured.

On motion of John Adams, who had first moved Washington's nomination as commander-in-chief, a unaminous vote of thanks to him was passed in Congress and it was ordered that a gold medal be struck commemorating the evacuation of Boston, bearing the effigy of Washington as its deliverer.

The British fleet bearing the army from Boston had disappeared from the coast. Washington conjectured their destination to be New York and made his arrangements accordingly, but he was mistaken. Howe steered for Halifax, there to await strong reinforcements from England and the fleet of his brother, Admiral Lord Howe, who was to be commander-in-chief of the naval forces on the North American station.

It was presumed the enemy, in the ensuing campaign, would direct their operations against the middle and southern colonies. Congress divided those colonies into two departments: one, comprehending New York, New Jersey, Pennsylvania, Delaware and Maryland, was to be under the command of a major-general and two brigadier-generals; the other, comprising Virginia, the Carolinas and Georgia, to be under the command of a major-general and four brigadiers.

In this new arrangement, the orders destining Lee to Canada were superseded, and he was appointed to the command of the southern department, where he was to keep watch upon the movements of Sir Henry Clinton. "As I am the only general officer on the continent," writes he to Washington, "who can speak or think in French, I confess I think it would have been more prudent to have sent me to Canada; but I shall obey with alacrity and I hope with success."

The command in Canada was given to Thomas, who had distinguished himself at Roxbury and was promoted to the rank of major-general. It would have been given to Schuyler but for the infirm state of his health. Still, as the very existence of the army in Canada would depend on supplies sent from these colonies across the lakes, he was required to fix his head-quarters at Albany, where, until his health was perfectly restored, he would be in a situation to forward supplies and to superintend the operations necessary for the defence of New York and the Hudson River and the affairs of the whole middle department.

On Lee's departure for the South, on the 7th of March, Brigadier-general Lord Stirling remained in temporary command at New York. Washington, presuming that the British fleet had steered for that port with the force which had evacuated Boston, hastened detachments thither under Heath and Sullivan and wrote for 3000 additional men to be furnished by Connecticut. The command of the whole he gave to Putnam, who was ordered to fortify the city and the passes of the Hudson, according to Lee's plans. In the mean time, Washington delayed to come on himself, until he should have pushed forward the main body of his army by divisions.

Washington came on by the way of Providence, Norwich and New London, expediting the embarkation of troops from these posts and arrived at New York on the 13th of April. Many of the works which Lee had commenced were by this time finished; others were in progress. It was apprehended the principal operations of the enemy would be on Long Island, the high grounds of which, in the neighborhood of Brooklyn, commanded the city. Washington saw that an able and efficient officer was needed at that place. Greene was accordingly stationed there with a division of the army. He immediately proceeded to complete the fortifications of that important post and to make himself acquainted with the topography and the defensive points of the surrounding country.

The aggregate force distributed at several posts in New York and its environs, on Long Island, Staten Island and elsewhere amounted to little more than 10,000 men. Some of those were on the sick list, others absent on command or on furlough; there were but about 8000 available and fit for duty. These, too, were without pay; those recently enlisted, without arms; and no one could say where arms were to be procured.

Washington saw the inadequacy of the force to the purposes required, and was full of solicitude about the security of a place, the central point of the confederacy and the grand deposit of ordnance and military stores. He was aware, too, of the disaffection to the cause among many of the inhabitants and apprehensive of treachery. The process of fortifying the place had induced the ships of war to fall down into the outer bay, within the Hook, but Tryon was still on board of one of them, keeping up an active correspondence with the tories on Staten and Long Islands and in other parts of the neighborhood.

Washington took an early occasion to address an urgent letter to the committee of safety, pointing out the dangerous, even treasonable nature of this correspondence. He procured the passage of a resolution prohibiting, under severe penalties, all intercourse with the king's ships.

(CHAPTER 20)

In addition to his cares about the security of New York, Washington had to provide for the perilous exigencies of the army in Canada. Since his arrival in the city, four regiments of troops, a company of riflemen and another of artificers had been detached under the command of Thompson and a further corps of six regiments under Sullivan with orders to join Thomas as soon as possible.

Still Congress inquired of him whether further reinforcements to the army in Canada would not be necessary and whether they could be spared from the army in New York. His reply shows the tormenting uncertainty in which he was kept as to where the next storm of war would break. "It is impossible, at present, to know the designs of the enemy. Should they send the whole force under General Howe up the river St. Lawrence to relieve Quebec and recover Canada, the troops gone and now going will be insufficient to stop their progress; and, should they think proper to send that, or an equal force, this way from Great Britain for the purpose of possessing this city and securing the navigation of Hudson's River, the troops left here will not be sufficient to oppose them; and yet, for any thing we know, I think it not improbable they may attempt both; both being of the greatest importance to them, if they have men. I could wish, indeed, that the army in Canada should be more powerfully reinforced; at the same time I am conscious that the trusting of this important post, which is now become the grand magazine of America, to the handful of men remaining here is running too great a risk. The securing of this post and Hudson's River is to us also of so great importance that I cannot, at present, advise the sending any more troops from hence; on the contrary, the general officers now here, whom I thought it my duty to consult, think it absolutely necessary to increase the army at this place."

Washington at that time was not aware of the extraordinary expedients England had recently resorted to against the next campaign. The Duke of Brunswick, the Landgrave of Hesse Cassel, and the Hereditary Prince of Cassel, Count of Hanau, had been subsidized to furnish troops to assist in the subjugation of her colonies: 4300 Brunswick troops and nearly 13,000 Hessians had entered the British service. Beside the subsidy exacted by the German princes, they were to be paid for every soldier furnished by them and as much more for every one slain.

It was not until the 17th of May, when he received letters from General Schuyler inclosing others from the commanders in Canada, that he knew in what direction some of these bolts of war were launched.

In a former chapter, we left Arnold before the walls of Quebec, wounded yet not disheartened, blockading that "proud town" with a force inferior, by half, in number to that of the garrison. For his gallant services, Congress promoted him in January to the rank of brigadier-general.

Throughout the winter he kept up the blockade, though had Carleton ventured upon a sortie, he might have been forced to decamp. That cautious general, however, remained within his walls.

Arnold, in truth, had difficulties of all kinds to contend with. His military chest was exhausted; his troops were in want of necessaries; as their terms of enlistment expired, his men claimed their discharge and returned home. Sickness also thinned his ranks, so that, at one time, his force was reduced to 500 men.

The failure of the attack on Quebec had weakened the cause among the Canadians; the peasantry had once welcomed them as deliverers; they now began to regard them as intruders.

Notwithstanding all these discouragements, Arnold still kept up a bold face, cut off supplies occasionally, and harassed the place with alarms. Having repaired his batteries, he opened a fire upon the town, but with little effect.

On the 1st day of April, Wooster arrived from Montreal with reinforcements and took command. The day after his arrival, Arnold, falling off his horse, received an injury on the leg recently wounded and was disabled for a week. Considering himself slighted by Wooster, who did not consult him in military affairs, he obtained leave until he should be recovered from his lameness and repaired to Montreal, where he took command.

Thomas arrived at the camp in the course of April and found the army in a forlorn condition, scattered at different posts and on the island of Orleans. It was numerically increased to 2000 men, but smallpox had made great ravages. In their debilitated state, they were without barracks and almost without medicine. A portion, whose term of enlistment had expired, refused to do duty and clamored for discharge.

The winter was over and the case would be desperate. Observing that the river about Quebec was clear of ice, Thomas determined to send up a fire-ship with the flood and, while the ships in the harbor were in flames and the town in confusion, to scale the walls.

Accordingly, on the third of May, the troops turned out with scaling ladders; the fire-ship came up the river and arrived near the shipping before it was discovered. The crew applied a slow match to the train and the ship was soon in a blaze, but the flames consumed the sails and she drifted off harmlessly with the ebbing tide. The rest of the plan was abandoned.

Nothing now remained but to retreat before the enemy should be reinforced. Preparations were made to embark the sick and the military stores. While this was taking place, five ships made their way into the harbor on the 6th of May and began to land troops. Thus reinforced, Carleton sallied forth with about 1000 men.

The Americans were in no condition to withstand Carleton's attack. They had no intrenchments and could not muster 300 men at any point. A precipitate retreat was the consequence, in which baggage, artillery, every thing was abandoned. Even the sick were left behind, many of whom took refuge in the woods or among the Canadian peasantry.

Thomas came to a halt at Point Deschambault, about 60 miles above Quebec, and called a council of war. The enemy's ships were hastening up the St. Lawrence. The camp was without cannon; powder forwarded by Schuyler had fallen into the enemy's hands; there were not provisions enough to subsist the army for more than three days; the men-of-war, too, might run up the river, intercept all their resources, and reduce them to the same extremity they had experienced before Quebec. It was resolved, therefore, to ascend the river still further. Thomas, however, determined to remain at Point Deschambault with about 500 men until he should receive orders from Montreal and learn whether such supplies could be forwarded as would enable him to defend his position.

The despatches of Thomas, setting forth the disastrous state of affairs, had a disheartening effect on Schuyler, who feared the army would be obliged to abandon Canada. Washington, on the contrary, spoke cheeringly on the subject. He regretted that the troops had not been able to make a stand at Point Deschambault, but hoped they would maintain a post as far down the river as possible.

The tidings of the reverses in Canada and the retreat of the American army had spread consternation throughout the New Hampshire Grants and the New England frontiers, which would now be laid open to invasion. Schuyler's enemies stigmatized him as the cause of the late reverses. He had neglected, they said, to forward reinforcements and supplies to the army in Canada. It was insinuated that he was untrue to his country, if not positively leagued with her enemies.

These imputations were not generally advanced; and when advanced, were not generally countenanced; but a committee of

King's County appears to have given them credence, addressing a letter to the commander-in-chief on the subject, accompanied by documents. Washington received the letter and documents with indignation and disgust.

While the imputations had merely floated in public rumor, Schuyler had taken no notice of them; "but it is now," writes he to Washington, "a duty which I owe myself and my country to . . . request . . . an immediate inquiry be made into the matter. . . . I am informed . . . that . . . persons, living on . . . the New Hampshire Grants . . . design to seize me as a tory."

We need only add that the Berkshire committees, which had given countenance to these imputations, investigated them and acknowledged, in a letter to Washington, that their suspicions respecting Schuyler were wholly groundless. "We sincerely hope," added they, "his name may be handed down, with immortal honor, to the latest posterity, as one of the great pillars of the American cause."

As the reverses in Canada would affect the fortunes of the Revolution elsewhere, Washington sent Gates to lay the despatches concerning them before Congress. Scarce had Gates departed on his mission (May 19th) when Washington received a summons to Philadelphia to advise with Congress concerning the opening campaign. He was informed also that Gates, on the 16th of May, had been promoted to major-general and Mifflin to brigadier-general, and a wish was intimated that they might take command of Boston.

Washington prepared to proceed to Philadelphia. His general orders issued on the 19th of May show the situation of affairs at New York. In his instructions to Putnam, who, as the oldest major-general in the city, would have command during his absence, Washington informed him of the intention of the Provincial Congress to seize the principal tories and disaffected persons in the city and the surrounding country, especially on Long Island, and authorized him to afford military aid, if required, to carry the same into execution. He was also to send Stirling, Colonel Putnam, and Colonel Knox, if he could be spared, up to the Highlands, to examine the forts and garrisons and report what was necessary to put them in a posture of defence.

The general, accompanied by Mrs. Washington, departed from New York on the 21st of May and they were invited by Hancock, the President of Congress, to be his guests during their sojourn at Philadelphia.

Washington, in his conferences with Congress, expressed his conviction that no accommodation could be effected with Great Britain, on acceptable terms. The sword being drawn, the most coercive measures would be persevered in until there was complete submission. The recent subsidizing of foreign troops indicated unsparing hostility. A protracted war, therefore, was inevitable, but it would be impossible to carry it on successfully with the scanty force actually embodied and with transient enlistments of militia.

In consequence, resolutions were passed in Congress that soldiers should be enlisted for three years, that the army at New York should be reinforced until the 1st of December with 13,800 militia, that gondolas and fire-rafts should be built to prevent the men-of-war and enemy's ships from coming into New York Bay or the Narrows, and that a flying camp of 10,000 militia, furnished by Pennsylvania, Delaware and Maryland and engaged until the 1st of December, should be stationed in the Jerseys for the defence of the middle colonies. Washington was, moreover, empowered, in case of emergency, to call on neighboring colonies for temporary aid with their militia.

Another important result of his conferences with Congress was the establishment of a war office. Military affairs, hitherto referred in Congress to committees casually appointed, had consequently been subject to great irregularity and neglect. Henceforth a permanent committee, entitled the Board of War and Ordnance, was to take cognizance of them. The first board was composed of five members: John Adams, Colonel Benjamin Harrison, Roger Sherman, James Wilson, and Edward Rutledge, with Richard Peters as secretary.

While at Philadelphia, Washington had frequent consultations with George Clinton, one of the delegates from New York, concerning the interior defences of that province, especially those connected with the security of the Highlands of the Hudson, where part of the regiment of Colonel James Clinton, the brother of the delegate, was stationed.

Despatches from Canada continued to be disastrous. Arnold, in command at Montreal, had established a post on the St. Lawrence, about 40 miles above that place, on a point of land called the Cedars where he had stationed Colonel Bedel with about 400 men to prevent goods being sent to the enemy and to guard against surprise from them or their Indians.

In the latter part of May, Bedel received intelligence that a large body of British, Canadians, and Indians were coming to attack him. Leaving Major Butterfield in command, he hastened to Montreal to obtain reinforcements. In the mean time, the post at the Cedars had been besieged and Butterfield intimidated into a surrender by a threat that resistance would provoke a massacre by the Indians. The reinforcements being sent were assailed by a large party of savages and captured after a sharp skirmish.

Arnold received word of these disasters while on the march. He instantly sent forward some Caughnawaga Indians to overtake the savages and demand a surrender of the prisoners. He embarked 400 of his men in bateaux and pushed on with the remainder by land. Arriving at St. Ann's, he discovered several of the enemy's bateaux taking the prisoners off an island, a league distant. It was a tormenting sight as it was not in his power to relieve them. His bateaux, were a league behind, coming up the rapids very slowly. In the mean time, his Caughnawaga messengers returned with an answer from the savages. They had 500 prisoners, they said; should he attack them, they would kill every prisoner.

In this situation, Arnold now pushed for Quinze Chiens, where the whole force of the enemy, civilized and savage, was intrenched and fortified. Arnold rowed near the land, but by this time it was too dark to distinguish anything on shore and he judged it prudent to return to St. Johns.

In the next few days Arnold negotiated an agreement by which the prisoners were to be exchanged for an equal number of British prisoners of the same rank.

The accounts which reached Washington of these affairs were vague and kept him in painful suspense. "The situation of our affairs in Canada," observes he in a letter to Schuyler, "is truly alarming. . . . The most vigorous exertions will be necessary to retrieve our circumstances there, and I hope you will strain every nerve for that purpose. Unless it can be done now, Canada will be lost to us for ever."

While his mind was agitated by these concerns, letters from Schuyler showed that mischief was brewing in another quarter.

Guy Johnson, accompanied by the Sachem Brant and the Butlers, had been holding councils with the Indians and designed, it was said, to come back to the Mohawk country at the head of a British and savage force. A correspondence was carried on between him and his cousin, Sir John Johnson, who was said to be preparing to co-operate with his Scotch dependants and Indian allies. Considering this a breach of Sir John's parole, Schuyler sent Colonel Dayton with a force to apprehend him. Sir John, with a number of his armed tenants, retreated for refuge among the Indians. Dayton took possesion of Johnson Hall, seized Sir John's papers, and subsequently conveyed her ladyship as a hostage to Albany.

Shortly afterwards came further intelligence of the designs of the Johnsons. Sir John, with his Scotch warriors and Indian allies, was coming down the valley of the Mohawk, bent on revenge and prepared to lay every thing waste; Schuyler was collecting a force at Albany to oppose him. Washington instantly wrote to Schuyler to detach Dayton with his regiment on that service, with instructions to secure a post where Fort Stanwix formerly stood. As to Schuyler, Washington directed him to hold a conference with the Six Nations and with any other Indians to secure their active services.

Stirling, who, by Washington's orders, had inspected the defences in the Highlands, rendered a report of their condition. Fort Montgomery, at the lower part of the Highlands, was on the west bank where the river was about half a mile wide. Opposite the fort was the promontory of Anthony's Nose, several hundred feet higher, where a body of riflemen might command the decks of vessels. Fort Montgomery appeared to Stirling the proper place for a guard post.

Fort Constitution, about six miles up the river on a rocky

island, was at a narrow strait where the Hudson, shouldered by precipices, makes a sudden bend round West Point. A redoubt, in the opinion of Stirling, would be needed on the point, not only for the preservation of Fort Constitution, but for its own importance.

The garrison of that fort consisted of two companies of Colonel James Clinton's regiment and Captain Wisner's company of minute men, in all 160 rank and file. Fort Montgomery was garrisoned by three companies of the same regiment, about 200 rank and file. Both garrisons were miserably armed. The general command of the posts required to be adjusted. In view of all these circumstances, Washington, on the 14th of June, ordered Colonel Clinton to take command of both posts.

Kingsbridge, and the heights adjacent, considered by Lee of utmost importance to communication between New York and the mainland and to the security of the Hudson, were reconnoitred by Washington about the middle of the month, ordering where works should be laid out. Breastworks were to be thrown up for the defence of the bridge, and an advanced work (subsequently called Fort Independence) was to be built beyond it on a hill commanding Spyt den Duivel Creek, as that inlet of the Hudson is called, which links it with Harlem River.

A strong work, a kind of citadel, was to crown a rocky height south of the bridge, commanding the channel of the Hudson; below it were to be redoubts on the banks at Jeffrey's Point. In honor of the general, the citadel received the name of Fort Washington. Putnam was the principal engineer who had the direction of the works. Mifflin, with part of the two battalions from Pennsylvania, was to be employed in their construction, aided by the militia.

While these preparations were made for the protection of the Hudson, the works about Brooklyn were carried on under Greene. In a word, the utmost exertions were made to put the city, its environs, and the Hudson River, in a state of defence before the arrival of another hostile armament.

Operations in Canada were drawing to a disastrous close. Thomas, finding it impossible to make a stand at Point Deschambault, had continued his retreat to the mouth of the Sorel, where he found Thompson with part of the troops detached by Washington from New York, who were making some preparations for defence. Shortly after his arrival, he was taken ill with the smallpox, and he died of that malady on the 2d of June. Sullivan, who had recently arrived with the main detachment of troops from New York, succeeded to the command, Wooster having been recalled. He advanced immediately to the mouth of the Sorel, where he found Thompson with very few troops to defend that post, having detached Colonel St. Clair with about 700 men to Three Rivers to check an advanced corps of the enemy of about 800 regulars and Canadians under Maclean.

Sullivan proceeded forthwith to complete the works on the Sorel; in the mean time he detached Thompson with additional troops to overtake St. Clair and assume command of the whole party, which would then amount to 2000 men. He was by no means to attack the encampment at Three Rivers, unless there was great prospect of success, as his defeat might prove the total loss of Canada.

Sagaciously perceiving that Sullivan was aiming at the command in Canada, Washington soberly weighed his merits for the appointment in a letter to the President of Congress. "He is active, spirited, and zealously attached to the cause. . . . He wants experience to move upon a grand scale"—a want overbalanced in Washington's estimate by sound judgment and an enterprising genius.

Scarce had Washington despatched this letter, when he received one from the President of Congress, dated the 18th of June, informing him that Gates had been appointed to command the forces in Canada and requesting him to expedite his departure. The appointment of Gates has been attributed to the influence of the Eastern delegates, with whom he was a favorite. He departed for his command on the 26th of June, vested with extraordinary powers for the regulation of affairs in that "distant, dangerous, and shifting scene."

Despatches received from Sullivan had indicated that the enemy in Canada had recently been augmented to about 13,000 men, several regiments having arrived from Ireland, one from England, another from General Howe, and a body of Brunswick troops under the Baron Riedesel. Of these, the greater part were on the way up from Quebec in divisions, by land and water, with

Carleton, Burgoyne, Philips and Riedesel, while a considerable number under Frazer had arrived at Three Rivers and others, under Nesbit, lay near them on board of transports.

Thompson had coasted in bateaux along the right bank of the river at that expanse called Lake St. Pierre and arrived at Nicolete, where he found St. Clair and his detachment. He crossed the river in the night and landed above Three Rivers, intending to surprise the enemy before daylight; he was not aware at the time that additional troops had arrived under Burgoyne.

After landing, he marched with rapidity towards Three Rivers, but was led by treacherous guides into a morass and obliged to return back nearly two miles. Day broke and he was discovered from the ships. A cannonade was opened upon his men as they made their way slowly through a swamp. At length they arrived in sight of Three Rivers, but it was to find a large force drawn up in battle array under Frazer, by whom they were warmly attacked and thrown in confusion. Thompson attempted to rally his troops and partly succeeded until a fire was opened upon them in rear by Nesbit, who had landed from his ships. Their rout now was complete. General Thompson, Colonel Irvine, and about 200 men were captured, 25 were slain; the rest, pursued for several miles, after great sufferings, were able to get on board of their boats, in which they made their way back to the Sorel, bringing Sullivan the alarming intelligence of the overpowering force coming up the river.

Sullivan had made the desperate resolve to defend the mouth of the Sorel but was induced to abandon it by the unanimous opinion of his officers and the evident unwillingness of his troops. Dismantling his batteries, therefore, he retreated just before the arrival of the enemy and was followed along the Sorel by a strong column under Burgoyne.

On the 18th of June he was joined by Arnold with 300 men, the garrison of Montreal, who had crossed at Longueil just in time to escape a large detachment of the enemy. The evacuation of Canada being determined on in a council of war, Sullivan succeeded in destroying every thing at Chamblee and St. Johns that he could not carry away, breaking down bridges, leaving forts and vessels in flames, and continued his retreat to the Isle la Motte, whence, on orders from Schuyler, he embarked with his forces, sick and well, for Crown Point.

Thus ended this famous invasion—an enterprise bold in its conception, daring and hardy in its execution, full of ingenious expedients, and hazardous exploits—which, had not unforeseen circumstances counteracted its well-devised plans, might have added all Canada to the American confederacy.

(CHAPTER 21)

The great aim of the British at present was to get possession of New York and the Hudson and make them the basis of military operations. This they hoped to effect on the arrival of a powerful armament, hourly expected and designed for operations on the seaboard.

At this critical juncture there was an alarm of a conspiracy among the tories in the city and on Long Island suddenly to take up arms and co-operate with the British troops on their arrival. Some of the tories were to break down King's Bridge, others were to blow up the magazines, and massacre all the field-officers. Washington was to be killed or delivered up to the enemy. Some of his own body guard were said to be in the plot. Several publicans of the city were pointed out, as having aided or abetted the plot. One of the most noted was Corbie, whose tavern was said to be to the south-east of Washington's house, the general being quartered at what was called Richmond Hill, a mansion surrounded by trees, at a short distance from the city, in rather an isolated situation.

A committee of the New York Congress, of which John Jay was chairman, traced the plot to Tryon, who, from his safe retreat on shipboard, acted through agents on shore. The most important of these was David Matthews, the tory mayor of the city. He was accused of disbursing money to enlist men, purchase arms, and corrupt the soldiery.

Washington was authorized and requested by the committee to cause the mayor to be apprehended and all his papers secured. Matthews was at that time residing at Flatbush on Long Island, at no great distance from Greene's encampment. Washington transmitted the warrant of the committee to the general on the 21st with directions that it should "be executed . . . exactly by one o'clock of the ensuing morning by a careful officer." Precisely at the hour of one, a detachment from Greene's brigade surrounded the house of the mayor and secured his person, but no papers were found though diligent search was made.

Numerous other arrests took place and, among the number, some of Washington's body-guard. A great dismay fell upon the tories. Some of those on Long Island who had proceeded to arm themselves, finding the plot discovered, sought refuge in woods and morasses. Washington directed that those arrested who belonged to the army should be tried by a court-martial and the rest handed over to the secular power.

Corbie's tavern was a rendezvous of the conspirators. There one Gilbert Forbes enlisted men, gave them money, and swore them on the book to secrecy. From this house a correspondence was kept up with Tryon on shipboard. At this tavern Washington's body-guards were tampered with. Thomas Hickey, one of the guards, was said to have aided in corrupting his comrades.

Much of the evidence given was of a dubious kind. It was certain that persons had secretly been enlisted and sworn to hostile operations, but Washington did not think that any regular plan had been digested by the conspirators.

According to the mayor's own admission before the committee, he had been cognizant of attempts to enlist tories and corrupt Washington's guards though he declared that he had discountenanced them. He had on one occasion, also, at the request of Tryon, paid money for him to Forbes for rifles and guns which he had already furnished and for others which he was to make. The mayor, with a number of others, were detained in prison to await a trial.

Thomas Hickey, the individual of Washington's guard, was tried before a court-martial, which found him guilty of mutiny and sedition and treacherous correspondence with the enemy, and

BAY OF NEW YORK

(From the Narrows)

Printed by W. Pate

NEW YORK G.P. PUTNAM & CO

sentenced him to be hanged. The sentence was approved by Washington and was carried promptly into effect, in the most solemn and impressive manner, to serve as a warning and example in this time of treachery and danger. He was hanged in the presence of near 20,000 persons.

While the city was brooding over this doleful spectacle, four ships of war appeared off the Hook, stood quietly in at the Narrows, and dropped anchor in the bay.

On the 29th of June, an express from the look-out on Staten Island announced that 40 sail were in sight. They were, in fact, ships from Halifax, bringing about 10,000 troops recently expelled from Boston, together with six transports filled with Highland troops which had joined the fleet at sea. At sight of this formidable armament in the harbor, Washington instantly sent notice of its arrival to Colonel Clinton, who had command of the posts in the Highlands and urged all possible preparation to give the enemy a warm reception should they push their frigates up the river.

The ramifications of the conspiracy lately detected extended up the Hudson. Many of the disaffected in the upper counties were enlisted in it. The committee of safety at Cornwall, in Orange County, sent word to Colonel Clinton of the mischief that was brewing. It was expected the British would push up the river and land at Verplanck's Point, whereupon the guns at the forts in the Highlands were to be spiked by soldiers of their own garrisons and the tories throughout the country were to be up in arms. Clinton received letters, also, from a meeting of committees in the precincts of Newburgh apprising him that persons dangerous to the cause were lurking in that neighborhood.

While city and country were thus agitated by apprehensions of danger, other arrivals swelled the number of ships in the bay of New York to 130 men-of-war and transports. They made no movement to ascend the Hudson but anchored off Staten Island, where they landed their troops; the hill sides were soon whitened with their tents.

In the frigate Greyhound, one of the four ships which first arrived, came General Howe. He had preceded the fleet in order to confer with Tryon and inform himself of the state of affairs. In a letter to his government he writes, "There is great reason to expect a numerous body of the inhabitants to join the army from the province of York, the Jerseys and Connecticut who, in this time of universal oppression, only wait for opportunities to give proofs of their loyalty and zeal."

Washington beheld the gathering storm with an anxious eye, aware that General Howe only awaited the arrival of his brother, the admiral, to commence hostile operations. He wrote to the President of Congress, urging a call on the Massachusetts government for its quota of continental troops and the formation of a flying camp of 10,000 men, to be stationed in the Jerseys as a central force ready to act in any direction as circumstances might require.

On the 2d of July, he issued a general order, calling upon the troops to prepare for a momentous conflict which was to decide their liberties and fortunes.

As Greene one day, on his way to Washington's head-quarters, was passing through a field, he paused to notice a Provincial company of artillery and was struck with its able performances and with the tact and talent of its commander. He was a mere youth, small in stature, but remarkable for his alert and manly bearing. It was Alexander Hamilton. Greene was quick to appreciate any display of military science; a little conversation sufficed to convince him that the youth before him had a mind of no ordinary grasp and quickness. He invited him to his quarters and from that time cultivated his friendship.

Hamilton, a native of the West Indies, entered King's (now Columbia) College, at New York, in the latter part of 1773 to fit himself for the medical profession. The contentions of the colonies with the mother country gave a different direction and impulse to his ardent and aspiring mind. On the 6th of July, 1774, there was a general meeting of the citizens to express their abhorrence of the Boston Port Bill. Hamilton was present and ventured to address the multitude.

The war approaching, he now devoted himself to military studies, especially pyrotechnics and gunnery, and formed an amateur corps of a number of his fellow students and young gentlemen of the city. In the month of March, 1776, he became captain of artillery in a Provincial corps, newly raised, and soon, by able drilling, rendered it conspicuous for discipline. It was while exercising his artillery company that he attracted the attention of Greene. Further acquaintance heightened the general's opinion of his extraordinary merits and he took an early occasion to introduce him to the commander-in-chief.

A valuable accession to the army at this anxious time was Washington's neighbor and former companion in arms, Hugh Mercer, the veteran of Culloden and Fort Duquesne. His military spirit was alert as ever; the talent he had shown in organizing the Virginia militia and his zeal as a member of the committee of safety had been appreciated by Congress and on the 5th of June he had received the commission of brigadier-general. The flying camp was about forming and Washington gave command of it to Mercer, of whose merits he felt sure, and sent him over to Paulus Hook in the Jerseys to make arrangements for the Pennsylvania militia as they should come in, recommending him to Brigadier-general William Livingston as an officer on whose experience and judgment great confidence might be reposed.

Livingston was a man inexperienced in arms, but of education, talent, sagacity and ready wit. Mercer and he were to consult together and concert plans to repel invasions; the New Jersey militia, however, were distinct from the flying camp and only called out for local defence. New Jersey's greatest danger of invasion was from Staten Island, where the British were throwing up works and whence they might attempt to cross to Amboy. The flying camp was therefore to be stationed in the neighborhood of that place.

PART V

(CHAPTERS 22–24)

The Decision for Independence
[1776]

While danger was gathering round New York, the General Congress at Philadelphia was discussing, with closed doors, what John Adams pronounced "the greatest question ever debated in America." The result was a resolution passed unanimously, on the 2d of July, "that these United Colonies are, and of right ought to be, free and independent States."

"The 2d of July," adds Adams, "will be the most memorable epoch in the history of America. . . . It ought to be commemorated as the day of deliverance, by solemn acts of devotion to Almighty God. It ought to be solemnized with pomp and parade, with shows, games, sports, guns, bells, bonfires and illuminations, from one end of this continent to the other, from this time forth for evermore."

The fourth of July is actually the day of national rejoicing, for on that day the "Declaration of Independence," that solemn and sublime document, was adopted. Tradition gives a dramatic effect to its announcement. It was known to be under discussion but the closed doors of Congress excluded the populace. They awaited in throngs an appointed signal. In the steeple of the state-house was a bell imported twenty-three years previously from London by the Pro-

THE ANNOUNCEMENT OF THE DECLARATION OF INDEPENDENCE.

(STATE HOUSE PHILADELPHIA.)

Engraved by J M⁰ Gofin at J M Butler's establishment, 84 Chesnut St

NEW YORK G.P. PUTNAM & C⁰

vincial Assembly of Pennsylvania. It bore the portentous text from scripture: "Proclaim liberty throughout all the land, unto all the inhabitants thereof." A joyous peal from that bell gave notice that the bill had been passed. It was the knell of British domination.

Washington hailed the declaration with joy. It is true, it was but a formal recognition of a state of things which had long existed but it put an end to all those temporizing hopes of reconciliation which had clogged the military action of the country.

On the 9th of July, he caused it to be read at the head of each brigade of the army. "The general hopes," said he in his orders, "that this important event will serve as a fresh incentive to every officer and soldier to act with fidelity and courage, as knowing that now the peace and safety of his country depend, under God, solely on the success of our arms; and that he is now in the service of a State possessed of sufficient power to reward his merit and advance him to the highest honors of a free country."

The exultation of the patriots of New York caused by the Declaration of Independence was soon overclouded. On the 12th of July, several ships stood in from sea and joined the naval force below. Every nautical movement was now a matter of speculation and alarm.

Two ships of war were observed getting under way and standing toward the city. One was the Phoenix of 40 guns, the other the Rose, of 20 guns, commanded by Captain Wallace, who had marauded the New England coast. The troops were immediately at their alarm posts. In the afternoon the ships and three tenders came sweeping up the bay with the advantage of wind and tide and shaped their course up the Hudson. The batteries of the city and of Paulus Hook on the Jersey shore opened fire upon them. They answered it with broadsides and continued up the Hudson. They sustained little damage, their decks having ramparts of sand-bags. The ships below remained at their anchors and showed no intention of following them. The firing ceased. The fear of a general attack upon the city died away and the agitated citizens breathed more freely.

Washington, however, apprehended this movement might be with a different object. They might land troops and seize upon the passes of the Highlands. Forts Montgomery and Constitution, far from complete, were scantily manned. A small force might be sufficient to surprise them. The ships might intend, also, to distribute arms among the tories and prepare them to cooperate in the apprehended attack upon New York.

Thus thinking, Washington sent off an express to alert Mifflin, who was stationed with his Philadelphia troops at Fort Washington and King's Bridge. The same express carried a letter from him to the New York Convention, at that time holding its sessions at White Plains, apprising it of the impending danger.

Fortunately George Clinton, the patriotic legislator, had recently been appointed brigadier-general of the militia of Ulster and Orange Counties. His native state in danger, he had only remained in Congress to vote for the declaration of independence and then hastened home. He was now at New Windsor, just above the Highlands. Washington wrote to him on the 12th, urging him to collect as great a force as possible of the New York militia for the protection of the Highlands and to solicit aid, if requisite, from western Connecticut.

Long before receipt of Washington's letter, Clinton had been put on the alert by an alarm gun from his brother at Fort Constitution. Shortly afterwards, two river sloops came to anchor before the general's residence and their captains informed him that New York had been attacked on the preceding afternoon.

The neighboring militia were forthwith put in motion. Three regiments were ordered out, one to Fort Montgomery, another to Fort Constitution, the third to Newburgh, ready to assist Fort Constitution should another signal be given. All other regiments under his command were to be prepared for service at a moment's notice.

Another of his sagacious measures was to send expresses to all owners of sloops and boats twenty miles up the west side of the river to haul them off so as to prevent their grounding. Part of them were to be ready to carry militia to the forts; the rest were ordered to Fort Constitution, where a chain of them might be drawn across the river, to be set on fire should enemy ships attempt to pass.

Having made these prompt arrangements, he proceeded on

the same day to Fort Montgomery, where he fixed his head-quarters, as being nearer the enemy and better situated to discover their motions.

Here, on the following day, he received Washington's letter but he had already anticipated its orders and stirred up the whole country. On that same evening, about 300 hardy Ulster yeomanry, part of one of the regiments he had ordered out, marched into Fort Montgomery; early the next morning 500 of another regiment arrived, and he was told that parts of two other regiments were on the way. On no one could this prompt and brave gathering of the yeomanry produce a more gratifying effect than upon the commander-in-chief.

While the vigilant Clinton was preparing to defend the passes of the Highlands, danger was growing more imminent at the mouth of the Hudson. The agitation into which New York was thrown on the 12th of July by the Phoenix and the Rose was followed by another on the same evening, when there was a great booming of cannon from the shipping at anchor at Staten Island. The British fleet were saluting a ship of the line, just arrived from sea. At her foretop mast-head she bore St. George's flag. "It is the admiral's ship!" was echoed from mouth to mouth and the word soon flew throughout the city, "Lord Howe is come!"

Lord Howe was indeed come and affairs now appeared to be approaching a crisis. In consequence of the recent conspiracy the Convention of New York, seated at White Plains, had a secret committee in New York for taking cognizance of traitorous machinations. To this committee Washington addressed a letter the day after his lordship's arrival, suggesting the policy of removing from the city and its environs "all persons of known disaffection and enmity to the cause of America," especially those in jail for treasonable offences. In consequence of his suggestion, thirteen persons in confinement for traitorous offences were removed to the jail of Litchfield in Connecticut. Among the number was the late mayor.

The proceedings of Lord Howe soon showed the policy of these precautions. His lordship had prepared a declaration addressed to the people at large, inviting all who had deviated from their al-legiance to the crown to receive pardon by a prompt return to their duty. His lordship really desired peace. It was a sore matter of regret to him, therefore, to find that, in consequence of his tardy arrival, his invitation to loyalty had been forestalled by the Declaration of Independence.

We have heretofore shown the tenacity with which Washington in his correspondence with Gage and Howe exacted the deference due to him as commander-in-chief of the American armies; he did this not from official pride and punctilio, but as the guardian of American rights and dignities. British officers, considering the Americans in arms as rebels without valid commissions, were in the habit of denying them all military title. Washington's officers urged him not to submit to this tacit indignity but to reject all letters directed to him without a specification of his rank.

An occasion now presented for the adjustment of this matter. A lieutenant of the British navy came with a flag from Lord Howe, seeking a conference with Washington. Colonel Reed, the adjutant-general, met him half way between Governor's and Staten Islands. The lieutenant informed him that he was the bearer of a letter from Lord Howe to Mr. Washington. Reed replied that he knew no such person in the American army. The lieutenant produced the letter, addressed to George Washington, Esquire. He was informed that it could not be received with such a direction. While the lieutenant was agitated, Reed politely declined to receive the letter, stating that the general's station in the army was well known and they could not be at a loss as to the proper mode of addressing him.

On the 19th, an aide-de-camp of General Howe came with a flag, and requested to know whether Colonel Patterson, the British adjutant-general, could be admitted to an interview with General Washington. Colonel Reed consented in the name of the general and pledged his honor for the safety of the adjutant-general during the interview, which was fixed for the following morning.

At the appointed time, Reed met the flag in the harbor, took Patterson into their barge, and escorted him to town. Washington received the adjutant-general at head-quarters with form and ceremony, in full military array, with his officers and guards about him.

Patterson, addressing him by the title of *your excellency*, endeavored to explain the address of the letter as consistent with propriety, and then produced, but did not offer, a letter addressed to George Washington, Esquire, &c. &c., hoping that the et ceteras, which implied every thing, would remove all impediments. Washington replied that the et ceteras implied every thing but they also implied any thing. A letter, he added, addressed to a person acting in a public character should have some inscription to designate it from a mere private letter, and he should absolutely decline any letter addressed to himself as a private person when it related to his public station.

Colonel Patterson, finding the letter would not be received, endeavored to communicate the scope of it in conversation. What he chiefly dwelt upon was that Lord Howe and his brother had been specially nominated commissioners for the promotion of peace, that they had great powers and would derive the highest pleasures from effecting an accommodation, and that he wished his visit to be considered as the first advance toward that object. Washington replied that their powers, it would seem, were only to grant pardons. Those who had committed no fault needed no pardon, and such was the case with the Americans, who were only defending their indisputable rights.

Patterson avoided a discussion of this matter and so the conference, which had been conducted with great courtesy, terminated. The colonel took his leave and was conducted to his boat.

Washington received the applause of Congress and of the public for sustaining the dignity of his station. His conduct in this particular was recommended as a model to all American officers in corresponding with the enemy.

In the mean time the irruption of the Phoenix and the Rose into the Hudson had roused a belligerent spirit along its borders. The lower part of that noble river is commanded on the east by the bold woody heights of Manhattan Island and Westchester County, on the west by the rocky cliffs of the Palisades. Beyond those cliffs, the river expands into a succession of what may almost be termed lakes, first the Tappan Sea, then Haverstraw Bay, then the Bay of Peekskill. Then come the Highlands, that strait, fifteen miles in length, where the river bends its course, narrow and deep, between rocky forest-clad mountains. "He who has command of that grand defile," said an old navigator, "may at any time throttle the Hudson."

The New York Convention, aware of the impending danger, despatched military envoys to stir up the yeomanry along the river and order out militia. Powder and ball were sent to Tarrytown, before which the hostile ships were anchored, and yeoman troops were stationed there and along the neighboring shores of the Tappan Sea. In a little while the militia of Dutchess County and Cortlandt's Manor were hastening, rudely armed, to protect the public stores at Peekskill and mount guard at the entrance of the Highlands.

No one showed more zeal in this time of alarm, than Colonel Pierre Van Cortlandt, of an old colonial family which held its manorial residence at the mouth of the Croton. With his regiment he kept watch along the eastern shore of the Tappan Sea and Haverstraw Bay. Sentinels were posted to keep a look-out from heights and headlands and marksmen were ready to assemble in a moment.

The ships of war lay quietly anchored in the broad expanses of the Tappan Sea and Haverstraw Bay, keeping out of musket shot of the shore, while their boats were out taking soundings up to the Highlands, evidently preparing for further operations. At night, too, their barges were heard rowing up and down the river on mysterious errands.

The ships, now acquainted with the channel, moved up within six miles of Fort Montgomery. General Clinton apprehended they might take advantage of a dark night and slip by him in the deep shadows of the mountains. Once above the Highlands, they might ravage the country and destroy certain vessels of war being constructed at Poughkeepsie.

To prevent this, he stationed a guard at night about two miles and a half below the fort, prepared to kindle a blazing fire should the ships appear in sight. Large piles of dry brushwood were prepared at various places down the shore and men stationed to set fire to them as soon as a signal should be given from the lower point. The fort, therefore, would have a fair chance with its batteries as the ships passed between it and these conflagrations.

The Decision for Independence (1776)

A committee sent up by the New York convention had a conference with the general to devise further means of obstructing the
passage of ships up the river. Fire rafts were to be brought from
Poughkeepsie and kept at hand ready for action. These were to be
lashed two together with chains between old sloops filled with
combustibles and sent down with a strong wind and tide to drive
upon the ships. An iron chain, also, was to be stretched obliquely
across the river from Fort Montgomery to the foot of Anthony's
Nose, thus chaining up the gate of the Highlands.

For protection below the Highlands, it was proposed to station
whale-boats about the Tappan Sea and Haverstraw Bay to reconnoitre the enemy, carry intelligence from post to post, seize river
craft that might bring the ships supplies, and cut off their boats when
attempting to land. Galleys, also, were prepared, with nine-
pounders mounted at the bows.

While the security of the Hudson was claiming the attention of
Washington, he was equally anxious to prevent an irruption of the
enemy from Canada. He was grieved, therefore, to find a clashing of
authorities between the generals who had charge of the northern
frontier. Gates, on his way to take command of the army in Canada,
had heard with surprise in Albany of its retreat across the New York
frontier. He still considered it under his orders and was proceeding
to act accordingly, when Schuyler observed that the resolution of
Congress and the instructions of Washington applied to the army
only while in Canada; the moment it retreated within the limits of
New York it came within his (Schuyler's) command.

The two generals agreed to refer the question of command to
Congress and in the mean time to act in concert. They accordingly
departed together for Lake Champlain to prepare against an anticipated invasion by Carleton. They arrived at Crown Point on the
6th of July and found there the wrecks of the army recently driven
out of Canada. They had no food but salt pork, often rancid, hard bis-
cuit or unbaked flour, and scarcely any medicine. Not more than
6000 men had reached Crown Point and half of those were on the
sick list, the shattered remains of very fine battalions. Some were
sheltered in tents, some under sheds, and others in huts formed of

bushes—scarce one of which but contained a dead or dying man.

In a council of war, it was determined that Crown Point was not tenable and that it was expedient to fall back and take a strong position at Ticonderoga.

Sullivan had been deeply hurt that Gates, his former inferior in rank, should have been appointed over him to the command of the army in Canada. He, therefore, requested leave of absence in order to wait on the commander-in-chief. It was granted with reluctance.

On the 9th of July, Schuyler and Gates returned to Ticonderoga, accompanied by Arnold. Arrangements were made to encamp the troops and land the artillery and stores as fast as they should arrive. Great exertions, also, were made to strengthen the defences of the place. Colonel Trumbull, who was to have accompanied Gates to Canada as adjutant-general, had been reconnoitring the neighborhood of Ticonderoga and had pitched upon a place for a fortification on the east side of the lake, opposite the east point of Ticonderoga, where Fort Independence was subsequently built. He also advised erection of a work on a lofty eminence, the termination of a mountain ridge which separates Lake George from Lake Champlain. His advice was unfortunately disregarded. The eminence, subsequently called Mount Defiance, commanded the narrow parts of both lakes.

Preparations were made, also, to augment the naval force on the lakes. Ship carpenters from the Eastern States were employed at Skenesborough to build the hulls of galleys and boats which, when launched, were to be sent to Ticonderoga for equipment and armament under the superintendence of Arnold.

Schuyler soon returned to Albany to superintend the general concerns of the northern department. He was indefatigable in procuring and forwarding the necessary materials and artillery for the fortification of Ticonderoga.

The question of command between him and Gates was apparently at rest. A letter from the President of Congress, dated July 8th, informed General Gates that his command was totally independent of Schuyler while the army was in Canada, but no longer. Gates professed himself entirely satisfied with the explanation he had received and perfectly disposed to obey the commands of Schuyler.

Schuyler, too, assured both Congress and Washington, "that the difference in opinion between Gates and himself had not caused the least ill-will."

As to Sullivan, who repaired to Philadelphia and tendered his resignation, the question of rank was explained in a manner that induced him to continue in service. It was universally allowed that his retreat had been ably conducted through all kinds of difficulties and disasters.

A greater source of solicitude to Washington than this jealousy between commanders, was the sectional jealousy springing up among the troops. Nowhere were these sectional jealousies more prevalent than in the motley army assembled from distant quarters under Washington's own command. Reed, the adjutant-general, speaking on this subject, observes: "The Southern troops, comprising the regiments south of the Delaware, looked with very unkind feelings on those of New England, especially those from Connecticut, whose pecularities of deportment made them the objects of ill-disguised derision among their fellow-soldiers."

As to the Connecticut infantry which had been furnished by Governor Trumbull in the present emergency, they were substantial farmers, men of simple rural manners from an agricultural State where great equality of condition prevailed; the officers, elected by the men out of their own ranks, were their own neighbors and every way their equals. All this, as yet, was but little understood by the troops from the South, among whom military rank was more defined and tenaciously observed and where the officers were men of the cities and of more aristocratic habits.

The sectional jealousies thus early springing up among the troops from different States show the difficulties with which Washington had to contend at the outset and which formed a growing object of solicitude throughout the rest of his career.

(CHAPTER 23)

Letters from Lee gave Washington intelligence of the fate of Sir Henry Clinton's expedition to the South, that expedition which had been the subject of so much surmise and perplexity. Sir Henry in his cruise along the coast had been repeatedly foiled by Lee. First, when he looked in at New York; next, when he paused at Norfolk in Virginia; and lastly, when he made a bold attempt at Charleston in South Carolina, for scarce did his ships appear off the bar of the harbor than the omnipresent Lee was marching his troops into the city.

Within a year past, Charleston had been fortified at various points. Fort Johnson, on James Island, three miles from the city, commanding the breadth of the channel, was garrisoned by a regiment of South Carolina regulars under Colonel Gadsden. A strong fort had recently been constructed nearly opposite, on the southwest point of Sullivan's Island about six miles below the city. It was garrisoned by 375 regulars and a few militia, commanded by Colonel William Moultrie of South Carolina, who had constructed it. This fort, in connection with that on James Island, was considered the key of the harbor. Cannon had also been mounted on Haddrell's Point on the mainland, to the north-west of Sullivan's Island, and along the bay in front of the town.

The arrival of Lee gave great joy to the people of Charleston from his high reputation for military skill and experience. According to his own account to Washington, the town on his arrival was "utterly defenceless." He was rejoiced, therefore, when the enemy, instead of attacking it, directed his whole force against the fort on Sullivan's Island.

The British ships, in fact, landed their troops on Long Island, situated to the east of Sullivan's Island and separated from it by a small creek called the Breach. Sir Henry meditated a combined attack with his land and naval forces on the fort commanded by Moultrie, the capture of which, he thought, would insure the reduction of Charleston.

The Americans immediately threw up works on the northeastern extremity of Sullivan's Island to prevent the passage of the enemy over the Breach, stationing a force of regulars and militia there under Colonel Thompson. Lee encamped on Haddrell's Point, on the mainland to the north of the island, whence he intended to keep up a communication by a bridge of boats so as to be ready at any moment to aid either Moultrie or Thompson.

Sir Henry Clinton, on the other hand, had to construct batteries on Long Island to oppose those of Thompson and cover the passage of his troops by boats or by the ford. Thus the enemy were, from the 1st to the 28th of June, preparing for the attack.

At length, on the 28th of June, the Thunder Bomb commenced the attack, throwing shells at the fort as the fleet under Sir Peter Parker advanced. About eleven o'clock the ships dropped their anchors directly before the front battery. "I was at this time in a boat," writes Lee, "endeavoring to make the island; but, the wind and tide being violently against us, drove us on the main. They immediately commenced the most furious fire I ever heard or saw. . . . The noble fellows who were mortally wounded conjured their brethren never to abandon the standard of liberty. Those who lost their limbs deserted not their posts."

The fire from the ships did not produce the expected effect. Through unskilful pilotage, several of the ships ran aground, where one, the frigate Acteon, remained; the rest were extricated with difficulty. Those which bore the brunt of the action were much cut up. One hundred and seventy-five men were killed and nearly as many wounded.

Sir Henry Clinton, with 2000 troops and about 600 seamen, attempted repeatedly to cross from Long Island and co-operate in the attack upon the fort, but was as often foiled by Thompson with his battery of two cannons and a body of South Carolina rangers and North Carolina regulars. The combat slackened before sunset and ceased before ten o'clock. Sir Peter Parker then slipped his cables and drew off his shattered ships to Five Fathom Hole. The Acteon remained aground. On the following morning Sir Henry made another attempt to cross from Long Island but was repulsed and obliged to take shelter behind his breastworks. Sir Peter Parker, too, giving up all hope of reducing the fort, ordered the Acteon set on fire and abandoned. The Americans boarded her in time to haul down her colors as a trophy and load three boats with stores. They then abandoned her and in half an hour she blew up.

Within a few days the troops were re-embarked from Long Island; the attempt upon Charleston was for the present abandoned and the fleet once more put to sea.

The tidings of this repulse of the enemy came most opportunely to Washington, when he was apprehending an attack upon New York. He announced it to the army in a general order of the 21st of July: "This generous example . . . will animate every officer and soldier to imitate and even outdo them. . . . With such a bright example before us of what can be done by brave men fighting in defence of their country, we shall be loaded with a double share of shame and infamy if we do not acquit ourselves with courage, and manifest a determined resolution to conquer or die."

(CHAPTER 24)

Putnam, beside his bravery in the field, was somewhat of a mechanical projector. The batteries at Fort Washington had proved ineffectual in opposing the passage of hostile ships up the Hudson. He was now engaged on a plan for obstructing the channel opposite the fort so as to prevent the passing of any more ships. A letter from him to Gates (July 26th) explains his project. "We are preparing chevaux-de-frise, at which we make great despatch by the help of ships, which are to be sunk—a scheme of mine which you may be assured is very simple, a plan of which I send you. The two ships' sterns lie towards each other, about 70 feet apart. Three large logs, which reach from ship to ship, are fastened to them. The two ships and logs stop the river 280 feet. The ships are to be sunk, and when hauled down on one side, the pricks will be raised to a proper height, and they must inevitably stop the river, if the enemy will let us sink them."

It so happened that Ephraim Anderson, adjutant to the second Jersey battalion, had recently submitted a project to Congress for destroying the enemy's fleet in the harbor of New York. He had attempted an enterprise of the kind against the British ships in the harbor of Quebec during the siege and, according to his own account, would have succeeded had not the enemy discovered his intentions and stretched a cable across the mouth of the harbor, and had he not accidentally been much burnt.

His scheme was favorably entertained by Congress, and Washington, by a letter dated July 10th, was instructed to aid him in carrying it into effect. Anderson, accordingly, was soon at work at New York constructing fire-ships with which the fleet was to be attacked. Simultaneous with the attack, a descent was to be made on the British camp on Staten Island from the nearest point of the Jersey shore by troops from Mercer's flying camp and by others stationed at Bergen under Major Knowlton.

Anderson, on the 31st of July, writes from New York to the President of Congress: "I have been for some time past very assiduous in the preparation of fire-ships. Two are already complete, . . . two more will be off to-morrow, and the residue in a very short time." Projectors are subject to disappointments. It was impossible to construct a sufficient number of fire-ships and galleys in time. The flying camp, too, recruited slowly and scarcely exceeded 3000 men. The combined attack had therefore to be given up.

In the course of a few days arrived a hundred sail with large reinforcements, among which were 1000 Hessians, and as many more were reported to be on the way. The troops were disembarked on Staten Island and fortifications thrown up on some of the most commanding hills.

All projects of attack upon the enemy were now out of the question. Indeed, some of Washington's advisers questioned remaining in New York, where they might be entrapped as the British had been in Boston. Reed, the adjutant-general, observed that there was nothing now to keep them at New York but a mere point of honor; in the mean time, they endangered the loss of the army and its military stores. Why should they risk so much in defending a city while the greater part of its inhabitants were plotting their destruction?

During the latter part of July, and the early part of August, ships of war with their tenders continued to arrive and Scotch Highlanders, Hessians, and other troops to be landed on Staten Island. At the beginning of August, the squadron with Sir Henry Clinton, recently repulsed at Charleston, anchored in the bay. He was accompanied by Cornwallis and brought 3000 troops.

In the mean time, Putnam's contrivances for obstructing the channel had reached their destined place. A letter dated Fort Washington, August 3d, says: "Four ships chained and boomed, with a number of amazing large chevaux-de-frise, were sunk close by the fort under command of General Mifflin, which fort mounts 32 pieces of heavy cannon. We are thoroughly sanguine that they never will be able to join the British fleet, nor assistance from the fleet be afforded to them." Another letter, written at the same date from Tarrytown, gives an account of an attack made by six row galleys upon the Phoenix and the Rose. They fought bravely for two hours, hulling the ships repeatedly, but sustaining great damage in return, until their commodore gave the signal to draw off. Such was the belligerent spirit prevailing up the Hudson.

The force of the enemy collected in the neighborhood of New York was about 30,000 men; that of the Americans a little more than 17,000, but was subsequently increased to 20,000, for the most part raw and undisciplined. One fourth were on the sick list; others were absent on furlough; the rest had to be distributed over posts and stations fifteen miles apart.

The sectional jealousies prevalent among them, were more and more a subject of uneasiness to Washington. In one of his general orders he observes: "It is with great concern that the general understands that jealousies have arisen among the troops from the different provinces, and reflections are frequently thrown out which can only tend to irritate each other, and injure the noble cause in which we are engaged, and which we ought to support with one hand and one heart. The general most earnestly entreats the officers and soldiers to consider the consequences; that they can no way assist our enemies more effectually than by making divisions among ourselves; that the honor and success of the army, and the safety of our bleeding country, depend upon harmony and good agreement with each other; that the provinces are all united to oppose the common enemy, and all distinctions sunk in the name of an American. . . . If there be any officers or soldiers so lost to virtue and a love of their country, as to continue in such practices after this order, the general assures them, and is authorized by Congress to declare to the whole army, that such persons shall be severely punished, and dismissed from the service with disgrace." The urgency of such a general order is apparent in that early period of our confederation when its various parts had not as yet been sufficiently welded together to acquire a thorough feeling of nationality.

Washington kept watchful eye upon the movements of the enemy. Beside their superiority in numbers as well as discipline to his own crude and scanty legions, they possessed a vast advantage in their fleet. "They would not be half the enemy they are," observed Reed, "if they were once separated from their ships." Every arrival and departure of these, therefore, was a subject of conjecture. Aaron Burr, at that time in New York, aide-de-camp to Putnam, speaks in a letter of 30 transports which, under convoy of three frigates, had put to sea on the 7th of August with the intention of sailing round Long Island and coming through the Sound, thus investing the city by the North and East Rivers. "They are then to land on both sides of the island," writes he, "join their forces, and draw a line across, which will hem us in, and totally cut off all communication; after which, they will have their own fun."

In this emergency, Washington wrote to Mercer for 2000 men from the flying camp. Smallwood's battalion was immediately furnished as a part of them. The Convention of the State ordered hasty levies of militia to form temporary camps on the shore of the Sound and on that of the Hudson above King's Bridge to annoy the enemy should they attempt to land from their ships on either of these waters. Others were sent to reinforce the posts on Long Island. As Kings County on Long Island was noted for being a stronghold of the disaffected, the Convention ordered that, should any of the militia of that county refuse to serve, they should be disarmed and secured and their possessions laid waste.

By the authority of the New York Convention, Washington had appointed General George Clinton to command of the levies on both sides of the Hudson. He ordered him to hasten down with them to the fort just erected on the north side of King's Bridge, leaving 200 men under the command of a brave and alert officer to throw up works at the pass of Anthony's Nose, where the main road to Albany crosses that mountain. Troops of horse also were to be posted by him along the river to watch the motions of the enemy.

Washington now made the last solemn preparations for the impending conflict. All suspected persons were removed to a distance. As to his domestic arrangement, Mrs. Washington had some time previously gone to Philadelphia with the intention of returning to Virginia, as there was no prospect of her being with him any part of the summer, which threatened to be one of turmoil and danger. The other wives of general officers, who used to grace and enliven head-quarters, had all been sent out of the way of the storm which was lowering over this devoted city.

Accounts of deserters and other intelligence informed Washington, on the 17th, that a great many of the enemy's troops had gone on board of the transports; that steps were taken indicating an intention of leaving Staten Island. Putnam, also, came up with word that at least one fourth of the fleet had sailed. Every thing indicated that affairs were tending to a crisis.

The "hysterical alarms" of the peaceful inhabitants of New York, which had provoked the impatience and satirical sneers of Lee, inspired different sentiments in the benevolent heart of Washington and produced the following letter to the New York Convention: "When I consider that the city of New York will, in all human probability, very soon be the scene of a bloody conflict, I cannot but view the great numbers of women, children, and infirm persons remaining in it, with the most melancholy concern. When the men-of-war (the Phoenix and Rose) passed up the river, the shrieks and cries of these poor creatures running every way with their children, were truly distressing, . . . Can no method be devised for their removal?" He listened to the suggestions of his own heart and, without awaiting the action of the Convention, issued a proclamation advising the inhabitants to remove and requiring the officers and soldiery to aid the helpless and the indigent. The Convention appointed a committee to effect these purposes in the most humane and expeditious manner.

A gallant little exploit at this juncture gave a fillip to the spirits of the community. Two of the fire-ships, recently constructed, went up the Hudson to attempt the destruction of the ships which had so long been domineering over its waters. One succeeded in grappling the Phoenix and would soon have set her in flames, but in the darkness got to leeward and was cast loose without effecting any damage. The other, in making for the Rose, fell foul of one of the tenders, grappled and burnt her. The enterprise was conducted with spirit and, though it failed of its main object, had an important effect. The commanders of the ships determined to abandon those waters. Taking advantage of a brisk wind and favoring tide, they made all sail early on the 18th of August and stood down the river, keeping close under the eastern shore, where they supposed the guns from Mount Washington could not be brought to bear upon them. Notwithstanding this precaution, the Phoenix was thrice hulled by shots from the fort and one of the tenders once. The Rose, also, was hulled once by a shot from Burdett's Ferry. The ships fired grape-shot as they passed but without effecting any injury. Unfortunately, a passage had been left open in the obstructions on which General Putnam had calculated so sanguinely; it was to have been closed in the course of a day or two. Through this they made their way, guided by a deserter, which alone, in Putnam's opinion, saved them from being utterly destroyed by the batteries.

PART VI

(CHAPTERS 25-30)

Disaster and Retreat
[1776]

The movements of the British fleet and of the camp on Staten Island gave signs of a meditated attack, but, as the nature of that attack was uncertain, Washington was obliged to retain the greater part of his troops in the city for its defence, ready, however, to be transferred to any point. Mifflin, with about 500 Pennsylvania troops, was at King's Bridge, ready to aid at a moment's notice. General George Clinton was also at that post, with about 1400 of his yeomanry of the Hudson.

As the Phoenix and Rose had explored the shores, Heath thought Howe might attempt an attack above King's Bridge rather than in the face of the strong works in and around the city. Reports from different quarters gave Washington reason to apprehend that the enemy might land part of their force on Long Island to get possession of the heights of Brooklyn, which overlooked New York, while another part should land above the city, as General Heath suggested. Thus, various points distant from each other had to be defended by raw troops against a superior force possessed of every facility for operating by land and water.

General Greene, with a considerable force, was stationed at

Brooklyn. He had acquainted himself with all the localities of the island and made his plan of defence accordingly. His troops were occupied on works he laid out about a mile beyond the village of Brooklyn, facing the interior of the island, whence a land attack might be attempted.

Brooklyn was immediately opposite to New York. The East River swept its rapid tides between them. The village stood on a peninsula formed by Wallabout Bay on the north and Gowanus Cove on the south. A line of intrenchments and strong redoubts extended across the neck of the peninsula from the bay to the cove. To protect the rear of the works from the enemy's ships, a battery was erected at Red Hook, the south-west corner of the peninsula, and a fort on Governor's Island, nearly opposite.

About two miles and a half in front of the line of intrenchments and redoubts, a range of hills, densely wooded, extended from south-west to north-east, forming a natural barrier across the island. It was traversed by three roads. One, on the left of the works, stretched from Bedford to Jamaica; another, central and direct, led through the heights to Flatbush; a third, on the right of the lines, passed by Gowanus Cove to the Narrows and Gravesend Bay. The occupation of the hills and the protection of its passes had been designed by Greene but in the midst of his toils, he was taken down by a fever which confined him to his bed; Sullivan, just returned from Lake Champlain, had temporary command.

Washington saw, that to prevent the enemy from landing on Long Island would be impossible, its great extent affording so many places favorable for that purpose. On the 21st came a letter written by Brigadier-general William Livingston of New Jersey. Movements of the enemy on Staten Island had been seen from his camp. He sent over a spy who brought back the following intelligence. Twenty thousand men had embarked to make an attack on Long Island and up the Hudson. Fifteen thousand remained on Staten Island to attack Bergen Point, Elizabethtown Point, and Amboy.

Washington sent a copy of the letter to the New York Convention. On the following morning (August 22d) the enemy appeared to be carrying their plans into execution. The reports of cannon and musketry were heard from Long Island and word soon came that several thousand men, with artillery and light-horse, were landed at Gravesend and that Colonel Hand, stationed there with the Pennsylvania rifle regiment, had retreated to the lines.

Washington apprehended an attempt of the foe to surprise the lines at Brooklyn. He immediately sent over a reinforcement of six battalions. It was all that he could spare, as with the next tide the ships might bring up the residue of the army and attack the city. Five battalions more, however, were ordered to be ready as a reinforcement, if required.

Nine thousand of the enemy had landed with 40 pieces of cannon. Sir Henry Clinton had the chief command and led the first division. His associate officers were the Earls of Cornwallis and Percy, General Grant, and General Sir William Erskine. As their boats approached the shore, Hand retreated to the chain of wooded hills and took post on a height commanding the central road from Flatbush. The enemy having landed without opposition, Cornwallis was detached with the reserve to Flatbush while the rest of the army extended itself from the Narrows through Utrecht and Gravesend to Flatland.

Cornwallis, with two battalions of light-infantry, Colonel Donop's corps of Hessians, and six field-pieces, advanced rapidly to seize the central pass through the hills. He found Hand and his riflemen ready to make a defence. This brought him to a halt, having been ordered not to attack should the pass be occupied. He took post for the night, therefore, in Flatbush.

It was evidently the aim of the enemy to force the lines at Brooklyn and get possession of the heights. Should they succeed, New York would be at their mercy. On the 24th Washington crossed over to Brooklyn to inspect the lines and reconnoitre the neighborhood. The American advanced posts were in the wooded hills. Hand kept watch over the central road and a strong redoubt had been thrown up in front of the pass to check any advance from Flatbush. Another road, leading from Flatbush to Bedford, by which the enemy might get round to the left of the works at Brooklyn, was guarded by two regiments, one under Colonel Williams on the north side of the ridge, the other by a Pennsylvania rifle regiment under Colonel Miles on the south side. The enemy were stretched along the country beyond the chain of hills.

As yet, nothing had taken place but skirmishing and irregular firing between the outposts. It was with deep concern Washington noticed a prevalent disorder in the camp. Unaccustomed to discipline and restraint, the men sallied forth whenever they pleased, singly or in squads, prowling about and firing upon the enemy, like hunters after game. Much of this was no doubt owing to the protracted illness of General Greene. On returning to the city, therefore, Washington gave command on Long Island to Putnam, warning him in his letter of instructions to summon the officers together and enjoin them to put a stop to the irregularities observed among the troops. Putnam crossed with alacrity to his post.

In the mean time, the enemy were augmenting their forces on the island. Two brigades of Hessians, under Lieutenant-general De Heister, were transferred from Staten Island on the 25th. This movement did not escape the vigilant eye of Washington, who concluded that the enemy were about to make a push with their main force for possession of Brooklyn Heights. He accordingly sent over reinforcements, among them Colonel John Haslet's well equipped and well disciplined Delaware regiment, which was joined to Stirling's brigade, chiefly composed of Southern troops and stationed outside of the lines.

On the 26th, Washington crossed over to Brooklyn, accompanied by Reed. There was much movement among the enemy's troops and their number was evidently augmented. In fact, De Heister had reached Flatbush with his Hessians and taken command of the centre; Sir Henry Clinton drew off to Flatlands in a diagonal line to the right of De Heister, while the left wing, commanded by Grant, extended to Gravesend Bay. In the evening, Washington returned to the city, full of anxious thought. It was a night of intense solicitude, and well might it be, for during that night a plan was carried into effect fraught with disaster to the Americans.

The plan was concerted by General Howe, the commander-in-chief. Sir Henry was, by a circuitous march in the night, to take the road leading from Jamaica to Bedford, seize a pass through the

Bedford Hills, and thus turn the left of the American advanced posts. It was preparatory to this march that Sir Henry during the day had fallen back to Flatlands and caused that movement which had attracted the notice of Washington.

To divert the attention of the Americans from this stealthy march on their left, Grant was to menace their right flank toward Gravesend before daybreak and De Heister to cannonade their centre. Neither, however, was to press an attack until Sir Henry had turned the left flank of the Americans; then the latter were to be assailed with utmost vigor.

About nine o'clock in the evening of the 26th, Sir Henry began his march from Flatlands with the vanguard, composed of light infantry. Percy followed with the grenadiers, artillery, and light dragoons, forming the centre. Cornwallis brought up the rear-guard with the heavy ordnance. Howe accompanied this division.

About two hours before daybreak, they arrived within half a mile of the pass through the Bedford Hills. At this juncture they captured an American patrol and learnt, to their surprise, that the Bedford pass was unoccupied. In fact, the whole road beyond Bedford, leading to Jamaica, had been left unguarded, excepting by some light volunteer troops. Colonels Williams and Miles sent out parties occasionally to patrol the road but no troops had been stationed at the Bedford pass. The neglect of the road and pass, however, proved fatal.

Sir Henry immediately detached a battalion of light infantry to secure the pass and, at the break of day, possessed himself of the heights. He was within three miles of Bedford and his march had been undiscovered. Having passed the heights, he halted for the soldiers to take refreshment, preparatory to the morning's hostilities. There we will leave them, while we note how the other divisions performed their part of the plan.

About midnight Grant moved from Gravesend Bay with two brigades and a regiment of regulars, a battalion of New York loyalists, and ten field-pieces. He proceeded along the road past the Narrows and Gowanus Cove, toward the right of the American works. A picket guard of Pennsylvanian and New York militia, under

Colonel Atlee, retired before him fighting to a position on the skirts of the wooded hills.

In the mean time, scouts had brought word that the enemy were approaching upon the right. Putnam instantly ordered Stirling to hasten with the two regiments nearest at hand and hold them in check. These were Haslet's Delaware and Smallwood's Maryland regiments; they turned out with alacrity, and Stirling pushed forward with them toward the Narrows. By the time he had passed Gowanus Cove, daylight began to appear. Here, he met Atlee and learned that the enemy were near. Stirling ordered Atlee to place himself in ambush on the left of the road and await their coming up, while he formed the Delaware and Maryland regiments along a ridge from the road up to a woods on the top of the hill.

Atlee gave the enemy two or three volleys as they approached and then retreated and formed in the wood on Stirling's left. By this time Stirling was reinforced by Kichline's riflemen, part of whom he placed along a hedge at the foot of the hill and part in front of the wood. Grant threw his light troops in the advance and posted them in an orchard and behind hedges, extending in front of the Americans about 150 yards distant.

A rattling fire commenced between the British light troops and the American riflemen, which continued for about two hours, when the former retired to their main body. In the mean time, Stirling's position had been strengthened by the arrival of Captain Carpenter with two field-pieces. These were placed on the side of the hill so as to command the road and the approach for some hundred yards. Grant, likewise, brought up his artillery and formed his brigades on opposite hills. There was occasional cannonading on both sides but neither party sought a general action. Stirling's object was merely to hold the enemy in check; the instructions of Grant were not to press an attack until aware that Sir Henry was on the left flank of the Americans.

During this time, De Heister commenced a cannonade from his camp at Flatbush upon the redoubt at the pass where Hand and his riflemen were stationed. On hearing this, Sullivan rode forth to Hand's post to reconnoitre. De Heister, however, did not advance from Flatbush, but kept up a brisk fire on the redoubt, which replied as briskly. At the same time, a cannonade from a British ship upon the battery at Red Hook contributed to distract the attention of the Americans.

Washington was still in doubt whether this was part of a general attack in which the city was to be included. Five ships of the line were endeavoring to beat up the bay. Were they to cannonade the city or to land troops above it? Fortunately, a strong head-wind baffled their efforts. Seeing no likelihood of an immediate attack upon the city, Washington hastened over to Brooklyn and galloped up to the works in time to witness the catastrophe for which all the movements of the enemy had been concerted.

The thundering of artillery in the direction of Bedford had given notice that Sir Henry had turned the left of the Americans. De Heister immediately ordered Donop to advance with his Hessian regiment and storm the redoubt, while he followed with his whole division. Sullivan did not remain to defend the redoubt. Sir Henry's cannon had appraised him that his flank was turned and he ordered a retreat to the lines, but it was too late. Scarce had he descended from the height, when he was met by the British light infantry and dragoons and driven back into the woods. By this time De Heister and his Hessians had come up, and now commenced a scene of confusion, consternation, and slaughter. Hemmed in and entrapped between the British and Hessians, the Americans under Williams and Miles fought for a time bravely, or rather desperately. Some were cut down and trampled by the cavalry, others bayoneted without mercy by the Hessians. The whole pass was a scene of carnage, resounding with the clash of arms, the tramp of horses, the volleying of firearms, and the cries of the combatants. Some of the Americans, by a desperate effort, cut their way through the host of foes and effected a retreat to the lines. Others took refuge among the woods of the hills, but a great part were either killed or taken prisoners. Among the latter was General Sullivan.

Washington arrived in time to witness this catastrophe, but was unable to prevent it. A deep column of the enemy was descending from the hills on the left; his choicest troops were all in action and he had none but militia to man the works. His solicitude was now awakened for the safety of Stirling and his corps, who had been all the morning exchanging cannonades with Grant. The forbearance of the latter in not advancing had been misinterpreted by the Americans. Washington saw the danger to which these brave fellows were exposed, though they could not. Stationed on a hill, he commanded a view of the whole field and saw the enemy's reserve, under Cornwallis, marching by a crossroad to get in their rear, and thus place them between two fires. With breathless anxiety he watched the result.

The sound of Sir Henry's cannon appraised Stirling that the enemy was between him and the lines. Grant, aware that the time had come for earnest action, was closing up and had already taken Atlee prisoner. Stirling now thought to effect a retreat to the lines by crossing the creek which empties into Gowanus Cove. The creek might be forded at low water but no time was to be lost, for the tide was rising. Leaving part of his men to face Grant, Stirling advanced with the rest to pass the creek but was suddenly checked by the appearance of Cornwallis and his grenadiers.

Washington, who watched every movement, supposed that Stirling and his troops, finding the case desperate, would surrender in a body without firing. On the contrary, his lordship boldly attacked Cornwallis with half of Smallwood's battalion while the rest of his troops retreated across the creek.

It was indeed, a desperate fight; Smallwood's macaronis showed their game spirit. They were repeatedly broken but as often rallied and renewed the fight. Only five companies of Smallwood's battalion were now in action. There was a warm and close engagement for nearly ten minutes. Broken and disordered, they rallied and made a second attack. They were again overpowered with numbers. Stirling had encouraged his young soldiers by his voice and example but, when all was lost, he sought out De Heister and surrendered himself as his prisoner. More than 250 brave fellows, most of them of Smallwood's regiment, perished in this deadly struggle, within sight of the lines of Brooklyn.

The enemy now concentrated their forces within a few hundred yards of the redoubts. The grenadiers were within musket shot. Washington expected they would storm the works and prepared for a desperate defence. The discharge of a cannon and volleys of musketry from the part of the lines nearest to them seemed to bring them to a pause. It was, in truth, the forbearance of the British commander that prevented a bloody conflict. His troops were eager to storm the works, but he was unwilling to risk the loss of life that must attend an assault when the object might be attained at a cheaper rate by regular approaches. Checking the ardor of his men, therefore, he drew them out of reach of the musketry and encamped there for the night.

The loss of the Americans in this disastrous battle is thought in killed, wounded and prisoners to have been nearly 2000, a large number considering that not above 5000 were engaged.

The success of the enemy was attributed, in some measure, to the doubt in which Washington was kept as to the nature of the intended attack and at what point it would chiefly be made. Much of the disaster has been attributed, also, to a confusion in the command, caused by the illness of Greene. Putnam, who had supplied his place in the emergency after the enemy had landed, had not time to make himself acquainted with the post and the surrounding country. Sullivan, though subordinate to Putnam, seems to have exercised an independent command and to have acted at his own discretion.

The fatal error, however, probably arising from all these causes, consisted in leaving the passes through the wooded hills too weakly fortified and guarded, especially in neglecting the eastern road, by which Sir Henry got in the rear of the advanced troops and subjected them to a cross fire of his own men and De Heister's Hessians.

The night after the battle was a weary, sleepless one to the Americans. Fatigued, dispirited, many of them sick and wounded, they were, for the most part, without shelter. Every thing boded a close and deadly conflict. The morning broke lowering and dreary. To appearance the enemy were 20,000 strong. As the day advanced, their ordnance began to play upon the works. They were proceeding to intrench themselves but were driven into their tents by a drenching rain.

Early in the morning Mifflin arrived in camp with part of the troops which had been stationed at Fort Washington and King's Bridge. He brought with him Shee's Philadelphia regiment and Magaw's Pennsylvania regiment, both well disciplined and officered. With Mifflin came also Glover's Massachusetts regiment, composed chiefly of Marblehead fishermen and sailors, hardy and weather-proof, trimly clad in blue jackets and trowsers. The detachment numbered about 1300 men, all fresh and full of spirits. Every eye brightened as they marched briskly along the line and were posted at the left extremity of the intrenchments towards the Wallabout. There were skirmishes throughout the day, but no decided attack was attempted.

On the 29th, there was a dense fog over the island, that wrapped every thing in mystery. In the course of the morning, Mifflin, Reed, and Grayson, one of Washington's aides-de-camp, rode to the western outposts, in the neighborhood of Red Hook. While they were there, a light breeze lifted the fog and revealed the British ships opposite Staten Island. There appeared to be an unusual bustle among them. Some movement was apparently in agitation. The idea occurred to the reconnoitring party that the fleet was preparing, should the wind hold and the fog clear away, to come up the bay at the turn of the tide, silence the feeble batteries at Red Hook and the city and anchor in the East River. In that case the army on Long Island would be completely surrounded and entrapped.

Alarmed at this perilous probability, they spurred back to head-quarters to urge the immediate withdrawal of the army. Washington instantly summoned a council of war. The difficulty was already apparent of guarding such extensive works with troops fatigued and dispirited. Other dangers now presented themselves. Their communication with New York might be cut off by the fleet from below. Other ships had passed round Long Island and were at Flushing Bay on the Sound; these might land troops on the east side of Harlem River and make themselves masters of King's Bridge, that key of Manhattan Island. Taking all things into consideration, it was resolved to cross with the troops to the city that very night.

Never did retreat require greater secrecy and circumspection. Nine thousand men, with all the munitions of war, were to be withdrawn from before a victorious army, encamped so near, that every stroke of spade and pickaxe from their trenches could be heard.

Verbal orders were sent to Colonel Hughes to impress all water craft from Spyt den Duivel on the Hudson round to Hell Gate on the Sound and have them on the east side of the city by evening. The order was issued at noon and so promptly executed that the vessels were all at Brooklyn at eight o'clock in the evening, and put under the management of Glover's amphibious Marblehead regiment.

According to Washington's plan, to keep the enemy from discovering the withdrawal until the main body should have embarked and pushed off from the shore, Mifflin was to remain at the lines with his Pennsylvania troops and the gallant remains of Haslet, Smallwood and Hand's regiments, with guards posted and sentinels alert as if nothing extraordinary was taking place; when the main embarkation was effected, they were to move off quietly, march briskly to the ferry, and embark.

It was late in the evening when the troops began to retire from the breastworks. As one regiment quietly withdrew from their station on guard, the troops on the right and left moved up and filled the vacancy. There was a stifled murmur in the camp, but it died away as the main body moved on in silence and order.

The embarkation went on with all possible despatch under the vigilant eye of Washington. In his anxiety for despatch, he sent Colonel Scammel, one of his aides-de-camp, to hasten forward all the troops that were on the march. Scammel blundered in executing his errand and gave the order to Mifflin likewise. The general instantly called in his pickets and sentinels and set off for the ferry.

By this time the tide had turned; there was a strong wind from the north-east; the boats with oars were insufficient to convey the troops; those with sails could not make headway against wind and tide. There was some confusion at the ferry and, in the midst of it, Mifflin came down with the whole covering party.

"It is a dreadful mistake," cried Washington to Mifflin, "and unless the troops can regain the lines before their absence is discovered by the enemy, the most disastrous consequences are to be apprehended."

Mifflin led back his men to the lines, which had been completely deserted. Fortunately, the dense fog had prevented the enemy from discovering that they were unoccupied. The men resumed their former posts.

The fog which prevailed all this time, seemed almost providential. It hung over Long Island and concealed the movements of the Americans. The whole embarkation of troops, artillery, ammunition, provisions, cattle, horses and carts, was happily effected, and by daybreak the greater part had safely reached the city, thanks to the aid of Glover's Marblehead men. Scarce any thing was abandoned to the enemy, excepting a few heavy pieces of artillery. At a proper time, Mifflin with his covering party left the lines and effected a silent retreat to the ferry. Washington refused to enter a boat until all the troops were embarked, and crossed the river with the last.

This extraordinary retreat, which, in its silence and celerity, equalled the midnight fortifying of Bunker's Hill, was one of the most signal achievements of the war, and redounded greatly to the reputation of Washington.

(CHAPTER 26)

The enemy had now possession of Long Island. British and Hessian troops garrisoned the works at Brooklyn, or were distributed at Bushwick, Newtown, Hell Gate and Flushing. Admiral Howe came up with the main body of the fleet and anchored close to Governor's Island, within cannon shot of the city. Matters seemed hurrying to a crisis.

On the night of Monday (Sept. 2d), a forty-gun ship passed between Governor's Island and Long Island, swept unharmed by the batteries which opened upon her, and anchored in Turtle Bay, above the city. In the morning, Washington despatched Major Crane of the artillery with two twelve-pounders and a howitzer to annoy her from the New York shore. They hulled her several times and obliged her to take shelter behind Blackwell's Island. Several other ships of war, with transports and store-ships, had made their appearance in the upper part of the Sound, having gone round Long Island.

As the city might speedily be attacked, Washington caused all the sick and wounded to be conveyed to Orangetown, in the Jerseys, and such military stores and baggage as were not immediately needed to be removed as fast as conveyances could be procured to a post partially fortified at Dobbs' Ferry, on the eastern bank of the Hudson, about twenty-two miles above the city.

The "shameful and scandalous desertions," as Washington termed them, continued. In a few days the Connecticut militia dwindled down from six to less than two thousand. Nor was this ill-timed yearning for home confined to the yeomanry of Connecticut. Some of the gentlemen volunteers from beyond the Delaware were likewise among the first to feel the homeward impulse. Present experience induced Washington to reiterate the opinion he had repeatedly expressed to Congress, that little reliance was to be placed on militia enlisted for short periods. The only means of protecting the national liberties from great hazard, if not utter loss, was, he said, an army enlisted for the war.

The 1000 men ordered from the flying camp were furnished by Mercer. They were Maryland troops and were a seasonable addition to his effective forces, but the ammunition carried off by the disbanding militia, was a serious loss at this critical juncture.

A work had been commenced on the Jersey shore, opposite Fort Washington, to aid in protecting Putnam's chevaux-de-frise which had been sunk between them. This work had received the name of Fort Constitution (a name already borne by one of the forts in the Highlands). Troops were drawn from the flying camp to make a strong encampment in the vicinity of the fort, with an able officer to command it and a skilful engineer to strengthen the works. It was hoped, by the co-operation of these opposite forts and the chevaux-de-frise, to command the Hudson and prevent the passing of hostile ships.

The British, in the mean time, forbore to press further hostilities. Lord Howe, desirous of a peaceful adjustment of the strife between the colonies and the mother country, sent General Sullivan on parole, charged with an overture to Congress. In this he declared himself empowered to compromise the dispute on the most favorable terms, and, though he could not treat with Congress as a legally organized body, he was desirous of a conference with some of its members. These, for the time, he should consider only as private gentlemen but, if any probable scheme of accommodation should be agreed upon, the authority of Congress would be acknowledged to render the compact complete.

The message caused some embarrassment in Congress. After much debate, Congress, on the 5th September, replied that, being the representatives of the free and independent States of America, they could not send any members to confer with his lordship in their private characters, but that, desirous of establishing peace on reasonable terms, they would send a committee of their body to ascertain what authority he had to treat with persons authorized by Congress and what propositions he had to offer. A committee was chosen on the 6th of September, composed of John Adams, Edward Rutledge, and Doctor Franklin.

Hope lingered in the breast of his lordship when he sought the proposed conference. It was to take place on the 11th at a house on Staten Island, opposite to Amboy, at which latter place Mercer was stationed with his flying camp. At Amboy, the committee found Howe's barge waiting to receive them, and the parties crossed together to Staten Island. The admiral met them on their landing and conducted them to his house.

On opening the conference, his lordship again intimated that he could not treat with them as a committee of Congress, but only confer with them as private gentlemen of influence in the colonies on the means of restoring peace between the two countries. The commissioners replied that, as their business was to hear, he might consider them in what light he pleased, but that they should consider themselves in no other character than that in which they were placed by order of Congress.

Lord Howe then entered into a discourse of considerable length but made no explicit proposition of peace nor promise of redress of grievances, excepting on condition that the colonies return to their allegiance. This, the commissioners replied, was not now to be expected. Their repeated humble petitions to the king and parliament having been treated with contempt and answered by additional injuries, and war having been declared against them, the colonies had declared their independence and it was not in the power of Congress to agree for them that they should return to their former dependent state. His lordship expressed his sorrow that no accommodation was likely to take place.

The result of this conference showed that his lordship had no power but what was given by the act of Parliament, and put an end to the popular notion that he was vested with secret powers to negotiate an adjustment of grievances.

Since the retreat from Brooklyn, Washington had watched the movements of the enemy to discover their further plans. Their whole force, excepting about 4000 men, had been transferred from Staten to Long Island. A great part was encamped on the peninsula between Newtown Inlet and Flushing Bay. A battery had been thrown up near the extremity of the peninsula to check an American battery at Horen's Hook opposite and to command the mouth of Harlem River. Troops were subsequently stationed on the islands about Hell Gate. "It is evident," writes Washington, "the enemy mean to inclose us on the island of New York by taking post in our rear while the shipping secures the front, and thus . . . oblige us to fight them on their own terms or surrender."

History, experience, the opinions of able friends in Europe, the fears of the enemy, even the declarations of Congress, all concurred in demonstrating that the war on the American side should be defensive and that, on all occasions, a general action should be avoided.

In a council of war, held on the 7th of September, the question was discussed, whether the city should be defended or evacuated. All admitted that it would not be tenable, should it be cannonaded and bombarded. Several of the council, among whom was Putnam, were for a total and immediate removal from the city; by removing, they would keep the army together to be recruited another year and preserve the unspent stores and the heavy artillery. Washington himself inclined to this opinion. Others, however, were unwilling to abandon a place which had been fortified with great cost and labor and seemed defensible, which, by some, had been considered the key to the northern country.

After much discussion a middle course was adopted. Putnam with 5000 men was to be stationed in the city. Heath, with 9000, was to guard the upper part of the island and oppose any attempt of the enemy to land. His troops were posted about King's Bridge and its vicinity. The third division, composed principally of militia, was under the command of Greene and Spencer, the former still unwell. It was stationed about the centre of the island, chiefly along Turtle Bay and Kip's Bay, where strong works had been thrown up to guard against any landing of troops from the ships or from the encampments on Long Island. It was also to hold itself ready to support either of the other divisions. Washington himself had his head-quarters at a short distance from the city. A resolution of Congress, passed the 10th of September, left the occupation or abandonment of the city entirely at Washington's discretion. Nearly the whole of his officers, in a second council of war, retracted their former opinion and determined that removal of his army was not only prudent but absolutely necessary. Three members of the council, however, Spencer, Heath, and Clinton, tenaciously held to the former decision.

Convinced of the propriety of evacuation, Washington prepared for it by ordering the removal of all stores, excepting such as were indispensable for the subsistence of the troops while they remained. On the 14th, Washington's baggage was removed to King's Bridge, where head-quarters were to be transferred the same evening, it being clear that the enemy were preparing to encompass him on the island.

About sunset of the same day, six more ships, two of them men-of-war, passed up the Sound and joined those above. Within half an hour came expresses to head-quarters, one from Mifflin at King's Bridge, the other from Sargent at Horen's Hook. Three or four thousand of the enemy were crossing at Hell Gate to the islands at the mouth of Harlem River, where numbers were already encamped. An immediate landing at Harlem, or Morrisania, was apprehended. Washington was instantly in the saddle, spurring to Harlem Heights. The night, however, passed away quietly. In the morning the enemy commenced operations. Three ships of war stood up the Hudson and anchored opposite Bloomingdale, a few miles above the city, and put a stop to the removal by water of stores and provisions to Dobbs' Ferry. About eleven o'clock, the ships in the East River commenced a heavy cannonade upon the breast-works between Turtle Bay and the city. At the same time two divisions of the troops encamped on Long Island, one British, under Sir Henry, the other Hessian, under Donop, under cover of fire from the ships, began to land at two points between Turtle and Kip's Bays. The breastworks were manned by militia who, disheartened by their late defeat, fled at the first advance of the enemy. Two brigades of Putnam's Connecticut troops caught the panic and joined in the general scamper.

At this moment Washington came galloping to the scene of confusion; riding in among the fugitives, he endeavored to rally and restore them to order. All in vain. At the first appearance of red coats, they fled in headlong terror. Losing all self-command at the sight of such dastardly conduct, he dashed his hat upon the ground in a transport of rage. "Are these the men," exclaimed he, "with whom I am to defend America!" It was one of the rare moments of his life when the vehement element of his nature was stirred up from its deep recesses. He soon recovered his self-possession, and took measures against the general peril. The enemy might land another force about Hell Gate, seize upon Harlem Heights, the strong central portion of the island, cut off all retreat of the lower divisions, and effectually sever his army. In all haste, therefore, he sent off an express to the forces encamped above, directing them to secure that position immediately, while another express to Putnam ordered an immediate retreat from the city to those heights.

It was indeed a perilous moment. Had the enemy seized upon the heights or had they extended themselves across the island, the result might have been disastrous to the Americans. Fortunately, they contented themselves for the present with sending a strong detachment down the road along the East River, leading to the city, while the main body, British and Hessians, rested on their arms.

In the mean time, Putnam, on receiving Washington's express, called in his pickets and guards and abandoned the city in all haste, leaving behind a large quantity of provisions and military stores and most of the heavy cannon. To avoid the enemy he took the Bloomingdale road, though this exposed him to be raked by the enemy's ships anchored in the Hudson. It was a forced march, under a burning sun, his army encumbered with women and children and all kinds of baggage. Many were overcome by fatigue and thirst, but Putnam rode backward and forward, hurrying every one on.

Tradition gives a circumstance which favored Putnam's retreat. The British generals, in passing by Murray Hill, the country residence of a patriot of that name, made a halt to seek some refreshment. The proprietor of the house was absent, but his wife set cake and wine before them in abundance. So grateful were these refreshments in the heat of the day, that they lingered over their wine quaffing and bantering their hostess about the ludicrous panic and discomfiture of her countrymen. In the mean time, before they were roused from their regale, Putnam and his forces had passed by, within a mile of them. It became a common saying among the American officers, that Mrs. Murray saved Putnam's division of the army.

The fortified camp, where the main body of the army was now assembled, was upon that neck of land several miles long and for the most part not above a mile wide, which forms the upper part of Manhattan Island. It forms a chain of rocky heights and is separated from the mainland by Harlem River, a narrow strait from Hell Gate on the Sound to Spyt den Duivel, an inlet of the Hudson. Fort Washington occupied the crest of one of the rocky heights, overlooking the Hudson; about two miles north of it was King's Bridge, crossing Spyt den Duivel and forming the only pass from Manhattan to the mainland.

About a mile and a half south of the fort, a double row of lines extended across the neck from Harlem River to the Hudson. They faced south and were defended by batteries.

There were strong advanced posts, about two miles south of the outer line; one on the left at Harlem, commanded by Spencer, the other on the right, at McGowan's Pass, commanded by Putnam.

About a mile and a half beyond these posts the British lines extended across the island from Horen's Hook to the Hudson. An open plain intervened between the hostile camps. Washington established his head-quarters about a quarter of a mile within the inner line, at a country-seat the owners of which were absent.

While thus posted, Washington was incessantly occupied in fortifying the approaches to his camp by redoubts, abatis, and deep intrenchments.

In the course of his rounds of inspection, he was struck with the skill displayed in the construction of some of the works which were thrown up under the direction of a youthful captain of artillery, Alexander Hamilton. After some conversation with him, Washington invited him to his marquee and thus commenced that relationship which has indissolubly linked their memories togethero.

On the morning of the 16th, word was brought to head-quarters that the enemy were advancing in three large columns. There had been so many false reports, that Reed obtained leave to sally out and ascertain the truth. Washington himself soon mounted his horse and rode toward the advanced posts. On arriving there he heard a brisk firing. There was evidently a sharp conflict. At length Reed came galloping back with information. A strong detachment of the enemy had attacked the most advanced post, situated on a hill skirted by a wood. It had been bravely defended by Knowlton and his Connecticut rangers, but they had been overpowered by numbers and the outpost was taken by the enemy. Reed supposed the latter to be about 300 strong, but they were much stronger, the main part having been concealed behind a rising ground in the wood.

Reed urged that troops be sent to support the brave fellows who had behaved so well. While he was talking with Washington, "the enemy," he says, "appeared in open view and sounded their bugles in the most insulting manner, as usual after a fox-chase. I never," adds he, "felt such a sensation before; it seemed to crown our disgrace." Washington, too, was stung by the taunting note of derision. Resolved to rouse the spirits of the army, he ordered out three companies from Colonel Weedon's regiment just arrived from Virginia and sent them, under Major Leitch, to join Knowlton's rangers. The troops thus united were to get in the rear of the enemy while a feigned attack was made upon them in front.

The plan was partially successful. As the force advanced to make the false attack, the enemy ran down the hill and took what they considered an advantageous position behind some fences and bushes. A firing commenced, but in the mean time Knowlton and Leitch, ignorant of this change in the enemy's position, having made a circuit, came upon them in flank instead of in rear. They were sharply received. Major Leitch received three bullets in his side and was borne off the field. Shortly afterward, a wound in the head from a musket ball brought Knowlton to the ground. The men, undismayed by the fall of their leaders, fought with unflinching resolution under the command of their captains. The enemy were reinforced by Hessians and chasseurs. Washington likewise sent reinforcements of New England and Maryland troops. The action waxed hotter and the enemy were pushed for some distance, when Washington, having effected the object of this encounter and unwilling to risk a general action, ordered a retreat. Knowlton did not long survive the action. He had the dying satisfaction of knowing that his men had behaved bravely and driven the enemy in an open field-fight.

Similarly, Leitch died of his wounds on the 1st of October, soothed in his last moments by that recompense so dear to a soldier's heart, the encomium of a beloved commander.

In the dead of night on the 20th September, a great light was beheld by the picket guards, looming up behind the hills in the direction of the city. It continued throughout the night and it was evident there had been a great conflagration in New York.

In the course of the morning Captain Montresor, aide-de-camp to General Howe, came out with a flag, bearing a letter to Washington on the subject of an exchange of prisoners. According to Montresor's account a great part of the city had been burnt down, and he implied it to be the act of American incendiaries, several of whom, he informed Reed, had been caught and instantly shot. The act was disclaimed by the Americans and it is certain their commanders knew nothing about it.

The enemy were now bringing up their heavy cannon, preparatory to an attack upon the American camp by troops and ships.

What was the state of Washington's army? The terms of engagement of many of his men would terminate with the year, nor did Congress hold out offers to encourage re-enlistments. "We are now, as it were, upon the eve of another dissolution of the army," writes he, "and unless some speedy and effectual measures are adopted by Congress, our cause will be lost." Under these gloomy apprehensions, on the night of the 24th of September, he penned a letter to the President of Congress, setting forth the inefficiency of the existing military system, the insubordination, waste, confusion, and discontent produced by it among the men, and the harassing cares and vexations to which it subjected the commanders. Nor did he content himself with complaining, but, in his clear and sagacious manner, pointed out the remedies. His representations, illustrated by sad experience, produced at length a reorganization of the army and the establishment of it on a permanent footing. It was decreed that 88 battalions should be furnished in quotas by the different States according to their abilities. The pay of the officers was raised. The troops which engaged to serve throughout the war were to receive a bounty of 20 dollars and 100 acres of land, besides a yearly suit of clothes while in service. Those who enlisted for but three years received no bounty in land. The bounty to officers was on a higher ratio. The States were to send commissioners to the army to arrange with the commander-in-chief as to the appointment of officers in their quotas, but, as they might be slow in complying with this regulation, Washington was empowered to fill all vacancies.

All this was a great relief to his mind. He was gratified, also, by effecting, after a long correspondence with the British commander, an exchange of prisoners in which those captured in Canada were included. Among those restored to the service were Stirling and Morgan.

About this time information was received that the enemy were enlisting great numbers of the loyalists of Long Island and collecting large quantities of stock for their support. Oliver De Lancey, a leading loyalist of New York, member of a wealthy family of honorable Huguenot descent, was a prime agent in the matter. Recently appointed brigadier-general in the royal service and authorized by

General Howe to raise a brigade of provincials, he was at Jamaica, on Long Island, offering officer's commissions to any person who should raise a company of seventy men.

A descent upon Long Island to counteract these projects was concerted by Clinton and Lincoln, but men and water craft were wanting to carry it into effect and the "tory enlistments continued." They were not confined to Long Island, but prevailed more or less on Staten Island, in the Jerseys, up the Hudson as far as Dutchess County, and in Westchester County more especially. Many of the loyalists were honorable men, conscientiously engaged in the service of their sovereign, and anxious to put down what they sincerely regarded as an unjustifiable rebellion, and among these may be clearly classed the De Lanceys. There were others, however, of a different stamp, the most notorious of whom was Robert Rogers of New Hampshire. He had been a comrade of Putnam and Stark during the French war, and had made himself famous as major of a corps called Rogers' Rangers. In 1775, Washington received notice that he was in Canada in the service of Carleton. On learning that Rogers was prowling about the country under suspicious circumstances, Washington had him arrested. He declared that he was on his way to offer his secret services to Congress. Congress liberated him on his pledging himself in writing not to bear arms against the American United Colonies in any manner whatever during the contest with Great Britain. Scarcely was he liberated when he offered his services to the enemy, received a colonel's commission, and was now raising a tory corps to be called the Queen's Rangers. Of all Americans enlisted under the royal standard, this man had rendered himself the most odious. His daring, adventurous spirit and habits of Indian warfare rendered him a formidable enemy.

Nothing perplexed Washington at this juncture more than the conduct of the enemy. He beheld before him a hostile army, superior in numbers, thoroughly disciplined, and abounding in the means of pushing a vigorous campaign, yet suffering day after day to elapse. What could be the reason of Sir William Howe?

In this uncertainty, Washington wrote to Mercer to keep vigilant watch from the Jersey shore on the movements of the enemy, by sea and land, and to give immediate intelligence should any of the

British fleet put to sea. He himself practised unceasing vigilance, visiting the different parts of his camp on horseback. Occasionally he crossed over to Fort Constitution, on the Jersey shore, of which Greene had charge, and, accompanied by him, extended his reconnoitrings down to Paulus Hook. Greene had recently been promoted to major-general and now had command of all troops in the Jerseys. He had liberty to shift his quarters to Baskingridge or Bergen, as circumstances might require, but was enjoined to keep up a communication with the main army, east of the Hudson, so as to secure a retreat in case of necessity.

The security of the Hudson was an object of great solicitude with Congress and much reliance was placed on Putnam's obstructions at Fort Washington. Four galleys, mounted with heavy guns and swivels, were stationed at the chevaux-de-frise, and two new ships were at hand which, filled with stones, were to be sunk where they would block up the channel. A sloop was also at anchor, having on board a machine for submarine explosion, with which to blow up the men-of-war. The obstructions were so commanded by batteries on either shore that it was thought no hostile ship would be able to pass.

On the 9th of October, however, the Roebuck and Phoenix, each of 44 guns, and the Tartar of 20 guns, which had been lying for some time opposite Bloomingdale, got under way with their three tenders in the morning and came up the river with an easy southern breeze. At their approach, the galleys and the two ships intended to be sunk got under way with all haste, as did a schooner laden with supplies for the army and the sloop with the submarine machine.

The Roebuck, Phoenix and Tartar, broke through the vaunted barriers as through a cobweb. Seven batteries kept up a constant fire upon them, yet the hostile ships kept on their course. The schooner was overhauled and captured; a well-aimed shot sent the sloop to the bottom of the river. The two new ships would have taken refuge in Spyt den Duivel Creek but, fearing there might not be water enough, they kept on and drove ashore at Philipps' Mills at Yonkers. Two of the galleys got into a place where they were protected from the shore; the other two trusted to outsail their pursuers. The breeze freshened, and the frigates gained on them fast; the galleys ran aground just above Dobbs' Ferry and lay exposed to a shower of grape-shot. The crews, without stopping to burn or bilge them, swam on shore, and the enemy took possession of the two galleys.

One express after another brought Washington word of these occurrences. First, he sent off a party of rifle and artillery men, with two twelve-pounders, to secure the new ships which had run aground at Yonkers. Next, he ordered Colonel Sargent to march up the eastern shore with 500 infantry, a troop of light-horse and a detachment of artillery to prevent the landing of the enemy. Before the troops arrived at Dobbs' Ferry, the ships' boats had plundered a store there, and set it on fire.

To prevent, if possible, the men-of-war up the river from coming down or others from below joining them, Washington gave orders to complete the obstructions. Two hulks which lay in Spyt den Duivel Creek, were hastily ballasted by men from Heath's division, and men were sent up to get the ships aground at Philipps' Mills that they might be brought down and sunk immediately.

While this agitation prevailed below, fugitive river crafts carried the news up to the Highlands that the frigates were already before Tarrytown in the Tappan Sea. Word was instantly despatched to Peter Livingston, president of the Provincial Congress, which was then seated at Fishkill just above the Highlands. The committee of safety wrote, on the spur of the moment, to Washington. "Nothing," say they, "can be more alarming than the present situation of our State. . . . We beg leave to suggest to your Excellency the propriety of sending a body of men to the Highlands or Peekskill, to secure the passes, prevent insurrection, and over-awe the disaffected."

Washington transmitted the letter to the President of Congress and ordered up part of the militia from Massachusetts under Lincoln. As a further precaution, an express was sent to Colonel Tash, who, with a regiment of New Hampshire militia, was on his way from Hartford to the camp, ordering him to repair with all possible despatch to Fishkill and there hold himself at the disposition of the committee of safety.

James Clinton, also, who had charge of the posts in the Highlands was put on the alert. That trusty officer was now a brigadier-general, having been promoted by Congress on the 8th of August. He was charged to have all boats rigidly searched and the passengers examined. Beside the usual sentries, a barge was to patrol the river opposite each fort every night; all craft between the forts in the Highlands and the army were to be secured in a place of safety to prevent their falling into the enemy's hands. A French engineer was sent up to aid in strengthening and securing the passes. The commanding officers of the counties of Litchfield and Fairfield in Connecticut, had orders to hold their militia in readiness to render assistance in case of insurrections in New York.

(CHAPTER 27)

The successes of Lee at the South were contrasted by many with the defeat on Long Island and evacuation of New York, and they began to consider him the main hope of the army. Lee was actually in the Jerseys on his way to camp. He writes from Amboy on the 12th to the President of Congress, informing him that the Hessians encamped on Staten Island had on the preceding night quit the island entirely and some great measure was believed to be in agitation. "I am confident," writes he, "they will not attack General Washington's lines; such a measure is too absurd for a man of Mr. Howe's genius. . . . They will infallibly proceed . . . up the river Delaware with their whole troops or . . . land somewhere about South Amboy or Shrewsbury and march straight to Trenton or Burlington. . . . What means have we to prevent their possessing themselves of Philadelphia? . . . For Heaven's sake, arouse yourselves! . . . I set out immediately for head-quarters, where I shall communicate my apprehension that such will be the next operation of the enemy."

On the morning that Lee was writing this letter, Washington received intelligence by express from Heath, stationed above King's

Bridge, that the enemy were landing with artillery on Throg's Neck in the Sound, about nine miles from the camp. Washington surmised that Howe was pursuing his original plan of getting into the rear of the American army, cutting off its supplies and interrupting its communication with the main country. Officers were ordered to their alarm-posts and the troops to be ready, under arms, to act as occasion might require. Word was sent to Heath to dispose the troops on his side of King's Bridge and the two militia regiments on the Harlem River opposite the camp in such manner as he should think necessary.

Having made all his arrangements as promptly as possible, Washington mounted his horse and rode over towards Throg's Neck to reconnoitre.

Throg's Neck is a peninsula in Westchester County, stretching two miles into the Sound, separated from the mainland by a creek and marsh and surrounded by water every high tide. A bridge across a creek connecting with a ruined causeway across the marsh led to the mainland, and the upper end of the creek was fordable at low water. Early in the morning, 80 or 90 boats full of men had landed troops to the number of 4000 on Throg's Point, the extremity of the neck. Thence their advance pushed toward the causeway and bridge to secure that pass to the mainland. Heath had been too rapid for them. Hand and his Philadelphia riflemen had taken up the planks of the bridge and posted themselves opposite the end of the causeway, whence they commenced firing with their rifles. They were soon reinforced by Prescott with his regiment and Bryant of the artillery with a three-pounder. Checked at this pass, the British moved toward the head of the creek; here they found the Americans in possession of the ford, reinforced by Graham with his regiment and Jackson of the artillery with a six-pounder. These skilful dispositions of his troops by Heath had brought the enemy to a stand.

Having surveyed the ground, Washington ordered works thrown up at the passes from the neck to the mainland. The British also threw up a work at the end of the causeway. In the afternoon nine ships, with a great number of schooners, sloops, and flat-bottomed boats full of men, passed through Hell Gate towards Throg's Point; information from two deserters gave Washington reason to believe that the greater part of the enemy's forces were gathering in that quarter. McDougall's brigade was sent in the evening to strengthen Heath's division at King's Bridge and to throw up works opposite the ford of Harlem River.

Greene, who had heard of the landing of the enemy at Throg's Neck, wrote over to Washington, from Fort Constitution, informing him that he had three brigades ready to join him if required. It was plain the whole scene of action was changing.

On the 14th, Lee arrived in camp, where he was welcomed as the harbinger of good luck. No one gave him a sincerer greeting than the commander-in-chief, who, diffident of his own military knowledge, had a high opinion of that of Lee. He immediately gave him command of the troops above King's Bridge, now the greatest part of the army, but desired that he not exercise it for a day or two until he had time to acquaint himself with the localities and arrangements of the post; Heath, in the interim, held command.

In the mean time, Congress, on the 11th of October, having heard of the ingress of the Phoenix, Roebuck and Tartar, passed a resolution that Washington be desired to obstruct effectually the navigation of the North River between Fort Washington and Mount Constitution, as well to prevent the regress of the enemy's vessels lately gone up as to hinder them from receiving succors.

Under so many conflicting circumstances, Washington held a council of war on the 16th, at Lee's headquarters, at which all the major-generals were present excepting Greene, and all the brigadiers, as well as Colonel Knox, who commanded the artillery. The policy was discussed of remaining in their present position of Manhattan Island and awaiting there the menaced attack; the strength of the position was urged, its being well fortified and difficult of access. Lee, in reply, scoffed at the idea of a position being good merely because its approaches were difficult. How could they hold a position where the enemy were so strong in front and rear, where ships had the command of the water on each side, and where King's Bridge was their only pass by which to escape?

"After much consideration and debate," says the record of the council, "the following question was stated: Whether . . . it is now deemed possible, in our situation, to prevent the enemy from

GEN. SIR WILLIAM HOWE

BRITISH COMMANDER IN CHIEF &c.&c.

(From an English print 1777.)

Printed by W Pate

NEW YORK G.P. PUTNAM & CO.

cutting off the communication with the country and compelling us to fight them at all disadvantages or surrender prisoners at discretion?" All agreed, with but one dissenting voice, that it was not possible to prevent the communication from being cut off, and that one of the consequences mentioned in the question must follow.

As the resolve of Congress seemed imperative with regard to Fort Washington, that post, it was agreed, should be "retained as long as possible." A strong garrison was accordingly placed in it, chiefly troops from Magaw's and Shee's Pennsylvania regiments, the latter under Lieutenant-colonel Lambert Cadwalader. Shee having obtained leave of absence, Colonel Magaw was put in command of the post and solemnly charged by Washington to defend it to the last extremity. The name of the opposite post on the Jersey shore, where Greene was stationed, was changed from Fort Constitution to Fort Lee, in honor of the general, the military idol of the day.

Previous to decamping from Manhattan, Washington formed four divisions of the army, which were assigned to Generals Lee, Heath, Sullivan (recently obtained in exchange for Prescott), and Lincoln. Lee was stationed on Valentine's Hill on the mainland, immediately opposite King's Bridge, to cover the transportation across it of the military stores and heavy baggage. The other divisions were to form a chain of fortified posts extending about thirteen miles along a ridge of hills on the west side of the Bronx from Lee's camp up to the village of White Plains.

Washington's head-quarters continued to be on Harlem Heights for several days during which time he was continually forming posts and choosing sites for breastworks and redoubts. By his skillful disposition of the army, it was protected in its whole length by the Bronx, a narrow but deep stream, fringed with trees, which ran along the foot of the ridge; at the same time his troops faced and outflanked the enemy and covered the roads along which the stores and baggage had to be transported. On the 21st, he shifted his head-quarters to Valentine's Hill and on the 23d to White Plains, where he stationed himself in a fortified camp.

General, now Sir William Howe (recently made a knight companion of the Bath) remained six days in his camp on Throg's Point, awaiting supplies and reinforcements instead of pushing across to the Hudson and throwing himself between Washington's army and the upper country. By the time his supplies arrived, the Americans had broken up the causeway leading to the mainland and taken positions too strong to be easily forced.

Sir William re-embarked part of his troops in flat boats on the 18th, crossed Eastchester Bay, and landed on Pell's Point, at the mouth of Hutchinson's River. Here he was joined in a few hours by the main body, with the baggage and artillery, and proceeded through Pelham towards New Rochelle, still with a view to get above Washington's army.

In their march, the British were harrassed by Glover of Massachusetts, with his own, Reed's and Shepard's regiments of infantry. Twice the British advance guard were driven back by a sharp fire from behind stone fences. A third time they advanced in solid columns. The Americans gave them repeated volleys and then retreated.

On the 21st, Howe was encamped about two miles north of New Rochelle, his outposts extending to Mamaroneck on the Sound. He was reinforced by a second division of Hessians under Knyphausen and a regiment of Waldeckers. He was joined by the seventeenth light-dragoons and a part of the sixteenth, which had arrived on the 3d from Ireland with Lieutenant-colonel Harcourt.

The Americans at first regarded these troopers with great dread. Washington, therefore, took pains to convince them that in a rough, broken country like the present, full of stone fences, no troops were so inefficient as cavalry. They could be waylaid and picked off by sharp-shooters from behind walls and thickets, while they could not leave the road to pursue their covert foe.

On the 25th, about two o'clock in the afternoon, intelligence was brought to head-quarters that three or four detachments of the enemy were on the march, within four miles of the camp, and the main army following in columns. The men were ordered to their posts; an attack was expected. The day passed away, however, without any demonstration of the enemy. Howe detached none of his force on lateral expeditions, evidently meditating a general engagement. To prepare for it, Washington drew all his troops from the posts along the Bronx into the fortified camp at White Plains. Here every thing remained quiet but expectant throughout the 26th. In the morning of the 27th, heavy booming of cannon was heard from a distance, seemingly in the direction of Fort Washington. Scouts galloped off to gain intelligence. We will anticipate their report.

Two British frigates, at seven o'clock in the morning, had moved up the Hudson and come to anchor near Bourdett's Ferry, apparently with the intention of cutting off the communication between Fort Lee and Fort Washington. At the same time, troops made their appearance on Harlem Plains, where Percy held command. Morgan immediately manned the lines with troops from the garrison of Fort Washington. The ships opened a fire to enfilade and dislodge them. Magaw got down an eighteen-pounder to the lines near the Morris House, and fired 50 or 60 rounds, two balls at a time. Two eighteen-pounders were likewise brought down from Fort Lee and planted opposite the ships. By the fire from both shores they were hulled repeatedly.

It was the thundering of these cannonades which had reached Washington's camp at White Plains. The ships soon hoisted all sail. The foremost could make no way though towed by two boats. The other ship, seeing her distress, sent two barges to her assistance and she was dragged out of reach of the American fire.

At the time that the fire from the ships began, Percy brought up his field-pieces and mortars and made an attack upon the lines. He was resolutely answered by the troops sent down from Fort Washington. An occasional firing was kept up until evening, when the ships fell down the river and the troops which had advanced on Harlem Plains drew within their lines again.

While these things were passing at Fort Washington, Lee had struck his tents, and with the rear division, 8000 strong, the baggage and artillery, and a train of waggons four miles long laden with stores and ammunition, was lumbering along the rough country roads to join the main army. It was not until the next morning, being on the road all night, that he arrived at White Plains.

Washington's camp was on high ground, facing the east. The right wing stretched towards the south along a rocky hill, at the foot of which the Bronx, making an elbow, protected it in flank and rear.

The left wing rested on a small, deep lake among the hills. The camp was strongly intrenched in front.

About a quarter of a mile to the right of the camp, separated by the Bronx and a marshy interval, was a corresponding height called Chatterton's Hill. As this partly commanded the right flank and as the intervening bend of the Bronx was easily passable, Washington stationed on its summit a militia regiment.

The whole encampment was a temporary one, to be changed as soon as the military stores collected there could be removed. Now that Lee was arrived, Washington rode out with him and other officers to reconnoitre a height which appeared more eligible, when a trooper came spurring up his panting horse. "The British are in the camp, sir!" cried he. "Then, gentlemen," said Washington, "we have other business to attend to than reconnoitring." He set off for the camp at full gallop, the others spurring after him.

Arrived at head-quarters, he was informed by Reed that the picket guards had all been driven in and the enemy were advancing, but that the whole American army was posted in order of battle.

Apprehensive that the enemy might attempt to get possession of Chatterton's Hill, he detached Haslet with his Delaware regiment to reinforce the militia posted there. To these he soon added General McDougall's brigade. McDougall had command of the whole force upon the hill, which did not exceed 1600 men.

These dispositions were scarcely made when the enemy appeared on the high grounds beyond White Plains. They advanced in two columns, the right commanded by Clinton, the left by De Heister. There was also a troop of horse, so formidable in the inexperienced eyes of the Americans. They halted in a wheat field, behind a rising ground, and the general officers rode up in the centre to hold a consultation. Washington supposed they were preparing to attack him in front, and such indeed was their intention, but Chatterton's Hill had caught Sir William's eye and he determined first to get possession of it.

Colonel Rahl was accordingly detached with a brigade of Hessians to make a circuit southwardly round a piece of wood, cross the Bronx about a quarter of a mile below, and ascend the south side of the hill; while General Leslie, with a large force, British and Hessian, should advance directly in front, throw a bridge across the stream, and charge up the hill.

A furious cannonade was now opened by the British from 15 or 20 pieces of artillery placed on high ground opposite the hill, under cover of which, the troops of Leslie hastened to construct the bridge. In so doing, they were severely galled by two field-pieces on Chatterton's Hill in charge of Alexander Hamilton. Smallwood's Maryland battalion, also, kept up a sharp fire of small arms.

As soon as the bridge was finished, the British and Hessians under Leslie rushed over it, formed, and charged up the hill to take Hamilton's two field-pieces. Three times the two field-pieces were discharged, ploughing the ascending columns from hill-top to river, while Smallwood's Marylanders kept up their volleys of musketry.

In the mean time, Rahl and his Hessian brigade forded the Bronx lower down, pushed up the south side of the hill, and endeavored to turn McDougall's right flank. The militia gave the general but little support. The opening of the engagement by a shot from a British cannon nearly put the whole to flight. With the utmost difficulty McDougall rallied them and posted them behind a stone wall, where they did some service until a troop of British cavalry, having gained the crest of the hill, came on, brandishing their sabres. At their first charge the militia broke and fled in complete confusion. A brave stand was made on the summit of the hill by Haslet, Ritzema, and Smallwood with their troops, until, greatly outnumbered, they slowly retreated down the north side of the hill, where there was a bridge across the Bronx. At the bridge the retreating troops were met by Putnam, who was coming to their assistance with Beall's brigade. In the rear of this they marched back into the camp. The loss on both sides, in this short but severe action, was nearly equal. That of the Americans was about 400 men killed, wounded, and taken prisoners.

The British army now rested with their left wing on the hill just taken, which they were busy intrenching. They were extending their right wing to the left of the American lines so that their two wings and centre formed nearly a semicircle. It was evidently their design to outflank the American camp, and get in the rear of it. The day, being far advanced, was suffered to pass without any further attack, but the morrow was looked forward to for a deadly conflict.

During this night, Washington was occupied throwing back his right wing to stronger ground, doubling his intrenchments and constructing three redoubts, with a line in front, on the summit of his post. These works, principally intended for defence against small arms, were thrown up with a rapidity that to the enemy must have savored of magic. They were, in fact, made of the stalks of Indian corn pulled up with the earth clinging in masses to the large roots. "The roots of the stalks," says Heath, "and earth on them placed in the face of the works, answered the purpose of sods and fascines."

In the morning, when Howe beheld how greatly Washington had improved his position by what appeared to be solidly constructed works, he postponed his meditated assault, ordered up Percy from Harlem with the fourth brigade and two battalions of the sixth, and proceeded to throw up lines and redoubts in front of the American camp as if preparing to cannonade it. As the enemy were endeavoring to outflank him, especially on his right wing, Washington apprehended one of their objects might be to seize Pine's Bridge over Croton River which would cut off his communication with the upper country. Beall, with three Maryland regiments, was sent off with all expedition to secure that pass. It was Washington's idea that, having possession of Croton River and the passes in the Highlands, his army would be safe from further pursuit, have time to repose after its late excessive fatigue, and be ready to harass the enemy should they think fit to winter up the country.

In the course of the night of the 31st, Washington, leaving a strong rear-guard on the heights and in the neighboring woods, retired with his main army a distance of five miles among the high, rocky hills about Northcastle. Here he immediately set to work to intrench and fortify himself. Howe did not attempt to dislodge him from this fastness. "All matters are as quiet as if the enemy were one hundred miles distant from us," writes one of Washington's aides on the 2d of November. During the night of the 4th this quiet was interrupted. A mysterious sound was heard, like the rumbling of waggons and artillery. At daybreak the meaning of it was discovered. The enemy were decamping. Long trains were observed,

defiling across the hilly country along the roads leading to Dobbs'
Ferry on the Hudson. The movement continued for three successive days until their whole force disappeared from White Plains.

(CHAPTER 28)

Various were the speculations at head-quarters on the sudden
movement of the enemy. Washington writes to General William
Livingston (now governor of the Jerseys): "They have gone toward
the North River and King's Bridge. Some suppose they are going
into winter quarters, and will sit down in New York without doing
more than investing Fort Washington. I cannot subscribe wholly to
this opinion myself. . . . I think there is a strong probability that
General Howe will detach a part of his force to make an incursion
into the Jerseys, provided he is going to New York." In the same
letter he expressed his determination, as soon as it should appear
that the present manoeuvre was a real retreat, to throw troops into
the Jerseys to assist in checking Howe's progress. He recommended
to the governor to have the militia of that State put on the best
possible footing.

In a letter of the same date, he charged Greene, should Howe
invest Fort Washington with part of his force, to give the garrison all
possible assistance.

On the following day (Nov. 8th), his aide-de-camp, Tilghman,
writes to Greene: "The enemy are at Dobbs' Ferry with a great
number of boats, ready to go into Jersey, or proceed up the river."
Greene doubted any intention of the enemy to cross the river; still,
as a precaution, he ordered troops up from the flying camp, posting
them opposite Dobbs' Ferry and at other passes where a landing
might be attempted, the whole being under the command of
Mercer.

Affairs at Fort Washington soon settled the question of the
enemy's intentions with regard to it. Percy took his station with a

body of troops before the lines to the South. Knyphausen advanced on the north. The Americans had previously abandoned Fort Independence, burnt its barracks, and removed the stores and cannon. Crossing King's Bridge, Knyphausen took a position between it and Fort Washington. The approach to the fort was exceedingly steep and rocky, as, indeed, were all its approaches excepting that on the south, where the ascent was more gradual. The fort could not hold within its walls above 1000 men; the rest of the troops were distributed about the lines and outworks. While the fort was thus menaced, the chevaux-de-frise again proved inefficient. On the night of the 5th, a frigate and two transports, bound up to Dobbs' Ferry with supplies for Howe's army, had broken through, though, according to Greene's account, not without being considerably shattered by the batteries.

Informed of these facts, Washington wrote to Greene on the 8th: "If we cannot prevent vessels from passing up the river and the enemy are possessed of all the surrounding country, what valuable purpose can it answer to hold a post from which the expected benefit cannot be had? I am, therefore, inclined to think, that it will not be prudent to hazard the men and stores at Mount Washington; but, as you are on the spot, I leave it to you to give such orders as to evacuating Mount Washington as you may judge best, and so far revoking the orders given to Colonel Magaw to defend it to the last."

Accounts had been received at head-quarters of considerable movement on the preceding evening (Nov. 7th) among the enemy's boats at Dobbs' Ferry with the intention, it was said, of penetrating the Jerseys and falling upon Fort Lee. Washington, therefore, in the same letter, directed Greene to have all the stores not necessary to the defence removed immediately.

Greene, in reply (Nov. 9th), adhered with tenacity to the policy of maintaining Fort Washington. "The enemy," said he, "must invest it with double the number of men required for its defence. They must keep troops at King's Bridge to cut off all communication with the country and in considerable force for fear of an attack." He did not consider the fort in immediate danger.

It is doubtful when or where Washington received this letter, as he left the camp at Northcastle at eleven o'clock of the following morning. There being still considerable uncertainty as to the intentions of the enemy, all his arrangements were made accordingly. All troops belonging to States west of the Hudson were to be stationed in the Jerseys under command of Putnam. Stirling had already been sent forward with the Maryland and Virginia troops to Peekskill to cross the river at King's Ferry. Another division composed of Connecticut and Massachusetts troops under Heath was to co-operate with the brigade of New York militia under Clinton in securing the Highland posts on both sides of the river. The troops which would remain at Northcastle were to be commanded by Lee.

On the 10th of November, Washington left Northcastle and arrived at Peekskill at sunset, where Heath, with his division, had preceded him by a few hours. Stirling was there, likewise, having effected the transportation of the Maryland and Virginia troops across the river, and landed them at the ferry south of Stony Point. He had thrown out a scouting party in the advance and 100 men to take possession of a gap in the mountain through which a road passed toward the Jerseys.

Washington was now at the entrance of the Highlands, that grand defile of the Hudson, the object of so much precaution and solicitude. On the following morning, accompanied by Heath, Stirling, James and George Clinton, Mifflin, and others, he made a military visit in boats to the Highland posts. Fort Montgomery was in a considerable state of forwardness and a work in the vicinity was projected to co-operate with it. Fort Constitution commanded a sudden bend of the river, but Stirling, in his report of inspection, intimated that the fort itself was commanded by West Point opposite. A glance of the eye was sufficient to convince Washington of the fact. A fortress subsequently erected on that point, has been considered the Key of the Highlands.

On the morning of the 12th, Washington rode out with Heath to reconnoitre the east side of the Hudson at the gorge of the Highlands. Henry Wisner, in a report to the New York Convention, had mentioned a hill north of Peekskill so situated, with the road winding along the side of it, that ten men on the top, by rolling down stones, might prevent ten thousand from passing.

Near Robinson's Bridge, about two miles from Peekskill,

Washington chose a place where troops should be stationed to cover the south entrance into the mountains; here, afterwards, was established an important military depot called Continental Village.

On the same day (12th), he wrote to General Lee, "I cannot conclude without reminding you of the military and other stores about your encampment and at Northcastle, and to press the removal of them above Croton Bridge or such other places of security as you may think proper." It was evidently Washington's desire that Lee should post himself, as soon as possible, beyond the Croton, where he would be safe from surprise and at hand to throw his troops promptly across the Hudson should the Jerseys be invaded.

Having made all these surveys and arrangements, Washington placed Heath in general command of the Highlands with written instructions to fortify the passes with all possible despatch and directions how the troops were to be distributed on both sides of the river. We shall find him faithful to his trust and scrupulous in obeying the letter of his instructions.

During his brief sojourn at Peekskill, Washington received important intelligence from the Northern army, especially that part of it on Lake Champlain under Gates.

The preparations for the defence of Ticonderoga and the nautical service on the lake had met with difficulties at every step. At length, by the middle of August, a small flotilla was completed, subsequently augmented, and command was given by Gates to Arnold.

Sir Guy Carleton, in the mean time, was straining every nerve for the approaching conflict. Vessels were brought from England in pieces and put together at St. Johns, boats of various kinds and sizes were transported over land or dragged up the rapids of the Sorel. Should he get command of Lakes Champlain and George, the northern part of New York would be at his mercy; before winter set in he might gain possession of Albany. He would then be able to co-operate with Howe in severing and subduing the northern and southern provinces, and bringing the war to a speedy and triumphant close.

Three months elapsed before his armament was completed.

Winter was fast approaching. Before it arrived, his plan required that he should fight his way across Lake Champlain, carry the posts of Crown Point and Ticonderoga, traverse Lake George, and pursue a long and dangerous march to Albany, where he expected to find winter quarters for his troops.

By October between 20 and 30 sail were afloat, and ready for action. The flag-ship (the Inflexible), mounted 18 twelve-pounders; the rest were gunboats, a gondola and a flat-bottomed vessel named the *Thunderer*, carrying a battery of 6 twenty-four and 12 six-pounders, besides howitzers. The gunboats mounted brass field-pieces and howitzers. In a word, according to British accounts, "no equipment of the kind was ever better appointed, or more amply furnished with every kind of provision necessary for the intended service."

Captain Pringle conducted the armament, but Sir Guy Carleton was too full of zeal not to head the enterprise; he accordingly took his station on the flag-ship. They made sail early in October in quest of the American squadron, which was said to be abroad upon the lake. Arnold, however, unwilling to encounter a superior force in the open lake, had taken his post under cover of Valcour Island, in the upper part of a deep strait between that island and the mainland. His force consisted of 3 schooners, 2 sloops, 3 galleys and 8 gondolas; carrying in all 70 guns, many of them eighteen-pounders.

The British ships, on the morning of the 11th, had left the southern end of Valcour Island astern when they discovered Arnold's flotilla anchored behind it in a line extending across the strait so as not to be outflanked. They immediately tried to beat up into the channel but the wind did not permit the largest of them to enter. Arnold took advantage of the circumstance. He was on the galley Congress, and, leaving the line, advanced with two other galleys and the schooner Royal Savage to attack the smaller vessels as they entered before the large ones could come up. Seeing the enemy's gunboats approaching, the Americans endeavored to return to the line but the Royal Savage ran aground; her crew set her on fire and abandoned her. In about an hour the British brought all their gunboats in a range across the lower part of the channel. They landed, also, a large number of Indians on the island to keep up a galling fire from the shore upon the Americans with their rifles. The action, now general, was severe and sanguinary. The Americans, finding themselves thus hemmed in by a superior force, fought with desperation. Arnold pressed with his galley into the hottest of the fight. He cheered on his men by voice and example, often pointing the guns with his own hands. The contest lasted throughout the day. The Indian whoops and yells, mingling with the rattling of the musketry and the thundering of the cannon, increased the horrors of the scene, and this lovely recess of a beautiful and peaceful lake was rendered a perfect pandemonium.

The evening drew nigh, yet the contest was undecided. Pringle, after a consultation with Carleton, anchored his whole squadron in a line as near as possible to the Americans so as to prevent their escape.

Arnold, however, took advantage of a dark, cloudy night and a strong north wind; his vessels slipped silently through the enemy's line without being discovered. Arnold's galley, the Congress, the Washington galley and four gondolas, all which had suffered severely in the fight, fell astern of the rest of the squadron in the course of the night. In the morning, when the sun lifted a fog, they beheld the enemy within a few miles of them in full chase, while their own comrades were nearly out of sight, making for Crown Point.

It was now an anxious trial of speed and seamanship. Arnold, with the crippled relics of his squadron, managed by noon to get within a few leagues of Crown Point, when they were overtaken. The Washington galley, already shattered and having lost most of her officers, was compelled to strike and General Waterbury and the crew were taken prisoners. Arnold had now to bear the brunt of the action. For a long time he was engaged until his galley was reduced to a wreck and one third of the crew were killed. The gondolas were nearly in the same desperate condition. Seeing resistance vain, Arnold determined that neither vessels nor crews should fall into the hands of the enemy. He ordered the gondolas run on shore, the men to set fire to them and keep off the enemy until they were consumed. He did the same with his own galley, remaining on board until she was in flames, lest the enemy get possession. He now set off with his gallant crew, many of whom were wounded, by a road through the woods to Crown Point, where he arrived at night, narrowly escaping an Indian ambush.

Two schooners, two galleys, one sloop and one gondola, the remnant which had escaped of this squadron, were at anchor at the Point; Waterbury and most of his men arrived there the next day on parole. Seeing that the place must soon fall to the enemy, they set fire to the houses, destroyed every thing they could not carry away, and made sail for Ticonderoga.

The conduct of Arnold in these naval affairs gained him new laurels. He was extolled for the judgment with which he chose his position and brought his vessels into action, for his masterly retreat, and for the self-sacrificing devotion with which he covered the retreat of part of his flotilla.

Carleton took possession of the ruined works at Crown Point, where he was soon joined by the army. He made several movements by land and water, as if meditating an attack upon Ticonderoga. Gates in the mean time, strengthened his works with incessant assiduity and made every preparation for an obstinate defence. A strong southerly wind prevented the enemy's ships from advancing to attack the lines and gave time for the arrival of reinforcements of militia to the garrison. It also afforded time for Carleton to calculate the chances of success. The post, from its strength, and the apparent number and resolution of the garrison, could not be taken without great loss of life. If taken, the season was now too far advanced to think of exposing the army to a winter campaign in the inhospitable wilds to the southward.

These and other prudential reasons induced Carleton to give up all attempt upon the fortress at present. Re-embarking his troops, he returned to St. Johns and cantoned them in Canada for the winter. About the 1st of November, a reconnoitring party sent out from Ticonderoga by Gates brought back intelligence that Crown Point was abandoned by the enemy. All apprehensions of an attack upon Ticonderoga during the present year were at an end. The news from the north, received by Washington at Peekskill, relieved him for the present from anxiety respecting Lake Champlain.

(CHAPTER 29)

On the morning of the 12th of November, Washington crossed the Hudson to the ferry below Stony Point with the residue of the troops destined for the Jerseys. Far below were to be descried the Phoenix, the Roebuck, and the Tartar at anchor in Haverstraw Bay and the Tappan Sea. The army, thus shut out from the nearer passes, was slowly winding its way through the gap in the mountains which Stirling had secured. Leaving the troops which had just landed to pursue the same route to the Hackensack, Washington, accompanied by Reed, struck a direct course for Fort Lee, being anxious about Fort Washington. He arrived there on the following day and found that Greene had taken no measures for the evacuation of that fortress, but, on the contrary, had reinforced it with a part of Durkee's regiment and the regiment of Rawlings, so that its garrison now numbered 2000 men; a great part were militia. Washington's orders for its evacuation had, in fact, been discretionary, and Greene as well as Magaw, who had charge of the fortress, were confident it might be maintained. The fort was now invested on all sides but one; the troops under Howe which had been encamped at Dobbs' Ferry were moving down toward it.

Washington was much perplexed. He could not think that Sir William was moving his whole force upon that fortress, to invest which, a part would be sufficient. He suspected an ulterior object, probably a Southern expedition, as he was told a large number of ships were taking in wood and water at New York. He resolved, therefore, to continue a few days in this neighborhood, during which the designs of the enemy would be more apparent; in the mean time he would distribute troops at Brunswick, Amboy, Elizabethtown and Fort Lee to check any incursions into the Jerseys.

Washington was mistaken in his conjecture as to Howe's design. The capture of Fort Washington was his main object; he was encamped on Fordham Heights, not far from King's Bridge, until preliminary steps should be taken. In the night of the 14th, 30 flat-bottomed boats stole quietly up the Hudson, passed the American forts undiscovered, and made their way through Spyt den Duivel Creek into Harlem River. The means were thus provided for crossing that river and landing before unprotected parts of the American works.

On the 15th, Howe sent in a summons to surrender. Magaw, in his reply, said, "I am determined to defend this post to the very last extremity."

Apprised by the colonel of his peril, Greene sent over reinforcements, with an exhortation to him to persist in his defence, and despatched an express to Washington, who was at Hackensack, where the troops which had crossed from Peekskill were encamped. It was nightfall when Washington arrived at Fort Lee. Greene and Putnam being at the besieged fortress, he threw himself into a boat and had partly crossed the river when he met those generals returning. They assured him that the garrison was capable of making a good defence. It was with difficulty, however, they could prevail on him to return with them to the Jersey shore.

Early the next morning (16th), Magaw made his dispositions for the expected attack. His forces amounted to nearly 3000 men. As the fort could not contain above a third of that number, most of them were stationed about the outworks.

Cadwalader, with 800 Pennsylvanians, was posted in the outer lines, about two miles and a half south of the fort, the side menaced by Percy with 1600 men. Rawlings with a body of troops, many of them riflemen, was stationed by a three-gun battery on a rocky precipitous hill north of the fort, between it and Spyt den Duivel Creek. Baxter, with his regiment of Pennsylvania militia, was posted east of the fort on rough woody heights bordering the Harlem River to watch the enemy, who had thrown up redoubts of high ground on the opposite side of the river, apparently to cover the crossing of troops.

Howe had planned four simultaneous attacks. One was on the north by Knyphausen, who, encamped on the York side of King's

Bridge, and separated from Fort Washington by high and rough hills covered with woods, was to advance in two columns, formed by detachments from the Hessians of his corps, the brigade of Rahl, and the regiment of Waldeckers. The second attack was to be by two battalions of light infantry and two battalions of guards under Mathew, who was to cross Harlem River in flat-boats under cover of the redoubts above mentioned and land on the right of the fort. This attack was to be supported by the first and second grenadiers and a regiment of light infantry under command of Cornwallis. The third attack, intended as a feint to distract the attention of the Americans, was to be by Stirling with the forty-second regiment, who was to drop down the Harlem River in bateaux, to the left of the American lines, facing New York. The fourth attack was to be on the south by Percy, with the English and Hessian troops under his command, on the right flank of the American intrenchments.

About noon, a heavy cannonade and sharp volleys of musketry proclaimed that the action was commenced. Knyphausen's division was pushing on from the north in two columns, the right led by Rahl, the left by himself. Rahl essayed to mount a steep woody height which rises from Spyt den Duivel Creek; Knyphausen undertook a hill rising from the King's Bridge road but soon found himself in a woody defile exposed to the fire of the three-gun battery and Rawlings' riflemen.

While this was going on north of the fort, Mathew, with his light infantry and guards, crossed the Harlem River in the flat-boats under cover of heavy fire from the redoubts. He made good his landing, after being severely handled by Baxter and his men. Baxter, while bravely encouraging his men, was killed and his troops, overpowered by numbers, retreated to the fort. Mathew now pushed on to cut off Cadwalader, who had gallantly defended the lines against the attack of Percy. Informed that Stirling was dropping down Harlem River in bateaux to flank the lines and take him in the rear, he sent off a detachment to oppose his landing. They did it manfully, but Stirling landed, forced his way up a steep height, gained the summit, forced a redoubt, and took nearly 200 prisoners. Thus doubly assailed, Cadwalader was obliged to retreat to the fort.

The defence on the north side of the fort was equally obstinate and unsuccessful. Rawlings for some time kept the left column under Knyphausen at bay. At length Rahl, with the right column of the division, having forced his way up the north side of the steep hill at Spyt den Duivel Creek, came upon Rawlings' men, drove them from their strong post, and followed them until within 100 yards of the fort, where he was joined by Knyphausen. They sent in a flag with a second summons to surrender.

Washington, surrounded by several of his officers, had been an anxious spectator of the battle from the opposite side of the Hudson. Much of it was hidden from him by intervening hills and forests, but the action to the south could be distinctly seen through a telescope. When he saw Cadwalader, overpowered by numbers, retreating to the fort, he gave up the game as lost. The worst sight of all was to behold his men cut down and bayoneted by the Hessians while begging quarter. It is said so completely to have overcome him that he wept "with the tenderness of a child."

Seeing the flag go into the fort and surmising it to be a summons to surrender, he wrote to Magaw that, if he could hold out until evening and the place could not be maintained, he would endeavor to bring off the garrison in the night. Captain Gooch, of Boston, a brave and daring man, offered to be the bearer of the note. Washington's message arrived too late. The enemy, in possession of the redoubts around, could have poured in showers of shells and ricochet balls that would have made dreadful slaughter. Magaw was compelled, therefore, to yield himself and his garrison prisoners of war.

The sight of the American flag hauled down and the British flag waving in its place told Washington of the surrender. His instant care was for the safety of the upper country, now that the lower defences of the Hudson were at an end. He wrote to Lee, informing him of the surrender and calling his attention to the passes of the Highlands and those which lay east of the river, begging him to have such measures adopted for their defence as his judgment should suggest to be necessary. "I do not mean," added he, "to advise abandoning your present post, contrary to your own opinion; but only to mention my own ideas of the importance of those passes."

Lee, in reply, objected to removing from his encampment at

Northcastle. "It would," said he, "expose a fine fertile country to their ravages; and I must add, that we are as secure as we could be in any position whatever. . . . In short, if we keep a good look-out, we are in no danger; but I must entreat your Excellency to enjoin the officers posted at Fort Lee to give us the quickest intelligence if they observe any embarkation on the North River." As to the affair of Fort Washington, Lee observed: "Oh, general, why would you be over-persuaded by men of inferior judgment to your own? It was a cursed affair." Lee's allusion to men of inferior judgment was principally aimed at Greene, whose influence with the commander-in-chief seems to have excited the jealousy of other officers of rank.

The correspondence of Washington with his brother Augustine is full of gloomy anticipations. "It is impossible for me, in the compass of a letter, to give you any idea of our situation, of my difficulties, and of the constant perplexities I meet with, derived from the unhappy policy of short enlistments . . . . Last fall . . . I represented in clear and explicit terms the evils which would arise from short enlistments, the expense which must attend the raising an army every year, and the futility of such an army when raised. . . . All the year since, I have been pressing Congress to delay no time in engaging men upon such terms as would insure success, telling them that the longer it was delayed, the more difficult it would prove . . . . I am wearied almost to death with the retrograde motion of things; . . . it is impossible, under such a variety of distressing circumstances, to conduct matters agreeably to public expectation."

With the capture of Fort Washington, obstructing navigation of the Hudson at that point was at an end. Fort Lee consequently became useless, and Washington ordered all ammunition and stores removed, preparatory to abandonment. This was effected with the whole of the ammunition and a part of the stores, when, early in the morning of the 20th, intelligence was brought that the enemy, with 200 boats, had crossed the river and landed a few miles above. Greene immediately ordered the garrison under arms, sent troops to hold the enemy in check, and sent an express to Washington at Hackensack.

The enemy had crossed the Hudson on a rainy night in two divisions, one diagonally upward from King's Bridge, landing on the west side about eight o'clock; the other marched up the east bank three or four miles and then crossed to the opposite shore. The whole corps, 6,000 strong under Cornwallis, were landed by ten o'clock at Closter Dock, five or six miles above Fort Lee and under that line of lofty cliffs known as the Palisades.

Washington arrived at the fort in three quarters of an hour. He at once saw that the enemy intended to form a line from the Hudson to the Hackensack and hem the whole garrison in between the two rivers. Nothing would save it but a prompt retreat to secure the bridge over the Hackensack. No time was to be lost. The troops sent out to check the enemy were recalled. The retreat commenced in all haste. A great quantity of baggage, stores and provisions was abandoned. So was all the artillery excepting two twelve-pounders. Even the tents were left standing. With all their speed they did not reach the Hackensack before the vanguard of the enemy was close upon them. The enemy, however, did not dispute the passage of the river. Cornwallis stated in his despatches that, had not the Americans been apprised of his approach, he would have surrounded them at the fort.

Washington wrote to Lee on the following day (Nov. 21st). "I am of opinion," said he, "and the gentlemen about me concur in it, that the public interest requires your coming over to this side of the Hudson with the Continental troops . . . . The enemy is evidently changing the seat of war to this side of the North River, and the inhabitants of this country will expect the Continental army to give them what support they can."

In this moment of agitation, Reed wrote to Lee, but in a spirit that may surprise the reader, knowing the devotion he had hitherto manifested for the commander-in-chief. After expressing the wish that Lee should be at the principal scene of action, he adds: "I do not mean to flatter or praise you, at the expense of any other; but I do think it is entirely owing to you, that this army, and the liberties of America, so far as they are dependent on it, are not entirely cut off. You have decision, a quality often wanting in minds otherwise valuable . . . . Nor am I singular in my opinion; every gentleman of the family, the officers and soldiers generally, have a confidence in you." Then alluding to the late affair at Fort Washington, he continues: "General Washington's own judgment, seconded by representations from us, would, I believe, have saved the men, and their arms; but, unluckily, General Greene's judgment was contrary. This kept the general's mind in a state of suspense, till the stroke was struck. Oh, general! An indecisive mind is one of the greatest misfortunes that can befall an army; how often have I lamented it this campaign . . . . As soon as the season will admit, I think yourself and some others should go to Congress and form the plan of the new army."

Reed had evidently been dazzled by the daring spirit and unscrupulous policy of Lee, who, in carrying out his measures, heeded but little the counsels of others or even the orders of government; Washington's respect for both, and the caution with which he hesitated in adopting measures in oppositon to them, was stamped by the bold soldier and his admirers as indecision.

At Hackensack the army did not exceed 3000 men. Dispirited by ill success and the loss of tents and baggage, they were without intrenching tools in a flat country where there were no natural fastnesses. Washington resolved, therefore, to avoid attack from the enemy, though, by so doing, he must leave a fertile region open to their ravages or a plentiful storehouse from which they would draw voluntary supplies. A second move was necessary, again to avoid the danger of being enclosed between two rivers. Leaving three regiments to guard the passes of the Hackensack and serve as covering parties, he again decamped and threw himself on the west bank of the Passaic, in the neighborhood of Newark.

His army, small as it was, would soon be less. The term of enlistment of those under Mercer, from the flying camp, was nearly expired; and it was not probable that they would longer forego the comforts of their homes to drag out the residue of a ruinous campaign.

In addition to the superiority of the force following him, the rivers gave the enemy facilities, by means of their shipping, to throw troops in his rear. In this extremity he cast about in every direction for assistance. Reed was despatched to Burlington with a letter to

Engraved by G.B.Hall.

MAJ. GEN. CHARLES LEE.

Printed by W.Pate.

Charles Lee

NEW YORK G.P.PUTNAM & CO.

Governor Livingston, entreating him to call out a portion of the New Jersey militia; Mifflin was sent to Philadelphia to implore immediate aid from Congress and the local authorities.

His main reliance for prompt assistance, however, was upon Lee. On the 24th came a letter from that general addressed to Reed. Washington opened it, as he was accustomed to do in the absence of that officer with letters addressed to him on the business of the army. Lee was at his old encampment at Northcastle. He had no means, he said, of crossing at Dobbs' Ferry and the round by King's Ferry would be so great that he could not get there in time to answer any purpose. "I have, therefore," added he, "ordered General Heath, who is close to the only ferry which can be passed, to detach 2000 men, to apprise his Excellency, and await his further orders; a mode which I flatter myself will answer better what I conceive to be the spirit of the orders, than should I move the corps from hence. Withdrawing our troops from hence would be attended with some very serious consequences, which at present would be tedious to enumerate; as to myself," adds he, "I hope to set out to-morrow."

A letter of the same date (Nov.23d), from Lee to James Bowdoin, president of the Massachusetts council, may throw some light on his motives for delaying to obey orders of the commander-in-chief. "Before the unfortunate affair of Fort Washington," writes he, "it was my opinion that the two armies—that on the east, and that on the west side of the North River—must rest each on its own bottom; that the idea of detaching and reinforcing from one side to the other, on every motion of the enemy, was chimerical; but to harbor such a thought in our present circumstances, is absolute insanity." In another letter to Bowdoin, dated on the following day, he writes: "Indecision bids fair for tumbling down the goodly fabric of American freedom, and, with it, the rights of mankind . . . . 'Twas indecision in our military councils which cost us the garrison at Fort Washington, the consequence of which must be fatal, unless remedied in time by a contrary spirit." It is evident Lee considered Washington's star to be on the decline and his own in the ascendant. The "affair of Fort Washington," and the "indecision of the commander-in-chief," were apparently his watchwords.

On the following day (24th), he writes to Washington from

Northcastle on the subject of removing troops across the Hudson. "I have received your orders, and shall endeavor to put them in execution, but question whether I shall be able to carry with me any considerable number; not so much from a want of zeal in the men, as from their wretched condition with respect to shoes, stockings, and blankets, which the present bad weather renders more intolerable. I sent Heath orders to transport 2000 men across the river, apprise the general, and wait for further orders; but that great man (as I might have expected), intrenched himself within the letter of his instructions, and refused to part with a single file, though I undertook to replace them with a part of my own."

Scarce had Lee sent this letter when he received one from Washington informing him that he had mistaken his views in regard to the troops required to cross the Hudson; it was his (Lee's) division he wanted to have over. The force under Heath must remain to guard the posts and passes through the Highlands, the importance of which was so infinitely great that there should not be the least possible risk of losing them.

Lee's reply, still from Northcastle, explained that his idea of detaching troops from Heath's division was merely for expedition's sake, intending to replace them from his own. From the force of the enemy remaining in Westchester County, he did not conceive the number of them in the Jerseys to be near so great as Washington believed. He had been making a sweep of the country to clear it of the tories. Part of his army had now moved on and he would set out on the following day.

Washington was at Newark when, on the 27th, he received Lee's letter of the 24th. He immediately wrote to Lee: "My former letters were so full and explicit, as to the necessity of your marching as early as possible, that it is unnecessary to add more on that head. I confess I expected you would have been sooner in motion."

The situation of the little army was daily becoming more perilous. In a council of war, several members urged a move to Morristown to form a junction with the troops expected from the Northern army. Washington, however, still cherished the idea of making a stand at Brunswick on the Raritan, or, at all events, of disputing the passage of the Delaware; in this resolution he was warmly seconded by Greene. Breaking up his camp once more, he continued his retreat towards New Brunswick. So close was Cornwallis that his advance entered one end of Newark just as the American rear-guard left the other.

From Brunswick, Washington wrote on the 29th, to William Livingston, governor of the Jerseys, requesting him to have all river craft, for 70 miles along the Delaware, removed to the western bank out of the reach of the enemy and put under guard. He was disappointed in his hope of making a stand at the Raritan. All the force he could muster at Brunswick, including the New Jersey militia, did not exceed 4000 men. Reed had failed in procuring aid from the New Jersey legislature. The term of the Maryland and New Jersey troops in the flying camp had expired; Mercer endeavored to detain them, but his remonstrances were fruitless. As to the Pennsylvania levies, they deserted in such numbers that guards were stationed on the roads and ferries to intercept them.

At this moment of care and perplexity, a letter, forwarded by express, arrived at head-quarters. It was from Lee to Reed in reply to the letter written by that officer from Hackensack on the 21st, which we have already laid before the reader. Supposing that it related to official business, Washington opened it and read as follows: "I received your most obliging, flattering letter; lament with you that fatal indecision of mind, which in war is a much greater disqualification than stupidity or even want of personal courage. Accident may put a decisive blunderer in the right; but eternal defeat and miscarriage must attend the man of the best parts, if cursed with indecision. . . . To confess a truth, I really think our chief will do better with me than without me."

A glance sufficed to show Washington that, at this dark moment, when he most needed support and sympathy, his character and conduct were the subject of disparaging comments between the friend in whom he had implicitly confided and a sarcastic and apparently self-constituted rival. Whatever may have been his feelings of wounded pride and outraged friendship, he restrained them and enclosed the letter to Reed, with the following note: "The enclosed was put into my hands by an express from White Plains.

Having no idea of its being a private letter, much less suspecting the tendency of the correspondence, I opened it; as I have done all other letters to you from the same place, and Peekskill, upon the business of your office, as I conceived, and found them to be. This, as it is the truth, must be my excuse for seeing the contents of a letter, which neither inclination nor intention would have prompted me to,"&c.

The very calmness and coldness of this note must have had a greater effect upon Reed, than could have been produced by the most vehement reproaches. In subsequent communications, he endeavored to explain away Lee's letter. Washington's magnanimous nature, however, was incapable of harboring long resentments. His personal respect for Reed continued; he consulted him, as before, on military affairs; but his hitherto affectionate confidence in him, as a sympathizing friend, had received an incurable wound.

Washington lingered at Brunswick until the 1st of December in the vain hope of being reinforced. The enemy, in the mean time, advanced through the country, impressing waggons and horses and collecting cattle and sheep. At length their vanguard appeared on the opposite side of the Raritan. Washington immediately broke down the end of the bridge next the village and after nightfall resumed his retreat. In the mean time, as the river was fordable, Hamilton planted his field-pieces on commanding ground and opened a spirited fire to check any attempt of the enemy to cross.

At Princeton Washington left 1200 men in two brigades, under Stirling and Stephen, to cover the country and watch the enemy.

The harassed army reached Trenton on the 2d of December. Washington immediately proceeded to remove his baggage and stores across the Delaware. In his letters from this place to the President of Congress, he writes, "Nothing but necessity obliged me to retire before the enemy, and leave so much of the Jerseys unprotected. . . . If the militia of this State had stepped forth in season (and timely notice they had), we might have prevented the enemy's crossing the Hackensack. We might, with equal possibility of success, have made a stand at Brunswick on the Raritan. But, as both these rivers were fordable in a variety of places, being knee deep only, it required many men to guard the passes, and these we had not."

In excuse for the people of New Jersey, it may be observed that, while many of them looked upon the Revolution as rebellion, others thought it a ruined enterprise, the armies engaged in it having been defeated and broken up. They beheld the commander-in-chief retreating with a handful of men, weary, dispirited, without tents, many of them barefooted, exposed to wintry weather, driven from post to post, by a well-clad, well-fed, triumphant force. Could it be wondered at, that peaceful husbandmen should, instead of flying to arms, seek for the safety of their wives and little ones and protection from the desolation?

Lord Howe and his brother sought to profit by this dismay and despondency. A proclamation, dated 30th of November, commanded all persons in arms against his majesty's government to disband and return home and all Congresses to desist from treasonable acts, offering a free pardon to all who should comply within fifty days. Many hastened to take advantage of this proclamation. Those who had most property to lose were the first to submit. The middle ranks remained generally steadfast in this time of trial.

Washington remained firm and undaunted. In casting about for some stronghold where he might make a desperate stand for the liberties of his country, his thoughts reverted to the mountain regions of his early campaigns. Mercer was at hand, who had shared his perils among these mountains. "What think you," said Washington, "if we should retreat to the back parts of Pennsylvania, would the Pennsylvanians support us?"

"If the lower counties give up, the back counties will do the same," was the discouraging reply.

"We must then retire to Augusta County in Virginia," said Washington. "Numbers will repair to us for safety and we will try a predatory war. If overpowered, we must cross the Alleganies." Such was the indomitable spirit, rising under difficulties and buoyant in the darkest moment, that kept our tempest-tost cause from foundering.

(CHAPTER 30)

Notwithstanding the repeated orders and entreaties of the commander-in-chief, Lee did not reach Peekskill until the 30th of November. In a letter of that date to Washington, who had complained of his delay, he simply alleged difficulties, which he would explain when both had leisure.

It was not until the 4th of December, that Lee crossed the Hudson and began a laggard march though aware of the peril of Washington and his army.

In the mean time, Washington, who was at Trenton, had profited by a delay of the enemy at Brunswick and removed most of the stores and baggage of the army across the Delaware. Being reinforced by 1500 of the Pennsylvania militia procured by Mifflin, he prepared to march back to Princeton, there to be governed by circumstances and the movements of Lee. Accordingly, on the 5th of December he sent about 1200 men in the advance to reinforce Stirling and the next day set off himself with the residue.

While on the march, Washington received a letter from Greene, who was at Princeton, informing him of a report that Lee was "at the heels of the enemy." "I should think," adds Greene, "he had better keep on the flanks than the rear, unless it were possible to concert an attack at the same instant of time in front and rear. . . . I think General Lee must be confined within the lines of some general plan or else his operations will be independent of yours. His own troops, General St. Clair's, and the militia, must form a respectable army."

Lee had no idea of conforming to a general plan; he had an independent plan of his own and was at that moment at Pompton, indulging speculations on military greatness and the lamentable want of it in his American contemporaries.

While Lee was thus speculating, Cornwallis, knowing how far he was in the rear and how weak was Washington's army, made a forced march from Brunswick and was within two miles of Princeton. Stirling, to avoid being surrounded, immediately set out with two brigades for Trenton. Washington, too, receiving intelligence of these movements, hastened back to that place and caused the stores and troops to be transported across the Delaware. He himself crossed with the rear-guard on Sunday morning and took up his quarters about a mile from the river, causing the boats to be destroyed and troops to be posted opposite the fords. He was conscious, however, that his small force could make no great opposition should the enemy bring boats with them. Fortunately they did not come thus provided.

Cornwallis was brought to a stand. He made some moves as if he would cross the Delaware above and below, either to push on to Philadelphia or to entrap Washington in the bend of the river opposite Bordentown. An able disposition of American troops along the upper part of the river and of a number of galleys below discouraged any attempt of the kind. Cornwallis, therefore, gave up the pursuit, distributed the German troops along the left bank of the river and stationed his main force at Brunswick, trusting to be able before long to cross the Delaware on the ice.

In further letters to Lee, Washington urged the peril of Philadelphia. "Do come on," writes he; "your arrival may be fortunate, and, if it can be effected without delay, it may be the means of preserving a city whose loss must prove of the most fatal consequence to the cause of America."

Putnam was now detached to take command of Philadelphia and put it in a state of defence and Mifflin to have charge of the munitions of war deposited there. By their advice Congress hastily adjourned on the 12th of December to meet again on the 20th at Baltimore.

Washington's whole force at this time, was about 5500 men; 1000 of them Jersey militia; 1500 militia from Philadelphia, and a battalion of 500 of the German yeomanry of Pennsylvania. Gates, he was informed, was coming on with seven regiments detached by Schuyler from the Northern department; reinforced by these and the troops under Lee, he hoped to be able to attempt a stroke upon the enemy's forces.

Lee, though nearly three weeks had elapsed since he had received Washington's orders to join him with all possible despatch, was no farther than Morristown, where, with militia recruits, his force was about 4000 men. In a letter on the 8th of December he writes from Chatham to Washington: "I am extremely shocked to hear that your force is so inadequate to the necessity of your situation. . . . Your last letters proposing a plan of surprises and forced marches convinced me that there was no danger of your being obliged to pass the Delaware; in consequence of which proposals, I have put myself in a position the most convenient to co-operate with you by attacking their rear. I cannot persuade myself that Philadelphia is their object at present. . . . It will be difficult, I am afraid, to join you; but cannot I do you more service by attacking their rear?"

This letter received an instant reply from Washington. "Philadelphia, beyond all question, is the object of the enemy's movements and nothing less than our utmost exertions will prevent General Howe from possessing it. The force I have is weak and utterly incompetent to that end. I must, therefore, entreat you to push on with every possible succor you can bring."

On the 9th Lee, still at Chatham, received information from Heath that three regiments under Gates had arrived from Albany at Peekskill. He instantly writes to him to forward them without loss of time to Morristown: "I am in hopes," adds he, "to re-conquer (if I may so express myself) the Jerseys."

On the 11th, Lee writes to Washington from Morristown, where he says his troops had been obliged to halt two days for want of shoes. He now talked of making his way to the ferry above Burlington, where boats should be sent up from Philadelphia to receive him.

"I am much surprised," writes Washington in reply, "that you should be in any doubt respecting the route you should take after the information you have received upon that head. A large number of boats . . . is still retained at Tinicum . . . to facilitate your passage across the Delaware. I have so frequently mentioned our situation, and the necessity of your aid, that it is painful for me to add a word on the subject. . . . Congress have directed Philadelphia to be defended to the last extremity. The fatal consequences that must attend its loss are but too obvious to every one; your arrival may be the means of saving it."

Three of the regiments under Gates, as we have shown, were ordered by Lee to Morristown and Gates landed the remaining four at Esopus, whence he took a back route by the Delaware and the Minisink. On the 11th of December, detained by a heavy snow storm and cut off from all information respecting the adverse armies, he detached Major Wilkinson to seek Washington's camp with a letter stating the force under his command and inquiring what route he should take. Wilkinson, finding obstacles in his way to the commander-in-chief, determined to seek the second in command and ask orders from Lee. Lee, who, having decamped from Morristown on the 12th, had marched no further than Vealtown, eight miles distant. There he left Sullivan with the troops while he took up his quarters three miles off at a tavern at Baskingridge. As there was not a British cantonment within twenty miles, he took but a small guard, thinking himself perfectly secure.

About four o'clock in the morning, Wilkinson arrived at his quarters. He was presented to the general as he lay in bed, and delivered into his hands the letter of Gates. Lee, naturally indolent, lingered in bed until eight o'clock. From various delays they did not sit down to breakfast before ten o'clock. After breakfast, while Lee sat writing a reply to Gates, Wilkinson was looking out of a window down a lane leading from the house to the main road. Suddenly a party of British dragoons turned a corner of the avenue at a full charge. "Here, sir, are the British cavalry!" exclaimed Wilkinson. "Where?" replied Lee. "Around the house!"—for they had opened file and surrounded it. The guards, alas, chilled by the frosty morning, had stacked their arms and repaired to the south side of a house on the opposite side of the road to sun themselves and were now chased by the dragoons in different directions. In fact, a tory, who had visited the general the evening before to complain of the loss of a horse taken by the army, having found where Lee was to lodge and breakfast, had ridden in the night to Brunswick and had piloted back Colonel Harcourt with his dragoons.

Wilkinson took his stand, a pistol in each hand, resolved to shoot the first and second assailant and then appeal to his sword. He heard a voice declare, "If the general does not surrender in five minutes, I will set fire to the house!" After a short pause the threat was repeated with a solemn oath. Within two minutes he heard it proclaimed, "Here is the general, he has surrendered."

The general, bareheaded and in his slippers and blanket coat, was mounted on Wilkinson's horse and the troop clattered off with their prisoner to Brunswick.

On the departure of the troops, Wilkinson, finding the coast clear, mounted the first horse he could find and rode full speed in quest of Sullivan, whom he found under march toward Pluckamin. Sullivan, having read Lee's letter to Gates, advised him to rejoin Gates without delay; for his own part, being now in command, he changed his route and pressed forward to join the commander-in-chief.

The loss of Lee was a severe shock to the Americans, many of whom looked to him as the man who was to rescue them from their desperate situation. Some at first suspected that he had exposed himself unguardedly by design, but this was soon disproved by the rigorous treatment by the British, who considered him a deserter, having formerly served in their army.

Lee was a man of brilliant talents, shrewd sagacity, and much knowledge and experience in the art of war, but he was wilful and uncertain in his temper, self-indulgent in his habits, and an egoist in warfare, boldly dashing for a soldier's glory rather than acting for a country's good. He wanted those great moral qualities which, in addition to military capacity, inspired such universal confidence in the wisdom, rectitude and patriotism of Washington, enabling him to direct legislative bodies as well as armies, to harmonize a wide and imperfect confederacy, and to cope with the varied exigencies of the Revolution.

In a letter to his brother Augustine, Washington speaks of the critical state of affairs: "If every nerve is not strained to recruit the army with all possible expedition, I think the game is pretty nearly up. . . . However, under a full persuasion of the justice of our cause, I cannot entertain an idea that it will finally sink, though it may remain for some time under a cloud."

PART VII

(CHAPTERS 31–40)

The Turning Point
[1776–1777]

—⟨∞⟩—

Fortunately, Congress, prior to adjournment, had resolved
that "until they should otherwise order, General Washington
should be possessed of all power to order and direct all things
relative to the department and to the operations of war." Thus
empowered, he proceeded immediately to recruit three battalions
of artillery. To those whose terms were expiring, he promised an
augmentation of twenty-five per cent upon their pay and a bounty of
ten dollars to the men for six weeks' service.

The promise of increased pay and bounties had kept together
for a time the dissolving army. The local militia began to turn out.
Cadwalader brought a large volunteer detachment, well equipped,
principally of Philadelphia troops. Washington assigned him an
important station at Bristol, with Reed as an associate, charged to
keep a watchful eye upon Donop's Hessians cantoned along the
opposite shore from Bordentown to the Black Horse.

On the 20th of December arrived Sullivan in camp with the
troops recently commanded by Lee. They were in a miserable
plight, destitute of almost every thing. About 400 of them, Rhode
Islanders, were sent to reinforce Cadwalader. On the same day

arrived Gates with the remnants of four regiments from the Northern army.

The time seemed propitious for the *coup de main* which Washington had of late been meditating. Every thing showed careless confidence on the part of the enemy. Howe was in winter quarters at New York. His troops, loosely cantoned about the Jerseys from the Delaware to Brunswick, could not readily act in concert on a sudden alarm. The Hessians were in the advance, stationed along the Delaware, facing the American lines along the west bank. Cornwallis had obtained leave of absence and was at New York preparing to embark for England. Washington had now about 6000 men fit for service; with these he meditated to cross the river at night at different points and make simultaneous attacks upon the Hessians.

He calculated upon the eager support of his troops, who were burning to revenge the outrages on their homes and families committed by these foreign mercenaries. They considered the Hessians mere hirelings, actuated by no sentiment of patriotism or honor, who had rendered themselves the horror of the Jerseys by rapine, brutality, and heartlessness.

A brigade of three Hessian regiments, those of Rahl, Lossberg, and Knyphausen, was stationed at Trenton. Rahl had command of the post in consequence of the laurels he had gained at White Plains and Fort Washington, but he, with all his bravery, was little fitted for such an important command. He lacked the necessary vigilance and forecast. Rahl was a boon companion; he made merry until a late hour in the night and then lay in bed until nine o'clock in the morning. He took no precautions against the possibility of being attacked. "An assault by the rebels!" he jested, "Let them come! We'll at them with the bayonet."

Such was the posture of affairs at Trenton at the time the *coup de main* was meditated. Whatever was to be done, however, must be done quickly, before the river was frozen. An intercepted letter convinced Washington of what he had before suspected, that Howe was only waiting to cross the river on the ice and push on triumphantly to Philadelphia.

He communicated his project to Gates and wished him to go to Bristol to take command there. Gates, however, pleaded ill health and requested leave to proceed to Philadelphia. The request may have surprised Washington, but Gates had a disinclination to serve immediately under the commander-in-chief; like Lee, he had an impatience of his supremacy. He had, moreover, an ulterior object in view. Disappointed and chagrined in finding himself subordinate to Schuyler in the Northern campaign, he was now intent on making interest among the members of Congress for an independent command. Washington urged that, on his way to Philadelphia, he would stop for a day or two at Bristol to concert a plan of operations with Reed and Cadwalader, but he does not appear to have complied even with this request. He set out for Baltimore on the 24th of December, the very day before that of the intended *coup de main*. He believed that, instead of attempting to stop Howe at the Delaware, Washington ought to retire to the south of the Susquehanna and there form an army. It was his intention to propose this measure to Congress at Baltimore. Here we have somewhat of a counterpart to Lee's project of eclipsing the commander-in-chief. Evidently the two military veterans considered the truncheon of command falling from his grasp.

The projected attack upon the Hessian posts was to be threefold: *1st*. Washington was to cross the Delaware with a considerable force at McKonkey's Ferry (now Taylorsville), and march nine miles down to Trenton, where Rahl's cantonment comprised a brigade of 1500 Hessians, a troop of British light-horse, and a number of chasseurs. *2d*. Ewing, with a body of Pennsylvania militia, was to cross at a ferry a mile below Trenton, secure the bridge over the Assunpink, a stream along the south side of the town, and cut off any retreat of the enemy in that direction. *3d*. Putnam, with the troops occupied in fortifying Philadelphia and those under Cadwalader, was to cross below Burlington and attack the lower posts under Donop. The several divisions were to cross the Delaware at night so as to be ready for simultaneous action by five o'clock in the morning.

Symptoms of an insurrection in Philadelphia obliged Putnam to remain with some force in that city, but he detached about 600 Pennsylvania militia under Colonel Griffin, to co-operate with Cadwalader.

It has been said that Christmas night was fixed upon for the enterprise because the Germans are prone to revel on that festival and it was supposed a great part of the troops would be intoxicated; but in truth Washington would have chosen an earlier day, had it been in his power. "We could not ripen matters for the attack before the time mentioned," said he in his letter to Reed.

Early on the eventful evening (Dec. 25th), the troops destined for Washington's part of the attack, about 2400 strong, with a train of 20 small pieces, were near McKonkey's Ferry, ready to pass as soon as it grew dark. Washington repaired to the ground accompanied by Greene, Sullivan, Mercer, Stephen, and Stirling. It was, indeed, an anxious moment for all.

Boats being in readiness, the troops began to cross about sunset. The weather was intensely cold; the wind was high, the current strong, and the river full of floating ice. Glover, with his amphibious regiment of Marblehead fisherman, was in the advance; with all their skill and experience, the crossing was difficult and perilous. Washington, who had crossed with the troops, stood anxiously on the eastern bank while one precious hour after another elapsed. The night was dark and tempestuous; the drifting ice drove the boats out of their course and threatened them with destruction.

It was three o'clock before the artillery was landed and nearly four before the troops took up their line of march. Trenton, nine miles distant, could not be reached before daylight. To surprise it, therefore, was out of the question. There was no making a retreat without being discovered and harassed in repassing the river. Beside, the troops from the other points might have crossed and co-operation was essential to their safety. Washington resolved to push forward and trust to Providence.

He formed the troops into two columns. The first he led himself, accompanied by Greene, Stirling, Mercer, and Stephen; it was to make a circuit by the upper road to the north of Trenton. The other led by Sullivan was to take the lower or river road, leading to the west end of the town. Sullivan's column was to halt a few moments at a cross-road leading to Howland's Ferry to give Washington's column time to effect its circuit so that the attack might be simultaneous. On arriving at Trenton, they were to force

WASHINGTON CROSSING THE DELAWARE.

From the original drawing in possession of the Publisher for "Irving's Life of Washington".

NEW YORK. G. P. PUTNAM.

the outer guards and push directly into the town before the enemy had time to form.

It began to hail and snow as the troops commenced their march, and increased in violence as they advanced, the storm driving the sleet in their faces. The day dawned by the time Sullivan halted at the cross-road. It was discovered that the storm had rendered many of the muskets wet and useless. "What is to be done?" inquired Sullivan of St. Clair. "Push on and use the bayonet," was the reply. Sullivan despatched an officer to apprise the commander-in-chief of the condition of their arms. He came back half-dismayed by an indignant burst of Washington, who ordered him to return instantly and tell Sullivan to "advance and charge."

It was about eight o'clock when Washington's column arrived in the vicinity of the village. Washington, who was in front, came to a man chopping wood by the roadside and inquired, "Which way is the Hessian picket?" "I don't know," was the surly reply. "You may tell," said Captain Forest of the artillery, "for that is General Washington." The aspect of the man changed in an instant. Raising his hands to heaven, "God bless and prosper you!" cried he. "The picket is in that house and the sentry stands near that tree."

The advance guard was led by Captain William Washington, seconded by Lieutenant James Monroe (in after years President of the United States). They received orders to dislodge the picket. The sentries were not alert enough and the enemy scarcely had time to scramble to their arms. "Der feind! der feind! heraus! heraus!" (the enemy! the enemy! turn out! turn out!) was now the cry. Seeing heavy battalions at hand, the Hessians fell back upon a company stationed to support the picket, which appears to have been no better prepared against surprise.

By this time the American artillery was unlimbered; Washington kept beside it and the column proceeded. The report of fire-arms told that Sullivan was at the lower end of the town. Stark led his advance guard and did it in gallant style. The attacks, as concerted, were simultaneous. The outposts were driven in; they retreated, firing from behind houses. The Hessian drums beat to arms; the trumpets of the light-horse sounded the alarm; the whole place was in an uproar. Some of the enemy made a wild and undirected fire from the windows of their quarters; others rushed forth in disorder and attempted to form in the main street, while dragoons hastily mounted and galloping about, added to the confusion. Washington advanced with his column to the head of King Street; when Forest's battery of six guns was opened the general kept on the left and advanced with it, giving directions to the fire. His position was an exposed one and he was repeatedly entreated to fall back; all such entreaties were useless.

The enemy were training a couple of cannon in the main street to form a battery, which might have given the Americans a serious check. Captain Washington and Lieutenant Monroe, with a part of the advance guard, rushed forward, drove the artillerists from their guns, and took the two pieces when on the point of being fired. Both officers were wounded, the captain in the wrist, the lieutenant in the shoulder.

While Washington advanced on the north of the town, Sullivan approached on the west and detached Stark to press on the south end of the town. The British light-horse and about 500 Hessians and chasseurs had been quartered in the lower part of the town. Seeing Washington's column pressing in front and hearing Stark thundering in their rear, they took headlong flight by the bridge across the Assunpink toward Donop's encampment at Bordentown. Had Washington's plan been carried into full effect, their retreat would have been cut off by Ewing, but that officer had been prevented from crossing the river by the ice.

Rahl completely lost his head in the confusion of the surprise. He was endeavoring to rally his panic-stricken and disordered men but was himself sorely bewildered. With some difficulty he succeeded in extricating his troops from the town; a rapid retreat by the Princeton road was apparently in his thoughts, but the idea of flying before the rebels was intolerable. Some one, too, exclaimed at the ruinous loss of leaving all their baggage to be plundered by the enemy. Changing his mind, he made a rash resolve. "All grenadiers, forward!" cried he and went back upon the town.

He led his grenadiers bravely but rashly on, when, in the midst of his career, he received a fatal wound from a musket ball. His men, left without their chief, were struck with dismay; heedless of the orders of the second in command, they retreated up the banks of the Assunpink, intending to escape to Princeton. Washington saw their design and threw Hand's Pennsylvania rifleman in their way, while a body of Virginia troops gained their left. Brought to a stand and perfectly bewildered, the Hessians grounded their arms and surrendered.

The skirmishing had now ceased in every direction. The number of prisoners taken in this affair was nearly 1000, of which 32 were officers. Washington's triumph, however, was impaired by the failure of the two simultaneous attacks. Ewing, who was to have crossed at Trenton Ferry and taken the bridge over which the light-horse and Hessians retreated, was prevented by the quantity of ice in the river. Cadwalader was hindered by the same obstacle. He got part of his troops over but found it impossible to embark his cannon and was obliged, therefore, to return to the Pennsylvania side of the river. Had he and Ewing crossed, Donop's quarters would have been beaten up and the fugitives from Trenton intercepted.

By the failure of this part of his plan, Washington had been exposed to the most imminent hazard. The force with which he had crossed, 2400 men, raw troops, was not enough to cope with the veteran garrison had it been on guard. Nothing saved him but the utter panic of the enemy. Even now that the place was in his possession he dared not linger in it. There was a superior force under Donop below him and a strong battalion of infantry at Princeton. His own troops were exhausted by the operations of the night and morning in cold, rain, snow and storm. Washington gave up, therefore, all idea of pursuing the enemy or keeping possession of Trenton and determined to recross the Delaware with his prisoners and captured artillery. Understanding that the brave but unfortunate Rahl was in a dying state, he paid him a visit before leaving Trenton, accompanied by Greene. They found him in the house of a Quaker family. The consideration and unaffected sympathy manifested by them soothed the feelings of the unfortunate soldier now stripped of his laurels and resigned to die rather than outlive his honor.

The Hessian prisoners were conveyed across the Delaware into

Pennsylvania to Newtown. They were subsequently transferred from place to place until they reached Winchester in the interior of Virginia. Wherever they arrived, people thronged to see these terrible beings of whom they had received such formidable accounts. They had to endure the hootings and revilings of the multitude for having hired themselves out to the trade of blood. "At length," writes a Hessian corporal in his journal, "General Washington had written notices put up . . . that we were innocent of this war and had joined in it . . . through compulsion. We should, therefore, be treated not as enemies but friends." From this time, adds he, things went better. "Every day came many out of the towns, old and young, rich and poor, and brought us provisions, and treated us with kindness and humanity."

Colonel Griffin, who had thrown himself into the Jerseys with his detachment of Pennsylvania militia, found himself, through the scanty number of his troops, unable to render efficient service in the proposed attack. He sent word to Cadwalader, therefore, that he should probably render him more aid by drawing Donop off so far as to be unable to support Rahl.

He accordingly presented himself in sight of Donop's cantonment on the 25th of December and succeeded in drawing him out with nearly his whole force of 2000 men. He then retired slowly, skirmishing but avoiding an action, until he had lured him as far as Mount Holly, when he left him to find his way back to his post.

The cannonade of Washington's attack in Trenton on the morning of the 26th was distinctly heard at Cawalader's camp at Bristol. Tidings of the result produced the highest exultation and excitement. Cadwalader made another attempt to cross the river and join Washington, whom he supposed to be still in the Jerseys. He could not effect the passage of the river until the 27th, when he received from Washington a detailed account of his success and of his having recrossed into Pennsylvania.

Cadwalader was now in a dilemma. Donop, he presumed, was still at Mount Holly, but he might soon march back. His forces were equal, if not superior, in number to his own and veterans instead of raw militia. But then there was the importance of the relief of the

Jerseys and the salvation of Philadelphia. Beside, Washington, in all probability, had again crossed into the Jerseys and might be acting offensively.

Reed relieved Cadwalader from his dilemma by proposing that they push on to Burlington and there determine whether to proceed to Bordentown or Mount Holly. The plan was adopted.

Reed and his companions spurred on to reconnoitre the enemy's outposts, about four miles from Burlington, but pulled up at the place where the picket was usually stationed. They found the place deserted. From the people in the neighborhood they received an explanation. Donop had returned from the pursuit of Griffin, only to hear of the disaster at Trenton. He immediately began a retreat in the utmost panic and confusion. The troops in the neighborhood of Burlington had decamped precipitately the preceding evening.

Reed sent back intelligence of this to Cadwalader and pushed on with his companions. At Bordentown not an enemy was to be seen; the fugitives from Trenton had spread a panic on the 26th and the Hessians and their refugee adherents had fled in confusion. One of Reed's companions returned to Cadwalader, who had halted at Burlington, and advised him to proceed.

Cadwalader wrote in the night to Washington, informing him of his whereabouts. "If you should think proper to cross over," added he, " . . . a pursuit would keep up the panic. . . . If we can drive them from West Jersey, the success will raise an army next spring and establish the credit of the Continental money to support it."

There was another letter from Cadwalader, dated the following day, from Bordentown. He had 1800 men with him. Five hundred more were on the way to join him. Mifflin, too, had sent over 500 from Philadelphia, and 300 from Burlington, and was to follow with about 800 more.

Reed, too, wrote from Trenton on the 28th. He had found that place without a single soldier and urged Washington to recross the river and pursue the advantages gained. Donop might be overtaken before he could reach Princeton or Brunswick, where the enemy were yet in force.

Washington needed no prompting of the kind. Bent upon

following up his blow, he had written to McDougall and Maxwell at Morristown to collect as large a body of militia as possible and harass the enemy in flank and rear. Heath, also, had been ordered to abandon the Highlands, which there was no need of guarding at this season of the year, and hasten down with the eastern militia as rapidly as possible by way of Hackensack, continuing until further orders. Men of influence also were despatched into different parts of the Jerseys to spirit up the militia to revenge the oppression, the ravage, and insults they had experienced from the enemy, especially from the Hessians.

On the 29th, Washington's troops began to cross the river. It would be a slow and difficult operation, owing to the ice; two parties of light troops therefore were detached in advance, whom Reed was to send in pursuit of the enemy. They marched into Trenton and were immediately put on the traces of Donop to harass him until other troops should come up. Cadwalader detached a party of riflemen from Bordentown with like orders. Donop, in retreating, divided his force, sending one part to Princeton and hurrying on with the remainder to Brunswick. It was a service of delight to the American troops to hunt back these Hessians over ground which they themselves had trodden so painfully and despondingly in their retreat.

While this was going on, Washington was effecting the passage of his main force to Trenton. He had crossed on the 29th of December, but it took two days more to get the troops and artillery over the icy river. And now came a perplexity. With the year expired the term of several regiments which had seen most service and become inured to danger. Knowing how indispensable were such troops to lead on those which were raw and undisciplined, Washington had them invited to re-enlist. They were haggard with fatigue and hardship, and their hearts yearned for home. By the persuasions of their officers, however, and a bounty of ten dollars, the greater proportion were induced to remain six weeks longer.

At this critical moment too, Washington received a letter from a committee of Congress, transmitting resolves dated the 27th of December, investing him with military powers quite dictatorial. "Happy is it for this country," write the committee, "that the general of their forces can safely be intrusted with the most unlimited power, and neither personal security, liberty or property be in the least degree endangered thereby."

Washington's acknowledgment of this great mark of confidence was noble and characteristic. "Instead of thinking myself freed from all civil obligations by this mark of their confidence, I shall constantly bear in mind that, as the sword was the last resort for the preservation of our liberties, so it ought to be the first thing laid aside when those liberties are firmly established."

(CHAPTER 32)

General Howe was taking his ease in winter quarters at New York, waiting for the freezing of the Delaware to pursue his triumphant march to Philadelphia when tidings were brought him of the surprise and capture of the Hessians at Trenton. He instantly stopped Cornwallis, who was embarking for England, and sent him back in all haste to resume command in the Jerseys.

The ice in the Delaware impeded the crossing of the American troops and gave the British time to draw in their scattered cantonments and assemble their force at Princeton. While his troops were yet crossing, Washington sent Reed to reconnoitre the position and movements of the enemy. Six of the Philadelphia light-horse volunteered to accompany Reed. Emerging from a wood almost within view of Princeton, they caught sight of red coats passing from a barn to a dwelling house. Here must be an outpost. They dashed up without being discovered and surrounded it. Twelve British dragoons within were so panic-stricken that they surrendered without making defence. Important information was obtained from the prisoners. Cornwallis had joined Grant the day before at Princeton with a reinforcement of chosen troops. They had now about 8000 men, and were pressing waggons for a march upon Trenton.

Word, too, was brought from other quarters that Howe was on

the march with 1000 light troops, with which he had landed at Amboy.

The situation of Washington was growing critical. The enemy were beginning to advance their large pickets towards Trenton. The force with him was small; to retreat across the river would destroy the hope awakened by the late exploit, but to make a stand without reinforcements was impossible. In this emergency, he called to his aid Cadwalader and Mifflin with their forces, amounting to about 3600 men. They promptly answered his call, and, marching in the night, joined him on the 1st of January.

Washington chose a position for his main body on the east side of the Assunpink. There was a narrow stone bridge across it, where the water was very deep. He planted his artillery so as to command the bridge and the fords. His advance guard was stationed three miles off in a wood, having in front a stream called Shabbakong Creek.

Early on the morning of the 2d, came word that Cornwallis was approaching. Strong parties were sent out under Greene, who skirmished with the enemy and harassed them in their advance. By twelve o'clock the enemy reached the Shabbakong and, crossing it and moving forward with rapidity, they pushed on until near the town. Here Hand's corps of several battalions was drawn up and held them for a time in check. All the parties in advance ultimately retreated to the main body on the east side of the Assunpink.

It was nearly sunset before Cornwallis with the head of his army entered Trenton. His rear-guard under Leslie rested at Maiden Head, about six miles distant. He made repeated attempts to cross the Assunpink at the bridge and the fords but was as often repulsed by the artillery. At length they drew off and lighted their camp fires. The Americans did the same. Sir William Erskine, who was with Cornwallis, urged him to attack Washington that evening, but his lordship declined; he felt sure he had at length got Washington into a situation from which he could not escape, but where he might make a desperate stand. He would be sure, he said, to "bag the fox in the morning."

A cannonade was kept up on both sides until dark. When night closed in, the two camps lay in sight of each other's fires. It was the most anxious night that had yet closed in on the American army throughout its series of perils and disasters, for there was no concealing the impending danger. What must have been the feelings of the commander-in-chief as he considered his desperate position? A small stream, fordable in several places, was all that separated his inexperienced army from an enemy vastly superior in numbers and discipline. A general action must be ruinous, but how was he to retreat? Behind him was the Delaware, impassable from floating ice. Granting even that a retreat across it could be effected, the Jerseys would be left in possession of the enemy, endangering Philadelphia and sinking the public mind into despondency.

In this dark moment a gleam of hope flashed upon his mind; a bold expedient suggested itself. Almost the whole enemy force must by this time be drawn out of Princeton, advancing toward Trenton, while their baggage and principal stores must remain weakly guarded at Brunswick. Was it not possible by a rapid night-march along the Quaker road, a different road from that on which Leslie with the rear-guard was resting, to come by surprise on those left at Princeton, capture or destroy what stores were left there, and then push on to Brunswick? This would save the army from being cut off and might draw the enemy away from Trenton, while some fortunate stroke might give additional reputation to the American arms.

Such was the plan which Washington laid before his officers in a council of war. It met with instant concurrence, being of that hardy, adventurous kind which seems congenial with the American character. The baggage of the army was silently removed to Burlington and every preparation was made for a rapid march. To deceive the enemy, men were to dig trenches near the bridge within hearing of the British sentries, working noisily until daybreak; others were to go the rounds, relieve guards at the bridge and fords, keep up the camp fires, and maintain the appearance of a regular encampment. At daybreak they were to hasten after the army.

In the dead of the night, the army quietly began its march. Mercer was in the advance with the remnant of his flying camp, now but about 350 men. The main body followed, under Washington's immediate command.

It was near sunrise of a bright, frosty morning when Washington reached the bridge over Stony Brook, three miles from Princeton. After crossing the bridge, he led his troops along the brook to the edge of a wood, where a by-road which led off on the right through low grounds was a short cut to Princeton and less exposed to view. By this road Washington defiled with the main body, ordering Mercer to continue along the brook with his brigade until he should arrive at the main road, where he was to secure and, if possible, destroy a bridge over which it passes so as to intercept fugitives from Princeton and check any retrograde movements of the British troops which might have advanced towards Trenton.

Three regiments of the enemy, the 17th, 40th, and 55th, with three troops of dragoons, had been quartered all night in Princeton, under marching orders to join Cornwallis in the morning. The 17th regiment, under Colonel Mawhood, was already on the march; the 55th regiment was preparing to follow. Mawhood had crossed the bridge by which the main road to Trenton passes over Stony Brook and was proceeding through a wood when, as he attained the summit of a hill, the glittering of arms betrayed Mercer's troops to the left, who were filing along the road to secure the bridge as they had been ordered. The woods prevented him from seeing their number. He supposed them to be some broken portions of the army flying before Cornwallis. With this idea, he made a retrograde movement to intercept them, while messengers spurred off to hasten forward the regiments still at Princeton so as completely to surround them.

The woods concealed him until he had recrossed the bridge of Stony Brook, when he came in full sight of the van of Mercer's brigade. Both parties pushed to get possession of a rising ground on the right. The Americans, being nearest, reached it first and formed behind a hedge fence, whence, being chiefly armed with rifles, they opened a destructive fire. It was returned with great spirit by the enemy. At the first discharge Mercer was dismounted, his horse being crippled by a musket ball in the leg. One of his colonels was mortally wounded and carried to the rear. Availing themselves of the confusion thus occasioned, the British charged with the bayonet; the American riflemen, having no weapon of the kind, were thrown into disorder and retreated. Mercer, who was on foot, endeavored to rally them, when a blow from the butt end of a musket felled him; he was bayoneted repeatedly and left for dead.

Mawhood pursued the retreating troops to the brow of the rising ground, when he beheld a large force advancing to the rescue. It was a body of Pennsylvania militia, which Washington, on hearing the firing, had detached to support Mercer. Mawhood ceased pursuit, drew up his artillery, and by a heavy discharge brought the militia to a stand.

At this moment Washington himself arrived at the scene of action, having galloped in advance of his troops. He beheld Mercer's troops retreating and the detachment of militia checked by Mawhood's artillery. He dashed past the hesitating militia, waving his hat and cheering them on. Galloping forward under the fire of Mawhood's battery, he called upon Mercer's broken brigade; the Pennsylvanians rallied and caught fire from his example. At the same time the 7th Virginia regiment emerged from the wood and moved forward with loud cheers, while a fire of grapeshot was opened by Captain Moulder of the American artillery from the brow of a ridge to the south.

Mawhood, who a moment before had thought his triumph secure, found himself assailed on every side and separated from the other British regiments. He forced his way at the point of the bayonet through gathering foes, though with heavy loss, back to the main road and was in full retreat towards Trenton to join Cornwallis. Washington detached Major Kelly with a party of Pennsylvania troops to destroy the bridge at Stony Brook over which Mawhood had retreated so as to impede the advance of Leslie from Maiden Head.

In the mean time the 55th regiment, which had been on the left and nearer Princeton, had been encountered by the American advance-guard under St. Clair and, after some sharp fighting, was retreating to Brunswick. The remaining regiment, the 40th, had not been able to come up in time for the action; part fled toward Brunswick; the residue took refuge in the college at Princeton. Artillery was brought to bear on the college and a few shot compelled those within to surrender.

Mercer was said to be either dead or dying in a house whither he had been conveyed by his aide-de-camp, who found him, after the retreat of Mawhood's troops, lying on the field gashed with several wounds. Washington would have ridden back to have Mercer conveyed to a place of greater security, but was assured that, if alive, he was too wounded to bear removal; in the mean time he was in good hands.

Under these circumstances Washington felt compelled to leave his old companion in arms to his fate. Indeed, he was called away by the exigencies of his command, having to pursue the regiments which were making a headlong retreat to Brunswick. In this pursuit he took the lead at the head of a detachment of cavalry. At Kingston, he held a council of war on horseback. Should he keep on to Brunswick or not? The capture of the British stores and baggage would make his triumph complete but, on the other hand, his troops were excessively fatigued by their rapid march all night and hard fight in the morning. All of them had been without sleep and many were half-starved. They were without blankets, thinly clad, some of them barefooted, in freezing weather. Cornwallis would be upon them before they could reach Brunswick. Under these considerations, it was determined to discontinue the pursuit and push for Morristown. There they would be in a mountainous country, heavily wooded, with various defiles by which they might change their position according to enemy movements.

Filing off to the left from Kingston, and breaking down the bridges behind him, Washington took the narrow road by Rocky Hill to Pluckamin, where he halted for a time to allow them a little repose and refreshment.

While they are taking breath we will cast our eyes back to the camp of Cornwallis. His lordship had retired at Trenton with the vaunt that he would "bag the fox in the morning." Nothing could surpass his surprise and chagrin when at daybreak the deserted camp of the Americans told him that the prize had evaded his grasp, that the general whose military skill he had decried had out-generaled him.

For a time he could not learn whither the army had directed its

Eng.d by R. Thew.

BATTLE OF PRINCETON — DEATH OF MERCER.

[From the original picture by Col. J. Trumbull]

Printed by W. Pate.

NEW YORK G.P. PUTNAM & CO.

stealthy march. By sunrise, however, there was the booming of cannon in the direction of Princeton. The idea flashed upon him that Washington was about to make a dash at Brunswick. Alarmed for the safety of his military stores, his lordship made a rapid march towards Princeton. As he arrived in sight of the bridge over Stony Brook, he beheld Kelly and his party busy in its destruction. A discharge of round shot from his field-pieces drove them away but the bridge was already broken. It would take time to repair it for the passage of the artillery, so Cornwallis urged his troops breasthigh through the turbulent and icy stream, and again pushed forward, eager to save his magazines. Crossing the bridge at Kingston, he kept on along the Brunswick road, supposing Washington still before him. The latter, however, had got far in the advance and the alteration of his course at Kingston had carried him completely out of the way of Cornwallis. His lordship reached Brunswick towards evening and endeavored to console himself by the safety of the military stores for being so completely foiled and out-manoeuvred.

Washington, in the mean time, was calling out aid to follow up his successes. In a letter to Putnam, he says: "The enemy appear to be panic-struck. I am in hopes of driving them out of the Jerseys. March the troops under your command to Crosswicks, and keep a strict watch upon the enemy in this quarter." To Heath, who was stationed in the Highlands of the Hudson, he wrote: "The enemy are in great consternation; . . . it has been determined in council that you should move down towards New York with a considerable force, as if you had a design upon the city. That being an object of great importance, the enemy will be reduced to the necessity of withdrawing a considerable part of their force from the Jerseys, if not the whole, to secure the city."

These letters despatched, he continued to Morristown, where he learnt that Mercer was still alive. He immediately sent his nephew, Major George Lewis, under the protection of a flag to attend upon him. Lewis found him in great pain; he had been treated with respect by the enemy and great tenderness by the benevolent family who had sheltered him. He expired in the arms of Major Lewis on the 12th of January, in the fifty-sixth year of his age.

From Morristown, Washington wrote to Heath, repeating his

former orders. To Lincoln, also, who was just arrived at Peekskill and had command of the Massachusetts militia, he writes on the 7th, "General Heath will communicate mine of this date to you, by which you will find that the greater part of your troops are to move down towards New York, to draw the attention of the enemy to that quarter. . . . If we can oblige them to evacuate the Jerseys, we must drive them to the utmost distress, for they have depended upon the supplies from that State for their winter's support."

Reed was ordered to send out rangers and bodies of militia to scour the country, waylay foraging parties, cut off supplies, and keep the cantonments of the enemy in a state of seige.

The expedition under General Heath toward New York, from which much had been anticipated by Washington, proved a failure. It arrived at the enemy's outposts at King's Bridge. There was some skirmishing, but the feature of the expedition was a pompous summons of Fort Independence to surrender. The garrison made no answer but an occasional cannonade. Heath failed to follow up his summons by corresponding deeds. He hovered and skirmished for some days about the outposts and Spyt den Duivel Creek, and then retired before a threatened snow-storm and the report of an enemy's fleet from Rhode Island, with troops under Percy, who might land in Westchester and take the besieging force in rear.

Though disappointed in this part of his plan, Washington, having received reinforcements of militia, continued to carry on his system of annoyance. The situation of Cornwallis, who, but a short time before, traversed the Jerseys so triumphantly, became daily more irksome. Spies were in his camp to give notice of every movement and foes without to take advantage of it; not a foraging party could sally forth without being waylaid. By degrees he drew in his troops and collected them at New Brunswick and Amboy so as to have a communication by water with New York, whence he was now compelled to draw nearly all his supplies.

The recent operations in the Jerseys had suddenly changed the whole aspect of the war and given a triumphant close to what had been a disastrous campaign. The troops, which had been driven from post to post, had all at once turned upon their pursuers and astounded them by brilliant stratagems and daring exploits. The commander, whose cautious policy had been sneered at by enemies and regarded with impatience by misjudging friends, had all at once shown that he possessed enterprise as well as circumspection and that beneath his wary coldness lurked a fire to break forth at the proper moment. This year's campaign, the most critical one of the war, especially the part which occurred in the Jerseys, was the ordeal that made his great qualities fully appreciated by his countrymen.

(CHAPTER 33)

The British, nearly driven out of the Jerseys, were now hemmed in and held in check by Washington and his handful of men castled among the heights of Morristown. So far from holding territory that they had overrun, they were fain to ask safe conduct across it for a convoy to their soldiers captured in battle. It must have been a severe trial to the pride of Cornwallis when he had to inquire by letter of Washington whether money and stores could be sent to the Hessians captured at Trenton and a surgeon and medicines to the wounded at Princeton. Washington's reply must have conveyed a reproof still more mortifying: No molestation would be offered to the convoy by the regular army under his command, but "he could not answer for the militia, who were resorting to arms in most parts of the State, and were excessively exasperated at the treatment they had met with from both Hessian and British troops."

In fact, the conduct of the enemy had roused the whole country against them. The Hessians plundered friend and foe alike. The British soldiery often followed their example and the plunderings were at times attended by brutal outrages on the weaker sex. The whole State was roused against its invaders. Washington ordered a safe conduct to be given to the Hessian baggage as far as Philadelphia and to the surgeon and medicines to Princeton.

Morristown, where the main army was encamped, had been chosen by Washington merely as a halting-place, but further considerations persuaded him that it was well situated for the system of warfare he meditated and induced him to remain there. It was protected by forests and rugged heights. All approach from the seaboard was rendered difficult and dangerous to a hostile force by a chain of sharp hills. It was nearly equidistant from Amboy, Newark, and Brunswick, the principal posts of the enemy, so that any movement could be met by a counter movement on his part.

He had three faithful generals with him: Greene, Sullivan, and Knox. Washington's military family was composed of his aides-de-camp, Colonels Meade and Tilghman of Philadelphia, and his secretary, Colonel Harrison of Maryland.

Washington's head-quarters at first were in what was called the Freemason's Tavern. His troops were encamped about the vicinity of the village, the main encampment being near Bottle Hill in a sheltered valley which was thickly wooded.

The enemy being now concentrated at New Brunswick and Amboy, Putnam, who had with him but a few hundred men, was ordered by Washington to move from Crosswicks to Princeton, with the troops under his command. He was instructed to draw his forage as much as possible from the neighborhood of Brunswick, thereby contributing to distress the enemy, to have good scouting parties continually on the lookout, and, if compelled to leave Princeton, to retreat towards the mountains to form a junction with the forces at Morristown. Cantonments were gradually formed between Princeton and the Highlands of the Hudson, where Heath had command.

To counteract the proclamation of the British commissioners promising amnesty to all in rebellion who should, in a given time, return to their allegiance, Washington issued a counter proclamation (Jan. 25th), commanding every person who had subscribed a declaration of fidelity to Great Britain, or taken an oath of allegiance, to repair within 30 days to the quarters of any general officer of the Continental army or the militia, there to take the oath of allegiance to the United States of America and give up any protection, certificate, or passport he might have received from the enemy; at the same time permitting all such as preferred the interest and protection of Great Britain to withdraw themselves and families within the enemy's lines. All who should neglect or refuse to comply with this order were to be considered adherents to the crown and treated as common enemies.

A striking contrast was offered throughout the winter and spring between Howe at New York and Washington at Morristown. Howe was a soldier by profession. War, with him, was a career. Easy and indolent by nature, of convivial and luxurious habits, he found himself in good quarters at New York. His officers, too, many of them young men of rank and fortune, gave a gayety and brilliancy to the place in a round of dinners, balls and assemblies.

Washington, on the contrary, was a patriot soldier, grave, earnest, thoughtful, self-sacrificing. War, to him, was a painful remedy, hateful in itself. To the prosecution of it all his pleasures, comforts, natural inclinations and private interests were sacrificed. His officers were earnest like himself, their whole thoughts directed to the struggle in which they were engaged.

So, too, the armies were contrasted. The British troops, all mere men of the sword, were well clad, well housed, and surrounded by all the conveniencies of a thoroughly appointed army. The American troops, for the most part were mere yeomanry, were ill sheltered, ill clad, ill fed and ill paid, with nothing to reconcile them to their hardships but love for the soil they were defending, and the inspiring thought that it was their country.

A cartel for the exchange of prisoners had been a subject of negotiation previous to the affair of Trenton, without being adjusted. The British commanders were slow to recognize the claims to equality of those they considered rebels; Washington was tenacious in holding them up as patriots ennobled by their cause.

Among the cases which came up for attention was that of Ethan Allen, the brave captor of Ticonderoga: thrown into irons as a felon, threatened with a halter, carried to England to be tried for treason, confined in Pendennis Castle, retransported to Halifax, and now a prisoner in New York. "I have suffered every thing short of death," writes he to the Assembly of Connecticut. Washington was instructed, considering his long imprisonment, to urge his exchange.

This had scarce been urged, when tidings of the capture of General Lee presented a case of still greater importance to be provided for. By direction of Congress, he had sent in a flag to inquire about Lee's treatment and to convey him a sum of money. Lee was reported to be in rigorous confinement in New York, and treated with harshness and indignity. The British considered him a deserter, he having been a lieutenant-colonel in their service, although he had resigned his commission before joining the American army.

On the 13th of January, Washington addressed the following letter to Howe. "I am directed by Congress to propose an exchange of five of the Hessian field-officers taken at Trenton for Major-general Lee; or if this proposal should not be accepted, to demand his liberty upon parole, within certain bounds, as has ever been granted to your officers in our custody. I am informed . . . that you . . . look upon him . . . as a deserter from the British service . . . and that you intend to try him as such by a court-martial. . . . I must give you warning that Major-general Lee is looked upon as an officer belonging to, and under the protection of the United Independent States of America, and that any violence you may commit upon his life and liberty will be severely retaliated upon the lives or liberties of the British officers or those of their foreign allies in our hands." In this letter he likewise adverted to the treatment of American prisoners in New York, several who had recently been released having given the most shocking account of the barbarities they had experienced.

Sir William, in reply, proposed to send an officer of rank to Washington, to confer upon a mode of exchange and subsistence of prisoners. "This expedient," observes he, "appearing to me effectual for settling all differences. . . . I trust that in this or in any other event in the course of my command, you will not have just cause to accuse me of inhumanity, prejudice, or passion." His proposal that all disputed points be adjusted by referees, led to the appointment of two officers for the purpose, Colonel Walcott by General Howe and Colonel Harrison by Washington. In the contemplated exchanges was that of one of the Hessian field-officers for Ethan Allen.

Lee's actual treatment was not so harsh as had been represented. He was in close confinement, it is true, but three rooms had been fitted up for him in the Old City Hall of New York, having nothing of the look of a prison excepting that they were secured by bolts and bars. Congress, in the mean time, resorted to their threatened measure of retaliation. On the 20th of February they resolved that the Board of War be directed to order the five Hessian field-officers and Lieutenant-colonel Campbell into safe and close custody, "it being the unalterable resolution of Congress to retaliate on them the same punishment as may be inflicted on the person of General Lee."

In a letter to the President of Congress on the following day, Washington gives his moderating counsels on retaliation. "Though I sincerely commiserate," writes he, "the misfortunes of General Lee, . . . with all possible deference to the opinion of Congress, I fear that these resolutions . . . will, if adhered to, produce consequences of an extensive and melancholy nature. . . . The balance of prisoners is greatly against us and a general regard to the happiness of the whole should mark our conduct. Can we imagine that our enemies will not mete the same punishments, the same indignities, the same cruelties, to those belonging to us in their possession that we impose on theirs in our power?"

Washington was not successful in instilling his wise moderation. Congress adhered to their vindictive policy, merely directing that no other hardships would be inflicted on the captive officers than such confinement as was necessary to carry their resolve into effect. There were other circumstances to produce indignant sensibility on the part of Congress. Accounts were rife of the cruelties and indignities almost invariably experienced by American prisoners at New York, and an active correspondence on the subject was going on between Washington and the British commanders.

The captive Americans who had been in the naval service were said to be confined, officers and men, in prison-ships, which, from their loathsome condition and the horrors and sufferings experienced on board of them, had acquired the appellation of "floating hells." Those who had been in the land service were crowded into jails and dungeons like the vilest malefactors and were represented as pining in cold, filth, hunger and nakedness.

It was denied that prisoners were ill treated but we have heard too many particulars from persons of unquestionable veracity who suffered in the cause to permit us to doubt about the fact. The Jersey Prisonship is proverbial in our revolutionary history; the bones of the patriots who perished on board form a monument on the Long Island shore. The horrors of the Sugar House converted into a prison are traditional in New York; and the brutal tyranny of the provost marshal over men of worth confined in the common jail for the sin of patriotism has been handed down from generation to generation.

That Lord Howe and Sir William were ignorant of the extent of these atrocities we really believe, but it was their duty to be well informed. There is not a doubt, too, that patriot prisoners were regarded as criminals rather than captives. The stigma of "rebels" seemed to take from them all the indulgences usually granted to prisoners of war. It was not until our countrymen had made themselves formidable by their successes that they were treated, when prisoners, with common decency and humanity.

The difficulties arising out of the case of Lee interrupted the operations with regard to the exchange of prisoners; gallant men, on both sides, suffered prolonged detention in consequence, among them Ethan Allen. Events, however, had diminished Lee's importance in the eyes of the enemy. "As the capture of the Hessians and the manoeuvres against the British took place after the surprise of General Lee," observes a London writer of the day, "we find that he is not the only efficient officer in the American service."

The early part of the year brought the annual embarrassments caused by short enlistments. The brief terms of service for which the Continental soldiery had enlisted, at most a year, were expiring; the men were hastening to their homes. Militia had to be the dependence until a new army could be raised and organized; Washington called on the council of safety of Pennsylvania speedily to furnish temporary reinforcements of the kind.

All officers that could be spared were ordered away, some to recruit, some to collect the scattered men of the different regiments who were dispersed. Knox was sent to Massachusetts to expedite raising a battalion of artillery. Different States were urged to levy and equip their quotas for the Continental army. "Nothing but the united efforts of every State in America," writes he, "can save us from disgrace, and probably from ruin."

While anxiously exerting himself to strengthen his own precarious army, the security of the Northern department was urged upon his attention. Schuyler represented it as in need of reinforcements and supplies. He apprehended that Carleton might attack Ticonderoga as soon as he could cross Lake Champlain on the ice; that important fortress was under the command of Colonel Anthony Wayne, but its garrison had dwindled down to about 700 men, chiefly New England militia. Schuyler feared that Carleton might not only succeed in an attempt on Ticonderoga, but might push his way to Albany.

He had written in vain, he said, to the Convention of New York and to the Eastern States for reinforcements, and he entreated Washington to aid him with his influence. Although Washington considered a winter attack too difficult and dangerous to be very probable, he urged reinforcements from Massachusetts and New Hampshire, whence they could be furnished most speedily. Massachusetts, in fact, had already determined to send four regiments to Schuyler's aid as soon as possible. The quota of Massachusetts, under the present arrangement of the army, was 15 regiments; Washington ordered Heath, who was in Massachusetts, to forward them to Ticonderoga as fast as they could be raised.

Notwithstanding all Washington's exertions in behalf of the army under his immediate command, it continued deplorably in want of reinforcements and it was necessary to maintain vigilance at all posts to prevent his camp from being surprised. He anticipated an attack as soon as the roads were passable and apprehended a disastrous result unless speedily reinforced.

As the season advanced, Washington was led to believe that Philadelphia would be their first object of the enemy campaign and that they would bring round all their troops from Canada by water to aid in the enterprise. Under this persuasion he wrote to Heath, ordering him to send eight of the Massachusetts battalions to

Peekskill instead of Ticonderoga, and he explained his reasons in a letter to Schuyler. At Peekskill, he observed, "they would be well placed to give support to any of the Eastern or Middle States; or to oppose the enemy should they design to penetrate the country up the Hudson; or to cover New England, should they invade it. . . . Even should the enemy invade from Canada, the troops at Peekskill would not be badly placed to reinforce Ticonderoga, and cover the country round Albany."

On the 18th of March he despatched Greene to Philadelphia to lay before Congress such matters as he could not venture to communicate by letter. Greene had scarce departed when the enemy began to give signs of life. General Howe now made preparations for the next campaign by detaching troops to destroy the American deposits of military stores. One of the chief of these was at Peekskill, the very place where Washington had directed Heath to send troops from Massachusetts and which he thought of making a central point of assemblage. McDougall had command of it in the absence of Heath but his force did not exceed 250 men.

As soon as the Hudson was clear of ice, a squadron of vessels, with 500 troops under Colonel Bird, ascended the river. McDougall had intelligence of the intended attack and, while the ships were making their way across the Tappan Sea and Haverstraw Bay, removed as much as possible of the provisions and stores to Forts Montgomery and Constitution in the Highlands. On the 23d, the squadron came to anchor in Peekskill Bay and 500 men landed on the south side of the bay, whence they pushed forward with four light field-pieces. On their approach, McDougall set fire to the barracks and principal storehouses and retreated two miles to a strong post commanding the entrance to the Highlands and the road to Continental Village, the place of the deposits. Hence McDougall sent an express to Willet, who had charge of Fort Constitution, to hasten to his assistance.

The British, finding the wharf in flames where they had intended to embark their spoils, completed the conflagration. They kept possession of the place until the following day, when a scouting party which had advanced toward the entrance of the Highlands was encountered by a detachment from Fort Constitution and driven back to the main body after a sharp skirmish. Finding the country around was getting under arms, the enemy re-embarked in the evening and swept down the Hudson.

(CHAPTER 34)

We now enter upon circumstances connected with the Northern department which will be found materially to influence the course of affairs in that quarter throughout the current year. To make these more clear, it is necessary to revert to events in the preceding year.

The question of command between Schuyler and Gates, when settled as we have shown by Congress, had caused no interruption to the harmony between these generals. Schuyler directed the affairs of the department from his head-quarters at Albany, where they had been fixed by Congress, while Gates, subordinate to him, commanded the post of Ticonderoga.

The disappointment of an independent command, however, still rankled in the mind of the latter, and was kept alive by the officious suggestions of meddling friends. In the autumn, his hopes in this respect revived. Schuyler was again disgusted with the service. In the discharge of his duties, he had been annoyed by sectional jealousies and ill-will. His motives and measures had been maligned. The failures in Canada had been attributed to him, and he had repeatedly entreated Congress to order an inquiry into the charges made against him.

On the 14th of September, he offered his resignation of his commission as major-general and of every other office and appointment, still claiming a court of inquiry on his conduct, and expressing his determination to fulfil the duties of a good citizen.

He immediately wrote to Gates, apprising him of his having sent in his resignation. As command of the department would devolve on Gates, he assured him of every assistance in his power to any officer whom Gates might appoint to command in Albany.

The hopes of Gates, inspired by this proffered resignation, were doomed to be overclouded. Schuyler was informed by President Hancock that Congress could not consent to accept his resignation, but "to put calumny to silence, they would at an early day appoint a committee to inquire fully into his conduct, which they trusted would establish his reputation in the opinion of all good men."

Schuyler received the resolve of Congress with grim acquiescence, but was but half soothed. He remained at his post, therefore, discharging the duties of his department with his usual zeal and activity; Gates, at the end of the campaign, had repaired, as we have shown, to the vicinity of Congress to attend the fluctuation of events.

About this time the office of adjutant-general, which had remained vacant ever since the resignation of Reed, to the great detriment of the service, especially now when a new army was to be formed, was offered to Gates, who had formerly filled it with ability; President Hancock informed him by letter of the earnest desire of Congress that he should resume it, retaining his present rank and pay. Gates almost resented the proposal. "I had, last year, the honor to command in the second post in America and had the good fortune to prevent the enemy from making their so much wished-for junction with General Howe. After this, to be expected to dwindle again to the adjutant-general, requires more philosophy on my part, and something more than words on yours."

He wrote to Washington to the same effect, but declared that, should it be his Excellency's wish, he would resume the office with alacrity. Washington promptly replied that he had often wished it in secret though he had never even hinted at it, supposing Gates might have scruples on the subject. "You cannot conceive the pleasure I feel," adds he, "when you tell me that, if it is my desire that you should resume your former office, you will with cheerfulness and alacrity proceed to Morristown." He assures him that he will be glad to receive a line from him mentioning the time he would leave Philadelphia. He received no such line. Gates had a higher object in view.

A letter from Schuyler to Congress informed that body that he should set out for Philadelphia about the 21st of March and should on his arrival require the promised inquiry into his conduct. Gates, who was acquainted with this circumstance, knew Schuyler had given offence to Congress and he knew that he had been offended and had repeatedly talked of resigning. Gates had active friends in Congress ready to push his interests.

While Schuyler was thus in partial eclipse, the House proceeded to appoint a general officer for the Northern department, of which he had stated it to be in need. On the 25th of March, Gates received the following note from President Hancock: "I have it in charge to direct that you repair to Ticonderoga immediately and take command of the army stationed in that department." Gates obeyed with alacrity. Again the vision of an independent command floated before his mind, and he was on his way to Albany at the time that Schuyler, ignorant of this new arrangement, was journeying to Philadelphia.

When Gates arrived in Albany, Colonel Varick, Schuyler's secretary, waited on him with a message from Mrs. Schuyler, inviting him to take up his quarters at the general's house. He declined, as the despatch of affairs required him to be continually in town, but remained in Albany, unwilling to depart for Ticonderoga until there should be sufficient troops there to support him.

Schuyler arrived in Philadelphia in the second week in April and found himself superseded in effect by Gates in the Northern department. He enclosed to the committee of Albany the recent resolutions of Congress, passed before his arrival. "By these," writes he, "you will readily perceive that I shall not return a general." Taking his seat in Congress as a delegate from New York, he demanded the investigation of his conduct during the time he had held a command in the army. It was his intention, when the scrutiny had taken place, to resign his commission and retire from the service. On the 18th, a committee of inquiry was appointed, as at his request, composed of a member from each State.

In the mean time, as second major-general of the United States (Lee being the first), he held active command at Philadelphia, forming a camp on the western side of the Delaware, completing the works on Fort Island, throwing up works on Red Bank, and accelerating the despatch of troops and provisions to the commander-in-chief. During his sojourn at Philadelphia, also, he essentially reorganized the commissary department, digesting rules for its regulation, which were mainly adopted by Congress.

The American struggle for independence was bringing foreign officers as candidates for admission into the patriot army and causing great embarrassment to the commander-in-chief. "They seldom," writes Washington, "bring more than a commission and a passport. . . . Their ignorance of our language and their inability to recruit men are insurmountable obstacles to their being engrafted in our Continental battalions, for our officers . . . would be disgusted if foreigners were put over their head."

Congress determined that no foreign officers should receive commissions who were not well acquainted with the English language and did not bring strong testimonials of their abilities. Still there was embarrassment.

Among the foreign candidates for appointments was Colonel Conway, a native of Ireland, who, according to his own account, had been 30 years in the service of France and claimed to be a chevalier of the order of St. Louis. Mr. Deane, the American commissioner at Paris, had recommended him to Washington as an officer of merit and had written to Congress that he considered him well qualified for the office of adjutant or brigadier-general and that he had given him reason to hope for one of these appointments. Conway pushed for that of brigadier-general. It had been conferred some time before by Congress on two French officers, De Fermoy and Deborre, who, he observed, had been inferior to him in the French service and it would be mortifying now to hold rank below them.

Conway received the rank of brigadier-general, of which he subsequently proved himself unworthy. He was boastful and presumptuous, and became noted for his intrigues and for a despicable cabal against the commander-in-chief, of which we shall have to speak hereafter.

A candidate of a different stamp had presented himself in the preceding year, the gallant Thaddeus Kosciuszko. He was a Pole and had been educated for the profession of arms at the military school at Warsaw and subsequently in France. He came with a letter of introduction from Dr. Franklin to Washington.

"What do you seek here?" inquired the commander-in-chief.

"To fight for American independence."

"What can you do?"

"Try me."

Washington was pleased with the curt, comprehensive reply and with his chivalrous spirit, and at once received him into his family as an aide-de-camp. Congress shortly afterwards appointed him an engineer, with the rank of colonel. He proved a valuable officer throughout the Revolution and won an honorable and lasting name in our country.

Questions of rank among his generals were perpetual sources of perplexity to Washington, too often caused by what Lee termed "the stumblings of Congress." Such was the case at present. In recent army promotions Congress had advanced Stirling, Mifflin, St. Clair, Stephen, and Lincoln to the rank of major-general while Arnold, their senior in service and distinguished by so many brilliant exploits, was passed over and left to remain a brigadier. Washington, supposing it might have been omitted through mistake, wrote to Arnold, who was in Rhode Island, advising him not to take any hasty step and promising his own endeavors to remedy any error that might have been made. He wrote also to Henry Lee in Congress inquiring whether the omission was owing to accident or design.

Arnold was, in truth, deeply wounded by the omission. "I am greatly obliged to your Excellency," writes he to Washington, "for interesting yourself so much in respect to my appointment. . . . Their promoting junior officers to the rank of major-generals, I view as a very civil way of requesting my resignation. . . . My commission was conferred unsolicited and received with pleasure only as a means of serving my country. With equal pleasure I resign it, when I can no longer serve my country with honor. . . . In justice, therefore, to my own character and for the satisfaction of my friends, I must request a court of inquiry into my conduct." He intimated that he should remain at his post until he could leave it without any damage to the public interest.

The principle upon which Congress had proceeded in their recent promotions was explained to Washington. The number of general officers promoted from each State was proportioned to the number of men furnished by it. Connecticut (Arnold's State) had already two major-generals, which was its full share. "I confess," writes Washington to Arnold, "this is a strange mode of reasoning. . . . Your determination not to quit your present command while any danger to the public might ensue . . . justly entitles you to the thanks of the country." An opportunity occurred before long for Arnold again to signalize himself.

The amount of stores destroyed at Peekskill had fallen far short of Howe's expectations. Accordingly, another expedition was set on foot against a still larger deposit at Danbury, within the borders of Connecticut. Ex-governor Tryon, recently commissioned major-general of provincials, conducted it. He had a force 2000 strong and made his appearance on the Sound in April, with a fleet of 26 sail; on the 25th, he landed his troops at the foot of Canepo Hill, near the mouth of the Saugatuck River. The troops set off for Danbury, 23 miles distant, galled at first by a scattering fire behind a stone fence. General Silliman of the Connecticut militia, who resided at Fairfield, sent out expresses to rouse the country. Arnold was at New Haven, on his way to Philadelphia for the purpose of settling his accounts, but at the alarm of a British inroad, he mounted his horse and, accompanied by General Wooster, hastened to join Silliman. As they spurred forward, every farm house sent out its warrior, until upwards of 100 were pressing on with them, full of the fighting spirit. Lieutenant Oswald, Arnold's secretary in the Canada campaign, was at this time at New Haven enlisting men for Lamb's regiment of artillery. He, too, mustering his recruits, marched off with three field-pieces for the scene of action.

In the mean while the British, marching all night with short haltings, reached Danbury in the afternoon of the 26th. There were but 50 Continental soldiers and 100 militia in the place. These retreated, as did most of the inhabitants. There was a great quantity of stores in the village, but no vehicles to convey them to the ships. The work of destruction commenced. Throughout the night there was revel, drunkenness, blasphemy, and devastation. Tryon, aware that the country was rising, ordered a retreat before daylight, setting fire to the magazines to complete the destruction of the stores. The flames spread to the other edifices and almost the whole village was soon in a blaze.

While these scenes had been transacted at Danbury, the Connecticut yeomanry had been gathering. Silliman had advanced at the head of 500. Wooster and Arnold joined him with their followers, as did a few more militia. When they reached Bethel, within 4 miles of Danbury, they halted to take a little repose and put their arms in order rendered almost unserviceable by the rain. Wooster took command as first major-general of the militia of the State. A plan was concerted to punish the enemy on their retreat. At dawn, Wooster detached Arnold with 400 men, to take post at Ridgefield, by which the British must pass, while he with 200 remained to harass them in flank and rear.

The British began their retreat early in the morning. As soon as they had passed his position, Wooster attacked the rear-guard with great spirit and effect; there was sharp skirmishing until within two miles of Ridgefield, when, as the veteran was cheering on his men, a musket ball finished his gallant career. On his fall his men retreated in disorder.

The delay which his attack had occasioned to the enemy had given Arnold time to throw up a barricade across the road at the north end of Ridgefield, protected by a house on the right and a high rocky bank on the left, where he took his stand with his force now increased to about 500 men. The enemy advanced in column with artillery and flanking parties. They received several volleys from the barricade, until it was outflanked and carried. Arnold ordered a retreat and was bringing off the rear-guard, when his horse was shot under him. Arnold remained in the saddle, one foot entangled in the stirrups. Extricating his foot from the stirrup, he threw himself into the thickets of a neighboring swamp and joined his retreating troops.

Tryon intrenched for the night in Ridgefield, his troops having suffered greatly in their harassed retreat. The next morning, after having set fire to four houses, he continued his march for the ships.

Colonel Huntingdon of the Continental army, with the troops which had been stationed at Danbury, the scattered forces of Wooster which had joined him, and a number of militia, hung on the rear of the enemy as soon as they were in motion. Arnold was again in the field, with his rallied forces, strengthened by Oswald with two companies of Lamb's artillery regiment and three field-pieces. With these he again posted himself on the enemy's route.

Difficulties and annoyances had multiplied upon the latter at every step. When they came in sight of the position where Arnold was waiting for them, they changed their route, wheeled to the left and made for a ford of Saugatuck River. Arnold hastened to cross the bridge and take them in flank but they were too quick for him. Lamb had now reached the scene of action, as had about 200 volunteers. Leaving to Oswald the charge of the artillery, he put himself at the head of the volunteers and led them up to Arnold's assistance.

The enemy, finding themselves hard pressed, pushed for Canepo Hill. They reached it in the evening and, as they were now within cannon shot of their ships, the Americans ceased the pursuit. The British landed a large body of marines and sailors, who drove the Americans back for some distance and covered the embarkation of the troops.

In this inroad the enemy destroyed a considerable amount of military stores and 1700 tents prepared for the use of Washington's army in the ensuing campaign. Arnold's gallantry in this affair gained him fresh laurels and Congress, to remedy their late error, promoted him to the rank of major-general. Still this promotion did not restore him to his proper position. He was at the bottom of the list of major-generals, with four officers above him, his juniors in service. Washington felt this injustice on the part of Congress, and wrote about it to the president. As an additional balm to Arnold's wounded pride, Congress voted that a horse, properly caparisoned, should be presented to him in their name as a token of their approbation of his gallant conduct in the late action. But he remained at the bottom of the list and the wound still rankled in his bosom.

The time was at hand for the committee of inquiry on Schuyler's conduct to make their report to Congress and he awaited it with impatience. "I propose in a day or two to resign my commission," writes he to Washington on the 3d of May.

Affairs, however, were taking a more favorable turn. The committee of inquiry made a report which placed the character of Schuyler higher than ever as an able and active commander and a zealous and disinterested patriot.

He made a memorial to Congress explaining away, or apologizing for, the expressions in one of his letters which had given offence to the House. His memorial was satisfactory and he was officially informed that Congress now "entertained the same favorable sentiments concerning him that they had entertained before that letter was received."

There were warm discussions in the House on the subject of the Northern department. Several important New York delegates observed that Gates misapprehended his position. He considered himself as holding the command formerly held by Schuyler. Such was not the intention of Congress in sending him to take command at Ticonderoga. There had been a question between sending him to that post or giving him the adjutancy general, and it had been decided for the former. It would be nonsense, they observed, to give him command of the Northern department and confine him to Ticonderoga and Mount Independence, where he could not have an extensive idea of the defence of the frontier of the Eastern States, but only of one spot.

The friends of Gates, on the other hand, chiefly delegates from New England, pronounced it an absurdity that an officer holding such an important post as Ticonderoga should be under the orders of another 100 miles distant.

A letter from Philadelphia by Mr. Lovell, dated the 22d of May, put an end to the suspense of the general with respect to his position. "Misconceptions of past resolves and consequent jealousies," writes he, "have produced a definition of the Northern department, and General Schuyler is ordered to take command of it. The resolve, also, which was thought to fix head-quarters at Albany, is repealed." Such a resolve had actually been passed and Albany,

Ticonderoga, Fort Stanwix and their dependencies were thenceforward to be considered as forming the Northern department.

Schuyler was received with open arms at Albany on the 3d of June. "I had the satisfaction," writes he, "to experience the finest feelings which my country expressed on my arrival and reappointment."

Gates, still in Albany, persisted in considering himself degraded. He declined serving under Schuyler, who would have given him the post at Ticonderoga in his absence and, obtaining permission to leave the department, set out on the 9th for Philadelphia to demand redress of Congress.

St. Clair was sent to take command at Ticonderoga, accompanied by Fermoy. As the whole force in the Northern department would not be sufficient to command the extensive works there on both sides of the lake, St. Clair was instructed to bestow his first attention in fortifying Mount Independence, on the east side, that it might be made capable of sustaining a long and vigorous siege. "I am fully convinced," writes he, "that between 2000 and 3000 men can effectually maintain Mount Independence and secure the pass." It would be imprudent, he thought, to station the greater part of the forces at Fort Ticonderoga; should the enemy be able to invest it and cut off communication with the country on the east side, it might experience a disaster similar to that at Fort Washington.

While Schuyler was providing for the security of Ticonderoga, Gates was wending his way to Philadelphia, his bosom swelling with imaginary wrongs. He arrived there on the 18th. The next day at noon, Gates was, by permission of Congress ushered in to its meeting, took his seat in an elbow chair, and proceeded to give some news concerning the Indians, their friendly dispositions, and other matters of the kind. Then, drawing forth some papers from his pocket, he opened upon the real object of his visit, stating from his notes in a flurried and disjointed manner the happy life he had left to take up arms for the liberties of America, how strenuously he had exerted himself in its defence, how he had been appointed to a command in the Northern department, but that a few days since, without having given any cause, he had received a resolution by which he was, in a most disgraceful manner, superseded in his command. Here his irritated feelings got the better of his judgment and he indulged in angry reproaches of Congress.

The conduct of the general was pronounced disrespectful to the House and unworthy of himself, and it was moved and seconded that he be requested to withdraw. Some of the Eastern delegates opposed the motion and endeavored to palliate his conduct. A wordy clamor ensued, during which the general stood endeavoring to be heard but, the clamor increasing, he withdrew with the utmost indignation. It was then determined that he should not again be admitted on the floor but should be informed that Congress were ready and willing to hear, by way of memorial, any grievances of which he might have to complain.

(CHAPTER 35)

The Highland passes of the Hudson, always objects of anxious thought to Washington, were especially so at this juncture. McDougall still commanded at Peekskill, and George Clinton, who resided at New Windsor, had command of the Highland forts. The latter, at the earnest request of the New York Convention, had received from Congress the command of brigadier-general in the Continental army.

When the "unhappy affair of Peekskill" had alarmed the Convention of New York for the safety of the forts on the Highlands, Clinton, authorized by that body, had ordered out part of the militia of Orange, Dutchess, and Westchester counties without waiting for Washington's approbation of the measure. He had strengthened, also, with anchors and cables, the chain across the river at Fort Montgomery.

A few days later came word that several transports were anchored at Dobbs' Ferry in the Tappan Sea. It might be intended to divert attention from a movement towards the Delaware; or to make incursions into the country back of Morristown, seize the passes through the mountains, and cut off communication between the army and the Hudson. Washington ordered Clinton to post as good a number of troops as he could spare on the mountains west of the river.

On the 12th of May, Greene received instructions from Washington to proceed to the Highlands and examine the condition of the forts, especially Fort Mongtomery. This done, and the general officers present having been consulted, he was to give such orders as might appear necessary for the greater security of the passes by land and water. When reconnoitring the Highlands in the preceding year, Washington had remarked a rugged pass on the west side of the Hudson round Bull Hill, a forest-clad mountain forming an advance rampart at the entrance to Peekskill Bay. "This pass," he observed, "should also be attended to, lest the enemy by a coup de main should possess themselves of it, before a sufficient force could be assembled to oppose them." Subsequent events will illustrate, though unfortunately, the foresight of this instruction.

Knox was associated with Greene in this visit of inspection. They examined the river and the passes of the Highlands in company with McDougall, George Clinton and Anthony Wayne. The latter, recently promoted to brigadier, had just returned from Ticonderoga. The five generals made a joint report to Washington, in which they recommended the completion of the obstructions in the river. These consisted of a boom, or heavy iron chain, across the river from Fort Montgomery to Anthony's Nose, with cables stretched in front to break the force of any ship under way, before she could strike it. The boom was to be protected by the guns of two ships and two row galleys stationed just above it and by batteries on shore. This, it was deemed, would prevent the enemy's ships from ascending the river. If these obstructions could be rendered effective, they did not think the enemy would attempt to operate by land; "the passes through the Highlands being so exceedingly difficult."

The general command of the Hudson was one of the most important in the service and required an officer of consummate energy and judgment. It was offered by Washington to Arnold, intending thus publicly to manifest his opinion of his deserts and hoping to appease his irritated feelings. Arnold, however, declined

MAJOR GENERAL NATHANIEL GREENE

Nath Greene

NEW YORK, G.P. PUTNAM & Cᵒ

to accept it. In an interview with Washington at Morristown, he alleged his anxiety to proceed to Philadelphia and settle his public accounts, which were of considerable amount. He intended, therefore, to wait on Congress and request a committee of inquiry into his conduct. Beside, he did not consider the promotion conferred on him by Congress sufficient to obviate their previous neglect, as it did not give him the rank he had a claim to from seniority in the line of brigadiers. With these considerations he proceeded to Philadelphia, bearing a letter from Washington to the President of Congress, countenancing his complaints and testifying to the excellence of his military character.

The command of the Hudson was given to Putnam, who repaired forthwith to Peekskill and set about promptly to carry into effect the measures Greene and Knox had recommended, especially the boom and chain at Fort Montgomery, about which George Clinton had busied himself. A large part of the New York and New England troops were stationed at this post, not merely to guard the Hudson, but to render aid either to the Eastern or Middle States in case of exigency.

Washington planned a night expedition for Putnam, who was to descend the Hudson in boats, surprise Fort Independence at Spyt den Duivel Creek, capture the garrison and sweep the road between that post and the Highlands. Movements on the part of the enemy, seemingly indicative of a design upon Philadelphia, however, obliged Washington to abandon the project and exert all his vigilance in watching hostile operations in the Jerseys.

Accordingly, towards the end of May, he broke up his cantonments at Morristown and shifted his camp to Middlebrook, within 10 miles of Brunswick. His whole force fit for duty was now about 7300 men, all from the States south of the Hudson. There were 43 regiments, forming 10 brigades, commanded by Brigadiers Muhlenberg, Weedon, Woodford, Scott, Smallwood, Deborre, Wayne, Dehaas, Conway, and Maxwell. These were apportioned into 5 divisions of 2 brigades each, under Major-generals Greene, Stephen, Sullivan, Lincoln and Stirling. The artillery was commanded by Knox. Sullivan, with his division, was stationed on the right at Princeton. With the rest of his force, Washington fortified himself in a position naturally strong, among hills, in the rear of Middlebrook. His camp was, on all sides, difficult of approach, and he rendered it still more so by intrenchments. The high grounds about it commanded a wide view of the country around Brunswick, the road to Philadelphia, and the course of the Raritan, so that the enemy could make no important movement on land without his perceiving it.

On the 31st of May, reports were brought to camp that a fleet of 100 sail had left New York and stood out to sea. Whither bound, and how freighted, was unknown. Eighteen transports, also, had arrived at New York, with troops in foreign uniforms who proved to be Anspachers and other German mercenaries; there were British reinforcements also and a supply of tents and camp equipage.

The country was now in full verdure, affording "green forage" in abundance, and all things seemed to Sir William propitious for the opening of the campaign. Early in June, therefore, he gave up gayety and luxurious life at New York and, crossing into the Jerseys, set up his head-quarters at Brunswick.

As soon as Washington ascertained that Sir William's attention was completely turned to this quarter, he determined to strengthen his position with all the force that could be spared from other parts to be able, in case opportunity presented, to attack the enemy; in the mean time, he would harass them with his light militia troops, aided by a few Continentals, so as to weaken their numbers by continual skirmishes. With this view, he ordered Putnam to send down most of the Continental troops from Peekskill, leaving only a number sufficient, in conjunction with the militia, to guard that post against surprise. They were to proceed in three divisions, under Parsons, McDougall, and Glover, at one day's march distant from each other.

Arnold, in this critical juncture, had been put in command of Philadelphia, a post he had been induced to accept, although the question of rank had not been adjusted to his satisfaction. His command embraced the western bank of the Delaware and he took up his station there with a strong body of militia, supported by a few Continentals, to oppose any attempt of the enemy to cross the river. He was instructed by Washington to give him notice by expresses if any fleet should appear in Delaware Bay and to concert signals with the camp of Sullivan at Princeton by alarm fires upon the hills.

On the night of the 13th of June, Howe sallied forth in great force from Brunswick, as if pushing directly for the Delaware, but his advanced guard halted at Somerset court-house, about nine miles distant. Apprised of this movement, Washington, at day-break, reconnoitred the enemy. He observed their front halting at the court-house while troops and artillery were grouped here and there along the road and the rear-guard was still at Brunswick. It was a question with Washington and his generals whether this was a real move toward Philadelphia or merely a lure to tempt them from their strong position. In this uncertainty, Washington drew out his army in battle array along the heights but kept quiet. It was his plan not to risk a general action, but, should the enemy really march toward the Delaware, to hang heavily upon their rear. Their principal difficulty would be in crossing that river, and there, he trusted, they would meet spirited opposition from the Continental troops and militia on the western side under Arnold and Mifflin.

The British took up a strong position, having Millstone Creek on their left, the Raritan all along their front, and their right resting on Brunswick, and proceeded to fortify themselves with bastions.

The American and British armies, strongly posted, the former along the heights of Middlebrook, the other beyond the Raritan, remained four days grimly regarding each other; both waiting to be attacked. The Jersey militia, which now turned out with alacrity, repaired, some to Washington's camp, others to that of Sullivan. The latter had fallen back from Princeton and taken a position behind the Sourland Hills.

Howe pushed out detachments and made several feints, as if to pass by the American camp and march to the Delaware, but Washington was not to be deceived. He kept on the heights and strengthened his intrenchments.

Baffled in these attempts to draw his cautious adversary into a general action, Howe, on the 19th, suddenly broke up his camp and pretended to return with some precipitation to Brunswick. Washington's light troops hovered round the enemy but the main army kept to its stronghold on the heights.

On the next day came warlike news from the North. A British spy had been seized and examined by Schuyler. Burgoyne was stated as being arrived at Quebec to command the forces in an invasion from Canada. While he advanced with his main force by Lake Champlain, a detachment led by Sir John Johnson was to penetrate by Oswego to the Mohawk River and place itself between Fort Stanwix and Fort Edward.

If this information was correct, Ticonderoga would soon be attacked. The force there might be sufficient for its defence, but Schuyler would have no troops to oppose the inroad of Sir John Johnson and he urged a reinforcement. Washington forthwith sent orders to Putnam to procure sloops and hold four Massachusetts regiments in readiness to go up the river at a moment's warning. Still, if the information of the spy was correct, he doubted the ability of the enemy to carry the reported plan into effect. In the mean time, he retained his mind unflurried by these new rumors, keeping from his heights a vigilant eye upon Howe.

On the 22d, Sir William again marched out of Brunswick, but this time towards Amboy, burning several houses on the way, hoping, perhaps, that the sight of a ravaged country would irritate the Americans and provoke an attack. Washington sent out three brigades under Greene to fall upon the rear of the enemy while Morgan hung upon their skirts with his riflemen. At the same time the army remained paraded on the heights ready to yield support if necessary.

Finding that Howe had actually sent his heavy baggage and part of his troops over to Staten Island, Washington, on the 24th, left the heights and descended to Quibbletown (now New Market), six miles on the road to Amboy, to be nearer at hand for the protection of his advanced parties, while Stirling with his division and some light troops was at Matouchin Church, closer to the enemy's lines to watch their motions and be ready to harass them while crossing to the island.

Howe now thought he had gained his point. Recalling those who had crossed, he formed his troops into two columns, the right led by Cornwallis, the left by himself, and marched back rapidly by different routes from Amboy. He had three objects in view: to cut off the principal advanced parties of the Americans; to bring the main body into an engagement near Quibbletown; or that Cornwallis, making a circuit to the right, should turn the left of Washington's position, get to the heights, take possession of the passes, and oblige him to abandon that stronghold where he had hitherto been so secure.

Washington, however, had timely notice of his movement and, penetrating his design, regained his fortified camp at Middlebrook and secured the passes of the mountains. He then detached a body of light troops under Scott, together with Morgan's riflemen, to hang on the flank of the enemy and watch their motions.

Cornwallis, in his circuitous march, dispersed the light parties of the advance, but fell in with Stirling's division, strongly posted in a woody country and well covered by artillery judiciously disposed. A sharp skirmish ensued, when the Americans gave way and retreated to the hills, while the British halted at Westfield, disappointed in the main objects of their enterprise. They remained at Westfield until the afternoon of the 27th, when they moved toward Spanktown (now Rahway), pursued and harassed the whole way by the American light troops.

Perceiving that every scheme of bringing the Americans to a general action was rendered abortive by the prudence of Washington and aware of the madness of attempting to march to the Delaware through a hostile country with such a force on his rear, Howe broke up his head-quarters at Amboy on the last of June and crossed over to Staten Island. His troops that were encamped opposite Amboy struck their tents on the following day and marched off to the old camping ground in the Bay of New York. The ships got under way and moved down round the island and it was soon apparent that, at length, the enemy had really evacuated the Jerseys.

The question now was, what would be their next move? A great stir among the shipping seemed to indicate an expedition by water. But whither?

(CHAPTER 36)

Scarce had the last transport disappeared from before Amboy when intelligence arrived from St. Clair, announcing the appearance of a hostile fleet on Lake Champlain and that Burgoyne with the whole Canada army was approaching Ticonderoga. The judgment and circumspection of Washington were never more severely put to the proof. Was this merely a diversion to occupy the attention of the American forces in that quarter while the main body of the army in Canada should come round by sea and form a junction with the army under Howe? Did Burgoyne really intend to break through by way of Ticonderoga? In that case it must be Howe's plan to co-operate with him. His next move, in such case, would be to ascend the Hudson, seize on the Highland passes before Washington could form a union with the troops stationed there, and thus open the way for the junction with Burgoyne. Should Washington, however, on such a presumption, hasten with his troops to Peekskill, leaving Howe on Staten Island, what would prevent the latter from pushing to Philadelphia by South Amboy or any other route?

Such were the perplexities and difficulties presenting themselves under every aspect of the case. In this dilemma he sent Parsons and Varnum with a couple of brigades in all haste to Peekskill. He wrote to George Clinton and Putnam, the former to call out the New York militia from Orange and Ulster counties, the latter to summon the militia from Connecticut; as soon as such reinforcements should be at hand, to despatch four Massachusetts regiments to Ticonderoga.

Sullivan, moreover, was ordered to advance with his division towards the Highlands as far as Pompton, while Washington moved his own camp back to Morristown to be ready either to push on to the Highlands or fall back upon his recent position at Middlebrook, according to the movements of the enemy.

Deserters from Staten Island and New York soon brought word that transports were being fitted up with berths for horses and taking in three weeks' supply of water and provender. This indicated some other destination than that of the Hudson. Lest an attempt on the Eastern States should be intended, Washington sent a circular to their governors to put them on their guard.

In the midst of his various cares, his yeoman soldiery, the Jersey militia, were not forgotten. It was their harvest time and, the State being evacuated, there was no immediate call for their services. He dismissed, therefore, almost the whole of them to their homes.

The armament advancing against Ticonderoga was not a diversion but a regular invasion. The junction of the two armies—that in Canada and that under Howe in New York—was considered the speediest mode of quelling the rebellion. As the security of Canada required the presence of Governor Sir Guy Carleton, 3000 men were to remain there with him; the residue of the army was to be employed upon two expeditions, one under Burgoyne to force his way to Albany, the other under St. Leger to make a diversion on the Mohawk River.

The invading army was composed of 3724 British rank and file, 3016 Germans, mostly Brunswickers, 250 Canadians, and 400 Indians; beside these there were 473 men, in all nearly 8000 men. The army was admirably appointed, its artillery perhaps the finest ever allotted to an army of the size. General Phillips, who commanded the artillery, had gained great reputation in the wars in Germany. Brigadiers-general Fraser, Powel, and Hamilton were officers of distinguished merit. So was Major-general the Baron Riedesel, a Brunswicker, who commanded the German troops.

While Burgoyne with the main force proceeded from St. Johns, St. Leger with 700 men was to land at Oswego and, guided by Sir John Johnson at the head of his loyalist volunteers, tory refugees, and Indians, was to enter the Mohawk country, draw Schuyler in that direction, attack Fort Stanwix, and, having ravaged the valley of the Mohawk, rejoin Burgoyne at Albany. There they would make a triumphant junction with the army of Sir William Howe.

General Burgoyne left St. Johns on the 16th of June. If information from scouts and a captured spy might be relied on, Ticonderoga would soon be attacked, but he trusted the garrison was sufficient to maintain it.

On the following day Schuyler was at Ticonderoga. The works were not in such a state of forwardness as he had anticipated, owing to the tardy arrival of troops and want of sufficient artificers. The works in question related chiefly to Mount Independence, a high hill east of the lake, opposite the old fort. A star fort with pickets crowned the summit of the hill, which was table land; half way down the hill was a battery and at its foot were strongly intrenched works well mounted with cannon. The French General de Fermois had charge of this fort.

As this part of Lake Champlain is narrow, a connection was kept up between the two forts by a floating bridge, supported on sunken piers in caissons, formed of strong timber. Between the piers were separate floats 50 feet long and 12 feet wide, strongly connected by iron chains and rivets. On the north side of the bridge was a boom composed of large pieces of timber; beside this was a double iron chain with links an inch and a half square. The bridge, boom, and chain were 400 yards in length. This immense work was intended, while it afforded communication between the two forts, to protect the upper part of the lake, presenting, under cover of their guns, a barrier which no hostile ship would be able to break through.

Schuyler hastened to Fort George, whence he sent on provisions for 60 days and, from the banks of the Hudson, additional carpenters and working cattle. "Business will now go on . . . with much more spirit," writes he to Congress, . . . although I expect they will approach with their fleet to keep us in alarm and to draw our attention from other quarters where they may mean a real attack."

In the mean time, Burgoyne was advancing up the lake. On the 21st of June, he encamped several miles north of Crown Point, where he gave a war feast to his savage allies and made them a speech in that pompous and half poetical vein in which it is the absurd practice to address our savages and which is commonly reduced to flat prose by their interpreters. It was a speech intended to excite their ardor but restrain their cruelty, a difficult medium to attain with Indian warriors.

The garrison at Ticonderoga, meanwhile, were anxiously on the look-out. By the 24th, scouts began to bring in word of the approaching foe. Bark canoes had been seen filled with white men and savages. Then three vessels under sail and one at anchor, above Split Rock, and behind it the radeau Thunderer. Anon came word of encampments sufficient for a large body of troops.

St. Clair wrote word of all this to Schuyler and that it was supposed the enemy were waiting the arrival of more force. Schuyler transmitted a copy of St. Clair's letter to Washington and urged reinforcements as soon as possible. This done, he hastened to Albany to forward reinforcements and bring up the militia.

While there, he received word from St. Clair that the enemy's fleet and army were arrived at Crown Point and had sent off detachments, one up Otter Creek to cut off the communication by Skenesborough and another on the west side of the lake to cut off Fort George. It was evident a real attack on Ticonderoga was intended. Claims for assistance came hurrying on from other quarters. A large force (St. Leger's) was said to be arrived at Oswego and Sir John Johnson on his way to attack Fort Schuyler.

Schuyler, amid the thickening alarms, writes urgent letters to the committee of safety of New York, to Putnam at Peekskill, to the Governor of Connecticut, to the President of Massachusetts, to the committee of Berkshire, and to Washington stating the impending dangers and imploring reinforcements. He exhorts Herkimer to keep the militia of Tryon County in readiness to protect the western frontier and to check the inroad of Johnson; he assures St. Clair he will move to his aid with the militia of New York as soon as he can collect them.

Dangers accumulate at Ticonderoga according to advices from St. Clair (28th). Seven of the enemy's vessels are at Crown Point; the rest of their fleet is probably a little lower down. Some troops have debarked and encamped at Chimney Point. There is no prospect, he says, of being able to defend Ticonderoga unless militia come in and he has thought of calling in those from Berkshire. "Should the enemy invest and blockade us," writes he, "we are infallibly ruined;

. . . nor do I see that a retreat will in any shape be practicable."

The enemy came up the lake on the 30th, their main body under Burgoyne on the west side, the German reserve under Riedesel on the east; communication was maintained by frigates and gunboats which kept pace between them. On the 1st of July, Burgoyne encamped four miles north of Ticonderoga and began to intrench and to throw a boom across the lake. His advanced guard under Fraser took post at Three Mile Point and the ships anchored just out of gunshot of the fort. Here he issued a proclamation denouncing woe to all who should persist in rebellion, laying particular stress upon his means, with the aid of the Indians, to overtake the hardiest enemies wherever they might lurk.

St. Clair beheld the force arrayed against him without dismay. It is true his garrison had no more than 3500 men, of whom 900 were militia. They were badly equipped and few had bayonets; yet they were in good heart. St. Clair trusted, however, in the strength of his position and the works constructed to resist any attempt to take it by storm.

Schuyler at this time was at Albany, sending up reinforcements of Continental troops and militia and awaiting the arrival of further reinforcements for which sloops had been sent to Peekskill. He was endeavoring also to provide for security in other quarters. The threatenings of Brant, the famous Indian chief, and the prospect of a British inroad by way of Oswego had spread terror through Tryon County, the inhabitants of which called upon him for support.

Such was the state of affairs in the north, of which Washington from time to time had been informed. An attack on Ticonderoga appeared to be impending, but as the garrison was in good heart, the commander resolute, and troops were on the way to reinforce him, a spirited and perhaps successful resistance was anticipated by Washington. His surprise may therefore be imagined, on receiving a letter from Schuyler dated July 7th, conveying the astounding intelligence that Ticonderoga was evacuated!

Schuyler had just received the news at Stillwater on his way with reinforcements for the fortress. The first account was so vague Washington hoped it might prove incorrect. It was confirmed by another letter from Schuyler, dated the 9th at Fort Edward. A part of the garrison had been pursued by a detachment of the enemy as far as Fort Anne, where the latter had been repulsed. As to St. Clair and his forces, they had thrown themselves into the forest and nothing was known what had become of them!

"I am here," writes Schuyler, "at the head of a handful of men, not above 1500, with little ammunition. . . . The country is in the deepest consternation; no carriages to remove the stores from Fort George, which I expect every moment to hear is attacked; and what adds to my distress is that a report prevails that I had given orders for the evacuation of Ticonderoga."

Washington was totally at a loss to account for St. Clair's movement. To abandon a fortress pronounced so defensible, apparently without firing a gun! and then the strange uncertainty as to his whereabouts and of his troops!

His first attention was to supply the wants of Schuyler. An express was sent to Springfield for musket cartridges, gunpowder, lead and cartridge papers. Ten pieces of artillery with proper officers were to be forwarded from Peekskill, as well as intrenching tools. Of tents he had none to furnish, neither could heavy cannon be spared from the defence of the Highlands. Six hundred recruits, on their march from Massachusetts to Peekskill, were ordered to reinforce Schuyler. This was all that Washington could send to his aid, but this addition to his troops, supposing those under St. Clair should have come in and any number of militia have turned out, would probably form an army equal, if not superior, to that said to be under Burgoyne. Beside, it was Washington's idea that the latter would suspend his operations until Howe should move in concert. Supposing that movement would be an attempt against the Highlands, he ordered Sullivan with his division to Peekskill to reinforce Putnam. At the same time he advanced with his main army to the Clove, a defile through the Highlands west of the Hudson. Here he encamped within 18 miles of the river to be at hand to oppose the designs of Howe, whatever might be their direction.

On the morning of the 14th came another letter from Schuyler, dated Fort Edward, July 10th. He had that morning received tidings of St. Clair and his missing troops being 50 miles east of him. We leave Washington at his encampment in the Clove, anxiously watching the movements of the fleet and the lower army, while we turn to the north to explain the mysterious retreat of General St. Clair.

In the approach of Burgoyne to Ticonderoga, he had encamped north of the fortress and intrenched himself. On the 2d of July, Indian scouts appeared in the vicinity of a block-house and some outworks about the channel leading to Lake George. As St. Clair did not think the garrison sufficient to defend all the outposts, these works were set on fire and abandoned. Because the extreme left of Ticonderoga might easily be turned, a post had been established in the preceding year on an eminence half a mile north of the old French lines. St. Clair, through singular remissness, had neglected to secure it. Burgoyne discovered this neglect and hastened Phillips and Fraser to take possession of this post. They did so without opposition. Heavy guns were mounted upon it and Fraser's whole corps was stationed there. The post commanded communication by land and water with Lake George so as to cut off all supplies from that quarter. Such were the advantages expected from this post that the British gave it the name of Mount Hope.

The enemy now proceeded to invest Ticonderoga. A line of troops was drawn from the western part of Mount Hope to Three Mile Point, where Fraser was posted with the advance guard, while Riedesel encamped with the German reserve in a parallel line on the opposite side of Lake Champlain at the foot of Mount Independence. For two days the enemy occupied themselves in making advances and securing positions, regardless of a cannonade by the American batteries.

With all the pains lavished by the Americans to render the works impregnable, they had neglected the master key by which they were all commanded. This was Sugar Hill, a rugged height, the termination of a mountain ridge which separates Lake Champlain from Lake George. It stood south of Ticonderoga, beyond the channel which connected the two lakes, and rose precipitously from the waters of Champlain to the height of 600 feet. It had been pronounced by the Americans too distant to be dangerous and inaccessible to an enemy. Washington's aide-de-camp, Trumbull, had insisted this was the true point for the fort, commanding the neighboring heights, the narrow parts of both lakes, and the communication between. His suggestions were disregarded.

Phillips, on taking his position, had regarded the hill with a practised eye. His engineer's report was that it overlooked and had entire command of Forts Ticonderoga and Independence. Measures were instantly taken to plant a battery on that height. British troops were busy throughout the day and night cutting a road through rocks and trees and up rugged defiles. Guns, ammunition, and stores were carried up the hill in the night; the cannon were hauled up and before morning the ground was levelled for the battery. To this work, they gave the name of Fort Defiance.

On the fifth of July, to their astonishment and consternation, the garrison beheld a legion of red-coats on the summit of this hill, constructing works which must soon lay the fortress at their mercy. In this sudden and appalling emergency, St. Clair called a council of war. What was to be done? The batteries from this new fort would probably be opened the next day; by that time Ticonderoga might be completely invested and the whole garrison exposed to capture. The danger was imminent; delay might prove fatal. It was unanimously determined to evacuate Ticonderoga and Mount Independence that very night and retreat to Skenesborough (now Whitehall), at the upper part of the lake, where there was a stockaded fort. The main body of the army, led by St. Clair, were to cross and take a circuitous route through the woods east of the lake by the way of Castleton.

The cannon, stores and provisions, together with the wounded and the women, were to be embarked on 200 bateaux and conducted to the upper extremity of the lake by Colonel Long with 600 men, 200 of whom in five armed galleys were to form a rear-guard. It was afternoon; yet all the preparations were to be made for the coming night, and that with as little bustle and movement as possible. As soon as the evening closed, they began in all haste to load the boats. Everything was conducted with such silence that the flotilla departed undiscovered and was soon under the shadows of mountains and overhanging forests.

The retreat by land was not conducted with equal mystery. St. Clair had crossed over the bridge to the Vermont side of the lake by three o'clock in the morning and set forward through the woods toward Hubbardton, but, before the rear-guard under Colonel Francis got in motion, the house at Fort Independence occupied by de Fermois was set on fire. The consequences were disastrous. The British sentries at Mount Hope were astonished by a conflagration suddenly lighting up Mount Independence and revealing the American troops in full retreat, for the rear-guard, disconcerted by this sudden exposure, pressed forward for the woods in the utmost haste and confusion.

Alarm guns were fired from Mount Hope. Fraser dashed into Ticonderoga with his pickets, giving orders for his brigade to arm in all haste and follow. By daybreak he had hoisted the British flag over the deserted fortress; before sunrise he had passed the bridge and was in full pursuit of the American rear-guard.

Burgoyne was roused on board of the frigate Royal George by the alarm guns from Fort Hope and a message from Fraser announcing the double retreat of the Americans by land and water. Burgoyne's measures were prompt. Riedesel was ordered to follow and support Fraser with a part of the German troops; garrisons were thrown into Ticonderoga and Mount Independence; the main part of the army was embarked on board of the frigates and gunboats; the floating bridge with its boom and chain was broken through and Burgoyne set out with his squadron in pursuit of the flotilla.

We left the latter making its retreat on the preceding evening towards Skenesborough, where, in the afternoon of the succeeding day, the heavily laden bateaux arrived. The disembarkation had scarcely commenced when the thundering of artillery was heard from below. The British gunboats, having pushed on in advance of the frigates, had overtaken and were firing upon the galleys. The latter defended themselves for a while, but at length two struck and three were blown up. The fugitives from them brought word that the British ships not being able to come up, troops and Indians were landing from them and scrambling up the hills, intending to get in the rear of the fort and cut off all retreat.

All now was consternation and confusion. The bateaux, the storehouses, the fort, the mill were all set on fire, and a general flight took place to Fort Anne, about 12 miles distant. It was a small picketed fort, about 16 miles from Fort Edward. Schuyler, hearing of Long's situation, immediately sent him a small reinforcement with provisions and ammunition and urged him to maintain his post resolutely.

On the same day Long's scouts brought in word of British red-coats approaching. Long sallied forth to meet them, posting himself at a rocky defile. As the enemy advanced he opened a heavy fire upon them in front, while part of his troops, availing themselves of their knowledge of the ground, kept up a shifting attack from the woods in flank and rear. Apprehensive of being surrounded, the British took post upon a high hill where they were warmly besieged and would have been forced, had not some of their Indian allies arrived. This changed the fortune of the day. The Americans had nearly expended their ammunition and retreated, therefore, to Fort Anne. Supposing the troops an advance guard of Burgoyne's army, they set fire to the fort and pushed on to Fort Edward, where they gave the alarm that the main force of the enemy was close after them.

St. Clair's retreat through the woods from Mount Independence continued the first day until night, when he arrived at Castleton, 30 miles from Ticonderoga. His rear-guard, halted at Hubbardton to await the stragglers, was composed of three regiments, under Colonels Seth Warner, Francis and Hale, in all about 1300 men. Early the next morning, their sentries discharged their muskets and came running in with word that the enemy were at hand.

It was Fraser, with his advance of 850 men, who had pressed forward in the night and now attacked the Americans with great spirit, notwithstanding their superiority in numbers. The Americans gave the British a warm reception, but at the very commencement of the action were deserted by Colonel Hale and his militia regiment, who fled toward Castleton, leaving Warner and Francis with but 700 men to bear the brunt of the battle. These posted themselves behind logs and trees, whence they kept up a destructive fire, when Riedesel came pressing into the action with his reinforcement troops in an impetuous charge with the bayonet. Francis was among the first who fell, gallantly fighting at the head of his men. The Americans fled, leaving the ground covered with their dead and wounded.

The noise of the firing had reached St. Clair at Castleton. He immediately sent two militia regiments in his rear to the assistance of his rear-guard. They refused to obey and hurried forward to Castleton. At this juncture St. Clair received information of Burgoyne's arrival at Skenesborough and the destruction of the American works there. Fearing to be intercepted at Fort Anne, he changed his route, struck into the woods on his left toward Rutland, leaving word for Warner to follow. The latter overtook him two days afterwards, his shattered force reduced to 90 men. Hale, who had so faithlessly deserted, and his men surrendered the same day to British soldiers without making any fight. He died while yet a prisoner and never had the opportunity which he sought to vindicate himself before a court-martial.

On the 12th St. Clair reached Fort Edward, his troops haggard and exhausted by their long retreat through the woods. Such is the story of the catastrophe at Fort Ticonderoga. The loss of artillery, ammunition, provisions and stores was prodigious, but the worst effect was the consternation spread throughout the country. The great barriers of the North, it was said, were broken through and there was nothing to check the triumphant enemy.

A spirited exploit to the eastward was performed during the prevalence of adverse news from the North. General Prescott had command of the British forces in Rhode Island. His harsh treatment of Ethan Allen and his arrogant conduct on various occasions had rendered him peculiarly odious to the Americans. Lieutenant-colonel Barton, stationed with a force of Rhode Island militia on the mainland, received word that Prescott was quartered at a house near the western shore of the island, about 4 miles from Newport, in a very exposed situation. He determined, if possible, to capture him. Forty resolute men joined him in the enterprise. Embarking at night in two boats at Warwick Neck, they pulled quietly across the bay, landed in silence, eluded the guard near the house, captured the sentry at the door, and surprised the general in his bed. His aide-de-camp leaped from the window, but was likewise taken. Barton returned with equal silence to Warwick with his prisoners.

Washington hailed the capture of Prescott as a peculiarly fortunate circumstance, furnishing him with an equivalent for Lee. He accordingly wrote to Sir William Howe, proposing the exchange. No immediate reply was received to this letter, Howe being at sea; in the mean time Prescott remained in durance. "I would have him genteelly accommodated but strongly guarded," writes Washington, "I would not admit him to parole, as General Howe has not thought proper to grant General Lee that indulgence."

Washington continued his anxious exertions to counteract the operations of the enemy, forwarding artillery and ammunition to Schuyler with all the camp furniture that could be spared from his own encampment and from Peekskill. A part of Nixon's brigade was all the reinforcement he could afford in his present situation.

Schuyler had desired the assistance of an officer well acquainted with the country. Washington sent him Arnold. The question of rank, about which Arnold was so tenacious, was yet unsettled and though, had his promotion been regular, he would have been superior in command to St. Clair, he assured Washington that, on the present occasion, his claim should create no dispute.

Schuyler, in the mean time, aided by Kosciuszko, who was engineer in his department, had selected two positions on Moses Creek, 4 miles below Fort Edward, where the troops which had retreated from Ticonderoga and part of the militia were throwing up works. To impede the advance of the enemy, he had caused trees to be felled into Wood Creek to render it unnavigable, the roads between Fort Edward and Fort Anne to be broken up, the cattle in that direction to be brought away, and the forage destroyed. He had drawn off the garrison from Fort George, who left the buildings in flames.

In circulars to the brigadier-generals of militia in western Massachusetts and Connecticut, he warned them that the evacuation of Ticonderoga had opened a door by which the enemy, unless vigorously opposed, might form a junction with General Howe and cut off the communication between the Eastern and Northern States. "It cannot be supposed," adds he, "that the small number of Continental troops assembled at Fort Edward is alone sufficient to check the progress of the enemy. . . . I trust that you will immediately . . . march with at least one third of the militia under your command and rendezvous at Saratoga, unless directed to some other place by General Schuyler or General Arnold."

Washington ordered all river craft not required at Albany to be sent down to New Windsor and Fishkill and kept in readiness, for he knew not how soon the movements of Howe might render it necessary to transport part of his forces up the Hudson.

Further letters from Schuyler urged the increasing exigencies of his situation. It was harvest time. The militia, impatient at being detained from their rural labors, were leaving him in great numbers. In this position of affairs, he urged to be reinforced as speedily as possible. Washington, in reply, informed him that he had ordered a further reinforcement of Glover's brigade, which was all he could possibly furnish in his own exigencies. He trusted that the Eastern States, who were so deeply concerned in the matter, would exert themselves, by effectual succors, to enable him to check the progress of the enemy. "I have directed General Lincoln to repair to you as speedily as the state of his health . . . will permit; this gentleman . . . is exceedingly popular in the State of Massachusetts, to which he belongs; he will have a degree of influence over the militia which cannot fail of being highly advantageous."

Washington highly approved of a measure suggested by Schuyler of stationing troops somewhere about the Hampshire Grants so as to be in the rear or on the flank of Burgoyne, should he advance. It would make the latter, he said, very circumspect in his advances, if it did not entirely prevent them. It would oblige him to leave the posts behind him much stronger than he would otherwise do. He advised that General Lincoln should have the command of the corps thus posted. He recommended, moreover, that in case the enemy should make any formidable movement in the neighborhood at Fort Schuyler (Stanwix), Arnold, or some other spirited officer, should take charge of that post, keep up the spirits of the inhabitants, and cultivate the favorable disposition of the Indians.

(CHAPTER 37)

But now the attention of the commander-in-chief is called to the seaboard. On the 23d of July, the fleet, so long the object of watchful solicitude, put to sea. The force embarked consisted of almost 18,000 men in all. The destination of the fleet was still a matter of conjecture. Just after it had sailed, a young man presented himself at one of Putnam's outposts. He had been a prisoner in New York, he said, but had received his liberty on undertaking to be the bearer of a letter from Howe to Burgoyne which his patriotism prompted him to deliver to Putnam. The letter was immediately transmitted to Washington. It was in the handwriting of Howe and bore his signature. In it he informed Burgoyne that he was bound to the east against Boston. Washington at once pronounced the letter a feint. "No stronger proof could be given," said he, "that Howe is not going to the eastward. The letter was evidently intended to fall into our hands. . . . I am persuaded, more than ever, that Philadelphia is the place of destination."

He set out with his army for the Delaware, ordering Sullivan and Stirling with their divisions to cross the Hudson from Peekskill and proceed towards Philadelphia. Every movement and order showed the circumspection with which he had to proceed. On the 30th, he writes from Coryell's Ferry, about 30 miles from Philadelphia, to Gates, who was in that city: "As we are yet uncertain as to the real destination of the enemy, though the Delaware seems the most probable, I have thought it prudent to halt the army at this place, Howell's Ferry, and Trenton, at least till the fleet actually enters the bay and puts the matter beyond a doubt. From hence we can be on the proper ground to oppose them before they can possibly make their arrangements and dispositions for an attack. . . . That the post in the Highlands may not be left too much exposed, I have ordered General Sullivan's division to halt at Morristown, whence it will march southward if there should be occasion, or northward upon the first advice that the enemy should be throwing any force up the North River."

On the 31st, he was informed that the enemy's fleet of 228 sail had arrived the day previous at the Capes of Delaware. He instantly wrote to Putnam to hurry on two brigades, which had crossed the river, and to let Schuyler and the commanders in the Eastern States know that they had nothing to fear from Howe and might bend all their forces against Burgoyne. In the mean time he moved his camp to Germantown, about 6 miles from Philadelphia, to be at hand for the defence of that city.

The very next day came word, by express, that the fleet had again sailed out of the Capes and apparently shaped its course eastward. "This surprising event gives me the greatest anxiety," writes he to Putnam (Aug. 1), " . . . The importance of preventing Mr. Howe's getting possession of the Highlands by a coup de main, is infinite to America; and, in the present situation of things, every effort that can be thought of must be used."

Under this impression Washington sent orders to Sullivan to hasten back with his division and the two brigades which had recently left Peekskill and to recross the Hudson to that post as speedily as possible, intending to forward the rest of the army with all the expedition in his power. He wrote, also, to General George Clinton who had just been installed Governor of the State of New York, to reinforce Putnam with as many of the New York militia as could be collected. He still continued in command of the militia and it was with great satisfaction that Washington subsequently learnt he had determined to resume command of Fort Montgomery in the Highlands.

Washington, moreover, requested Putnam to send an express to Governor Trumbull urging assistance from the militia of his State without a moment's loss of time. There could be no surer reliance for aid in time of danger than the patriotism of Trumbull, nor were there men more ready to obey a sudden appeal to arms than the yeomanry of Connecticut. Washington avowed, when the great struggle was over, that "if all the States had done their duty as well as the little State of Connecticut, the war would have been ended long ago."

The command of the Northern department seemed to Gates again within his reach. The evacuation of Ticonderoga had been imputed by many either to cowardice or treachery on the part of St. Clair and the enemies of Schuyler had, for some time past, been endeavoring to involve him in the disgrace. It is true he was absent from the fortress at the time, zealously engaged in forwarding reinforcements and supplies, but it was alleged that the fort had been evacuated by his order and that, while there, he had made such dispositions as plainly indicated an intention to deliver it to the enemy. To excite popular feeling against him, the failure of the invasion of Canada and all the subsequent disasters in that quarter were again laid to his charge as commanding-general of the Northern department.

These charges, which for some time existed merely in popular clamor, had recently been taken up in Congress and a strong demonstration had been made against him by some New England delegates. Schuyler expressed the most ardent wish that Congress would order him to give an account of his conduct. He wished his friends to push for the closest scrutiny, confident it would redound to his honor. "I would not, however, wish the scrutiny to take place immediately," adds he, "as we shall probably soon have an engagement, if we are so reinforced with militia as to give us a probable chance of success."

It seemed to be the object of Schuyler's enemies to forestall his having such a chance of distinguishing himself. The business was pushed in Congress urgently. The consequence was, that after long and ardent debates, in which some of the most eminent delegates from New York stood up in his favor, it was resolved (Aug. 1st) that both Schuyler and St. Clair be summoned to head-quarters to account for the misfortunes in the North and that Washington should be directed to order such general officer as he should think proper to succeed Schuyler in command of the Northern department.

The very next day a letter was addressed to Washington by several leading Eastern members, men of unquestionable good faith, such as Samuel and John Adams, urging the appointment of Gates. Washington excused himself from making any nomination, alleging that the Northern department had, in a great measure, been considered a separate one and that the situation of the department might involve delicate consequences. The nomination, therefore, was made by Congress; the Eastern influence prevailed and Gates received the appointment, so long the object of his aspirations, if not intrigues.

Washington deeply regretted the removal of a noble-hearted man, whose exertions had been so energetic and unwearied and who was so peculiarly fitted for the varied duties of the department. He consoled himself, however, with the thought that the excuse of want of confidence in the general officers, hitherto alleged by the Eastern States for withholding reinforcements, would be obviated by the presence of this man of their choice.

He officially announced to Gates his appointment, and desired him to proceed immediately to the place of his destination, wishing him success.

About this time took effect a measure of Congress making a complete change in the commissariat. This important and complicated department had hitherto been under the management of one commissary-general, Colonel Joseph Trumbull of Connecticut. By the new arrangement there were to be two commissaries-general, one of purchases, the other of issues, each to be appointed by Congress. They were to have several deputy commissaries under them but accountable to Congress and to be appointed and removed by that body. These, and many subordinate arrangements, had been adopted in opposition to the opinion of Washington, and, unfortunately, were brought into operation in the midst of this critical campaign.

Their first effect was to cause the resignation of Trumbull, who had been nominated commissary of purchases, and the entrance into office of a number of inexperienced men. The ultimate effect was to paralyze the organization of this vital department, to cause delay and confusion in furnishing and forwarding supplies, and to retard the operations of the different armies throughout the year. Washington had many dangers and difficulties to harass and perplex him throughout this complicated campaign, not among the least the "stumblings of Congress."

GOVERNOR GEORGE CLINTON.

Printed by W.Pate

NEW YORK. G.P. PUTNAM & CO.

For several days Washington remained at Germantown in painful uncertainty about the British fleet, whether gone to the south or to the east. Concluding, at length, that the fleet had gone to the east, he was on the way to recross the Delaware, when an express overtook him on the 10th of August, with tidings that three days before the fleet had been seen off Sinepuxent Inlet, south of the Capes of Delaware.

He came to a halt and waited for further intelligence. Might it not be Howe's plan, by thus appearing with his ships at different places, to lure the army after him and thereby leave the country open for Sir Henry Clinton with the troops at New York to form a junction with Burgoyne? Washington wrote forthwith to Putnam to be on the alert, collect all the force he could to strengthen his post at Peekskill, and send spies to ascertain whether Sir Henry was at New York and what troops he had there.

The old general was already on the alert. A spy had been detected collecting information of the force and condition of the post at Peekskill and had undergone a military trial. A vessel of war came up the Hudson in all haste and landed a flag of truce by which a message was transmitted to Putnam from Sir Henry, claiming Edmund Palmer as a lieutenant in the British service. The reply of the old general was brief but emphatic.

HEAD-QUARTERS, 7th Aug., 1777

Edmund Palmer, an officer in the enemy's service, was taken as a spy lurking within our lines; he has been tried as a spy, condemned as a spy, and shall be executed as a spy; and the flag is ordered to depart immediately.

Israel Putnam

P.S. He has, accordingly, been executed.

Governor Clinton, the other guardian of the Highlands, at his post at Fort Montgomery, was equally alert. He had faithfully followed Washington's directions in ordering out militia from different counties to reinforce his own garrison and the army under Schuyler. At the same time, the governor expressed surprise that the Northern army had not been reinforced from the eastward. "Common gratitude to a sister State, as well as duty to the continent at large, conspire in calling on our eastern neighbors to step forth on this occasion."

One measure more was taken by Washington during this interval in aid of the Northern department. The Indians who accompanied Burgoyne were objects of great dread to the American troops, especially the militia. As a counterpoise to them, he sent up Colonel Morgan with five hundred riflemen to fight them in their own way. "I expect the most eminent services from them, and I shall be mistaken if their presence does not go far towards producing a general desertion among the savages." Putnam was directed to have sloops ready to transport them up the Hudson; Gates was informed of their being on the way and when he might expect them, as well as two regiments from Peekskill, under Colonels Van Courtlandt and Livingston.

"With these reinforcements, besides the militia under General Lincoln," writes Washington to Gates, "I am in hopes you will find yourself at least equal to stop the progress of Mr. Burgoyne, and, by cutting off his supplies of provisions, to render his situation very ineligible." Washington was thus carrying on two games at once, with Howe on the seaboard and with Burgoyne on the upper Hudson, endeavoring by skilful movements to give check to both.

His measures to throw a force in the rear of Burgoyne, were now in a fair way of being carried into effect. Lincoln was at Bennington. Stark had joined him with a body of New Hampshire militia, and a corps of Massachusetts militia was arriving. "Such a force in his rear," observed Washington, "will oblige Burgoyne to leave such strong posts behind as must make his main body very weak and extremely capable of being repulsed by the force we have in front."

During his encampment in the neighborhood of Philadelphia, Washington was repeatedly at that city, making himself acquainted with the military capabilities of the place and its surrounding country and directing the construction of fortifications on the river. In one of these visits he became acquainted with the young Marquis de

Lafayette, who had recently arrived from France. The marquis, not quite twenty years of age, had already been married three years to a lady of rank and fortune. He had torn himself from his youthful bride, turned his back upon the gayeties of a court, and had made his way to America to join its hazardous fortunes.

He sent in his letters of recommendation to the Committee of Foreign Affairs but received little encouragement; Congress was embarrassed by the foreign applications, many without merit. Lafayette immediately sent the following note: "After my sacrifices, I have the right to ask two favors: one is to serve at my own expense; the other to commence by serving as a volunteer." This simple appeal called attention to his peculiar case and Congress resolved on the 31st of July that, in consideration of his zeal and his illustrious family, he should have the rank of major-general in the army of the United States.

It was at a public dinner that Lafayette first saw Washington. When the party was breaking up, Washington took him aside, complimented him on his disinterested zeal and the generosity of his conduct, and invited him to make head-quarters his home.

Many days had now elapsed without further tidings of the fleet. What had become of it? Had Howe gone against Charleston? What, under these uncertainties, was to be done? Proceed to the Hudson to oppose Burgoyne or make an attempt upon New York? The latter was unanimously determined in a council of war, Congress approved the decision, and the army was about to march when all these uncertainties were brought to an end by intelligence that the fleet had entered the Chesapeake and anchored at Swan Point, at least 200 miles within the capes. "By General Howe's coming so far up the Chesapeake," writes Washington, "he must mean to reach Philadelphia by that route, though to be sure it is a strange one."

The several divisions of the army had been summoned to the immediate neighborhood of Philadelphia, and the militia of Pennsylvania, Delaware, and the northern parts of Virginia were called out. Many of the militia with Proctor's corps of artillery had been ordered to rendezvous at Chester on the Delaware, 12 miles below Philadelphia; and by Washington's orders, Wayne left his brigade under the next in command and repaired to Chester to arrange the troops assembling there.

As there had been much disaffection to the cause evinced in Philadelphia, Washington, in order to encourage its friends and dishearten its enemies, marched with the whole army through the city. Great pains were taken to make the display as imposing as possible. All were charged to keep to their ranks, carry their arms well, and step in time to the music of the drums and fifes collected in the centre of each brigade. To give them something of a uniform appearance, they had sprigs of green in their hats.

Washington rode at the head of the troops attended by his numerous staff, with the Marquis Lafayette by his side. The long column of the army, broken into divisions and brigades, the pioneers with their axes, the squadrons of horse, the trains of artillery, the bray of trumpet and the spirit-stirring sound of drum and fife, all had an imposing effect on a peaceful city unused to the sight of marshalled armies. The disaffected were astonished as they gazed on the procession which, to their unpractised eyes, appeared innumerable; the whigs, gaining fresh hope and animation from the sight, cheered the patriot squadrons as they passed.

The army continued on to Wilmington, at the confluence of Christiana Creek and the Brandywine, where Washington set up his head-quarters, his troops being encamped on the neighboring heights.

(CHAPTER 38)

We last left Burgoyne, early in July, at Skenesborough, of which he had just gained possession. He remained there nearly three weeks, awaiting the arrival of the residue of his troops, with tents, baggage and provisions, and preparing for his grand move toward the Hudson. Many royalists flocked to his standard. One of the most important was Major Skene, from whom the place was named, being its founder; Burgoyne considered him a valuable adjunct and frequently took advice from him in his campaign through this part of the country.

The progress of the army towards the Hudson was slow and difficult, in consequence of the impediments which Schuyler had multiplied in his way. Bridges had to be rebuilt and great trees to be removed which had been felled across roads and into Wood Creek. It was not until the latter part of July that Burgoyne reached Fort Anne. At his approach, Schuyler retired from Fort Edward to Fort Miller, a few miles lower down the Hudson.

The Indian allies who had hitherto accompanied the British army, had been more troublesome than useful. The Indians were of the tribes of Lower Canada, corrupted by intercourse with white men. It had been found difficult to draw them from plunder or to restrain their murderous propensities.

A party had recently arrived of a different stamp, braves of the Ottawa and other tribes from the upper country. They were the very Indians who had aided the French in the defeat of Braddock and were under the conduct of two French leaders; one, Langlade, had command of them on that very occasion; the other, St. Luc, was one of the best partisans of the French in the war of 1756. Burgoyne trusted these Indians to check Schuyler, knowing the terror they inspired throughout the country. He thought also to employ them in a foray to the Connecticut River to force a supply of provisions and intercept reinforcements to the American army. He was a humane man and disliked Indian allies, but these had heretofore served with civilized troops and he trusted St. Luc and Langlade to keep them within the usages of war.

A marauding party of these Indians, sent out by Burgoyne to harass the country, took a young American woman, Jane McCrea, captive, killed her, and completed the savage act by bearing off her scalp as a trophy. Burgoyne was reluctantly brought to spare the offender, but thenceforth made it a rule that no party of Indians should be permitted to go on a foray unless under the conduct of a British officer or some other person responsible for their behavior.

The murder of Miss McCrea resounded throughout the land. Those peoples of the frontiers, who had hitherto remained quiet, now flew to arms to defend their families and firesides. They abhorred an army, which, professing to be civilized, could league itself with such barbarians. The blood of this unfortunate girl, therefore, was not shed in vain. Armies sprang up from it. Her name passed as a note of alarm along the Hudson: it was a rallying word among the Green Mountains of Vermont and brought down all their hardy yeomanry.

As Burgoyne advanced to Fort Edward, Schuyler fell back to Saratoga, or rather Stillwater, about 30 miles from Albany. He had been joined by Lincoln, who, in pursuance of Washington's plans, proceeded to Manchester in Vermont to take command of the militia collecting at that point. He found about 500 militia assembled at Manchester under Colonel Seth Warner; others were coming on from New Hampshire and Massachusetts to protect their uncovered frontier. With these, according to Washington's plan, he was to hang on the flank and rear of Burgoyne's army, cramp its movements, and watch for an opportunity to strike a blow.

Burgoyne was now at Fort Edward. The enthusiasm of the general was checked, however, by ill-humor among his Indian allies. They were impatient under the restraint to which they were subjected. At the request of St. Luc, he called a council of the chiefs; to his astonishment, the tribe declared their intention of returning home and demanded his concurrence and assistance.

Burgoyne was greatly embarrassed. Should he acquiesce, it would be to relinquish the aid of a force which was especially serviceable in furnishing scouts and outposts. Yet he saw that a reconciliation with them could only be effected by indulging their propensities to blood and rapine. To his credit, he refused their proposition and persisted in the restraints he had imposed upon them. His speech appeared to have a good effect. Perfect harmony seemed restored. The next day, however, the chivalry of the wilderness deserted by scores, laden with such spoil as they had collected in their maraudings. These desertions continued from day to day until there remained in camp scarce a vestige of the savage warriors that had joined the army at Skenesborough.

New difficulties beset Burgoyne at Fort Edward. The horses contracted for in Canada arrived slowly and scantily, having to come a long distance through the wilderness. Artillery and munitions, too, had to be brought from Ticonderoga by the way of Lake George. These, with a vast number of boats for freight or to form bridges, it was necessary to transport over the carrying places between the lakes and by land from Fort George to Fort Edward. So far from being able to bring provisions for a march, it was with difficulty that enough could be furnished to feed the army from day to day.

While thus situated, Burgoyne received intelligence that the part of his army he had detached from Canada under St. Leger to proceed by Lake Ontario and Oswego and make a diversion on the Mohawk, had penetrated to that river and were investing Fort Stanwix, the stronghold of that part of the country.

It now behooved him to make a rapid move down the Hudson to be at hand to co-operate with St. Leger on his approach to Albany. But how was he to do this, deficient as he was in horses and vehicles? In this dilemma Colonel (late Major) Skene, the royalist of Skenesborough, informed him that at Bennington, about 24 miles east of the Hudson, the Americans had a great depot of horses, carriages, and supplies intended for their Northern army. This place might easily be surprised, being guarded by only a small militia force.

An expedition was immediately set on foot, not only to surprise this place, but to scour the country and return by the great road to Albany, there to meet Burgoyne. They were to make prisoners of all officers, civil and military, acting under Congress, to tax the towns where they halted with every thing they stood in need of, and bring off all horses fit for service. They were every where to give out that this was the vanguard of the British army on its way to Boston, to be joined by the army from Rhode Island.

Before relating the events of this expedition, we will turn to the detachment under St. Leger, with which it was intended to co-operate and which was investing Fort Schuyler.

This fort, built in 1756 on the site of an old French fortification, and formerly called Fort Stanwix, was situated on the right bank of the Mohawk River, commanding the carrying place between it and Wood Creek, whence the boats passed to Oneida Lake, Oswego River, and Lake Ontario. It was thus a key to the intercourse between Upper Canada and the valley of the Mohawk. The fort was square, with four bastions, and was originally a place of strength having bomb-proof magazines, a deep moat and drawbridge, a sally port, and covered way. In the interval of peace subsequent to the French war, it had fallen to decay. Recently it had been repaired by Schuyler and received his name. It was garrisoned by 750 Continental troops from New York and Massachusetts under Colonel Gansevoort of New York, who had served under General Montgomery in Canada.

It was a motley force which appeared before it—British, Hessian, Royalist, Canadian and Indian, about 1700 in all. Among them were St. Leger's rangers, Sir John Johnson's royalist corps, Indians led by the famous Brant.

On the 3d of August, St. Leger sent in a flag with a summons to surrender, which was disregarded. He now set his troops to work to fortify his camp and clear obstructions from Wood Creek and the roads, and he sent scouting parties of Indians in all directions to cut off the communication of the garrison with the surrounding country.

On the 6th of August, three men made their way into the fort through a swamp and brought the intelligence that General Herkimer was at Oriskany, about 8 miles distant, with upwards of 800 men. He had requested Gansevoort, through his two messengers, to fire three signal-guns on receiving word of his vicinage; upon hearing which, he would endeavor to force his way to the fort, depending upon the co-operation of the garrison.

The messengers had been despatched by Herkimer on the evening of the 5th and he had calculated they would reach the fort very early in the morning. Through some delay, they did not reach it until almost eleven o'clock. Gansevoort instantly complied with the message; signal-guns were fired and Colonel Willett, with 250 men and an iron three-pounder, was detached to make a diversion by attacking that part of the enemy's camp occupied by Johnson and his royalists.

The delay of the messengers in the night, however, disconcerted the plan of Herkimer. He marshalled his troops by daybreak and waited for the signal-guns. Hour after hour elapsed, but no gun was heard. His officers, impatient of delay, urged an immediate march. High words ensued between him and two of his officers. He had relatives among the enemy and hence there were some doubts of his fidelity, subsequently proved to be unmerited. Colonels Cox and Paris were particularly urgent for an advance and suspicious of the motives for holding back. Paris, a prominent man in Tryon County, losing his temper in the dispute, accused Herkimer of being either a tory or a coward. Herkimer's discretion, however, was overpowered by repeated taunts and he at length, about nine o'clock, gave the word to march, intimating, however, that those who were most eager to advance would be first to run away.

The march was dogged and irregular. There was ill-humor between the general and his officers. Colonels Paris and Cox advised him to throw out a reconnoitring party in the advance, but he disregarded their advice and neglected so necessary a precaution. About ten o'clock they came to a place where the road crossed a marshy ravine. They had scarcely crossed, when enemies suddenly sprang up in front and on either side with deadly volleys of musketry and deafening yells and war-whoops. St. Leger, apprised by his scouts of their approach, had sent a force to waylay them. This force was composed of a division of Johnson's men, a company of rangers, and a strong body of Indians under Brant. The plan of the ambuscade was to let the van of the Americans pass the ravine, when the attack was to be commenced by the troops in front, after which the Indians were to fall on the Americans in rear and cut off all retreat.

The savages, however, could not restrain their ferocity and discharged their rifles simultaneously with the troops and instantly rushed forward, commencing a dreadful butchery. The rear-guard, which had not entered the ravine, retreated. The main body defended themselves bravely in one of those conflicts common in Indian warfare, where the combatants take post with their rifles behind rock and tree or come to deadly struggle with knife and tomahawk.

The veteran Herkimer was wounded early in the action. He made his men place him at the foot of a large tree and he continued to give his orders.

The regulars attempted to charge with the bayonet, but the Americans formed themselves in circles back to back and repelled them. Old neighbors met in deadly feud; war was literally carried to the knife, for bodies were afterwards found grappled in death, the hand still grasping the knife plunged in a neighbor's heart. The Indians, at length, having lost many of their bravest warriors, fled to the woods. The other troops, hearing a firing in the direction of the fort, feared an attack upon their camp and hastened to its defence. The Americans did not pursue them, but returned to Oriskany. It would seem as if each party gladly abandoned this scene of one of the most savage conflicts of the Revolution. We may add, that Cox was shot down at the first fire and so was a son of Colonel Paris; the colonel himself was taken prisoner and fell beneath the tomahawk of the famous Red Jacket. As to Herkimer, he was conveyed to his residence and died nine days after the battle, sinking gradually through loss of blood from an unskilful amputation. He died like a philosopher and a Christian, smoking his pipe and reading his Bible to the last.

The sortie of Colonel Willett had been spirited and successful. He attacked the encampments of Sir John Johnson and the Indians, strong detachments of which were absent on the ambuscade. Sir John and his men were driven to the river; the Indians fled to the woods. Willett sacked their camps; loaded waggons with camp equipage, clothing, blankets, and stores, seized the baggage and papers of Sir John and several of his officers, and retreated to the fort just as St. Leger was coming up with a powerful reinforcement.

St. Leger now endeavored to operate on the fears of the garrison. His prisoners, it is said, were compelled to write a letter giving dismal accounts of the affair of Oriskany and advising surrender to prevent inevitable destruction. St. Leger accompanied the letter with warnings that, should the garrison persist in resistance, he would not be able to restrain the savages who threatened to slaughter the garrison and lay waste the whole valley of the Mohawk.

All this failing to shake the resolution of Gansevoort, St. Leger next issued an appeal to the inhabitants of Tryon County, signed by their old neighbors, Sir John Johnson, Colonel Claus and Colonel Butler, promising pardon and protection to all who should submit to royal authority. The people of the county, however, were as little moved as the garrison.

St. Leger now began to lose heart. The fort proved more capable of defence than he had anticipated. He was obliged to resort to the slow process of sapping and mining.

Gansevoort, seeing the siege was likely to be protracted, resolved to send to Schuyler for succor. Willett volunteered to undertake the perilous errand, accompanied by Lieutenant Stockwell, who served as a guide. They left the fort on the 10th, after dark, and made their way through bog and morass and pathless forests until they reached the camp of General Schuyler at Stillwater. A change had come over the position of that commander four days previous to the arrival of Willett.

Schuyler was in Albany in early August, making appeals in every direction for reinforcements. Burgoyne was advancing upon him, he had received news of the disastrous affair of Oriskany, and Tryon County was crying to him for assistance. One of his appeals was to John Stark, the comrade of Putnam in the French war and the battle of Bunker's Hill. He had his farm in the Hampshire Grants and his name was a tower of strength among the Green Mountain Boys. But Stark had retired from service, his name having been omitted in the list of promotions. Hearing that he was on a visit to Lincoln's camp at Manchester, Schuyler wrote, "Assure General Stark that I have acquainted Congress of his situation, and that I trust and entreat he will, in the present alarming crisis, waive his right; . . . entreat him to march immediately to our army."

Schuyler was about to mount his horse on the 10th, to return to the camp at Stillwater, when a despatch from Congress was put into his hand containing the resolves which called him to a court of inquiry about the affair of Ticonderoga and requested Washington to appoint an officer to succeed him.

Schuyler felt deeply the indignity of being thus recalled, but endeavored to console himself with the certainty that investigation of his conduct would prove how much he was entitled to the thanks of his country. He intimated the same in his reply to Congress; in the mean time, he considered it his duty to remain at his post until his successor should arrive. Returning, therefore, to the camp at Stillwater, he continued to conduct the affairs of the army with unremitting zeal.

His first care was to send relief to Gansevoort and his beleaguered garrison. Eight hundred men were all he could spare from his army in its threatened state. A spirited and effective officer was wanted to lead them. Arnold was in camp, recently sent as an efficient coadjutor by Washington, and promptly volunteered to lead the enterprise.

After the departure of this detachment, it was unanimously determined in a council of war that the post at Stillwater was untenable with their actual force; part of the army, therefore, retired to the islands where the Mohawk River empties into the Hudson, while a brigade was posted above the Falls of the Mohawk, called the Cohoes, to prevent the enemy from crossing there. It was considered a strong position, where they could not be attacked without great disadvantage to the assailant.

We will now take a view of occurrences on the right and left of Burgoyne, and show the effect of Schuyler's measures, poorly seconded as they were, in crippling and straitening the invading army. First, we will treat of the expedition against Bennington, whence the American army derived its supplies. It was to be surprised. Phillips and Riedesel demurred strongly to the expedition, but their counsels were outweighed by those of Skene. He knew, he said, all the country thereabout. The inhabitants were in favor of the royal cause and would be prompt to turn out on the first appearance of a protecting army. He was to accompany the expedition, and much was expected from his personal influence and authority.

Lieutenant-colonel Baum was to command the detachment. He had under him 200 dismounted dragoons of the regiment of Riedesel, Fraser's marksmen, all the Canadian volunteers, a party of provincials who knew the country, 100 Indians, and 2 light pieces of cannon. The whole detachment amounted to about 500 men. The dragoons, it was expected, would supply themselves with horses in the course of the foray, and a skeleton corps of royalists would be filled up by recruits.

To be nearer at hand in case assistance should be required, Burgoyne encamped east of the Hudson, nearly opposite Saratoga, throwing over a bridge of boats by which Fraser, with the advanced guard, crossed to that place.

Baum set out from camp at break of day, on the 13th of August but he was too slow a man to take a place by surprise. The people of Bennington heard of his approach and were on the alert. Stark was there with about 900 troops. During the late alarms the militia of the State had been formed into two brigades, one commanded by General William Whipple; Stark had been prevailed upon to accept command of the other, upon the express condition that he should not be obliged to join the main army, but should be left to make war in his own partisan style and accountable to none but the authorities of New Hampshire.

Lincoln had informed Stark of the orders of Schuyler that all militia should repair to Stillwater, but the veteran refused to comply. He had taken up arms, he said, to defend the neighborhood, which would be exposed to the enemy should he leave it, and he held himself accountable solely to the authorities of New Hampshire. This act of insubordination might have involved the doughty old general in difficulty had not his sword carved out an ample excuse for him.

Having heard that Indians had appeared at Cambridge, 12 miles to the north of Bennington, on the 13th, he sent out 200 men under Gregg in quest of them. In the course of the night he learnt that they were mere scouts in advance of a force marching upon Bennington. He immediately rallied his brigade, called out the militia of the neighborhood, and sent off for Warner and his regiment of militia, who were with Lincoln at Manchester. Lincoln instantly detached them, and Warner and his men marched all night through drenching rain, arriving at Stark's camp in the morning.

Stark left them at Bennington to dry and rest and then to follow on; in the mean time, he pushed forward with his men to support the party sent out the preceding day under Gregg in quest of the Indians. He met them in full retreat, Baum and his force a mile in their rear.

Stark halted and prepared for action. Baum also halted, posted himself on a high ground, and began to intrench himself. Stark fell back a mile to wait for reinforcements and draw Baum from his strong position.

An incessant rain on the 15th prevented an attack on Baum's camp, but there was continual skirmishing. The colonel strengthened his intrenchments and, finding he had a larger force to contend with than he had anticipated, sent off in all haste to Burgoyne for reinforcements. Breyman marched off immediately with 500 Hessian grenadiers and infantry and 2 six-pounders. "So foolishly attached were they to forms of discipline," writes a British historian, "that in marching through thickets they stopped ten times an hour to dress their ranks." It was here, in fact, that they most dreaded the American rifle. "In the open field," said they, "the rebels are not much; but they are redoubtable in the woods."

In the mean time the alert Americans had been mustering from all quarters to Stark's assistance with such weapons as they had at hand. During the night of the 15th, Colonel Symonds arrived with a body of Berkshire militia.

On the following morning Stark prepared to attack Baum in his intrenchments though he had no artillery and his men, for the most part, had only their ordinary brown firelocks without bayonets. Two hundred of his men, under Colonel Nichols, were detached to the rear of the enemy's left; 300 under Colonel Herrick, to the rear of his right; they were to join forces and attack him in the rear while Colonels Hubbard and Stickney, with 200 men, diverted his attention in front.

At the first sound of fire-arms, Stark, who had remained with the main body in camp, mounted his horse and gave the word, "Forward!" He had promised his men the plunder of the British camp. The homely speech made by him when in sight of the enemy, has often been cited. "Now, my men! There are the red coats! Before night they must be ours or Molly Stark will be a widow!"

Baum soon found himself assailed on every side, but he defended his works bravely. His two pieces of artillery, advantageously planted, were very effective, and his troops, if slow in march, were steady in action. For two hours the discharge of fire-arms was said to have been like the constant rattling of the drum. Stark inspired his men with his own impetuosity. They drove the royalist troops upon the Hessians and, pressing after them, stormed the works with irresistible fury. The artillerists were slain, the cannon captured. The royalists and Canadians escaped to the woods. The Germans kept their ground and fought bravely until there was not a cartridge left. Baum and his men then took to their broadswords and bayonets, but in vain; many were killed, more wounded, and all who survived were taken prisoners.

The victors now dispersed, some to collect booty, some to attend to the wounded, some to guard the prisoners, and some to seek refreshment, being exhausted by hunger and fatigue. At this juncture, Breyman's tardy reinforcement came, making its way heavily and slowly to the scene of action, joined by many of the enemy who had fled. Attempts were made to rally the militia, but they were in complete confusion. Nothing would have saved them from defeat, had not Colonel Seth Warner's corps fortunately arrived from Bennington and advanced to meet the enemy, while the others regained their ranks. It was four o'clock in the afternoon when this second action commenced, fought from wood to wood and hill to hill for several miles until sunset. The last stand of the enemy was at Van Schaick's mill, where, having expended all their ammunition, they retreated under favor of night, leaving two field-pieces and all their baggage in the hands of the Americans. Stark ceased to pursue them, lest in the darkness his men should fire upon each other.

Burgoyne was awakened in his camp towards daylight of the 17th, by tidings that Baum had surrendered. Next came word that Breyman was engaged in severe and doubtful conflict. The whole army was roused, preparing to hasten to his assistance, when one report after another gave assurance he was on his way back in safety. The main body, therefore, remained in camp, but Burgoyne forded that stream with the 47th regiment and pushed forward until he met Breyman and his troops, weary and haggard. In the evening all returned to their old encampments.

General Schuyler was encamped at the mouth of the Mohawk River when a letter from Lincoln informed him of "the capital blow given the enemy by General Stark." "I trust," replies he, "that the severity with which they have been handled will retard General

Burgoyne's progress. Part of his force was yesterday afternoon about three miles and a half above Stillwater. If the enemy have entirely left that part of the country you are in, I think it would be advisable for you to move towards Hudson River tending towards Stillwater."

Tidings of the affair of Bennington reached Washington just before he moved his camp to Wilmington. In a letter to Putnam he writes, "As there is not now the least danger of General Howe's going to New England, I hope the whole force of that country will turn out, and, by following the great stroke struck by General Stark near Bennington, entirely crush General Burgoyne."

We will now give the fate of Burgoyne's detachment, under St. Leger, sent to capture Fort Stanwix and ravage the valley of the Mohawk.

Arnold's march to the relief of Fort Stanwix was slower than suited his ardent and impatient spirit. He was detained in the valley of the Mohawk by bad roads, by the necessity of waiting for baggage and ammunition waggons, and for militia recruits who turned out reluctantly.

Conscious of the smallness of his force, Arnold resorted to sending emissaries ahead to spread exaggerated reports of the number of his troops. The most important of these emissaries was Yan Yost Cuyler, an eccentric fellow known throughout the country as a rank tory. He had been convicted as a spy and spared on condition that he would go into St. Leger's camp and spread alarming reports among the Indians, by whom he was well known. To insure faithful discharge of his mission, Arnold detained his brother as a hostage.

On his way up the Mohawk Valley, Arnold was joined by a New York regiment under Colonel James Livingston, sent by Gates to reinforce him. In a letter to Gates, written from the German Flats (August 21st), Arnold says, "I leave this place this morning with 1200 Continental troops and a handful of militia for Fort Schuyler, still besieged by a number equal to ours. You will hear of my being victorious—or no more."

All this while St. Leger was advancing his parallels and pressing the siege while provisions and ammunition were rapidly decreasing within the fort. St. Leger's Indian allies, however, were growing sullen. They had been led to expect little fighting, many scalps, and much plunder; whereas they had fought hard, lost many of their best chiefs, been checked in their cruelty, and gained no booty.

At this juncture, scouts brought word that a force 1000 strong was marching to the relief of the fort. Eager to put his savages in action, St. Leger offered to their chiefs to place himself at their head, with 300 of his best troops, and meet the enemy as they advanced. It was agreed, and they sallied forth together to choose a fighting ground. By this time rumors stole into the camp doubling the number of the approaching enemy. Burgoyne's whole army were said to have been defeated. Lastly came Yan Yost Cuyler, with his coat full of bullet holes, giving out that he had escaped from the hands of the Americans. His story was believed, for he was known to be a royalist. Mingling among his old acquaintances, the Indians, he assured them that the Americans were close at hand and "numerous as the leaves on the trees."

Arnold's stratagem succeeded. The Indians began to desert. In a little while 200 had decamped and the rest threatened to do so likewise unless St. Leger retreated instantly. St. Leger still refused to depart before nightfall. The savages now became ungovernable. In a word, St. Leger was obliged to decamp about noon, in such hurry and confusion that he left his tents standing, and his artillery with most of his baggage, ammunition and stores fell into the hands of the Americans.

A detachment from the garrison pursued and harassed him for a time, but his greatest annoyance was from his Indian allies, who plundered the boats which conveyed such baggage as had been brought off, murdered all stragglers, and amused themselves by giving false alarms to keep up the panic of the soldiery. It was not until he reach Onondaga Falls that St. Leger discovered by a letter from Burgoyne and reports brought by the bearer that he had been the dupe of a *ruse de guerre* and that, at the time the advancing foe were reported to be close upon his haunches, they were not within 40 miles of him.

Such was the second blow to Burgoyne's invading army, but before the news of it had reached that doomed commander, he had already been half paralyzed by the disaster at Bennington.

The moral effect of these two blows was such as Washington had predicted. Fortune, so long adverse, seemed at length to have taken a favorable turn. People were roused from their despondency. There was a sudden exultation throughout the country.

Means were now augmenting in Schuyler's hands. Colonels Livingston and Pierre van Cortlandt, forwarded by Putnam, arrived. Governor Clinton was daily expected with New York militia from the Highlands. The arrival of Arnold was anticipated with troops and artillery, and Lincoln with the New England militia. At this propitious moment Gates arrived in the camp. Schuyler received him with noble courtesy. After acquainting him with all the affairs of the department, he informed him of his intention to render every service in his power and entreated Gates to call upon him for counsel and assistance whenever he thought proper.

Gates was in high spirits. His letters to Washington show how completely he was aware that an easy path of victory had been opened for him. Not a word does he say of consulting Schuyler, who, more than any one else, had co-operated in effecting the measures which had produced the present promising situation of affairs. So far was he from responding to Schuyler's magnanimity and profiting by his counsel and assistance that he did not even ask him to be present at his first council of war.

Gates opened hostilities against Burgoyne with the pen. He had received a letter from that commander, complaining of the harsh treatment experienced by the royalists captured at Bennington. "Duty and principle," writes Burgoyne, "made me a public enemy to the Americans who have taken up arms; but I seek to be a generous one; nor have I the shadow of resentment against any individual who does not induce it by acts derogatory to those maxims upon which all men of honor think alike."

There was nothing in this that was not borne out by the conduct and character of Burgoyne; but Gates seized upon the occasion to assail that commander in no measured terms in regard to his Indian allies.

"That the savages," said he, "should in their warfare mangle the unhappy prisoners who fall into their hands, is neither new nor extraordinary; but that the famous General Burgoyne, in whom the fine gentleman is united with the scholar, should hire the savages of America to scalp Europeans: nay more, that he should pay a price for each scalp so barbarously taken, is more than will be believed in Europe, until authenticated facts shall in every gazette confirm the horrid tale."

Burgoyne, in a manly reply, declared that he would have disdained to justify himself from such fiction and calumny but his silence might be construed into an admission of their truth. We have already shown what was the real conduct of Burgoyne, and Gates could and should have ascertained it before "he presumed to impute" to a gallant antagonist and a humane and cultivated gentleman, such base and barbarous policy. It was the government under which Burgoyne served that was chargeable with the murderous acts of the savages. He was rather to be pitied for being obliged to employ such hell-hounds, whom he endeavored in vain to hold in check. Great Britain reaped the reward of her policy in the odium which it cast upon her cause and the determined and successful opposition which it provoked in the American bosom.

(CHAPTER 39)

We now shift the scene to Washington's camp at Wilmington, where we left him watching the operations of the British fleet and preparing to oppose the army under Sir William Howe in its designs upon Philadelphia.

On the 25th of August the British army under General Howe began to land from the fleet in Elk River, at the bottom of Chesapeake Bay. The place where they landed was below the Head of Elk (now Elkton), the capital of Cecil County. This was 70 miles from Philadelphia. Sir William had chosen this route in the expectation of finding among the people of Cecil County and of the lower counties of Pennsylvania many Quakers, noncombatants, and persons disaffected to the patriot cause.

Early in the evening, Washington received intelligence that the enemy were landing. There was a quantity of stores at the Head of Elk which he feared would fall into their hands. Every attempt was to be made to check them. The divisions of Greene and Stephen were within a few miles of Wilmington; orders were sent to march thither immediately. The two other divisions, which had halted at Chester to refresh, were to hurry forward. Major-general Armstrong, who commanded the Pennsylvania militia, was urged to send all the men he could muster.

General Rodney, who commanded the Delaware militia, was ordered to throw out scouts and patrols toward the enemy to watch their motions; and to move near them as soon as he should be reinforced by the Maryland militia.

The country was in a great state of alarm. The inhabitants were hurrying off their most valuable effects, so that it was difficult to procure cattle and vehicles to remove the public stores. The want of horses and the annoyances given by American light troops, however, kept Howe from advancing promptly and gave time for the greater part of the stores to be saved.

To allay public alarm, Howe issued a proclamation on the 27th, promising security of person and property to all who remained quietly at home and pardon to those under arms who should promptly return to their obedience.

The divisions of Greene and Stephen were now stationed several miles in advance of Wilmington, about 10 miles from the Head of Elk. Smallwood and Gist had been directed by Congress to take command of the militia of Maryland, who were gathering on the western shore, and Washington sent them orders to cooperate with Rodney and get in the rear of the enemy.

Washington now felt the want of Morgan and his riflemen, whom he had sent to assist the Northern army; to supply their place, he formed a corps of light troops by drafting 100 men from each brigade. Command was given to Maxwell, who was to hover about the enemy and give them continual annoyance.

The army about this time was increased by the arrival of Sullivan and his division of 3000 men. He had recently, while encamped at Hanover in Jersey, made a gallant attempt to surprise a corps of 1000 provincials on Staten Island. The attempt was partially successful, but the regulars came to the rescue. Sullivan had not brought sufficient boats to secure a retreat and his rear-guard was captured while waiting for the boats, yet not without sharp resistance. Congress directed Washington to appoint a court of inquiry to investigate the matter; in the mean time, Sullivan, whose gallantry remained undoubted, continued in command.

There were now in camp several of those officers from Europe the suitable employment of whom had been a source of much perplexity to Washington. General Deborre, the French veteran, commanded a brigade in Sullivan's division. Brigadier-general Conway, the Gallicized Hibernian, was in the division of Stirling. There was Louis Fleury, a French engineer who had come at the opening of the Revolution to offer his services; Washington had obtained for him a captain's commission. Another officer of distinguished merit was the Count Pulaski, a Pole, an officer famous throughout Europe for his bravery in defence of the liberties of his country against Russia, Austria, and Prussia. He served at present as a volunteer in the light-horse and Washington suggested to Congress the expediency of giving him the command of it.

At this time Henry Lee of Virginia, of military renown, makes his first appearance. He was in the twenty-second year of his age and in the preceding year had commanded a company of Virginia volunteers. He had recently signalized himself in scouting parties, harassing the enemy's pickets. His adventurous exploits soon won him notoriety and the popular appellation of "Light-horse Harry." He was favorably noticed by Washington throughout the war. Perhaps there was something beside his bold, dashing spirit, which won him this favor, for Lee was the son of the lady who first touched Washington's heart in his school-boy days, the one about whom he wrote rhymes at Mount Vernon.

Several days were now passed by the commander-in-chief making himself acquainted with the surrounding country, which was much intersected by rivers and streams, running chiefly from northwest to southeast. He had now made up his mind to risk a battle in the open field although his troops were inferior to those of the enemy in number, equipment, and discipline. The divisions of the army had acquired facility at moving in large masses and were considerably improved in military tactics. At any rate, it would never do to let Philadelphia, at that time the capital of the States, fall without a blow.

The British army, having effected a landing, was formed into two divisions. One, under Howe, was at Elkton, with its advanced guard at Gray's Hill two miles off. The other, under Knyphausen, was on the opposite side of the ferry, at Cecil Court House. On the third of September the enemy advanced in considerable force, with three field-pieces, moving with great caution. About three miles in front of White Clay Creek, their vanguard was encountered by Maxwell and his light troops, and a severe skirmish took place. The fire of the American sharpshooters and riflemen was very effective but, being inferior in number and having no artillery, Maxwell was compelled to retreat across White Clay Creek.

The main body of the American army was encamped east of Red Clay Creek, on the road from Elkton to Philadelphia. The light-infantry were in the advance, at White Clay Creek. The armies were 8 to 10 miles apart. In this position, Washington determined to await the threatened attack.

On the 5th of September he made a stirring appeal to the army, stating the object of the enemy, the capture of Philadelphia. They had tried it before, from the Jerseys, and had failed. He trusted they would be again disappointed. Now was the time for the most strenuous exertions. "Two years," said he, "have we . . . struggled with difficulties innumerable, but the prospect has brightened. Now is the time to reap the fruit of all our toils and dangers." Washington's force was about 15,000 men, but from sickness and other causes the effective force, militia included, did not exceed 11,000. The strength of the British was computed at 18,000 men, but, it is thought, not more than 15,000 were brought into action.

On the 8th, the enemy advanced in two columns, one appeared preparing to attack the Americans in front, while the other extended its left up west of the creek halting at Milltown, somewhat to the right of the American position. Washington suspected an intention on the part of Howe to march by his right, suddenly pass the Brandywine, gain the heights north of that stream, and cut him off from Philadelphia. He summoned a council of war that evening, in which it was determined to change their position and move to the river in question. In the morning the army was under march and by the next evening was on the high grounds in the rear of the Brandywine. The enemy on the same evening moved to Kennet Square, seven miles from the American position.

The Brandywine commences with two branches which unite in one stream, flowing from west to east 22 miles and emptying into the Delaware 25 miles below Philadelphia. It has several fords; one, called Chadd's Ford, the most practicable, was in the direct route from the enemy's camp to Philadelphia. As the principal attack was expected here, Washington made it the centre of his position, where he stationed the main body of his army, composed of Wayne's, Weedon's, and Muhlenberg's brigades, with the light-infantry under Maxwell. An eminence immediately above the ford had been intrenched in the night, and was occupied by Wayne and Proctor's artillery. Weedon's and Muhlenberg's brigades, which formed Greene's division, were posted in the rear on the heights as a reserve to aid either wing of the army. With these Washington took his stand. Maxwell's light-infantry were thrown in the advance, south of the Brandywine, and posted on high ground each side of the road leading to the ford.

The right wing of the army commanded by Sullivan, composed of his division and those of Stephen and Stirling, extended up the Brandywine two miles beyond Washington's position. Its light troops and videttes were distributed up to the forks. The left wing, the Pennsylvania militia under Armstrong, was stationed about a mile and a half below the main body to protect the lower fords, where the least danger was apprehended. The Brandywine was now the only obstacle between the two armies.

Early on the morning of the 11th, a great column of troops was descried advancing on the road to Chadd's Ford. It was supposed to be the main body of the enemy; if so, a general conflict was at hand. The Americans were immediately drawn out in order of battle.

Washington rode along the front of the ranks and was every where received with acclamations. A sharp firing of small arms soon told that Maxwell's light-infantry were engaged with the vanguard of the enemy. The skirmishing was kept up for some time with spirit, when Maxwell was driven across the Brandywine below the ford. The enemy did not follow but halted on commanding ground and appeared to reconnoitre the American position with a view to an attack. A heavy cannonading commenced on both sides about ten o'clock. The enemy made repeated dispositions to force the ford, which brought on frequent skirmishes on both sides of the river, for detachments of the light troops occasionally crossed over. All this while, there was the noise and uproar of a battle, but little of the reality. The enemy made a great thundering of cannon but no vigorous onset.

Towards noon came an express from Sullivan, reporting that Howe, with a large body of troops and artillery, was pushing up the Lancaster road, doubtless to cross at the upper fords and turn the right flank of the American position. Startled by the information, Washington instantly sent off Colonel Bland to reconnoitre above the forks and ascertain the truth of the report. In the mean time, he resolved to cross the ford, attack the division in front of him with his whole force, and rout it before the other could arrive. He gave orders for both wings to co-operate.

Colonel Bland, whom Washington had sent to reconnoitre above the forks, had seen the enemy two miles in the rear of Sullivan's right, marching down at a rapid rate, while a cloud of dust showed that there were more troops behind them.

The old Long Island stratagem had been played over again. Knyphausen had engrossed the Americans by a feigned attack at Chadd's Ford, kept up with great noise and prolonged by skirmishes, while the main body of the army under Cornwallis had made a circuit of 17 miles, crossed the forks of the Brandywine, and arrived two miles to the right of Sullivan. It was a capital stratagem, successfully conducted.

Finding Cornwallis had gained the rear of the army, Washington sent orders to Sullivan to oppose him with the whole right wing, each brigade attacking as soon as it arrived upon the ground. Wayne, in the mean time, was to keep Knyphausen at bay at the ford, and Greene, with the reserve, to hold himself ready to aid wherever required. Lafayette, seeing there was likely to be warm work with the right wing, obtained permission to join Sullivan and spurred off to the scene of action.

Sullivan, on receiving Washington's orders, advanced with his own, Stephen's and Stirling's divisions, and began to form a line in front of an open piece of wood. The time expended in transmitting intelligence, receiving orders, and marching had enabled Cornwallis to choose his ground and prepare for action. Still more time was given him by a delay of the Americans arising from a mere point of etiquette. Stirling's division had accidentally formed on the right of Sullivan's; this was taking rank of him; the position had to be changed, and this change was taking place when Cornwallis advanced rapidly with his troops and opened a brisk fire of musketry and artillery. The Americans made an obstinate resistance, but, taken at a disadvantage, the right and left wings were broken and driven into the woods. The centre stood firm for a while, but gave way at length also. The British, following up their advantage, got entangled in the wood. Lafayette was endeavoring to rally the troops, when he was shot through the leg with a musket ball. The Americans rallied on a height north of Dilworth and made a spirited resistance but were again obliged to retreat with a heavy loss.

While this was occurring with the right wing, Knyphausen, as soon as he learnt that Cornwallis was engaged, made a push to force his way across Chadd's Ford in earnest. He was vigorously opposed by Wayne with Proctor's artillery, aided by Maxwell and his infantry. Greene was preparing to second him with the reserve, when he was summoned by Washington to support the right wing, which the commander-in-chief had found in imminent peril.

Greene advanced to the relief with such celerity that his division accomplished the march, or rather run, of 5 miles in less than 50 minutes. He arrived too late to save the battle but in time to protect the broken masses of the left wing, which he met in full flight. Opening his ranks for the fugitives and closing them the moment they had passed, he covered their retreat by a sharp and well-directed fire from his field-pieces. His grand stand was made at a place a mile beyond Dilworth, which, in reconnoitring the neighborhood, Washington had pointed out to him as well calculated for a second position, should the army be driven out of the first. Weedon's brigade was drawn up in a narrow defile, flanked by woods and commanding the road, while Greene, with Muhlenberg's brigade, passing to the right took his station on the road. The British came on impetuously, expecting faint opposition. They met with a desperate resistance and were repeatedly driven back. The check given to the enemy by these two brigades allowed time for the broken troops to retreat. Greene gradually drew off the whole division in face of the enemy, who, checked by this vigorous resistance and seeing the day far spent, gave up all further pursuit.

The brave stand made by these brigades had, likewise, been a great protection to Wayne. He had withstood the attacks of the enemy at Chadd's Ford, until the approach of some of the enemy's troops who had been entangled in the woods showed him that the right wing had been routed. He gave up the defence of his post and retreated by the Chester road. Knyphausen's troops were too fatigued to pursue him. So ended the varied conflict of the day.

Lafayette gives an animated picture of the general retreat. All around him was headlong terror and confusion. Chester road, the common retreat of the broken fragments of the army, was crowded with fugitives, with cannon, with baggage cars, all hurrying forward pell-mell. The thundering of cannon and volleying of musketry by the contending parties in the rear added to the confusion and panic of the flight. At Chester, however, there was a deep stream with a bridge over which the fugitives would have to pass. Here Lafayette set a guard to prevent their further flight. The commander-in-chief arrived soon after with Greene and his division; some order was restored and the whole army took its post behind Chester for the night.

The scene of this battle, which decided the fate of Philadelphia, was 26 miles from that city and each discharge of cannon could be heard there. The two parties of the inhabitants, whig and tory, awaited the event in anxious silence. At length a courier arrived. His tidings spread consternation among the friends of liberty. Many left their homes; entire families abandoned every thing in terror and despair. Congress, that same evening, determined to repair to Lancaster, whence they subsequently removed to Yorktown. Before leaving Philadelphia, however, they summoned the militia of Pennsylvania and the adjoining States to join the main army without delay, and they ordered down 1500 Continental troops from Putnam's command on the Hudson.

Notwithstanding the retreat of the American army, Howe did not press the pursuit, but passed the night on the field of battle and remained the two following days at Dilworth, sending out detachments to take post at Concord and Chester and seize on Wilmington, whither the sick and wounded were conveyed.

Washington profited by the inactivity of Howe, quietly retreating through Derby (on the 12th) across the Schuylkill to Germantown, within a short distance of Philadelphia, where he gave his troops a day's repose. Finding them in good spirits, he resolved to seek the enemy again and give him battle. As preliminary measures, he left some of the Pennsylvania militia in Philadelphia to guard the city; others, under Armstrong, were posted at the various passes of the Schuylkill with orders to throw up works; the floating bridge on the lower road was to be unmoored and the boats collected and taken across the river.

Having taken these precautions against any hostile movement by the lower road, Washington recrossed the Schuylkill on the 14th and advanced along the Lancaster road with the intention of turning the left flank of the enemy. Howe, apprised of his intention, made a similar disposition to outflank him. The two armies came in sight of each other 23 miles from Philadelphia and were on the point of engaging, but were prevented by a violent rain which lasted for 24 hours.

This inclement weather was particularly distressing to the Americans, scantily clothed, destitute of blankets, and separated from their tents and baggage. The rain penetrated their cartridge boxes and the ill-fitted locks of their muskets, rendering the latter useless, being deficient in bayonets. In this plight, Washington gave up for the present all thought of attacking the enemy. The only aim, at present, was to get to some dry and secure place, where the army might repose and refit. All day and for a great part of the night they marched under a pelting rain through miry roads to the Yellow Springs, thence to Warwick, on French Creek. At Warwick furnace, ammunition and a few muskets were obtained to aid in disputing passage of the Schuylkill and the advance of the enemy on Philadelphia.

From French Creek, Wayne was detached with his division to get in the rear of the enemy, form a junction with Smallwood and the Maryland militia, and, keeping concealed, watch for an opportunity to cut off Howe's baggage and hospital train; in the mean time, Washington crossed the Schuylkill at Parker's Ford and took a position to defend that pass of the river.

Wayne set off in the night, and, by a circuitous march, got within three miles of the left wing of the British encamped at Trydraffin and, concealing himself in a wood, waited the arrival of Smallwood and his militia. At daybreak he reconnoitred the camp, where Howe, checked by the severity of the weather, remained under shelter. Wayne sent repeated messages to Washington, describing the situation of the enemy and urging him to attack them in their camp. He writes: "The enemy are very quiet. . . . I expect General Maxwell on the left flank every moment, and, as I lay on the right, we only want you in their rear to complete Mr. Howe's business. I believe he knows nothing of my situation, as I have taken every precaution to prevent any intelligence getting to him."

His motions, however, had not been so secret as he imagined. He was in a part of the country full of the disaffected and Sir William had received accurate information of his force. Gray, with a strong detachment, was sent to surprise him at night in his lair. Late in the evening, when Wayne had set his pickets and sentinels and thrown out his patrols, a countryman brought him word of the meditated attack. He doubted the intelligence but strengthened his pickets and patrols and ordered his troops to sleep upon their arms.

At eleven o'clock, the pickets were driven in at the point of the bayonet—the enemy were advancing in column. Wayne instantly took post on the right of his position to cover the retreat of the left, led by Hampton, the second in command. The latter was tardy and incautiously paraded his troops in front of their fires so as to be in full relief. The enemy rushed on without firing a gun; all was the silent but deadly work of the bayonet and the cutlass. Nearly 300 of Hampton's men were killed or wounded and the rest put to flight. Wayne, retreating a small distance, rallied his troops and prepared for further defence. The British, however, contented themselves with the blow they had given.

Smallwood, who was to have co-operated with Wayne, was within a mile of him at the time of his attack, but his raw militia fled in panic at first sight of the enemy.

Wayne, mortified by this affair, demanded a court-martial, which pronounced his conduct every thing that was to be expected from a brave and vigilant officer; whatever blame was in the matter fell upon his second in command, who, by delay and an unskilful position of his troops, had exposed them to be massacred.

On the 21st, Howe made a rapid march up the Schuylkill, on the road leading to Reading, as if he intended either to capture the military stores there or to turn the right of the American army. Washington kept pace with him on the opposite side of the river up to Pott's Grove, about 30 miles from Philadelphia.

The movement on the part of Howe was a feint. No sooner had he drawn Washington far up the river, than, by a rapid counter-march on the night of the 22d, he got to the ford below, threw his troops across on the next morning, and pushed forward for Philadelphia. By the time Washington was apprised of this counter-movement, Howe was too far on his way to be overtaken by harassed, barefooted troops, worn out by constant marching. He wrote on the same day to Putnam at Peekskill, "The situation . . . calls for every aid and for every effort. I therefore desire, that, without a moment's loss of time, you will detach as many effective rank and file, under proper generals and officers, as will . . . amount to 2500 privates and non-commissioned fit for duty."

On the next day (24th) he wrote to Gates. "This army has not been able to oppose General Howe's with the success that was wished, and needs a reinforcement. I therefore request . . . that you will order Colonel Morgan to join me again with his corps. . . . If his services can be dispensed with now, you will direct his immediate return."

Having called a council of officers, which concurred, Washington determined to remain at Pott's Grove to give repose to his troops and await the arrival of reinforcements.

Howe halted at Germantown, within a short distance of Philadelphia, detaching Cornwallis with a large force to take formal possesion of the city. That general marched into Philadelphia on the 26th with a brilliant staff and escort, followed by splendid legions of British and Hessian grenadiers, long trains of artillery and squadrons of light-dragoons, the finest troops in their best array. Stepping to the swelling music of the band playing, "God Save the King," they presented with their scarlet uniforms, their glittering arms and flaunting feathers a striking contrast to the poor patriot troops, weary, war-worn, and happy if they could cover their raggedness with a brown linen hunting frock and decorate their caps with a sprig of evergreen.

Washington maintained his characteristic equanimity. "This is an event," writes he to Governor Trumbull, "which we have reason to wish had not happened, . . . but I hope . . . that a little time and perseverance will give us some favorable opportunity of recovering our loss and of putting our affairs in a more flourishing condition."

(CHAPTER 40)

Washington had heard of the prosperous situation of affairs in the Northern Department and the repeated checks given to the enemy. We will now revert to the course of the campaign in that quarter, the success of which he trusted would have a beneficial influence on the operations in which he was personally engaged. Indeed the operations in the Northern Department formed but a part of his general scheme. His generals had each his own enterprise or department to think about; Washington had to think for the whole.

The checks which Burgoyne had received in a great measure

through the spontaneous rising of the country had opened his eyes to the difficulties of his situation. "Wherever the kings forces point, militia, to the amount of three or four thousand, assemble in twenty-four hours: they bring with them their subsistence, etc., and, the alarm over, they return to their farms. The Hampshire Grants, in particular, . . . abounds in the most active and most rebellious race of the continent and hangs like a gathering storm upon my left."

He complains, too, that no operation had yet been undertaken in his favor; the Highlands of the Hudson had not even been threatened.

Burgoyne declared that, had he any latitude in his orders, he would remain where he was or fall back to Fort Edward, where his communication with Lake George would be secure; his orders, however, were to force a junction with Howe. He did not feel at liberty, therefore, to remain inactive longer than necessary to receive the reinforcements of additional companies and to collect provisions enough for twenty-five days. These reinforcements were indispensable because, from the hour he should pass the Hudson River and proceed towards Albany, all safety of communication would cease.

The American army had received various reinforcements; the most efficient was Morgan's corps of riflemen sent by Washington. He had also furnished it with artillery. It was now about 10,000 strong. Schuyler, finding his proffered services slighted by Gates, had returned to Albany. His patriotism was superior to personal resentments. He continued to exert his influence over the Indian tribes to win them from the enemy. At Albany, he held talks with deputations of Oneida, Tuscarora, and Onondaga warriors and procured scouting parties of them, which he sent to the camp and which proved of great service.

As Gates threw out no harassing parties, his information concerning the enemy was vague. Burgoyne, however, was diligently collecting his forces from Skenesborough, Fort Anne and Fort George and collecting provisions; he had completed a bridge by which he intended to pass the Hudson and force his way to Albany, where he expected co-operation from below. On the 11th of September, a report was circulated in the American camp that Burgoyne had made a speech to his soldiers telling them that the fleet had returned to Canada and their only safety was to fight their way to New York.

As General Gates was to receive an attack, it was thought he ought to choose the ground where to receive it. Arnold, therefore, in company with Kosciuszko, reconnoitred the neighborhood and at length fixed upon a ridge of hills called Bemis's Heights, which Kosciuszko proceeded to fortify.

In the mean time, Colonel Colburn was sent off with a small party to ascend the hills east of the Hudson and watch the movements of the enemy, sending word to camp of all he espied.

On the 11th there were the first signs of movement among Burgoyne's troops. On the 13th and 14th, they slowly passed over a bridge of boats they had thrown across the Hudson and encamped near Fish Creek. The Hessians remained encamped east of the river. There was not the usual stir of military animation in the camps.

On the 15th, both English and Hessian camps began to march. Colburn neglected to notice the route taken by the Hessians; his attention was absorbed by the British, who made their way laboriously down the west side of the river along a wretched road. The division had with it 85 baggage waggons and a great train of artillery, with two unwieldy twenty-four-pounders acting like drag anchors. It was a silent, dogged march. A body of light troops, new levies, and Indians struck off from the rest and disappeared in the forest up Fish Creek. From the silence observed by Burgoyne and the care he took in keeping his men together, Colburn apprehended that he meditated an attack. Having seen the army advance two miles on its march, therefore, he hastened to the American camp to make his report.

On the following morning, the army was under arms at daylight; the enemy, however, remained encamped, repairing bridges in front and sending down guard boats to reconnoitre; the Americans, therefore, went on to fortify their position. Bemis's Heights rises abruptly from the narrow flat bordering the west side of the river. Kosciuszko had fortified the camp with intrenchments three quarters of a mile in extent, having redoubts and batteries which commanded the valley and even the hills on the opposite side of the river, for the Hudson in this part is comparatively narrow. From the foot of the height, an intrenchment extended to the river, ending with a battery at the water edge, commanding a floating bridge.

The right wing of the army, under the immediate command of Gates and composed of Glover's, Nixon's, and Patterson's brigades, occupied the brow of the hill nearest to the river, with the flats below.

The left wing, commanded by Arnold, was on the side of the camp furthest from the river, distant from the latter about three quarters of a mile. It was composed of the New Hampshire brigade of Poor, Van Courtlandt's and Livingston's regiments of New York militia, the Connecticut militia, Morgan's riflemen, and Dearborn's infantry. The centre was composed of Massachusetts and New York troops.

Burgoyne gradually drew nearer to the camp, throwing out large parties of pioneers and workmen. The Americans disputed every step. Burgoyne now encamped about two miles from Gates, disposing his army in two lines: the left on the river, the right extending at right angles to it, about 600 yards across the low grounds to a range of steep rocky hills; a ravine formed by a rivulet from the hills passed in front of the camp. The low ground between the armies was cultivated; the hills were covered with woods. Beside the ravines which fronted each camp there was a third one, midway between them, also at right angles to the river.

On the morning of the 19th, Gates received intelligence that the enemy were advancing in great force on his left. It was, in fact, their right wing, composed of the British line and led by Burgoyne in person. It was covered by the grenadiers and light-infantry under Fraser and Breyman, who kept along the high grounds on the right, while they, in turn, were covered in front and on the flanks by Indians, provincial royalists and Canadians. The left wing and artillery were advancing at the same time, under Phillips and Riedesel, along the great road and meadows by the river side. It was the plan of Burgoyne, that the Canadians and Indians should attack the central outposts of the Americans and draw their attention in that direction while he and Fraser, making a circuit through the woods, should join forces and fall upon the rear of the American camp. As the forests hid them from each other, signal guns were to regulate their movements.

The American pickets sent repeated accounts to Gates of the movements of the enemy, but he remained as if determined to await an attack. The American officers grew impatient. Arnold especially urged repeatedly that a detachment be sent forth to check the enemy in their advance and drive the Indians out of the woods. At length he succeeded in getting permission to detach Morgan with his riflemen and Dearborn with his infantry from his division. They soon fell in with the Canadians and Indians, the advance guard of the enemy's right, and attacking them with spirit, dispersed them. Morgan's riflemen, following up their advantage with too much eagerness, became scattered and a strong reinforcement of royalists arriving on the scene of action, the Americans were obliged to give way.

Other detachments now arrived from the American camp, led by Arnold, who attacked Fraser on his right to check his attempt to get in the rear of the camp. Finding the position of Fraser too strong to be forced, he sent to head-quarters for reinforcements, but they were refused by Gates, who declared his camp might be attacked by the enemy's left wing. Arnold now made a rapid counter-march, and, his movement masked by the woods, attempted to turn Fraser's left. Here he came in full conflict with the British line, and threw himself upon it with boldness and impetuosity. The grenadiers and Breyman's riflemen hastened to its support. Phillips broke his way through the woods with four pieces of artillery and Riedesel came on with his heavy dragoons. Reinforcements came likewise to Arnold's assistance; his force, however, never exceeded 3000 men and with these, for nearly four hours, he kept up a conflict with the whole right wing of the British army.

Night alone put an end to the conflict. Though the British remained on the field of battle, they had failed in their object; they had been assailed instead of being the assailants. The American troops had accomplished the purpose for which they had sallied forth; they had checked the advance of the enemy, frustrated their plan of attack, and returned exulting to their camp.

Arnold was excessively indignant at Gates's withholding the

reinforcements he required in the heat of the action; had they been furnished, he said, he might have severed the line of the enemy and gained a complete victory. He was urgent to resume the action on the succeeding morning and follow up the advantage he had gained, but Gates declined, to his additional annoyance. Gates subsequently gave as a reason the great deficiency of powder and ball in the camp, which he kept secret until a supply was sent from Albany.

Burgoyne strengthened his position with intrenchments and batteries, part of them across the meadows which bordered the river, part on the brow of the heights which commanded them. The Americans extended and strengthened their line of breastworks on the left of the camp; the right was already unassailable. The camps were within gunshot, but with ravines and woods between them.

Washington's predictions of the effect to be produced by Morgan's riflemen approached fulfilment. The Indians, dismayed at the severe treatment by these veteran bush fighters, were disappearing from the British camp. The Canadians and royal provincials, too, were deserting in great numbers.

Burgoyne's situation was growing more and more critical. On the 21st, he heard shouts in the American camp. News had been received from Lincoln that a detachment of New England troops under Brown had surprised the carrying place, mills, and French lines at Ticonderoga, captured an armed sloop, gunboats and bateaux, made 300 prisoners, beside releasing 100 American captives, and were laying siege to Fort Independence.

Fortunately for Burgoyne, while affairs were darkening in the North, a ray of hope dawned from the South. While the shouts from the American camp were yet ringing in his ears, came a letter from Sir Henry Clinton, dated the 12th of September, announcing his intention in about 10 days to attack the forts in the Highlands of the Hudson.

Burgoyne, the same night, despatched messages informing Sir Henry of his perilous situation, urging a diversion that might oblige Gates to detach a part of his army, adding that he would endeavor to maintain his present position and await favorable events until the 12th of October.

The jealousy of Gates had been intensely excited at finding the whole credit of the late affair given to Arnold: in his despatches to government he made no mention of him. This increased the schism between them. Wilkinson, the adjutant-general, who was a sycophantic adherent of Gates, pandered to his pique by withdrawing from Arnold's division Morgan's rifle corps and Dearborn's light infantry, its arm of strength; they were henceforth subject to head-quarters.

Arnold called on Gates on the evening of the 22d to remonstrate. High words passed between them and matters came to an open rupture. Gates told Arnold that he did not consider him a major-general, he having sent his resignation to Congress; that he had never given him the command of any division of the army; that as Lincoln would arrive in a day or two, he would have no further occasion for him and would give him a pass to go to Philadelphia whenever he chose. Arnold returned to his quarters in a rage, but determined to remain in camp and abide the anticipated battle.

Lincoln, in the mean time, arrived in advance of his troops, which soon followed to the amount of 2000. Part of the troops, detached by him under Brown, were besieging Ticonderoga and Fort Independence. Brown himself, with part of his detachment, had embarked on Lake George in an armed schooner and a squadron of captured gunboats and bateaux and was threatening the enemy's deposit of baggage and heavy artillery at Diamond Island. The toils so skilfully spread were encompassing Burgoyne more and more; the gates of Canada were closing behind him.

A morning or two after Lincoln's arrival, Arnold observed him giving some directions in the left division and quickly inquired whether he was doing so by orders of Gates; being answered in the negative, he observed that the left division belonged to him and that he believed Lincoln's proper station was on the right, and that of Gates ought to be in the centre. He requested him to mention this to Gates and have the matter adjusted.

Arnold was in a bellicose vein; Gates, he said, could not refuse him his command and he would not yield it now that a battle was expected.

Some proposed that the general officers should endeavor to produce a reconciliation between the jarring parties, but, in the end, no measure was taken through fear of offending Gates. In the mean time Arnold remained in camp, treated, he said, as a cipher and never consulted.

On the 30th, he gave vent to his feelings in an indignant letter to Gates. "Notwithstanding I have reason to think your treatment proceeds from a spirit of jealousy," writes he, ". . . I am determined to sacrifice my feelings . . . and continue in the army at this critical juncture when my country needs every support. I hope you will not impute this hint to a wish to command the army or to outshine you when I assure you it proceeds from my zeal for the cause of my country in which I expect to rise or fall."

All this time the Americans were harassing the British camp with frequent night alarms and attacks on its pickets and outposts. Still Burgoyne kept up a resolute mien, telling his soldiers that he was determined to leave his bones on the field or force his way to Albany. He yet clung to the hope that Sir Henry Clinton might relieve him from his perilous position.

We will now cast a look toward New York and ascertain the cause of Sir Henry's delay in his anxiously expected operations on the Hudson.

The expedition of Sir Henry Clinton had awaited the arrival of reinforcements from Europe, which arrived after a three month's voyage. There was a stir of warlike preparation at New York; the streets were full of soldiery, the bay full of ships. About 4000 men were to be embarked. A southern destination was given out but shrewd observers surmised the real one.

The defences of the Highlands, on which the security of the Hudson depended, were at this time weakly garrisoned, some of the troops having been sent off to reinforce the armies on the Delaware and in the North. Putnam, who had general command of the Highlands, had but 1100 continental and 400 militia troops with him at Peekskill, his head-quarters. There was a feeble garrison at Fort Independence, in the vicinity of Peekskill, to guard the public stores and workshops at Continental Village.

The Highland forts—Clinton, Montgomery, and Constitution —situated among the mountains and forming their main defence were no better garrisoned. George Clinton, who had command of them, was absent from his post, attending the State Legislature at Kingston (Esopus) in his capacity of governor.

On the 29th of September Putnam writes to the governor: "I have received intelligence on which I can fully depend that the enemy had received a reinforcement at New York last Thursday, . . . that Clinton has called in guides who belong about Croton River, . . . and the whole troops are now under marching orders. I think it highly probable the designs of the enemy are against the posts of the Highlands, or some part of the counties of Westchester or Dutchess." Under these circumstances, he begged a reinforcement of the militia and intimated a wish for the personal assistance of the governor.

On receiving this letter the governor forthwith hastened to his post in the Highlands with such militia force as he could collect. We have heretofore spoken of Fort Montgomery and of the obstructions of chain, boom and chevaux-de-frise between it and the opposite promontory of Anthony's Nose with which it had been hoped to barricade the Hudson. The chain had repeatedly given way under the pressure of the tide but the obstructions, still considered efficient, were protected by the guns of the fort and of two frigates and two armed galleys anchored above.

Fort Clinton had subsequently been erected within rifle shot of Fort Montgomery to occupy ground which commanded it. A deep ravine and stream intervened between the two forts, across which there was a bridge. The governor had his head-quarters in Fort Montgomery, the northern and largest fort, but its works were unfinished. His brother James had charge of Fort Clinton, which was complete. The whole force to garrison the associate forts did not exceed 600 men, chiefly militia, but they had the veteran Lamb of the artillery with them.

The armament of Sir Henry Clinton, which had been waiting for a wind, set sail in the course of a day or two and continued across the Tappan Sea and Haverstraw Bay to Verplanck's Point, where, on the 5th, Sir Henry landed with 3000 men about 8 miles below Peekskill.

Putnam drew back to the hills in the rear of the village, to prepare for the expected attack and sent off to Governor Clinton for all the troops he could spare. So far the manoeuvres of Sir Henry had been successful. It was his plan to threaten an attack on Peekskill and Fort Independence, and, when he had drawn the attention of the American commanders to that quarter, to land troops on the western shore of the Hudson below the Dunderberg, make a rapid march through the defiles behind that mountain to the rear of Forts Montgomery and Clinton, come down on them by surprise, and carry them by a *coup de main*.

Accordingly at an early hour of the following morning, taking advantage of a thick fog, he crossed with 2000 men to Stony Point, on the west shore of the river, leaving about 1000 men, chiefly royalists, at Verplanck's Point, to keep up a threatening aspect towards Peekskill. Three frigates, also, were to station themselves within cannon-shot of Fort Independence.

Having accomplished his landing, Sir Henry set out on a forced and circuitous march round the western base of the Dunderberg, which, by eight o'clock in the morning, he had effected and halted on the northern side in a ravine, between it and a conical mount called Bear Hill.

In the ravine between the Dunderberg and Bear Hill, Sir Henry divided his forces. One division, 900 strong led by Campbell, was to make a circuit round the west of Bear Hill so as to gain the rear of Fort Montgomery. After Sir Henry had allowed sufficient time for them to make the circuit, he was to proceed with the other division down the ravine, towards the river, turn to the left, pass along a narrow strip between Sinipink Pond and the Hudson, and advance upon Fort Clinton. Both forts were to be attacked at the same time.

The detachment under Campbell set off in high spirits; it was composed partly of royalists led by Colonel Beverley Robinson of New York, partly of Emerick's chasseurs, and partly of grenadiers under Lord Rawdon, who had already seen service at Bunker's Hill. Every thing had been conducted with celerity and apparent secrecy and a complete surprise of both forts was anticipated. Sir Henry had indeed outwitted one of the guardians of the Highlands but the other was aware of his designs. Governor Clinton, on receiving intelligence of ships of war coming up the Hudson, had sent scouts to watch their movements. Early on the present morning, word had been brought him that boats were landing a large force at Stony

Point. He apprehended an attack and sent to Putnam for reinforcements, preparing in the mean time to make such defence as his scanty means afforded.

A lieutenant was sent out with thirty men from Fort Clinton to proceed along the river-road and reconnoitre. He fell in with the advance guard of Sir Henry's division and retreated skirmishing to the fort. A larger detachment was sent out to check the approach of the enemy on this side, while about 100 men took post with a brass field-piece in the Bear Hill defile. It was a narrow pass, bordered by shagged forests. As Campbell's division came forward, they were checked by the fire-arms and the brass field-piece which swept the defile. The British troops then filed off on each side into the woods to surround the Americans. The latter, finding it impossible to extricate their field-piece in the rugged pass, retreated into the fort.

Sir Henry had met with equally obstinate opposition in his approach to Fort Clinton; the narrow strip between Sinipink and the Hudson being fortified by an abatis. By four o'clock the Americans were driven within their works and both forts were assailed. The defence was desperate. Governor Clinton was a hard fighter and he was in hopes of reinforcements from Putnam, not knowing that the messenger he sent had turned traitor and deserted to the enemy.

About five o'clock, he was summoned to surrender; the reply was a refusal. About ten minutes afterwards, there was a general attack on both forts. It was resisted with obstinate spirit until dusk but the works were too extensive to be manned by the scanty garrisons. They were entered at different places and carried at the point of the bayonet; the Americans fought desperately from one redoubt to another; some were slain, some taken prisoners, and some escaped under cover of the night to the river or the mountains.

His brother James, who had received a flesh-wound in the thigh, slid down a precipice into the ravine between the forts and escaped to the woods. The governor leaped down the rocks to the river side, where a boat was putting off with a number of the fugitives. The boat crossed the Hudson and before midnight the governor was with Putnam at Continental Village concerting further measures.

Putnam had been completely outmanoeuvred by Sir Henry. He had continued until late in the morning in the belief that

Peekskill and Fort Independence were to be the objects of attack. After reconnoitring the ground near the enemy, he was alarmed, he says, by "a very heavy and hot firing both of small arms and cannon, at Fort Montgomery." Aware of the real point of danger, he immediately detached 500 men to reinforce the garrison. They had 6 miles to march along the eastern shore and then to cross the river; before they could do so the fate of the forts was decided.

On the capture of the forts, the American frigates and galleys stationed for the protection of the chevaux-de-frise endeavored to escape up the river. The wind, however, proved adverse; there was danger of their falling into the hands of the enemy; the crews, therefore, set them on fire and abandoned them.

On the following morning, the obstructions between Fort Montgomery and Anthony's Nose were cleared away, the Americans evacuated Forts Independence and Constitution, and passage up the Hudson was open for the British ships. Sir Henry proceeded no further in person but left the rest to be accomplished by Sir James Wallace and General Vaughan with a squadron of light frigates and a considerable detachment of troops.

Putnam had retreated to a pass in the mountains, on the east side of the river, near Fishkill, having removed as much as possible from the post he had abandoned. The old general was mortified at having been outwitted by the enemy. In a letter to Washington (Oct. 8th), he writes: "My . . . sincere opinion is that they now mean to join General Burgoyne with the utmost despatch. Governor Clinton is exerting himself in collecting the militia of this State. . . . Parsons I have sent off to forward in the Connecticut militia, which are now arriving in great numbers. I therefore hope and trust, that . . . I shall be able to oppose the progress of the enemy."

He had concerted with Governor Clinton that they should move to the northward with their forces, along opposite shores of the Hudson, endeavoring to keep pace with the enemy's ships and cover the country from their attacks.

The governor was in the neighborhood of New Windsor, just above the Highlands, where he had posted himself to rally what he termed his "broken but brave troops," and to call out the militia of Ulster and Orange. The militia, however, were not as prompt as usual in answering to the call of their popular and brave-hearted governor.

As soon as the governor could collect a little force, he pressed forward to protect Kingston, the seat of the State legislature. The enemy in the mean time landed from their ships, routed about 150 militia collected to oppose them, marched to the village, set fire to it, and then retreated to their ships.

Having laid Kingston in ashes, the enemy proceeded in their ravages, destroying the residences of conspicuous patriots at Rhinebec, Livingston Manor, and elsewhere, trusting to close their desolating career by a triumphant junction with Burgoyne at Albany.

While Sir Henry Clinton had been thundering in the Highlands, Burgoyne and his army had been wearing out hope within their intrenchments, vigilantly watched, but unassailed by the Americans. Gates saw the desperate situation of Burgoyne, and bided his time.

On the 7th of October, but four or five days remained of the time Burgoyne had pledged himself to await the co-operation of Sir Henry Clinton. He now determined to make a grand movement on the left of the American camp to discover whether he could force a passage, should it be necessary to advance, or dislodge it from its position, should he have to retreat. Another object was to cover a forage of the army, which was suffering from the great scarcity. For this purpose 1500 of his best troops were to be led by himself, seconded by Phillips, Riedesel, and Fraser.

On leaving his camp, Burgoyne committed the guard of it on the high grounds to Hamilton and Specht and of the redoubts on the low grounds near the river to Gall. Forming his troops within three quarters of a mile of the left of the Americans, he sent out a corps of rangers, provincials and Indians to skulk through the woods, get in their rear, and give them an alarm at the time the attack took place in front.

The movement, though carried on behind the screen of forests, was discovered. In the afternoon the advanced guard of the American centre beat to arms; the alarm was repeated throughout the line. Gates ordered his officers to their alarm posts, and sent forth Wilkinson, the adjutant-general, to inquire the cause.

The Turning Point (1776–1777)

Returning to the camp, Wilkinson reported the position and movements of the enemy: that their front was open, their flanks rested on woods, under cover of which they might be attacked, and their right was skirted by a height; that they were reconnoitring the left and he thought offered battle.

A plan of attack was soon arranged. Morgan with his riflemen and a body of infantry was sent to make a circuit through the woods and get possession of the heights on the right of the enemy, while Poor with his brigade of New York and New Hampshire troops and a part of Learned's brigade were to advance against the enemy's left. Morgan was to make an attack on the heights as soon as he should hear the fire opened below.

Burgoyne now drew out his troops in battle array. The grenadiers, under Ackland, with the artillery, under Williams, formed his left and were stationed on a rising ground, with a rivulet called Mill Creek in front. Next to them were the Hessians, under Riedesel, and British, under Phillips, forming the centre. The light infantry, under Lord Balcarras, formed the extreme right, having in the advance a detachment of 500 picked men under Fraser, ready to flank the Americans as soon as they should be attacked in front.

He had scarce made these arrangements when he was astonished by a thundering of artillery on his left and a rattling fire of rifles on his right. The troops under Poor advanced steadily up the ascent where Ackland's grenadiers and Williams' artillery were stationed, received their fire, and then rushed forward. Ackland's grenadiers received the first brunt but it extended along the line and was carried on with inconceivable fury. The artillery, repeatedly taken and retaken, at length remained in possession of the Americans, who turned it upon its former owners. Ackland was wounded in both legs and taken prisoner; Williams of the artillery was also captured. The headlong impetuosity of the attack has been ascribed to the presence and example of Arnold. That daring officer, exasperated at having no command assigned him, could restrain no longer his warlike impulse. Putting spurs to his horse, he dashed into the scene of action and was received with acclamation. Being the superior officer in the field his orders were obeyed of course. Putting himself at the head of the troops of Learned's brigade, he attacked the Hessians in the enemy's centre and broke them with repeated charges, riding hither and thither, brandishing his sword, and cheering on the men to acts of desperation.

Morgan, in the mean time, was harassing the enemy's right wing with an incessant fire of small-arms, preventing it from sending assistance to the centre. Fraser with his chosen corps for some time rendered great protection to this wing. Mounted on an iron-gray charger, his uniform of a field-officer made him a conspicuous object for Morgan's sharp-shooters. Shot down by a marksman posted in a tree, his fall was as a death-blow to his corps. The arrival of a large reinforcement of New York troops under General Ten Broeck completed the confusion. Burgoyne saw that the field was lost and now only thought of saving his camp. The troops nearest to the lines were ordered to throw themselves within them, while Phillips and Riedesel covered the retreat of the main body, which was in danger of being cut off. The troops, though hard pressed, retired in good order. Scarcely had they entered the camp when it was stormed with great fury, the Americans, with Arnold at their head, rushing to the lines under a severe discharge of grape-shot and small-arms. Balcarras defended the intrenchments bravely. After an ineffectual attempt to make his way into the camp in this quarter, Arnold spurred his horse toward the right flank of the camp occupied by the German reserve, where Brooks was making a general attack with a Massachusetts regiment. Here, he forced his way into a sally-port, but a shot from the retreating Hessians wounded him in the leg. He was borne off from the field but not until the victory was complete.

The night was now closing in. The victory of the Americans was decisive. They had routed the enemy, killed and wounded a great number, made many prisoners, taken their field-artillery, and gained possession of a part of their works which laid open the right and the rear of their camp. They lay all night on their arms, within half a mile of the scene of action, prepared to renew the assault upon the camp in the morning.

Burgoyne shifted his position during the night to heights about a mile to the north, close to the river and covered in front by a ravine. Early in the morning, the Americans took possession of the camp he had abandoned. A random fire of artillery and small-arms was kept up on both sides during the day. Gates took measures to cut off the retreat and insure a surrender. General Fellows, with 1400 men, had already been sent to occupy the high ground east of the Hudson opposite Saratoga Ford. Other detachments were sent higher up the river in the direction of Lake George.

Burgoyne saw that nothing was left for him but a prompt retreat to Saratoga, yet in this he was delayed by a melancholy duty of friendship: to attend the obsequies of the gallant Fraser who, according to his dying request, was to be interred at six o'clock in the evening within a redoubt which had been constructed on a hill.

Preparations had been made to decamp immediately after the funeral and at nine o'clock at night the retreat commenced. It was a dismal retreat. The rain fell in torrents; the roads were deep and broken and the horses weak and half-starved. At daybreak there was a halt to refresh the troops and give time for the bateaux laden with provision to come abreast. In three hours the march was resumed but before long there was another halt, to guard against an American reconnoitring party which appeared in sight.

It rained terribly throughout the 9th and in consequence of repeated halts they did not reach Saratoga until evening. A detachment of Americans had arrived there before them and were throwing up intrenchments on a commanding height at Fish Kill. They abandoned their work, forded the Hudson, and joined a force under Fellows, posted on the hills east of the river. The bridge over the Fish Kill had been destroyed; the artillery could not cross until the ford was examined. Exhausted by fatigue, the men had not strength to cut wood nor make fire but threw themselves upon the wet ground in their wet clothes and slept under the continuing rain.

At daylight on the 10th, the artillery and the last of the troops passed the fords of the Fish Kill and took a position upon the heights and in the redoubts formerly constructed there. To protect the troops from being attacked in passing the ford by the Americans, who were approaching, Burgoyne ordered fire to be set to the farm-houses and other buildings on the south side of the Fish Kill.

The force under Fellows, posted on the opposite hills of the Hudson, now opened a fire from a battery commanding the ford of that river. Thus prevented from crossing, Burgoyne thought to retreat along the west side as far as Fort George, on the way to Canada, and sent out workmen under a strong escort to repair the bridges and open the road toward Fort Edward. The escort was soon recalled and the work abandoned, for the Americans under Gates appeared in great force on the heights south of the Fish Kill and seemed preparing to cross and bring on an engagement.

Burgoyne called a general council of war in which it was resolved, since the bridges could not be repaired, to abandon the artillery and baggage, let the troops carry a supply of provisions upon their backs, push forward in the night, and force their way across the fords at or near Fort Edward. Before the plan could be put in execution, scouts brought word that the Americans were intrenched opposite those fords and encamped in force with cannon on the high ground between Fort Edward and Fort George. In fact, by this time the American army, augmented by militia and volunteers from all quarters, had posted itself in strong positions on both sides of the Hudson so as to extend three fourths of a circle round the enemy.

Giving up all further attempt at retreat, Burgoyne fortified his camp on the heights to the north of Fish Kill, still hoping that succor might arrive from Sir Henry or that an attack upon his trenches might give him some chance of cutting his way through. In this situation his troops lay continually on their arms. His camp was subjected to cannonading from Fellows' batteries on the opposite side of the Hudson, Gates's batteries on the south of Fish Kill, and a galling fire from Morgan's riflemen, stationed on heights in the rear.

Burgoyne was now reduced to despair. His forces were diminished by losses, by the desertion of Canadians and royalists, and the total defection of the Indians; the provision on hand, even upon short allowance, would not suffice for more than three days. A council of war, therefore, was called of all the generals, field-officers and captains. All concurred in the necessity of opening a treaty with Gates for a surrender on honorable terms.

Negotiations were accordingly opened on the 13th under sanction of a flag. Lieutenant Kingston, Burgoyne's adjutant-general, was the bearer of a note proposing a cessation of hostilities until terms could be adjusted.

LT. GEN. BURGOYNE.

J. Burgoyne

Printed by W. Pate

NEW YORK G.P. PUTNAM & CO.

The Turning Point (1776–1777)

The first terms offered by Gates were that the enemy should lay down their arms within their intrenchments and surrender themselves prisoners of war.

Counter proposals were then made by Burgoyne and finally accepted by Gates. According to these, the British troops were to march out of the camp with artillery and all the honors of war to a fixed place, where they were to pile their arms at a command from their own officers. They were to be allowed a free passage to Europe upon condition of not serving again in America, during the present war. The capitulation was accordingly signed by Burgoyne on the 17th of October.

The British army, at the time of its surrender, was reduced by capture, death, and desertion, from 9000 to 5752 men. That of Gates, regulars and militia, amounted to 10,554 men on duty, about 3000 being on the sick list or absent on furlough.

By this capitulation, the Americans gained a fine train of artillery, 7000 stand of arms, and a great quantity of clothing, tents, and military stores.

When the British troops marched forth to deposit their arms at the appointed place, Wilkinson was the only American soldier to be seen. Gates had ordered his troops to keep rigidly within their lines that they might not add to the humiliation of a brave enemy. In fact, throughout all his conduct, British writers, and Burgoyne himself, give him credit for acting with great humanity and forbearance.

The surrender of Burgoyne was soon followed by the evacuation of Ticonderoga and Fort Independence, the garrisons retiring to the Isle aux Noix and St. Johns. As to the armament on the Hudson, the commanders in charge of it received the astounding intelligence of the capture of the army with which they had come to co-operate. Nothing remained for them, therefore, but to return to New York.

The whole expedition, though it had effected much damage to the Americans, failed to be of essential service to the royal cause. The fortresses in the Highlands could not be maintained, and the plundering and burning of defenceless towns and villages had given to the whole enterprise the character of a maraud, disgraceful in civilized warfare and calculated only to inflame more deadly enmity and determined opposition.

The War Shifts Southwards
[1777–1780]

Having given the catastrophe of the British invasion from the North, we will revert to that part of the year's campaign under the immediate eye of Washington. We left him encamped at Pott's Grove towards the end of September, giving his troops a few days' repose. Rejoined by Wayne and Smallwood with their brigades and other troops being arrived from the Jerseys, his force amounted to about 8000 Continentals and 3000 militia; with these he advanced, on the 30th of September, to Skippack Creek, about 14 miles from Germantown, where the main body of the British army lay encamped, a detachment under Cornwallis occupying Philadelphia.

Immediately after the battle of Brandywine, Admiral Lord Howe with great exertions had succeeded in getting his ships of war and transports round from the Chesapeake into the Delaware and had anchored them along the Pennsylvania shore from Reedy Island to Newcastle. They were prevented from approaching nearer by obstructions the Americans had placed in the river. The lowest of these were at Billingsport, where *chevaux-de-frise* in the channel of the river were protected by a strong redoubt on the Jersey shore.

Higher up were Fort Mifflin on Mud Island and Fort Mercer on the Jersey shore, with *chevaux-de-frise* between them. Washington had exerted himself to throw a garrison into Fort Mifflin and keep up the obstructions of the river.

Sir William Howe was perfectly aware of this and had concerted operations with his brother by land and water to reduce the forts and clear away the obstructions of the river. With this view he detached a part of his force into the Jerseys to proceed, in the first instance, against the fortifications at Billingsport. Washington had been for some days on the look-out for opportunity to strike a blow of consequence, when two intercepted letters gave him intelligence of this movement. He immediately determined to make an attack upon the British camp at Germantown, while weakened by the absence of this detachment. To understand the plan of the attack, some description of the British place of encampment is necessary.

Germantown, at that time, was little more than one street, extending two miles north and south. The houses were mostly of stone, low and substantial. Beyond the village, about 100 yards east of the road, stood a spacious stone edifice, the country seat of Benjamin Chew, chief justice of Pennsylvania previous to the Revolution.

Four roads approached the village from the north. The Skippack, which was the main road, led over Chestnut Hill and Mount Airy down to and through the village toward Philadelphia, forming the street of which we have just spoken. On its right, and nearly parallel, was the Monatawny or Ridge Road, passing near the Schuylkill and entering the main road below the village.

On the left of the Skippack was the Limekiln Road, running nearly parallel to it for a time and then turning towards it, almost at right angles, so as to enter the village at the market-place. Still further to the left or east, and outside of all, was the Old York Road, falling into the main road some distance below the village.

The main body of the British forces lay encamped across the lower part of the village, divided into almost equal parts by Skippack Road. The right wing, commanded by Grant, was to the east of the road, the left wing to the west. Each wing was covered by strong detachments and guarded by cavalry. Howe had his head-quarters in the rear.

The advance of the army, composed of the 2d battalion of British light-infantry, with a train of artillery, was more than two miles from the main body, on the west of the road, with an outlying picket stationed with two six-pounders at Allen's house on Mount Airy. About three quarters of a mile in rear of the light-infantry lay encamped in a field opposite "Chew's House" the 40th regiment of infantry under Musgrave.

According to Washington's plan for the attack, Sullivan was to command the right wing, composed of his own division, principally Maryland troops and the division of Wayne. He was to be sustained by a *corps de reserve* under Stirling, composed of Nash's North Carolina and Maxwell's Virginia brigades and to be flanked by the brigade of Conway. He was to march down the Skippack Road and attack the left wing; at the same time Armstrong, with the Pennsylvania militia, was to pass down the Monatawny or Ridge Road and get upon the enemy's left and rear.

Greene with the left wing, composed of his own division and the division of Stephen, flanked by MacDougall's brigade, was to march down the Limekiln Road so as to enter the village at the market-house. The two divisions were to attack the enemy's right wing in front, MacDougall with his brigade to attack it in flank while Smallwood's division of Maryland militia and Forman's Jersey brigade, making a circuit by the Old York Road, were to attack it in the rear. Two thirds of the forces were thus directed against the enemy's right wing under the idea that, if it could be forced, the whole army must be pushed into the Schuylkill or compelled to surrender. The attack was to begin on all quarters at daybreak.

About dusk, on the 3d of October, the army left its encampment at Matuchen Hills by its different routes. Washington accompanied the right wing. It had 15 miles of weary march to make over rough roads, so that it was after daybreak when the troops emerged from the woods on Chestnut Hill. A detachment advanced to attack the enemy's out picket stationed at Allen's House. The alarm, however, was given; the picket guard retreated down the south side of Mount Airy to the battalion of light-infantry who were forming in order of battle. As their pursuers descended into the valley, the sun rose but was soon obscured. Wayne led the attack upon the light-infantry. "They broke at first," writes he, "without waiting to receive us but soon formed again, when a heavy and well-directed fire took place on both sides."

They again gave way but, being supported by the grenadiers, returned to the charge. Sullivan's division and Conway's brigade formed on the west of the road and joined in the attack; the rest of the troops were too far to the north to render any assistance. The infantry, after fighting bravely for a time, broke and ran, leaving their artillery behind. They were hotly pursued by Wayne. The whole of the enemy's advance were driven from their camping ground, leaving their tents standing with all their baggage. Musgrave, with six companies of the 40th regiment, threw himself into Chew's House, barricaded the doors and lower windows, and took post above stairs; the main torrent of the retreat passed by pursued by Wayne into the village.

As the residue of this division of the army came up to join in the pursuit, Musgrave and his men opened a fire of musketry upon them from the upper windows of his citadel. This brought them to a halt. Some of the officers were for pushing on, but Knox, insisting on the old military maxim, never to leave a garrisoned castle in the rear, unluckily prevailed. Half an hour was thus spent in vain; scarce any of the defenders of the house were injured though many of the assailants were slain. At length a regiment was left to keep guard upon the mansion and the rear division again pressed forward.

This delay, however, of nearly half the army, disconcerted the action. The divisions and brigades, separated from each other by the attack upon Chew's House, could not be reunited. The fog and smoke rendered all objects indistinct and the different parts of the army knew nothing of the position or movements of each other, and the commander-in-chief could take no view nor gain any information of the situation of the whole. The original plan of attack was only effectively carried into operation in the centre. The flanks and rear of the enemy were nearly unmolested; still

the action, though disconnected, irregular and partial, was animated in various quarters. Sullivan, being reinforced by Nash's
North Carolina troops and Conway's brigade, pushed on a mile beyond Chew's House, where the left wing of the enemy gave way
before him.

Greene and Stephen, with their divisions, having had to make a
circuit, were late in coming into action and became separated from
each other, part of Stephen's division being arrested by a heavy fire
from Chew's House and pausing to return it: Greene, however, with
his division, comprising the brigades of Muhlenberg and Scott,
pressed rapidly forward, drove an advance regiment of light-
infantry before him, and made his way to the centre of the village,
where he encountered the right wing of the British drawn up to
receive him. The impetuosity of his attack had an evident effect
upon the enemy, who began to waver. Forman and Smallwood, with
the Jersey and Maryland militia, were just showing themselves on
the right flank of the enemy and our troops seemed on the point of
carrying the whole encampment. At this moment a singular panic
seized our army. Various causes are assigned for it. Sullivan alleges
that his troops had expended all their cartridges and were alarmed
by seeing the enemy gathering on their left and by the cry of a
light-horseman that the enemy were getting round them. Wayne's
division, which had pushed the enemy nearly three miles, was
alarmed by the approach of a large body of American troops on its
left flank which it mistook for foes and fell back in defiance of every
effort of its officers to rally it. In its retreat it came upon Stephen's
division and threw it into a panic, being, in its turn, mistaken for the
enemy; thus all fell into confusion and our army fled from their own
victory.

In the mean time, the enemy, having recovered from the first
effects of the surprise, advanced in their turn. Grey brought up the
left wing and pressed upon the American troops as they receded.
Cornwallis, with a squadron of light-horse from Philadelphia, arrived just in time to join in the pursuit. The retreat of the Americans
was attended with less loss than might have been expected, and they
carried off all their cannon and wounded. The retreat continued
through the day to Perkiomen Creek, a distance of 20 miles.

Speaking of Washington's conduct amidst the perplexities of this confused battle, Sullivan writes, "I saw, with great concern, our brave commander-in-chief exposing himself to the hottest fire of the enemy in such a manner that regard for my country obliged me to ride to him and beg him to retire. He, to gratify me and some others, withdrew to a small distance but his anxiety for the fate of the day soon brought him up again, where he remained till our troops had retreated."

The sudden retreat of the army gave him surprise, chagrin and mortification. "Every account," said he, subsequently, in a letter to the President of Congress, "confirms the opinion I at first entertained, that our troops retreated at the instant when victory was declaring herself in our favor. The tumult, disorder, and even despair, which, it seems, had taken place in the British army, were scarcely to be paralleled. I can discover no other cause for not improving this happy opportunity, than the extreme haziness of the weather."

In fact, as has been observed by an experienced officer, the plan of attack was too widely extended and too complicated for precise co-operation, as it had to be conducted in the night and with a large proportion of undisciplined militia. Yet, a bewildering fog alone appears to have prevented its complete success. But although the Americans were balked of the victory which seemed for a moment within their grasp, the impression made by the audacity of this attempt upon Germantown was greater, we are told, than that caused by any single incident of the war after Lexington and Bunker's Hill.

Washington remained a few days at Perkiomen Creek to give his army time to rest and recover from the disorder incident to a retreat. Having been reinforced by the arrival of 1200 Rhode Island troops from Peekskill under Varnum and nearly 1000 Virginia, Maryland and Pennsylvania troops, he gradually drew nearer to Philadelphia and took a strong position at White Marsh, within 14 miles of that city. Washington detached large bodies of militia to scour the roads above the city and between the Schuylkill and Chester to intercept all supplies going to the enemy.

On the forts and obstructions in the river Washington mainly counted to complete the harassment of Philadelphia. These defences had been materially impaired. The works at Billingsport had been attacked and destroyed; some of the enemy's ships had forced their way through the *cheavaux-de-frise* placed there. The American frigate Delaware, stationed in the river between the upper forts and Philadelphia, had run aground before a British battery and been captured.

It was now the great object of the Howes to reduce and destroy, and of Washington to defend and maintain, the remaining forts and obstructions. Fort Mifflin, erected on a reedy island in the Delaware a few miles below Philadelphia and below the mouth of Schuylkill, consisted of a strong redoubt with extensive outworks and batteries. There was but a narrow channel between the island and the Pennsylvania shore. The main channel, practicable for ships, was on the other side. In this were sunk strong *chevaux-de-frise*, difficult either to be weighed or cut through and dangerous to any ships that might run against them, subjected as they would be to the batteries of Fort Mifflin on one side, and on the other to those of Fort Mercer, a strong work at Red Bank on the Jersey shore.

Fort Mifflin, garrisoned by troops of the Maryland line under Lieutenant-colonel Samuel Smith of Baltimore, had kept up a brave defence against batteries erected by the enemy on the Pennsylvania shore. A reinforcement of Virginia troops made the garrison about 400 strong.

Floating batteries, galleys, and fire-ships, commanded by Commodore Hazelwood, were stationed under the forts and about the river.

Fort Mercer had hitherto been garrisoned by militia but Washington now replaced them by 400 of Varnum's Rhode Island Continentals. Colonel Christopher Greene was put in command, a brave officer, who had accompanied Arnold in his rough expedition to Canada and fought valiantly under the walls of Quebec.

Greene was accompanied by Captain Mauduit Duplessis, who was to have the direction of the artillery. He was a young French engineer who had volunteered in the American cause and received a commission from Congress.

Greene, aided by Duplessis, made all haste to put Fort Mercer in a state of defence, but, before the outworks were completed, he was surprised (October 22) by a large force emerging from a wood within cannon shot of the fort. Their uniforms showed them to be Hessians. There were, in fact, four battalions 1200 strong of grenadiers, picked men, beside light-infantry and chasseurs, all commanded by Donop.

Greene, in nowise dismayed by the superiority of the enemy, prepared for a stout resistance. The Hessians were seen at work throwing up a battery within half a mile of the outworks. It was finished by four o'clock and opened a heavy cannonade, under cover of which the enemy were preparing to approach.

As the American outworks were but half finished and too extensive to be manned by the garrison, it was determined by Greene and Duplessis that the troops should make but a short stand there and then retire within the redoubt, which was defended by a deep intrenchment, boarded and fraised.

Donop led on his troops in gallant style under cover of a heavy fire from his battery. They advanced in two columns to attack the outworks in two places. They were galled by a flanking fire from the American galleys and batteries and by sharp volleys from the outworks. The latter, however, as had been concerted, were quickly abandoned by the garrison. The enemy entered at two places, and, imagining the day their own, the two columns pushed on with shouts to storm different parts of the redoubt. As yet, no troops were to be seen but, as one of the columns approached the redoubt on the north side, a tremendous discharge of grape-shot and musketry burst forth from the embrasures in front and a half-masked battery on the left. The slaughter was prodigious; the column was driven back in confusion. Donop, with the other column, in attempting the south side of the redoubt, had advanced considerably, when a tempest of artillery and musketry burst upon them. Some were killed on the spot, many were wounded, and the rest were driven out. Donop himself was mortally wounded, and other of the best officers were slain or disabled. The troops retreated in confusion, hotly pursued, and were again cut up in their retreat by the flanking fire from the galleys and floating batteries.

According to the plan of the enemy, Fort Mifflin, opposite Fort Mercer, was to have been attacked at the same time by water. The force employed was the Augusta of 64 guns, the Roebuck of 44, two frigates, the Merlin sloop of 18 guns, and a galley. They forced their way through the lower line of *chevaux-de-frise*, but the Augusta and Merlin ran aground below the second line and every effort to get them off proved fruitless. The other vessels drew as near to Fort Mifflin as they could and opened a cannonade, but the obstructions in the river had so altered the channel that they could not get within very effective distance. They kept up a fire upon the fort throughout the evening and recommenced it early in the morning, as did likewise the British batteries on the Pennsylvania shore, hoping that under cover of it the ships might be got off. A strong adverse wind, however, kept the tide from rising sufficiently to float them.

The Americans discovered their situation and sent down four fire-ships to destroy them, but without effect. In the course of the action, a red-hot shot set the Augusta on fire. It was impossible to check the flames, and she blew up. The Merlin was set on fire and abandoned, the Roebuck and the other vessels dropped down the river, and the attack on Fort Mifflin was given up.

These signal repulses of the enemy had an animating effect on the public mind and were promptly noticed by Congress.

We have heretofore had occasion to advert to the annoyances and perplexities occasioned to Washington by the foreign officers who had entered into the service. Among the officers who came out with Lafayette was the Baron De Kalb, a German who had long been employed in the French service. In September, Congress had given him the commission of major-general to date with that of Lafayette.

This instantly produced a remonstrance from Brigadier-general Conway, the Gallic Hibernian, who claimed, therefore, the rank of major-general and was supported in his pretensions by persons in and out of Congress, especially by Mifflin, the quartermaster-general.

Washington had already been disgusted by the overweening presumption of Conway and was surprised to hear that his application was likely to be successful. He wrote on the 17th of October to Richard Henry Lee, then in Congress, warning him that such an appointment would be as unfortunate a measure as ever was adopted. "General Conway's merit as an officer," writes he, "and his importance in this army, exist more in his own imagination than in reality. For it is a maxim with him to leave no service of his own untold, nor to want any thing which is to be obtained by importunity."

This opposition to his aspirations at once threw Conway into a faction forming under the auspices of Mifflin. This gentleman, who had recently tendered his resignation of the commission of major-general and quartermaster-general on the plea of ill health, was busily engaged in intrigues against the commander-in-chief, towards whom he had long cherished a secret hostility. Conway now joined with him and soon became so active a member of the faction that it acquired the name of Conway's Cabal. The object was to depreciate the military character of Washington in comparison with that of Gates, to whom was attributed the whole success of the Northern campaign. Gates, perfectly ready for such an elevation, seemed to forget that the defeat of Burgoyne had been insured by plans put in operation before his arrival in the Northern Department.

In fact, Gates appears to have forgotten that there was a commander-in-chief to whom he was accountable. He neglected to send him any despatch on the surrender of Burgoyne, contenting himself with sending one to Congress, then sitting at Yorktown. Washington was left to hear of the important event by rumor until he received a copy of the capitulation in a letter from Putnam.

Gates was equally neglectful to inform him of the disposition he intended to make of the army under his command. He delayed even to forward Morgan's rifle corps, though their services were no longer needed in his camp and were so much required in the South. It was determined, therefore, in a council of war, that one of Washington's staff should be sent to Gates to represent the critical state of affairs and that a large reinforcement from the Northern army would, in all probability, reduce Howe to the same situation with Burgoyne. Alexander Hamilton, his aide-de-camp, was charged with this mission. He bore a letter from Washington to Gates, dated October 30th, of which the following is an extract: "By this opportunity, I do myself the pleasure to congratulate you on the signal success of the army under your command in compelling General Burgoyne and his whole force to surrender themselves prisoners of war. . . . At the same time, I cannot but regret that a matter of such magnitude . . . should have reached me by report only or through the channel of letters not bearing that authenticity which . . . it would have received . . . under your signature."

A fortuitous circumstance apprised Washington about this time that a correspondence derogatory to his military character and conduct was going on between Conway and Gates. Washington let Conway know, by the following brief note, dated November 9th, that his correspondence was detected.

Sir: A letter which I received last night contained the following paragraph—"In a letter from General Conway to General Gates, he says, 'Heaven has determined to save your country, or a weak general and bad counsellors would have ruined it.'" I am, sir, your humble servant,

George Washington.

The brevity of this note rendered it the more astounding. It seems, at first, to have prostrated Conway. He immediately sent in his resignation. His resignation, however, was not accepted by Congress; on the contrary, he was advanced to further honors, which we shall specify hereafter.

In the mean time, the cabal went on to make invidious comparisons between the achievements of the two armies, deeply derogatory to that under Washington. Publicly he took no notice of them, but they drew from him the following apology for his army in a letter to Patrick Henry, then governor of Virginia. "The design of this," writes he, "is only to inform you . . . that the army which I have had under my immediate command, has not, at any one time, since General Howe's landing at the Head of Elk, been equal in point of numbers to his. . . . How different the case in the Northern Department! There the States of New York and New England, resolving to crush Burgoyne, continued pouring in their troops till the surrender of that army. . . . Had the same spirit pervaded the people of this and the neighboring States, we might before this time have had General Howe nearly in the situation of General Burgoyne. . . . My own difficulties, in the course of the campaign, have been not a little increased by the extra aid of Continental troops, which the gloomy prospect of our affairs in the North immediately after the reduction of Ticonderoga, induced me to spare from this army. But it is to be hoped that all will yet end well. If the cause is advanced, indifferent is it to me where or in what quarter it happens."

The last sentence speaks the whole soul of Washington. Glory with him is a secondary consideration. Let those who win, wear the laurel—sufficient for him is the advancement of the cause.

The non-arrival of reinforcements from the Northern army continued to embarass Washington's operations. The enemy were making preparations for further attempts upon Forts Mercer and Mifflin. Howe was constructing redoubts and batteries on Province Island, on the west side of the Delaware, within 500 yards of Fort Mifflin and mounting them with heavy cannon. Washington consulted with his general officers what was to be done. Had the army received the expected reinforcements from the North, it might have detached sufficient force to the west side of the Schuylkill to dislodge the enemy from Province Island, but at present it would require almost the whole of the army for the purpose. This would leave the public stores at Easton, Bethlehem and Allentown uncovered, as well as several of the hospitals. It would also leave the post at Red Bank unsupported, through which Fort Mifflin was reinforced and supplied. It was determined, therefore, to await the arrival of the expected reinforcements from the North. In the mean time, the garrisons of Forts Mercer and Mifflin were increased and Varnum was stationed at Red Bank with his brigade to be at hand to render reinforcements to either of them as occasion might require.

On the 10th of November, Howe commenced a heavy fire upon Fort Mifflin from his batteries, which mounted eighteen, twenty-four, and thirty-two pounders. Smith doubted the competency of his feeble garrison to defend the works against a force so terribly effective and wrote to Washington accordingly. The latter in reply represented the great importance of the works and trusted they would be maintained to the last extremity. Varnum was instructed to send over fresh troops occasionally to relieve those in the garrison and to prevail upon as many as possible of the militia to go over.

Washington's orders and instructions were faithfully obeyed. Major Fleury, a brave French officer, acquitted himself with intelligence and spirit as engineer, but an incessant cannonade and bombardment for several days defied all repairs. The block-houses were demolished, the palisades beaten down, the guns dismounted, the barracks reduced to ruins. Smith himself was disabled by severe contusions and obliged to retire to Red Bank.

The fort was in ruins. There was danger of its being carried by storm but the gallant Fleury thought it might yet be defended with the aid of fresh troops; such were furnished from Varnum's brigade. Lieutenant-colonel Russell of the Connecticut line replaced Colonel Smith. He, in turn, obliged to relinquish command through fatigue and ill health, was succeeded by Major Thayer of Rhode Island, aided by Captain Talbot.

On the fourth day the enemy brought a large Indiaman, cut down to a floating battery, to bear upon the works, but, though it opened a terrible fire, it was silenced before night. The next day several ships-of-war got within gunshot. Two prepared to attack it in front; others brought their guns to bear on Fort Mercer; two made their way into the narrow channel between Mud Island and the Pennsylvania shore to operate with the British batteries erected there. At a concerted signal a cannonade was opened from all quarters. The heroic little garrison stood the fire without flinching; the danger, however, was growing imminent.

The scene now became awful—incessant firing from ships, forts, gondolas and floating batteries, with clouds of sulphurous smoke, and the deafening thunder of cannon. Before night there was

hardly a fortification to defend; palisades were shivered, guns dismounted, the whole parapet levelled. There was terrible slaughter;
most of the company of artillery was destroyed. Fleury himself
was wounded. Captain Talbot received a wound in the wrist
but continued bravely fighting until disabled by another wound
in the hip.

To hold out longer was impossible. Colonel Thayer made preparations to evacuate the fort in the night. Every thing was removed
in the evening. The wounded were taken over to Red Bank accompanied by part of the garrison. Thayer remained with 40 men until
eleven o'clock, when they set fire to the fort and crossed to Red
Bank.

Washington still hoped to keep possession of Red Bank and
thereby prevent the enemy from weighing the chevaux-de-frise
before the frost obliged their ships to quit the river. "I am anxiously
waiting the arrival of the troops from the northward," writes he,
"who ought, from the time they have had my orders, to have been
here before this. Colonel Hamilton, one of my aides, is doing all he
can to push them forward, but he writes me word that he finds many
unaccountable delays thrown in his way."

The delays in question will best be explained by a few particulars concerning the mission of Hamilton. On his way to the head-
quarters of Gates, at Albany, he found Governor Clinton and Putnam encamped on the opposite sides of the Hudson, the governor at
New Windsor, Putnam at Fishkill. About a mile from New Windsor,
Hamilton met Morgan and his riflemen, early in the morning of the
2d of November, on the march for Washington's camp, having been
thus tardily detached by Gates. The colonel had expected to find
that he would have little to do but hurry on ample reinforcements
already on the march, whereas he found that a large part of the
Northern army was to remain in and about Albany, about 4000 men
to be spared to the commander-in-chief; the rest were to be
stationed on the east side of the Hudson with Putnam, who had for
some time past been haunted by a project of an attack upon New
York. Hamilton disconcerted his project by directing him, in Washington's name, to hurry forward two Continental brigades to the

latter, together with Warner's militia brigade; also, to order Red Bank a body of Jersey militia about to cross to Peekskill.

Having given these directions, Hamilton hastened on to Albany. He found still less disposition on the part of Gates to furnish the troops required. There was no certainty, he said, that Sir Henry had gone to join Howe. There was a possibility of his returning up the river, which would expose Albany to destruction. The New England States, too, would be left open to the ravages of the enemy; besides, it would put it out of his power to attempt any thing against Ticonderoga. In a word, Gates had schemes of his own, to which those of the commander-in-chief must give way.

It was with the greatest difficulty that Hamilton prevailed on Gates to detach the brigades of Poor and Patterson to the aid of the commander-in-chief; finding reinforcements fall thus short from this quarter, he wrote to Putnam to forward an additional 1000 of Continental troops from his camp.

Hamilton returned to the camp of Governor Clinton, the general officer best disposed in this quarter to promote the public weal, independent of personal considerations. He had recently expressed his opinion to Gates that the army under Washington ought at present to be the chief object of attention, "for on its success every thing worth regarding depended."

Putnam, on the contrary, wished to keep as much force as possible under his control. The old general was once more astride of what Hamilton termed his "hobby-horse," an expedition against New York. He had neglected to forward the troops which had been ordered to the South.

Hamilton, in his perplexity, consulted Governor Clinton. The latter agreed with him that an attempt against New York would be a "suicidal parade," wasting time and men. The governor, however, understood the character and humors of his old coadjutor and advised Hamilton to send an order in the most emphatical terms to Putnam to despatch all the Continental troops under him to Washington's assistance and to detain the militia instead of them. The "emphatical" letter of Hamilton had the effect the governor intended. The project against New York was given up, and the reinforcements reluctantly ordered to the South.

"I cannot but say," writes Washington to Putnam, "there has been more delay in the march of the troops than I think necessary; and I could wish, that in future my orders may be immediately complied with, without arguing upon the propriety of them."

Washington found it more necessary than usual, at this moment, to assert his superior command, from the attempts which were being made to weaken his stand in the public estimation. Still he was not aware of the extent of the intrigues that were in progress around him, in which we believe Putnam had no share. The surrender of Burgoyne, though mainly the result of Washington's far-seeing plans, had suddenly trumped up Gates into a quasi rival.

In the mean time, Sir William Howe was following up the reduction of Fort Mifflin by an expedition against Fort Mercer, which still impeded the navigation of the Delaware. On the 17th of November, Cornwallis was detached with 2000 men to cross from Chester into the Jerseys, where he would be joined by a force advancing from New York.

Apprised of this movement, Washington detached Huntington, with a brigade, to join Varnum at Red Bank. Greene was also ordered to repair thither with his division and an express was sent off to Glover, who was on his way through the Jerseys with his brigade, directing him to file off to the left towards the same point. These troops, with such militia as could be collected, Washington hoped would be sufficient to save the fort. Before they could reach their destination, however, Cornwallis appeared before it. A defence against such superior force was hopeless. The works were abandoned and taken possession of by the enemy, who proceeded to destroy them. After the destruction had been accomplished, the reinforcements from the North, so long and so anxiously expected, and so shamefully delayed, made their appearance. "Had they arrived but ten days sooner," writes Washington to his brother, "it would, I think, have put it in my power to save Fort Mifflin, which defended the chevaux-de-frise, and consequently have rendered Philadelphia a very ineligible situation for the enemy this winter."

The evil which Washington had so anxiously striven to prevent had now been effected. The American vessels stationed in the river had lost all protection. Some of the galleys took refuge in the upper part of the Delaware; the rest were set on fire by their crews and abandoned.

Washington advised the navy board, now that the enemy had the command of the river, to have all the American frigates scuttled and sunk immediately. The board objected to sinking them, but said they should be ballasted and plugged, ready to be sunk in case of attack. Washington warned them that an attack would be sudden, so as to get possession of them before they could be sunk or destroyed; his advice and warning were unheeded.

(CHAPTER 42)

On the evening of the 24th of November Washington reconnoitred the lines and defences about Philadelphia from the opposite side of the Schuylkill. His army was now considerably reinforced; the garrison was weakened by the absence of a large body of troops under Cornwallis in the Jerseys. Some of the general officers thought this an advantageous moment for an attack upon the city.

With an anxious eye Washington scrutinized the enemy's works. They appeared to be exceeding strong. A chain of redoubts extended along the most commanding ground from the Schuylkill to the Delaware. They were framed, planked, and of great thickness, and were surrounded by a deep ditch, enclosed and fraised. The intervals were filled with an abatis.

The idea of those in favor of an attack, was that it should be at different points at daylight; the main body to attack the lines to the north of the city, while Greene, embarking his men in boats at Dunk's Ferry and passing down the Delaware, and Potter, with a body of Continentals and militia moving down the west side of the Schuylkill, should attack the eastern and western fronts.

Washington saw that there was an opportunity for a brilliant blow that might satisfy the impatience of the public and silence the sarcasms of the press, but he saw that it must be struck at the expense of a fearful loss of life. Returning to camp, he held a council of war in which the matter was debated at great length but without coming to a decision. At breaking up, Washington requested that each member of the council would give his opinion the next morning in writing, and he sent off a messenger in the night for the written opinion of Greene.

Only four members of the council were in favor of an attack. Eleven were against it, objecting, among other things, that the enemy's lines were too strong and their force too numerous, well disciplined and experienced to be assailed without great loss and the hazard of a failure.

Had Washington been actuated by personal ambition, he might have disregarded the loss and hazarded the failure, but his patriotism was superior to his ambition; the idea of an attack was abandoned.

A letter from Greene, received about this time, gave Washington some gratifying intelligence about the Marquis de Lafayette. Though not quite recovered from the wound received at the battle of Brandywine, he had accompanied Greene as a volunteer in his expedition into the Jerseys, and had been indulged by him with an opportunity of gratifying his belligerent humor in a brush with Cornwallis's outposts. "The marquis," writes Greene, "is charmed with the spirited behavior of the militia and rifle corps; they drove the enemy above half a mile and kept the ground until dark."

Washington had repeatedly written to Congress in favor of giving the marquis a command equal to his nominal rank in consideration of his illustrious connections, the attachment he manifested to the cause, and the good sense he had displayed on various occasions.

Washington availed himself of the present occasion to support his former recommendations by transmitting to Congress an account of Lafayette's youthful exploit. He received, in return, an intimation from that body, that it was their pleasure he should appoint the marquis to the command of a division in the Continental army. The division of Stephen at this time was vacant, that officer having been dismissed for misconduct at the battle of Germantown. Lafayette was forthwith appointed to the command of that division.

At this juncture (November 27th), a modification took place in the Board of War, indicative of the influence which was operating in Congress. It was increased from three to five members: General Mifflin, Joseph Trumbull, Richard Peters, Colonel Pickering, and General Gates. Mifflin's resignation of the commission of quartermaster-general had been accepted, but that of major-general was continued to him. Gates was appointed president of the board and the President of Congress was instructed to express to him the high sense which that body entertained of his abilities and peculiar fitness to discharge the duties of that important office, upon the right execution of which the success of the American cause so eminently depended; to inform him it was their intention to continue his rank as major-general, and that he might officiate at the board or in the field, as occasion might require; furthermore, that he should repair to Congress with all convenient despatch to enter upon the duties of his appointment. It was evidently the idea of the cabal that Gates was henceforth to be the master spirit of the war.

While busy faction was thus at work to undermine the fame and authority of Washington, General Howe, according to his own threat, was preparing to "drive him beyond the mountains."

On the 4th of December, Captain Allen McLane of Maryland brought word to head-quarters that an attack was to be made that very night on the camp at White Marsh. Washington made his dispositions to receive the assault and, in the mean time, detached McLane with 100 men to reconnoitre. The latter met the van of the enemy about eleven o'clock at night on the Germantown Road, attacked it at the Three Mile Run, forced it to change its line of march, and impeded it throughout the night. The enemy appeared at daybreak and encamped on Chestnut Hill, within three miles of Washington's right wing. Brigadier-general James Irvine, with 600 Pennsylvania militia, was sent out to skirmish with their light advanced parties. He encountered them at the foot of the hill but, after a short conflict, his troops gave way and fled in all directions, leaving him and some of his men wounded on the field, who were taken prisoners.

Howe passed the day in reconnoitring, and at night changed his ground and moved to a hill on the left within a mile of the American line. He had scrutinized Washington's position and pronounced it inaccessible. For three days he manoeuvred to draw him from it, shifting his own position occasionally but still keeping on advantageous ground. Washington was not to be decoyed. He knew the vast advantages which superior science, discipline and experience gave the enemy in open field fight and remained within his lines. All his best officers approved of his policy. Several sharp skirmishes occurred at Edge Hill and elsewhere. There was loss on both sides but the Americans gave way before a great superiority of numbers.

On the 7th there was every appearance that Howe meditated an attack on the left wing. Washington prepared for a warm and decisive action. He rode through every brigade, giving directions how the attack was to be met. His men were inspirited by his words but still more by his looks, so calm and determined.

The day wore away with nothing but skirmishes, in which Morgan's riflemen and the Maryland militia under Gist rendered good service. An attack was expected in the night or early in the morning, but no attack took place. The spirit manifested by the Americans, in their recent contests, had rendered the British commanders cautious.

The next day, in the afternoon, the enemy were again in motion, but, instead of advancing, filed off to the left, halted, and lit up a long string of fires on the heights, behind which they retreated, silently and precipitately, in the night. By the time Washington received intelligence of their movement, they were in full march for Philadelphia. He immediately detached light parties to fall upon their rear but they were too far on the way for any but light-horse to overtake them.

Here was another occasion of which the enemies of Washington availed themselves to deride his cautious policy. Yet it was clearly dictated by true wisdom. In his despatch to the President of Congress, he writes, "I sincerely wish that they had made an attack; as the issue, in all probability, from the disposition of our troops and the strong situation of our camp, would have been fortunate and happy. At the same time I must add, that reason, prudence, and every principle of policy forbade us from quitting our post to attack them."

At this time, one of the earliest measures recommended by the Board of War and adopted by Congress showed the increasing influence of the cabal: two inspectors-general were to be appointed for the promotion of discipline and reformation of abuses in the army; one of the persons chosen for this important office was Conway, with the rank, too, of major-general! This was tacitly in defiance of the opinion so fully expressed by Washington. Conway, however, was the secret colleague of Gates, and Gates was now the rising sun.

Winter had now set in with all its severity. The troops, worn down by long and hard service, had need of repose. Poorly clad and almost destitute of blankets, they required a warmer shelter than mere tents against the inclemencies of the season. The nearest towns which would afford winter-quarters were Lancaster, York and Carlisle, but, should the army retire to either of these, a large and fertile district would be exposed to be foraged by the foe.

The plan adopted by Washington, after holding a council of war, was to hut the army for the winter at Valley Forge in Chester County, on the west side of the Schuylkill, about 20 miles from Philadelphia. Here he would be able to keep a vigilant eye on that city and at the same time protect a great extent of country.

Sad and dreary was the march to Valley Forge. Hungry and cold were the poor fellows who had so long been keeping the field, for provisions were scant, clothing worn out and, so badly off were they for shoes, that the footsteps of many might be tracked in blood. Such were the consequences of the derangement of the commissariat.

Arrived at Valley Forge on the 17th, the troops had still to brave the wintry weather in their tents until they could cut down trees and construct huts for their accommodation.

Scarce had the troops been two days employed in these labors, when, before daybreak on the 22d, word was brought that a body of the enemy had made a sortie toward Chester apparently on a foraging expedition. Washington issued orders to Huntington and Varnum to hold their troops in readiness to march against them. "Fighting will be far preferable to starving," writes Huntington. "My brigade are out of provisions nor can the commissary obtain any meat."

"It's a very pleasing circumstance to the division under my command," writes Varnum, "that there is a probability of their marching; three days successively we have been destitute of bread. Two days we have been entirely without meat. The men must be supplied or they cannot be commanded." In fact, a dangerous mutiny had broken out among the famishing troops in the preceding night, which their officers had had great difficulty in quelling.

Washington instantly wrote to the President of Congress on the subject. "I do not know from what cause this . . . total failure of supplies arises; but unless more vigorous exertions and better regulations take place . . . immediately, the army must dissolve. I have done all in my power by remonstrating, by writing, by ordering the commissaries on this head, from time to time; but without any good effect, or obtaining more than a present scanty relief."

Scarce had Washington despatched this letter, when he learnt that the Legislature of Pennsylvania had addressed a remonstrance to Congress against his going into winter-quarters instead of keeping in the open field. This letter, received in his forlorn situation, surrounded by an unhoused, scantily clad, half-starved army, shivering in the midst of December's snow and cold, put an end to his forbearance and drew from him another letter to the President of Congress, dated on the 23d.

"Though I have been tender, heretofore," writes he, "of giving any opinion, or lodging complaints, . . . it is time to speak plain in exculpation of myself. . . . "Since the month of July, we have had no assistance from the quartermaster-general; . . . as a proof . . . of the inability of an army, under the circumstances of this, to perform the common duties of soldiers (besides a number of men confined to hospitals for want of shoes, and others in farmers' houses on the same account), we have, by a field return this day made, no less than 2898 men now in camp unfit for duty because they are barefoot and otherwise naked. By the same return, it appears that our whole strength in Continental troops, including the eastern brigades which have joined us since the surrender of General Burgoyne, exclusive of the Maryland troops sent to Wilmington, amounts to no more than 8200 in camp fit for duty; notwithstanding which, and that since the 4th instant, our numbers fit for duty, from the hardships and exposures they have undergone, particularly on account of blankets (numbers having been obliged, and still are, to sit up all night by fires, instead of taking comfortable rest in a natural and common way), have decreased near 2000 men.

"We find gentlemen, without knowing whether the army was really going into winter-quarters or not, . . . reprobating the measure as much as if they thought the soldiers were made of stocks or stones, and equally insensible of frost and snow; and moreover, as if they conceived it easily practicable for an inferior army, under the disadvantages I have described ours to be—which are by no means exaggerated—to confine a superior one, in all respects well appointed and provided for a winter's campaign, within the city of Philadelphia, and to cover from depredation and waste the States of Pennsylvania and Jersey. . . . I can assure those gentlemen that it is a much easier and less distressing thing to draw remonstrances in a comfortable room by a good fireside than to occupy a cold, bleak hill, and sleep under frost and snow, without clothes or blankets."

To save his camp from desolation, and to relieve his starving soldiery, he was compelled to exercise the authority given him by Congress, to forage the country round, seize supplies wherever he could find them, and pay for them in money or in certificates redeemable by Congress. He exercised these powers with great reluctance. "Such procedures," writes he to the President of Congress, "may give a momentary relief but, if repeated, will prove of the most pernicious consequence. Beside spreading disaffection, jealousy and fear among the people, they never fail, even in the most veteran troops, under the most rigid and exact discipline, to raise in the soldiery a disposition to licentiousness, to plunder and robbery, difficult to suppress afterward."

With these appeals to Congress, we close Washington's operations for 1777, one of the most arduous and eventful years of his military life. He began it with an empty arm-chest and a force dwindled down to 4000 half-disciplined men. Throughout the year he had had to contend not merely with the enemy but with the parsimony and meddlesome interference of Congress. In his most critical times that body had left him without funds and without reinforcements. It had made promotions contrary to his advice and contrary to military usage, thereby wronging and disgusting some of his bravest officers. It had changed the commissariat in the very midst of a campaign and thereby thrown the whole service into confusion.

Among so many cross-purposes and discouragements, it was a difficult task for Washington to "keep the life and soul of the army together." Yet he had done so. Marvellous indeed was the manner in which he had soothed the discontents of his aggrieved officers and reconciled them to an ill-requiting service; still more marvellous the manner in which he had breathed his own spirit of patience and perseverance into his yeoman soldiery.

All this time, too, while endeavoring to ascertain and counteract the operations of Lord Howe upon the ocean and his brother upon the land, he was directing and aiding military measures against Burgoyne in the North. The operations of the commander-in-chief are not always obvious to the public eye; most of the moves which ended in giving a triumphant check to Burgoyne may be traced to Washington's shifting camp in the Jerseys.

It has been an irksome task to notice the intrigue by which part of this year's campaign was disgraced. We have shown how successful they were in displacing Schuyler from the head of the Northern department; the same machinations were now at work to undermine the commander-in-chief and elevate the putative hero of Saratoga. He was painfully aware of them; yet in no part of the war did he more thoroughly evince that magnanimity which was his grand characteristic than in the last scenes of this campaign, where he rose above the tauntings of the press, the sneerings of the cabal, the murmurs of the public, the suggestions of some of his friends, and the throbbing impulses of his own courageous heart, and adhered to that policy which he considered essential to the safety of the cause.

(CHAPTER 43)

While censure and detraction had dogged Washington throughout his harassing campaign, Gates was held up by the cabal as the only one capable of retrieving the desperate fortunes of the South. Letters from his friends in Congress urged him to hasten on, take his seat at the head of the Board of War, assume the management of military affairs, and save the country!

Gates, however, while feasting on the sweets of adulation, received an epistle from his friend Mifflin. "My dear General," writes he, "an extract from Conway's letter to you has been procured and sent to head-quarters. . . . General Washington enclosed it to Conway without remarks." Nothing could surpass the trouble and confusion of mind of Gates on the perusal of this letter. In fact Mifflin knew nothing in particular when he wrote; nor did any of the cabal. The laconic nature of Washington's note to Conway had thrown them all in confusion.

Gates in his perplexity suspected that his portfolio had been stealthily opened and his letters copied. But by whom? He wrote to Conway and Mifflin, anxiously inquiring what part of their correspondence had been thus surreptitiously obtained. He made rigid inquiries among the gentlemen of his staff; all disavowed any knowledge of the matter. In this state of mental trepidation Gates wrote, on the 8th of December, to Washington. ". . . I conjure your Excellency to give me all the assistance you can in tracing the author of the infidelity which puts extracts from General Conway's letters to me into your hands. Those letters have been stealingly copied, but which of them, when, and by whom, is to me as yet an unfathomable secret. . . . It is, I believe, in your Excellency's power to do me and the United States a very important service, by detecting a wretch who may betray me, and capitally injure the very operations under your immediate directions."

A copy of this letter was transmitted by Gates to the President of Congress. Washington replied with characteristic dignity and candor. "Colonel Wilkinson, on his way to Congress, in the month of October last, fell in with Lord Stirling at Reading, and, not in confidence, that I ever understood, informed his aide-de-camp, Major McWilliams, that General Conway had written this to you; 'Heaven has been determined to save your country, or a weak general and bad counsellors would have ruined it.' Lord Stirling, from motives of friendship, transmitted the account with this remark: 'The enclosed was communicated by Colonel Wilkinson to Major McWilliams.'"

Washington adds, that the letter written by him to Conway was merely to show that gentleman that he was not unapprised of his intriguing disposition. " . . . I never knew that General Conway, whom I viewed in the light of a stranger to you, was a correspondent of yours; much less did I suspect that I was the subject of your confidential letters. . . . I considered the information as coming from yourself, and given with a view to forewarn, and consequently to forearm me, against a . . . dangerous incendiary; in which character sooner or later this country will know General Conway."

A few days after writing the above letter, Washington received the following warning from his old and faithful friend, Dr. Craik, dated from Maryland, Jan. 6th. "The morning I left camp, I was informed that a strong faction was forming against you in the new Board of War, and in the Congress. . . . The method they are taking is by holding General Gates up to the people, and making them believe that you have had a number three or four times greater than the enemy, and have done nothing; that Philadelphia was given up by your management, and that you have had many opportunities of defeating the enemy. It is said they dare not appear openly as your enemies; but that the new Board of War is composed of such leading men, as will throw such obstacles and difficulties in your way as to force you to resign."

Gates was disposed to mark his advent to power by a striking operation. A notable project had been concerted by him and the Board of War for a winter irruption into Canada. An expedition was to proceed from Albany, cross Lake Champlain on the ice, burn the British shipping at St. Johns and press forward to Montreal. Washington was not consulted in the matter; the project was submitted to Congress and sanctioned by them without his privity.

One object of the scheme was to detach the Marquis de Lafayette from Washington, to have command of the expedition; Conway was to be second in command. The first notice that Washington received of the project was in a letter from Gates, enclosing one to Lafayette informing the latter of his appointment and requiring his attendance at Yorktown to receive instructions.

Gates in his letter to Washington asked his opinion and advice, evidently as a matter of form. The cabal, however, had overshot their mark. Lafayette, aware of their intrigues, was so disgusted by the want of deference and respect to the commander-in-chief that he would have declined the appointment had not Washington himself advised him strongly to accept it.

He accordingly proceeded to Yorktown, where Gates was profuse of promises. Every thing was to be made smooth and easy for Lafayette. He was to have at least 2500 fighting men under him. Stark was ready to co-operate with a body of Green Mountain Boys.

Lafayette, in accepting the command, considered himself detached from the main army and under the immediate orders of the commander-in-chief. He had a favorable opinion of the military talents of Conway, but he was aware of the game he was playing. He made a point, therefore, of having de Kalb appointed to the expedition; his commission, being of older date than that of Conway, would give him the precedence of that officer and make him second in command. Lafayette set out for Albany without any very sanguine expectations.

Washington's letter of the 4th of January on the Conway correspondence had not reached Gates until the 22d of January, after his arrival at Yorktown. No sooner did Gates learn from its context that all Washington's knowledge of that correspondence was confined to a single paragraph of a letter (and that merely as quoted in conversation by Wilkinson) than the whole matter appeared easily to be explained or shuffled off. He accordingly took pen in hand and addressed Washington on the 23d of January: "The letter which I had the honor to receive yesterday from your Excellency, has relieved me from unspeakable uneasiness. I now anticipate the pleasure it will give you when you discover that what has been conveyed to you for an extract of General Conway's letter to me . . . is spurious. It was certainly fabricated to answer the most selfish and wicked purposes." He then goes on to declare that the genuine letter of Conway was perfectly harmless. "Honor forbids it, and patriotism demands that I should return the letter into the hands of the writer. I will do it; but, at the same time, I declare that the paragraph conveyed to your Excellency as a genuine part of it, was, in words as well as in substance, a wicked forgery."

Conway, in a letter to Washington (dated January 27th), informs him that the letter had been returned to him by Gates and that he found with great satisfaction that "the paragraph so much spoken of did not exist in the said letter nor any thing like it."

On the 9th of February, Washington wrote Gates a long and searching reply to his letters of the 8th, and 23d of January, showing how, in spirit and import, they contradicted each other and how sometimes the same letter contradicted itself: In the first letter, the reality of the extracts was by implication allowed and the only solicitude shown was to find out the person who brought them to light; while, in the second letter, the whole was pronounced "in word as well as in substance a wicked forgery." "Were it necessary," writes Washington, with reference to Conway, "more instances than one might be adduced, from his behavior and conversation, to manifest that he is capable of all the malignity of detraction, and all the meanness of intrigue, to gratify the absurd resentment of disappointed vanity, or to answer the purposes of personal aggrandizement, and promote the interest of faction."

Gates evidently quailed beneath this letter. In his reply, he earnestly hoped that no more time might be lost upon the subject of General Conway's letter. In a dignified but freezing note Washington closed this correspondence: "I am as averse to controversy as any man; . . . Your repeatedly and solemnly disclaiming any offensive views in those matters . . . makes me willing to close with the desire you express of burying them hereafter in silence, and, as far as future events will permit, oblivion. My temper leads me to peace and harmony with all men; and it is peculiarly my wish to avoid any personal feuds or dissensions with those who are embarked in the same great national interest with myself, as every difference of this kind must, in its consequences, be very injurious."

Letters received at this juncture from Lafayette gave Washington tidings concerning the expedition against Canada. Conway had arrived at Albany before the marquis and his first word when they met was that the expedition was quite impossible. Schuyler, Lincoln and Arnold had written to Conway to that effect. The marquis at first was inclined to hope the contrary but his hope was soon demolished. Instead of the 2500 men that had been promised him, not 1200 in all were to be found fit for duty. As to Stark, the marquis received at Albany a letter from the veteran asking what number of men, for what time, and for what rendezvous he was to raise them. Another officer, who was to have enlisted men, would have done so had he received money.

The project of an irruption into Canada was at length formally suspended by a resolve of Congress; Washington was directed to recall the marquis and de Kalb, the presence of the latter being deemed absolutely necessary to the army at Valley Forge. Gladly the young marquis hastened back to Valley Forge to enjoy the companionship and find himself once more under the paternal eye of Washington, leaving Conway for the time in command at Albany.

The Conway letter was destined to be a further source of trouble to the cabal. Stirling, in whose presence Wilkinson had cited the letter and who had sent information of it to Washington, was told that Wilkinson, on being questioned by Conway, had declared that no such words as those reported, nor any to the same effect, were in the letter.

His lordship immediately wrote to Wilkinson, reminding him of the conversation at Reading and telling him of what he had recently heard. Wilkinson found that his tongue had again brought him into a difficulty; but he wrote in reply, "Brigadier-general Conway informed me that he had been charged by General Washington with writing a letter to Major-general Gates, which reflected on the general and the army. The particulars of this charge, which Brigadier-general Conway then repeated, I cannot now recollect."

When Wilkinson was subsequently on his way to Yorktown to enter upon his duties as secretary of the Board of War, he learnt at Lancaster that Gates had denounced him as the betrayer of that letter in the grossest language. Wilkinson proceeded to Yorktown, where he met with Lieutenant-colonel Ball, of the Virginia line, who willingly became bearer of the following note from Wilkinson to Gates: "Sir,—I have discharged my duty to you, and to my conscience; meet me to-morrow morning behind the English church, and I will there stipulate the satisfaction which you have promised to grant," etc.

Colonel Ball was received with complaisance by the general. The meeting was fixed for eight o'clock in the morning, with pistols.

At the appointed time Wilkinson and his second, having put their arms in order, were about to sally forth when Captain Stoddart informed Wilkinson that Gates desired to speak with him. "The surprise robbed me of circumspection," continues Wilkinson. ". . . I found General Gates unarmed and alone and was received with tenderness but manifest embarrassment; . . . he burst into tears, took me by the hand, and asked me 'how I could think he wished to injure me?' I was too deeply affected to speak; . . . and he added, 'Besides, there was no cause for injuring you, as Conway acknowledged his letter, and has since said much harder things to Washington's face.' Such language left me nothing to require," continues Wilkinson. "It was satisfactory beyond expectation, and rendered me more than content."

A change soon came over the spirit of this maudlin scene. Wilkinson attended as secretary at the War Office. "My reception from the president, General Gates," writes he, "did not correspond with his recent professions; he was civil, but barely so, and I was at a loss to account for his coldness, yet had no suspicion of his insincerity." Wilkinson soon found his situation at the Board of War uncomfortable; and after the lapse of a few days set out for Valley Forge.

At Valley Forge Wilkinson had an interview with Washington,

in which the subject of Conway's letter was discussed and the whole correspondence between Gates and the commander-in-chief laid before him.

"This exposition," writes Wilkinson, "unfolded to me a scene of perfidy and duplicity of which I had no suspicion." A few days afterwards, Wilkinson addressed the following letter to the President of Congress: "Sir,—While I make my acknowledgements to Congress for the appointment of secretary to the Board of War and Ordnance, I am sorry I should be constrained to resign that office; but, after the acts of treachery and falsehood in which I have detected Major-general Gates, the president of that board, it is impossible for me to reconcile it to my honor to serve with him."

Throughout all the intrigues and manoeuvres of the cabal, Washington conducted himself with calmness and self-command, speaking on the subject to no one but a very few of his friends, lest a knowledge of those internal dissensions should injure the service.

In a letter to Patrick Henry he gives his closing observations concerning them. "I cannot precisely mark the extent of their views, but it appeared in general, that General Gates was to be exalted on the ruin of my reputation and influence. This I am authorized to say, from undeniable facts in my own possession, from publications the evident scope of which could not be mistaken, and from private detractions industriously circulated. General Mifflin, it is commonly supposed, bore the second part in the cabal, and General Conway, I know, was a very active and malignant partisan, but I have good reason to believe that their machinations have recoiled most sensibly upon themselves."

Wanting as the intrigues of the cabal might be in plan or design, they were fraught with mischief to the public service, inspiring doubts of its commanders. They harassed Washington in the latter part of his campaign, contributed to the dark cloud that hung over his gloomy encampment at Valley Forge and might have effected his downfall had he been less firmly fixed in the affections of the people. Jealous rivals he might have in the army, bitter enemies in Congress, but the soldiers loved him, and the large heart of the nation always beat true to him.

The War Shifts Southwards (1777–1780)

During the winter's encampment in Valley Forge, Washington sedulously applied himself to the formation of a new system for the army. At his solicitation Congress appointed the Committee of Arrangement (General Reed, Nathaniel Folsom, Francis Dana, Charles Carroll, and Gouverneur Morris) to repair to the camp and assist him. Before their arrival he collected the opinions and suggestions of his officers, and from these, and his own observations, prepared a document exhibiting the actual state of the army and the alterations and reforms that were necessary. The committee remained three months with him in camp, and then made a report to Congress founded on his statement. The reforms therein recommended were generally adopted.

The reforms adopted were slow in going into operation. In the mean time, the distresses of the army continued to increase. The surrounding country for a great distance was exhausted and had the appearance of having been pillaged. In some places where the inhabitants had provisions and cattle they denied it, intending to take them to Philadelphia, where they could obtain greater prices.

The parties sent out to forage too often returned empty-handed. "For some days past there has been little less than a famine in the camp," writes Washington, on one occasion. "A part of the army has been a week without any kind of flesh and the rest three or four days."

The committee, in their report, declared that "sickness and mortality have spread through their quarters in an astonishing degree. Nothing can equal their sufferings, except the patience and fortitude with which the faithful part of the army endure them."

A British historian cites as proof of the great ascendency of Washington over his "raw and undisciplined troops," that so many remained with him throughout the winter in this wretched plight—almost naked, often on short allowance, with great sickness and mortality, and a scarcity of medicines, their horses perishing by hundreds from hunger and the severity of the season.

The army for a part of the winter, while it held Philadelphia in siege, was in as perilous a situation as that which kept a bold front before Boston without ammunition to serve its cannon.

On one occasion there was a flurry at the most advanced post, where Captain Henry Lee (Light-horse Harry) with a few of his troops was stationed. He had made himself formidable to the enemy by harassing their foraging parties. A party of about 200 dragoons, taking a circuitous route in the night, came upon him by daybreak. He had but a few men with him at the time and took post in a large store-house. The dragoons attempted to force their way into the house, but were bravely repulsed, and sheered off, leaving two killed and four wounded. Washington, whose heart evidently warmed more and more to this young Virginian officer, not long afterwards strongly recommended Lee for the command of two troops of horse, with the rank of major, to act as an independent partisan corps. Congress made this appointment, accompanying it with encomiums on Lee as a brave and prudent officer who had rendered essential service to the country.

A very important arrival in the camp was that of the Baron Steuben towards the latter part of February. He was a seasoned soldier from the old battlefields of Europe, having served in the seven years' war, been aide-de-camp to the great Frederick, and connected with the quartermaster-general's department. Honors had been heaped upon him in Germany; he had declined liberal offers from the King of Sardinia and the Emperor of Austria. He was persuaded by the French Minister of War and others of the French cabinet to come out to America and engage in the cause they were preparing to befriend. Their object was to secure for the American armies the services of an officer of experience and a thorough disciplinarian to aid a half-disciplined people in their struggle for liberty.

The baron had brought strong letters from Dr. Franklin and Mr. Deane, our envoys at Paris. Landing in Portsmouth in New Hampshire, Dec. 1st, he had forwarded copies of his letters to Washington. "The object of my greatest ambition," writes he, "is to render your country all the service in my power and to deserve the title of a citizen of America by fighting for the cause of your liberty."

By Washington's direction, the baron proceeded direct to Congress. His letters procured him a distinguished reception from the president. A committee was appointed to confer with him. He offered his services as a volunteer, making no condition for rank or

Forrest

GEN. BARON STEUBEN

(From an original picture in the New York City Hall.)

Printed by W. Pate

Le Baron de Steuben

NEW YORK G.P. PUTNAM & CO.

pay. His proffered services were accepted with a vote of thanks and he was ordered to join the army at Valley Forge. That army, in its ragged condition and squalid quarters, presented a sorry aspect to a strict disciplinarian from Germany, accustomed to the order and appointments of European camps; the baron often declared that under such circumstances no army in Europe could be kept together for a single month.

The evils arising from a want of uniformity in discipline and manoeuvres throughout the army had long caused Washington to desire a well organized inspectorship. Conway had been appointed to that office but had never entered upon its duties. Washington proposed to the baron to undertake the office of inspector-general. The latter cheerfully agreed.

In a little while the whole army was under drill, for a great part, made up of raw militia, scarcely knew the manual exercise. Many of the officers, too, knew little of manoeuvring and the best of them had much to learn. He took a company of soldiers under his immediate training and, after he had sufficiently schooled it, made it a model for the others, exhibiting the manoeuvres they had to practise.

He was sadly worried for a time with the militia, especially when any manoeuvre was to be performed. The men blundered in their exercise; the baron blundered in his English; his French and German were of no avail; he lost his temper, which was rather warm; swore in all three languages at once. Still he had a kind generous heart that soon made him a favorite with the men. His discipline extended to their comforts. He inquired into their treatment by the officers. He examined the doctor's reports, visited the sick, and saw that they were well lodged and attended.

The strong good sense of the baron was evinced in the manner in which he adapted his tactics to the nature of the army and the situation of the country instead of adhering with bigotry to the systems of Europe. His instructions were appreciated by all. The officers received them gladly and conformed to them. The men soon became active and adroit. The army gradually acquired a proper organization and began to operate like a great machine.

Another great satisfaction to Washington was the appointment by Congress (March 3d) of Greene to the office of quartermaster-general, still retaining his rank of major-general in the army. The confusion and derangement of this department during the late campaign, while filled by General Mifflin, had been a source of perpetual embarrassment.

Greene undertook the office with reluctance, but, by extraordinary exertions and excellent system, so arranged it as to put the army in a condition to take the field and move with rapidity the moment it should be required.

(CHAPTER 44)

The Highlands of the Hudson had been carefully reconnoitred in the course of the winter by Putnam, Governor Clinton, his brother James, and several others, and subsequently by a committee from the New York Legislature, to determine upon the most eligible place to be fortified. West Point was ultimately chosen and Putnam was urged by Washington to have the works finished as soon as possible. The general being called to Connecticut by his private affairs, McDougall was ordered to the Highlands to take command and to press forward the construction of the works, in which he was to be assisted by Kosciuszko as engineer.

The spring opened without any material alteration in the dispositions of the armies. Washington at one time expected an attack upon his camp, but Sir William contented himself with sending out parties which foraged the surrounding country for many miles and scoured part of the Jerseys, bringing in considerable supplies. These forays were in some instances accompanied by wanton excesses and needless bloodshed. Another ravaging party ascended the Delaware in flat-bottomed boats and galleys, set fire to public store-houses in Bordentown containing provisions and munitions of war, and burnt two frigates, several privateers, and a number of vessels of various classes, some of them laden with military stores.

A circular letter was sent by Washington on the 20th to all the general officers in camp requesting their opinions in writing, which of three plans to adopt for the next campaign: to attempt the recovery of Philadelphia; to transfer the war to the north and make an attempt on New York; or to remain quiet in a secure and fortified camp, disciplining and arranging the army until the enemy should begin their operations, then to be governed by circumstances.

Just after the issue of this circular, intelligence received from Congress showed that the ascendency of the cabal was at an end. By a resolution of that body on the 15th, Gates was directed to resume command of the Northern department and to proceed forthwith to Fishkill for that purpose. He was invested with powers for completing the work on the Hudson and authorized to carry on operations against the enemy should any favorable opportunity offer, but he was not to undertake any expedition against New York without previously consulting the commander-in-chief. Washington was requested to assemble a council of major-generals to determine upon a plan of operations, and Gates and Mifflin, by a subsequent resolution, were ordered to attend that council. This arrangement, putting Gates under Washington's order, evinced the determination of Congress to sustain the latter in his proper authority.

And here we may note the downfall of the intriguing individual who had given his name to the extinguished cabal. Conway, after a short time in command at Albany, was ordered to join the army under McDougall at Fishkill. Thence he was soon ordered back to Albany, whereupon he wrote an impertinent letter to the President of Congress complaining that he was "boxed about in a most indecent manner." In a word, he intimated a wish that the president would make his resignation acceptable to Congress. To his surprise and consternation his resignation was immediately accepted. He instantly wrote to the president, declaring that his meaning had been misapprehended; all his efforts to get reinstated were unavailing, though he went to Yorktown to make them in person. Disappointed in his aims, he became irritable in his temper, and offensive in his manners. In consequence of some dispute he became involved in a duel with General John Cadwalader, in which he was severely wounded. He recovered from the wound and embarked for France in the course of the year.

The capture of Burgoyne and his army was now operating with powerful effect on the cabinets of both England and France. With the former it was coupled with the apprehension that France was about to espouse the American cause. The consequence was Lord North's "Conciliatory Bills," submitted by him to Parliament and passed with but slight opposition. One of these bills regulated taxation in the American colonies in a manner which, it was trusted, would obviate every objection. The other authorized the appointment of commissioners clothed with powers to negotiate with the existing governments, to proclaim a cessation of hostilities, to grant pardons, and to adopt other measures of a conciliatory nature.

Intelligence that a treaty between France and the United States had actually been concluded at Paris induced the British minister to hurry off a draft of the bills to America to forestall the effects of the treaty upon the public mind. Tryon caused copies of it to be printed in New York and circulated through the country. He sent several of them to Washington, 15th April, with a request that they should be communicated to the officers and privates of his army. Washington felt the singular impertinence of the request. He transmitted them to Congress, observing that the time to entertain such overtures was past. Congress unanimously resolved that no conference could be held and no treaty made with Great Britain until that power should have withdrawn its fleets and armies, or acknowledged in positive and express terms the independence of the United States.

The tidings of the capitulation of Burgoyne had been equally efficacious in quickening the action of the French cabinet. The negotiations, which had gone on slowly, were brought to a happy termination and, on the 2d of May, a messenger arrived express from France with two treaties, one of amity and commerce, the other of defensive alliance, signed in Paris on the 6th of February by Benjamin Franklin, Silas Deane, and Arthur Lee on the part of the United States. This last treaty stipulated that, should war ensue between France and England, it should be made a common cause by the contracting parties, in which neither should make truce or peace with Great Britain without the consent of the other nor either lay down their arms until the independence of the United States was established. These treaties were unanimously ratified by Congress and their promulgation was celebrated by public rejoicings throughout the country.

On the 8th, the council of war ordered by Congress was convened; present were Gates, Greene, Stirling, Mifflin, Lafayette, De Kalb, Armstrong, Steuben, Knox and Duportail. After the state of the forces, British and American, their number and distribution, had been laid before the council by the commander-in-chief, it was unanimously determined to remain on the defensive and not attempt any offensive operation until some opportunity should occur to strike a successful blow.

The military career of Sir William Howe in the United States was now drawing to a close. His conduct of the war had given much dissatisfaction in England. His enemies observed that every thing gained by the troops was lost by the general, that he had suffered an enemy with less than 4000 men to reconquer a province he had recently reduced and lay siege to his army in their winter-quarters, and that he had brought a sad reverse upon the British arms by failing to co-operate vigorously and efficiently with Burgoyne.

Sir William, on his part, considered himself slighted by the ministry. His suggestions, he said, were disregarded and the reinforcements withheld which he considered indispensable for the successful conduct of the war. He had therefore tendered his resignation, which had been promptly accepted, and Sir Henry Clinton ordered to relieve him. Clinton arrived in Philadelphia on the 8th of May and took command of the army on the 11th. At this time, the number of British chivalry in Philadelphia was 19,530, cooped up in a manner by an American force at Valley Forge, amounting, according to official returns, to 11,800 men.

Soon after Sir Henry Clinton had taken command, there were symptoms of an intention to evacuate Philadelphia. Lafayette was therefore detached by Washington with 2100 chosen men and five pieces of cannon to take a position nearer the city, where he might be at hand to gain information, watch the movements of the enemy, check their predatory excursions, and fall on their rear when in the act of withdrawing.

The marquis crossed the Schuylkill on the 18th of May and proceeded to Barren Hill, about half way between Washington's camp and Philadelphia. Here he planted his cannon facing the south, with rocky ridges bordering the Schuylkill on his right, woods and stone houses on his left. Behind him the roads forked, one branch leading to Matson's Ford of the Schuylkill, the other by Swedes' Ford to Valley Forge. In advance of his left wing was McLane's company and about 50 Indians. Pickets and videttes were placed in the woods to the south, through which the roads led to Philadelphia, and a body of 600 Pennsylvania militia were stationed to keep watch on the roads leading to White Marsh.

In the mean time Sir Henry Clinton, having received intelligence of this movement of Lafayette, concerted a plan to entrap the young French nobleman. Five thousand men were sent out at night under Grant to make a circuitous march by White Marsh and get in the rear of the Americans; another force under Grey was to cross to the west side of the Schuylkill and take post below Barren Hill, while Sir Henry in person was to lead a third division along the Philadelphia road.

The plan came near being completely successful through the remissness of the Pennsylvania militia, who had left their post of observation. Early in the morning, word was brought that red coats had been descried in the woods near White Marsh; Lafayette sent out an officer to reconnoitre. The latter soon came spurring back at full speed. A column of the enemy had pushed forward on the road from White Marsh, were within a mile of the camp, and had possession of the road leading to Valley Forge. Another column was advancing on the Philadelphia road. In fact, the young French general was on the point of being surrounded by a greatly superior force.

Lafayette saw his danger, but maintained his presence of mind. Throwing out small parties of troops to show themselves at various points of the intervening wood, as if an attack on Grant was meditated, he brought that general to a halt to prepare for action, while he with his main body pushed forward for Matson's Ford on the Schuylkill.

The alarm-guns at sunrise had apprised Washington that the detachment under Lafayette was in danger. Washington, with his aides-de-camp and some general officers, galloped to the summit of a hill and reconnoitred the scene of action with a glass. His solicitude for the marquis was soon relieved. The youthful warrior had completely gained the march upon Grant, reached Matson's Ford in safety, crossed it and taken a strong position on high grounds that commanded it. Seeing that Lafayette had extricated himself from their hands and was so strongly posted, the enemy returned somewhat disconcerted to Philadelphia, while the youthful marquis rejoined the army at Valley Forge, where he was received with acclamations.

The exchange of Lee for Prescott, delayed by various impediments, had recently been effected and Lee was reinstated in his position of second in command. Ethan Allen, also, had been released from his long captivity. He paid a visit to the camp at Valley Forge, and then left for his home in Vermont, where he hung up his sword.

Indications continued to increase of the departure of troops from Philadelphia. Was the whole army to leave the city, or only a part? The former was probable. A war between France and England appeared to be impending; in that event, Philadelphia would be an ineligible position for the British army.

New York, it was concluded, would be the place of destination, either as a rendezvous or a post whence to attempt the occupation of the Hudson. Would they proceed thither by land or water? Supposing the former, Washington held his army ready to march toward the Hudson at a moment's warning and sent Maxwell with a brigade of Jersey troops to co-operate with Dickinson and the militia of that State in breaking down the bridges and harassing the enemy should they actually attempt to march through it. At the same time he wrote to Gates, who was now at his post on the Hudson, urging him to call in as large a force of militia as he could find subsistence for and to be on the alert for the protection of that river.

In the mean time, the commissioners empowered under the new Conciliatory Bills to negotiate the restoration of peace between Great Britain and her former colonies arrived in the Delaware. These were Frederick Howard, Earl of Carlisle; William Eden, brother of the last colonial governor of Maryland; and George Johnstone, commonly known as Governor Johnstone, having held that office in Florida.

The commissioners landed at Philadelphia on the 6th of June and discovered, to their astonishment, that they had come out on a mission in which but half confidence had been reposed in them by government. Three weeks before their departure from England, orders had been sent to Sir Henry to evacuate Philadelphia and concentrate his forces at New York; yet these orders were never imparted to them.

The commissioners had prepared a letter for Congress inform- ing that body of their arrival and powers and their disposition to promote a reconciliation, intending quietly to await an answer, but the unexpected situation of affairs occasioned by the order for evacuation obliged them to write one of a different character, bring- ing forward at once all the powers delegated to them.

On the 9th June, Sir Henry informed Washington of the arrival of the commissioners and requested a passport for their secretary to proceed to Yorktown bearing a letter to Congress. Washington sent to Congress a copy of Sir Henry's letter but did not consider himself at liberty to grant the passport until authorized by them.

Without waiting the result, the commissioners forwarded, by the ordinary military post, their letter, accompanied by the "Con- ciliatory Acts" and other documents. They were received by Con- gress on the 13th. The letter of the commissioners, addressed to the president and the members of Congress, came near being indig- nantly rejected, on account of expressions disrespectful to France, charging it with being the insidious enemy of both England and her colonies and interposing its pretended friendship to the latter "only to prevent reconciliation and prolong this destructive war."

In their reply, signed by the president (June 17th), the Congress expressed a readiness to treat as soon as the King of Great Britain should demonstrate a sincere disposition for peace either by an explicit acknowledgement of the independence of the States or by the withdrawal of his fleets and armies.

The commissioners, disappointed in their hopes of influencing Congress, attempted to operate on the feelings of the public, at one time by conciliatory appeals, at another by threats and denunciations. Their last measure was to publish a manifesto recapitulating their official proceedings, stating the refusal of Congress to treat with them, and offering to treat within 40 days with deputies from all or any of the colonies or provincial Assemblies, holding forth at the same time the usual offers of conditional amnesty. This measure, like all which had preceded it, proved ineffectual. The commissioners embarked for England and so terminated this tardy and blundering attempt of the British Government and its agents to effect a reconciliation—the last attempt that was made.

The delay of the British to evacuate Philadelphia tasked the sagacity of Washington but he supposed it to have been caused by the arrival of the commissioners from Great Britain. The force in the city in the mean time had been much reduced. The effective force remaining with Sir Henry was now about 10,000 men; that under Washington was a little more than 12,000 Continentals and about 1300 militia.

Early in June, it was evident that a total evacuation of the city was on the point of taking place and circumstances convinced Washington that the march of the main body would be through the Jerseys. Some of his officers thought differently, especially Lee, who had now the command of a division composed of Poor, Varnum, and Huntington's brigades.

Washington called a general council of war on the 17th to consider what measures to adopt: whether to undertake any enterprise against the enemy in their present circumstances—whether the army should remain in its actual position until the final evacuation had taken place or move immediately toward the Delaware— whether, should the enemy march through the Jerseys, it would be advisable to attack them while on the way or to push on directly to the Hudson and secure that important communication between the Eastern and Southern States?

Lee opposed an attack of any kind. The enemy were nearly equal in number to the Americans, far superior in discipline; an attack would endanger the cause. He advised merely to follow the enemy and prevent them from committing any excesses.

Lee's opinions had great weight with the army; most of the officers concurred with him. Greene, Lafayette, Wayne and Cadwalader thought differently. They could not brook that the enemy should evacuate the city and make a long march through the country unmolested. Washington's heart was with this latter counsel but, seeing such want of unanimity among his generals, he requested their opinions in writing. Before these were given in, word was brought that the enemy had actually evacuated the city.

On the first intelligence of this movement, Washington detached Maxwell with his brigade, to co-operate with Dickinson and the New Jersey militia in harassing the enemy on their march. He sent Arnold with a force to take command of Philadelphia. Then, breaking up his camp at Valley Forge, he pushed forward with his main force in pursuit of the enemy.

As the route of the latter lay along the eastern bank of the Delaware as high as Trenton, Washington was obliged to make a considerable circuit so as to cross the river higher up at Coryell's Ferry. Heavy rains and sultry summer heat retarded his movements, but the army crossed on the 24th. The British were now at Moorestown and Mount Holly. Thence they might take the road on the left for Brunswick and on to Staten Island and New York; or the road to the right, through Monmouth, by the Heights of Middletown to Sandy Hook. Uncertain which they might adopt, Washington detached Morgan with 600 picked men to reinforce Maxwell and hang on their rear, while he himself pushed forward with the main body toward Princeton, cautiously keeping along the mountainous country to the left of the most northern road.

The march of Sir Henry was very slow. His army was encumbered with baggage and provisions; bridges and causeways had to be built where they had been destroyed by the Americans.

Washington suspected Sir Henry of a design to draw him down

into the level country and then, by a rapid movement on his right, to gain possession of the strong ground above him and bring him to a general action on disadvantageous terms. Washington halted, therefore, at Hopewell and held another council of war while his troops were reposing and refreshing themselves. The purport was to keep at a distance from the enemy, and annoy them by detachments. Lee was the prime mover of this plan, in pursuance of which a detachment of 1500 men was sent off under Scott, to join the other troops near the enemy's line.

Greene, Wayne, and Lafayette were in the minority in the council and subsequently gave the opinion that the rear of the enemy should be attacked by a strong detachment while the main army should be so disposed as to give a general battle should circumstances render it advisable. As this opinion coincided with his own, Washington determined to act upon it.

Sir Henry in the mean time had advanced to Allentown, on his way to Brunswick, to embark on the Raritan. Finding the passage of that river likely to be strongly disputed by the forces under Washington and by others from the north under Gates, he changed his plan and turned to the right by a road leading through Freehold to Navesink and Sandy Hook to embark at the latter place.

Washington, no longer in doubt as to the route of the enemy's march, detached Wayne with 1000 men to join the advanced corps which, thus augmented, was upwards of 4000 strong. The command of the advance properly belonged to Lee as senior major-general, but it was eagerly solicited by Lafayette. Lee ceded the command without hesitation, observing that he was pleased to be freed from all responsibility in executing plans which he was sure would fail. Lafayette set out on the 25th to form a junction as soon as possible with the force under Scott.

Scarce, however, had Lee relinquished the command when he changed his mind. In a note to Washington, he declared that, in assenting to the arrangement, he had considered the command of the detachment one more fitting a young general then a veteran like himself, second in command in the army. He now viewed it in a different light. Lafayette would be at the head of all the Continental parties already in the line, 6000 men at least, a command next to that of the commander-in-chief. Should the detachment march, therefore, he entreated to have command of it.

Washington was perplexed how to satisfy Lee's punctilious claims without wounding Lafayette. A change in the disposition of the enemy's line of march furnished an expedient. Sir Henry, harassed by light troops on the flanks and in danger of an attack in the rear, placed all his baggage in front under the convoy of Knyphausen while he threw the main strength of his army in the rear under Cornwallis. This made it necessary for Washington to strengthen his advanced corps; he took this occasion to detach Lee, with Scott's and Varnum's brigades, to support the force under Lafayette. As Lee was the senior major-general, this gave him the command of the whole advance.

That evening the enemy encamped on high ground near Monmouth Court House. Lee encamped with the advance at Englishtown, about five miles distant. The main body was three miles in his rear.

About sunset Washington rode forward to the advance and reconnoitred Sir Henry's position. It was protected by woods and morasses, too strong to be attacked with success. Should the enemy, however, proceed further unmolested, they would gain the heights of Middletown and be on ground still more difficult. To prevent this, he resolved that an attack should be made on their rear early in the morning as soon as their front should be in motion. This plan he communicated to Lee, ordering him to make dispositions for the attack.

Early in the morning, Washington received an express from Dickinson, informing him that the enemy were in motion. He instantly sent orders to Lee to push forward and attack them, adding that he was coming on to support him. For that purpose he immediately set forward with his own troops.

Knyphausen, with the British vanguard, had begun about daybreak to descend into the valley between Monmouth Court House and Middletown. To give the waggons and pack horses time to get well on the way, Sir Henry with his choice troops remained in camp until eight o'clock, when he likewise resumed the march toward Middletown.

Darley

G.R.Hall

WASHINGTON AT MONMOUTH.

NEW YORK G.P.PUTNAM.

Entered according to act of Congress A.D. 1858 by G.P.PUTNAM in the clerks office of the District court for the Southern District of New York.

Printed by W. Pate.

In the mean time Lee, on hearing of the early movement of the enemy, advanced with the brigades of Wayne and Maxwell, to support the light troops engaged in skirmishing. Being joined by Lafayette with the main body of the advance, he had now about 4000 men at his command, independent of those under Morgan and Dickinson.

Arriving on the heights of Freehold, Lee caught sight of a force, under march, partly hidden from view by intervening woods. Supposing it to be a mere covering party of about 2000 men, he detached Wayne with 700 men and two pieces of artillery, to skirmish in its rear and hold it in check, while he, with the rest of his force, would get in front of it and cut it off from the main body. He sent a message to Washington apprising him of this movement and of his certainty of success.

Washington in the mean time was on his march with the main body to support the advance, as he had promised. The booming of cannon at a distance indicated that the attack had commenced. Arrived near Freehold church, where the road forked, he detached Greene with part of the forces to the right to flank the enemy in the rear of Monmouth Court House while he, with the rest of the column, would press forward by the other road.

Washington had alighted while giving these directions and was standing with his arm thrown over his horse, when a countryman rode up and said the Continental troops were retreating. Springing on his horse, Washington had moved forward but a short distance when he met other fugitives who all concurred in the report. He sent forward Colonels Fitzgerald and Harrison to learn the truth, while he himself spurred past Freehold meeting house. Between that edifice and the morass beyond it, he met Grayson's and Patton's regiments in disorderly retreat, jaded with heat and fatigue. Riding up to the officer at their head, Washington demanded whether the whole advanced corps were retreating. The officer believed they were.

It seemed incredible. There had been scarce any firing— Washington had received no notice of the retreat from Lee. It was too evident—the whole advance was falling back on the main body and no notice had been given to him. One of the first officers that came up was Colonel Shreve, at the head of his regiment; Washington asked the meaning of this retreat. The colonel smiled significantly—he did not know—he had retreated by order. There had been no fighting excepting a slight skirmish with the enemy's cavalry, which had been repulsed. A suspicion flashed across Washington's mind of wrongheaded conduct on the part of Lee to mar the plan of attack adopted contrary to his counsels. Ordering Shreve to march his men over the morass, halt them on the hill beyond and refresh them, Washington galloped forward to stop the retreat of the rest of the advance. At the rear of the regiment he met Howard; he, too, could give no reason for the retreat.

Arriving at a rising ground, Washington beheld Lee approaching with the residue of his command in full retreat. By this time he was thoroughly exasperated.

"What is the meaning of all this, sir?" demanded he in the sternest and even fiercest tone as Lee rode up to him.

Lee, stung by the manner of the demand, made an angry reply and provoked still sharper expressions, which have been variously reported.

"I am very sorry," replied Washington, "that you undertook the command unless you meant to fight the enemy."

"I did not think it prudent to bring on a general engagement."

"Whatever your opinion may have been," replied Washington, disdainfully, "I expected my orders would have been obeyed."

Washington's appearance had stopped the retreat. The fortunes of the day were to be retrieved, if possible, by instant arrangements. The place was favorable for a stand; it was a rising ground to which the enemy could approach only over a narrow causeway. The rallied troops were hastily formed upon this eminence. Stewart and Ramsey, with two batteries, were stationed in a covert of woods on their left to protect them and keep the enemy at bay. Oswald was posted for the same purpose on a height with two field-pieces. The promptness with which every thing was done showed the effects of Steuben's discipline.

In the interim, Lee, being asked about the disposition of some of the troops, replied that he could give no orders as he supposed Washington intended he should have no further command. Washington, having made all his arrangements with great despatch, rode back to Lee and inquired, "Will you retain the command on this height or not? If you will, I will return to the main body and have it formed on the next height."

"It is equal to me where I command," replied Lee.

"I expect you will take proper means for checking the enemy," rejoined Washington.

"Your orders shall be obeyed and I shall not be the first to leave the ground," was the reply.

A warm cannonade by Oswald, Stewart, and Ramsey had the desired effect. The enemy were brought to a stand and Washington had time to gallop back and bring on the main body. This he formed on an eminence, with a wood in the rear and the morass in front. The left wing was commanded by Stirling, who had with him a detachment of artillery and several field-pieces. Greene was on his right.

Lee had maintained his advanced position with great spirit but was at length obliged to retire. He brought off his troops in good order across a causeway which traversed the morass in front of Stirling. Washington saw that the poor fellows were exhausted by marching, hard fighting and intolerable heat; he ordered Lee, therefore, to repair with them to the rear of Englishtown and assemble there all the scattered fugitives he might meet with.

The batteries under the direction of Stirling opened a brisk and sustained fire upon the enemy, who, finding themselves warmly opposed in front, attempted to turn the left flank of the Americans but were driven back by detached parties of infantry stationed there. They then attempted the right but here were met by Greene, who had planted his artillery under Knox on a commanding ground and not only checked them but enfiladed those who were in front of the left wing. Wayne too, with an advanced party posted in an orchard, kept up a severe fire upon the enemy's centre. Repeated attempts were made to dislodge him, but in vain.

The enemy at length fell back to the ground which Lee had occupied in the morning. Here their flanks were secured by woods and morasses and their front could only be approached across a narrow causeway.

Notwithstanding the difficulties of the position, Washington prepared to attack it, ordering Poor with his own and the Carolina brigade to move round upon their right and Woodford on their left, while the artillery should gall them in front. Before these orders could be carried into effect the day was at an end. Washington lay on his cloak at the foot of a tree, Lafayette beside him, talking over the strange conduct of Lee. Some, who recollected his previous opposition to all plan of attack, almost suspected him of wilfully aiming to procure a defeat. It would appear, however, that he had been really surprised and thrown into confusion by a move of Sir Henry, who had suddenly turned upon Lee's forces, so that Lee found himself front to front with the whole rear division of the British army—and that too, on unfavorable ground, with a deep ravine and a morass in his rear. Mistakes occurred; orders were misunderstood; one corps after another fell back, until the whole retreated, almost without a struggle, before an inferior force. Lee, himself, seemed to partake of the confusion, failing to send notice of it to the main body upon which they were falling back.

At daybreak the troops prepared for action. To their surprise, the enemy had disappeared. Sir Henry, it appeared, had allowed his wearied troops but short repose on the preceding night and was far on the road to Middletown.

The distance the enemy must have attained, the extreme heat, and the fatigued condition of the troops, deterred Washington from continuing a pursuit through the country. Besides, persons well acquainted with the country assured him that it would be impossible to annoy the enemy in their embarkation, as he must approach the place by a narrow passage capable of being defended by a few men against his whole force. Detaching Maxwell's brigade and Morgan's rifle corps, therefore, to hang on the rear of the enemy, prevent depredation and encourage desertions, he determined to shape his course with his main body by Brunswick toward the Hudson, lest Sir Henry should have any design upon the posts there.

After giving his troops a day's repose Washington decamped on the 30th. His march lay through a country destitute of water, with deep sandy roads, wearying to the feet and reflecting the intolerable heat and glare of a July sun. Washington, ever considerate of the health and comfort of his men, encamped near Brunswick on open airy grounds and gave them time to repose; Lieutenant-Colonel Aaron Burr, at that time a young and enterprising officer, was sent on a reconnoitring expedition to learn the movements and intentions of the enemy. He was authorized to despatch trusty persons into New York, Bergen, Weehawk and Hoboken, to observe the situation of the enemy's forces and note whether any movement gave signs of an expedition up the Hudson.

Sir Henry with the royal army had arrived at the Highlands of Navesink, in the neighborhood of Sandy Hook, on the 30th of June. The storms of the preceding winter had cut off the peninsula of Sandy Hook from the main land. Fortunately the squadron of Lord Howe had arrived the day before and was at anchor within the Hook. A bridge was immediately made across the channel with the boats of the ships, over which the army passed to the Hook on the 5th of July. It was now encamped in three divisions on Staten Island, Long Island, and the island of New York, apparently without any immediate design of offensive operations.

General Lee's pride had been deeply wounded by the rebuke he had received on the field of battle. On the following day (June 29th) he addressed a note to Washington on the subject. "Your making use of so very singular expressions as you did on my coming up to the ground where you had taken post . . . implied that I was guilty either of disobedience of orders, want of conduct, or want of courage. Your Excellency will therefore infinitely oblige me by letting me know on which of these three articles you ground your charge. . . . I think, sir, I have a right to demand some reparation for the injury committed. . . ."

In reply, Washington wrote, " . . . I am not conscious of making use of any very singular expressions at the time of meeting you, as you intimate. What I recollect to have said was dictated by duty and warranted by the occasion. As soon as circumstances will permit, you shall have an opportunity of justifying yourself to the army, to Congress, to America, and to the world in general; or of convincing them that you were guilty of a breach of orders and of misbehavior before the enemy on the 28th instant, in not attacking them as you had been directed and in making an unnecessary, disorderly, and shameful retreat."

Shortly after, Lee addressed another note to Washington. "It will be for our mutual convenience that a court of inquiry should be immediately ordered, but I could wish that it might be a court-martial and that on the first halt I may be brought to a trial."

Washington in reply wrote, "I have sent Colonel Scammel and the adjutant-general to put you under arrest, who will deliver you a copy of the charges on which you will be tried."

The following were the charges: *1st*. Disobedience of orders in not attacking the enemy on the 28th June agreeably to repeated instructions. *2d*. Misbehavior before the enemy on the same day by making an unnecessary, disorderly, and shameful retreat. *3d*. Disrespect to the commander-in-chief in two letters, dated the 1st of July and the 28th of June.

A court-martial was accordingly formed on the 4th of July at Brunswick, the first halting place. It was composed on one major-general, four brigadiers, and eight colonels, with Stirling as president. It moved with the army and convened subsequently at Paramus, Peekskill, and Northcastle, the trial lasting until the 12th of August.

Lee defended himself with ability. He contended that, after the troops had commenced to fall back in consequence of a retrograde movement of Scott, he had intended to form them on the first advantageous ground he could find and that none such presented itself until he reached the place where he met Washington, on which very place he had intended to make battle. He denied that in the whole course of the day he had uttered the word "retreat." But this retreat, said he, though necessary, was brought about contrary to his orders, contrary to his intention.

The result of the prolonged and tedious investigation was, that he was found guilty of all the charges against him. He was sentenced to be suspended from all command for one year, the sentence to be approved or set aside by Congress. Congress were more than three months in coming to a decision on the proceedings of the court-martial. At length, the sentence was approved.

From that time Lee was unmeasured in his abuse of Washington and his reprobation of the court-martial, which he termed a "court of inquisition."

Lee's aggressive tongue at length involved him in a quarrel with Colonel Laurens, one of Washington's aides, who felt himself bound to vindicate the honor of his chief. A duel took place and Lee was wounded in the side. Towards spring he retired to his estate in Berkely County in Virginia.

The term of his suspension had expired when a rumor reached him that Congress intended to take away his commission. Without attempting to ascertain the truth of the report, he scrawled the following note to the President of Congress: "Sir, I understand that it is in contemplation of Congress, on the principle of economy, to strike me out of their service. Congress must know very little of me, if they suppose that I would accept of their money, since the confirmation of the wicked and infamous sentence which was passed upon me."

Though bitter in his enmities, Lee had his friendships. There was nothing crafty or mean in his character nor do we think he ever engaged in the low intrigues of the cabal, but he was a disappointed and embittered man. Weary of his Virginia estate, he entered into negotiations to dispose of his property, in the course of which he visited Philadelphia. On arriving there, he was taken with chills, followed by a fever, which went on increasing in violence and terminated fatally.

The magnanimity exhibited by Washington in regard to Lee while living continued after his death. He never spoke of him with asperity, but did justice to his merits, acknowledging that "he possessed many great qualities."

(CHAPTER 45)

While encamped at Paramus, Washington, in the night of the 13th of July, received a letter from Congress informing him of the arrival of a French fleet on the coast and instructing him to concert measures with the commander, the Count D'Estaing, for offensive operations by sea and land, empowering him to call on the States from New Hampshire to New Jersey inclusive to aid with their militia.

The fleet in question was composed of 12 ships of the line and 6 frigates, with a land force of 4000 men. After struggling against adverse winds for 88 days, it had made its appearance off the northern extremity of the Virginia coast and anchored at the mouth of the Delaware on the eighth of July. Thence the count despatched a letter to Washington, dated at sea. "I have the honor of imparting to your Excellency," writes he, "the arrival of the king's fleet, charged by his majesty with the glorious task of giving his allies, the United States of America, the most striking proofs of his affection."

Finding the enemy had evacuated both city and river, the count, putting to sea, continued along the coast. When he arrived with his fleet outside of Sandy Hook, he descried the British ships quietly anchored inside of it.

A cordial correspondence took place between the count and Washington and a plan of action was concerted between them by the intervention of confidential officers—Washington's aides-de-camp, Laurens and Hamilton, boarding the fleet while off the Hook and Major Chouin, a French officer, repairing to the American head-quarters.

The first idea of the count was to enter at Sandy Hook and capture or destroy the British fleet composed of 6 ships of the line, 4 fifty-gun ships, and a number of frigates and smaller vessels; should he succeed in this, which his greatly superior force rendered probable was to proceed against the city with the co-operation of the American forces. To be at hand for such purpose, Washington crossed the Hudson with his army at King's Ferry and encamped at White Plains about the 20th of July.

Several experienced American pilots and masters of vessels, however, who had accompanied Laurens and Hamilton, declared that there was not sufficient depth of water on the bar to admit the safe passage of the largest ships; the attempt, therefore, was reluctantly abandoned and the ships anchored about four miles off, near Shrewsbury on the Jersey coast, taking in provisions and water.

The enterprise which the American and French commanders deemed next worthy of a combined operation, was the recapture of Rhode Island proper, that is to say, the island which gives its name to the State, and which the enemy had made one of their military depots and strongholds. In anticipation of such an enterprise, Washington on the 17th of July wrote to Sullivan, who commanded at Providence, ordering him to make the necessary preparations for a descent from the main land upon the island and authorizing him to call in reinforcements of New England militia. He subsequently sent to his aid Lafayette with two brigades (Varnum's and Glover's). Greene also was detached for the service, being a native of the island. Sullivan was instructed to form his whole force into two equal divisions, one to be commanded by Greene, the other by Lafayette.

On the 22d of July, the French fleet, having finished taking in its supplies, appeared again in full force off the bar at Sandy Hook. D'Estaing, however, had already determined his course. He stood away to the eastward and, on the 29th, arrived off Point Judith, coming to anchor within five miles of Newport.

Rhode Island (proper), the object of this expedition, is about 16 miles long, running deep into Narraganset Bay. Seaconnet Channel separates it on the east from the main land; on the west the main channel passes between it and Conanicut Island. The town of Newport is situated near the south end of the island, facing west, with Conanicut Island in front of it. It was protected by batteries and a small naval force. Here General Sir Robert Pigott, who commanded in the island, had his head-quarters. The force under him was about 6000 strong, variously posted about the island, the greater part within strongly intrenched lines extending across the island, about three miles from the town. Greene hastened from Providence on hearing of the arrival of the fleet of Count D'Estaing and went on board of it at the anchorage to concert a plan of operations. It was agreed that the fleet should force its way into the harbor at the same time that the Americans approached by land and that the landing of the troops from the ships on the west side of the island should take place at the same time that the Americans should cross Seaconnet Channel and land on the east side near the north end. This combined operation was to have been carried promptly into effect, but was postponed until the 10th of August to give time for the reinforcements sent by Washington to arrive. The delay was fatal to the enterprise.

On the 8th the Count D'Estaing entered the harbor and passed up the main channel, exchanging a cannonade with the batteries as he passed, and anchored a little above the town, between Goat and Conanicut Islands. Sullivan, to be ready for the concerted attack, had moved down from Providence to the neighborhood of Howland's Ferry, on the east side of Seaconnet passage.

The British troops stationed opposite on the north end of the island, fearful of being cut off, evacuated their works in the night of the 8th and drew into the lines at Newport.

Sullivan, seeing the works thus abandoned, could not resist the temptation to cross the channel on the morning of the 9th and take possession of them.

This sudden movement, a day in advance of the concerted time, without due notice given to the count, surprised and offended him. He, however, prepared to co-operate, when, about two o'clock in the day, his attention was called to a great fleet of ships standing toward Newport. It was, in fact, the fleet of Lord Howe, who had heard of the danger of Newport and, being reinforced by part of a squadron under Admiral Byron, had hastened to its relief, though still inferior in force to the French admiral. The delay of the concerted attack had enabled him to arrive in time. The wind set directly into the harbor. Had he entered promptly, the French would have been placed between two fires, from his ships and the batteries, and cramped up in a confined channel. His lordship, however, merely having informed himself exactly of the situation of the French fleet, came to anchor at Point Judith, some distance from the southwest entrance of the bay.

In the night the wind changed to the northeast. Favored by the wind, the count stood out of the harbor at eight o'clock in the morning to give the enemy battle where he should have good sea room, previously sending word to Sullivan, who had advanced to about ten miles north of Newport, that he would land his promised troops and marines and co-operate with him on his return.

The French ships were severely cannonaded as they passed the batteries but without material damage. Forming in order of battle, they bore down upon the fleet of Lord Howe. The British ships likewise formed in line of battle but his lordship avoided an encounter while the enemy had the weathergage. The two fleets manoeuvred throughout the day, standing to the southward, and gradually disappearing from the anxious eyes of the forces on Rhode Island.

The army of Sullivan, now left to itself before Newport, amounted to 10,000 men, having received the militia reinforcements. Lafayette advised the delay of hostile operations until the return of D'Estaing but the American commander, piqued and chagrined at the departure of his allies, determined to commence the siege. Expecting the prompt return of the French, they took post on Honeyman's Hill, about two miles from the British lines, and began to construct batteries, form lines of communication, and make regular approaches. The British were equally active in strengthening their defences. The situation of the besiegers was growing critical when, on the evening of the 19th, they descried the expected fleet standing toward the harbor. All now was exultation in the camp. Should the French with their ships and troops attack the town by sea and land on the one side while the Americans assailed it on the other, the surrender of the place was inevitable.

These sanguine anticipations, however, were short-lived. The French fleet was in a shattered and forlorn condition. After sailing from before Newport, on the 20th, it had manoeuvred for two days with the British fleet, each unwilling to enter into action without having the weathergage. While thus manoeuvring, a furious storm dispersed them with fearful ravage. Some single encounters of scattered ships subsequently took place but without definite result. All were too much tempest-tost and disabled to make good fight. Howe bore away to New York to refit and the French admiral was now before Newport, but in no plight or mood for fighting.

In a letter to Sullivan, he informed him that pursuant to the orders of his sovereign and the advice of his officers, he was bound for Boston, being instructed to repair to that port should he meet with misfortune or a superior British force.

Dismayed at this intelligence, Sullivan wrote a letter to the count, and Greene and Lafayette repaired with it on board of the admiral's ship. They represented to the count the certainty of carrying the place in two days by a combined attack and the discouragement and reproach that would follow a failure on their first attempt at co-operation. The count was inclined to remain and pursue the enterprise, but was overruled by the principal officers of his fleet, who insisted on his complying with his letter of instructions and sailing for Boston.

At the sailing of the ships there was a feeling of exasperation throughout the camp and a general feeling of irritation against the French continued to prevail in the army.

The departure of the fleet was a death-blow to the enterprise. Volunteers abandoned the camp and desertions occurred among the militia; in a few days the number of besiegers did not exceed that of the beseiged.

All thoughts of offensive operations were now at an end. The question was how best to extricate the army from its perilous position. To prepare for rapid retreat, if necessary, all the heavy artillery that could be spared was sent off from the island. On the 28th it was determined in a council of war to fall back to the military works at the north end of the island until it should be known whether the French fleet would soon return to their assistance, Lafayette setting off with all speed to have an interview with D'Estaing.

Sullivan broke up his camp and commenced his retreat that very night, the rear covered by light troops under Livingston and Laurens. Their retreat was not discovered until daylight, when a pursuit was commenced. The covering parties behaved gallantly, keeping up a retreating fire that checked the advance of the enemy. They were pressed back to the fortified grounds on the north end of the island; Sullivan had already taken post there, on Batt's Hill, the main body of his army being drawn up in order of battle, with strong works in their rear and a redoubt in front of the right wing.

The British now took post on an advantageous height called Quaker Hill, a little more than a mile from the American front, whence they commenced a cannonade which was briskly returned. Skirmishing ensued until about ten o'clock, when two British sloops-of-war and some small vessels having gained a favorable position, the enemy's troops, under cover of their fire, advanced in force to turn the right flank of the American army and capture the redoubt which protected it. This was bravely defended by Greene; the British at length drew back to Quaker Hill and a mutual cannonade was resumed.

In the mean time, Sullivan had received intelligence that Lord Howe had again put to sea with the design, no doubt, to attempt the relief of Newport; then followed another report that a fleet with troops was actually off Block Island.

Under these circumstances it was determined to abandon Rhode Island. To do so with safety, however, required the utmost caution. Any suspicious movements would be easily discovered and reported to the British commander. The position on Batt's Hill favored a deception, so successfully managed, that the whole army had crossed to the mainland unperceived by the enemy, and had reason to congratulate themselves, for the very next day Sir Henry arrived at Newport with a reinforcement of 4000 men, a naval and land force that might effectually have cut off Sullivan's retreat had he lingered on the island.

Sir Henry returned to New York, but first detached Major-general Sir Charles Grey with the troops on a ravaging expedition to the eastward, chiefly against ports which were the haunts of privateers. In the course of his expedition he destroyed more than 70 vessels in Acushnet River, some of them privateers with their prizes, others peaceful merchant ships. New Bedford and Fair Haven, having been made military and naval deposits, were laid waste, wharves demolished, store-houses and mills, with several private dwellings, wrapped in flames. Similar destruction was effected at the Island of Martha's Vineyard, a resort of privateers. Having thus ravaged the coasts of New England, the squadron returned laden with inglorious spoil to New York.

Lord Howe, also, had sailed for Boston in the hope of intercepting D'Estaing, but he found the French fleet safely sheltered in Nantasket Road, protected by American batteries erected on commanding points. He returned to New York and, shortly afterward, availing himself of a permission granted him some time before by government, resigned the command of the fleet to Admiral Gambier, to hold it until the arrival of Admiral Byron, and returned to England.

The failure of the combined enterprise against Rhode Island was a cause of universal chagrin and disappointment, but to none more so than to Washington. Washington regarded the irritation between the French naval officers and the American army officers which had so suddenly sprung up with the most poignant anxiety. He wrote to Sullivan and Greene, urging them to suppress the feuds and jealousies which had already arisen, to conceal from the soldiery and public the misunderstandings which had occurred between the officers of the two nations, and to cultivate the utmost harmony and good will.

While hostilities were carried on in the customary form along the Atlantic borders, Indian warfare, with all its atrocity, was going on in the interior. The British post at Niagara was the common rallying place of tories, refugees, savage warriors, and other desperadoes of the frontiers. Here was concerted the memorable incursions into the Valley of Wyoming, a beautiful region lying along the Susquehanna, which had been the scene of sanguinary feuds prior to the Revolution, between the people of Pennsylvania and Connecticut, who both laid claim to it. Seven rural forts or block-houses had been strongholds during these territorial contests, and remained as places of refuge in times of Indian ravage.

The expedition set on foot, in June, was composed of Butler's rangers, Johnson's royal greens, and Brant, the noted Indian chief, with his Indian braves. Their united force, about 1100 strong, was conducted by Colonel John Butler, renowned in Indian warfare. Passing down in canoes, they landed at Three Islands, struck through the wilderness to a gap by which they entered the Valley of Wyoming. Butler made his head-quarters at one of the strongholds already mentioned, called Wintermoot's Fort.

Rumors of this intended invasion had reached the valley some time before the appearance of the enemy and had spread great consternation. Most of the sturdy yeomanry were absent in the army. A company of 60 men, enlisted under an act of Congress, hastily and imperfectly organized, took post at one of the strongholds called Forty Fort, where they were joined by about 300 of the most efficient of the yeomanry, armed and equipped in rude rustic style. Colonel Zebulon Butler, an officer of the continental army, took general command. Several officers from the army brought word that a reinforcement sent by Washington was on its way.

In the mean time marauding parties sent out by Butler and Brant were spreading desolation through the valley. What was to be done? Wait for the arrival of the promised reinforcement or attempt to check the ravage? The latter was rashly determined on.

Leaving the women and children in Forty Fort, Zebulon Butler with his men sallied forth on the 3d of July and made a rapid move upon Wintermoot Fort, hoping to come upon it by surprise. They found the enemy drawn up in front of it in a line extending from the river to a marsh, Colonel John Butler and his rangers, with Johnson's royal greens, on the left, Indians and tories on the right.

The Americans formed a line of the same extent, the regulars under Butler on the right flank, resting on the river, the militia under Denison on the left wing, on the marsh. A sharp fire was opened and the enemy in front of Butler began to give way. The Indians, however, throwing themselves into the marsh, turned the left flank of the Americans and attacked the militia in rear. Denison, finding himself exposed to a cross fire, sought to change his position and gave the word to fall back. It was mistaken for an order to retreat. In an instant the left wing turned and fled; all attempts to rally it were vain; the panic extended to the right wing. A horrible massacre ensued. Some of the Americans escaped to Forty Fort, but the greater number were slaughtered.

The desolation of the valley was now completed; fields were laid waste, houses burnt, and their inhabitants murdered. After completing this horrible work of devastation, the enemy retired before the arrival of the troops detached by Washington.

For a great part of the summer, Washington remained encamped at White Plains, watching the movements of the enemy at New York. Early in September he observed a great stir of preparation; cannon and military stores were embarked and a fleet of 140 transports were ready to make sail. What was their destination?

There were but two capital objects which they could have in view, beside the defeat and dispersion of his army. One was to get possession of the forts and passes of the Highlands; the other, by a junction of their land and naval forces, to attempt the destruction of the French fleet at Boston and regain possession of that town. These points were so far asunder, that it was difficult to protect the one without leaving the other exposed. To do the best that the case would admit, Washington strengthened the works and reinforced the garrison in the Highlands, stationing Putnam with two brigades in the neighborhood of West Point. Gates was sent with three brigades to Danbury in Connecticut, where he was joined by two brigades under McDougal, while Washington moved his camp to a rear position at Fredericksburg on the borders of Connecticut, about 30 miles from West Point, so as to be ready for a movement to the eastward or a speedy junction for the defence of the Hudson.

Scarce had Washington moved from White Plains, when Sir Henry threw a detachment of 5000 men under Cornwallis into the Jerseys between the Hackensack and Hudson Rivers and another of 3000 under Knyphausen into Westchester County between the Hudson and the Bronx. These detachments, by the aid of flat-bottomed boats, could unite their forces in 24 hours on either side of the Hudson.

Washington considered these mere foraging expeditions and detached troops into the Jerseys to co-operate with the militia in checking them, but, as something more might be intended, he ordered Putnam to cross the river to West Point for its immediate security while he himself moved with a division of his army to Fishkill.

Wayne, who was with the detachment in the Jerseys, took post with a body of militia and a regiment of light-horse in front of the division of Cornwallis. The militia were quartered at the village of New Tappan, but Lieutenant-colonel Baylor, who commanded the light-horse, chose to encamp apart in Old Tappan, where his men lay unguardedly in barns. Cornwallis had intelligence of their exposed situation and laid a plan to cut off the whole detachment. A body of troops from Knyphausen's division was to cross the Hudson in the night and come by surprise upon the militia in New Tappan; at the same time Grey was to attack Baylor and his dragoons in Old Tappan.

Fortunately the militia were apprised by deserters of their danger in time to escape. Not so with Baylor's party. Grey surrounded with his troops three barns in which the dragoons were sleeping. With bayonets fixed, his men rushed forward, and, deaf for a time to all cries for mercy, made a savage slaughter of naked and defenceless men.

This whole movement of troops, on both sides of the Hudson, was designed to cover an expedition against Little Egg Harbor, on the east coast of New Jersey, a noted rendezvous of American privateers. Three hundred regular troops and a body of royalist volunteers from the Jerseys, headed by Captain Patrick Ferguson, embarked at New York on board of galleys and transports and made for Little Egg Harbor under convoy of vessels of war. The country heard of their coming; four privateers put to sea and escaped; others took refuge up the river. The wind prevented the transports from entering. The troops embarked in row galleys and small craft and pushed up the river to the village of Chestnut Neck. Here the batteries and storehouses were demolished, the prize ships burnt, saltworks destroyed, and private dwellings sacked and laid in ashes.

The vessels which brought this detachment being wind-bound for several days, Ferguson had time for another enterprise. Among the forces detached by Washington into the Jerseys to check these ravages was Pulaski's legionary corps, composed of three companies of foot and a troop of horse, officered principally by foreigners. A deserter brought word that the legion was cantoned about 12 miles up the river, the infantry in three houses by themselves, Count Pulaski with the cavalry at some distance apart.

Captain Ferguson, with 250 men, ascended the river in the night and surrounded the houses in which the infantry were sleeping. "It being a night attack," says the captain in his report, "little quarter . . . could be given, so there were only five prisoners."

The clattering of hoofs gave note of the approach of Pulaski and his horse, whereupon the British made a rapid retreat to their boats and pulled down the river; thus ended the marauding expedition of Captain Ferguson.

The detachment on the east side of the Hudson likewise made a foray from their lines at King's Bridge towards the American encampment at White Plains, plundering the inhabitants without discrimination. None were more efficient in this ravage than a party of about 100 of Donop's Hessian yagers. They were in full maraud between Tarrytown and Dobbs' Ferry when a detachment of infantry under Colonel Richard Butler and of cavalry under Major Henry Lee came upon them by surprise, killed ten of them on the spot, captured a lieutenant and eighteeen privates, and would have taken or destroyed the whole, had not the extreme roughness of the country impeded the action of the cavalry and enabled the yagers to escape by scrambling up hill-sides or plunging into ravines. The British detachments, having accomplished the main objects of their movements, returned to New York.

About the middle of September Admiral Byron arrived at New York with the residue of the scattered armament which had sailed from England in June to counteract the designs of D'Estaing. Finding that the count was still repairing his fleet in Boston, he set sail for that port to entrap him. He arrived off Boston on the 1st of November; his rival was still in port. Scarce had he entered the bay, however, when a violent storm drove him out to sea, disabled his ships, and compelled him to put into Rhode Island to refit. Meanwhile the count, having his ships in good order, put to sea and made his way for the West Indies. Previous to his departure he issued a proclamation addressed to the French inhabitants of Canada inviting them to resume allegiance to their former sovereign. This measure, not authorized by his government, awakened a jealousy in the

American mind as to the ultimate views of France in taking a part in this contest. It added to the chagrin occasioned by the failure of the expedition against Rhode Island and the complete abandonment by the French of the coasts of the United States.

The force at New York, which had been an object of watchful solicitude, was gradually dispersed in different directions. Immediately after the departure of Admiral Byron for Boston, another naval expedition had been set on foot by Sir Henry Clinton. All being ready, a fleet of transports with 5000 men, under Grant, convoyed by Commodore Hotham with a squadron of six ships of war, set sail on the third of November with the secret design of an attack on St. Lucia.

Towards the end of the same month, another body of troops under Lieutenant-colonel Campbell sailed for Georgia in the squadron of Commodore Hyde Parker, the British cabinet having determined to carry the war into the Southern States. At the same time General Prevost, who commanded in Florida, was ordered by Sir Henry to march to the banks of the Savannah River and attack Georgia in flank while the expedition under Campbell should attack it in front on the seaboard.

An American force of about 600 regulars and a few militia under General George Howe were encamped near Savannah, being the remnant of an army with which that officer had invaded Florida in the preceeding summer but had been obliged to evacuate it by a mortal malady which desolated his camp.

Campbell landed his troops on the 29th of December, about three miles below the town. The whole country bordering the river is a deep morass, cut up by creeks, and only to be traversed by causeways. Campbell advanced, while Sir James Baird was detached with the light infantry along a path through the morass, by which troops might get unobserved to the rear of the Americans. The Americans, thus suddenly attacked in front and rear, were completely routed. Savannah, the capital of Georgia, was taken possession of by the victors, with cannon, military stores and provisions.

While Campbell thus invaded Georgia in front, Prevost, who

commanded the British forces in Florida, received orders from Sir Henry to take it in flank. He accordingly took Sunbury, the only remaining fort of importance, and marched to Savannah, where he assumed general command, detaching Campbell against Augusta. By the middle of January (1779) all Georgia was reduced to submission.

By this time Major-general Lincoln, who had gained such reputation in the campaign against Burgoyne and whose appointment to this station had been solicited by the delegates from South Carolina and Georgia, arrived to take command of the Southern Department.

(CHAPTER 46)

About the beginning of December, Washington distributed his troops for the winter in a line of cantonments from Long Island Sound to the Delaware. Putnam commanded at Danbury, McDougall in the Highlands, while the headquarters of the commander-in-chief were near Middlebrook in the Jerseys.

Washington was now doomed to experience great loss in the narrow circle of those about him on whose attachment and devotion he could place implicit reliance. Lafayette, seeing no immediate prospect of active employment in the United States and anticipating a war on the continent of Europe, was disposed to return to France to offer his services to his sovereign. Desirous, however, of preserving a relation with America, he merely solicited from Congress the liberty of going home for the next winter, engaging himself not to depart until certain that the campaign was over. Washington backed his application for a furlough as an arrangement that would still link him with the service, expressing his reluctance to part with an officer who united "to all the military fire of youth an uncommon maturity of judgment." Congress in consequence granted the marquis an unlimited leave of absence, to return to America whenever he should find it convenient.

Much of the winter was passed by Washington in Philadelphia, occupied in devising and discussing plans for the campaign of 1779. Circumstances which inspired others with confidence, filled him with solicitude. The alliance with France had produced a feeling of security which, it appeared to him, was paralyzing the energies of the country. England, it was thought, would be too occupied in securing her position in Europe to extend her operations in America. Many, therefore, considered the war as virtually at an end.

Dissensions, too, and party feuds were breaking out in Congress, owing to the relaxation of that external pressure of a common and imminent danger. That body had, in fact, greatly deteriorated since the commencement of the war. Many of those whose names had been as watchwords at the Declaration of Independence, had withdrawn from the national councils, occupied either by their individual affairs or by the affairs of their individual States. Washington deplored the dawning of this sectional spirit. America, he declared, had never stood in more imminent need of the wise, patriotic, and spirited exertions of her sons than at this period. The States, separately, were too much engaged in their local concerns and had withdrawn too many of their ablest men from the general council for the good of the common weal.

In discussing the policy to be observed in the next campaign, Washington presumed the enemy would maintain their present posts, and conduct the war as heretofore, in which case he was for remaining entirely on the defensive with the exception of such operations as might be necessary to check the ravages of the Indians. The ravages and massacres perpetrated by the Indians and their tory allies at Wyoming had been followed by similar atrocities at Cherry Valley in New York and called for signal vengeance to prevent a repetition. Washington knew by experience that Indian warfare should never be merely defensive but must be carried into the enemy's country. The Six Nations, the most civilized of the savage tribes, had proved themselves the most formidable. His idea was to lay waste their villages and settlements and at the same time destroy the British post at Niagara, that nestling place of tories and refugees. The policy thus recommended was adopted by Congress.

The first act of the Indian campaign was an expedition from Fort Schuyler by Colonel Van Schaick, Lieutenant-colonel Willett, and Major Cochran, with about 600 men, who, on the 19th of April, surprised the towns of the Onondagas, destroyed the whole settlement, and returned to the fort without the loss of a single man.

The great expedition of the campaign, however, was in revenge of the massacre of Wyoming. Early in the summer 3000 men, conducted by Sullivan, moved up the west branch of the Susquehanna into the Seneca country. On the way, they were joined by a part of the western army under General James Clinton, who had come from the valley of the Mohawk by Otsego lake and the east branch of the Susquehanna. The united forces amounted to about 5000 men, of which Sullivan had the general command.

The Indians and tories had received information of the invasion and appeared in arms to oppose it. They were much inferior in force, however, being about 1500 Indians and 200 white men, commanded by the two Butlers, Johnson, and Brant. A battle took place at Newtown on the 29th of August in which they were easily defeated. Sullivan then pushed forward into the heart of the Indian country, penetrating as far as the Genesee River, laying every thing waste, the design being to starve the Indians out of the country. The latter retreated before him with their families and at length took refuge under the protection of the British garrison at Niagara. Having completed his errand, Sullivan returned to Pennsylvania. He shortly afterward resigned his commission on account of ill health and retired from the service.

A similar expedition was undertaken by Colonel Brodhead from Pittsburg up the Allegany against the Mingo, Muncey, and Seneca tribes with similar results. The wisdom of Washington's policy of carrying the war against the Indians into their country was apparent from the general intimidation produced among the tribes and the subsequent infrequency of their murderous incursions, the instigation of which by the British had been the most inhuman feature of the war.

The situation of Sir Henry Clinton must have been mortifying in the extreme to an officer of lofty ambition and generous aims. His force, about 17,000 strong, was superior in number, discipline, and equipment to that of Washington; yet his instructions confined him to a predatory warfare carried on by attacks and marauds at distant points. Such was the nature of an expedition set on foot against the commerce of the Chesapeake by which the armies were supplied and the credit of the government sustained. On the 9th of May, a squadron under Sir George Collier, convoying transports and galleys, with 2500 men, commanded by General Mathews, entered these waters, took possession of Portsmouth without opposition, sent out armed parties against Norfolk, Suffolk, Gosport, Kemp's Landing, and other neighboring places, where were immense quantities of provisions, naval and military stores, and merchandise of all kinds; with numerous vessels, some on the stocks, others richly laden. Wherever they went, a scene of plunder, conflagration, and destruction ensued. A few days sufficed to ravage the whole neighborhood.

While this was going on at the South, Washington received intelligence of movements at New York and in its vicinity which made him apprehend an expedition against the Highlands of the Hudson.

Since the loss of Forts Montgomery and Clinton, the main defences of the Highlands had been established at the bend of the river where it winds between West Point and Constitution Island. Two opposite forts commanded this bend and an iron chain which was stretched across it.

Washington had projected two works also just below the Highlands, at Stony Point and Verplanck's Point, to serve as outworks of the mountain passes and to protect King's Ferry, the most direct and convenient communication between the Eastern and Middle States.

A small but strong fort had been erected on Verplanck's Point, garrisoned by 70 men under Captain Armstrong. A more important work was in progress at Stony Point. When completed, these two forts on opposite promontories would form as it were the lower gates of the Highlands. To be at hand in case of any real attempt upon the Highlands, Washington drew up with his forces in that direction, moving by the way of Morristown.

An expedition up the Hudson was really the object of Sir Henry's movements; for this he was strengthened by the return of Sir George Collier with his marauding ships and forces from Virginia. On the 30th of May, Sir Henry set out on his second grand cruise up the Hudson with an armament of about 70 sail great and small and 150 flatboats. Collier commanded the armament and there was a land force of about 5000 men under General Vaughan.

The first aim of Sir Henry was to get possession of Stony and Verplanck's Points. On the morning of the 31st, the forces were landed in two divisions, the largest under Vaughan, on the east side of the river, about seven or eight miles below Verplanck's Point; the other, commanded by Sir Henry in person, landed in Haverstraw Bay, about three miles below Stony Point. There were but about 30 men in the unfinished fort; they abandoned it on the approach of the enemy, having first set fire to the block-house. The British took possession of the fort in the evening, dragged up cannon and mortars in the night, and at daybreak opened a furious fire upon Fort Lafayette. It was cannonaded at the same time by the armed vessels and a demonstration was made on it by the division under Vaughan. Thus surrounded, the little garrison of 70 men was forced to surrender.

Sir Henry stationed garrisons in both posts and set to work with great activity to complete the fortification of Stony Point. The fleet generally fell down a little below King's Ferry; some of the vessels, however, having troops on board, dropped down Haverstraw Bay and finally disappeared behind the promontories which advance across the upper part of the Tappan Sea.

Some of the movements of the enemy perplexed Washington exceedingly. He presumed, however, that the main object of Sir Henry was to get possession of West Point, the guardian fortress of the river, and that the capture of Stony and Verplanck's Points were preparatory steps. He would fain have dislodged him from these posts, but they were too strong; he had not the force nor military apparatus necessary. Deferring any attempt on them for the present, he took measures for the protection of West Point. Leaving

Putnam and the main body of the army at Smith's Clove, a mountain pass in the rear of Haverstraw, he removed his head-quarters to New Windsor, to be near West Point in case of need and to press for completion of its works. McDougall was transferred to command of the point. Three brigades were stationed at different places on the opposite side of the river, under Heath, from which fatigue parties crossed daily to work on the fortifications.

This strong disposition of the American forces checked Sir Henry's designs against the Highlands. Contenting himself, for the present, with the acquisition of Stony and Verplanck's Points, he returned to New York, where he soon set on foot a desolating expedition along the seaboard of Connecticut. That State had hitherto experienced nothing of the horrors of war within its borders. Sir Henry was now about to give it a scourging lesson and he entertained the hope that, in so doing, he might draw down Washington from his mountain fastnesses and lay open the Hudson to a successful incursion.

General (late Governor) Tryon was the officer selected by Sir Henry for this inglorious service. About the beginning of July he embarked with 2600 men, in a fleet convoyed up the Sound by Collier with two ships of war.

On the 5th of July the troops landed near New Haven in two divisions, one led by Tryon, the other by Brigadier-general Garth. They came upon the neighborhood by surprise; the militia assembled in haste and made a resolute though ineffectual opposition. The British captured the town, dismantled the fort, and took or destroyed all the vessels in the harbor, with all the artillery, ammunition and public stores. Several private houses were plundered; this, it was said, was done by the soldiery contrary to orders.

They next proceeded to Fairfield, where, meeting with greater resistance, they thought the moment arrived for severity. Accordingly, they not merely ravaged and destroyed the public stores and the vessels in the harbor but laid the town itself in ashes. The sight of their homes laid desolate only served to produce a more determined opposition to the progress of the destroyers, whereupon the ruthless ravage of the latter increased as they advanced.

At Norwalk, where they landed on the 11th of July, they

burned dwelling-houses, barns, store-houses, shops, mills, places of worship, and five vessels which were in the harbor. These acts of devastation were accompanied by atrocities, inevitable where the brutal passions of the soldiery are aroused.

It was intended to crown this grand ravage by a descent on New London, a noted rendezvous of privateers but, as greater opposition was expected there than at either of the other places, the squadron returned to Huntington Bay on Long Island to await reinforcements and Collier proceeded to Throg's Neck, to confer with Sir Henry about further operations. In this conference Sir Henry was assured that the principal inhabitants were incensed at the apathy of Washington in remaining encamped near the Hudson while their country was ravaged and their homes laid in ashes.

Washington, however, was not culpable of the apathy ascribed to him. On hearing of the departure of the expedition to the eastward, he detached Heath with two brigades of Connecticut militia to counteract the movements of the enemy. This was all that he could spare from the force stationed for the protection of the Highlands. Any weakening of his posts there might bring the enemy suddenly upon him, such was their facility in moving from one place to another by means of their shipping.

As a kind of counter-check to Sir Henry, he had for some days been planning the recapture of Stony Point and Fort Lafayette. Stony Point, having been recently strengthened by the British, was now the most important. It was a rocky promontory advancing far into the Hudson. A deep morass, covered at high water, separated it from the main land but at low tide might be traversed by a narrow causeway and bridge. The promontory was crowned by strong works, furnished with heavy ordnance, commanding the morass and causeway. Lower down were two rows of abatis and the shore at the foot of the hill could be swept by vessels of war anchored in the river. The garrison was about 600 strong, commanded by Lieutenant-colonel Johnson.

To attempt the surprisal of this post, thus strongly fortified, was a perilous enterprise. Wayne was the officer to whom Washington proposed it and he engaged in it with avidity. According to Washington's plan, it was to be attempted by light-infantry only, at night

BRIG^R. GEN. ANTHONY WAYNE.

Printed by W. Pate

NEW YORK. G.P.PUTNAM & CO.

and with the utmost secrecy. Between one and two hundred chosen men and officers were to make the surprise, preceded by a vanguard of determined men to remove obstructions, secure sentries, and drive in the guards. The whole were to advance with fixed bayonets and unloaded muskets; all was to be done with the bayonet. These parties were to be followed by the main body, at a small distance, to support and reinforce them or to bring them off in case of failure.

On getting possession of Stony Point, Wayne was to turn its guns upon Fort Lafayette and the shipping. A detachment was to march down from West Point to Peekskill, to the vicinity of Fort Lafayette, and hold itself ready to join in the attack upon it as soon as the cannonade began from Stony Point.

On the 15th of July, about mid-day, Wayne set out with his light-infantry from Sandy Beach, 14 miles distant from Stony Point. The roads were rugged, across mountains, morasses, and narrow defiles. Midnight was the time recommended by Washington for the attack. About half-past eleven, the whole moved forward, and overcame the two sentinels so that no alarm was given. The causeway, however, was overflowed and it was some time after twelve o'clock before the troops could cross, leaving 300 men under General Muhlenberg on the western side of the morass as a reserve.

At the foot of the promontory, the troops were divided into two columns, for simultaneous attacks on opposite sides of the works. One hundred and fifty volunteers, led by Lieutenant-colonel Fleury, seconded by Major Posey, formed the vanguard of the right column. One hundred volunteers under Major Stewart, the vanguard of the left. In advance of each was a forlorn hope of 20 men, one led by Lieutenant Gibbon, the other by Lieutenant Knox; it was their desperate duty to remove the abatis. So well had the whole affair been conducted that the Americans were close upon the outworks before they were discovered. There was then severe skirmishing at the pickets. The reports roused the garrison. Stony Point was instantly in an uproar. The drums beat to arms; every one hurried to his alarm post; the works were hastily manned, and a tremendous fire of grape shot and musketry opened upon the assailants.

The two columns forced their way with the bayonet, at opposite points, surmounting every obstacle. Fleury was the first to enter the fort and strike the British flag. Wayne, who had received a contusion on the head from a musket ball, was borne in between his aides. The garrison surrendered.

At daybreak, the guns of the fort were turned on Fort Lafayette and the shipping. The latter cut their cables and dropped down the river. Through a series of blunders, the detachment from West Point did not arrive in time and came unprovided with suitable ammunition for their battering artillery. This part of the enterprise, therefore, failed; Fort Lafayette held out.

The storming of Stony Point stands out in high relief as one of the most brilliant achievements of the war. The Americans had effected it without firing a musket; it was the silent, deadly work of the bayonet.

Tidings of the capture of Stony Point and the imminent danger of Fort Lafayette reached Sir Henry just after his conference with Collier at Throg's Neck. The expedition against New London was instantly given up; the transports and troops were recalled; a forced march was made to Dobbs' Ferry on the Hudson; a detachment was sent up the river in transports to relieve Fort Lafayette, and Sir Henry followed with a greater force, hoping Washington might quit his fastnesses and risk a battle for the possession of Stony Point.

Again the Fabian policy of the American commander-in-chief disappointed the British general. Having examined the post with an engineer and several general officers, he found that at least 1500 men would be required to maintain it, a number not to be spared from the army at present.

The works, too, were only calculated for defence on the land side and were open towards the river, where the enemy depended upon protection from their ships. The army, also, would have to be in the vicinity, too distant from West Point to aid in completing or defending its fortifications and exposed to the risk of a general action on unfavorable terms.

For these considerations, Washington evacuated the post on the 18th, removing the cannon and stores and destroying the works; after which he drew his forces together in the Highlands and established his quarters at West Point, not knowing but that Sir Henry might attempt a stroke on that fortress. The latter retook possession of Stony Point and fortified and garrisoned it more strongly than ever, but was too wary to risk an attempt upon the strongholds of the Highlands. Finding Washington was not to be tempted out of them, he returned to his former encampment at Philipsburg.

The brilliant storming of Stony Point was somewhat over-shadowed by an enterprise at the eastward undertaken without consulting Washington. A British detachment from Halifax, of about 800 men, had founded in June a military post on the eastern side of the Bay of Penobscot, and were erecting a fort there to protect Nova Scotia, control the frontiers of Massachusetts, and command the vast wooded regions of Maine.

The people of Boston undertook, on their own responsibility, a naval and military expedition to drive off the invaders. All Boston was in a military bustle, enrolling militia and volunteers. A squadron of armed ships and brigantines under Commodore Saltonstall put to sea, convoying transports, on board of which were near 4000 land troops under General Lovel.

Arriving in the Penobscot on the 25th of May, they found Colonel Maclean posted on a peninsula, steep and precipitous to-ward the bay, and deeply trenched on the land side, with three ships of war anchored before it.

Lovel was repulsed in an attempt to effect a landing on the peninsula but finally succeeded on the 28th. The moment was propitious for a bold and vigorous blow but, unfortunately, Lovel proceeded by regular siege. He threw up works and opened a cannonade, which was continued for a fortnight. Distrustful of the efficiency of the militia, Lovel sent to Boston for Continental troops to carry the place by storm. A golden opportunity was lost by this excess of caution. It gave time for Collier at New York to hear of this enterprise and take measures for its defeat.

On the 13th of August, Lovel was astounded by intelligence that the admiral was arrived before the bay with a superior arma-ment. Thus entrapped, he endeavored to extricate his force with as little loss as possible. Before news of Collier's arrival could reach the fort, he re-embarked his troops in the transports to make their escape up the river. His armed vessels were drawn up to hold the enemy in check, but they soon gave way; some were captured, others were set on fire, or blown up and abandoned by their crews. The transports disgorged the troops and seamen on the wild shores of the river: whence they had to make the best of their way to Boston, struggling through a pathless wilderness.

If Washington was chagrined by the signal failure of this expedition, undertaken without his advice, he was cheered by the better fortune of one set on foot about the same time under his own eye by his young friend, Major Henry Lee of the Virginia dragoons. This daring officer had frequently been employed by him in scouring the country on the west side of the Hudson to collect information, keep an eye upon the enemy's posts, cut off their supplies and check their foraging parties. In the course of his reconnoitring, he had discovered that the British post at Paulus Hook, immediately opposite New York, was very negligently guarded. Paulus Hook is a long, low point, of the Jersey shore, stretching into the Hudson and connected to the main land by a sandy isthmus. A fort had been erected on it and garrisoned with about 500 men, under the command of Major Sutherland. A creek fordable only in two places rendered the hook difficult of access. Within this, a deep trench had been cut across the isthmus, traversed by a drawbridge with a barred gate; within this was a double row of abatis, extending into the water.

Confident in the strength of his position and its distance from any American force, Major Sutherland had become remiss in his military precautions. Major Lee proposed surprising the fort at night and thus striking an insulting blow "within cannon shot of New York." Washington was disposed to favor the adventurous schemes of this young officer. The chief danger would be in the evacuation and retreat after the blow had been effected, owing to the proximity of the enemy's force at New York. In consenting to the enterprise, therefore, he stipulated that Lee should "surprise the post, bring off the garrison immediately, and effect a retreat."

On the 18th of August Lee set out on the expedition, at the head of 300 men of Stirling's division and a troop of dismounted dragoons under Captain McLane. The attack was to be made that night.

It was between two and three in the morning when Lee arrived at the creek which rendered Paulus Hook difficult of access. It happened fortunately that the British commander had, the day before, detached a foraging party to a part of the country called the English Neighborhood. As Lee and his men approached, they were mistaken in the darkness by the sentinel for this party on its return. They passed the creek and ditch, entered the works unmolested, and had made themselves masters of the post before the garrison were roused from sleep. Major Sutherland and about 60 Hessians threw themselves into a small block-house on the left of the fort and opened an irregular fire. To attempt to dislodge them would have cost too much time. Alarm guns from the ships in the river and the forts at New York threatened speedy reinforcements to the enemy. Having made 159 prisoners, Lee commenced his retreat without tarrying to destroy either barracks or artillery. He had achieved his object: a coup de main of signal audacity.

His retreat was attended by perils. Through blunder or misapprehension, the boats which he was to have found at Dow's Ferry on the Hackensack disappointed him and he had to make his way with his weary troops up the neck of land between that river and the Hudson. Fortunately Stirling heard of his peril and sent out a force to cover his retreat, which was effected in safety.

Washington was now at West Point, diligently providing for the defence of the Highlands against any farther attempts of the enemy. During the time that he made this his head-quarters, the most important works were completed, especially the fort at West Point, which formed the citadel of those mountains.

The arrival of Admiral Arbuthnot, with a fleet, bringing 3000 troops and a supply of provisions and stores, strengthened the hands of Sir Henry. Still he had not sufficient force to warrant any further attempt up the Hudson, Washington, by his diligence in fortifying West Point, having rendered that fastness of the Highlands apparently impregnable. Sir Henry turned his thoughts, therefore, towards the South. As this would require large detachments, he threw up additional works on New York Island and at Brooklyn, to render his position secure with the diminished force that would remain with him.

At this juncture news was received of the arrival of D'Estaing with a formidable fleet on the coast of Georgia, having made a successful cruise in the West Indies. A combined attack upon New York was again talked of. In anticipation of it Washington called upon several of the Middle States for supplies of all kinds and reinforcements of militia. Sir Henry changed his plans, caused Rhode Island to be evacuated, the troops and stores to be brought away, the garrisons brought off from Stony and Verplanck's Points, and all his forces to be concentrated at New York, which he endeavored to put in the strongest posture of defence.

Intelligence recently received, too, that Spain had joined France in hostilities against England contributed to increase the solicitude and perplexities of the enemy, while it gave fresh confidence to the Americans.

Washington's anticipations of a combined operation with D'Estaing against New York were disappointed. The French admiral, on arriving on the coast of Georgia, had been persuaded to co-operate with the Southern army under Lincoln in an attempt to recover Savannah, which had fallen into the hands of the British during the preceding year. For three weeks a siege was carried on with great vigor by regular approaches on land and cannonade and bombardment from the shipping. On the 9th of October, although no sufficient breach had been effected, Lincoln and D'Estaing, at the head of their choicest troops, advanced before daybreak to storm the works. The assault was gallant but unsuccessful; both Americans and French had planted their standards on the redoubts but were finally repulsed. After the repulse, both armies retired from before the place, the French having lost in killed and wounded upwards of 600 men, the Americans about 400. D'Estaing himself was among the wounded and the gallant Count Pulaski among the slain. The loss of the enemy was trifling, being protected by their works. The Americans recrossed the Savannah River into South Carolina, the militia returned to their homes, and the French re-embarked.

The tidings of this reverse, which reached Washington late in November, put an end to all prospect of co-operation from the

French fleet; a consequent change took place in all his plans. The militia of New York and Massachusetts, recently assembled, were disbanded and arrangements were made for the winter. The army was thrown into two divisions; one was to be stationed under Heath in the Highlands for the protection of West Point and the neighboring posts; the other and principal division was to be hutted near Morristown, where Washington was to have his headquarters. The cavalry were to be sent to Connecticut.

Understanding that Sir Henry was making preparations at New York for a large embarkation of troops and fearing they might be destined against Georgia and Carolina, he resolved to detach the greater part of his Southern troops for the protection of those states; the North Carolina brigade took up its march for Charleston in November, and the whole of the Virginia line in December.

Notwithstanding the recent preparations at New York, the ships remained in port and the enemy held themselves in collected force there. Sir Henry, however, was regulating his movements by those the French fleet might make after the repulse at Savannah. Intelligence at length arrived that it had been dispersed by a violent storm. D'Estaing, with a part, had shaped his course for France; the rest had proceeded to the West Indies.

Sir Henry now lost no time in carrying his plans into operation. Leaving the garrison of New York under Knyphausen, he embarked several thousand men on board of transports, to be convoyed by five ships-of-the-line and several frigates under Admiral Arbuthnot, and set sail on the 26th of December, accompanied by Cornwallis, on an expedition intended for the capture of Charleston and the reduction of South Carolina.

(CHAPTER 47)

The dreary encampment at Valley Forge has become prover-bial for its hardships, yet they were scarcely more severe than those suffered by Washington's army during the present winter while hutted among the heights of Morristown. The winter set in early and was uncommonly rigorous. The transportation of supplies was obstructed, the magazines were exhausted, and the commissaries had neither money nor credit to enable them to replenish them. For weeks at a time the army was on half allowance, sometimes without meat, sometimes without bread, sometimes without both. There was a scarcity, too, of clothing and blankets so that the poor soldiers were starving with cold as well as hunger.

The root of the evil lay in the derangement of the currency. Congress had commenced the war without adequate funds and without the power of imposing direct taxes. To meet emergencies it had emitted paper money, which sank in value as further emissions succeeded. Thus the country gradually became flooded with a "con-tinental currency," as it was called, irredeemable and of no intrinsic value. The consequence was a general derangement of trade and finance. Congress attempted to put a stop to this depreciation by making paper money a legal tender at its nominal value in the discharge of debts, however contracted. The commissaries now found it difficult to purchase supplies for the immediate wants of the army and impossible to provide any stores in advance. They were left destitute of funds and the public credit was prostrated by the accumulating debts suffered to remain uncancelled.

Washington was reluctantly compelled by the distresses of the army to call upon the counties of the State for supplies of grain and cattle, proportioned to their respective abilities. These supplies were to be brought into the camp within a certain time, the grain to be measured and the cattle estimated by any two of the magistrates

WASHINGTON AT VALLEY FORGE.

NEW YORK, G. P. PUTNAM & Cº

of the county in conjunction with the commissary, certificates to be given by the latter specifying the quantity of each and the terms of payment. Wherever a compliance with this call was refused, the articles required were to be impressed; it was a painful alternative, yet nothing else could save the army from dissolution or starving.

As the winter advanced, the cold increased in severity, the most intense ever remembered in the country. The great bay of New York was frozen over. No supplies could come to the city by water. The ships of war, immovably icebound in its harbor, no longer gave it protection. The insular security of the place was at an end. An army with its heaviest artillery and baggage might cross the Hudson on the ice. Washington was aware of the opportunity but was not in a condition to profit by it. His troops were half fed, half clothed, and inferior in number to the garrison of New York. Still, some minor blow might be attempted, sufficient to cheer the spirits of the people. Having ascertained that the ice formed a bridge across the strait between the Jersey shore and Staten Island, he projected a descent upon the latter by Stirling with 2500 men to surprise and capture a British force of about 1200.

His lordship crossed on the night of the 14th of January from De Hart's Point to the island. His approach was discovered; the troops took refuge in the works, which were too strongly situated to be attacked; a channel remaining open through the ice across the bay, a boat was dispatched to New York for reinforcements.

The surprise having thus proved a failure, Stirling recrossed to the Jersey shore with a number of prisoners he had captured. He was pursued by a party of cavalry, which he repulsed, and effected a retreat to Elizabethtown.

By way of retort, Knyphausen, on the 25th of January, sent out two detachments to harass the American outposts. One crossed to Paulus Hook and, joined by part of its garrison, pushed on to Newark, surprised and captured a company stationed there, set fire to the academy, and returned without loss.

The other detachment, consisting of dragoons and infantry, crossed from Staten Island to Trembly's Point, surprised the picket-guard at Elizabethtown, and captured 2 majors, 2 captains, and 42 privates. The disgraceful part of the expedition was the burning of the town house, a church, and the plundering of the inhabitants.

The church destroyed was a Presbyterian place of worship, whose pastor, the Rev. James Caldwell, had rendered himself an especial object of hostility to both Briton and tory. He was a zealous patriot and his church had at times served as hospital to the American soldier or shelter to the hastily assembled militia. Its bell was the tocsin of alarm; from its pulpit he had many a time stirred up the patriotism of his countrymen.

Another noted maraud was in the lower part of Westchester County, in a hilly region between the British and American lines which had been the scene of part of the past year's campaign. In this region, not far from White Plains, the Americans had established a post of 300 men at a stone building commonly known as Young's house. It commanded a road from north to south down along the narrow valley of the Sawmill River. On this road the garrison kept a vigilant eye to intercept the convoys of cattle and provisions collected or plundered by the enemy. The country was covered with snow and troops could be rapidly transported on sleighs; it was determined that Young's house should be surprised and this rebel nest broken up.

On the evening of the 2d of February, an expedition set out for the purpose from King's Bridge, consisting of four flank companies of guards, two companies of Hessians, and a party of Yagers, all in sleighs, as well as a body of Yager cavalry and mounted Westchester refugees with two three-pounders.

The snow, newly fallen, was deep and the sleighs broke their way through it with difficulty. The troops at length abandoned them and pushed forward on foot. The cannon were left behind for the same reason. To surprise the post was out of the question. Before they could reach the house the country had taken the alarm and the Westchester yeomanry were hastening to aid the garrison.

The British light infantry and grenadiers invested the mansion, the cavalry posted themselves on a neighboring eminence to prevent retreat or reinforcement, and the house was assailed. It made a brave resistance, but the garrison was overpowered and the house was sacked and set in flames.

The War Shifts Southwards (1777–1780)

We give this affair as a specimen of the *petite guerre* carried on in the southern part of Westchester County, foraged by the royal forces and plundered and insulted by refugees and tories. No part of the Union was more harried and trampled down by friend and foe during the Revolution than this "neutral ground," as it was called, and the Jerseys.

The most irksome duty Washington had to perform during this winter's encampment at Morristown regarded Arnold and his military government of Philadelphia in 1778. To explain it requires a glance back to that period.

At the time of entering upon this command, Arnold's accounts with government were yet unsettled, the committee appointed by Congress, at his own request, to examine them, having considered some of his charges dubious and others exorbitant.

The command of Philadelphia, at this time, was a delicate and difficult one. The boundaries between the powers vested in the military commander and those inherent in the State government were ill defined. Disaffection to the American cause prevailed among the residents and required to be held in check with firmness but toleration. By a resolve of Congress, no goods, wares, or merchandise were to removed, transferred, or sold until the ownership of them could be ascertained by a joint committee of Congress and of the Council of Pennsylvania; any public stores belonging to the enemy were to be seized and converted to the use of the army.

One of Arnold's first measures was to issue a proclamation enforcing the resolve of Congress. The measure excited great dissatisfaction and circumstances attending the enforcement of it gave rise to scandal. It was alleged that, while by the proclamation he shut up the stores and shops so that even the officers of the army could not procure necessary articles of merchandise, he was privately making large purchases for his own enrichment. His style of living gave point to this scandal. He occupied one of the finest houses in the city, had his carriage and four horses and a train of domestics, gave expensive entertainments, and indulged in luxury condemned as little befitting a republican general.

In the exercise of his military functions, he had become involved in disputes with the president and executive council of Pennsylvania and, by his conduct, which was deemed arbitrary and arrogant, had drawn upon himself the hostility of that body.

He had not been many weeks in Philadelphia before he became attached to one of its reigning belles, Margaret Shippen, whose family were not considered well affected to the American cause. The young lady herself, during the occupation of the city by the enemy, had been a "toast" among the British officers. Arnold paid his addresses in an open and honorable style but his connection with the Shippen family increased his disfavor with the president and executive council, who were whigs to a man.

In the beginning of December, Reed became president of the executive council of Pennsylvania; under his administration the ripening hostility to Arnold was brought to a crisis. His public conduct was discussed in the executive council and it was resolved unanimously that his military command in the city had been in many respects oppressive, unworthy of his rank, highly discouraging to the liberties and interests of America, and disrespectful to the supreme executive authority of the State.

As he was an officer of the United States, the complaints of Pennsylvania were set forth by the executive council in eight charges and forwarded to Congress, accompanied by documents and a letter from Reed.

Information of these facts, with a printed copy of the charges, reached Arnold at Washington's camp on the Raritan, which he had visited on the way to Albany. His first solicitude was about the effect they might have upon Miss Shippen, to whom he was now engaged. On the following day he issued an address to the public, recalling his faithful services of nearly four years and inveighing against the president and council, who had ordered copies of their charges to be printed and dispersed throughout the several States. In conclusion, Arnold informed the public that he had requested Congress to direct a court-martial to inquire into his conduct and trusted his countrymen would suspend judgment until he should have an opportunity of being heard.

Arnold's appeal to Congress was referred to the committee

MAJ. GEN. BENEDICT ARNOLD.

Engraved by H.B.Hall.

Printed by W Pate.

NEW YORK. G.P.PUTNAM & CO.

which had under consideration the letter of Reed and its accompanying documents.

Arnold, in January, had obtained permission from Washington to resign the command of Philadelphia, but deferred to act upon it until the charges against him should be examined, lest his enemies ascribe his resignation to fear of a disgraceful suspension. In March, the committee brought in a report exculpating him from all criminality in the matters charged against him. As soon as the report was brought in, he considered his name vindicated and resigned.

Whatever exultation he may have felt was shortlived. Congress did not act upon the report, as, in justice to him, they should have done, but referred the subject anew to a joint committee of their body and the assembly and council of Pennsylvania. Arnold was, at this time, on the eve of marriage with Miss Shippen, and it must have been peculiarly galling to his pride to be kept under the odium of imputed delinquencies.

The report of the joint committee brought up animated discussions in Congress. Several resolutions intended to soothe the wounded sensibilities of Pennsylvania were passed without dissent; it was contended that certain charges were only cognizable by a court-martial and it was resolved (April 3d) that the commander-in-chief should appoint such a court for consideration of them.

Arnold inveighed bitterly against the injustice of subjecting him to a trial before a military tribunal for alleged offences of which he had been acquitted by the committee of Congress. He urged Washington to appoint a speedy day for the trial that he might not linger under the odium of an unjust public accusation. The woman on whom he had placed his affections remained true to him and his marriage with Miss Shippen took place just five days after the mortifying vote of Congress.

Washington sympathized with Arnold's impatience and appointed the 1st of May for the trial. But it was repeatedly postponed: first, at the request of the Pennsylvania council, to allow time for the arrival of witnesses from the South; afterwards, in consequence of threatening movements of the enemy which obliged every officer to be at his post. Arnold, in the mean time, continued to reside at Philadelphia, holding his commission in the army but filling no public office, getting deeper and deeper in debt, and becoming more and more unpopular.

At length, when the army had gone into winter-quarters, the long delayed court-martial was assembled at Morristown. Of the eight charges advanced by the Pensylvania council, only four came under cognizance of the court. Of two of these he was entirely acquitted. The remaining two were:

First. While in the camp at Valley Forge, he, without the knowledge of the commander-in-chief or the sanction of the State government, had granted permission for a vessel belonging to disaffected persons to proceed from the port of Philadelphia, then in possession of the enemy, to any port of the United States.

Second. Availing himself of his official authority, he had appropriated the public waggons of Pennsylvania to the transportation of private property of persons who were disaffected to the interests and independence of America.

In regard to the first of these charges, Arnold alleged that the person who applied for the protection of the vessel had taken the oath of allegiance to the State of Pennsylvania required by the laws and that the intentions of that person and his associates appeared to be upright. As to his having granted the permission without the knowledge of the commander-in-chief, Arnold alleged that it was customary for general officers to grant passes and protections to inhabitants of the United States, friendly to the same, and that the protection was given to prevent the soldiery from plundering the vessel and cargo, coming from a place in possession of the enemy, until the proper authority could take cognizance of the matter.

In regard to the second charge, while it was proved that under his authority public waggons had been so used, it was allowed that they had been employed at private expense and without any design to defraud the public or impede the military service.

In regard to both charges, nothing fraudulent on the part of Arnold was proved, but the transactions involved in the first were pronounced irregular and contrary to one of the articles of war, and, in the second, imprudent and reprehensible, considering the high station occupied by the general at the time. The court sentenced him to be reprimanded by the commander-in-chief and the sentence was confirmed by Congress on the 12th of February (1780).

The reprimand was administered by Washington with consummate delicacy. It was so mild and considerate, accompanied by such high eulogiums and generous promises, that it might have had a favorable effect upon Arnold, but he had persuaded himself that the court would acquit him altogether and he resented deeply a sentence he protested as unmerited. His resentment was aggravated by delays in the settlement of his accounts, as he depended upon the sums he claimed as due to him for the payment of debts by which he was harassed.

In March, we find Arnold intent on a new and adventurous project: an expedition requiring several ships of war and about 400 land troops. Washington was disposed to favor his proposition but the scheme fell through from the impossibility of sparing the requisite number of men from the army. On the failure of the project, he obtained from Washington leave of absence from the army for the summer, his wounds unfitting him for the field.

The return of spring brought little alleviation to the sufferings of the army at Morristown. All means of supplying its wants or recruiting its ranks were paralyzed by the continued depreciation of the currency. While Washington saw his forces gradually diminishing, his solicitude was intensely excited for the safety of the Southern States.

The reader will recall the departure from New York, in the latter part of December, of the fleet of Admiral Arbuthnot with the army of Sir Henry Clinton, destined for the subjugation of South Carolina. It was presumed that the subjugation of it would be an easy task. Some of the foreign elements of the population might be hostile to British domination but others would be favorable. There was a large class too, that had been born or had passed much of their lives in England, who retained for it a filial affection, spoke of it as home, and sent their children to be educated there. Little combination of militia and yeomanry need be apprehended from a population sparsely scattered, where the settlements were widely separated by swamps and forests. Washington was in no condition to render relief, his army being at a vast distance. Such were some of the considerations which prompted the enemy to this expedition and which gave Washington great anxiety concerning it.

The voyage of Sir Henry proved long and tempestuous. The ships were dispersed; several fell into the hands of the Americans; one ordnance vessel foundered; most of the artillery horses and all those of the cavalry perished. The scattered ships rejoined each other about the end of January at Tybee Bay on Savannah River. The loss of the cavalry horses was especially felt by Sir Henry. There was a corps of 250 dragoons on which he depended greatly in the kind of guerilla warfare he was likely to pursue in a country of forests and morasses. Lieutenant-colonel Banastre Tarleton, who commanded them, repaired with his dragoons in some boats to Port Royal Island, on the seaboard of South Carolina, "to collect . . . from friends or enemies, by money or by force, all the horses . . . in the neighborhood." He succeeded in procuring horses, though of an inferior quality, but consoled himself that he would secure better ones in the course of the campaign.

In the mean time, the transports sailed under convoy on the 10th of February from Savannah to North Edisto Sound, where the troops disembarked on the 11th on St. Johns Island, about 30 miles below Charleston. Thence, Sir Henry set out for the banks of Ashley River opposite the city, while a part of the fleet proceeded round by sea for the purpose of blockading the harbor. The advance of Sir Henry was slow and cautious. Much time was consumed in fortifying intermediate ports to keep a secure communication with the fleet. He ordered from Savannah all the troops that could be spared and wrote to Knyphausen at New York for reinforcements. Every precaution was taken to insure against a second repulse from Charleston, which might prove fatal to his military reputation.

Lincoln took advantage of this slowness to extend and strengthen the works. Charleston stands at the end of an isthmus formed by the Ashley and Cooper Rivers. Beyond the main works on the land side he cut a canal between the swamps which border these rivers. In advance of the canal were two rows of abatis and a double picketed ditch. Within the canal, and between it and the main works, were strong redoubts and batteries to open a flanking fire on any approaching column, while an inclosed hornwork of masonry formed a kind of citadel.

A squadron, commanded by Commodore Whipple, composed of 9 vessels of war, the largest mounting forty-four guns, was to co-operate with Forts Moultrie and Johnston and the various batteries in defence of the harbor. They were to lie before the bar so as to command the entrance of it. Great reliance also was placed on the bar itself, which it was thought no ship-of-the-line could pass.

Governor Rutledge, a man eminent for talents, patriotism, and decision, called out the militia of the State. Large reinforcements of troops were expected from the North. Under all these circumstances, Lincoln yielded to the entreaties of the inhabitants and, instead of remaining with his army in the open country as he had intended, shut himself up with them in the place for its defence, leaving merely his cavalry and 200 light troops outside to hover about the enemy and prevent small parties from marauding.

On the 12th of March Sir Henry took up a position on Charleston Neck, a few miles above the town. Admiral Arbuthnot soon showed an intention of introducing his ships into the harbor. Commodore Whipple had by this time ascertained that his ships could not anchor nearer than within three miles of the bar, so that it would be impossible for him to defend the passage of it. He therefore took a position where his ships might be abreast and form a cross-fire with the batteries of Fort Moultrie, where Colonel Pinckney commanded.

Washington was informed of these facts by letters from his former aide-de-camp, Colonel Laurens, who was in Charleston at the time. "The impracticability of defending the bar, I fear, amounts to the loss of the town and garrison," writes he in reply. The same opinion was expressed in a letter to Baron Steuben: "I have the greatest reliance in General Lincoln's prudence, but I cannot forbear dreading the event."

His solicitude for the safety of the South was increased by hearing of the embarkation at New York of 2500 British and Hessian troops, under Lord Rawdon, reinforcements for Sir Henry Clinton. It seemed evident the enemy intended to push their operations with vigor at the South, perhaps to make it the principal theatre of the war.

At this moment his utmost vigilance was required to keep watch upon New York and maintain the security of the Hudson, the vital part of the confederacy. The weak state of the American means of warfare in both quarters presented a choice of difficulties. The South needed support. Could the North give it without exposing itself to ruin, since the enemy, by means of their ships, could suddenly unite their forces and fall upon any point that they might consider weak? Such were the perplexities to which he was continually subjected, in having scanty means to provide for the security of a vast extent of country, and with only land forces to contend with an amphibious enemy.

He determined to leave something at hazzard in the Middle States, where the country was internally so strong, and yield further succor to the Southern States, which had not equal military advantages. With the consent of Congress, therefore, he put the Maryland line under marching orders, together with the Delaware regiment, which acted with it, and the first regiment of artillery. Baron de Kalb, now at the head of the Maryland division, was instructed to conduct this detachment with all haste to the aid of General Lincoln. He might not arrive in time to prevent the fall of Charleston but he might assist to arrest the progress of the enemy and save the Carolinas.

Washington's feelings at the present juncture are admirably expressed in a letter to Steuben. "The prospect, my dear Baron, is gloomy and the storm threatens but I hope we shall extricate ourselves and bring every thing to a prosperous issue. I have been so inured to difficulties in the course of this contest that I have learned to look upon them with more tranquillity than formerly. Those which now present themselves no doubt require vigorous exertions to overcome them and I am far from despairing of doing it."

(CHAPTER 48)

We have cited the depreciation of the currency as a main cause of the difficulties and distresses of the army. Congress, being destitute of the power of levying taxes, which vested in the State governments, devolved upon those governments, in their separate capacities, the business of supporting the army. This produced a great inequality in the condition of the troops, according to the means and liberality of their respective States. Some States furnished their troops amply; others were more contracted in their supplies; others left their troops almost destitute. Some of the States undertook to make good to their troops the loss in their pay caused by the depreciation of the currency; as this was not general, it increased the inequality of condition. Those who fared worse than others were incensed not only against their own State but against the confederacy.

These and other defects in the military system were pressed by Washington upon the attention of Congress in a letter to the President: "It were devoutly to be wished," observed he, "that a plan could be devised by which every thing relating to the army could be conducted on a general principle, under the direction of Congress. This alone can give harmony and consistency to our military establishment."

In consequence of this letter it was proposed in Congress to send a committee of three of its members to consult with the commander-in-chief. Chosen by ballot, it consisted of General Schuyler, John Mathews, and Nathaniel Peabody. The committee found the disastrous state of affairs had not been exaggerated. For five months the army had been unpaid. Every department was destitute of money or credit; there were rarely provisions for six days in advance; on some occasions the troops had been for several successive days without meat; there was no forage.

To soothe the discontents of the army, Congress engaged to make good to the Continental and independent troops the difference in the value of their pay caused by depreciation; all moneys or other articles heretofore received by them should be considered as advanced on account and comprehended at their just value in the final settlement.

At this gloomy crisis came a letter from Lafayette, dated April 27th, announcing his arrival at Boston. Washington's eyes, we are told, were suffused with tears as he read this most welcome epistle. The marquis arrived at head-quarters on the 12th of May, where he was welcomed with acclamations, for he was popular with both officers and soldiers. Washington folded him in his arms in a truly paternal embrace and they were soon closeted to talk over the state of affairs. Lafayette made known the result of his visit to France. His efforts at court had been crowned with success: a French fleet under the Chevalier de Ternay was to put to sea early in April, bringing a body of troops under the Count de Rochambeau, to co-operate with the American forces; this, however, he was at liberty to make known only to Washington and Congress. Remaining but a day at head-quarters, he hastened on to the seat of government, where he met the reception his generous enthusiasm in the cause of American Independence had so fully merited.

Within three days after the departure of the marquis from Morristown, Washington, in a letter to him, gave his idea of the plan for the French fleet and army to pursue on their arrival upon the coast. The reduction of New York he considered the first enterprise to be attempted by the co-operating forces. The effective land force of the enemy he estimated at about 8000 regulars and 4000 refugees, with some militia on which no great dependence could be placed. Their naval force consisted of one seventy-four gun-ship and three or four small frigates. The French fleet might gain possession of the harbor without difficulty and, with the co-operation of the American army, oblige the city to capitulate. He advised Lafayette, therefore, to urge the French commanders, on their arrival on the coast, to proceed to Sandy Hook and there await further advices; should they learn, however, that the expedition under Sir Henry Clinton had returned from the South to New York, they were to proceed to Rhode Island.

General Arnold was at this time in Philadelphia and his connection with subsequent events requires a few words concerning his career, daily becoming more perplexed. He had again petitioned Congress on the subject of his accounts; the Board of Treasury had made a report far short of his wishes. He had appealed and his appeal, together with all the documents connected with the case, was referred to a committee of three. The old doubts and difficulties continued and there was no prospect of a speedy settlement; he was in extremity.

When Arnold heard of the expected arrival of aid from France, and the talk of an active campaign, his military ambition was once more aroused. To Schuyler, who was about to visit the camp as one of the committee, he wrote expressing a determination to rejoin the army, although his wounds still made it painful to walk or ride, and intimated, that the command at West Point would be best suited to him. In reply, Schuyler wrote that he had put Arnold's letter into Washington's hands and added: "He expressed a desire to do whatever was agreeable to you, . . . and intimated, that as soon as his arrangements for the campaign should take place, he would properly consider you."

In the mean time, the army with which Washington was to co-operate in the projected attack upon New York was so reduced by the departure of troops whose term had expired and the tardiness in furnishing recruits that it did not amount quite to 4000 rank and file fit for duty. Among these was a prevalent discontent; their pay was five months in arrear; if now paid it would be in Continental currency without allowance for depreciation.

A long interval of scarcity and several days of actual famine brought matters to a crisis. On the 25th of May, two regiments of the Connecticut line declared their intention to march home "or, at best, to gain subsistence at the point of the bayonet." Colonel Meigs, while endeavoring to suppress the mutiny, was struck by one of the soldiers. Every argument and expostulation was used with the mutineers. It was with difficulty they could be prevailed upon to return to their huts. This mutiny, Washington declared, had given him infinitely more concern than any thing that had ever happened.

In this alarming state of destitution, Washington looked round anxiously for bread for his famishing troops. Virginia was sufficiently tasked to supply the South. New York, by legislative coercion, had already given all that she could spare from the subsistence of her inhabitants. Jersey was exhausted by the long residence of the army. Maryland had made great exertions and might still do something more, and Delaware might contribute handsomely in proportion to her extent. But Pennsylvania was now the chief dependence, for that State was represented to be full of flour. Washington's letter of the 16th of December to Reed had obtained temporary relief from that quarter; he now wrote to him a second time. "Every idea you can form of our distresses, will fall short of the reality. There is such a combination of circumstances to exhaust the patience of the soldiery that it begins at length to be worn out, and we see in every line of the army features of mutiny and sedition." He urges Reed to press upon the legislature of Pennsylvania the policy of investing its executive with plenipotentiary powers. His letter procured relief for the army from the legislature and a resolve empowering the president and council, during its recess, to declare martial law should circumstances render it expedient.

In like manner, Washington endeavored to rouse the dormant fire of Congress. "Certain I am," writes he to a member of that body, "unless Congress speak in a more decisive tone, unless they are vested with powers by the several States . . . or assume them as matters of right, and they and the States . . . act with more energy than they have hitherto done, that our cause is lost. . . . I see one army branching into thirteen which, instead of looking up to Congress as the supreme controlling power of the United States, are considering themselves dependent on their respective States. In a word, I see the powers of Congress declining too fast for the consideration and respect which are due to them as the great representative body of America and I am fearful of the consequences."

In a preceding chapter we left the British fleet under Arbuthnot preparing to force its way into the harbor of Charleston. Several days elapsed before the ships were able to pass the bar. They did so on the

20th of March with but slight opposition from several galleys. Commodore Whipple, seeing the vast superiority of their force, made a second retrograde move, stationing some of his ships in Cooper River and sinking the rest at its mouth to prevent the enemy from cutting off communication with the country on the east; the crews and heavy cannon were landed to aid in the defence of the town.

The reinforcements expected from the North were not yet arrived, the militia of the State did not appear at Governor Rutledge's command, and other reliances were failing.

At this time the reinforcements which Sir Henry had ordered from Savannah were marching toward the Cambayee under Patterson. On his flanks moved Ferguson with a corps of riflemen and Cochrane with the infantry of the British legion. Being arrived in the neighborhood of Port Royal, where Tarleton had succeeded in remounting his dragoons, Patterson sent orders to that officer to join him. Tarleton hastened to obey the order. The Carolina militia, having heard that the British horses had perished at sea, made an attack on Patterson's force, supposing it to be without cavalry. To their surprise, Tarleton charged them with his dragoons, routed them, and took several prisoners and a number of horses.

Tarleton had soon afterwards to encounter a worthy antagonist in Colonel William Washington, the cavalry officer who had distinguished himself at Trenton and was destined to distinguish himself still more in this Southern campaign. He was now at the head of a body of Continental cavalry consisting of his own, Bland's lighthorse, and Pulaski's hussars. A brush took place in the neighborhood of Rantoul's Bridge. Colonel Washington took several prisoners and drove back the dragoons of the British legion.

On the 7th of April, Woodford with 700 Virginia troops, after a forced march of 500 miles in thirty days, crossed from the east side of Cooper River by the only passage open into Charleston. It was a timely reinforcement and joyfully welcomed.

About the same time Arbuthnot, in the Roebuck, passed Sullivan's Island at the head of a squadron of 7 armed vessels and 2 transports. Pinckney opened a heavy cannonade from the batteries of Fort Moultrie. The ships thundered in reply; clouds of smoke were raised, under the cover of which they slipped by. The ships took a position near Fort Johnston, just without the range of the shot from the American batteries. After the passage of the ships, Pinckney and part of the garrison withdrew from Fort Moultrie.

The enemy had by this time completed his first parallel and, the town being almost entirely invested by sea and land, received a summons from the British general and admiral to surrender. Lincoln refused.

The British batteries were now opened. The siege was conducted on a magnitude scarcely warranted by the moderate strength of the place. A great object with the besieged was to keep open the channel of communication with the country by the Cooper River, the last by which they could receive reinforcements and supplies or retreat if necessary. For this purpose, Governor Rutledge, leaving the town in the care of Lieutenant-governor Gadsden, set off to rouse the militia between the Cooper and Santee Rivers. His success was limited. Two militia posts were established by him, one between these rivers, the other at a ferry on the Santee. Brigadier-general Huger with a force of militia and Continental cavalry, including those of Colonel Washington, was stationed at Monk's Corner, about 30 miles above Charleston, to guard the passes at the head waters of Cooper River.

Sir Henry, when proceeding with his second parallel, detached Lieutenant-colonel Webster with 1400 men to break up these posts. The most distant one was that of Huger's cavalry at Monk's Corner. The surprisal of this was entrusted to Tarleton who, with his dragoons, was in Webster's advanced guard. He was to be seconded by Ferguson with his riflemen.

On the evening of the 13th of April, Tarleton moved toward Monk's Corner. It was made in profound silence and by unfrequented roads. The surprisal of Huger's camp was complete. Several officers and men were killed or wounded. General Huger, Colonel Washington, with many others, escaped in the darkness to the neighboring swamps. One hundred officers, dragoons and hussars, were taken, with about 400 horses and near 50 waggons, laden with arms, clothing and ammunition.

Biggins Bridge on Cooper River was likewise secured and the

way opened for Webster to advance nearly to the head of the passes in such a manner as to shut up Charleston entirely.

During the progress of the siege, Lincoln held repeated councils of war in which he manifested a disposition to evacuate the place. The inhabitants, however, implored Lincoln not to abandon them to the mercies of an infuriated and licentious soldiery, and the general yielded to their entreaties.

The American cavalry had gradually reassembled on the north of the Santee under Colonel White of New Jersey, where they were joined by some militia infantry and by Colonel Washington with such of his dragoons as had escaped at Monk's Corner. Cornwallis had committed the country between Cooper and Wando Rivers to Tarleton's charge with orders to be continually on the move with the cavalry and infantry of the legion. Hearing of the assemblage of American troops, Tarleton came suddenly upon them by surprise at Laneau's Ferry. It was one of his bloody exploits. Colonels White, Washington and Jamieson, with other officers and men, threw themselves into the river and escaped by swimming.

The arrival of a reinforcement of 3000 men from New York, enabled Sir Henry to throw a powerful detachment under Cornwallis east of Cooper River to complete the investment of the town. Fort Moultrie surrendered. The batteries of the third parallel were opened upon the town. This fire was kept up for two days. The besiegers crossed the canal and prepared to make an assault by sea and land.

All hopes of successful defence were at an end. The works were in ruins, the guns almost all dismounted, the garrison exhausted with fatigue, the provisions nearly consumed. The inhabitants, dreading an assault, joined in a petition to Lincoln and prevailed upon him to offer a surrender. The capitulation was signed on the 12th of May. The prisoners taken by the enemy, exclusive of the sailors, amounted to 5618 men, comprising every male adult in the city. The Continental troops did not exceed 2000; the rest were citizens and militia.

Sir Henry Clinton considered the fall of Charleston decisive of the fate of South Carolina. To complete the subjugation of the country, he planned three expeditions into the interior. One, under

Lieutenant-colonel Brown, was to move up the Savannah River to Augusta, on the borders of Georgia. Another, under Lieutenant-colonel Cruger, was to proceed up the southwest side of the Santee River to a region between the Savannah and the Saluda rivers. A third, under Cornwallis, was to cross the Santee, march up the northeast bank, and strike at a corps of troops under Colonel Buford which were retreating to North Carolina with artillery and waggons laden with arms, ammunition and clothing.

Buford, in fact, had arrived too late for the relief of Charleston and was now making a retrograde move; he had come on with 380 troops of the Virginia line and two field-pieces, and had been joined by Colonel Washington with a few of his cavalry that had survived the surprisal by Tarleton. As Buford was moving with celerity and had the advantage of distance, Cornwallis detached Tarleton in pursuit of him, with 170 dragoons, 100 mounted infantry, and a three pounder. The bold partisan pushed forward with his usual ardor and rapidity. After a day and night of forced march he arrived about dawn at Rugeley's Mills. Buford, he was told, was 20 miles in advance of him, pressing on with all diligence to join another corps of Americans. Tarleton continued forward, anxious to overtake Buford before he could form a junction with the force he was seeking.

Tarleton came upon Buford's rear-guard and Buford hastily drew up his men in order of battle, in an open wood, on the right of the road. His artillery and waggons, which were in the advnace escorted by part of his infantry, were ordered to continue on their march.

There appears to have been some confusion on the part of the Americans and they were attacked in front and on both flanks by cavalry and mounted infantry. The American battalion was broken; most of the men threw down their arms and begged for quarter but were cut down without mercy. Buford and a few of the cavalry escaped, as did about 100 of the infantry who were with the baggage in the advance.

The two other detachments sent out by Clinton met with nothing but submission. The people in general accepted the proffered protection and conformed to its humiliating terms.

Sir Henry now persuaded himself that South Carolina was subdued and proceeded to station garrisons in various parts to maintain subjection. In the fulness of his confidence, he issued a proclamation on the 3d of June discharging all military prisoners from their paroles after the 20th of the month excepting those captured in Fort Moultrie and Charleston. All thus released were reinstated in the rights and duties of British subjects but, at the same time, they were bound to take an active part in support of the government hitherto opposed by them. All who should neglect to return to their allegiance or should refuse to take up arms against the independence of their country were to be considered as rebels and treated accordingly.

Having struck a blow which, as he conceived, was to ensure the subjugation of the South, Sir Henry embarked for New York on the 5th of June with a part of his forces, leaving the residue under the command of Cornwallis, who was to carry the war into North Carolina and thence into Virginia.

(CHAPTER 49)

On the 6th of June came a new alarm. The enemy were landing in force at Elizabethtown Point to carry fire and sword into the Jerseys!

Knyphausen was persuaded that a sudden show of military protection, following up news of the capture of Charleston, would produce general desertion among Washington's troops and rally back the inhabitants of the Jerseys to the crown.

In this belief he projected a descent into the Jerseys with about 5000 men and some light artillery, who were to cross in the night of the 5th of June from Staten Island to Elizabethtown Point.

The first division, led by Stirling, landed before dawn and advanced as silently as possible. The tramp of the troops, however, caught the ear of an American sentinel; he challenged the dimly descried mass as it approached and, receiving no answer, fired into it. That shot wounded Stirling in the thigh and ultimately proved mortal. The wounded general was carried back and Knyphausen took his place.

This delayed the march until sunrise and gave time for the troops of the Jersey line under Colonel Elias Dayton, stationed in Elizabethtown, to assemble. They were too weak in numbers, however, and retreated in good order, skirmishing occasionally.

Signal guns and signal fires were rousing the country. The militia and yeomanry hastened to their alarm posts and fired upon the enemy from behind walls and thickets as they advanced.

At Connecticut Farms, the retreating troops under Dayton fell in with the Jersey brigade under Maxwell and, a few militia joining them, the Americans were enabled to hold the enemy in check. The latter, however, brought up several field-pieces and, reinforced by a second division from Staten Island, compelled the Americans again to retreat.

In the mean time Knyphausen was pressing on with his main force towards Morristown. The booming of alarm guns had roused the country; every valley was pouring out its yeomanry.

Within half a mile of Springfield Knyphausen halted to reconnoitre. Springfield, which had been made the American rallying point, stands at the foot of the Short Hills, on the west side of Rahway River. On the bank of the river, Maxwell's Jersey brigade and the militia of the neighborhood were drawn up; on the Short Hills in the rear was Washington with the main body of his forces, on the alert expecting to be assailed in the morning. But in the morning no enemy was to be seen. Knyphausen, convinced that he had been misinformed as to the disposition of the Jersey people and of the army, had retreated under cover of night, intending to recross to Staten Island.

Knyphausen, impeded in crossing to Staten Island by the low tide and deep muddy shore, had time to reflect on the ridicule that would await him in New York. He lingered with his troops at Elizabethtown and the Point beyond, obliging Washington to exercise unremitting vigilance for the safety of the Jerseys and of the Hudson.

On the 17th of June the fleet from the South arrived in the bay of New York and Sir Henry Clinton landed his troops on Staten Island but almost immediately re-embarked them, as if meditating an expedition up the river.

Fearing for the safety of West Point, Washington set off on the 21st June with the main body of his troops towards Pompton, while Greene, with Maxwell and Stark's brigades, Lee's dragoons and the militia of the neighborhood remained on the Short Hills to cover the country and protect the stores at Morristown.

Washington's movements were slow and wary, unwilling to be far from Greene until better informed of the designs of the enemy. At Rockaway Bridge, about 11 miles beyond Morristown, he received word on the 23d that the enemy were advancing from Elizabethtown against Springfield. Supposing Morristown to be their ultimate object, he detached a brigade to assist Greene and fell back to be in supporting distance of him.

The re-embarkation of the troops at Staten Island had, in fact, been a stratagem of Sir Henry to divert the attention of Washington and enable Knyphausen to carry out his original enterprise. No sooner did the latter ascertain that the American commander-in-chief had moved off towards the Highlands than he sallied from Elizabethtown 5000 strong with a large body of cavalry and 15 or 20 pieces of artillery, hoping to destroy the public stores at Morristown and get possession of those hills and defiles among which Washington's army had been so securely posted.

Early on the morning of the 23d Knyphausen pushed forward toward Springfield. Beside the main road which passes directly through the village, there is another, north of it, called the Vauxhall road, crossing several streams, the confluence of which forms the Rahway. These two roads unite beyond the village in the principal pass of the Short Hills. The enemy's troops advanced rapidly in two columns, the right one by the Vauxhall road, the other by the main road. Greene was stationed among the Short Hills, about a mile above the town.

At five o'clock in the morning, signal-guns gave notice of the approach of the enemy. The troops were hastily called in from their posts among the mountain passes and preparations were made to defend the village.

Major Lee, with his dragoons and a picket-guard, was posted on the Vauxhall road to check the right column of the enemy in its advance. Colonel Dayton with his regiment of New Jersey militia was to check the left column on the main road. Colonel Angel of Rhode Island, with about 200 picked men and a piece of artillery, was to defend a bridge over the Rahway, a little west of the town. Colonel Shreve, stationed with his regiment at a second bridge over a branch of the Rahway east of the town, was to cover, if necessary, the retreat of Colonel Angel. Those parts of Maxwell and Stark's brigades not thus detached were drawn up on high grounds in the rear of the town, having the militia on their flanks.

There was some sharp fighting at a bridge on the Vauxhall road, where Major Lee with his dragoons and picket-guard held the right column at bay; a part of the column, however, forded the stream above the bridge and obliged Lee to retire. The left column met with similar opposition from Dayton and his Jersey regiment.

The severest fighting of the day was at the bridge over the Rahway. Angel defended it against a vastly superior force, but he was at length compelled to retire. His retreat was bravely covered by Shreve, but he too was obliged to give way before the over-whelming force of the enemy and join the brigades of Maxwell and Stark upon the hill.

Greene, finding his front too much extended for his small force, and in danger of being outflanked on the left by the column pressing forward on the Vauxhall road, took post with his main body on the first range of hills, where the roads were brought near to a point and passed between him and the height occupied by Stark and Maxwell. He then threw out a detachment which checked the further advance of the right column of the enemy along the Vauxhall road and secured that pass through the Short Hills. Now strongly posted, he awaited with confidence the expected attempt of the enemy to gain the height. No such attempt was made. The enemy commander saw that, should he persist in pushing for Morristown, the enterprise, even if successful, might cost too much, beside taking him too far from New York at a time when a French armament might be expected.

Before the brigade detached by Washington arrived at the

scene of action, the enemy had retreated. Previous to their retreat, Springfield was reduced to ashes. They were pursued and harassed the whole way to Elizabethtown by light scouting parties, by the militia and yeomanry of the country, and by Lee and his dragoons.

During the night the enemy passed over to Staten Island by their bridge of boats. By morning, the State of New Jersey, so long harassed by the campaignings of either army, was finally evacuated by the enemy. It had proved a school of war to the American troops; it had brought the patriot soldier nearly on a level with the European mercenary in the habitudes and usages of arms, while he had the superior incitements of home, country, and independence. At the same time the conflagration of villages by which they sought to cover or revenge their repeated failures and their precipitate retreat formed an ignominious close to the British campaigns in the Jerseys.

Apprehensive that the next move of the enemy would be up the Hudson, Washington resumed his measures for the security of West Point, moving towards the Highlands in the latter part of June. Circumstances soon convinced him that the enemy had no present intention of attacking that fortress, but merely menaced him at various points, thereby interrupting agriculture, distressing the country, and rendering his cause unpopular.

He now exerted himself to the utmost to procure from the different State Legislatures their quotas and supplies for the regular army. The basis of every thing was the completion of the Continental battalions to their full establishment; otherwise, nothing decisive could be attempted. The desired relief, however, had to be effected through the ramifications of General and State governments and their committees. The operations were tardy and unproductive.

The capture of Lincoln at Charleston had left the Southern department without a commander-in-chief. As there were likely to be important military operations in that quarter, Washington intended to recommend Greene for the appointment. Congress, however, with unbecoming precipitancy, gave that command to Gates (June 13th) without waiting to consult Washington. Gates accepted the appointment with avidity, anticipating new triumphs.

On the 10th of July a French fleet under the Chevalier de Ternay arrived at Newport. It was composed of 7 ships of the line, 2 frigates and 2 bombs and convoyed transports on board of which were 5000 troops. This was the first division of the forces promised by France of which Lafayette had spoken. The second division had been detained at Brest for want of transports but might soon be expected.

Count de Rochambeau, Lieutenant-general of the royal armies, was commander-in-chief of this force. He was a veteran who had gained laurels in various battles and had risen from one post of honor to another. Another officer of distinction in this force was Major-general the Marquis de Chastellux, a friend and relative of Lafayette.

The French troops presented a gallant and martial appearance. A feeling of adventure and romance associated with the American struggle had caused many of the young nobility to seek this new field of achievement. They brought with them the ancient French politeness, for it was remarkable how soon they accommodated themselves to all the privations and inconveniences of a new country and conformed to the familiar simplicity of republican manners.

The instructions of the French ministry to Rochambeau placed him entirely under the command of General Washington. This considerate arrangement, adopted at the suggestion of Lafayette, was intended to prevent the recurrence of those questions of rank and etiquette which had heretofore disturbed the combined service.

Washington, in general orders, congratulated the army on the arrival of this timely and generous succor, which he hailed as a new tie between France and America, anticipating that the only contention between the two armies would be to excel each other in the display of military virtue.

Washington was still unprovided with the troops and military means requisite for the combined operations meditated. Still he took upon himself the responsibility of immediate action and forthwith despatched Lafayette to the French commanders to concert plans for the attack upon New York.

The arrival, however, of the British Admiral Graves at New

The count de ROCHAMBEAU.

(As Marshal of France. 1791)

Printed by W. Pate.

NEW YORK G.P. PUTNAM & CO.

York on the 13th of July with 6 ships-of-the-line gave the enemy such a superiority of naval force that the design on New York was postponed until the second French division should make its appearance, or a squadron under the Count de Guichen expected from the West Indies.

In the mean time, Sir Henry Clinton determined to attack the French quarters on Rhode Island. This he was to do in person at the head of 6000 men, aided by Arbuthnot with his fleet. Sir Henry proceeded with his troops to Throg's Neck on the Sound, there to embark on transports which Arbuthnot was to provide. No sooner did Washington learn that so large a force had left New York than he crossed the Hudson to Peekskill and prepared to move towards King's Bridge with the main body of his troops. His intention was either to oblige Sir Henry to abandon his project against Rhode Island or to strike a blow at New York during his absence.

As Washington was observing the crossing of his troops, Arnold approached, having just arrived in camp. Arnold, asking whether any place had been assigned to him, was told that he was to command the left wing. The chagrin with which the reply was received surprised Washington and he was still more surprised when he learned that Arnold was more desirous of a garrison post than a command in the field. Arnold's excuse was that his wounded leg still unfitted him for action, but that at West Point he might render himself useful.

The expedition of Sir Henry was delayed by the tardy arrival of transports. In the mean time he heard of the sudden move of Washington and learned that the French at Newport had been strengthened by the militia from the neighboring country. These tidings disconcerted his plans. He left Arbuthnot to proceed with his squadron to Newport, blockade the French fleet and endeavor to intercept the second division, supposed to be on its way, while he with his troops hastened back to New York. In consequence, Washington again withdrew his forces to the west side of the Hudson, first establishing a post and throwing up some small works at Dobbs' Ferry, about 10 miles above King's Bridge, to secure a communication across the river for the transportation of troops and ordnance should the design upon New York be prosecuted.

Arnold now received the command he had so earnestly coveted, the fortress at West Point and the posts from Fishkill to King's Ferry, together with the infantry and cavalry advanced towards the enemy on the east side of the river. He was ordered to have the works at the Point completed as expeditiously as possible and to keep all posts on guard against surprise.

Having made these arrangements, Washington recrossed to the west side of the Hudson and took post at Tappan, opposite Dobbs Ferry, to be at hand for any attempt upon New York.

The execution of this cherished design, however, was again postponed by intelligence that the second division of the French reinforcements was blockaded in the harbor of Brest by the British. Washington still had hopes that it might be carried into effect by the aid of the squadron of the Count de Guichen from the West Indies or of a fleet from Cadiz.

At this critical juncture, an embarrassing derangement took place in the quartermaster-general's department, of which General Greene was the head. The reorganization of this department had long been in agitation. A system had been digested by Washington, Schuyler and Greene, adapted, as they thought, to the situation of the country. Congress devised a different scheme, which Greene considered likely to be attended with calamitous results; he therefore tendered his resignation. Washington endeavored to prevent its being accepted. The tone and manner, however, assumed by Greene in offering his resignation were deeply offensive to Congress. His resignation was promptly accepted; there was talk even of suspending him from his command in the line.

Colonel Pickering was appointed to succeed Greene as quartermaster-general but the latter continued for some time, at the request of Washington, to aid in conducting the business of the department. Pickering acquitted himself in his new office with zeal, talents and integrity but there were radical defects in the system which defied all ability and exertion.

The commissariat was equally in a state of derangement. In his emergencies Washington was forced to empty the magazines at West Point. These afforded but temporary relief; scarcity continued to prevail to a distressing degree. The anxiety of Washington at this moment of embarrassment was heightened by the receipt of disastrous intelligence from the South.

Lord Cornwallis, when left in military command at the south by Sir Henry Clinton, was charged with the invasion of North Carolina. It was an enterprise in which much difficulty was to be apprehended. The original settlers, mostly men who had experienced political or religious oppression, had brought with them a stern appreciation of their rights and an indomitable spirit of freedom and independence.

It was this spirit which gave rise to the confederacy, called the Regulation, formed to withstand the abuses of power. The first blood shed in our country in resistance to arbitrary taxation was in North Carolina in a conflict between the regulators and Governor Tryon. Above all, at Mecklenburg, in the heart of North Carolina, was fulminated the first declaration of independence of the British crown, a year before a like declaration by Congress.

A population so characterized presented formidable difficulties to the invader. The physical difficulties arising from the nature of the country consisted in its mountain fastnesses in the north-western part, its vast forests, its sterile tracts, its long rivers, destitute of bridges and which, though fordable in fair weather, were liable to be swollen by sudden storms and rendered deep, turbulent and impassable.

Cornwallis forbore to attempt the invasion of North Carolina until the summer heat should be over and the harvest gathered in. In the mean time he disposed his troops to cover the frontiers of South Carolina and Georgia and maintain internal quiet. The command of the frontiers was given by him to Lord Rawdon, who made Camden his principal post. This town, situated on the east bank of the Wateree River on the road leading to North Carolina, was to be the grand military depot for the projected campaign. Cornwallis set up his head-quarters at Charleston, where he occupied himself in regulating the civil and commercial affairs of the province, in organizing the militia of the lower districts, and in forwarding provisions and munitions of war to Camden.

The proclamation of Sir Henry putting an end to all neutrality had for a time quelled the spirit of the country. By degrees, however, the dread of British power gave way to impatience of British exactions. Symptoms of revolt were encouraged by intelligence that DeKalb was advancing through North Carolina at the head of 2000 men and that the militia of that State and of Virginia were joining his standard. This was soon followed by tidings that Gates was on his way to take command of the Southern forces.

The prospect of such aid from the North reanimated the Southern patriots. One of the most eminent of these was Thomas Sumter, who had served against the Indians in his boyhood during the French war, had been present at the defeat of Braddock, and in the present war held the rank of lieutenant-colonel of riflemen in the Continental line. After the fall of Charleston, when patriots took refuge in the natural fastnesses of the country, he had retired with his family into one of the latter. A handful of his fellow-sufferers who had taken refuge in North Carolina chose him as a leader and resolved on a desperate struggle for the deliverance of their native State.

When Sumter led this gallant band of exiles over the border, he attacked and routed a well-armed body of British troops and tories, the terror of the frontier. His followers supplied themselves with weapons from the slain. In a little while his band was augmented by recruits. Parties of militia, also, recently under the compelling measures of Cornwallis, deserted to the patriot standard. Thus reinforced to the amount of 600 men, he made, on the 30th of July, a spirited attack on the British post at Rocky Mount, near the Catawba, but was repulsed. A more successful attack was made by him eight days afterwards on another post at Hanging Rock. The regiment which defended it was nearly annihilated and a large body of loyalists was routed and dispersed. The gallant exploits of Sumter were emulated in other parts of the country; the partisan war thus commenced soon obliged the enemy to call in their outposts and collect their troops in large masses.

The advance of De Kalb with reinforcements from the North had been retarded by various difficulties, the most important of which was want of provisions. This had been especially the case since his arrival in North Carolina. His troops were reduced for a time to short allowance and, on the 6th of July, brought to a positive halt at Deep River. The North Carolina militia under General Caswell were already on the road to Camden, beyond the Pedee River. He was anxious to form a junction with them and with some Virginia troops under Colonel Porterfield, but a wide and sterile region lay between him and them, difficult to be traversed unless magazines were established in advance or he were supplied with provisions to take with him. For three weeks he remained in this encampment, foraging an exhausted country for a meagre subsistence, when, on the 25th of July, Gates arrived at the camp.

The baron received him with the ceremony and deference due to a superior officer who was to take the command. Gates, at the first review of the troops, to the astonishment of the baron, gave orders for them to hold themselves in readiness to march at a moment's warning. It was in vain the destitute situation of the troops was represented to him. His reply was that waggons laden with supplies were coming on and would overtake them in two days.

On the 27th, he put the army in motion over the Buffalo Ford, on the direct road to Camden. Colonel Williams, the adjutant-general of De Kalb, warned him of the sterile nature of that route, but Gates persisted in taking the direct route, observing that he should the sooner form a junction with Caswell and the North Carolina militia; as to the sterility of the country, his supplies would soon overtake him. The route proved all that had been represented. The supplies never overtook him. His army had to subsist itself on lean cattle, green Indian corn, unripe apples, and peaches. The consequence was a distressing prevalence of dysentery.

Having crossed the Pedee River on the 3d of August, the army was joined by a handful of Virginia regulars under Porterfield; and, on the 7th, the much-desired junction took place with the North Carolina militia. On the 13th they encamped at Rugeley's Mills, otherwise called Clermont, 12 miles from Camden, and on the following day were reinforced by a brigade of 700 Virginia militia under Stevens.

On the approach of Gates, Rawdon concentrated his forces at Camden. The post was flanked by the Wateree River and Pine-tree Creek and strengthened with redoubts. Cornwallis hastened hither from Charleston on learning that affairs in this quarter were drawing to a crisis and arrived on the 13th. The British effective force thus collected was more than 2000, including officers. About 500 were militia and tory refugees from North Carolina. The forces under Gates, according to the return of his adjutant-general, were 3052 fit for duty; more than two-thirds of them, however, were militia.

On the 14th, Gates received an express from Sumter who, harassing the enemy at various points, was endeavoring to cut off their supplies from Charleston. The object of the express was to ask a reinforcement of regulars to aid him in capturing a large convoy of clothing, ammunition and stores on its way to the garrison and which would pass Wateree Ferry, about a mile from Camden.

Gates accordingly detached Colonel Woolford of the Maryland line, with 100 regulars, a party of artillery, and two brass field-pieces. On the same evening he moved with his main force to take post at a deep stream 7 miles from Camden, intending to attack Rawdon or his redoubts should he march out to repel Sumter.

By a singular coincidence, Cornwallis on the very same evening sallied forth from Camden to attack the American camp at Clermont. About two o'clock at night, the two forces blundered on each other about half way. A skirmish took place between their advanced guards in which Porterfield of the Virginia regulars was mortally wounded. Some prisoners were taken on either side. From these the respective commanders learnt the nature of the forces each had stumbled upon. Both halted, formed their troops for action, but deferred further hostilities until daylight.

Gates was astounded at being told that the enemy at hand was Cornwallis with 3000 men. Calling a council of war, he demanded what was best to be done? For a moment there was blank silence, broken by Stevens of the Virginia militia with the question, "Gentlemen, is it not too late now to do any thing but fight?" No other advice was asked or offered and all were required to repair to their commands.

In forming the line, the first Maryland division, including the Delawares, was on the right, commanded by De Kalb. The Virginia militia under Stevens were on the left. Caswell with the North Carolinians formed the centre. The artillery was in battery on the road. Each flank was covered by a marsh. The second Maryland brigade formed a reserve a few hundred yards in rear of the first.

At daybreak (Aug. 16th), the enemy were descried advancing in column; they appeared to be displaying to the right. The deputy adjutant-general ordered the artillery to open a fire upon them and then rode to Gates to inform him of the cause of the firing. Gates ordered Stevens to advance briskly with his brigade of Virginia militia and attack them while in the act of displaying. No sooner did Stevens receive the order than he put his brigade in motion, but discovered that the right wing of the enemy was already in line. The British rushed on, shouting and firing. The inexperienced militia, dismayed by this impetuous assault, threw down their muskets and fled. The panic spread to the North Carolina militia. Part of them made a temporary stand but soon joined with the rest in flight, rendered headlong and disastrous by the pursuit of Tarleton and his cavalry.

Gates, seconded by his officers, made several attempts to rally the militia but was borne along with them. Supposing that the regular troops were dispersed like the militia, Gates gave all up for lost and retreated from the field.

The regulars, however, had not given way. The Maryland brigades and the Delaware regiment stood their ground and bore the brunt of the battle. Though repeatedly broken, they as often rallied. At length a charge of Tarleton's cavalry on their flank drove them into the woods and swamps. None showed more gallantry on this disastrous day than de Kalb; he fought on foot with the second Maryland brigade and fell exhausted after receiving eleven wounds. His aide-de-camp supported him in his arms and was repeatedly wounded in protecting him. He announced the rank and nation of his general and both were taken prisoners. De Kalb died in the course of a few days.

Gates had hoped to rally a sufficient force at Clermont to cover the retreat of the regulars but the further they fled, the more the militia were dispersed, until the generals were abandoned by all but their aids. To add to the mortification of Gates, he learned that Sumter had been completely successful and, having reduced the enemy's redoubt on the Wateree, was marching off with his booty on the opposite side of that river. Gates sent orders to him to retire in the best manner he could, while he himself proceeded with Caswell towards Charlotte, about 60 miles distant.

Cornwallis was apprehensive that Sumter's corps might form a rallying point to the routed army. On the morning of the 17th of August, therefore, he detached Tarleton in pursuit with a body of cavalry and light infantry, about 350 strong. Sumter was retreating up the western side of the Wateree, much encumbered by his spoils and prisoners. Tarleton pushed up by forced and concealed marches on the eastern side. At dusk Tarleton descried the fires of the American camp about a mile from the opposite shore. In the morning his sentries gave word that the Americans were quitting their encampment. Tarleton crossed the Wateree; the infantry with a three-pounder passed in boats; the cavalry swam their horses where the river was not fordable. The delay in crossing and the diligence of Sumter's march increased the distance between the pursuers and the pursued. Tarleton pushed on with about 100 dragoons, the freshest and most able. As he entered a valley, a discharge of small-arms from a thicket tumbled a dragoon from his saddle. A sergeant and five dragoons rode up to the summit of a neighboring hill to reconnoitre. Crouching on their horses they made signs to Tarleton. He cautiously approached the crest of the hill and beheld the American camp on a neighboring height, apparently in a most negligent condition. Sumter, his patrols having scoured the road without discovering any signs of an enemy, considered himself secure from surprise. The troops, having for the last four days been almost without food or sleep, were now indulged in complete relaxation.

Tarleton prepared for instant attack. His cavalry and infantry dashed forward and, before the Americans could recover from their surprise, got between them and the parade ground on which the muskets were stacked. All was confusion and consternation in the American camp. There was skirmishing in various quarters but in a little while there was a universal flight to the river and the woods. Sumter with about 350 of his men effected a retreat.

Gates, joined by some fugitives from his army, continued on to Hillsborough, 180 miles from Camden, where he endeavored to rally his scattered forces. His regular troops, however, were little more than 1000 and, as to the militia, they had dispersed to their homes.

It was not until the beginning of September that Washington received word of the disastrous reverse at Camden. It was evident to Washington that the course of war must ultimately tend to the Southern States, yet the situation in the North did not permit him to detach sufficient force for their relief. All that he could do for the present was to endeavor to hold the enemy in check in that quarter. For this purpose he gave orders that some regular troops enlisted in Maryland for the war and intended for the main army should be sent southward. He wrote to Governor Rutledge of South Carolina (12th September) to raise a permanent, compact, well-organized body of troops instead of depending upon a numerous army of militia. He was still more urgent in his letters to the President of Congress (Sept. 15th). "Regular troops alone," said he, "are equal to the exigencies of modern war, . . . No militia will ever acquire the habits necessary to resist a regular force."

He had scarce written the foregoing when he received a letter from Gates, dated at Hillsborough, Aug. 30th and Sept. 3d. No longer vaunting and vainglorious, he pleads nothing but his patriotism. The appeal he makes to Washington's magnanimity to support him in this day of his reverse is the highest testimonial he could give to the exalted character of the man whom he once affected to underrate and aspired to supplant. Washington in his reply, while he acknowledged the shock caused by the first account of the unexpected event, did credit to the behavior of the Continental troops. "It would add no good purpose," writes he, "to take a position near the enemy while you are so far inferior in force."

Washington still cherished the idea of a combined attack upon New York as soon as a French naval force should arrive. The destruction of the enemy here would relieve this part of the Union from an internal war and enable its troops and resources to be united with those of France in vigorous efforts against the common enemy elsewhere. Hearing that de Guichen, with his West India squadron, was approaching the coast, Washington prepared to proceed to Hartford in Connecticut, to confer with Rochambeau and Ternay on a plan for future operations, of which the attack on New York was to form the principal feature.

The Shadow of Treason
[1780]

We now enter upon a sad episode of our revolutionary history—the treason of Arnold. Of the military skill, enterprise, and courage of this man, ample evidence has been given in the foregoing pages. Of the confidence reposed in his patriotism by Washington, sufficient proof is manifested in the command with which he was entrusted. But Arnold, at the very time of seeking that command, had been for months in traitorous correspondence with the enemy.

The first idea of proving recreant to the cause he had vindicated so bravely appears to have entered his mind when the charges preferred against him by the council of Pennsylvania were referred by Congress to a court-martial. Before that time he had been incensed against Pennsylvania; now his wrath was excited against his country, which appeared so insensible to his services. Disappointment in regard to the settlement of his accounts added to his irritation and resentment and he began to think how, while he wreaked vengeance on his country, he might do it with advantage to his fortunes. With this view he commenced a correspondence with Sir Henry Clinton under the signature of Gustavus, representing himself as a person of importance in the American service who was desirous of joining the cause of Great Britain, could he be certain of personal security and indemnification for whatever loss of property he might sustain. His letters occasionally communicated articles of intelligence which proved true and induced Sir Henry to keep up the correspondence, conducted on his part by his aide-de-camp, Major John André, under the signature of John Anderson.

Months elapsed before Sir Henry discovered who was his secret correspondent. Even after discovering it he did not hold out strong inducements to Arnold for desertion. The latter was out of command and had nothing to offer but his services.

In the mean time the circumstances of Arnold were daily becoming more desperate. Debts were accumulating, and creditors becoming more and more importunate. The public reprimand he had received filled his heart with bitterness. His desperate decision was to get some important command, the betrayal of which to the enemy might obtain for him a munificent reward. Such certainly was the secret of his eagerness to obtain command of West Point, the great object of British and American solicitude, on the possession of which were supposed by many to hinge the fortunes of war.

He took command of the post and its dependencies about the beginning of August, fixing his head-quarters at Beverley, a country-seat below West Point on the eastern side of the river. It was commonly called the Robinson House, having formerly belonged to Washington's early friend, Colonel Beverley Robinson, who had obtained a large part of the Phillipse estate in this neighborhood by marrying one of the heiresses. Robinson, a royalist, had entered into the British service and was now residing in New York; Beverley with its surrounding lands had been confiscated.

From this place Arnold carried on a secret correspondence with Major André. Their letters, in disguised hands and under the names of Gustavus and John Anderson, purported to treat merely of commercial operations, but the real matter in negotiation was the betrayal of West Point and the Highlands. This stupendous piece of treachery was to be consummated at the time when Washington, with the main body of his army, would be drawn down towards

King's Bridge and the French troops landed on Long Island, in the projected co-operation against New York. At such time, a flotilla under Rodney, having on board a large land force, was to ascend the Hudson to the Highlands, which would be surrendered by Arnold almost without opposition under pretext of insufficient force to make resistance. The immediate result of this surrender, it was anticipated, would be the defeat of the combined attempt upon New York; its ultimate effect might be the dismemberment of the Union and the dislocation of the whole American scheme of warfare.

His correspondence had now done its part; for completion of the plan and adjustment of the traitor's recompense, a personal meeting was necessary between Arnold and André. It was arranged that the meeting should take place on neutral ground, near the American out-posts at Dobbs Ferry on the 11th of September at 12 o'clock. André attended at the appointed place and time, accompanied by Robinson, who was acquainted with the plot. An application of the latter for the restoration of his confiscated property in the Highlands seems to have been used as a blind in these proceedings.

Arnold had passed the preceding night at the residence of Joshua Hett Smith, on the west side of the Hudson in Haverstraw Bay. He set off thence in his barge for the place of rendezvous but, not being protected by a flag, was fired upon and pursued by British guard-boats stationed near Dobbs Ferry. He took refuge at an American post on the western shore, whence he returned in the night to his quarters in the Robinson House.

New arrangements were made for an interview but it was postponed until after Washington should depart for Hartford to hold the proposed conference with Rochambeau and the other French officers. In the mean time, the British sloop of war, Vulture, anchored a few miles below Teller's Point to be at hand in aid of the negotiation. On board was Robinson who, pretending to believe that Putnam still commanded in the Highlands, addressed a note to him requesting an interview on the subject of his confiscated property. This letter he sent by a flag, enclosed in one addressed to Arnold, soliciting of him the same boon should Putnam be absent.

H.B Hall

MAJOR JOHN ANDRE

Major Andre

(From a Miniature by himself)

NEW YORK . G. P. PUTNAM

On the 18th Sept., Washington crossed the Hudson in Arnold's barge on his way to Hartford. Arnold accompanied him as far as Peekskill and on the way laid before him the letter of Colonel Robinson and asked his advice. Washington disapproved of any such interview, observing that civil authorities alone had cognizance of questions of confiscated property.

Arnold now openly sent a flag on board of the Vulture as if bearing a reply to the letter he had communicated to the commander-in-chief. By this occasion he informed Robinson that a person with a boat and flag would be alongside of the Vulture on the night of the 20th and that any matter he might wish to communicate would be laid before Washington on the following Saturday, when he might be expected back from Newport.

On the information thus conveyed, André proceeded up the Hudson on the 20th and went on board of the Vulture, where he found Robinson and expected to meet Arnold. The latter, however, had made other arrangements, probably with a view to his personal security. About half-past eleven, of a still and starlight night (the 21st), a boat was descried from on board, rowed by two men with muffled oars. She was hailed by an officer on watch and a man, seated in the stern, gave out that they were from King's Ferry, bound to Dobbs Ferry. Ordered on board, he proved to be Joshua Hett Smith, whom Arnold had prevailed upon to board the Vulture and bring a person from New York with important intelligence. He had made him the bearer of a letter addressed to Robinson. "This will be delivered to you by Mr. Smith, who will conduct you to a place of safety. Neither Mr. Smith nor any other person shall be made acquainted with your proposals; if they (which I doubt not) are of such a nature that I can officially take notice of them, I shall do it with pleasure. I take it for granted Colonel Robinson will not propose any thing that is not for the interest of the United States as well as of himself." All this use of Robinson's name was intended as a blind should the letter be intercepted.

Robinson introduced André to Smith as John Anderson, who was to go in his place (he being unwell) to Arnold. André wore a blue great coat which covered his uniform and Smith always declared that at the time he was totally ignorant of his name and military character. André, embarking in the boat with Smith, was rowed to the western side of the river, about 6 miles below Stony Point, at the foot of a shadowy mountain called the Long Clove.

Arnold had come hither on horseback from Smith's house, attended by one of Smith's servants, likewise mounted. The midnight negotiation between André and Arnold was carried on in darkness among the trees. Smith remained in the boat and the servant drew off to a distance with the horses. One hour after another passed away, when Smith gave warning that it was near daybreak and the boat would be discovered.

The nefarious bargain was not yet completed and Arnold feared the sight of a boat going to the Vulture might cause suspicion. He prevailed therefore upon André to remain until the following night and André, mounting the servant's horse, set off with Arnold for Smith's house.

They had scarcely arrived at Smith's house when the booming of cannon was heard from down the river. It gave André uneasiness, with reason. Livingston, who commanded at Verplanck's Point, learning that the Vulture lay within shot of Teller's Point, had sent a party with cannon to that point in the night and they were now firing upon the sloop of war. André watched the cannonade from an upper window of Smith's house and saw the vessel drop down the river out of reach of cannon shot.

After breakfast, the plot for the betrayal of West Point and its dependent posts was adjusted and the sum agreed upon that Arnold was to receive should it be successful. André was furnished with plans of the works and explanatory papers, which he placed between his stockings and his feet, promising, in case of accident, to destroy them.

All matters being thus arranged, Arnold prepared to return in his own barge to his head-quarters at the Robinson House. As the Vulture had shifted her ground, he suggested to André a return to New York by land as most safe and expeditious; the latter, however, insisted upon being put on board of the sloop of war on the ensuing night. Arnold consented but, to provide against the possible necessity of a return by land, he gave André the following pass, dated from the Robinson House:

Permit Mr. John Anderson to pass the guards to the White Plains, or below if he chooses; he being on public business by my direction.

B. Arnold, M. Genl.

Smith also, who was to accompany him, was furnished with passports to proceed either by water or by land.

Arnold departed about ten o'clock. André passed a lonely day, casting many a wistful look toward the Vulture. As evening approached he spoke to Smith about departure. To his surprise he found Smith, fearing for his own safety in getting André to the Vulture, had discharged his boatmen, who had gone home. He offered, however, to cross the river with André at King's Ferry, put him in the way of returning to New York by land, and accompany him some distance on horseback.

André was in an agony at finding himself forced within the American lines but there seemed to be no alternative and he prepared for the journey. He wore, as we have noted, a military coat under a long blue surtout; he was now persuaded to lay it aside and put on a citizen's coat of Smith's, thus adding disguise to the other hazardous circumstances of the case.

It was about sunset when André and Smith crossed to Verplanck's Point. After proceeding about 8 miles on the road toward White Plains, they were stopped by a patrolling party. The captain of it warned them against proceeding further in the night. Cow Boys from the British lines had recently marauded the neighborhood. Smith's fears were again excited and André was obliged to yield to them. A bed was furnished them in a neighboring house, where André passed an anxious night under the very eye, as it were, of an American patrol. At daybreak he awoke Smith, and hurried their departure.

They were now approaching that part of the country, the "Neutral Ground," extending north and south about 30 miles, between the British and American lines—a beautiful region of forest-clad hills, fertile valleys, and abundant streams, now almost desolated by the scourings of Skinners and Cow Boys, the former professing allegiance to the American cause, the latter to the British, but both arrant marauders.

About two and a half miles from Pine's Bridge, on the Croton-River, André and his companion parted, Smith to return home, André to pursue his journey to New York. His spirits were cheerful for, having got beyond the patrols, he considered the most perilous part of his route accomplished.

About 6 miles beyond Pine's Bridge he came to a place where the road forked, the left branch leading toward White Plains, the right inclining toward the Hudson. He had originally intended to take the left-hand road, the other being said to be infested by Cow Boys. These, however, were not apprehended by him and since the road led more directly to New York, he took his course along the river road.

He had not proceeded far when a man stepped out from the trees, levelled a musket and brought him to a stand while two other men, similarly armed, showed themselves prepared to second their comrade.

The man who had first stepped out wore a refugee uniform. At sight of it André's heart leapt; he felt himself secure and exclaimed eagerly: "Gentlemen, I hope you belong to our party?" "What party?" was asked. "The lower party," said André. "We do," was the reply. André declared himself to be a British officer and that he had been up the country on particular business and must not be detained a single moment. To his consternation, the supposed refugee now avowed himself and his companions to be Americans and told André he was their prisoner!

The sacking and burning of Young's House and carrying of its defenders into captivity had roused the spirit of the Neutral Ground. The yeomanry had turned out to intercept freebooters from the British lines, who might be returning to the city with their spoils. One of these parties, composed of seven men of the neighborhood, had divided itself. Four took post on a hill above Sleepy Hollow to watch the road which crossed the country; the other three, John Paulding, Isaac Van Wart, and David Williams, stationed themselves on the road parallel to the Hudson.

The Shadow of Treason (1780)

The one in refugee garb who brought André to a stand was John Paulding, a stout-hearted youngster who, like most of the young men of this outraged neighborhood, had been repeatedly in arms to repel aggressions and now belonged to the militia. He had twice been captured and confined in the loathsome military prisons in New York; both times he had made his escape, the last time only four days previous to the event of which we are treating. The ragged refugee coat, which had deceived André, had been given to Paulding by one of his captors, in exchange for a good yeoman garment of which they stripped him. This slight circumstance produced the whole discovery of the treason.

André, recovering his self-possession, endeavored to pass off his previous account of himself as a mere subterfuge. He now declared himself a Continental officer going to Dobbs Ferry to get information from below; so saying he showed them the pass of General Arnold.

This, in the first instance, would have been sufficient but his unwary tongue had ruined him. The suspicions of his captors were completely roused. Seizing the bridle of his horse, they ordered him to dismount.

Paulding asked whether he had any letters about him. He answered, no. They proceeded to search him, found 80 dollars in Continental money but nothing to warrant suspicion and were disposed to let him proceed when Paulding exclaimed: "Boys, I am not satisfied—his boots must come off."

At this André changed color. His boots, he said, came off with difficulty and he begged he might not be subjected to the inconvenience and delay. His remonstrances were in vain. He was obliged to sit down; his boots were drawn off and the concealed papers discovered. Hastily scanning them, Paulding exclaimed, "My God! He is a spy!"

He demanded of André where he had gotten these papers.

"Of a man at Pine's Bridge, a stranger to me," was the reply.

While dressing himself, André endeavored to ransom himself from his captors, rising from one offer to another. He would give any reward they might name in goods or money and would remain with two of their party while one went to New York to get it. Here

Paulding declared with an oath, that if he would give 10,000 guineas he should not stir one step.

The unfortunate André now submitted to his fate and the captors set off with their prisoner for North Castle, the nearest American post, distant 10 or 12 miles. Lieutenant-colonel Jameson, who was in command there, recognized the handwriting of Arnold in the papers found upon André and, perceiving that they were of a dangerous nature, sent them off by express to General Washington at Hartford.

André, still adhering to his assumed name, begged that the commander at West Point be informed that John Anderson, though bearing his passport, was detained. Jameson wrote to Arnold, stating the circumstances of the arrest and that the papers found upon the prisoner had been despatched to the commander-in-chief; at the same time, he sent the prisoner himself, under a strong guard, to accompany the letter.

Shortly afterwards, Major Tallmadge, next in command to Jameson, arrived at North Castle, having been absent on duty to White Plains. When the circumstances of the case were related to him, he at once suspected treachery on the part of Arnold. At his earnest entreaties, an express was sent after the officer who had André in charge, ordering him to bring the latter back to Noth Castle but, by singular perversity or obtuseness in judgment, Jameson neglected to countermand the letter he had written to Arnold.

André was brought back and Tallmadge saw at once by his air and movements that he was a military man. By his advice and under his escort, the prisoner was conducted to Colonel Sheldon's post at Lower Salem as more secure than North Castle.

Here André, being told that the papers found upon his person had been forwarded to Washington, addressed to him immediately the following lines:

   "I beg your Excellency will be persuaded that . . . the step of addressing you . . . is to secure myself from the imputation of having assumed a mean character for treacherous purposes or self-interest. . . . The person in your possession is Major John André, adjutant-general of the British Army. The influence of one commander in the army of his adversary is an advantage taken in war. . . . I agreed to meet upon ground not within the posts of either army a person who was to give me intelligence. I came up in the Vulture for this effect and was fetched from the shore to the beach. Being there, I was told that the approach of day would prevent my return and that I must be concealed until the next night. I was in my regimentals and had fairly risked my person. Against my stipulation, my intention, and without my knowledge beforehand, I was conducted within one of your posts. Thus was I betrayed into the vile condition of an enemy within your posts. . . . The request I have made to your Excellency . . . is, that in any rigor policy may dictate, a decency of conduct towards me may mark, that, though unfortunate, I am branded with nothing dishonorable. . . ."

On the very day that the treasonable conference between Arnold and André took place, Washington had his interview with the French officers at Hartford. It led to no important result. Intelligence was received that the squadron of de Guichen, on which they had relied to give them superiority by sea, had sailed for Europe. This disconcerted their plans and Washington, in consequence, set out two or three days sooner than had been anticipated on his return to his head-quarters on the Hudson. He was accompanied by Lafayette and Knox and, part of the way, by Count Matthew Dumas, aide-de-camp to Rochambeau.

On approaching the Hudson Washington took a more circuitous route than the one he had originally intended, striking the river at Fishkill just above the Highlands that he might visit West Point and show the marquis the works which had been erected there during his absence in France. Circumstances detained them a night at Fishkill. Their baggage was sent on to Arnold's quarters in the Robinson House, with a message that they would breakfast there the next day. In the morning (Sept. 24th) they were in the saddle before break of day, having a ride to make of 18 miles through the mountains.

When within a mile of the Robinson House, Washington turned down a cross road leading to the banks of the Hudson. Lafayette apprised him that he was going out of the way. "Ah, marquis!" replied he good humoredly, "you young men are all in love with Mrs. Arnold. Go and breakfast with her and tell her not to wait for me. I must ride down and examine the redoubts on this side of the river but will be with her shortly."

The marquis and Knox, however, turned off and accompanied him down to the redoubts, while Hamilton and Lafayette's aide-de-camp continued along the main road to the Robinson House.

The family with the two aides-de-camp sat down to breakfast. Mrs. Arnold was bright and amiable as usual. Arnold was silent and gloomy. This was the day appointed for the consummation of the plot, when the enemy's ships were to ascend the river. The return of the commander-in-chief from the East two days sooner than had been anticipated and his proposed visit to the forts threatened to disconcert every thing. An interval of fearful imaginings was soon brought to a direful close. In the midst of the repast a horseman alighted, bearing Jameson's letter to Arnold, stating the capture of André and that dangerous papers found on him had been forwarded to Washington.

Controlling the dismay that must have smitten him to the heart, he beckoned Mrs. Arnold from the breakfast table, signifying a wish to speak with her in private. When alone with her in her room up stairs, he announced in hurried words that he was a ruined man and must instantly fly for his life! Overcome by the shock, she fell senseless on the floor. Without pausing to aid her, he hurried down stairs, returned to the breakfast room, and informed his guests that he must haste to West Point to prepare for the reception of the commander-in-chief. Mounting the horse of the messenger, which stood saddled at the door, he galloped down where his six-oared barge was moored. Throwing himself into it, he ordered his men to pull out into the middle of the river and then made down with all speed for Teller's Point.

Washington arrived at the Robinson House shortly after the flight of the traitor. Being informed that Mrs. Arnold was in her room, unwell, and that Arnold had gone to West Point to receive him, he took a hasty breakfast and repaired to the fortress, leaving word that he would return to dinner.

In crossing the river he noticed that no salute was fired from the fort nor was there any preparation to receive him on his landing. Colonel Lamb, the officer in command, manifested surprise at seeing him, and apologized for this want of military ceremony, by assuring him he had not been apprised of his intended visit.

"Is not General Arnold here?" demanded Washington.

"No, sir. He has not been here for two days past nor have I heard from him in that time."

This was strange and perplexing but no sinister suspicion entered Washington's mind. He remained at the Point throughout the morning inspecting the fortifications.

In the mean time, the messenger whom Jameson had despatched to Hartford with a letter covering the papers taken on André arrived at the Robinson House. He had learnt, while on the way to Hartford, that Washington had left that place, whereupon he turned to overtake him but missed him in consequence of the general's change of route. Coming by the lower road, the messenger had passed through Salem, where André was confined, and brought with him the letter written to the commander-in-chief. These letters were opened and read by Hamilton, as Washington's aide-de-camp and confidential officer. He maintained silence as to their contents, met Washington as he and his companions were coming up from the river on their return from West Point, spoke to him a few words in a low voice, and they retired together into the house. Taking Knox and Lafayette aside, Washington communicated to them the intelligence and placed the papers in their hands. "Whom can we trust now?" was his only comment.

Conjecturing the direction of Arnold's flight, he despatched Hamilton on horseback with all speed to Verplanck's Point, with orders to the commander to intercept Arnold should he not already have passed that post.

In the mean time, Arnold, panic-stricken, had sped his flight through the Highlands. He passed through the Highlands in safety but there were the batteries at Verplanck's Point yet to fear. Fortunately for him, Hamilton, with the order for his arrest, had not arrived there.

His barge was known by the garrison. A white handkerchief displayed gave it the sanction of a flag of truce; it was suffered to pass without question, and the traitor effected his escape to the Vulture anchored a few miles below.

Hamilton returned to the Robinson House and reported the escape of the traitor. He brought two letters also to Washington, which had been sent on shore from the Vulture under a flag of truce. One was from Arnold, in which he wrote: "I ask no favor for myself. I have too often experienced the ingratitude of my country to attempt it; but, from the known humanity of your Excellency, I am induced to ask your protection for Mrs. Arnold from every insult and injury that a mistaken vengeance of my country may expose her to. It ought to fall only on me; she is as good and as innocent as an angel and is incapable of doing wrong. I beg she may be permitted to return to her friends in Philadelphia or to come to me as she may choose; from your Excellency I have no fears on her account but she may suffer from the mistaken fury of the country."

The other letter was from Robinson, interceding for the release of André on the plea that he was on shore under the sanction of a flag of truce at the request of Arnold.

Notwithstanding Washington's apparent tranquillity and real self-possession, it was a time of appalling distrust. Arnold knew every thing about the posts: might he not persuade the enemy to attempt a coup de main? Washington instantly despatched a letter to Colonel Wade, who was in temporary command at West Point. "General Arnold is gone to the enemy," writes he. ". . . I request that you will be as vigilant as possible, and as the enemy may have it in contemplation to attempt some enterprise, even to-night, against these posts, I wish you to make, immediately after the receipt of this, the best disposition you can of your force so as to have a proportion of men in each work on the west side of the river."

A regiment stationed in the Highlands was ordered to the same duty, as well as a body of the Massachusetts militia from Fishkill. Washington wrote to Greene, who in his absence, commanded the army at Tappan, urging him to put the left division in motion as soon as possible with orders to proceed to King's Ferry where, or before they should arrive there, they would be met with further orders.

His next thought was about André. On the same evening, therefore, Washington wrote to Jameson, charging that every precaution should be taken to prevent André from making his escape. "That he may be less liable to be recaptured by the enemy, who will no doubt make every effort to regain him, he had better be conducted to this place by some upper road, rather than by the route of Crompond."

In the mean time, Mrs. Arnold remained in her room in a state bordering on frenzy. Washington regarded her with the sincerest commiseration, acquitting her of all previous knowledge of her husband's guilt. He informed her that he had done all that depended upon himself to have him arrested but, not having succeeded, he experienced a pleasure in assuring her of his safety. During the brief time she remained at the Robinson House she was treated with the utmost deference and delicacy but soon set off, under a passport of Washington, for her father's house in Philadelphia.

On the 26th of September, the day after the treason of Arnold had been revealed to Washington, André arrived at the Robinson House, having been brought under escort and in charge of Major Tallmadge. Washington made many inquiries of the major but declined to have the prisoner brought into his presence. The same evening he transmitted him to West Point and, shortly afterwards, Joshua Smith, who had likewise been arrested. Still, not considering them secure even there, he determined on the following day to send them on to the camp. Major Tallmadge continued to have charge of André. Early on the morning of the 28th, the prisoners were embarked in a barge to be conveyed from West Point to King's Ferry.

After disembarking at King's Ferry near Stony Point, they set off for Tappan under the escort of a body of horse. André, who rode beside Tallmadge, became solicitous to know the opinion of the latter as to what would be the result of his capture. Tallmadge evaded the question as long as possible but, being urged to a reply, gave it in the following words. "I had a much-loved classmate in Yale College, by the name of Nathan Hale, who entered the army in 1775. Immediately after the battle of Long Island, General Washington wanted information respecting the strength, position, and probable movements of the enemy. Captain Hale tendered his services, went over to Brooklyn and was taken just as he was passing the outposts of the enemy on his return. Do you remember the sequel of the story?"

"Yes," said André, "He was hanged as a spy! But you surely do not consider his case and mine alike?" "Yes, precisely similar, and similar will be your fate."

The capture of André caused a great sensation at New York. He was universally popular with the army and an especial favorite of Sir Henry Clinton. The latter addressed a letter to Washington on the 26th, claiming the release of André on the ground that he had visited Arnold at the request of that officer under the sanction of a flag of truce and that he had been stopped while travelling under Arnold's passports. The same letter inclosed one addressed by Arnold to Sir Henry, intended as a certificate of the innocence of André. "I commanded at the time at West Point," writes the renegade, "had an undoubted right to send my flag of truce to Major André, who came to me under that protection, and, having held conversation with him, I delivered him confidential papers in my own handwriting to deliver to your Excellency. . . . All which I had then a right to do, being in the actual service of America, under the orders of General Washington and commanding-general at West Point and its dependencies."

Neither the official demand of Sir Henry Clinton nor the impudent certificate of Arnold had any effect on the steady mind of Washington. He determined to refer the case to a board of general officers, which he convened on the 29th of September, the day after his arrival at Tappan. It was composed of six major-generals, Greene, Stirling, St. Clair, Lafayette, R. Howe, and Steuben, and eight brigadiers, Parsons, James Clinton, Knox, Glover, Paterson, Hand, Huntingdon, and Stark. Greene, who was well versed in military law, was president and Colonel John Lawrence judge advocate-general.

The report of the board briefly stated the circumstances of the case and concluded with the opinion that Major André ought to be considered a spy from the enemy and, agreeably to the law and usage of nations, ought to suffer death.

Even in this situation of gathering horrors, André thought of others more than of himself. "There is only one thing that disturbs

WASHINGTON'S HEAD QUARTERS AT TAPPAN.

(The house where André was tried)

NEW YORK G.P. PUTNAM & CO.

Printed by W. Pate.

my tranquillity," said he to Hamilton. "Sir Henry Clinton has been too good to me. . . . I am bound to him by too many obligations and love him too well to bear the thought that he should reproach himself, or others should reproach him, on the supposition of my having conceived myself obliged, by his instructions, to run the risk I did. . . . I wish to be permitted to assure him that I did not act under this impression." His request was complied with, and he wrote a letter to Sir Henry Clinton to the above purport.

This letter accompanied one from Washington to Sir Henry Clinton, stating the report of the board of inquiry, omitting the sentence. "From these proceedings," observes he, "it is evident that Major André was employed in the execution of measures very foreign to the objects of flags of truce . . . and this gentleman confessed with the greatest candor . . . that it was impossible for him to suppose that he came on shore under the sanction of a flag."

Captain Aaron Ogden, a worthy officer of the New Jersey line, was selected by Washington to bear these despatches to the enemy's post at Paulus Hook, thence to be conveyed across the Hudson to New York. Before his departure, he called by Washington's request on the Marquis Lafayette, who gave him instructions to sound the officer commanding that post whether Sir Henry might be willing to deliver up Arnold in exchange for André. Ogden arrived at Paulus Hook in the evening and made the suggestion. The officer crossed the river before morning and communicated the matter to Sir Henry Clinton, but the latter instantly rejected the expedient as incompatible with honor and military principle.

The execution was to have taken place on the 1st of October but in the interim Washington received a second letter from Sir Henry Clinton, dated September 30th, expressing an opinion that the board of inquiry had not been rightly informed of all the circumstances and that he should send a commission on the following day to wait near Dobbs Ferry for permission to meet Washington, or such persons as he should appoint to converse with them on the subject. This letter caused a postponement of the execution and Greene was sent to meet the commissioners at Dobbs Ferry. They came up in the morning of the 1st of October in a schooner, with a flag of truce, accompanied by Beverley Robinson. A long conference took place without any agreement upon the issue. Greene returned to camp promising to report faithfully to Washington and to inform the commission of the result.

A letter also was delivered to Greene for Washington which Arnold had sent by the commissioners, in which the traitor asserted that "should André suffer the severity of their sentence, I shall think myself bound, by every tie of duty and honor, to retaliate on such unhappy persons of your army as may fall within my power." Beside this impudent and despicable letter, there was another from Arnold containing the farce of a resignation. The letters of Arnold were regarded with merited contempt.

Greene, in a brief letter to the British commission, stated that he had made full report to the commander-in-chief but that it had made no alteration in Washington's opinion and determination. It being announced to André that one o'clock on the following day was fixed on for his execution, he addressed a note to Washington in which he wrote, "Let me hope, sir, that if aught in my character impresses you with esteem towards me, if aught in my misfortunes marks me as the victim of policy and not of resentment, I shall experience the operation of these feelings in your breast by being informed that I am not to die on a gibbet."

Washington regarded the peculiar circumstances of the case: the insidious operations pursued to undermine the loyalty of one of his most trusted officers; the great evil which the treason would have effected; the uncertainty how far the enemy had carried, or might still be carrying, their scheme of corruption, for anonymous intimations spoke of treachery in other quarters. All these considerations pointed this out as a case in which a signal example was required.

Although André's request as to the mode of his death was not to be granted, it was thought best to let him remain in uncertainty on the subject; no answer, therefore, was returned to his note. On the morning of the 2d, he maintained a calm demeanor though all around him were gloomy and silent. He walked to the place of execution between two subaltern officers, arm in arm, with a serene countenance. When he came within sight of the gibbet, he appeared to be startled and inquired with emotion whether he was not to be shot. He was informed that the mode first appointed for his death could not be altered.

All things being ready, he stepped into the waggon. Taking off his hat and stock and opening his shirt collar, he adjusted the noose to his neck, after which he took out a handkerchief and tied it over his eyes. Being told by the officer in command that his arms must be bound, he drew out a second handkerchief with which they were pinioned. The waggon moved from under him and left him suspended. He died almost without a struggle. He remained suspended for half an hour, during which time a stillness prevailed over the surrounding multitude. His remains were interred within a few yards of the place of his execution, whence they were transferred to England in 1821 and buried in Westminster Abbey.

Joshua Smith, who aided in bringing André and Arnold together, was tried by a court-martial on a charge of participating in the treason but was acquitted, no proof appearing of his having had any knowledge of Arnold's plot.

Arnold was now made brigadier-general in the British service and put on an official level with honorable men who scorned to associate with the traitor. What golden reward he was to have received had his treason been successful is not known, but 6315 pounds sterling were paid to him as a compensation for losses in going over to the enemies of his country.

Shortly after his arrival in New York, Arnold published an address to the inhabitants of America in which he endeavored to vindicate his conduct. Beside this address, he issued a proclamation inviting the officers and soldiers of the American army to rally under the royal standard and fight for true American liberty, holding out promises of large bounties and liberal subsistence, with compensation for all the implements and accoutrements of war they might bring with them. Both the address and the proclamation were regarded by Americans with contempt.

In a letter to Reed, Washington writes, "Arnold's conduct is so villanously perfidious that there are no terms that can describe the baseness of his heart. That overruling Providence which has so often and so remarkably interposed in our favor never manifested itself

more conspicuously than in the timely discovery of his horrid intention to surrender the post and garrison of West Point into the hands
of the enemy."

Mrs. Arnold, on arriving at her father's house in Philadelphia,
had decided on a separation from her husband, to whom she could
not endure the thoughts of returning after his dishonor. This course,
however, was not allowed her. The executive council ordered her to
leave the State within fourteen days and not to return during the
war. Strongly against her will, she rejoined her husband in New
York.

She returned home but once, about five years after her exile,
and was treated with such coldness and neglect that she declared she
never could come again. In England her charms and virtues, it is
said, procured her sympathy and friendship and helped to sustain
the social position of her husband. She died in London in the winter
of 1796.

(CHAPTER 51)

As the enemy would now possess the means, through Arnold,
of informing themselves thoroughly about West Point, Washington
hastened to have the works completed and strongly garrisoned.
Greene was ordered to march with the Jersey, New York, New
Hampshire, and Stark's brigades and take temporary command.
Washington himself took post with his main army, at Prakeness in
New Jersey.

At the same time, a plan was formed at Washington's suggestion to get possession of the person of Arnold. The agent pitched
upon by Lee for the purpose was the sergeant-major of cavalry in his
legion, John Champe, a young Virginian. Champe was to make a
pretended desertion to the enemy at New York. There he was to
enlist in a corps which Arnold was raising, and, watching for a
favorable moment, was, with the aid of a confederate from Newark,

to seize and bring him across the Hudson into Bergen woods in the Jerseys. Washington, in approving the plan, stipulated that Arnold should be brought to him alive.

The pretended desertion of the sergeant took place on the night of October 20th. It was almost midnight when the officer of the day, hurrying into Lee's quarters, gave word that one of the patrols had fallen in with a dragoon who, on being challenged, put spurs to his horse and escaped. Lee was now compelled to order out a party in pursuit, but in so doing, he contrived so many delays that Champe had an hour's start. At daybreak they descried Champe not more than half a mile in front. The sergeant at the same moment caught sight of his pursuers; the chase became desperate. Champe had originally intended to make for Paulus Hook but changed his course and succeeded in getting abreast of two British galleys at anchor near the shore beyond Bergen. Throwing himself off his horse, he plunged into the river and called to the galleys for help. A boat was sent to his assistance and he was conveyed on board of one of those vessels.

For a time, the plan promised to be successful. Champe enlisted in Arnold's corps, and an arrangement was made to surprise Arnold at night in a garden in the rear of his quarters, convey him to a boat, and ferry him across the Hudson. On the appointed night, Lee, with three dragoons, was on the Jersey shore waiting to receive the captive. Hour after hour passed; day broke; and the major returned perplexed and disappointed to the camp. It subsequently proved that, on the day preceding the night fixed on for the capture, Arnold had removed his quarters to another part of the town to superintend the embarkation of troops and that the American legion, consisting chiefly of American deserters, had been transferred to one of the transports. Among the troops transferred was John Champe—nor was he able for a long time to effect his escape and resume his real character of a loyal and patriotic soldier.

We have here to note the altered fortunes of General Gates. His defeat at Camden had withered the laurels snatched at Saratoga. The sudden annihilation of the army and the retreat of the general before the field was absolutely lost appeared to demand investigation. Congress therefore passed a resolution (October 5th) requiring Washington to order a court of inquiry into the conduct of Gates as commander of the Southern army and to appoint some other officer to the command until the inquiry should be made. Washington at once selected Greene for the important trust, whom he would originally have chosen had his opinion been consulted when Congress so unadvisedly gave the command to Gates.

With regard to the court of inquiry, it was to be conducted in the quarter in which Gates had acted, where all the witnesses were and where alone the requisite information could be obtained. Steuben, who was to accompany Greene to the South, was to preside and the members of the court were to be such officers as were not present at the battle of Camden, or, having been present, were persons to whom Gates had no objection. The affair was to be conducted with the greatest impartiality and despatch.

Ravaging incursions from Canada had harassed the northern parts of the State of New York of late and laid desolate some parts of the country from which Washington had hoped to receive great supplies of flour for the armies. Major Carleton, at the head of a motley force, had captured Forts Anne and George. Sir John Johnson and Joseph Brant, with a mongrel half-savage crew, had laid waste the fertile region of the Mohawk River and burned the villages of Schoharie and Caughnawaga. The greatest alarm prevailed throughout the neighboring country. Washington now put Brigadier-general James Clinton (the governor's brother) in command of the Northern department.

The state of the army was growing more and more a subject of solicitude to the commander-in-chief. He felt weary of struggling on with such scanty means and such vast responsibility. The campaign which, at its commencement, had seemed pregnant with favorable events had proved sterile and was drawing to a close. The short terms for which most of the troops were enlisted must soon expire and the present army would be reduced to a mere shadow. The saddened state of his mind may be judged from a letter addressed to Sullivan. "We have been half of our time without provisions," writes he, "and are likely to continue so. We have no magazines nor money to form them; and in a little time we shall have no men if we have no money to pay them. . . . To suppose that this great Revolution can be accomplished by a temporary army, that this army will be subsisted by State supplies, and that taxation alone is adequate to our wants is in my opinion absurd. . . . An annual army . . . is . . . more expensive than a permanent body of men under good organization and military discipline."

We will here add, that the repeated reasonings of Washington, backed by dear-bought experience, slowly brought Congress to adopt a system suggested by him for the organization and support of the army according to which troops were to be enlisted to serve throughout the war and all officers who continued in service until the return of peace were to receive half pay during life.

Lafayette at this time commanded the advance guard of Washington's army, composed of six battalions of light-infantry. He had a young man's ardor for active service and the inactivity which had prevailed for some time past was intolerable to him.

The marquis was urgent with Washington that the campaign should be terminated by some brilliant stroke. Complaints, he hinted, had been made in France of the prevailing inactivity. "If any thing could decide the ministry to yield us the succor demanded," writes he, "it would be our giving the nation a proof that we are ready."

The brilliant stroke, suggested with some detail by the marquis, was a general attack upon Fort Washington and the other posts at the north end of the island of New York, and, under certain circumstances which he specified, to make a push for the city.

Washington regarded the project with a more sober and cautious eye. "It is impossible, my dear marquis," replies he, "to desire more ardently than I do to terminate the campaign by some happy stroke; but we must consult our means rather than our wishes . . . . It would, in my opinion, be imprudent to throw an army of 10,000 men upon an island against 9000, exclusive of seamen and militia. . . . All we can do at present, therefore, is to endeavor to gain a more certain knowledge of their situation and act accordingly."

The British posts in question were accordingly reconnoitred from the opposite banks of the Hudson by Colonel Gouvion, an able French engineer. Preparations were made to carry the scheme into effect should it be determined upon, in which case Lafayette was to lead the attack at the head of his light troops and be supported by Washington with his main force, while a strong foraging party sent by Heath from West Point to White Plains to draw the attention of the enemy in that direction was, on preconcerted signals, to advance rapidly to King's Bridge and co-operate.

Unfortunately, news was received of the unexpected appearance of several British armed vessels in the Hudson; the effect was to disconcert the complicated plan of a coup-de-main upon the British posts and, finally, to cause it to be abandoned.

Some parts of the original scheme, however, were attended with success. Stark, with a detachment of 2500 men, made an extensive forage in Westchester county. Major Tallmadge with 80 men, chiefly dismounted dragoons of Sheldon's regiment, crossed in boats from the Connecticut shore to Long Island, traversed the island on the night of the 22d of November, surprised Fort George at Coram, captured the garrison of 52 men, demolished the fort, set fire to magazines of forage, and recrossed the Sound without the loss of a man.

At the end of November the army went into winter-quarters: the Pennsylvania line in the neighborhood of Morristown, the Jersey line about Pompton, the New England troops at West Point and the other posts of the Highlands, and the New York line at Albany to guard against any invasion from Canada.

The French army remained stationed at Newport, excepting the Duke of Lauzun's legion, which was cantoned at Lebanon in Connecticut. Washington's head-quarters were established at New Windsor on the Hudson.

PART X

(CHAPTERS 52–58)

The War in the South
[1780–1782]

———————•◦∞◦•———————

Cornwallis having, as he supposed, crushed the "rebel cause" in South Carolina by the defeats of Gates and Sumter, remained at Camden, detained by the excessive heat and by the sickness of part of his troops. He awaited also supplies and reinforcements.

Immediately after the victory at Camden, he ordered the friends to royalty in North Carolina "to intercept the beaten army of General Gates," promising that he would march directly in their support; he detached Major Patrick Ferguson to its western confines to keep the war alive in that quarter. This resolute partisan had a corps of light infantry and a body of royalist militia. His whole force was about 1200 men, noted for activity and alertness and unincumbered with baggage or artillery.

His orders were to skirr the mountain country between the Catawba and the Yadkin, harass the whigs, inspirit the tories, and embody the militia under the royal banner. This done, he was to repair to Charlotte, where he would find Cornwallis, who intended to make it his rendezvous. Should he, however, be threatened by a superior force, he was immediately to return to the main army. No great opposition, however, was apprehended, the Americans being considered totally broken up and dispirited.

During the suspense of his active operations in the field, Cornwallis instituted rigorous measures against Americans who continued under arms, or, by any other acts, manifested what he termed "a desperate perseverance in opposing His Majesty's Government." Estates and property were often seized; inhabitants whose "treasonable" correspondence was found in the baggage of captured American generals were imprisoned; some prisoners who had British protections in their pockets were deemed arrant runagates and hanged, almost without an inquiry. These measures were not in keeping with the character for moderation and benevolence usually given to Cornwallis, but they accorded with the rancorous spirit manifested toward each other by whigs and tories in Southern warfare.

Cornwallis decamped from Camden and set out for North Carolina. In the subjugation of that province, he counted on the co-operation of the troops which Sir Henry was to send to Virginia, which, after reducing the Virginians to obedience, were to join his lordship's standard in North Carolina.

Advancing into the latter province Cornwallis took post at Charlotte, where he had given rendezvous to Ferguson. Mecklenburg, of which this was the capital, was, as the reader may recollect, the county where the first declaration of independence had been made and his lordship soon pronounced Charlotte "the Hornet's nest of North Carolina."

The surrounding country was wild and rugged, covered with close and thick woods, and crossed in every direction by narrow roads. The inhabitants were staunch whigs. Instead of receiving the king's money for their produce, they turned out with their rifles, stationed themselves in covert places, and fired upon the foraging parties. Convoys from Camden had to fight their way and expresses were shot down and their despatches seized.

The capture of his expresses was a sore annoyance to Cornwallis, depriving him of all intelligence concerning the movements of Ferguson, whose arrival he was anxiously awaiting. Ferguson had a loyal hatred of whigs and to his standard flocked many rancorous tories. He was on his way to join Cornwallis when a chance for a signal exploit presented itself. An American force under Colonel Elijah Clarke of Georgia was retreating to the mountain districts of North Carolina after an unsuccessful attack upon the British post at Augusta. Ferguson resolved to cut off their retreat. Turning towards the mountains, he made his way through a rugged wilderness and took post at Gilbert-town, a small frontier village. All of a sudden, a numerous, fierce and unexpected enemy sprung up. These, in fact, were the people of the mountains which form the frontiers of the Carolinas and Georgia; subject to inroads from the Chickasaws, Cherokees and Creeks, a league existed among them for mutual defence and it only needed an alarm circulated by swift messengers to bring them at once to the point of danger. Beside these, a band of inhabitants of Kentucky, with men from other settlements west of the Alleghanies, which had crossed the mountains, led by Colonels Campbell and Boone, to pounce upon a quantity of Indian goods at Augusta, had pulled up on hearing of the repulse of Clarke. The stout yeomen, also, of the district of Ninety-Six, roused by the marauds of Ferguson, had taken the field under Colonel James Williams of Granville County. Here, too, were hard-riders and sharp-shooters, from various parts of Virginia, commanded by Colonels Campbell, Cleveland, Shelby and Sevier. Such were the different bodies of mountaineers and backwoodsmen, suddenly drawing together from various parts to the number of 3000.

Threatened by a force so superior in numbers and fierce in hostility, Ferguson remembered the instructions of Cornwallis that he rejoin him should he find himself threatened by a superior force; breaking up his quarters, therefore, he sent messengers ahead to apprise his lordship of his danger. Unfortunately for him, his missives were intercepted.

Gilbert-town had not long been vacated by Ferguson and his troops, when the motley host we have described thronged in. Some were on foot but the greater part on horseback. Some were in homespun garb but the most part in hunting-shirts, occasionally decorated with fringe and tassels. Each man had his long rifle and hunting-knife, his knapsack and blanket, and either a buck's tail or sprig of evergreen in his hat. Here and there an officer appeared in the Continental uniform, but most preferred the half-Indian hunting-dress. There was neither tent nor tent equipage, neither baggage nor baggage waggon to encumber the movements of that host.

Being told that Ferguson had retreated by the Cherokee road toward North Carolina, about 900 of the hardiest and best mounted set out in pursuit, leaving those on foot or weakly mounted to follow as fast as possible. Colonel William Campbell of Virginia was allowed to have command of the whole party but there was not much order nor subordination. Each colonel led his own men in his own way.

A rapid march was kept up in murky darkness and through heavy rain. The rainy night had been succeeded by a bright October morning and all were in high spirits. Ferguson, they learnt, had taken the road towards King's Mountain, about 12 miles distant. When within 3 miles of it scouts brought word that he had taken post on its summit. The officers held a short consultation and then proceeded. The position taken by Ferguson was a strong one. King's Mountain rises out of a broken country and is detached, on the north, by a deep valley, so as to resemble a promontory about half a mile in length, with sloping sides excepting on the north. The mountain was covered for the most part with lofty trees, free from underwood, interspersed with boulders and masses of gray rock. The forest was sufficiently open to give free passage to horsemen.

Dismounting at a small stream which runs through a ravine, the Americans picketed their horses or tied them to trees and gave them in charge of a small guard. They then formed themselves into three divisions of nearly equal size and prepared to storm the heights on three sides. Campbell, seconded by Shelby, was to lead the centre division; Sevier with McDowell, the right; and Cleveland and Williams, the left. The divisions were to scale the mountain at the same time. The fighting directions were in frontier style. Once in action, every one must act for himself. The men were not to wait for the word of command but to take good aim and fire as fast as possible. When they could no longer hold their ground they were to get behind trees or retreat a little and return to the fight, but never to go quite off.

Campbell allowed time for the flanking divisions to move to the right and left along the base of the mountain and take their proper distances; he then pushed up in front with the centre division, he and Shelby each at the head of his men. The first firing was about four o'clock, when a picket was driven in by Cleveland and Williams on the left and pursued up the mountain. Campbell soon arrived within rifle distance of the crest of the mountain, whence a sheeted fire of musketry was opened upon him. He instantly deployed his men, posted them behind trees, and returned the fire with deadly effect.

Ferguson, exasperated at being thus hunted into this mountain fastness, now rushed out with his regulars, made an impetuous charge with the bayonet and, dislodging his assailants from their coverts, began to drive them down the mountain. He had not proceeded far when a flanking fire was opened by one of the other divisions. Facing about and attacking this he was again successful, when a third fire was opened from another quarter. Thus, as fast as one division gave way before the bayonet another came to its relief, while those who had given way rallied and returned to the charge. Ferguson found that he was completely in the hunter's toils, beset on every side, but he stood bravely at bay, the ground around him strewed with the killed and wounded, picked off by the fatal rifle. His men at length retreated in confusion along the ridge. He endeavored to rally them when a rifle ball brought him to the ground.

This closed the bloody fight. Ferguson's second in command, seeing all further resistance hopeless, hoisted a white flag. One hundred and fifty of the enemy had fallen and as many been wounded; of the Americans, but 20 were killed though a considerable number were wounded. Among those slain was Colonel James Williams, who had proved himself one of the most daring of the partisan leaders.

Eight hundred and ten men were taken prisoners, one hundred of whom were regulars, the rest royalists. The rancor awakened by civil war was shown in the treatment of some of the prisoners. A court-martial was held the day after the battle and a number of tory prisoners were hanged. This was to revenge the death of American prisoners hanged at Camden and elsewhere.

The army of mountaineers and frontier men thus fortuitously congregated did not attempt to follow up their signal blow. They had no plan of campaign; having effected their purpose, they returned to their homes. They were little aware of the importance of their achievement. The battle of King's Mountain turned the tide of Southern warfare. The destruction of Ferguson and his corps gave a complete check to the expedition of Cornwallis. He began to fear for the safety of South Carolina, liable to such sudden irruptions from the mountains. He resolved, therefore, to return with all speed to that province and provide for its security.

On the 14th of October he commenced his retrograde march, conducting it with such hurry and confusion that 20 waggons laden with baggage and supplies were lost. As he proceeded, the rainy season set in; the brooks and rivers became swollen and almost impassable, the roads deep and miry, provisions and forage scanty, the troops generally sickly, having no tents. Cornwallis himself was seized with a fever which obliged him to halt two days and afterwards to be conveyed in a waggon, giving up the command to Rawdon.

In the course of this desolate march, the British suffered from the vengeance of an outraged country, fired upon from behind trees and other coverts by the yeomanry, their sentries shot down at their encampments, their foraging parties cut off. At length, the army arrived at Winnsborough in South Carolina, where his lordship took post. Hence, by order of Cornwallis, Rawdon wrote on the 24th of October to Brigadier-general Leslie, who was in the Chesapeake with the force detached by Sir Henry for a descent upon Virginia, suggesting the expediency of his advancing to North Carolina for co-operation with Cornwallis, who feared to proceed far from South Carolina, lest it should be again in insurrection.

The victory at King's Mountain had set the partisan spirit throughout the country in a blaze. Francis Marion was soon in the field. He had been made a brigadier-general by Governor Rutledge but his brigade, formed of neighbors and friends, was continually fluctuating in numbers. He had his haunts and strongholds in the morasses of the Pedee and Black River. Sallying forth from his morasses, he would beat up the small posts in the vicinity of Charleston, cut up the communication between that city and Camden, and, having roused the vengeance of the enemy, would retreat into his fenny fastnesses. Hence the British gave him the name of the "Swamp Fox."

Tarleton, who was on duty in that part of the country, undertook to draw the swamp fox from his cover. He accordingly marched cautiously down the east bank of the Wateree with dragoons and infantry. The fox kept close but he saw that the enemy was too strong for him. Tarleton changed his plan. By day he broke up his force into small detachments, giving them orders to keep near enough to each other to render mutual support if attacked and to gather together at night.

The artifice had its effect. Marion sallied forth just before daybreak to make an attack upon one of these detachments when, to his surprise, he found himself close upon the British camp. Perceiving the snare spread for him, he made a rapid retreat. For seven hours Marion was hunted from one swamp and fastness to another. Tarleton was in strong hope of bringing him into action, when an express came spurring from Cornwallis, calling for the immediate services of himself and his dragoons in another quarter.

Sumter was again in the field! That indefatigable partisan, having recruited a strong party in the mountainous country, had reappeared on the west side of the Santee, repulsed a British party sent against him, and then, crossing Broad River, effected a junction with Colonels Clark and Brannan, and now menaced the British posts in the district of Ninety-Six.

It was to disperse this head of partisan war that Tarleton was called. Advancing with celerity he thought to surprise Sumter on the Enoree River. A deserter apprised the latter of his danger. He pushed across the river but was hotly pursued. He now made for the Tyger River, noted for turbulence and rapidity; once beyond this, he might disband his followers in the woods. Tarleton, to prevent his passing it unmolested, spurred forward in advance of his main body with 170 dragoons and 80 mounted men of the infantry. Before five o'clock (Nov. 20) his advanced guard overtook and charged the rear of the Americans, who retreated to the main body. Sumter, finding it impossible to cross the Tyger River in safety, took post on Black Stock Hill, with a rivulet and rail fence in front, the Tyger River in the rear and on the right flank, a large log barn on the left. The barn was turned into a fortress and a part of the force stationed in it.

Tarleton halted to await the arrival of his infantry and part of his men dismounted to ease their horses. Sumter seized this moment for an attack, but he was driven back after some sharp fighting. Tarleton charged with his cavalry, but found it impossible to dislodge the Americans from their rustic fortress. At the approach of night he fell back to join his infantry.

Sumter, who had received a severe wound in the breast, understanding the enemy would be reinforced in the morning, crossed the Tyger River in the night. He was then placed on a litter between two horses and thus conducted across the country by a few adherents. The rest of his little army dispersed themselves through the woods. Tarleton, finding his enemy had disappeared, claimed the credit of a victory but those who considered the affair rightly declared that he had received a severe check.

While the attention of the enemy was thus engaged by Sumter and Marion, Gates was gathering the scattered fragments of his army at Hillsborough. When collected, his whole force, exclusive of militia, did not exceed 1400 men. His troops, disheartened by defeat, were without clothing, without pay, and sometimes without provisions.

The vanity of Gates was completely cut down by his late reverses. To add to his depression of spirits, Gates received the melancholy intelligence of the death of an only son, and, while yet writhing under the blow, came official despatches informing him of his being superseded in command. A letter from Washington accompanied them, sympathizing with him in his domestic misfortunes, adverting with delicacy to his reverses in battle, assuring him of his undiminished confidence. The effect of this letter was overpowering. Gates declared that its tender sympathy and considerate delicacy had conveyed more consolation and delight to his heart than he had believed it possible ever to have felt again.

General Greene arrived at Charlotte on the 2d of December. On his way from the North, he had made arrangements for supplies from the different States and had left Steuben in Virginia to defend that State and procure and send on reinforcements and stores for the Southern army. On the day following his arrival, Greene took formal command. Consulting with his officers as to the court of inquiry on the conduct of Gates ordered by Congress, it was agreed that, among other considerations, the state of Gates's feelings, in consequence of the death of his son, disqualified him from entering upon the task of his defence and that it would be desirable to make such representations as may obtain a revision of the order of Congress directing an inquiry into his conduct.

Gates was ultimately brought to acquiesce in the postponement but declared that he could not think of serving until the matter should have been investigated. He determined to pass the interim on his estate in Virginia.

The whole force at Charlotte, to which Gates had moved his quarters for the winter, when Greene took command did not much exceed 2300 men, more than half of them militia. It had been broken in spirit by the recent defeat.

The state of the country in which Greene was to act was equally discouraging. "War here," observes he, "is . . . every where; and the country is so full of deep rivers and impassable creeks and swamps that you are always liable to misfortunes of a capital nature."

The first care of General Greene was to reorganize his army. He went to work quietly but resolutely; the army soon began to assume what he termed a military complexion. He was equally studious to promote harmony among his officers, of whom a number were young, gallant, and intelligent. The manly benignity of his manners diffused itself and a common affection for their chief united the young men in a kind of brotherhood.

Finding the country round Charlotte exhausted by repeated foragings, he separated the army into two divisions. One, about 1000 strong, commanded by Morgan of rifle renown, was composed of 400 Continental infantry under Lieutenant-colonel Howard of the Maryland line, two companies of Virginia militia under Captains Triplet and Tate, and 100 dragoons under Lieutenant-colonel Washington. With these Morgan was detached towards the district of Ninety-Six, in South Carolina, to take a position near the confluence of the Pacolet and Broad Rivers and to assemble the militia of the country. With the other division, Greene made a march of toilful difficulty to Hicks' Creek in Chesterfield district, on the east side of the Pedee River, opposite the Cheraw Hills. There he posted himself on the 26th, partly to discourage the enemy from attempting to possess themselves of Cross Creek, which would give them command of the greatest part of the provisions of the lower country, partly to form a camp of repose.

(CHAPTER 53)

Recent occurrences made Washington apprehend a design on the part of the enemy to carry the war into the Southern States. Conscious that he was the man who was, in a manner, responsible for the general course of military affairs, he deeply felt the actual impotency of his position.

In a letter to Franklin, who was minister-plenipotentiary at the court of Versailles, he strongly expresses his chagrin. "We have been obliged to become spectators of a succession of detachments from the army at New York in aid of Lord Cornwallis, while our naval weakness and the political dissolution of a great part of our army put it out of our power to counteract them at the southward or to take advantage of them here."

The last of these detachments to the South took place on the 20th of December, but was not destined, as Washington had supposed, for Carolina. This detachment was to take their place in Virginia. It was composed of British, German, and refugee troops, about 1700 strong, commanded by Benedict Arnold, now a brigadier-general in his majesty's service. Sir Henry Clinton, who distrusted the man he had corrupted, sent with him Colonels Dundas and Simcoe, by whose advice he was to be guided in every important measure. He was to make an incursion into Virginia, destroy the public magazines, assemble and arm the loyalists, and hold himself ready to co-operate with Cornwallis. He departed on his enterprise animated by the rancorous spirit of a renegade.

As Washington beheld one hostile armament after another winging its way to the South and received applications from that quarter for assistance, which he had not the means to furnish, it became painfully apparent to him that the efforts to carry on the war had exceeded the natural capabilities of the country. The patience of the army was nearly exhausted, the people were dissatisfied with the mode of supporting the war, and there was reason to apprehend that, under impositions of a new and odious kind, they might imagine they had only exchänged one kind of tyranny for another.

Washington was continually urging upon Congress his opinion that a foreign loan was indispensably necessary to a continuance of the war. His counsels and entreaties were at length successful in determining Congress to seek aid in men and money from abroad. Accordingly on the 28th of December they commissioned Lieutenant-colonel John Laurens as special minister at the court of Versailles to apply for such aid. He was instructed to confer with Washington previous to his departure. Washington advised him to solicit a loan sufficiently large to be a foundation for substantial arrangements of finance, to revive public credit, and give vigor to future operations. Next to a loan of money, a naval force was to be desired, sufficient to maintain superiority on the American coast; also additional troops. In a word, a means of co-operation by sea and land, with purse and sword, competent to attain the liberty and independence of the United States.

Scarce had Laurens been appointed to this mission, when a painful occurrence proved the urgent necessity of the required aid. In the arrangement for winter-quarters, the Pennsylvania line, consisting of six regiments, was hutted near Morristown. These troops had experienced the hardships and privations common to the whole army, but they had an additional grievance peculiar to themselves. Many had enlisted to serve "for three years or during war," that is to say, for less than three years should the war cease in less time. When, however, having served for three years, they sought their discharge, the officers interpreted the terms of enlistment to mean three years or to the end of the war should it continue for a longer time. This naturally produced great exasperation.

The first day of the New Year arrived and the men were excited by an extra allowance of ardent spirits. In the evening, at a preconcerted signal, a great part of the Pennsylvania line turned out under arms, declaring their intention to march to Philadelphia and demand redress from Congress. Wayne endeavored to pacify them; they were no longer to be pacified by words. In an attempt to suppress the mutiny there was a bloody affray, in which numbers were wounded on both sides.

Three regiments which had taken no part in the mutiny were paraded under their officers. The mutineers compelled them to join their ranks. Their number being increased to about 1300, they seized six field-pieces and set out in the night for Philadelphia under command of their sergeants.

Fearing the enemy might take advantage of this outbreak, Wayne detached a Jersey brigade to Chatham and ordered the militia to be called out there. Alarm fires were kindled upon the hills; alarm guns boomed from post to post; the country was soon on the alert.

Wayne sent provisions after the mutineers, lest they should supply their wants from the country people by force. Two officers of rank spurred to Philadelphia to apprise Congress of the approach of the insurgents. Wayne sent a despatch with news of the outbreak to Washington; he then mounted his horse and, accompanied by Butler and Stewart, two officers popular with the troops, set off after the mutineers, either to bring them to a halt or to keep with them and seek every occasion to exert a favorable influence over them.

Having visited the Highland posts of the Hudson and satisfied himself of the fidelity of the garrisons, Washington ordered a detachment of 1100 men to be ready to march at a moment's warning. Knox was despatched by him to the Eastern States to represent to their governments the alarming crisis and to urge them to send immediately money, clothing, and other supplies for their lines.

In the mean time, Sir Henry received intelligence at New York of the mutiny and hastened to profit by it. Emissaries were despatched to the mutineers, holding out offers of pardon, protection, and ample pay if they would return to their allegiance to the crown. On the 4th of January, troops and cannon were transported to Staten Island, Sir Henry accompanying them. There they were to be held in readiness either to land at Amboy in the Jerseys, should the revolters be drawn in that direction, or to make a dash at West Point, should the departure of Washington leave that post assailable.

Wayne and his companions, Butler and Stewart, had overtaken the insurgent troops on the 3d of January at Middlebrook. They were proceeding in military form under the control of a board of sergeants, whose orders were implicitly obeyed. Conferences were held by Wayne with sergeants delegated from each regiment. They appeared to be satisfied with the mode and promises of redress held out to them but the main body of the mutineers persisted in revolt and proceeded on the next day to Princeton. Their proceedings continued to be orderly; they behaved well to the people of the country and committed no excesses.

Wayne, Butler and Stewart remained with them in an equivocal position—popular but without authority. The insurgents professed themselves still ready to march under them against the enemy.

The news of the revolt caused great consternation in Philadelphia. A committee of Congress set off to meet the insurgents, accompanied by Reed, president of Pennsylvania, and one or two other officers. The committee halted at Trenton, whence Reed wrote to Wayne requesting a personal interview at four o'clock in the afternoon at four miles' distance from Princeton. Wayne was told to inform the troops that he (Reed) would be there to receive any propositions from them and redress any injuries they might have sustained.

Wayne, knowing that the letter was intended for his troops more than for himself, read it publicly on the parade. It had a good effect upon the men. The idea that the president of their State should leave the seat of government to treat with them touched their pride and their home feelings. Wayne promised to meet him on the following day (7th), though it seemed uncertain whether he was master of himself or a kind of prisoner.

At this critical juncture, two of Sir Henry's emissaries arrived in the camp and delivered to the leaders of the malcontents a paper containing his seductive proposals and promises. The mutineers spurned the idea of turning "Arnolds," as they termed it. The emissaries were seized and conducted to Wayne, who placed them in confinement. This incident had a great effect in inspiring hope of the ultimate loyalty of the troops; the favorable representations of the temper of the men, made by Wayne in a personal interview, determined Reed to venture among them.

As he approached Princeton, he found guards regularly posted, who turned out and saluted him in military style. The sergeants saluted the president as he passed; never were mutineers more orderly and decorous.

The propositions now offered to the troops were: (1) to discharge all those who had enlisted indefinitely for three years or during the war; (2) to give immediate certificates for the deficit in their pay caused by the depreciation of the currency, the arrearages to be settled as soon as circumstances would permit; (3) to furnish them immediately with specified articles of clothing which were most wanted. These propositions proving satisfactory, the troops set out for Trenton, where the negotiation was concluded.

The accommodation entered into with the mutineers appeared to Washington of doubtful policy and likely to have a pernicious effect on the whole army. His apprehensions were soon justified by events. On the night of the 20th of January, a part of the Jersey troops stationed at Pompton rose in arms, claiming the same terms just yielded to the Pennsylvanians. Sir Henry was again on the alert. Troops were sent to Staten Island to be ready to cross into the Jerseys and an emissary was despatched to tempt the mutineers with seductive offers.

In this instance, Washington adopted a more rigorous course than in the other. A detachment from the Massachusetts line was sent under Howe, who was instructed to compel the mutineers to unconditional submission; to grant them no terms while in a state of resistance; and, on their surrender, instantly to execute a few of the most incendiary leaders. Howe had the good fortune, after a night-march, to surprise the mutineers napping just at daybreak.

Five minutes were allowed them to parade without their arms and give up their ringleaders. This was instantly complied with and two of them were executed on the spot. Thus the mutiny was quelled.

A great cause of satisfaction to Washington was the ratification of the articles of confederation between the States, which took place not long after this agitating juncture. A set of articles had been submitted to Congress by Dr. Franklin as far back as 1775. A form had been prepared and digested by a committee in 1776 and agreed upon, with some modifications in 1777, but had ever since remained in abeyance in consequence of objections made by individual States. The confederation was now complete and Washington, in a letter to the President of Congress, congratulated him and the body over which he presided on an event long wished for and which he hoped would have the happiest effects upon the politics of this country and be of essential service to our cause in Europe. It served an important purpose in binding the States together as a nation and keeping them from falling asunder into individual powers after the pressure of external danger should cease to operate.

The armament with which Arnold boasted he was "to shake the continent" met with that boisterous weather which often rages along our coast in the winter. His ships were tempest-tost and scattered and half of his cavalry horses and several of his guns had to be thrown overboard. It was the close of the year when he anchored in the Chesapeake.

Virginia, at the time, was almost in a defenceless state. Steuben, who had general command there, had recently detached such of his regular troops as were clothed and equipped to the South to reinforce Greene. The remainder, deficient in clothing, blankets, and tents, were scarcely fit to take the field, and the volunteers and militia had been disbanded. Governor Jefferson, on hearing of the arrival of the fleet, called out the militia but few could be collected on the spur of the moment.

Having land and sea forces at his command, Arnold opened the new year with a buccaneering ravage. Ascending James River with some small vessels he had captured, he landed on the fourth of

Janurary with 900 men at Westover, 25 miles below Richmond, and pushed for the latter place, the metropolis of Virginia.

It was Arnold's hope to capture the governor but the latter, after providing for the security of as much as possible of the public stores, had left Richmond the evening before on horseback. Jefferson got back by noon to Manchester on the opposite side of the James River in time to see Arnold's marauders march into the town. Many of the inhabitants had fled to the country; not more than 200 men were in arms for the defence of the place; these, after firing a few volleys, retreated to Richmond and Shockoe Hills, whence they were driven by the cavalry. Arnold had possession of the capital. He sent some citizens to the governor, offering to spare the town provided his ships might come up James River to be laden with tobacco from the warehouses. His offer was indignantly rejected, whereupon fire was set to the public edifices, stores, and workshops; private houses were pillaged and a great quantity of tobacco consumed.

While this was going on, Simcoe had been detached to Westham, six miles up the river, where he destroyed a cannon foundry and sacked a public magazine; after effecting a complete devastation, he rejoined Arnold at Richmond.

Having completed his ravage at Richmond, Arnold re-embarked at Westover, landing occasionally to burn, plunder, and destroy, pursued by Steuben with a few Continental troops and all the militia he could muster. General Nelson, also, with similar levies opposed him. Some skirmishing took place, but Arnold made his way to Portsmouth, opposite Norfolk, where he took post on the 20th of January and proceeded to fortify.

Collecting all the force that could be mustered, Steuben so disposed it as to hem the traitor in, prevent his making further incursions, and drive him back to his intrenchments should he attempt any.

About this time an important resolution was adopted in Congress. Washington had repeatedly attributed much of the distress and disasters of the war to the congressional mode of conducting business through committees and boards, thus causing irregularity and delay, preventing secrecy and augmenting expense. He was greatly rejoiced, therefore, when Congress decided to appoint heads of departments; secretaries of foreign affairs, of war and of marine, and a superintendent of finance.

General Sullivan, who was in Congress, was a warm friend of Washington's aide-de-camp, Colonel Hamilton; he sounded the commander-in-chief as to the qualifications of Hamilton to take charge of the department of finance. "I am unable to answer," replied Washington, "because I never entered upon a discussion with him but . . . there are few men to be found of his age who have more general knowledge than he possesses, and none whose soul is more firmly engaged in the cause or who exceeds him in probity and sterling virtue."

It was but a few days after Washington had penned the eulogium just quoted, when a scene took place between him and the man he had praised so liberally that caused him deep chagrin. We give it as related by Hamilton himself in a letter to Schuyler, one of whose daughters he had recently married.

"An unexpected change has taken place in my situation," writes Hamilton (Feb. 18). ". . . Two days ago the general and I passed each other on the stairs:—he told me he wanted to speak to me. I answered that I would wait on him immediately. . . . Returning to the general, I was stopped on the way by the Marquis de Lafayette and we conversed about a minute on a matter of business. . . . Instead of finding the general, as is usual, in his room, I met him at the head of the stairs, where accosting me in an angry tone, 'Colonel Hamilton (said he), you have kept me waiting at the head of the stairs these ten minutes;—I must tell you, sir, you treat me with disrespect.' I replied, 'I am not conscious of it, sir, but since you have thought it necessary to tell me so, we part.' 'Very well, sir (said he), if it be your choice,' and we separated. . . . In less than an hour after, Tilghman came to me in the general's name, assuring me of his . . . desire, in a candid conversation, to heal a difference which could not have happened but in a moment of passion. I requested Mr. Tilghman to tell him . . . that, as a conversation could serve no other purpose than to produce explanations mutually disagreeable, though I certainly would not refuse an interview, if he desired it, yet I would be happy if he would permit me to decline it . . . . And that, in the mean time, it depended on him to let our behaviour to each other be the same as if nothing had happened. He consented to decline the conversation."

In considering this occurrence, as stated by Hamilton himself, we think he was in the wrong. His hurrying past the general on the stairs without pausing, although the latter expressed a wish to speak with him; his giving no reason for his haste; his tarrying below with Lafayette, the general all this time remaining at the head of the stairs, had certainly an air of great disrespect and we do not wonder that the commander-in-chief was deeply offended at being so treated by his youthful aide-de-camp. His expression of displeasure was measured and dignified, however irritated he may have been. Washington's subsequent overture, intended to soften the recent rebuke, by assurances of confidence and esteem, strikes us as noble and gracious, and furnishes another instance of that magnanimity which governed his whole conduct.

The following passage in Hamilton's letter to Schuyler gives the real key to his conduct on this occasion: "I always disliked the office of an aide-de-camp, as having in it a kind of personal dependence."

Hamilton, in fact, had long been ambitious of an opportunity, as he said, "to raise his character above mediocrity." When an expedition by Lafayette against Staten Island had been meditated in 1780, he had applied for the command of a battalion. Washington had declined on the ground that giving him a whole battalion might be a subject of dissatisfaction. He had next been desirous of the post of adjutant-general, which Colonel Scammel was about to resign, and was recommended for that office by Lafayette and Greene, but, before their recommendations reached Washington, he had already sent in to Congress the name of Brigadier-general Hand, who received the nomination. These disappointments may have rendered Hamilton doubtful of his being properly appreciated by the commander-in-chief.

We are happy to add that, though a temporary coolness took place between the commander-in-chief and his aide-de-camp, it was but temporary. The friendship between these men was destined to survive the revolution and to signalize itself through many eventful years.

(CHAPTER 54)

The stress of war, as Washington apprehended, shifted to the South. Greene, in the latter part of December, took post with one division of his army on the east side of the Pedee river in North Carolina, having detached Morgan with the other division, 1000 strong, to take post near the confluence of the Pacolet and Broad rivers in South Carolina.

Cornwallis lay encamped 70 miles south-west of Greene, at Winnsborough. General Leslie had recently arrived at Charleston from Virginia and was advancing to reinforce him with 1500 men. This would give Cornwallis such a superiority of force that he prepared for a second invasion of North Carolina. His plan was to leave Rawdon at the central post of Camden with a considerable body of troops to keep all quiet, while his lordship by rapid marches would throw himself between Greene and Virginia, cut him off from all reinforcements from that quarter and oblige him either to make battle or retreat precipitately.

By recent information, he learnt that Morgan had passed both the Catawba and Broad Rivers and was 70 miles northwest of him on his way to the district of Ninety-six. As he might prove formidable if left in his rear, Tarleton was sent in quest of him with about 350 of his cavalry, a corps of legion and light infantry and a number of the royal artillery with two field-pieces—about 1100 choice troops in all. His instructions were either to strike at Morgan and push him to the utmost or to drive him out of the country.

Cornwallis moved with his main force on the 12th of December in a northwest direction between the Broad River and the Catawba toward the back country. This was for the purpose of crossing the great rivers at their fords near their sources, for they are apt, when storms of rain prevail, to become impassable below their forks. He took this route also to cut off Morgan's retreat or prevent his junction with Greene, should Tarleton's expedition fail of its object. Leslie, whose arrival was daily expected, was to move up along the eastern side of the Wateree and Catawba, keeping parallel with his lordship and joining him above. Every thing seemed to promise a successful campaign.

Tarleton, after several days' hard marching, came upon the traces of Morgan, who was posted on the north bank of the Pacolet to guard the passes of that river. He sent word to Cornwallis of his intention to force a passage across the river and compel Morgan either to fight or retreat and suggested that his lordship should proceed up the eastern bank of Broad River so as to be at hand to co-operate. His lordship, in consequence, took up a position at Turkey Creek on Broad River.

Morgan had been recruited by North Carolina and Georgia militia so that his force was nearly equal in number to that of Tarleton but, in point of cavalry and discipline, vastly inferior. Cornwallis was on his left and might get in his rear. Checking his impulse to dispute the passage of the Pacolet, he crossed that stream and retreated towards the upper fords of Broad River.

Tarleton reached the Pacolet on the evening of the 15th, and crossed the river before daylight. He proceeded warily, until he learnt that Morgan was in full march toward Broad River. Tarleton now pressed on in pursuit. At ten o'clock at night he reached an encampment which Morgan had abandoned a few hours previously, apparently in great haste. Tarleton allowed his exhausted troops but a brief repose and resumed his dogged march in the night through swamps and rugged broken grounds. A little before daylight of the 17th, he captured two videttes, from whom he learnt to his surprise that Morgan, instead of a headlong retreat, had taken a night's repose and was preparing to give him battle.

Morgan, in fact, had been urged by his officers to retreat across Broad River, but, being nearly equal in number to the enemy, military pride would not suffer him to avoid a combat.

The place where he came to halt was known by the name of Hannah's Cowpens. It was in an open wood, favorable to the action of cavalry. There were two eminences of unequal height, separated by an interval about 80 yards wide. To the first eminence, which was the highest, there was an easy ascent of about 300 yards. On these heights Morgan had posted himself. His flanks were unprotected and the Broad River, running on his rear about 6 miles distant and winding round on the left, would cut off retreat should the day prove unfortunate.

In arranging his troops for action, he drew out his infantry in two lines. The first was composed of the North and South Carolina militia under Pickens, having an advanced corps of volunteer riflemen. This line was charged to wait until the enemy were within dead shot, then to fire two volleys and fall back.

The second line, drawn up a moderate distance in the rear of the first, was composed of Howard's light infantry and the Virginia riflemen, all Continental troops. They were informed of the orders given to the first line, lest they mistake their falling back for a retreat. Howard had command of this line, on which the greatest reliance was placed.

About 150 yards in the rear of the second line, on the slope of the lesser eminence, was Colonel Washington's troop of cavalry, about 80 strong, with about 50 mounted Carolinian volunteers under McCall, armed with sabres and pistols.

It was about eight o'clock in the morning, (Jan. 17th) when Tarleton came up. The position of the Americans seemed to give advantage to his cavalry and he made hasty preparation for immediate attack. Part of his infantry he formed into a line, dragoons on each flank. The rest of the infantry and cavalry were to be a reserve.

Tarleton did not even wait until the reserve could be placed but led his first line to the attack. The American riflemen in the advance delivered their fire with effect and fell back to the flanks of Pickens' militia. These waited until the enemy were within 50 yards and then made a destructive volley, but soon gave way before the bayonet. The British infantry pressed up to the second line while 40 of their cavalry attacked it on the right. Howard, seeing himself in danger of being outflanked, endeavored to change his front to the right. His orders were misunderstood and his troops were falling into confusion when Morgan rode up and ordered them to retreat over the hill, where Colonel Washington's cavalry were hurried forward for their protection.

The British rushed forward in pursuit of what they deemed a routed foe. To their astonishment, they were met by Washington's dragoons, who spurred on them impetuously while Howard's infantry, facing about, gave them an effective volley of musketry and then charged with the bayonet.

The enemy now fell into complete confusion. A panic seized upon the British troops and general flight took place. Tarleton endeavored to bring his cavalry into action to retrieve the day but, infected by the panic, they galloped off through the woods.

On the approach of Howard's infantry Tarleton gave up all for lost and spurred off with his few faithful adherents, trusting to the speed of their horses for safety.

Morgan did not linger on the field of battle. Leaving Pickens with a body of militia to bury the dead and provide for the wounded of both armies, he set out the same day with his prisoners and spoils. Cornwallis, with his main force, was at Turkey Creek, 25 miles distant, and must soon hear of the late battle. His object was to get to the Catawba before he could be intercepted by his lordship, who lay nearer than he did to the fords of that river. Before nightfall he crossed Broad River at the Cherokee ford and halted for a few hours on its northern bank. Before daylight of the 18th he was again on the march. Colonel Washington rejoined him in the course of the day, as also did Pickens.

Cornwallis was confidently waiting for tidings of a new triumph when, towards evening, some of his dragoons came straggling into camp to tell the tale of defeat. Tarleton defeated! It seemed incredible. It was confirmed the next morning by the arrival of Tarleton himself, discomfited and crest-fallen. Supposing that Morgan would linger near the scene of his triumph or advance toward Ninety-six, Cornwallis remained at Turkey Creek to collect the scattered remains of Tarleton's forces and to await the arrival of Leslie.

On the 19th, rejoined by Leslie, his lordship moved towards King's Creek and thence in the direction of King's Mountain until informed of Morgan's retreat toward the Catawba. Cornwallis now altered his course in that direction and, trusting that Morgan, encumbered by prisoners and spoils, might be overtaken before he could cross that river, detached a part of his force in pursuit of him while he followed on with the remainder.

Morgan succeeded in reaching the Catawba and crossing it in the evening just two hours before those in pursuit of him arrived on its banks. A heavy rain fell all night and by daybreak the river was so swollen as to be impassable. This sudden swelling continued for several days and gave Morgan time to send off his prisoners, who had crossed several miles above, and to call out the militia of Mecklenburg and Rowan Counties to guard the fords of the river.

Cornwallis moved slowly with his main body. He was encumbered by an immense train of baggage; the roads were through deep red clay and the country was cut up by streams and morasses. It was not until the 25th that he assembled his whole force at Ramsour's Mills on the Little Catawba, as the south fork of that river is called, and learnt that Morgan had crossed the main stream. Now he felt the loss he had sustained in the defeat of Tarleton's light troops, which are especially efficient in a thinly peopled country of swamps, streams, and forests.

In this crippled condition, he determined to relieve his army of every thing that could impede rapid movement in his future operations. Two days, therefore, were spent by him in destroying all such baggage and stores as could possibly be spared. His lordship was preparing for a trial of speed, where it was important to carry as light weight as possible.

Greene was gladdened by a letter from Morgan shortly after his defeat of Tarleton and transmitted the news to Washington with his own generous comments.

Greene had recently received intelligence of the landing of troops at Wilmington from a British squadron, supposed to be a force under Arnold destined to push up Cape Fear River and co-operate with Cornwallis; he had to prepare, therefore, not only to succor Morgan but to prevent this co-operation. He accordingly detached Stevens with his Virginian militia to conduct Morgan's prisoners to Charlottesville. At the same time he wrote to the Governors of North Carolina and Virginia for all the aid they could furnish, to Steuben to hasten forward his recruits, and to Shelby, Campbell and others to take arms once more and rival their achievements at King's Mountain.

This done, he left Huger in command of the division on the Pedee with orders to hasten on by forced marches to Salisbury to join the other division. In the mean time he set off on horseback for Morgan's camp, attended merely by a guide, an aide-de-camp, and a sergeant's guard of dragoons. His object was to aid Morgan in assembling militia and checking the enemy until the junction of his forces could be effected. On the last day of January he reached Morgan's camp at Sherrard's ford on the east side of the Catawba. The British army, on the opposite side of the river, appeared to be making preparations to force a passage across, as it would soon be fordable. Greene supposed Cornwallis had in view a junction with Arnold at Cape Fear; he wrote, therefore, to Huger to hurry on so that, with their united forces, they could give his lordship a defeat before he could effect the junction.

More correct information relieved him from the apprehension of a co-operation of Arnold and Cornwallis. The British troops which had landed at Wilmington were merely a small detachment from Charleston to establish a military depot for the use of Cornwallis in his southern campaign. Greene changed his plans. He was aware of the ill-provided state of the British army; his plan now was to tempt the enemy with the prospect of a battle but to elude one, to draw them higher into the country, and to gain time for the division advancing under Huger to join him. It was the Fabian policy he had learnt under Washington.

As the subsiding of the Catawba would enable Cornwallis to cross, Greene ordered Morgan to move off silently with his division, on the evening of the 31st, and to press his march all night so as to gain a good start in advance, while he (Greene) would remain to bring on the militia. The militia, which did not exceed 500, were partly distributed at different fords; the remaining 300, forming a corps of mounted riflemen under Davidson, were to watch the movements of the enemy and attack wherever he should make his attempt to cross. When the enemy should have actually crossed, the militia were to make their way to a rendezvous 16 miles distant, on

GEN. LORD CORNWALLIS

Printed by W.Pate

Cornwallis

NEW YORK G.P. PUTNAM & CO.

the road to Salisbury, where Greene would be waiting to conduct their further movements.

While these dispositions were being made by the American commander, Cornwallis was preparing to cross the river. The night of the 31st was chosen for the attempt. To divert the attention of the Americans, he detached Webster and Tarleton with part of the army to Beattie's ford, where he supposed Davidson to be stationed and where they were to make a feint of forcing a passage. The main attempt, however, was to be made 6 miles lower down, at McGowan's ford, where little if any opposition was anticipated.

Cornwallis set out for that ford with the main body of his army, at one o'clock in the morning. The night was dark and rainy. His artillery stuck fast; the line passed on without them. It was near daybreak by the time the head of the column reached the ford. To their surprise, they beheld that the ford was guarded by Davidson with his riflemen.

His lordship would have waited for his artillery but the rain was still falling and might render the river unfordable. The troops entered the river and were ordered not to fire until they should gain the opposite bank. Colonel Hall, of the light infantry of the guards, led the way directly across the river, whereas the true ford inclined diagonally further down. Hall had to pass through deeper water but he reached a part of the bank where it was unguarded. The American pickets, too, which had turned out at the alarm given by the sentinel, had to deliver a distant and slanting fire. Hall pushed on gallantly but was shot down as he ascended the bank. The horse on which Cornwallis rode was wounded, but the brave animal carried his lordship to the shore.

Davidson hastened with his men towards the place where the British were landing. The latter formed as soon as they found themselves on firm ground, charged Davidson's men before he had time to get them in order, killed and wounded about 40, and put the rest to flight. Davidson, last to leave the ground, was killed just as he was mounting his horse.

When the enemy had effected the passage, Tarleton was detached with his cavalry in pursuit of the militia. Eager to avenge his late disgrace, he scoured the country and fell upon some unsuspecting troops, who ran to their horses, delivered a hasty fire, and then dispersed in the woods. Tarleton, satisfied with his achievement, rejoined the main body. Had he scoured the country a few miles further, Greene and his suite might have fallen into his hands.

The general, informed that the enemy had crossed the Catawba at daybreak, awaited anxiously at the rendezvous the arrival of the militia. It was not until after midnight that he heard of their utter dispersion and of the death of Davidson. Apprehending the rapid advance of Cornwallis, he hastened to rejoin Morgan, who was pushing forward for the Yadkin, first sending orders to Huger to conduct the other division by the most direct route to Guilford Court-house, where the forces were to be united. At mid-day he alighted, weary and travel-stained, at the inn at Salisbury, where the landlady, Elizabeth Steele, entered the room and drew from under her apron two bags of money. "Take these," said the noble-hearted woman, "you will want them and I can do without them." This is one of the numberless instances of the devoted patriotism of our women during the revolution. Their patriotism was apt to be purer and more disinterested than that of the men.

Cornwallis did not advance so rapidly as had been appre-hended. After crossing the Catawba he had to wait for his waggons and artillery, which had remained on the other side in the woods; by nightfall of the 1st of February he was not more than 5 miles on the road to Salisbury. Eager to come up with the Americans, he mounted some of the infantry upon the baggage horses, joined them to the cavalry, and sent the whole forward under General O'Hara. They arrived on the banks of the Yadkin at night, between the 2d and 3d of February. There were no boats with which to cross; the Americans had secured them on the other side. The rain had over-flooded the ford by which the American cavalry had passed. After some delay, Cornwallis took his course up the south side of the Yadkin and crossed by the Shallow ford, while Greene continued to Guilford Court-house, where he was joined by Huger and his divi-sion on the 9th.

Cornwallis encamped 25 miles above them at the old Moravian town of Salem. Greene summoned a council of war and submitted the question whether or not to offer battle. There was an unanimous vote in the negative. It was determined to continue the retreat.

The great object of Greene now was to get across the river Dan and throw himself into Virginia. With the reinforcements and assistance he might there expect to find, he hoped to effect the salvation of the South and prevent the dismemberment of the Union. The object of Cornwallis was to get between him and Virginia, force him to a combat before he could receive those reinforcements or to enclose him between the great rivers on the west, the sea on the east, and the British army on the north and south. His lordship had been informed that the lower part of the Dan, at present, could only be crossed in boats; he trusted, therefore, to cut him off from the upper part of the river where alone it was fordable. Greene, however, had provided against such a contingency; boats had been secured at various places by his agents and he shaped his course for fords just above the confluence of the Dan and Staunton rivers, 70 miles from Guilford Court-house. This would give him 25 miles advantage of Cornwallis at the outset. Kosciuszko was sent with a party in advance to collect the boats and throw up breastworks at the ferries.

In ordering his march, Greene took the lead with the main body, the baggage, and stores. Morgan would have had the command of the rear-guard, composed of 700 of the most alert troops, cavalry and light infantry but, being disabled by a violent attack of ague and rheumatism, it was given to Colonel Otho Williams, who had with him Colonels Howard, Washington, and Lee. This corps, detached some distance in the rear, did infinite service. Being lightly equipped, it could manoeuvre in front of the British line of march, break down bridges, sweep off provisions, and impede its progress in a variety of ways, while the main body moved forward unmolested. It was now that Cornwallis most felt the severity of the blow he had received at the battle of the Cowpens in the loss of his light troops, having so few to cope with the élite corps under Williams.

Great abilities were shown by the commanders on either side in this momentous trial of activity and skill. Tarleton himself bears witness in his narrative that every measure of the Americans was judiciously designed and vigorously executed. So much had

Cornwallis been misinformed that he pushed on in the firm conviction that he was driving the American army into a trap and would give it a signal blow before it could cross the Dan.

In the mean time, Greene, with the main body, reached the banks of the river and succeeded in crossing over with ease in a single day, sending back word to Williams, who with his covering party was in the rear. That officer encamped, as usual, in the evening at a wary distance in front of the enemy, but, leaving his camp fires burning, pushed on all night, arrived at the river in the morning of the 15th, and made such despatch in crossing that his last troops had landed on the Virginia shore by the time the astonished enemy arrived on the opposite bank.

For a day the two armies lay panting within sight of each other on the opposite banks of the river, which had put an end to the race. On the 16th, the river began to subside; the enemy might soon be able to cross. Greene prepared for a further retreat to Halifax, where he was resolved to make a stand because an enemy position on the Roanoke would favor their designs on Virginia and the Carolinas. With a view to its defence, intrenchments had already been thrown up under the direction of Kosciuszko.

Cornwallis, however, did not deem it prudent to venture into Virginia, where Greene would be sure of powerful reinforcements. After giving his troops a day's repose, he put them once more in motion along the road by which he had pursued Greene. The latter was informed of this retrograde move by a preconcerted signal: the waving of a handkerchief by a female patriot.

This changed the game. Lee with his legion, strengthened by two Maryland companies, and Pickens, with a corps of South Carolina militia, all light troops, were transported across the Dan in the boats with orders to gain the front of Cornwallis to cut off his intercourse with the royalists. Greene, in the meanwhile, remained with his main force on the northern bank of the Dan, waiting to ascertain his lordship's real designs.

Cornwallis, on the 20th, took post at Hillsborough. Here he erected the royal standard and invited all loyal subjects to hasten to this standard with arms and provisions to assist in suppressing the rebellion. By another instrument, all who could raise independent companies were called upon to give in their names at head-quarters and a bounty in money and lands was promised to those who should enlist under them. These appeals produced little effect on the people of the surrounding districts. Many hundreds rode into the camp to talk over the proclamation and view the king's troops. The generality acknowledged that the Continentals had been chased out but apprehended they would soon return. Tarleton was detached with the cavalry and a small body of infantry to a region between the Haw and Deep Rivers to bring on loyalists said to be assembling there.

Rumor, in the mean time, had magnified the effect of his lordship's proclamations. Word was brought to Greene that the tories were flocking to the royal standard. At this time reinforcements to the American camp had been little more than 600 Virginia militia under Stevens. Greene saw that at this rate, Cornwallis would soon have complete command of North Carolina; he determined, therefore, to recross the Dan and give his lordship check; he broke up his camp and crossed the river on the 23d.

In the mean time, Lee and Pickens, scouting the country about Hillsborough, received information of Tarleton's recruiting expedition. They resolved to give him a surprise. Having forded the Haw one day about noon, they prepared to give the bold partisan a blow after his own fashion. On the way, however, they had an encounter with a body of about 400 mounted royalists, commanded by a Colonel Pyle, marching in quest of Tarleton. As Lee with his cavalry was in the advance, he was mistaken for Tarleton and hailed with acclamations. He favored the mistake and was taking measures to capture the royalists when some of them, seeing the infantry under Pickens, discovered their error and fired upon the rear-guard. The cavalry instantly charged upon them; 90 were slain and a great number wounded.

After all, Lee and Pickens missed the object of their enterprise. The approach of night and the fatigue of their troops made them defer their attack upon Tarleton until morning. In the mean time, the latter had received an express from Cornwallis, informing him Greene had passed the Dan and ordering him to return to Hillsborough as soon as possible. Lee was in the saddle before daybreak but Tarleton's troops were already on the march. Before sunrise, Tarleton had forded the Haw and "Light Horse Harry" gave over the pursuit.

The re-appearance of Greene and his army in North Carolina, heralded by the scourings of Lee and Pickens, disconcerted the schemes of Cornwallis. He found himself, he said, "amongst timid friends and adjoining to inveterate rebels." On the 26th, therefore, he threw himself across the Haw and encamped near Alamance Creek, in a country favorable to supplies and with a tory population. His position was commanding, at the point of concurrence of roads from Salisbury, Guilford, High Rockford, Cross Creek, and Hillsborough. It covered also the communication with Wilmington, where a dépôt of military stores, so important to his half-destitute army, had recently been established.

Greene, with his main army, took post 15 miles above him on the heights between Troublesome Creek and Reedy Fork. His plan was to harass the enemy by skirmishes but to avoid a general battle, thus gaining time for the arrival of reinforcements. He kept his light troops under Pickens and Williams between him and the enemy, intercepting intelligence, attacking foraging parties, and engaging in sharp cavalry skirmishes.

On the 6th of March, Cornwallis, learning that the light troops under Williams were carelessly posted, suddenly crossed the Alamance to drive them in upon the main army and bring Greene to action should he come to their assistance. His movement was discovered by the American patrols and the alarm given. Williams hastily retreated across Reedy Fork while Lee manoeuvred in front of the enemy. A stand was made by the Americans at Wetzell's Mill but they were obliged to retire. Cornwallis did not pursue; he had failed in his object of bringing Greene to action. The latter, resolved to avoid a conflict, retreated across the Haw to the roads by which he expected supplies and reinforcements.

Shortly after Greene's retreat, the long expected reinforcements arrived. They consisted of a brigade of Virginia militia under General Lawson, two brigades of North Carolina militia under Generals Butler and Eaton, and 400 regulars enlisted for eighteen months. His whole effective force amounted to 4243 foot and 161 cavalry. Of his infantry, not quite 2000 were regulars, three-fourths being new levies. His force nearly doubled in number that of Cornwallis, which did not exceed 2400 men, but many of Greene's troops were raw and inexperienced while those of the enemy were veterans. Greene knew the inferiority of his troops in this respect; yet he determined to accept the battle so long offered. The corps of light troops under Williams was now incorporated with the main body and all detachments were ordered to assemble at Guilford, within 8 miles of the enemy, where he encamped on the 14th, sending his waggons and heavy baggage to the Iron Works at Troublesome Creek, 10 miles in his rear.

Cornwallis had an exaggerated idea of the American force, rating it as high as 8000 men: still he determined to attack Greene now that he seemed disposed for a general action. He sent his carriages and baggage to Bell's Mills, on Deep River, and set out at daybreak on the 15th for Guilford.

Within four miles of that place, Tarleton with the advanced guard of cavalry, infantry, and yagers came upon the American advance-guard, composed of Lee's legion and some mountaineers and Virginia militia. Tarleton and Lee were well-matched in military prowess and the skirmish between them was severe. Lee's horses were superior to those of his opponent and Tarleton, seeing that his mounted men fought to a disadvantage, sounded a retreat. Lee endeavored to cut him off, until the appearance of the main body of the enemy obliged him to retire.

During this time Greene was preparing for action on a woody eminence, a mile south of Guilford Court House. The neighboring country was covered with forest, excepting some cultivated fields about the court house and along the Salisbury road, which passed through the centre of the place from south to north.

Greene had drawn out his troops in three lines. The first, composed of North Carolina militia, volunteers and riflemen under Butler and Eaton, was posted behind a fence, with an open field in front and woods on the flanks and in the rear. About 300 yards behind this, was the second line, composed of Virginia militia under

Stevens and Lawson, drawn up across the road and covered by a wood. The third line, about 400 yards in the rear of the second, was composed of Continental troops or regulars, those of Virginia under Huger on the right, those of Maryland under Williams on the left. Colonel Washington with a body of dragoons, Kirkwood's Delaware infantry, and a battalion of Virginia militia covered the right flank. Lee's legion, with the Virginia riflemen under Campbell, covered the left. Two six pounders were in the road in advance of the first line, two field pieces with the rear line near the court house, where Greene took his station.

About noon the head of the British army was descried advancing spiritedly from the south along the Salisbury road and defiling into the fields. The enemy advanced steadily in three columns: the Hessians and Highlanders under Leslie on the right, the Royal artillery and guards in the centre, and Webster's brigade on the left.

The North Carolinians, who formed the first line, waited until the enemy were within 150 yards, when, agitated by their martial array and undaunted movement, they took to flight. Some fled to the woods, others fell back upon the Virginians, who formed the second line. Stevens, who commanded the latter, ordered his men to open and let the fugitives pass. Under his spirited command and example, the Virginians kept their ground and fought bravely. The British bayonet again succeeded; the second line gave way and Stevens, who had kept the field for some time, ordered a retreat.

The enemy pressed with increasing ardor against the third line, composed of Continental troops supported by Washington's dragoons and Kirkwood's Delawares. Greene counted on these to retrieve the day. They were regulars; they were fresh and in perfect order. He rode along the line, calling on them to give the enemy a warm reception.

The first Maryland regiment, which was on the right wing, was attacked by Webster with the British left. It stood the shock bravely and, seconded by some Virginia troops and Kirkwood's Delawares, drove Webster across a ravine. The second Maryland regiment was not so successful. Impetuously attacked by Stewart, it faltered, gave way, and fled. Stewart was pursuing, when the first regiment, which had driven Webster across the ravine, came to the rescue with fixed bayonets while Colonel Washington spurred up with his cavalry. The fight now was fierce and bloody. Stewart was slain; the enemy gave way and were pursued with slaughter until a destructive fire of grape shot from the enemy's artillery checked the pursuit. Two regiments approached on the right and left; Webster recrossed the ravine and fell upon Kirkwood's Delawares. There was intrepid fighting in different parts of the field, but Greene saw that the day was lost; there was no retrieving the effect produced by the first flight of the North Carolinians. Unwilling to risk the destruction of his army, he directed a retreat to the place of rendezvous at Speedwell's Iron Works on Troublesome Creek. The British were too much cut up and fatigued to follow up their victory. Two regiments with Tarleton's cavalry attempted a pursuit but were called back. It was a dismal night even to the victors, a night of unusual darkness with torrents of rain. The cries of the disabled and dying who remained on the field of battle during the night exceeded all description.

The loss of the Americans in this hard-fought affair was never fully ascertained. Their official returns, made immediately after the action, give little more than 400 killed and wounded, about nine hundred missing. The loss sustained by his lordship, even if numerically less, was far more fatal. Of his small army, 93 had fallen, 413 were wounded, and 26 missing. Thus, one-fourth of his army was either killed or disabled; his troops were exhausted by fatigue and hunger. His victory, in fact, was almost as ruinous as a defeat.

Greene lay for two days within 10 miles of him, gathering up his scattered troops. He had imbibed the spirit of Washington and remained undismayed by hardships or reverses.

In Washington he had a friend whose approbation was dearer to him than the applause of thousands. To Greene's account of the battle he sent a cheering reply: "The motives which induced you to risk an action with Lord Cornwallis are supported upon the best military principle, and the consequence, if you can prevent the dissipation of your troops, will no doubt be fortunate."

The consequence was such as Washington predicted. Cornwallis could not even hold the ground he had won but was obliged to retreat to some position where he might obtain supplies for his famished army.

Leaving, therefore, some of his officers and men who were too severely wounded to bear travelling, together with a number of wounded Americans, under a flag of truce, he set out, on the third day after the action, for Cross Creek (the Haw), an eastern branch of Cape Fear River, where he expected to be supplied with provisions and to have his sick and wounded taken care of. Hence, too, he could open communication with Wilmington and obtain from the depot there such supplies as the country about Cross Creek did not afford.

No sooner did Greene learn that Cornwallis was retreating than he set out to follow him, determined to bring him again to action. His troops, however, suffered greatly in this pursuit from wintry weather, deep, wet, clayey roads, and scarcity of provisions, but they harassed the enemy's rear-guard with frequent skirmishes.

On the 28th, Greene arrived at Ramsay's Mills, on Deep River, hard on the traces of Cornwallis, who had left the place a few hours previously with precipitation.

At Deep River, Greene was brought to a stand. Cornwallis had broken down the bridge by which he had crossed and further pursuit for the present was impossible. The militia had been continually on the march with little to eat, less to drink, and obliged to sleep in the woods in the midst of smoke. The term for which most of them had enlisted was expired and they now demanded their discharge, which Greene felt compelled to grant. His force thus reduced, it would be impossible to pursue the enemy further. In this situation, remote from reinforcements, inferior to the enemy in numbers, and without hope of support, what was to be done? Suddenly he determined to change his course and carry the war into South Carolina. This would oblige the enemy either to follow him, and thus abandon North Carolina, or to sacrifice all his posts in the upper part of North Carolina and Georgia.

He apprised Sumter, Pickens, and Marion of his intentions and called upon them to be ready to co-operate with all the militia they could collect, promising to send forward cavalry and small detachments of light infantry to aid them in capturing outposts before the army should arrive.

To Lafayette he writes at the same time. "I expect by this movement to draw Cornwallis out of this State, and prevent him from forming a junction with Arnold. If you follow to support me, it is not impossible that we may give him a drubbing, especially if General Wayne comes up with the Pennsylvanians."

In pursuance of his plan, Greene, on the 30th of March, discharged all his militia with many thanks for the courage and fortitude with which they had endured peril and hardship. Then, after giving his army a short repose and having collected a few days' provision, he set forward on the 5th of April toward Camden, where Rawdon had his head-quarters.

Cornwallis, in the mean time, was grievously disappointed in the hopes of obtaining provisions at Cross Creek and reinforcements from the royalists in that neighborhood. Neither could he open communication by Cape Fear River for the conveyance of his troops to Wilmington. The distance by water was about 100 miles, the breadth of the river seldom above 100 yards, and the inhabitants on each side generally hostile. He was compelled, therefore, to continue his retreat by land to Wilmington, where he arrived on the 7th of April.

It was his lordship's intention, as soon as he should have equipped his own corps and received reinforcement from Ireland, to return to the upper country in hopes of giving protection to the royal interest in South Carolina and of concerting new measures with Sir Henry Clinton. His plans were all disconcerted, however, by intelligence of Greene's rapid march toward Camden. Never, we are told, was his lordship more affected than by this news. It was too late for his lordship to render aid by a move towards Camden. All thoughts of offensive operations against North Carolina were at an end. Sickness, desertion, and the loss sustained at Guilford Courthouse had reduced his army to 1435 men.

In this sad predicament, after several days of irresolution, he determined to take advantage of Greene's having left the back part of Virginia open to march directly into that province, and attempt a junction with the force there under Phillips.

By this move he might draw Greene back northward, and by the reduction of Virginia he might promote the subjugation of the

South. The move, however, he felt to be perilous. His troops were worn down by marching through an inhospitable country; they had now more marching before them under still worse circumstances.

There was no time for hesitation or delay; Greene might return and render the junction with Phillips impracticable. Having sent an express to the latter, informing him of his coming and appointing a meeting at Petersburg, his lordship set off on the 25th of April on his fated march into Virginia.

(CHAPTER 55)

We must now step back in dates to bring up events in the more northern parts of the Union.

In a former chapter we left Arnold fortifying himself at Portsmouth after his ravaging incursion. At the solicitation of Governor Jefferson, backed by Congress, the Chevalier de la Luzerne had requested the French commander to send a ship of the line and some frigates to Chesapeake Bay to oppose the traitor. Fortunately a severe snow storm (Jan. 22d) scattered Arbuthnot's blockading squadron and enabled the French fleet at Newport to look abroad. Rochambeau wrote to Washington that the Chevalier Destouches, who commanded the fleet, proposed to send 3 or 4 ships to the Chesapeake.

Washington feared the position of Arnold might enable him to withstand a mere attack by sea. Anxious to ensure his capture, he advised that Destouches send his whole fleet and that Rochambeau embark about 1000 men on board of it with artillery and apparatus for a siege, engaging, on his own part, to send off immediately a detachment of 1200 men to co-operate.

The French commanders, acting on their own impulse, had, about the 9th of February, detached M. de Tilly with a sixty gun ship and two frigates to make a dash into the Chesapeake. Washington was apprised of their sailing just as he was preparing to send off the

1200 men. He gave command of this detachment to Lafayette, instructing him to act in conjunction with the militia and the ships sent by Destouches against the enemy's corps in Virginia. As the case was urgent, he was to suffer no delay for want of provisions, forage, or waggons, but, where ordinary means did not suffice, he was to resort to military impress.

Washington wrote at the same time to Steuben, informing him of the arrangements, requesting him to be on the alert. "Arnold, on the appearance of the fleet, may endeavor to retreat through North Carolina. . . . Should you be able to capture this detachment with its chief, it will be an event as pleasing as it will be useful."

Lafayette set out on his march on the 22d of February and Washington was indulging the hope that, scanty as was the naval force sent to the Chesapeake, the combined enterprise might be successful when, on the 27th, he received a letter from Rochambeau announcing its failure. De Tilly had made his dash into Chesapeake Bay but Arnold had been apprised by Arbuthnot of his approach and had drawn his ships high up Elizabeth River. The water was too shallow for the largest French ship to get within four leagues of him. One of De Tilly's frigates ran aground and was got off with difficulty, and that commander, fearing to be blockaded should he linger, put to sea and returned to Newport, having captured during his cruise a British frigate of forty-four guns and two privateers with their prizes.

The French commanders now determined to follow the plan suggested by Washington and operate in the Chesapeake with their whole fleet and a detachment of land troops, being, as they said, disposed to risk every thing to hinder Arnold from establishing himself at Portsmouth.

Washington set out for Newport to concert operations with the French commanders. Before his departure, he wrote to Lafayette, on the 1st of March, giving him intelligence of these intentions, and desiring him to transmit it to Steuben.

Washington arrived at Newport on the 6th of March, and found the French fleet ready for sea, the troops 1100 strong, commanded by General the Baron de Viomenil, being already embarked. On board of the admiral's ship, Washington had an interview with Rochambeau and arranged the plan of the campaign.

On the 8th of March, he writes to Lafayette: "I have the pleasure to inform you that the whole fleet went out with a fair wind this evening about sunset." The British fleet made sail in pursuit on the morning of the 10th but, as the French had so much the start, it was hoped they would reach Chesapeake Bay before them.

On returning to his head-quarters at New Windsor, Washington on the 20th of March found letters from Greene, informing him that he had saved all his baggage, artillery, and stores, notwithstanding the hot pursuit of the enemy and was now in his turn following them, but that he was greatly in need of reinforcements. "My regard for the public good, and my inclination to promote your success," writes Washington in reply, "will prompt me to give every assistance, . . . but what can I do if I am not furnished with the means?"

In the mean time, Lafayette was pressing forward by forced marches for Virginia. Arriving at the Head of Elk on the 3d of March, he halted until he should receive tidings respecting the French fleet. On the 7th he received Washington's letter of the 1st, apprising him of the approaching departure of the whole fleet with land forces. Lafayette now conducted his troops by water to Annapolis and, concluding the French fleet must be already in the Chesapeake, he crossed the bay in an open boat to Virginia and pushed on to confer with the American and French commanders, to get a convoy for his troops, and to concert matters for a vigorous co-operation. Arriving at York on the 14th, he found Steuben in the bustle of military preparations and confident of having 5000 militia ready to operate. These, with Lafayette's detachment, would be sufficient for the attack by land; but the French fleet had not yet appeared though double the time necessary for the voyage had elapsed.

On the 20th, word was brought that a fleet had come to anchor within the capes. It was supposed of course to be the French and now the capture of the traitor was certain. An officer of the French navy bore down to visit the fleet but returned with the astounding intelligence that it was British!

Arbuthnot had in fact overtaken Destouches on the 16th of

March off the capes of Virginia. Their forces were nearly equal: 8 ships of the line and 4 frigates on each side, the French having more men and the English more guns. An engagement took place which lasted about an hour. The British van at first took the brunt of the action; the centre came up to its relief. The French line gave way but rallied and formed again at some distance. The crippled state of some of his ships prevented the British admiral from bringing on a second encounter, nor did the French seek one but shaped their course the next day back to Newport. Both sides claimed a victory. The British certainly effected the main objects they had in view: the French were cut off from the Chesapeake, the combined enterprise against Portsmouth was disconcerted, and Arnold was saved.

Washington's anxiety was now awakened for the safety of Greene. Two thousand troops had sailed from New York under Phillips, probably to join with the force under Arnold and proceed to reinforce Cornwallis. Should they form a junction, Greene would be unable to withstand them. With these considerations Washington wrote to Lafayette, urging him, since he was already half the distance to push on with all possible speed to join the southern army.

The detachment from New York under Phillips arrived at Portsmouth on the 26th of March. That officer immediately took command, greatly to the satisfaction of the British officers who had been acting under Arnold. The force now collected there amounted to 3500 men. The garrison of New York had been greatly weakened in furnishing this detachment, but Cornwallis had urged the policy of transferring the seat of war to Virginia, even at the expense of abandoning New York.

The disparity in force was now so great that Steuben had to withdraw his troops and remove the military stores into the interior. Many of the militia, their term of three months being expired, stacked their arms and set off for their homes.

Phillips had hitherto remained quiet in Portsmouth, completing the fortifications but evidently making preparations for an expedition. On the 16th of April, he left 1000 men in garrison and, embarking the rest in small vessels of light draught, proceeded up

James River, destroying armed vessels, public magazines, and a ship-yard belonging to the State.

Landing at City Point, he advanced against Petersburg, a place of deposit of military stores and tobacco. He was met about a mile below the town by about 1000 militia under General Muhlenberg, who, after disputing the ground inch by inch, retreated across the Appomattox, breaking down the bridge behind them.

Phillips entered the town, set fire to the tobacco warehouses, and destroyed all the vessels in the river. Repairing the bridge over the Appomattox, he proceeded to Chesterfield Court-house, where he destroyed barracks and public stores, while Arnold with a detachment laid waste the magazines of tobacco in the direction of Warwick.

This destructive course was pursued until they arrived at Manchester, opposite Richmond, where the tobacco warehouses were immediately in a blaze. Richmond was a leading object of this desolating enterprise for there a great part of the military stores of the State had been collected. Fortunately, Lafayette with his detachment of 2000 men, had arrived there by forced marches the evening before and, being joined by about 2000 militia and 60 dragoons, had posted himself strongly on the high banks on the north side of the river.

There being no bridge across the river, Phillips did not think it prudent to attempt a passage in face of such a force so posted. Returning down the river to the place where his vessels awaited him, Phillips re-embarked on the 2d of May and dropped slowly down the river below the confluence of the Chickahomony. He was followed cautiously and his movements watched by Lafayette, who posted himself behind the last-named river.

Despatches from Cornwallis now informed Phillips that his lordship was advancing with all speed from the South to effect a junction with him. The general immediately made a rapid move to regain possession of Petersburg, where the junction was to take place. Lafayette attempted by forced marches to get there before him but was too late. Falling back, therefore, he recrossed James River and stationed himself some miles below Richmond to be at hand for the protection of the public stores collected there.

During this main expedition of Phillips, some of his smaller vessels had carried on plunder and devastation in other rivers emptying into the Chesapeake Bay, setting fire to houses where they met with resistance. One had ascended the Potomac and menaced Mount Vernon. Lund Washington, who had charge of the estate, met the flag which the enemy sent on shore and saved the property from ravage by furnishing the vessel with provisions. Washington received a letter from Lund himself and had immediately written him a reply. He was stung to the quick that his agent should "commune with a parcel of plundering scoundrels." He continued, "It would have been a less painful circumstance to me to have heard that, in consequence of your noncompliance with their request, they had burnt my house and laid my plantation in ruins."

In the mean time, the desolating career of Phillips was brought to a close. He had been ill for some days previous to his arrival at Petersburg, and died four days after he reached there. What made his death more sensibly felt was that it put Arnold once more in general command.

He held it, however, but for a short time, as Cornwallis arrived at Petersburg on the 20th of May, after nearly a month's weary marching from Wilmington. His lordship found his force augmented by a considerable detachment of royal artillery, two battalions of light infantry, two British regiments, a Hessian regiment, Simcoe's corps of Queen's rangers, cavalry and infantry, 100 yagers, Arnold's royalists, and the garrison of Portsmouth. He was cheered also by intelligence that Rawdon had obtained an advantage over Greene before Camden and that three British regiments had sailed from Cork for Charleston. His mind was now at ease with regard to Southern affairs; his spirits were again lifted and he indulged in hope of a glorious campaign in those parts of America where he commanded.

While affairs were approaching a crisis in Virginia, troubles were threatening from the north. There were rumors of invasion from Canada, of war councils among the savage tribes, and of a revival of the territorial feuds between New York and Vermont.

Such, however, was the deplorable inefficiency of the military system that though, according to the resolves of Congress, there were to have been 37,000 men under arms, Washington's whole force on the Hudson in May did not amount to 7000 men, of whom little more than 4000 were effective.

He still had his head-quarters at New Windsor, within a few miles of West Point. Here he received intelligence that the enemy were in force on the opposite side of the Hudson, marauding the country north of Croton River, and he ordered a hasty advance of Connecticut troops in that direction.

The Croton River, flowing from east to west across Westchester County, formed the barrier of the American lines. The advanced posts of Washington's army protected the upper country from the incursions of foraging parties and marauders. The incursions most to be guarded against were those of Colonel Delancey's Loyalists, a horde of tories and refugees which had their stronghold in Morrisania and who swept off forage and cattle for the British army at New York. Hence they were sometimes stigmatized by the opprobrious appellation of Cow Boys.

The object of their present incursion was to surprise an outpost near a fordable part of the Croton River not far from Pine's Bridge. The post was commanded by Colonel Christopher Greene of Rhode Island. Colonel Delancey, who led this foray, was successor to the unfortunate André as Adjutant-general of the British army. He conducted it at the head of 100 horse and 200 foot. The Croton was forded at daybreak and the farm houses were surprised in which the Americans were quartered. That occupied by Colonel Greene and Major Flagg was first surrounded. The Major discharged his pistols from a window but was shot through the head and afterwards despatched by sabre.

The door of Greene's room was burst open. He defended himself vigorously with his sword but he was overpowered by numbers and barbarously mangled. A massacre was going on in other quarters. It is said that Colonel Delancey was not present at the carnage but remained on the south side of the Croton to secure the retreat of his party.

Before the troops ordered out by Washington arrived, the

marauders had made a retreat. They attempted to carry off Greene a prisoner but he died within three quarters of a mile of the house. The commander-in-chief heard with anguish and indignation the tragical fate of his faithful friend and soldier.

At this juncture, Washington's attention was called in another direction. A frigate had arrived at Boston, bringing the Count de Barras to take command of the French naval force. He brought the cheering intelligence that 20 ships of the line, with land forces, were to sail from France under the Count de Grasse for the West Indies and that 12 of these ships were to relieve the squadron at Newport and might be expected in July or August.

Rochambeau, having received despatches from the court of France, requested an interview with Washington. They met in Weathersfield in Connecticut on the 22d of May, hoping to settle a definitive plan of the campaign. Both being as yet ignorant of the arrival of Cornwallis in Virginia, policy of a joint expedition to relieve the Carolinas was discussed. As the French ships in Newport were still blockaded by a superior force, a march to the Southern States would have to be made in the heat of summer. The difficulties and expenses of land transportation presented a formidable objection.

On the other hand, an effective blow might be struck at New York; that important post might be wrested from the enemy, or, if not, might be obliged to recall a part of their force from the South.

It was determined, therefore, that the French troops should march from Newport as soon as possible and form a junction with the American army on the Hudson and that both should move down to the vicinity of New York to make a combined attack, in which de Grasse should be invited to co-operate with his fleet and a body of land troops.

A vessel was despatched by Rochambeau, to inform de Grasse of this arrangement; letters were addressed by Washington to the authorities of New Jersey and the New England States urging them to fill up their battalions and furnish their quotas of provisions. Notwithstanding all his exertions however, when he mustered his forces at Peekskill, he was mortified to find not more than 5000 effective men. Notwithstanding, too, all the resolutions passed in the various States for supplying the army, it would, at this critical moment, have been destitute of provisions had it not been for Robert Morris, a delegate to Congress from the State of Pennsylvania and recently appointed superintendent of finance. This patriotic man, when public means failed, pledged his own credit in transporting military stores and feeding the army.

Rochambeau and Lauzun being arrived with their troops in Connecticut, Washington prepared for spirited operations, quickened by the intelligence that part of the garrison of New York had been detached to forage the Jerseys. Two objects were contemplated by him: one, the surprisal of the British works at the north end of New York Island; the other, the capture or destruction of Delancey's corps in Morrisania. The attack upon the posts was to be conducted by Lincoln with a detachment from the main army, which he was to bring down by water; that on Delancey's corps by Lauzun with his legion, aided by Sheldon's dragoons and a body of Connecticut troops. Both operations were to be carried into effect on the 3d of July. Should any thing prevent Lincoln from attempting the works on New York Island, he was to land above Spyt den Duivel Creek, march to the high grounds in front of King's Bridge, lie concealed there until Lauzun's attack on Delancey's corps should be announced by firing or other means, then to dispose his force to make the enemy think it larger than it really was, thereby deterring troops from coming over the bridge to turn Lauzun's right while he prevented the escape over the bridge of Delancey's refugees.

In pursuance of the plan, Lincoln left Peekskill on the 1st, with 800 men and artillery and proceeded to Teller's Point, where they were embarked and rowed silently at night down the Tappan Sea. At daylight they kept concealed under the land. Lauzun was supposed, at the same time, to be on the way from Connecticut. Washington, on the morning of the 2d, commenced his march with his main force, without baggage, to Valentine's Hill, 4 miles above King's Bridge, where he arrived about sunrise.

Lincoln, on the morning of the 2d, had left his flotilla concealed under the eastern shore and crossed to Fort Lee to reconnoitre Fort Washington from the cliffs on the opposite side of the Hudson. To his surprise, he discovered a British force on the north end of New York Island and a ship-of-war in the river. In fact, the troops detached into the Jerseys had returned. Surprisal of the forts was out of the question.

Lincoln's thoughts now were to aid Lauzun's part of the scheme. Before daylight of the 3d, he landed his troops above Spyt den Duivel Creek and took possession of the high ground north of Harlem River. Discovered by a foraging party of the enemy, 1500 strong, a skirmish ensued. The firing was heard by Lauzun, just arrived at East Chester; finding the country alarmed and hope of surprising Delancey's corps at an end, he hastened to support Lincoln. Washington also advanced with his troops from Valentine's Hill. The British, perceiving their danger, retreated to their boats on the Harlem River and crossed to New York Island.

Disappointed in both objects, Washington retired to Valentine's Hill and the next day marched to Dobbs Ferry, where he was joined by Rochambeau on the 6th of July. The two armies now encamped; the American in two lines, resting on the Hudson at Dobbs Ferry, covered by batteries and extending eastward toward the Sawmill River; the French in a single line on the hills further east, reaching to the Bronx River.

The two armies lay thus encamped for three or four weeks. In the mean time letters urged Washington's presence in Virginia. Richard Henry Lee advised that he should come with about 3000 good troops and be clothed with dictatorial powers. "I am fully persuaded," writes Washington in reply, ". . . that the measures I have adopted will give more effectual and speedy relief to the State of Virginia than my marching thither. . . . My present plan . . . will produce one of two things, either the fall of New York or a withdrawal of troops from Virginia, excepting a garrison at Portsmouth, at which place I have no doubt of the enemy's intention of establishing a permanent post."

After this letter was written, Washington crossed the river at Dobbs Ferry, accompanied by Rochambeau, Beville, and Duportail, to reconnoitre the British posts on the north end of New York Island. Their next movement was to reconnoitre the enemy's posts at King's Bridge and on the east side of New York Island, to cut off, if possible, such of Delancey's corps as should be found without the British lines. Five thousand troops, French and American, led by Chastellux and Lincoln, were to protect this reconnoissance and menace the enemy's posts. On the 21st of July, in the evening, the troops began their march in separate columns; the whole detachment arrived at King's Bridge about daylight and formed on the height back of Fort Independence. The enemy's forts on New York Island did not appear to have the least intelligence of what was going on until the Americans and French displayed themselves in full array, their arms flashing in the morning sunshine and their banners unfolded to the breeze.

Washington and Rochambeau, accompanied by engineers, set out under the escort of a troop of dragoons to reconnoitre the enemy's position and works from every point of view. It was a wide reconnoissance, extending from the Hudson to the Sound. The whole was done slowly and scientifically, exact notes and diagrams being made of every thing that might be of importance in future operations.

While the enemy's works had been thoroughly reconnoitred, light troops and lancers had performed their duty in scouring the neighborhood. Having effected the purposes of their expedition, the two generals set off with their troops, on the 23d, for their encampment, where they arrived about midnight.

The immediate effect of this threatening movement of Washington appears in a letter of Sir Henry Clinton to Cornwallis, dated July 26th, requesting him to order three regiments to New York from Carolina.

(CHAPTER 56)

The first object of Cornwallis on the junction of his forces at Petersburg in May was to strike a blow at Lafayette. The marquis was encamped on the north side of James River, between Wilton and Richmond, with about 1000 regulars, 2000 militia, and 50 dragoons. He was waiting for reinforcements of militia and for the arrival of General Wayne with the Pennsylvania line.

His lordship, hoping to draw him into an action, marched on the 24th of May to James River, which he crossed at Westover, about 30 miles below Richmond. Here he was joined on the 26th by a reinforcement from New York, part of which he sent under Leslie to strengthen the garrison at Portsmouth.

Strongly reinforced, Cornwallis moved to dislodge Lafayette from Richmond. The latter, conscious of the inferiority of his forces, decamped as soon as he heard his lordship had crossed James River. He directed his march toward the north to a junction with Wayne. Cornwallis followed Lafayette, but soon found it impossible either to overtake him or prevent his junction with Wayne; he turned his attention, therefore, to other objects.

Greene, in his passage through Virginia, had urged the importance of removing horses out of the way of the enemy but his caution had been neglected. Great numbers of fine horses in the stables of Virginia gentlemen enabled Cornwallis to mount many of his troops in first-rate style. These he employed in scouring the country and destroying public stores.

The State legislature had been removed for safety to Charlottesville, where it was assembled for the purpose of levying taxes and drafting militia. Tarleton, with 180 cavalry and 70 mounted infantry, was ordered by Cornwallis to dash there, break up the legislature, and carry off members. On his way thither, he surprised several persons of note at the house of a Dr. Walker but lingered so long breakfasting that a person on a fleet horse had time to reach Charlottesville before him and spread the alarm. Tarleton galloped into the town thinking to capture the whole assembly. Seven fell into his hand but the rest had made their escape. No better success attended a party of horse under Captain McLeod, detached to surprise the Governor (Thomas Jefferson) at his residence in Monticello, where several members of the Legislature were his guests. The guests dispersed and the family was hurried off, while the governor made a rapid retreat on horseback to Carter's Mountain.

Having set fire to all the public stores at Charlottesville, Tarleton pushed for the point of Fork at the confluence of the Rivanna and Fluvanna to aid a detachment sent under Simcoe to destroy military stores collected at that post. Steuben, who was stationed there with 500 Virginia regulars and a few militia and had heard of the march of Tarleton, had succeeded in transporting the greater part of the stores as well as his troops across the river. The unexpected appearance of Simcoe's infantry, however, designedly spread out on the opposite heights, deceived him into the idea that it was the van of the British army. In his alarm he made a night retreat of 30 miles, leaving the greater part of the stores scattered along the river bank, which were destroyed the next morning by a detachment of the enemy sent across in canoes.

On the 10th of June, Lafayette was at length gladdened by the arrival of Wayne with about 900 of the Pennsylvania line. Thus reinforced he changed his whole plan and ventured on the aggressive. Cornwallis had gotten between him and a large deposit of military stores at Albemarle Old Court House. The marquis, by a rapid march at night, threw himself between the British army and the stores, and, being joined by numerous mountain militia, took a strong position to dispute the advance of the enemy. Cornwallis did not think it advisable to pursue this enterprise, and turned toward the lower part of Virginia and made a retrograde march to Richmond and afterwards to Williamsburg.

Lafayette, joined by Steuben and his forces, had about 4000 men under him, half of whom were regulars. He now followed the British army at the distance of 20 miles, throwing forward his light troops to harass their rear.

An express was received by Cornwallis at Williamsburg, where he had arrived on the 25th, which obliged him to change his plans. The movements of Washington in the neighborhood of New York menacing an attack had produced the desired effect. Sir Henry had written to Cornwallis requiring a part of his troops for its protection. His lordship prepared to comply with this requisition but, as it would leave him too weak to continue at Williamsburg, he set out on the 4th of July for Portsmouth.

Lafayette followed him on the ensuing day and took post within

9 miles of his camp, intending, when the main body of the enemy should have crossed the ford to the island of Jamestown, to fall upon the rear guard. Cornwallis suspected his design and prepared to take advantage of it. The wheel carriages, bat horses and baggage were passed over to the island under the escort of the Queen's rangers, making a great display, as if the main body had crossed. His lordship, however, with the greater part of his forces, remained on the main land, his right covered by ponds, the centre and left by morasses over which a few narrow causeways of logs connected his position with the country, and James Island lay in the rear. His camp was concealed by a skirt of woods and covered by an outpost.

In the morning of the 6th, as the Americans were advancing, two of Tarleton's men, pretending to be deserters, informed them that the king's troops had passed James River in the night, leaving nothing behind but the rear guard. Lafayette with his troops crossed the morass on the left of the enemy by a narrow causeway of logs and halted beyond about sunset. Wayne was detached with a body of riflemen, dragoons and continental infantry to make the attack while the marquis with 900 continentals and some militia stood ready to support him.

Wayne easily routed a patrol of cavalry and drove in the pickets, who had been ordered to give way readily. Wayne pushed forward with the Pennsylvania line, 800 strong, and three field-pieces to attack it. At the first discharge of a cannon more than 2000 of the enemy emerged from concealment, and Wayne found the whole British line in battle array before him. To retreat was more dangerous than to go on. So thinking, he ordered a charge to be sounded and threw horse and foot with shouts upon the enemy. Fortunately the heaviness of the fire had awakened the suspicions of Lafayette: it was too strong for the outpost of a rear-guard. Spurring to a point of land which commanded a view of the British camp, he discovered the actual force of the enemy and the peril of Wayne. Galloping back, he sent word to Wayne to fall back to Muhlenberg's brigade, which had just arrived and was forming within half a mile of the scene of conflict. Wayne did so in good order.

The whole army then retired across the morass. The enemy's cavalry would have pursued them but Cornwallis forbade it. He thought the Americans more strong than they really were and the retreat a mere feint to draw him into an ambuscade.

Lafayette retreated to Green Springs, where he rallied and reposed his troops. Cornwallis crossed over to Jamestown Island after dark and proceeded to Portsmouth. His object was in conformity to instructions from the ministry to establish on the Chesapeake a permanent post to serve as a central point for naval and military operations.

We will now turn to resume the course of General Greene's campaigning in the Carolinas. It will be recollected that Greene, on the 5th of April, set out from Deep River on a march into South Carolina. Sumter and Marion had been keeping alive the revolutionary fire in that State; on the re-appearance of Greene they stood ready to aid.

On his way to attack Lord Rawdon's post at Camden, Greene detached Lee to join Marion with his legion and make an attack upon Fort Watson by way of diversion. For himself, he appeared before Camden but, finding it too strong and too well garrisoned, fell back and took post at Hobkirk's Hill, hoping to draw his lordship out. His lordship attacked him on the 25th of April. There was a hard-fought battle; Greene was obliged to retreat. His lordship did not pursue but shut himself up in Camden, waiting to be rejoined by part of his garrison which was absent.

Greene, Lee, and Marion had hoped to intercept these reinforcements, but efforts were unavailing. Rawdon was rejoined by the other part of his troops. His superior force now threatened to give him the mastery. Greene felt the hazardous nature of his situation; he prepared for another of his long and stubborn retreats.

The very next morning there was a joyful reverse. His lordship had heard of the march of Cornwallis into Virginia and that all hope of aid from him was at an end. His garrison was out of provisions. All supplies were cut off by the Americans; he had no choice but to evacuate. He left Camden in flames.

Rapid successes now attended the American arms. Fort Motte, the middle post between Camden and Ninety Six, was taken by Marion and Lee. Lee next captured Granby and marched to aid

Pickens in the siege of Augusta. Greene sat before the fortress of Ninety Six on the 22d of May. It was principally garrisoned by royalists from New Jersey and New York, commanded by Colonel Cruger. The siege lasted nearly a month. The place was valiantly defended. Lee arrived with his legion, having failed before Augusta, and invested a stockaded fort which formed part of the works.

Word was brought that Rawdon was pressing forward with reinforcements. The troops being eager to storm the works before his lordship should arrive, a partial assault was made on the 18th of June. The stockaded fort was taken but the troops were repulsed from the main works. Greene retreated and halted at Bush River, at 20 miles distance, to observe the motion of the enemy.

Rawdon entered Ninety Six on the 21st but sallied forth again on the 24th, taking with him two thousand troops, hoping by a rapid move to overtake Greene. Want of provisions soon obliged him to give up the pursuit and return to Ninety Six. Leaving half of his force there under Cruger, he sallied a second time at the head of 1100, marching by the south side of the Saluda for the Congaree.

He was now pursued in his turn by Greene and Lee. At Orangeburg, where he arrived on the 8th of July, his lordship was joined by a large detachment under Colonel Stuart.

Greene had followed him closely; having collected all his detachments and being joined by Sumter, he appeared within 4 miles of Orangeburg on the 10th of July and offered battle. The offer was not accepted and the position of Rawdon was too strong to be attacked. Greene remained there two or three days when, learning that Cruger was advancing with forces from Ninety Six, which would again give his lordship a superiority of force, he moved off with his infantry on the night of the 13th of July, crossed the Saluda, and posted himself on the east side of the Wateree, at the high hills of Santee, awaiting the arrival of continental troops and militia from North Carolina.

At the time when he moved from Orangeburg, (July 13th) he detached Sumter with about 1000 light troops to scour the lower country and attack the British posts in the vicinity of Charleston. Under Sumter acted Marion, Lee, the Hamptons, and other enterprising partisans. They were to act separately in breaking up the minor posts at and about Dorchester but to unite at Monk's Corner, where Lieutenant-colonel Coates was stationed with the ninth regiment. This post carried, they were to reunite with Greene's army on the high hills of Santee.

Scarce was Sumter on his march when he received a letter from Greene, dated July 14th, stating that Cruger had formed a junction with Rawdon the preceding night; no time therefore was to be lost. "Push your operations night and day; station a party to watch the enemy's motions at Orangeburg. Keep Colonel Lee and General Marion advised of all matters from above, and tell Colonel Lee to thunder even at the gates of Charleston."

Colonel Henry Hampton with a party was posted to keep an eye on Orangeburg. Lee with his legion, accompanied by Lieutenant-colonel Wade Hampton and a detachment of cavalry, was sent to carry Dorchester and then press forward to the gates of Charleston, while Sumter, with the main body, took up his line of march along the road on the south side of the Congaree towards Monk's Corner.

As Lee approached Dorchester, Colonel Wade Hampton, with his cavalry, passed to the east of that place to a bridge on Goose Creek to cut off all communication between the garrison and Monk's Corner. His sudden appearance gave the alarm and, when Lee arrived there, he found it deserted. Hampton feared that the alarm would spread through the country and the dash into the vicinity of Charleston be prevented—or perhaps that Lee might intend to make it by himself. Abandoning the bridge at Goose Creek, he set off with his cavalry, clattered down to the neighborhood of the lines and threw the city into confusion. Hampton captured a patrol of dragoons and a guard and then retired, carrying off 50 prisoners, several of them officers.

Lee arrived in the neighborhood on the following day; both now hastened to rejoin Sumter, who was waiting to collect his detachments before he made an attack on Coates at Monk's Corner. The assault was to be made on the following morning. During the night Coates decamped in silence; pursuit was commenced; Lee with his legion and Hampton with the State cavalry took the lead. Sumter followed with the infantry. The rear-guard of the British was overtaken and, on being charged by the cavalry sword in hand, threw down their arms without firing a shot, and cried for quarter, which was granted. Meanwhile, Captain Armstrong with the first section of cavalry pushed on in pursuit of Coates and the main body. That officer had crossed a wooden bridge over Quimby Creek, loosened the planks, and was only waiting to be rejoined by his rear-guard, to throw them off and cut off all pursuit. He knew nothing of an enemy being at hand until he saw Armstrong, who dashed across the bridge with his section. Armstrong's party in crossing the bridge had displaced some of the planks and formed a chasm. Lieutenant Carrington with the second section of dragoons leaped over it; the chasm being thus enlarged, the horses of the third section refused. A pell-mell fight took place between the handful of dragoons who had crossed and some of the enemy. Armstrong, seeing the foe too strong in front and no reinforcement coming on in rear, wheeled off with his men to the left, galloped into the woods and pushed up along the stream to ford it and seek the main body.

During the melée Lee had come up and endeavored to replace the planks of the bridge. While they were thus occupied, Coates opened fire upon them from the other end of the bridge; having no fire arms to reply with, they were obliged to retire. The remainder of the planks were then thrown from the bridge, after which Coates took post on an adjacent plantation, and awaited the arrival of Sumter with the main body, determined to make a defence.

It was not until three o'clock in the afternoon that Sumter with his forces appeared upon the ground. By four o'clock the attack commenced. Sumter, with part of the troops, advanced in front under cover of a line of huts, which he wished to secure. Marion, with his brigade, approached on the right of the enemy, where there was no shelter but fences; the cavalry, not being able to act, remained at a distance as a reserve, and, if necessary to cover a retreat.

Sumter's brigade soon got possession of the huts, where they used their rifles with sure effect. Marion and his men rushed up through a galling fire to the fences on the right. The enemy retired within the house and garden and kept up a sharp fire from doors and windows and picketed fence. The Americans, having repaired the bridge, sent off for the artillery. The evening was at hand and their ammunition was exhausted; they retired in good order, intending to renew the combat with artillery in the morning. Leaving the cavalry to watch and control the movements of the enemy, they drew off and encamped at the distance of 3 miles.

Here, when they came to compare notes, it was found that Marion's men, from their exposed situation, had borne the brunt of the battle, while Sumter's had suffered but little, being mostly sheltered in the huts. Jealousy and discord reigned in the camp. Lee, accustomed to act independently, and unwilling, perhaps, to acknowledge Sumter as his superior officer, took up his line of march for head-quarters without consulting him. Sumter still had force enough, now that he was joined by the artillery, to have held the enemy in a state of siege, but he apprehended the approach of Rawdon. He therefore retired across the Santee and rejoined Greene at his encampment.

So ended this foray. One of the best effects of the incursion was drawing down Lord Rawdon from Orangeburg with 500 of his troops. He returned no more to the upper country, but sailed not long after from Charleston for Europe.

Colonel Stuart, who was left in command at Orangeburg, moved forward from that place and encamped within 16 miles of Greene's position on the high hills of Santee. The two armies lay in sight of each other's fires but two large rivers intervened to secure each party from sudden attack. Both armies, however, needed repose and military operations were suspended, as if by mutual consent, during the sultry summer heat.

The campaign had been a severe and trying one, but Greene had succeeded in regaining the greater part of Georgia and the two Carolinas, and, as he said, only wanted a little assistance from the North to complete their recovery.

(CHAPTER 57)

After the grand reconnoissance of New York Island, the confederate armies remained encamped about Dobbs Ferry and the Greenburg hills, awaiting augmentation for their meditated attack. To Washington's great disappointment, his army was but tardily and scantily recruited, while the garrison of New York was augmented by the arrival of 3000 Hessian troops from Europe. In this predicament he despatched letters to the governments of the Eastern States, representing his delicate and embarrassed situation. "Our allies," writes he, "who were made to expect a very considerable augmentation of force by this time . . . must conjecture, upon good grounds, that the campaign will waste fruitlessly away. It will be no small degree of triumph to our enemies and will have a pernicious influence upon our friends in Europe, should they find such a failure of resource or such a want of energy to draw it out that our boasted and extensive preparations end only in idle parade."

In a few days came letters from Lafayette, dated 26th and 30th of July, speaking of the embarkation of the greatest part of Cornwallis's army at Portsmouth. "There are in Hampton Roads 30 transport ships full of troops, most of them red coats, and eight or ten brigs with cavalry on board." He supposed their destination to be New York, yet, though wind and weather were favorable, they did not sail. "Should a French fleet now come into Hampton Roads, the British army would, I think, be ours."

At this juncture arrived the French frigate Concorde at Newport, bringing despatches from de Grasse. He was to leave St. Domingo on the 3d of August with between 25 and 30 ships of the line and a considerable body of land forces and steer immediately for the Chesapeake.

This changed the face of affairs. All attempt upon New York was postponed; the whole of the French army and as large a part of the Americans as could be spared were to move to Virginia and co-operate with de Grasse for the redemption of the Southern States.

Washington after being disappointed so often by the incompetency of his means, and, above all, thwarted by the enemy's naval potency, now had the possibility of coping with them on land and sea. The contemplated expedition was likely to consummate his plans and he determined to lead it in person. He would take with him something more than 2000 of the American army; the rest were to remain with Heath, who was to command West Point and other posts of the Hudson.

Perfect secrecy was maintained as to this change of plan. Preparations were carried on as if for an attack upon New York. The American troops themselves were kept in ignorance of their destination.

Previous to his decampment, Washington sent a party to clear the roads towards King's Bridge, as if the posts recently reconnoitred were to be attempted. On the 19th of August his troops were marched up along the Hudson river road towards King's Ferry.

Rochambeau, in like manner, broke up his encampment and took the road by White Plains, North Castle, Pine's Bridge, and Crompond toward the same point. All Westchester County was alive with the tramp of troops, the gleam of arms, and the lumbering of artillery and baggage waggons along its roads.

On the 20th, Washington arrived at King's Ferry and his troops began to cross the Hudson with their baggage, stores, and cannon and to encamp at Haverstraw. He himself crossed in the evening. Thence he wrote confidentially to Lafayette apprising him of his being on the march with the expedition. He wrote also to de Grasse, urging him to send up all his frigates and transports to the Head of Elk by the 8th of September for the transportation of the combined army. He informed him, also, that de Barras had resolved to join him in the Chesapeake with his squadron.

On the 22d, the French troops arrived and began to cross to Stony Point with their artillery, baggage, and stores. The operation occupied several days. The two armies commenced on the 25th their

lines of march towards the Jerseys, the Americans for Springfield on
the Rahway, the French for Whippany towards Trenton. Both armies were still kept in the dark as to the ultimate object of their
movement.

Washington reached the Delaware with his troops before Sir
Henry was aware of their destination. It was too late to oppose their
march, even had his forces been adequate. As a kind of counterplot,
therefore, he hurried off an expedition to the eastward, to insult
Connecticut and attack New London. The command of this expedition, which was to be one of ravage and destruction, was given to
Arnold.

On the 6th of September he appeared off the harbor of New
London with a fleet of ships and transports and a force of 2000
infantry and 300 cavalry.

New London stands on the west bank of the river Thames. The
approach was defended by two forts on opposite sides of the river,
about a mile below the town: Fort Trumbull on the west and Fort
Griswold on the east. The troops landed in two divisions of about 800
men each, one under Lieutenant Colonel Eyre on the east, the
other under Arnold on the west. Arnold met with little opposition;
the few militia which manned Fort Trumbull abandoned their posts
and crossed the river to Fort Griswold; he pushed on and took
possession of the town.

Colonel Eyre had a harder task. The militia, about 157 strong,
had collected in Fort Griswold. Eyre forced the pickets, made his
way into the fosse and attacked the fort on three sides; it was bravely
defended; the enemy were repeatedly repulsed but they returned
to the assault, effected a lodgment on the fraise, and made their way
with fixed bayonets through the embrasures. Eyre received a mortal
wound near the works; Major Montgomery took his place but was
killed as he mounted the parapet; Major Bromfield succeeded to the
command and carried the fort at the point of the bayonet.

Arnold in the mean time had carried on the work of destruction
at New London. Some of the American shipping had effected their
escape up the river but a number were burnt. Fire too was set to the
public stores; in a little while, the whole place was wrapped in
flames. Having completed his ravage, Arnold retreated to his boats,

leaving the town still burning. The traitor was pursued by the exasperated yeomanry but he escaped their vengeance. So ended his career of infamy in his native land.

The expedition failed of its main object: it had not diverted Washington. On the 30th of August he arrived at Philadelphia about noon and was hospitably entertained at the house of Mr. Morris, the patriotic financier. The greatest difficulty with which he had to contend in his present enterprise was the want of funds, part of his troops not having received any pay for a long time and having occasionally given evidence of great discontent. In this emergency he was accommodated by Rochambeau with a loan of 20,000 hard dollars, which Morris engaged to repay by the first of October. This pecuniary pressure was relieved by the arrival in Boston of Colonel Laurens from his mission to France, bringing with him 2,500,000 livres in cash, being part of a subsidy of 6,000,000 livres granted by the French King.

At Philadelphia Washington received despatches from Lafayette, dated the 21st and 24th of August, from his camp in Virginia. The embarkation at Portsmouth, which the Marquis had supposed might be intended for New York, was merely for Yorktown, where Cornwallis had determined to establish the permanent post ordered in his instructions.

Yorktown was a small place on a projecting bank on the south side of York River, opposite a promontory called Gloucester Point. The river was not more than a mile wide but deep enough to admit ships of a large size. Here Cornwallis proceeded to fortify the opposite points, calculating to have the works finished by the beginning of October, at which time Sir Henry Clinton intended to recommence operations on the Chesapeake. Believing that he had no present enemy but Lafayette to guard against, Cornwallis wrote to Sir Henry on the 22d of August offering to detach men to strengthen New York against the apprehended attack.

While Cornwallis felt thus secure, Lafayette was taking measures to cut off any retreat by land which his lordship might attempt on the arrival of de Grasse. Thus a net was quietly drawn round Cornwallis by the youthful general.

Washington left Philadelphia on the 5th of September on his way to the head of Elk. Below Chester he was met by an express bearing tidings of the arrival of de Grasse in the Chesapeake with 28 ships of the line. Washington instantly rode back to Chester to rejoice with Rochambeau, who was coming down to that place from Philadelphia by water.

Washington reached the Head of Elk on the 6th. Thence he wrote to de Grasse felicitating him on his arrival and informing him that the van of the two armies were about to embark and form a junction with the troops under the Count de St. Simon and the Marquis de Lafayette to co-operate in blocking up Cornwallis in York River so as to prevent his retreat by land or his getting any supplies from the country.

Unfortunately, there were not vessels enough at the Head of Elk for the transportation of all the troops, ordnance and stores; a part of the troops would have to proceed to Baltimore by land. Leaving Heath to bring on the American forces and de Viomenil the French, Washington, accompanied by Rochambeau, crossed the Susquehanna early on the 8th and pushed forward for Baltimore.

On the 9th he left Baltimore a little after daybreak, to visit Mount Vernon. Six years had elapsed since last he was under its roof, six wearing years of toil, of danger and constant anxiety. It was a late hour when he arrived at Mount Vernon. He was joined by his suite at dinner time on the following day and by Rochambeau in the evening. Chastellux and his aides-de-camp arrived there on the 11th and Mount Vernon was now crowded with guests, who were all entertained with Virginian hospitality. On the 12th, tearing himself away from the home of his heart, Washington with his military associates continued onward to join Lafayette at Williamsburg.

Cornwallis had been completely roused from his dream of security by the appearance on the 28th of August, of the fleet of de Grasse within the capes of the Delaware. Three French ships of the line and a frigate soon anchored at the mouth of York River. The boats of the fleet were immediately busy conveying 3300 land forces under the Marquis de St. Simon up James River to form the preconcerted junction with those under Lafayette.

Awakened to his danger, Cornwallis meditated a retreat to the Carolinas. It was too late. York River was blocked up by French ships; James River was filled with armed vessels covering the transportation of the troops. His lordship reconnoitred Williamsburg; it was too strong to be forced and Wayne had crossed James River to join his troops to those under the marquis. Seeing his retreat cut off in every direction, Cornwallis proceeded to strengthen his works, sending off repeated expresses to apprise Sir Henry Clinton of his perilous situation.

De Grasse had been but a few days anchored within the Chesapeake, and 1500 of his seamen were absent conveying troops up James River, when Admiral Graves, who commanded the British naval force on the American coast, appeared with 20 sail off the capes of Virginia. De Grasse, anxious to protect the squadron of de Barras, which was expected from Rhode Island, immediately put to sea with 24 ships, leaving the rest to blockade York and James Rivers.

Washington received information of the sailing of the fleet from the capes shortly after his departure from Mount Vernon and he remained in anxious uncertainty, until, at Bowling Green, he was relieved by rumors concerning the fleet, confirmed on his arriving at Williamsburg on the 14th.

Graves, on the sallying forth of the French fleet, immediately prepared for action although he had 5 ships less than de Grasse. The latter, however, was not disposed to accept the challenge, his force being weakened by the absence of so many of his seamen. His plan was to occupy the enemy by partial actions and skilful manoeuvres so as to retain his possession of the Chesapeake and cover the arrival of de Barras.

The vans of the two fleets and some ships of the centre engaged in the afternoon of the 7th of September. Several ships were damaged and many men killed and wounded on both sides.

De Grasse, who had the advantage of the wind, drew off after sunset; the British admiral was not inclined to push the engagement so near night on a hostile coast. For four days the fleets remained in sight of each other, repairing damages and manoeuvring; the French, still having the advantage of the wind, maintained their prudent policy of avoiding a general engagement. At length de Grasse, learning that de Barras was arrived within the capes, formed a junction and returned with him to his former anchoring ground. Graves, disappointed in his hope of intercepting de Barras and finding the Chesapeake guarded by a superior force, bore away for New York. Under convoy of the squadron of de Barras came a fleet of transports, conveying land forces under de Choisy with siege artillery and military stores.

From Williamsburg, Washington sent forward Count Fersen, one of the aides-de-camp of Rochambeau, to hurry on the French troops with all possible dispatch. It was with great satisfaction Washington learned that de Barras had anticipated his wishes, in sending transports and prize vessels up the bay to assist in bringing on the French troops. In the mean time he and Rochambeau, with Chastellux, Knox, and Duportail, embarked on the 18th, for a meeting with de Grasse on the following day aboard the admiral's ship. A plan of co-operation was soon arranged to be carried into effect on the arrival of the American and French armies from the north.

About sunset Washington and his companions took their leave of the admiral and returned, owing to storms and contrary winds, to Williamsburg on the 22d, when intelligence was received that threatened to disconcert all the plans. Admiral Digby, it appeared, had arrived in New York with 6 ships of the line and a reinforcement of troops. This intelligence Washington instantly transmitted to de Grasse who, in reply, expressed great concern, observing that the position of affairs was changed by the arrival of Digby. He proposed, therefore, to leave two vessels at the mouth of York River and the corvettes and frigates in James River, which, with the French troops on shore, would be sufficient assistance and to put to sea with the rest, either to intercept and fight the enemy where there was good sea room or to blockade them in New York should they not have sailed.

On reading this letter, Washington dreaded that the present plan of co-operation might fall through. With the assistance of the fleet the reduction of Yorktown was demonstrably certain and the surrender of the garrison must go far to terminate the war. Even a momentary absence of the French fleet might enable Cornwallis to evacuate Yorktown and effect a retreat. These and other considerations were urged in a letter to the count, remonstrating against his putting to sea. Lafayette, the bearer of the letter, argued the case so eloquently that the count consented to remain.

By the 25th the American and French troops were mostly arrived near Williamsburg and preparations were made for the decisive blow.

Yorktown is on the south side of York River, immediately opposite Gloucester Point. Cornwallis had fortified the town by seven redoubts and six batteries on the land side, connected by intrenchments; there was a line of batteries along the river. The town was flanked on each side by deep ravines and creeks emptying into York River, their heads, in front of the town, being not more than half a mile apart. The enemy had availed themselves of these natural defences in the arrangement of extensive outworks, with redoubts strengthened by abatis, field-works mounted with cannon, and trees cut down and left with the branches pointed outward.

Gloucester Point had likewise been fortified. Its batteries, with those of Yorktown, commanded the intervening river. Ships of war were stationed on it, protected by the guns of the forts, and the channel was obstructed by sunken vessels. The defence of Gloucester Point was confided to Lieutenant Colonel Dundas, with about 700 men. The enemy's main army was encamped about Yorktown.

That evening Cornwallis received dispatches from Sir Henry Clinton informing him of the arrival of Admiral Digby and that a fleet of 23 ships of the line with above 5000 troops would sail to his assistance probably on the 5th of October. Cornwallis immediately wrote in reply: "I shall retire this night within the works and have no doubt, if relief arrives in any reasonable time, York and Gloucester will be both in the possession of His Majesty's troops."

That night his lordship accordingly abandoned his outworks and drew his troops within the town. The abandoned outworks, seized the next morning by American and French troops, served to cover the troops employed in throwing up breastworks.

The War in the South (1780–1782)

The combined French and American forces were now 12,000 strong, exclusive of the Virginia militia which Governor Nelson had brought into the field. On the morning of the 28th of September the combined armies marched from Williamsburg toward Yorktown and encamped at night within 2 miles of it, driving in the pickets and some patrols of cavalry. General de Choisy was sent across York River, with Lauzun's legion and Weedon's brigade of militia, to watch the enemy on the side of Gloucester Point.

By the first of October the line of the besiegers formed a semicircle, each end resting on the river so that the investment by land was complete, while de Grasse with the main fleet remained in Lynn Haven Bay to keep off assistance by sea.

The besieged army began now to be greatly distressed for want of forage. In the evening of the 2d of October, Tarleton with his legion and the mounted infantry were passed over the river to Gloucester Point to assist in foraging. At daybreak Dundas led out part of his garrison to forage the neighboring country. About ten o'clock the waggons and bat horses laden with Indian corn were returning, covered by a party of infantry, with Tarleton and his dragoons as a rear-guard. The waggons and infantry had nearly reached York River, when, from a cloud of dust, emerged Lauzun and the French hussars and lancers.

Tarleton, with part of his legion, advanced to meet them; the rest, with Simcoe's dragoons, remained as a rear-guard in a skirt of woods. A skirmish ensued but the superiority of Tarleton's horses gave him the advantage. Choisy hastened up with a corps of cavalry and infantry to support the hussars. Tarleton scrambled out of the melée and ordered a retreat to enable his men to recover from their confusion. Dismounting 40 infantry, he placed them in a thicket. Their fire checked the hussars in their pursuit. The British dragoons rallied and were about to charge when the hussars retired behind their infantry and a fire was opened upon the British by some militia from behind a fence. Tarleton ordered a retreat to be sounded and the conflict came to an end.

The next day Choisy, reinforced by a detachment of marines from the fleet of de Grasse, cut off all communication by land between Gloucester and the country.

At this momentous time, Washington received dispatches from General Greene giving him important intelligence of his co-operations in the South, to consider which we will suspend for a moment our narrative of affairs before Yorktown.

For some weeks in July and August, General Greene had remained encamped on the hills of Santee, awaiting the promised reinforcements. In the mean time Marion with his light troops, aided by Colonel Washington with his dragoons, held control over the lower Santee. Lee was detached to operate with Sumter's brigade on the Congaree and Colonel Harden with his mounted militia was scouring the country about the Edisto. The enemy was thus harrassed in every quarter.

Greene prepared for a bold effort to drive the enemy from their remaining posts. On the 22d of August he broke up his encampment to march against Colonel Stuart, who meanwhile moved down to the vicinity of Eutaw Springs, where he was reinforced by a detachment from Charleston with provisions.

Greene followed on. He had been joined by Pickens with a party of the Ninety Six militia and by State troops under Lieut. colonel Henderson; Marion, who was scouring the country, re-joined him on the 5th of September. On the seventh the army pushed on within 7 miles of the Eutaws, where it bivouacked for the night. At four o'clock in the morning his little army was in motion. His whole force at that time did not exceed 2000 men; that of the enemy he was seeking about 2300. The Americans, however, were superior in cavalry.

Within 4 miles of Eutaw they met with a British detachment sent forward to reconnoitre; it was put to flight after a severe skirmish. Supposing this to be the van of the enemy, Greene halted his columns and formed. The South Carolinians in equal divisions formed the right and left of the first line, the North Carolinians the centre. Marion commanded the right; Pickens, the left; Malmedy, the centre. Henderson with the State troops covered the left of the line; Lee with his legion, the right.

Of the second line, composed of regulars, the North Carolinians under Sumner were on the right; the Marylanders under Williams on the left; the Virginians under Campbell in the centre. Colonel Washington with his cavalry followed in the rear as a corps de reserve. In this order the troops moved forward.

Within a mile of the camp they encountered a body of infantry thrown forward by Stuart, to check their advance while he formed his troops in order of battle. These were drawn up in line in a wood west of Eutaw Springs. The right rested on Eutaw Creek and was covered by a battalion of grenadiers and infantry under Major Majoribanks, partly concealed among thickets. The left of the line extended across the Charleston road, with a reserve corps covering the road. About 50 yards in the rear of the British line was their encampment, with the tents all standing. Adjoining it was a brick house with a palisadoed garden.

The advanced party of infantry, which had retired firing before the Americans, formed on the flanks of Stuart's line. The Carolinian militia pressed after them. About nine o'clock the action was commenced by the left of the American line and soon became general. The militia fought until they had expended 17 rounds, when they gave way, covered by Lee and Henderson who fought bravely on the flanks of the line.

Sumner, with the regulars who formed the second line, advanced to take the place of the first. The enemy likewise brought their reserve into action; the conflict continued to be bloody and severe. Henderson was severely wounded; this caused some confusion and his brigade, formed partly of recruits, gave way under the superior fire of the enemy. The British rushed forward to secure their fancied victory. Greene instantly ordered Williams with his Marylanders to "sweep the field with the bayonet." Williams was seconded by Campbell with the Virginians. The order was gallantly obeyed. They advanced at a brisk rate, with loud shouts, prepared to make the deadly thrust. The British recoiled. While the Marylanders and Virginians attacked them in front, Lee turned their left flank and charged them in rear. Colonel Hampton with the State cavalry made a great number of prisoners and Colonel Washington, coming up with his reserve, completed their defeat. They were driven back through their camp; many fled along the Charleston road and others threw themselves into the brick house.

Major Majoribanks and his troops could still enfilade the left flank of the Americans from their covert. Greene ordered Washington's dragoons and Kirkwood's Delaware infantry to dislodge them, Wade Hampton to assist with the State troops. Colonel Washington, without waiting for the infantry, dashed forward with his dragoons. It was a rash move. Horse and riders were shot down or bayoneted; Washington was bayoneted and would have been slain had not a British officer interposed and taken him prisoner.

By the time Hampton and Kirkwood came up the cavalry were routed. While Hampton rallied the scattered cavalry, Kirkwood's Delawares charged with bayonet upon the enemy in the thickets. Majoribanks fell back with his troops to the palisadoed garden of the brick house.

Victory now seemed certain on the side of the Americans. The soldiers, thinking the day their own, fell to plundering the tents, devouring the food and carousing on the liquors found there. All was riot and disorder.

The enemy in the mean time recovered from their confusion and opened fire from the house and the palisadoed garden. Greene, finding his ammunition nearly exhausted, determined to give up the attempt to dislodge the enemy since he could not do it without severe loss. The enemy decamped in the night after destroying a large quantity of provisions and arms.

In the morning Greene, who knew not that the enemy had decamped, detached Lee and Marion to intercept any reinforcements coming to Stuart and to retard the latter should he be retreating. Stuart met with reinforcements, but continued his retreat to Monk's Corner.

Greene had followed with his main force almost to Monk's Corner; finding the enemy now too strong to be attacked with prudence, he fell back to his old position near the heights of Santee.

(CHAPTER 58)

We will now resume our narrative of the siege of Yorktown.

Lincoln had the honor, on the night of the 6th of October, of opening the first parallel before Yorktown. It was within 600 yards of the enemy, nearly 2 miles in extent, and the foundations were laid for two redoubts. The work was conducted with such silence that the enemy were not aware of it until daylight. A severe cannonade was then opened from the fortifications, but the men were under cover and continued working; by the afternoon of the 9th the parallel was completed and several batteries were ready to fire upon the town. "General Washington put the match to the first gun," says an observer who was present. "A furious discharge of cannon and mortars immediately followed."

The cannonade was kept up almost incessantly for three or four days from the batteries and from three others managed by the French. The half-finished works of the enemy suffered severely, the guns were dismounted or silenced, and many men killed. The red-hot shot from the French batteries northwest of the town reached the English shipping. The Charon, a forty-four gun ship, and 3 large transports were set on fire by them.

On the night of the 11th the second parallel was opened by Steuben's division within 300 yards of the works. The British now made new embrasures and kept up a galling fire upon those at work. The latter were still more annoyed by the flanking fire of two redoubts, 300 yards in front of the British works. As they enfiladed the intrenchments, it was resolved to storm them both on the night of the 14th, the one nearest the river by a detachment of Americans commanded by Lafayette, the other by a French detachment led by de Viomenil.

In the arrangements for the American assault, Lafayette had given the honor of leading the advance to his own aide-de-camp,

Lieutenant-colonel Gimat. This instantly touched the pride of Hamilton, who exclaimed against it as an unjust preference, it being his tour of duty. It was arranged that Gimat's battalion should lead the van and be followed by that of Hamilton, but that the latter should command the whole advanced corps.

About eight o'clock in the evening rockets were sent up as signals for the simultaneous attacks. Hamilton led the advance of the Americans and was the first to mount the parapet. Not a musket was fired. The redoubt was carried at the point of the bayonet.

The French stormed the other redoubt, which was more strongly garrisoned, with equal gallantry.

The abatis being removed, the troops rushed to the assault. The Chevalier de Lameth, Lafayette's adjutant-general, was the first to mount the parapet of the redoubt; shot through both knees he was conveyed away under care of his friend, the Count de Dumas.

The redoubts thus taken were included the same night in the second parallel and howitzers were mounted upon them the following day. The capture of them reduced Cornwallis almost to despair.

The second parallel was now nearly ready to open. Cornwallis dreaded the effect of its batteries on his works. To retard the danger, he ordered an attack on two of the batteries that were in the greatest state of forwardness, their guns to be spiked. It was made a little before daybreak of the 16th by about 350 men under Lieutenant-colonel Abercrombie. The redoubts which covered the batteries were forced in gallant style and several pieces of artillery hastily spiked. By this time the supporting troops from the trenches came up and the enemy were obliged to retreat. The spikes were easily extracted and, before evening, all the batteries and the parallel were nearly complete.

At this time the garrison could not show a gun on the side of the works exposed to attack and the shells were nearly expended; the place was no longer tenable. Rather than surrender, Cornwallis determined to attempt an escape. His plan was to cross over in the night to Gloucester Point, attack Choisy's camp before daybreak, mount his infantry on the captured cavalry horses and on such other as could be collected on the road, push for the upper country by rapid marches, then turn suddenly northward, and join Sir Henry Clinton in New York.

In pursuance of this design 16 large boats were secretly prepared; a large part of the troops were transported to the Gloucester side of the river before midnight and the second division had actually embarked when a violent storm scattered the boats a considerable distance down the river. They were collected with difficulty. It was now too late to effect the passage of the second division before daybreak and an effort was made to get back the division which had already crossed. It was not done until the morning was far advanced and the troops in recrossing were exposed to the fire of the American batteries.

The hopes of Cornwallis were now at an end. His works were tumbling in ruins about him, under an incessant cannonade; unwilling to expose troops which had stood by him so faithfully to the assault, which could not fail to be successful, he ordered a parley to be beaten about ten o'clock on the morning of the 17th and despatched a flag with a letter to Washington proposing a cessation of hostilties for 24 hours and that two officers be appointed by each side to meet and settle terms for the surrender of the posts of York and Gloucester.

Washington felt unwilling to grant such delay when reinforcements might be on the way for Cornwallis from New York. In reply, therefore, he requested that, previous to the meeting of commissioners, his lordship's proposals be sent in writing to the American lines, for which purpose a suspension of hostilities during two hours from the delivery of the letter would be granted. This was complied with but, as the proposals offered by Cornwallis were not all admissible, Washington drew up a schedule of such terms as he would grant and transmitted it to his lordship.

The armistice was prolonged. Commissioners met, de Noailles and Laurens on the part of the allies, Dundas and Ross on the part of the British. After much discussion, a draught was made of the terms of capitulation to be submitted to the British general. These Washington sent to Cornwallis early in the morning of the 19th with a note expressing his expectation that they would be signed by eleven o'clock and that the garrison would be ready to march out by two o'clock in the afternoon. Cornwallis was fain to comply. Accordingly, on the same day, the posts of Yorktown and Gloucester were surrendered to General Washington as commander-in-chief of the combined army, and the ships of war, transports and other vessels to the Count de Grasse as commander of the French fleet. The garrison of Yorktown and Gloucester, including the officers of the navy and seamen of every denomination, were to surrender as prisoners of war to the combined army, the land force to remain prisoners to the United States and the seamen to the King of France.

The garrison was allowed the same honors granted to the garrison of Charleston when it surrendered to Sir Henry Clinton. The officers were to retain their side arms, both officers and soldiers their private property, and no part of their baggage or papers was to be subject to search or inspection. The soldiers were to be kept as much by regiments as possible and supplied with the same rations as the American soldiers. The officers were to be permitted to proceed, upon parole, to Europe or to any maritime port on the continent of America in possession of British troops.

It was arranged in the allied camp that Lincoln should receive the submission of the royal army precisely in the manner in which the submission of his own army had been received on the surrender of Charleston.

On the following morning, Washington in general orders congratulated the allied armies on the recent victory, awarding high praise to the officers and troops, French and American, for their conduct during the siege and specifying by name several of the generals and other officers who had especially distinguished themselves.

Cornwallis felt deeply the humiliation of this close to all his campaigning and was made the more sensitive by circumstances of which he soon became apprised. On the very day that he had been compelled to lay down his arms before Yorktown, the lingering armament intended for his relief sailed from New York. It consisted of 25 ships of the line, 2 fifty-gun ships and 8 frigates, with Sir Henry Clinton and 7000 of his best troops. Sir Henry arrived off the Capes of Virginia on the 24th and gathered information which led him to apprehend that Cornwallis had capitulated. He hovered off the mouth of the Chesapeake until the 29th when, having fully ascertained that he had come too late, he turned toward New York.

In the mean time the rejoicings which Washington had commenced in the victorious camp, had spread throughout the Union. "Cornwallis is taken!" was the universal acclaim. It was considered a death-blow to the war.

Congress gave way to transports of joy. Thanks were voted to the commander-in-chief, to Rochambeau and de Grasse, to the officers of the allied armies generally, and to the corps of artillery and engineers especially. It was decreed that a marble column, commemorative of the alliance between France and the United States and of the victory achieved by their associated arms should be erected in Yorktown.

Washington would have followed up the reduction of Yorktown by a combined operation against Charleston and addressed a letter to de Grasse on the subject, but the count alleged in reply that it was impossible to remain the necessary time for the operation.

The prosecution of the Southern war, therefore, upon the scale which Washington had contemplated, had to be relinquished. He had to content himself, for the present, with detaching 2000 Continental troops under General St. Clair for the support of General Greene, trusting that, with this aid, he would be able to command the interior of South Carolina and confine the enemy to Charleston.

A dissolution of the combined forces now took place. St. Simon embarked his troops on the last of October and de Grasse made sail on the 4th of November. Lafayette resolved to return to France on a visit to his family, and, with Washington's approbation, set out for Philadelphia to obtain leave of absence from Congress. The British prisoners were marched to Winchester in Virginia and Frederickstown in Maryland; Lord Cornwallis and his principal officers sailed for New York on parole. The main part of the American army embarked for the Head of Elk and returned northward under Lincoln, to be cantoned for the winter in the Jerseys and on the Hudson. The French army were to remain for the winter in Virginia and Rochambeau established his head-quarters at Williamsburg.

Having attended in person to the distribution of ordnance and stores, the departure of prisoners, and the embarkation of the troops under Lincoln, Washington left Yorktown on the 5th of November and arrived the same day at Eltham, the seat of his friend Colonel Basset. He arrived just in time to receive the last breath of John Parke Custis, the son of Mrs. Washington. He had been an object of Washington's care from childhood and been cherished by him with paternal affection. He had acquitted himself with credit as a member of the Virginia legislature. But twenty-eight years old, he left a widow and four young children. It was an unexpected event and Washington remained several days at Eltham to comfort them in their afflictions. As a consolation to Mrs. Washington in her bereavement, he adopted the two youngest children of the deceased, a boy and girl, who thenceforth formed part of his immediate family.

From Eltham, Washington proceeded to Mount Vernon, but public cares gave him little leisure to attend to his private concerns. He had now to guard against an overweening confidence inspired by the recent triumph. In a letter to Greene he writes: "I shall attempt to stimulate Congress to the best improvement of our late success, by taking the most vigorous and effectual measures to be ready for an early and decisive campaign the next year. My greatest fear is, that Congress, viewing this stroke in too important a point of light, may think our work too nearly closed, and will fall into a state of languor and relaxation."

Towards the end of November Washington was in Philadelphia, where Congress received him with distinguished honors. His views were met by the military committee of Congress and by the secretaries of war, finance, and public affairs, who attended their conferences. The military arrangements for 1782 were made with unusual despatch. On the 10th of December resolutions were passed in Congress for requisitions of men and money from the several States; exertions, too, were made by Dr. Franklin, then minister in France, to secure a continuance of aid from that power and a loan of six millions had been promised by the king after hearing of the capitulation of Yorktown.

The persuasion that peace was at hand was, however, too prevalent for the public to be roused to new sacrifices. The States were slow in furnishing a small part of their quotas of troops and still slower in answering to the requisitions for money.

After four months in Philadelphia, Washington set out in March to rejoin the army at Newburg on the Hudson and again established his head-quarters there. The solicitude felt by him on account of the universal relaxation of the sinews of war was not allayed by reports of pacific speeches and motions made in the British parliament, which might be delusive. "Even if the nation and parliament," said he, "are really in earnest to obtain peace with America, it will, undoubtedly, be wisdom in us to meet them with great caution and circumspection."

Sir Guy Carleton arrived in New York early in May to take the place of Sir Henry Clinton, who had solicited his recall. In a letter dated May 7th, Sir Guy informed Washington of his being joined with Admiral Digby in the commission of peace; he transmitted copies of the proceedings in the House of Commons on the 4th of March respecting an address to the king in favor of peace and of a bill authorizing the king to conclude a peace or truce with the provinces of North America. As this bill, however, had not passed into a law when Sir Guy left England, it presented no basis for a negotiation and was only cited by him to show the pacific disposition of the British nation. Still, though circumstances gradually persuaded Washington of a real disposition on the part of Great Britain to terminate the war, he did not relax his preparations for hostilities.

Great discontents prevailed at this time in the army, both among officers and men. The neglect of the States to furnish their proportions of the sum voted by Congress for the prosecution of the war had left the army almost destitute. There was scarce money sufficient to feed the troops from day to day. The pay of the officers, too, was greatly in arrear; many of them doubted whether they would ever receive the half pay decreed to them by Congress for a term of years after the conclusion of the war.

On the 2d of August, Sir Guy Carleton and Admiral Digby wrote a joint letter to Washington, informing him that negotiations for a general peace had already been commenced at Paris and that the independence of the United States would be proposed by the

British commissioner instead of being made a condition of a general treaty.

Even yet, Washington was wary. "From the former infatuation, duplicity, and perverse system of British policy," said he, "I confess I am induced to doubt every thing; to suspect every thing."

What gave force to this policy was that, as yet, no offers had been made on the part of Great Britain for a general cessation of hostilities and, although the British commanders were in a manner tied down by the resolves of the House of Commons to a defensive war only in the United States, they might be at liberty to transport part of their force to the West Indies to act against the French possessions in that quarter. With these considerations he wrote to Rochambeau, then at Baltimore, advising him, for the good of the common cause, to march his troops to the banks of the Hudson and form a junction with the American army.

The junction took place about the middle of September. The French army crossed the Hudson at King's Ferry to Verplanck's Point, where the American forces were paraded under arms to welcome them.

After the meeting with the French army at Verplanck's Point, Washington had drawn up his forces to his former encampment at Newburg, where he established his head-quarters for the winter. In the leisure of a winter camp the discontents of the army had time to ferment. The arrearages of pay became a topic of constant and angry comment, as well as the question of whether the resolution of Congress granting half pay to officers who should serve to the end of the war would be carried into effect. Whence were the funds to arise for such half pay? The national treasury was empty; the States were slow to tax themselves; the resource of foreign loans was nearly exhausted.

The result was a memorial to Congress in December from the officers in camp on behalf of the army, representing the hardships of the case and proposing that a specific sum should be granted them for the money actually due and as a commutation for half pay. Three officers were deputed to present the memorial to Congress and watch over and promote its success.

Drawn & Engraved by James Smillie.

Printed by W. Pate

HEAD QUARTERS AT NEWBURGH.

FOR IRVING'S LIFE OF WASHINGTON

The memorial gave rise to animated and long discussions in Congress. Some members were for admitting the claims as founded on engagements entered into by the nation; others were for referring them to the respective States of the clamants. The winter passed away without any definite measures on the subject.

On the 10th of March, 1783, an anonymous paper was circulated through the camp, calling a meeting at eleven o'clock the next day of the general and field-officers, of an officer from each company, and a delegate from the medical staff to consider a letter just received from their representatives in Philadelphia and what measures, if any, should be adopted to obtain that redress of grievances which they seemed to have solicited in vain.

On the following morning an anonymous address to the officers of the army was privately put into circulation. It professed to be from a fellow-soldier who had shared in their toils and mingled in their dangers and who till very lately had believed in the justice of his country.

"After a pursuit of seven long years," observed he, "the object for which we set out is at length brought within our reach. Yes, my friends, that suffering courage of yours . . . has conducted the United States of America through a . . . bloody war; it has placed her in the chair of independency and peace returns to bless—whom? a country willing to redress your wrongs, cherish your worth, and reward your services? a country courting your return to private life with tears of gratitude and smiles of admiration, longing to divide with you that independency which your gallantry has given and those riches which your wounds have preserved? Is this the case? or is it rather a country that tramples upon your rights, disdains your cries, and insults your distresses?"

With a view to counteract inflammatory effects of the anonymous papers, Washington requested a meeting of officers on the 15th to hear the report of the committee deputed to Congress.

On Saturday, the 15th of March, the meeting took place. Washington rose and said the diligence which had been used in circulating anonymous writings rendered it necessary he give his sentiments to the army on the nature and tendency of them. He then proceeded to read a forcible and feeling address, pointing out

the impropriety of the recent anonymous summons and the dangerous nature of the anonymous address—a production, as he observed, addressed more to the passions than to the judgment,
calculated to impress the mind with an idea of premeditated injustice in the sovereign power of the United States and to rouse all
those resentments which must unavoidably flow from such a belief.

"For myself," observes he, "a recollection of the cheerful assistance and prompt obedience I have experienced from you under
every vicissitude of fortune and the sincere affection I feel for an
army I have so long had the honor to command will oblige me to
declare in this public and solemn manner that, for the attainment of
complete justice for all your toils and dangers and the gratification
of every wish, so far as may be done consistently with the great
duty I owe my country and those powers we are bound to respect,
you may fully command my services to the utmost extent of my
abilities.

"While I give you these assurances and pledge myself in the
most unequivocal manner to exert whatever abilities I am possessed
of in your favor, let me entreat you, gentlemen, on your part, not to
take any measures which, viewed in the calm light of reason, will
lessen the dignity and sully the glory you have hitherto maintained;
let me request you to rely on the plighted faith of your country and
place a full confidence in the purity of the intentions of Congress;
that, previous to your dissolution as an army, they will cause all your
accounts to be fairly liquidated, as directed in the resolutions which
were published to you two days ago; and that they will adopt the
most effectual measures in their power to render ample justice to
you for your faithful and meritorious services."

The moment Washington retired from the assemblage, a
resolution was passed unanimously assuring him that the officers
reciprocated his affectionate expressions with the greatest sincerity.
Then followed resolutions, declaring that no circumstances of distress or danger should induce conduct calculated to sully the reputation and glory acquired at the price of their blood and eight years'
faithful services; that they continued to have an unshaken confidence in the justice of Congress and their country; and that the
commander-in-chief should be requested to write to the President

of Congress earnestly entreating a speedy decision on the late address forwarded by a committee of the army.

A letter was accordingly written by Washington, breathing that generous yet well-tempered spirit with which he ever pleaded the cause of the army. This letter to the president was accompanied by other letters to members of Congress. The subject was again taken up in Congress, nine States concurred in a resolution commuting the half pay into a sum equal to five years' whole pay. The whole matter, through the temperate wisdom of Washington, was happily adjusted.

PART XI

(CHAPTERS 59–60)

The Coming of Peace
[1783–1788]

———⸻◦⟨∞⟩◦⸻———

At length arrived the wished-for news of peace. A general treaty had been signed at Paris on the 20th of January. An armed vessel, the Triumph, arrived at Philadelphia from Cadiz, on the 23d of March, bringing a letter from Lafayette to the President of Congress, communicating the intelligence. In a few days Sir Guy Carleton informed Washington by letter that he was ordered to proclaim a cessation of hostilities by sea and land.

A similar proclamation issued by Congress was received by Washington on the 17th of April. Being unaccompanied by any instructions respecting the discharge of the part of the army with him, should the measure be deemed necessary, he found himself in a perplexing situation.

The accounts of peace had raised an expectation in those of his troops that had engaged "for the war" that a speedy discharge must be the consequence of the proclamation. Most of them could not distinguish between a proclamation of a cessation of hostilities and a declaration of peace and might consider any further claim on their military services an act of injustice. Washington represented these circumstances in a letter to the president and earnestly entreated a prompt determination on the part of Congress as to what was to be the period of the services of these men and how he was to act respecting their discharge.

One suggestion of his letter urged that, in discharging those who had been engaged "for the war," the non-commissioned officers and soldiers should be allowed to take with them as their own property and as a gratuity their arms and accoutrements.

This letter despatched, he notified in general orders that the cessation of hostilities should be proclaimed at noon on the following day, and read in the evening at the head of every regiment and corps of the army.

The letter which he had written to the president produced a resolution in Congress that the service of the men engaged in the war did not expire until the ratification of the definitive articles of peace, but that the commander-in-chief might grant furloughs to such as he thought proper and that they should be allowed to take their arms with them.

Washington availed himself freely of this permission; furloughs were granted without stint; the men set out for their rustic homes. The men on furlough were never called upon to rejoin the army. Once at home, they sank into domestic life; their weapons were hung up over their fire-places, military trophies of the Revolution to be prized by future generations.

In the mean time Sir Guy Carleton was making preparations for the evacuation of the City of New York. As early as the 27th of April a fleet had sailed for different parts of Nova Scotia, carrying off about 7000 persons with all their effects. A great part of these were troops but many were royalists and refugees exiled by the laws of the United States.

On the 6th of May a conference took place between Washington and Sir Guy at Orangetown about the transfer of posts held by the British troops and the delivery of property stipulated by the treaty to be given up to the Americans. On the 8th of May Egbert Benson, William Smith, and Daniel Parker were commissioned by Congress to superintend at New York the embarkation of persons and property in fulfilment of the provisional treaty.

While sadness prevailed among the tories and refugees in New York, the officers in the patriot camp on the Hudson were not without gloomy feelings at the thought of their approaching separation from each other. Eight years of dangers and hardships, shared in common, had welded their hearts together. Prompted by such feelings, General Knox suggested, as a mode of perpetuating the friendships thus formed, the formation of a society composed of the officers of the army. The suggestion met with universal concurrence and the hearty approbation of Washington.

Meetings were held, at which Steuben, as senior officer, presided. A plan was drafted by a committee and the society was organized on the 13th of May at the baron's quarters in the old Verplanck House, near Fishkill. In memory of the illustrious Roman, Lucius Quintius Cincinnatus, who retired from war to the peaceful duties of the citizen, it was to be called "The Society of the Cincinnati." The objects proposed by it were to preserve inviolate the rights and liberties for which they had contended, to promote and cherish national honor and union between the States, to maintain brotherly kindness toward each other, and to extend relief to such officers and their families as might stand in need of it.

The general society, for the sake of frequent communications, was to be divided into State societies, and these again into districts. Washington was chosen unanimously to officate as president of it until the first general meeting, to be held in May, 1784.

On the 8th of June, Washington addressed a letter to the governors of the several States on the subject of the dissolution of the army. "The great object," said he, "for which I had the honor to hold an appointment in the service of my country being accomplished, I am now preparing to return to that domestic retirement which, it is well known, I left with the greatest reluctance." His letter then described the enviable condition of the citizens of America. "Sole lords and proprietors of a vast tract of continent, comprehending all the various soils and climates of the world and abounding with all the necessaries and conveniences of life; and acknowledged possessors of 'absolute freedom and independency.'"

He then proceeded to discuss what he considered the four

things essential to the well-being, and even the existence of the United States as an independent power:

First. An indissoluble union of the States under one federal head and a perfect acquiescence of the several States in the full exercise of the prerogative vested in such a head by the constitution.

Second. A sacred regard to public justice in discharging debts and fulfilling contracts made by Congress for the purpose of carrying on the war.

Third. The adoption of a proper peace establishment, in which care should be taken to place the militia throughout the Union on a regular, uniform and efficient footing.

Fourth. A disposition among the people of the United States to forget local prejudices and policies, to make mutual concessions, and to sacrifice individual advantages to the interests of the community.

We cannot omit its affecting close, addressed as it was to each individual governor:

"I have thus freely declared what I wished to make known before I surrendered up my public trust to those who committed it to me. The task is now accomplished. I now bid adieu to your Excellency, as the chief magistrate of your State, at the same time I bid a last farewell to the cares of office and all the employments of public life. . . . I now make it my earnest prayer, that God . . . incline the hearts of the citizens to cultivate a spirit of subordination and obedience to government, to entertain a brotherly affection and love for one another . . . and finally that he . . . dispose us all to do justice, to love mercy, and to demean ourselves with . . . charity, humility and pacific temper of mind."

Washington now found his situation at head-quarters irksome; there was little to do and he resolved, therefore, to while away part of the time that must intervene before the arrival of the definitive treaty by making a tour to the northern and western parts of the State, visiting the places which had been the theatre of important military transactions. He had another object in view; he desired to facilitate as far as in his power the operations which would be necessary for occupying, as soon as evacuated by British troops, the posts ceded by the treaty of peace. Governor Clinton accompanied him on the expedition. Washington returned to head-quarters at Newburg on the 5th of August, after a tour of at least 750 miles, performed in 19 days, and for the most part on horseback.

By a proclamation of Congress, dated 18th of October, all officers and soldiers absent on furlough were discharged from further service; all others who had engaged to serve during the war were to be discharged from and after the 3d of November. A small force only, composed of those who had enlisted for a definite time, were to be retained in service until the peace establishment should be organized.

In general orders of November 2d, Washington, after adverting to this proclamation, adds: "It only remains for the commander-in-chief to address himself once more, and that for the last time, to the armies of the United States, however widely dispersed the individuals who compose them may be, and to bid them an affectionate and a long farewell."

He then goes on to make them one of those paternal addresses which so eminently characterize his relationship with his army. He takes a brief view of the glorious but painful struggle from which they had just emerged; the unpromising circumstances under which they had undertaken it; the unparalleled perserverance of the American armies for eight long years, through almost every possible suffering and discouragement.

Adverting then to the prospects of happiness opened by the confirmation of national independence and the ample employments held out in a Republic so happily circumstanced, he exhorts them to maintain the strongest attachment to the Union, and to carry with them into civil society the most conciliatory dispositions; proving themselves not less virtuous and useful as citizens than they had been victorious as soldiers.

After a warm expression of thanks to the officers and men for the assistance he had received from every class, and in every instance, he adds: "And being now to conclude these his last public orders, . . . may the choicest of Heaven's favors, both here and hereafter, attend those who, under the Divine auspices, have secured innumerable blessings for others. With these wishes and this benediction,

WASHINGTON TAKING LEAVE OF HIS OFFICERS

NEW YORK G. P. PUTNAM

Painted by W. Pela

the commander-in-chief is about to retire from service. The curtain of separation will soon be drawn and the military scene to him will be closed for ever."

Notwithstanding every exertion had been made for the evacuation of New York, such was the number of persons and the quantity of effects to be conveyed away that the month of November was far advanced before it could be completed. Sir Guy Carleton had given notice to Washington of the time he supposed the different posts would be vacated so that the Americans might take possession of them. In consequence of this notice General George Clinton, at that time Governor of New York, had summoned the members of the state council to convene at East Chester on the 21st of November for the purpose of establishing civil government in the districts hitherto occupied by the British and a detachment of troops was marched from West Point to take possession of the posts as they were vacated.

On the 21st the British troops were drawn in from the oft-disputed post of King's Bridge and from M'Gowan's Pass, also from the various posts on the eastern part of Long Island. Paulus Hook was relinquished on the following day, and the afternoon of the 25th of November was appointed by Sir Guy for the evacuation of the city and the opposite village of Brooklyn.

Washington, in the mean time, had taken his station at Harlem, accompanied by Governor Clinton, who was to take charge of the city. They found there General Knox with the detachment from West Point. Sir Guy Carleton had intimated a wish that Washington would be at hand to take immediate possession of the city and prevent all outrage, as he had been informed of a plot to plunder the place whenever the king's troops should be withdrawn. Although Washington doubted the existence of any such plot, he took precautions accordingly. On the 25th the American troops, moved from Harlem to the Bowery at the upper part of the city. There they remained until the troops in that quarter were withdrawn, when they marched into the city and took possession, the British embarking from the lower parts.

A formal entry then took place of the military and civil authorities. General Washington and Governor Clinton, with their suites, on horseback, led the procession, escorted by a troop of

Westchester cavalry. Then came the lieutenant-governor and members of the council, General Knox and the officers of the army, the speaker of the Assembly, and a large number of citizens on horseback and on foot.

In the course of a few days Washington prepared to depart for Annapolis, where Congress was assembling, with the intention of asking leave to resign his command. A barge was in waiting about noon on the 4th of December at Whitehall ferry to convey him across the Hudson to Paulus Hook. The principal officers of the army assembled at Fraunces' Tavern in the neighborhood of the ferry to take a final leave of him. On entering the room and finding himself surrounded by his old companions in arms, his feelings overcame his usual self-command. Filling a glass of wine and turning upon them his benignant but saddened countenance, "With a heart full of love and gratitude," said he, "I now take leave of you, most devoutly wishing that your latter days may be as prosperous and happy as your former ones have been glorious and honorable."

Having drunk this farewell benediction, he added with emotion, "I cannot come to each of you to take my leave but shall be obliged if each of you will come and take me by the hand."

General Knox, who was nearest, was the first to advance. Washington, affected even to tears, grasped his hand and gave him a brother's embrace. In the same affectionate manner he took leave severally of the rest. The deep feeling and manly tenderness of these veterans in the parting moment could find no utterance in words. Silent and solemn they followed as he left the room, passed through a corps of light infantry, and proceeded on foot to Whitehall ferry. Having entered the barge he turned to them, took off his hat and waved a silent adieu. They replied in the same manner and, having watched the barge until the intervening point of the Battery shut it from sight, returned still silent to the place where they had assembled.

On his way to Annapolis, Washington stopped for a few days at Philadelphia, where with his usual exactness in matters of business, he adjusted with the Comptroller of the Treasury his accounts from the commencement of the war down to the 13th of the actual month of December. These were all in his own handwriting, and kept in the cleanest and most accurate manner, each entry being accompanied by a statement of the occasion and object of the charge. The gross amount included moneys expended for secret intelligence and service and in various incidental charges. All this was an account of money actually expended in the progress of the war—not for arrearage of pay, for it will be recollected Washington accepted no pay.

Being arrived at Annapolis, he addressed a letter to the President of Congress, on the 20th of December, requesting to know in what manner it would be most proper to offer his resignation, whether in writing or at an audience. The latter mode was adopted and the Hall of Congress appointed for the ceremonial.

A letter from Washington to Steuben, written on the 23d, concludes as follows: "The hour of my resignation is fixed at twelve to-day, after which, I shall become a private citizen on the banks of the Potomac."

At twelve o'clock the gallery and a great part of the floor of the Hall of Congress were filled with ladies, with public functionaries of the state, and with general officers. The members of Congress were seated and covered, as representatives of the sovereignty of the Union. The gentlemen present as spectators were standing and uncovered.

Washington entered, conducted by the secretary of Congress, and took his seat in a chair appointed for him. After a brief pause, the president (General Mifflin) informed him, that "the United States in Congress assembled, were prepared to receive his communications."

Washington then rose and delivered a short address.

"The great events," said he, "on which my resignation depended, having at length taken place, I now have the honor of offering my sincere congratulations to Congress, and of presenting myself before them, to surrender into their hands the trust committed to me, and to claim the indulgence of retiring from the service of my country. . . . Having now finished the work assigned me, I retire from the great theatre of action and, bidding an affectionate farewell to this august body, under whose orders I have long acted, I here offer my commission and take my leave of all the employments of public life."

Having delivered his commission into the hands of the president, the latter bore testimony to the patriotism with which he had answered to the call of his country and defended its invaded rights before it had formed alliances and while it was without funds or a government to support him; to the wisdom and fortitude with which he had conducted the great military contest, invariably regarding the rights of the civil power, through all disasters and changes. "You retire," added he, "from the theatre of action with the blessings of your fellow-citizens; the glory of your virtues will not terminate with your military command; it will continue to animate remotest ages."

(CHAPTER 60)

The very next morning Washington hastened to his beloved Mount Vernon, where he arrived the same day, on Christmas-eve, in a frame of mind suited to enjoy the sacred and genial festival.

For some time after his return to Mount Vernon, Washington was in a manner locked up by the ice and snow of an uncommonly rigorous winter, but it was enough for him at present that he was at length at home at Mount Vernon.

In a letter to Lafayette he writes: "I have not only retired from all public employments but I am retiring within myself and shall be able to view the solitary walk and tread the paths of private life with heartfelt satisfaction." During the winter storms, he anticipates the time when the return of the sun will enable him to welcome his friends to partake of his hospitality.

Some degree of economy was necessary, for his financial concerns had suffered during the war and the products of his estate had fallen off during his long absence. The supreme council of Pennsylvania, aware that popular love and curiosity would attract visitors to Mount Vernon and subject him to extraordinary expenses, instructed their delegates in Congress to call attention to these circumstances with a view to produce some national reward for his eminent services. Before acting upon these instructions, the delegates were directed to send a copy of them to Washington for his approbation. He received the document while buried in accounts and calculations, but he most gratefully and respectfully declined it, maintaining the satisfaction of having served his country at the sacrifice of his private interests.

As spring advanced, Mount Vernon, as had been anticipated, began to attract numerous visitors. They were received in the frank, unpretending style Washington had determined upon. Mrs. Washington, too, presided with amenity and grace at the simple board of Mount Vernon. She had a cheerful good sense that always made her an agreeable companion and was an excellent manager.

In entering upon the management of his estate, Washington was but doing in person what he had long been doing through others. Throughout all his campaigns, by means of maps on which every field was numbered, he was enabled to give directions for their cultivation and receive accounts of their crops. Thus the agriculturist was mingled with the soldier. Yet as spring returned and he resumed his rides about the beautiful neighborhood, he must have been mournfully sensible, now and then, of the changes which time and events had effected there.

The Fairfaxes, the kind friends of his boyhood and social companions of his riper years, were no longer at hand to share his pleasures and lighten his cares. He paid a sad visit to that happy resort of his youth and contemplated with a mournful eye its charred ruins and the desolation of its once ornamented grounds. George William Fairfax, its former possessor, was in England; his political principles had detained him there during the war and part of his property had been sequestered; still, though an exile, his hand had been open to relieve the distresses of Americans in England and he had kept up a cordial correspondence with Washington.

Old Lord Fairfax, Washington's early friend and patron, with whom he had first learned to follow the hounds, had lived on at his sylvan retreat in the valley of the Shenandoah, popular with his neighbors although frank in his adherence to Great Britain. He had attained his ninety-second year, when tidings of the surrender of Yorktown snapped the attenuated thread of his existence.

Washington now prepared for a tour to the west of the Apalla-
chian Mountains to visit his lands on the Ohio and Kanawha rivers.
Dr. Craik, the companion of his various campaigns, who had accompanied him in 1770 on a similar tour, was to be his fellow-traveller.
This soldier-like tour, made in hardy military style, with tent,
pack-horses, and frugal supplies, took him once more among the
scenes of his youthful expeditions when a land surveyor in the
employ of Lord Fairfax, a leader of Virginia militia, or an aide-de-
camp of the unfortunate Braddock. His intention had been to survey
and inspect his lands on the Monongahela River; then to descend
the Ohio to the great Kanawha, where also he had large tracts of wild
land. On arriving on the Monongahela, however, he heard such
accounts of discontent among the Indian tribes that he did not
consider it prudent to venture among them. Some of his land on the
Monongahela was settled; the rest was in the wilderness and of little
value in the present unquiet state of the country. He therefore
proceeded no further west than the Monongahela, ascended that
river, and struck southward through the wild, unsettled regions of
the Alleganies until he came out into the Shenandoah Valley near
Staunton. He returned to Mount Vernon on the 4th of October.

During all this tour he had carefully observed the course and
character of the streams flowing from the west into the Ohio, and the
distance of their navigable parts from the head navigation of the
rivers east of the mountains with the nearest and best portage
between them. For many years he had been convinced of the
practicability of an easy and short communication between the
Potomac and James River and the waters of the Ohio and thence on
to the great chain of lakes as well as of the vast advantages that would
result therefrom to the States of Virginia and Maryland.

The retention by the British government of the posts of Detroit, Niagara and Oswego, though contrary to the spirit of the
treaty, shut up the channel of trade in that quarter. These posts,
however, would eventually be given up and then, he was persuaded, the people of New York would lose no time in removing
every obstacle in the way of a water communication.

It behooved Virginia, therefore, to lose no time in availing herself of the present favorable conjuncture to secure a share of western trade by connecting the Potomac and James rivers with the waters beyond the mountains.

Such were some of the ideas set forth by him in a letter to Benjamin Harrison, Governor of Virginia, who laid the letter before the State legislature. The favor with which it was received induced Washington to repair to Richmond and give his personal support to the measure. The suggestions of Washington in his letter to the governor, and his representations during this visit to Richmond, gave the first impulse to the great system of internal improvement since pursued throughout the United States.

In a letter to Richard Henry Lee, recently chosen President of Congress, Washington urged that the western waters be explored, their navigable capabilities ascertained, and that a complete map be made of the country: that in all grants of land by the United States, there should be a reserve made for special sale of all mines, mineral and salt springs: that a medium price should be adopted for the western lands sufficient to prevent monopoly but not to discourage useful settlers.

In the latter part of December he was at Annapolis at the request of the Assembly of Virginia to arrange matters with the Assembly of Maryland respecting the communication between the Potomac and the western waters. Two companies were formed under the patronage of the governments of these States for opening the navigation of the Potomac and James rivers and he was appointed president of both. By a unanimous vote of the Assembly of Virginia, fifty shares in the Potomac and one hundred in the James River company were appropriated for his benefit.

Washington was exceedingly embarrassed by the appropriation. To decline so noble a testimonial of the good will of his countrymen might be construed into disrespect, yet he wished to be perfectly free to exercise his judgment and express his opinions without being liable to the least suspicion of interested motives. While, however, he declined to receive the proffered shares for his own benefit, he intimated a disposition to receive them in trust and the shares were ultimately appropriated by him to institutions devoted to public education.

We find in his diary noted down with curious exactness each day's labor and the share he took in it; his frequent rides to places along the Potomac in quest of young elms, ash trees, white thorn, crab-apples, maples, mulberries, willows and lilacs; the winding walks which he lays out, and the trees and shrubs which he plants along them. Now he sows acorns and buck-eye nuts brought by himself from the Monongahela; now he opens vistas through the Pine Grove, commanding distant views through the woodlands; and now he twines round his columns scarlet honeysuckles, which his gardener tells him will blow all the summer.

The ornamental cultivation was confined to the mansion-house farm but his estate included four other farms, all contiguous and containing 3260 acres, each farm having its overseer with a house for his accommodation, barns and outhouses for the produce, and cabins for the negroes.

In addition to these five farms there were several hundred acres of fine woodland so that the estate presented a beautiful diversity of land and water. In the stables near the mansion-house were the carriage and saddle horses, of which he was very choice; on the four farms there were 54 draught horses, 12 mules, 317 head of black cattle, 360 sheep, and a great number of swine, which last ran at large in the woods.

The children of Parke Custis formed a lively part of his household. He was fond of children and apt to unbend with them. Miss Custis, recalling in after life the scenes of her childhood, writes, "I have sometimes made him laugh most heartily from sympathy with my joyous and extravagant spirits;" she observes, however, that "he was a silent, thoughtful man. He spoke little generally; never of himself. I never heard him relate a single act of his life during the war. I have often seen him perfectly abstracted, his lips moving; but no sound was perceptible."

The reverential awe which his deeds and elevated position threw around him was often a source of annoyance to him in private life, especially when he perceived its effect upon the young and gay. Washington in fact, though habitually grave and thoughtful, was of a social disposition and loved cheerful society. He was fond of the dance and it was the boast of many ancient dames in our day, who had been belles in the time of the Revolution, that they had danced minuets with him or had him for a partner in contra-dances.

While Washington was thus calmly enjoying himself came a letter from Henry Lee, who was now in Congress, conveying a mournful piece of intelligence: "Your friend and second, the patriot and noble Greene, is no more. Universal grief reigns here." Greene died on the 18th of June at his estate of Mulberry Grove on Savannah River, presented to him by the State of Georgia. His last illness was brief, caused by a stroke of the sun; he was but 44 years of age. The news of his death struck heavily on Washington's heart to whom, in the most arduous trials of the Revolution, he had been a second self. Other deaths pressed upon Washington's sensibility about the same time. That of General McDougall, who had served his country faithfully through the war and since with equal fidelity in Congress. That, too, of Colonel Tilghman, for a long time one of Washington's aides-de-camp.

From his quiet retreat of Mount Vernon Washington, though ostensibly withdrawn from public affairs, was watching with intense solicitude the working together of the several parts in the great political confederacy, anxious to know whether the thirteen distinct States, under the present organization, could form a sufficiently efficient general government. He was daily becoming more and more doubtful of the solidity of the fabric he had assisted to raise. The form of confederation which had bound the States together and met the exigencies during the Revolution was daily proving more and more incompetent to the purposes of a national government. Congress had devised a system of credit to provide for the national expenditure and the extinction of the national debts, but the system experienced neglect from some States and opposition from others, each consulting its local interests instead of the interests and obligations of the whole. In like manner treaty stipulations which bound the good faith of the whole, were slighted, if not violated by individual States.

In a letter to James Warren, formerly President of the Massachusetts provincial Congress, Washington writes: "The confederation appears to me to be little more than a shadow without the substance . . . It is . . . extraordinary . . . that we should confederate as a nation and yet be afraid to give the rulers of that nation (who are creatures of our own making, appointed for a limited and short duration, and who are amenable for every action and may be recalled at any moment, and are subject to all the evils which they may be instrumental in producing) sufficient powers to order and direct the affairs of the same."

From a letter, written two or three months subsequently, we gather some of the ideas on national policy which were occupying Washington's mind. "I have ever been a friend to adequate powers in Congress, without which it is evident to me we never shall establish a national character or be considered as on a respectable footing by the powers of Europe. We are either a united people under one head and for federal purposes or we are thirteen independent sovereignties, eternally counteracting each other. If the former, whatever such a majority of the States as the constitution points out conceives to be for the benefit of the whole, should, in my humble opinion, be submitted to by the minority."

An earnest correspondence took place some months subsequently between Washington and the illustrious patriot, John Jay, at that time Secretary of Foreign Affairs, wherein the signs of the times were feelingly discussed. "I do not conceive we can exist long as a nation," writes Washington, "without lodging, somewhere, a power which will pervade the whole Union in as energetic a manner as the authority of the State governments extends over the several States. To be fearful of investing Congress, constituted as that body is, with ample authorities for national purposes, appears to me the very climax of popular absurdity and madness. . . . I am told that even respectable characters speak of a monarchical form of government without horror. . . . What a triumph for the advocates of despotism to find that we are incapable of governing ourselves, and that systems, founded on the basis of equal liberty, are merely ideal and fallacious!"

His anxiety on this subject was quickened by accounts of discontents and commotions in the Eastern States produced by the pressure of the times, the public and private indebtedness, and the imposition of heavy taxes at a moment of financial embarrassment.

JOHN JAY

First Chief Justice. U.S.

NEW YORK, G.P.PUTNAM.

The Coming of Peace (1783–1788)

General Knox, now Secretary at War, who had been sent by Congress to Massachusetts to inquire into these troubles, thus writes about the insurgents: "Their creed is that the property of the United States has been protected from the confiscation of Britain by the joint exertions of all, and therefore ought to be the common property of all, and he that attempts opposition to this creed is an enemy to equity and justice and ought to be swept from off the face of the earth."

In reply to Col. Henry Lee in Congress, who had addressed several letters to him on the subject, Washington writes: "You talk, my good sir, of employing influence to appease the present tumults in Massachusetts. . . . Influence is not government. Let us have a government by which our lives, liberties and properties will be secured. . . . Know precisely what the insurgents aim at. If they have real grievances, redress them, if possible or acknowledge the justice of them and your inability to do it at the moment. If they have not, employ the force of government against them at once."

A letter to him from his former aide-de-camp, Colonel Humphreys, dated November 1st, says: "The troubles in Massachusetts still continue. Government is prostrated in the dust and it is much to be feared that there is not energy enough in that State to re-establish the civil powers. The leaders of the mob, whose fortunes and measures are desperate, are strengthening themselves daily and it is expected that they will soon take possession of the Continental magazine at Springfield, in which there are from ten to fifteen thousand stand of arms in excellent order." Close upon the receipt of this letter came intelligence that the insurgents of Massachusetts, far from being satisfied with the redress which had been offered by their general court, were still acting in open violation of law and government and that the chief magistrate had been obliged to call upon the militia of the State to support the constitution.

To James Madison, he writes: "The consequences of a lax or inefficient government are too obvious to be dwelt upon. Thirteen sovereignties pulling against each other, and all tugging at the federal head, will soon bring ruin on the whole; whereas a liberal and energetic constitution, well checked and well watched to prevent encroachments, might restore us to that degree of respectability and consequence to which we had the fairest prospect of attaining."

Thus Washington, even though in retirement, was almost unconsciously exercising a powerful influence on national affairs; no longer the soldier, he was now becoming the statesman. The opinions and counsels given in his letters were widely effective. Federate organization had been extended and ripened in legislative Assemblies and ended in a plan of a convention composed of delegates from all the States to meet in Philadelphia for the sole purpose of revising the federal system, the proceedings to be subsequently reported to Congress and the several Legislatures, for approval and confirmation.

Washington was unanimously put at the head of the Virginia delegation but for some time objected to accept the nomination. He feared to be charged with inconsistency in again appearing in a public situation after his declared resolution to the contrary. These considerations were strenuously combated, for the influence of his name and counsel were felt to be all-important to the delegation. Two things contributed to bring him to a favorable decision: First, an insinuation that the opponents of the convention were monarchists who wished the distractions of the country should continue until a monarchical government might be resorted to as an ark of safety. The other was the insurrection in Massachusetts.

Before the time arrived for the convention, which was the second Monday in May, his mind was relieved by learning that the insurrection in Massachusetts had been suppressed with but little bloodshed and that the principals had fled to Canada.

On the 9th of May, Washington set out in his carriage from Mount Vernon to attend the convention. It was not until the 25th of May that a sufficient number of delegates were assembled to form a quorum; they proceeded to organize the body and by a unanimous vote Washington was called up to the chair as President.

This memorable convention occupied from four to seven hours each day for four months and every point was the subject of able and scrupulous discussion by the best talent and noblest spirits of the country. The result was the formation of the constitution of the United States.

"The business being closed," says Washington in his diary (Sept. 17), "the members adjourned to the city tavern, dined together, and took a cordial leave of each other. After which I returned to my lodgings, did some business with, and received the papers from, the secretary of the convention and retired to meditate on the momentous work which had been executed."

"It appears to me little short of a miracle," writes he to Lafayette, "that the delegates from so many States, different from each other, as you know, in their manners, circumstances and prejudices, should unite in forming a system of national government so little liable to well-founded objections. Nor am I such an enthusiastic, partial, or undiscriminating admirer of it as not to perceive it is tinctured with some real though not radical defects. With regard to the two great points, the pivots upon which the whole machine must move, my creed is simply, First, that the general government is not invested with more powers than are indispensably necessary to perform the functions of a good government; and consequently, that no objection ought to be made against the quantity of power delegated to it. Secondly, that these powers, as the appointment of all rulers will for ever arise from, and at short, stated intervals recur to, the free suffrages of the people, are so distributed among the legislative, executive, and judicial branches into which the general government is arranged, that it can never be in danger of degenerating into a monarchy, an oligarchy, an aristocracy, or any other despotic or oppressive form, so long as there shall remain any virtue in the body of the people."

The constitution thus formed was forwarded to Congress and thence transmitted to the State Legislatures, each of which submitted it to a State convention composed of delegates chosen for that express purpose by the people. The ratification of the instrument by nine States was necessary to carry it into effect; as the several State conventions would assemble at different times, nearly a year must elapse before the decisions of the requisite number could be obtained.

During this time, Washington resumed his retired life at

Mount Vernon but kept informed by his numerous correspondents of the progress of the constitution through its various ordeals and of the strenuous opposition which it met with in different quarters.

The testimonials of ratification having been received by Congress from a sufficient number of States, an act was passed by that body on the 13th of September, appointing the first Wednesday in January, 1789 for the people of the United States to choose electors of a President according to the constitution and the first Wednesday in the month of February following for the electors to meet and make a choice. The meeting of the government was to be on the first Wednesday in March in the City of New York.

The Presidency
[1789–1795]

The adoption of the Federal constitution was another epoch in the life of Washington. Before the official forms of an election could be carried into operation a unanimous sentiment throughout the Union pronounced him the nation's choice to fill the presidential chair. He looked forward to the possibility of his election with characteristic modesty and unfeigned reluctance.

Colonel Lee had written to him warmly and eloquently on the subject. "My anxiety is extreme that the new government may have an auspicious beginning. To effect this and to perpetuate a nation formed under your auspices, it is certain that again you will be called forth. The same principles of devotion to the good of mankind which have invariably governed your conduct will no doubt continue to rule your mind, however opposite their consequences may be to your repose and happiness."

In a letter to Colonel Alexander Hamilton he writes: "You will, I am well assured, believe the assertion . . . that, if I should receive the appointment and if I should be prevailed upon to accept it, the acceptance would be attended with more diffidence and reluctance than ever I experienced before in my life. It would be, however, with a fixed and sole determination of lending whatever assistance might be in my power to promote the public weal in hopes that, at a convenient and early period, my services might be dispensed with and that I might be permitted once more to retire, to pass an unclouded evening, after the stormy day of life, in the bosom of domestic tranquillity."

The election took place at the appointed time and it was soon ascertained that Washington was chosen President for the term of four years from the 4th of March. By this time the arguments and entreaties of his friends and his own convictions of public expediency had determined him to accept; he made preparations to depart for the seat of government as soon as he should receive official notice of his election.

From a delay in forming a quorum of Congress the votes of the electoral college were not counted until early in April, when they were found to be unanimous in favor of Washington. At length on the 14th of April he received a letter from the president of Congress, duly notifying him of his election and he prepared to set out immediately for New York, the seat of government. An entry in his diary, dated the 16th, says, "About ten o'clock I bade adieu to Mount Vernon, to private life, and to domestic felicity; and with a mind oppressed with more anxious and painful sensations than I have words to express, set out for New York with the best disposition to render service to my country in obedience to its call, but with less hope of answering its expectations."

His progress to the seat of government was a continual ovation. The ringing of bells and roaring of cannonry proclaimed his course through the country. The old and young, women and children, thronged the highways to bless and welcome him. Deputations of the most respectable inhabitants from the principal places came forth to meet and escort him. His carriage was attended by a numerous cavalcade of citizens, and he was saluted by the thunder of artillery.

In respect to his reception at New York, Washington had signified in a letter to Governor Clinton that none could be so congenial to his feelings as a quiet entry devoid of ceremony but his modest wishes were not complied with. At Elizabethtown Point, a committee of both Houses of Congress, with various civic functionaries, waited to receive him. He embarked on board of a splendid barge, manned by thirteen branch pilots, masters of vessels, in white uniforms, and commanded by Commodore Nicholson. Other barges fancifully decorated followed, having on board the heads of departments and other public officers, and several distinguished citizens. As they passed through the strait between the Jerseys and Staten Island, other boats decorated with flags fell in their wake, until the whole, forming a nautical procession, swept up the broad and beautiful bay of New York, to the sound of instrumental music. The ships at anchor in the harbor, dressed in colors, fired salutes as it passed.

He approached the landing-place of Murray's Wharf amid the ringing of bells, the roaring of cannonry, and the shouting of multitudes collected on every pier-head. On landing, he was received by Governor Clinton. General Knox, too, who had taken such affectionate leave of him on his retirement from military life, was there to welcome him in his civil capacity. Other of his fellow-soldiers of the Revolution were likewise there, mingled with the civic dignitaries.

Carpets had been spread to a carriage prepared to convey him to his destined residence but he preferred to walk. He was attended by a long civil and military train. In the streets through which he passed the houses were decorated with flags, silken banners, garlands of flowers and evergreens, and bore his name in every form of ornament. The streets were crowded with people so that it was with difficulty a passage could be made by the city officers. Washington frequently bowed to the multitude as he passed, taking off his hat to the ladies who thronged every window, waving their handkerchiefs, throwing flowers before him, and many of them shedding tears of enthusiasm.

The inauguration was delayed for several days by a question which had risen as to the form or title by which the President elect was to be addressed; this had been deliberated in a committee of both Houses. It was a relief to him, therefore, when it was finally resolved that the address should be simply "the President of the United States," without any addition of title.

The inauguration took place on the 30th of April. At nine o'clock in the morning there were religious services in all the churches. At twelve o'clock the city troops paraded before Washington's door; soon after the committees of Congress and heads of departments came in their carriages. At half-past twelve the procession moved forward preceded by the troops; next came the committees and heads of departments in their carriages; then Washington in a coach of state, his aide-de-camp, Colonel Humphreys, and his secretary, Mr. Lear, in his own carriage. The foreign ministers and a long train of citizens brought up the rear.

About 200 yards before reaching the hall, Washington and his suite alighted from their carriages and passed through the troops, who were drawn up on each side, into the hall and senate-chamber where the Vice President, the Senate and House of Representatives were assembled. The Vice President, John Adams, recently inaugurated, advanced and conducted Washington to a chair of state at the upper end of the room. A solemn silence prevailed when the Vice President rose and informed him that all things were prepared for him to take the oath of office required by the constitution.

The oath was to be administered by the Chancellor of the State of New York in a balcony in front of the senate chamber, in full view of an immense multitude occupying the street, the windows, and even roofs of the adjacent houses. In the centre of the balcony was a table with a covering of crimson velvet, upon which lay a superbly bound Bible on a crimson velvet cushion.

All eyes were fixed upon the balcony when, at the appointed hour, Washington made his appearance, accompanied by various public functionaries and members of the Senate and House of Representatives. He was clad in a full suit of dark-brown cloth, with a steel-hilted dress sword, white silk stockings, and silver shoe-buckles. His hair was dressed and powdered in the fashion of the day and worn in a bag and solitaire.

His entrance on the balcony was hailed by universal shouts. He was evidently moved by this demonstration of public affection. Advancing to the front of the balcony he laid his hand upon his heart, bowed several times, and then retreated to an arm-chair near the table. The populace appeared to understand that the scene had

H.B.Hall.

ROBERT R. LIVINGSTON

Printed by W.Pate.

NEW YORK · G.P.PUTNAM

overcome him and were hushed at once into profound silence.

After a few moments Washington rose and again came forward. John Adams, the Vice President, stood on his right; on his left the Chancellor of the State, Robert R. Livingston; somewhat in the rear were Roger Sherman, Alexander Hamilton, Generals Knox, St. Clair, Baron Steuben and others.

The chancellor advanced to administer the oath prescribed by the constitution and Mr. Otis, the secretary of the Senate, held up the Bible on its crimson cushion. The oath was read slowly and distinctly, Washington at the same time laying his hand on the open Bible.

The chancellor now stepped forward and exclaimed, "Long live George Washington, President of the United States!" At this moment a flag was displayed on the cupola of the hall, on which signal there was a general discharge of artillery on the battery. All the bells in the city rang out a joyful peal and the multitude rent the air with acclamations.

Washington again bowed to the people and returned into the senate chamber, where he delivered to both Houses of Congress his inaugural address, characterized by his usual modesty, moderation and good sense. After this he proceeded with the whole assemblage on foot to St. Paul's church, where prayers suited to the occasion were read by the Bishop of the Protestant Episcopal Church in New York. So closed the ceremonies of the inauguration.

The whole day was one of sincere rejoicing, and in the evening there were brilliant illuminations and fireworks.

The eyes of the world were upon Washington at the commencement of his administration. He had won laurels in the field; would they continue to flourish in the cabinet?

He had a high-spirited people to manage, in whom a passion for freedom and independence had been strengthened by war and who might bear with impatience even the restraints of self-imposed government. The constitution which he was to inaugurate had met with vehement opposition when under discussion in the General and State governments. Only New Jersey, Delaware and Georgia had accepted it unanimously. Several of the States had adopted it by a mere majority, five of them under an expectation of specified modifications. Two States, Rhode Island and North Carolina, still stood aloof.

A diversity of opinions still existed concerning the new government. Some feared that it would have too little control over the individual States and that the political connection would prove too weak to preserve order and prevent civil strife; others, that it would be too strong for their separate independence and would tend toward consolidation and despotism.

The very extent of the country he was called upon to govern must have pressed upon Washington's mind. It presented to the Atlantic a front of 1500 miles, divided into individual States, differing in the forms of their local governments, differing in interests, territorial magnitudes, amount of population, manners, soils, climates, productions, and the characteristics of their peoples.

Beyond the Alleghanies extended regions almost boundless, for the most part wild and uncultivated. Vast tracts, however, were rapidly being peopled and would soon be portioned into sections requiring local governments. The natural outlet for the export of the products of this region was the Mississippi, but Spain opposed a barrier to the free navigation of this river. Washington had heard that the hardy yeomanry of the far West were becoming impatient of this barrier and indignant at the apparent indifference of Congress to their prayers for its removal. He had heard, moreover, that British emissaries were fostering these discontents and offering assistance to the Western people to seize New Orleans and fortify the mouth of the Mississippi, while, on the other hand, the Spanish authorities at New Orleans were represented as intriguing to effect a separation of the Western territory from the Union with a hope of attaching it to Spain.

Great Britain, too, was giving grounds for solicitude by retaining possession of the Western posts, the surrender of which had been stipulated by treaty. Her plea was that debts due to British subjects, for which by the same treaty the United States were bound, remained unpaid. This, the Americans alleged, was a mere pretext, the real object of their retention being the monopoly of the fur trade.

While these causes of anxiety existed at home, the foreign commerce of the Union was on a most unsatisfactory footing and required prompt attention. It was subject to maraud, even by the corsairs of Algiers, Tunis and Tripoli, who captured American merchant vessels and carried their crews into slavery, no treaty having yet been made with any of the Barbary powers excepting Morocco.

To complete the perplexities which beset the new government, the finances of the country were in a lamentable state. There was no money in the treasury. The efforts of the former government to pay or fund its debts had failed; there was a universal state of indebtedness, foreign and domestic, and public credit was prostrate.

Such was the condition of affairs when Washington entered upon his new field of action. As yet he was without constitutional advisers, the departments under the new government not being organized; he could turn with confidence, however, for counsel to John Jay, who still remained at the head of affairs, where he had been placed in 1784. He was sure of sympathy also in his old comrade, General Knox, who continued to officiate as secretary of war, while the affairs of the treasury were managed by a board consisting of Samuel Osgood, Walter Livingston and Arthur Lee. Among the personal friends not in office to whom Washington felt he could have recourse for aid in initiating the new government was Alexander Hamilton. It is true, many had their doubts of his sincere adhesion to it but Washington, who knew Hamilton's character, had implicit confidence in his sincerity and felt assured that he would loyally aid in carrying into effect the constitution as adopted.

It was a great satisfaction to Washington, on looking round for reliable advisers, to see James Madison among the members of Congress—Madison whose talents as a calm, dispassionate reasoner and whose extensive information and legislative experience destined him to be a leader in the House. Highly appreciating his intellectual and moral worth, Washington would often turn to him for counsel.

Knox, of whose sure sympathies we have spoken, was cordially appreciated by Washington, who now looked to him as an energetic man of business, capable of giving practical advice in time of peace, and cherished for him that strong feeling of ancient companionship in toil and danger.

The moment the inauguration was over, Washington was made to perceive that he was no longer master of himself or of his home. How was he to be protected from intrusions? What were to be the forms and ceremonials in the presidential mansion that would maintain the dignity of his station, allow him time for the performance of official duties, and yet be in harmony with the feelings of the people and the prevalent notions of equality and republican simplicity?

Looking round, therefore, upon the able men at hand, such as Adams, Hamilton, Jay, Madison, he propounded to them a series of questions as to a line of conduct proper for him to observe. In regard to visitors, for instance, would not one day in the week be sufficient for 'visits of compliment and one hour every morning for visits on business? Washington was resolved not to give general entertainments, but he asked whether he might not invite, informally or otherwise, small groups of officials, including in rotation the members of both Houses of Congress, to dine with him on the days fixed for receiving company without exciting clamors in the rest of the community.

Adams in his reply talked of chamberlains, aides-de-camp, masters of ceremony, and evinced a high idea of the presidential office and the state with which it ought to be maintained. According to Adams, two days in a week would be required for visits of compliment. Persons desiring an interview with the President should make application through the minister of state; the name, quality or business of the visitor should be communicated to a chamberlain, who should judge whom to admit. The time for receiving visits ought to be limited, lest the whole morning be taken up. The President might invite what officials, members of Congress, strangers, or citizens of distinction he pleased in small parties without exciting clamors, but this should always be done without formality. In his official character, he should have no intercourse with society but upon public business or at his levees.

Hamilton, in his reply, while he considered that the dignity of

Martha Washington

the presidential office should be supported, advised that care should be taken to avoid so high a tone in the demeanor of the occupant as to shock the prevalent notions of equality. The President, he thought, should hold a levee at a fixed time once a week, remain half an hour, converse cursorily with such persons as invited his attention, and then retire. He should accept no invitations, give formal entertainments twice, or at most, four times in the year. The President on levee days should give informal invitations to dinners, not more than six or eight to be asked at a time, confined essentially to members of the legislature and other official characters and the President never to remain long at table. The heads of departments and members of the Senate should, of course, have access to the President on business. Foreign ministers of some descriptions should also be entitled to it.

Colonel Humphreys, formerly one of Washington's aides-de-camp and recently secretary of Jefferson's legation at Paris, was at present a resident in the presidential mansion. Knox was frequently there; to these Washington assigned the task of considering the minor forms and ceremonies to be observed on public occasions. Some of the forms proposed by them were adopted; others were so highly strained that Washington absolutely rejected them.

On the 17th of May, Mrs. Washington, accompanied by her grandchildren, Eleanor Custis and George Washington Parke Custis, set out from Mount Vernon in her travelling carriage, with a small escort of horse, to join her husband at the seat of government.

Throughout the journey she was greeted with public testimonials of respect and affection. At Elizabethtown she alighted at the residence of Governor Livingston, whither Washington came from New York to meet her. They proceeded thence by water in the same splendid barge in which the general had been conveyed for his inauguration. It was manned, as on that occasion, by 13 master pilots, arrayed in white, and had several persons of note on board. There was a salute of 13 guns as the barge passed the battery at New York. The landing took place not far from the presidential residence amid the enthusiastic cheers of an immense multitude.

On the following day, Washington gave a dinner, of which Mr.

Wingate, a senator from New Hampshire, who was present, writes as follows: "The guests consisted of the Vice President, the foreign ministers, the heads of departments, the Speaker of the House of Representatives and the Senators from New Hampshire and Georgia, the then most Northern and Southern States. It was the least showy dinner that I ever saw at the President's table. . . . After dinner and dessert were finished, the President rose and all the company retired to the drawing-room, from which the guests departed, as every one chose, without ceremony."

On the evening of the following day, (Friday, May 29th) Mrs. Washington had a general reception, attended by all who were distinguished in official and fashionable society. Henceforward there were similar receptions every Friday evening, to which all persons of respectability had access without special invitation and at which the President was always present. These assemblages were as free from ostentation and restraint as the ordinary receptions of polite society, yet they were soon cavilled at as "court-like levees" and "queenly drawing-rooms."

Beside these public receptions, the presidential family had its private circle of social intimacy; the President, moreover, was always ready to receive visits by appointment on public or private business.

The sanctity of Sunday was strictly observed by Washington. He attended church in the morning and passed the afternoon alone. No visitors were admitted, excepting perhaps an intimate friend in the evening, which was spent by him in the bosom of his family.

In regard to the deportment of Washington, he still retained a military air of command which had become habitual to him. At levees and drawing-rooms he sometimes appeared cold and distant, but his reserve had nothing repulsive in it, and, where he was no longer under the eye of critical supervision, soon gave way to frankness and cordiality. At all times his courtesy was genuine and totally free from that stately condescension sometimes mistaken for politeness. Nothing we are told could surpass the noble grace with which he presided at a ceremonial dinner, kindly attentive to all his guests but particularly attentive to put those at their ease who appeared to be most diffident.

As to Mrs. Washington, those who really knew her speak of her as free from pretension or affectation, undazzled by her position, and discharging its duties with the truthful simplicity and real good-breeding of one accustomed to preside over a hospitable mansion.

Much has been said of Washington's equipages when at New York and of his having four and sometimes six horses before his carriage, with servants and outriders in rich livery. Such style was usual at the time both in England and the colonies; it was still prevalent among the wealthy planters of the South and sometimes adopted by rich individuals at the North. It does not appear that Washington ever indulged in it through ostentation. If there was any thing he was likely to take a pride in, it was horses; he was passionately fond of that noble animal and mention is occasionally made of four white horses of great beauty which he owned while in New York. His favorite exercise when the weather permitted it was on horseback, accompanied by one or more of the members of his household, and he was noted always for being one of the best horsemen of his day.

As soon as Washington could command sufficient leisure to inspect papers and documents, he called unofficially upon the heads of departments to furnish him with such reports in writing as would aid him in gaining a distinct idea of the state of public affairs. He was interrupted in his task by a virulent attack of anthrax, which for several days threatened mortification. His sufferings were intense and his recovery was slow. For six weeks he was obliged to lie on his right side.

While yet in a state of convalescence, Washington received intelligence of the death of his mother. The event, which took place at Fredericksburg on the 25th of August, was not unexpected. She was 82 years of age and had for some time been sinking under an incurable malady, so that when he last parted with her he had apprehended that it was a final separation.

Mrs. Mary Washington is represented as a woman of strong plain sense, strict integrity, and an inflexible spirit of command. The deference for her continued throughout her life and was manifested by Washington when at the height of his power and reputation. Even his success and renown never dazzled, however much they may have gratified her. When others congratulated her and were enthusiastic in his praise, she listened in silence and would temperately reply that he had been a good son and had done his duty as a man.

Hitherto the new government had not been properly organized but its several duties had been performed by the officers who had them in charge at the time of Washington's inauguration. It was not until the 10th of September that laws were passed instituting a department of Foreign Affairs (afterwards termed Department of State), a Treasury department, and a department of War. On the following day, Washington nominated Knox to the department of War, the duties of which that officer had hitherto discharged.

The post of Secretary of the Treasury was one of far greater importance at the present moment. It was a time of financial exigency. As yet no statistical account of the country had been attempted; its fiscal resources were wholly unknown; its credit was almost annihilated, for it was obliged to borrow money even to pay the interest of its debts. Under all these circumstances, he needed an able and zealous coadjutor in the Treasury department. Such a person he considered Alexander Hamilton, whom he nominated as Secretary of the Treasury. Within a few days after Hamilton's appointment, the House of Representatives (Sept. 21) passed a resolution that an adequate provision should be made for the support of public credit, instructing the Secretary of the Treasury to prepare a plan for the purpose and report it at their next session.

The arrangement of the Judicial department was one of Washington's earliest cares. On the 27th of September, he wrote unofficially to Edmund Randolph of Virginia, informing him that he had nominated him Attorney-General of the United States and would be highly gratified with his acceptance of that office. Randolph promptly accepted the nomination but did not take his seat in the cabinet until some months after Knox and Hamilton.

By the judicial system established for the Federal Government, the Supreme Court of the United States was to be composed of a chief justice and five associate judges. There were to be district courts with a judge in each State and circuit courts held by an associate judge and a district judge. John Jay received the appointment of Chief Justice and, in a letter enclosing his commission, Washington expressed the singular pleasure he felt in addressing him "as the head of that department which must be considered as the keystone of our political fabric." Jay's associate judges were, John Rutledge of South Carolina, James Wilson of Pennsylvania, William Cushing of Massachusetts, John Blair of Virginia, and James Iredell of North Carolina.

On the 29th of September, Congress adjourned to the first Monday in January, after an arduous session in which many important questions had been discussed and powers organized and distributed. The Congress was inferior in shining talent to the first Congress of the revolution but it possessed men well fitted for the momentous work before them, sober, solid, upright, and well informed. An admirable harmony had prevailed between the legislature and the executive and the utmost decorum had reigned over the public deliberations.

The cabinet was still incomplete; the department of State was yet to be supplied with a head. John Jay would have received the nomination had he not preferred the bench. Washington next thought of Thomas Jefferson who had so long filled the post of Minister Plenipotentiary at the Court of Versailles, but had recently obtained permission to return, for a few months, to the United States for the purpose of arranging his private affairs, which had suffered from his absence. It was at this time that Washington wrote to Jefferson, offering him the situation of Secretary of State, forbearing to nominate a successor to his post at the Court of Versailles until he should be informed of his determination.

At the time of writing the letter to Jefferson, Washington was on the eve of a journey through the Eastern States, with a view to observe the situation of the country and with a hope of reestablishing his health, which a series of indispositions had much impaired. Having made all his arrangements, he set out from New York on the 15th of October, accompanied by his official secretary and his private secretary. Though averse from public parade, he could not but be deeply affected and gratified at every step by the manifestations of a people's love. Wherever he came, all labor was suspended; business neglected. The bells were rung, the guns were fired; there were civic processions and military parades and triumphal arches. All classes poured forth to testify their gratitude and affection for the man whom they hailed as the Father of his country—and well did his noble stature, his dignified demeanor, his matured years, and his benevolent aspect suit that venerable appellation.

After remaining in Boston for a week, fêted in the most hospitable manner, he appointed eight o'clock, on Thursday the 29th, for his departure. His journey eastward terminated at Portsmouth, whence he turned homeward by a route through the interior of the country to Hartford and thence to New York, where he arrived on the 13th of November.

On his return, Washington learned that Jefferson had embarked for America and, it was probable, had already landed in Virginia. Washington immediately forwarded to him his commission as Secretary of State, requesting to know his determination on the subject.

Jefferson, in reply, expressed himself flattered by the nomination but dubious of his being equal to its extensive and various duties. Washington, in answer, informed him that he regarded the office of Secretary of State very important and that he knew of no person who, in his judgment, could better execute the duties of it.

Jefferson accordingly accepted the nomination but observed that the matters which had called him home would probably prevent his setting out for New York before March.

(CHAPTER 62)

Congress reassembled on the 4th of January (1790) but a quorum of the two Houses was not present until the 8th, when the session was opened by Washington with an address delivered in the Senate chamber.

Among the most important objects suggested in the address for the deliberation of Congress were: provisions for national defence; provisions for facilitating intercourse with foreign nations and defraying the expenses of diplomatic agents; laws for the naturalization of foreigners; uniformity in the currency, weights, and measures of the United States; facilities for the advancement of commerce, agriculture, and manufactures; attention to the post-office and post-roads; measures for the promotion of science and literature; and measures for the support of public credit.

This last object was the one which Washington had more immediately at heart. The government was now organized apparently to the satisfaction of all parties, but its efficiency would essentially depend on the success of a system of finance adapted to revive the national credit and place the public debt in a condition to be paid off. The confederacy, by its articles, had the power of contracting debts but no control over the means of payment. Thirteen independent legislatures could grant or withhold the means. At the close of the war the debt had swollen, through arrears of interest, to upwards of $54,000,000. Of this nearly $12,000,000 were due abroad. The debt contracted at home amounted to upwards of $42,000,000 and was due to officers and soldiers of the war, farmers who had furnished supplies, and capitalists who had adventured their fortunes. The domestic debt had a sacred and patriotic origin, but the paper which represented these claims had sunk to less than a sixth of its nominal value and the larger portion of it had been parted with at that depreciated rate, either in the course of trade or to speculative purchasers.

Beside the foreign and domestic debt of the federal government, the States individually were involved in liabilities contracted for the common cause to an aggregate amount of about $25,000,000; of which more than one-half was due from Massachusetts, South Carolina, and Virginia. The reputation and the well-being of the government were, therefore, at stake upon the issue of some plan to retrieve the national credit and establish it upon a firm and secure foundation.

The Secretary of the Treasury had been directed by Congress to prepare such a plan during its recess. In the one thus prepared, he asserted what none were disposed to question the propriety of paying the foreign debt according to its terms. He asserted, also, the equal validity of the claims of American creditors, whether those creditors were the original holders of its certificates or subsequent purchasers of them at a depreciated value. The idea of any distinction between them, which some were inclined to advance, he repudiated as unjust, impolitic, and impracticable. He urged, moreover, the assumption by the general government of the separate debts of the States contracted for the common cause. They were all contracted in the struggle for national independence, not for the independence of any particular part. He recommended, therefore, that the entire mass of debt be funded, the Union made responsible for it, and taxes imposed for its liquidation.

The plan was reported to the House by Hamilton, the 14th of January, but did not undergo consideration until the 8th of February, when it was opposed with great earnestness, especially the point of assuming the State debts. This financial union of the States was reprobated as fraught with political evil. The Northern and Eastern States generally favored the plan, as did South Carolina, but Virginia manifested a determined opposition. The measure, however, passed in Committee of the Whole on the 9th of March by a vote of 31 to 26.

At this juncture (March 21st), Jefferson arrived in New York to undertake the duties of the Department of State. He had just been in Virginia, where the forms and ceremonials of our government were subjects of cavil and sneer and where it was reported that Washington affected a monarchical style, that he held court-like levees and Mrs. Washington queenly drawing-rooms at which none but the aristocracy were admitted, that the manners of both were haughty and their personal habits reserved and exclusive. The impressions thus made on Jefferson's mind received a deeper stamp on his arrival in New York from conversations with his friend Madison, in the course of which the latter observed that "the satellites and sycophants which surrounded Washington had wound up the ceremonials of the government to a pitch of stateliness which nothing but his personal character could have supported and which no character after him could ever maintain."

Thus prepossessed and premonished, Jefferson looked round him with an apprehensive eye and appears to have seen something to startle him at every turn. "I was astonished," he writes, "to find the general prevalence of monarchical sentiments insomuch that, in maintaining those of republicanism, I had always the whole company on my hands, never scarcely finding among them a single co-advocate in that argument unless some old member of Congress happened to be present. The furthest that any one would go in support of the republican features of our new government would be to say, 'the present constitution is well as a beginning and may be allowed a fair trial, but it is in fact only a stepping stone to something better.' "

This picture, is probably over-charged but, allowing it to be true, we can hardly wonder at it, viewed in connection with the place and times. As yet, the history of the world had furnished no favorable examples of popular government. Jay, one of the calmest thinkers of the Union, expressed himself dubiously on the subject. "Whether any people could long govern themselves in an equal, uniform, and orderly manner was a question of vital importance to the cause of liberty, but a question which . . . could only be determined by experience—now, as yet, there had been very few opportunities of making the experiment."

Hamilton, though pledged and sincerely disposed to support the republican form with regard to our country, preferred, theoretically, a monarchical form; and may have spoken openly in favor of that form as suitable to France. Opinions of the kind may have been uttered in unguarded hours with no sinister design by men who had no thought of paving the way for a monarchy. They made, however, a deep impression on Jefferson's apprehensive mind, which sank deeper and deeper until it became a fixed opinion with him that there was the desire and aim of a large party, of which Hamilton was the leader, to give a regal form to the government.

The question of the assumption of the State debts was resumed in Congress on the 29th of March on a motion to commit, which was carried by a majority of two; the five members from North Carolina (now a State of the Union) who were strongly opposed to assumption reversed the position of parties on the question. An intemperate discussion was revived, much to the chagrin of Washington, who considered the assumption of the State debts, under proper restrictions and scrutiny into accounts, to be just and reasonable. On the 12th of April, when the question to commit was taken, there was a majority of two against the assumption.

On the 26th the House was discharged, for the present, from proceeding on so much of the report as related to the assumption. Jefferson, who had arrived in New York in the midst of what he terms "this bitter and angry contest," had taken no concern in it. We give his own account of an earnest effort by Hamilton to resuscitate, through his influence, his almost hopeless project. "As I was going to the President's one day, I met him [Hamilton] in the street. . . . He painted pathetically the temper into which the legislature had been wrought; the disgust of those who were called the creditor States; the danger of the secession of their members, and the separation of the States. He observed that . . . the question having been lost by a small majority only, it was probable that an appeal from me to the judgment . . . of some of my friends might effect a change in the vote and the machine of government, now suspended, might be again set into motion. . . . I proposed to him . . . to dine with me the next day and I would invite another friend or two. . . . I thought it impossible that reasonable men, consulting together coolly, could fail, by some mutual sacrifices of opinion, to form a compromise which was to save the Union. The discussion took place. . . . It was finally agreed that, whatever importance had been attached to the rejection of this proposition, the preservation of the Union and of concord among the States was more important and that, therefore, it would be better that the vote of rejection should be rescinded, to effect which some members should change their votes. But it was observed that this pill would be peculiarly bitter to the Southern States and that some concomitant measure should be adopted to sweeten it a little to them. There had before been projects to fix the seat of government either at Philadelphia or at Georgetown . . . and it was thought that, by giving it to Philadelphia for ten years and to Georgetown permanently afterwards, this might . . . calm in some degree the ferment which might be excited by the other measure alone. So two of the Potomac members . . . agreed to change their votes and Hamilton undertook to carry the other point. In doing this, the influence he had established over the eastern members, with the agency of Robert Morris with those of the Middle States, effected his side of the engagement."

The decision of Congress was ultimately in favor of assumption, though the form in which it finally passed differed somewhat from the proposition of Hamilton. A specific sum was assumed ($21,500,000) and distributed among the States in specific portions. Thus modified, it passed the Senate by 14 to 12 and the House by 34 to 28.

It was agreed that Congress should continue for ten years to hold its sessions at Philadelphia, during which time the public buildings should be erected at some place on the Potomac, to which the government should remove at the expiration of the above term. A territory, ten miles square, selected for the purpose on the confines of Maryland and Virginia, was ceded by those States to the United States, subsequently designated the District of Columbia.

One of the last acts of the Executive during this session was the conclusion of a treaty of peace and friendship with the Creek nation of Indians, represented at New York by Mr. M'Gillivray and thirty of the chiefs and head men. By this treaty (signed August 7th), an extensive territory claimed by Georgia was relinquished greatly to the discontent of that State.

Congress adjourned on the 12th of August. Jefferson, commenting on the discord that had prevailed for a time among the members, observes that, in the latter part of the session, they had reacquired the harmony which had always distinguished their proceedings before the introduction of the two disagreeable subjects of the Assumption and the Residence.

Washington, however grieved he may have been by the dissensions in Congress, consoled himself by the fancied harmony of his cabinet. He had sought the ablest men to assist him in his arduous task and supposed them influenced by the same unselfish spirit.

Yet, at this very moment, a spirit of rivalry between Jefferson and Hamilton was already existing and daily gaining strength. Jefferson, who considered Hamilton a monarchist, regarded all his financial schemes with suspicion as intended to strengthen the influence of the treasury and make its chief the master of every vote in the legislature, "which might give to the government the direction suited to his political views."

Under these impressions, Jefferson looked back with an angry and resentful eye to the manner in which Hamilton had procured his aid in effecting the measure of assumption. He regarded it as a finesse by which he had been entrapped.

Two days after the adjournment of Congress, Washington, accompanied by Jefferson, departed by water on a visit to Rhode Island, which had recently acceded to the Union. He was cordially welcomed by the inhabitants and returned to New York, after an absence of ten days, whence he again departed for his beloved Mount Vernon, there to cast off public cares as much as possible and enjoy the pleasures of the country during the residue of the recess of Congress.

Frequent depredations had of late been made on our frontier settlements by Indians from the north-west side of the Ohio. Some of our people had been massacred and others carried into deplorable captivity.

Strict justice and equity had always formed the basis of Washington's dealings with the Indian tribes, but his efforts were often thwarted by the conduct of our own people—the encroachments of land speculators and the lawless conduct of our frontiersmen—and jealousies thus excited were fomented by the intrigues of foreign agents.

An act had been provided for emergencies, by which the President was empowered to call out the militia for the protection of the frontier; this act he put in force and an expedition began its march on the 30th of September from Fort Washington (the site of the present city of Cincinnati). Brigadier General Harmer led the expedition, having under him 320 regulars, with militia detachments from Pennsylvania and Virginia (or Kentucky), making in all 1453 men. After a march of seventeen days they approached the principal village of the Miamis. The Indians did not await an attack but set fire to the village and fled to the woods. The destruction of the place, with large quantities of provisions, was completed.

An Indian trail being discovered, Colonel Harden, a continental officer who commanded the Kentucky militia, was detached to follow it at the head of 150 of his men and about 30 regulars under Captain Armstrong and Ensign Hartshorn. They were crossing a plain covered by thickets when suddenly there were volleys of rifles on each side from unseen marksmen. The trail had, in fact, decoyed them into an ambush of 700 savages under the famous warrior Little Turtle. The militia fled without firing a musket. The savages now turned upon the handful of regulars, who made a brave resistance until all were slain, excepting Armstrong, Hartshorn, and five privates, who escaped narrowly and found their way back to the camp about 6 miles distant.

The army commenced its march back to Fort Washington. On the 21st of October, when it was about 10 miles west of Chillicothe, an opportunity was given Hardin to wipe out the late disgrace of his arms. He was detached with a larger body of militia than before and 60 regulars under Major Willys to seek and bring the savages to action. He had another encounter with Little Turtle and his braves, a bloody battle, fought well on both sides. The militia behaved bravely and lost many men and officers, as did the regulars; Willys fell at the commencement of the action. Hardin was at length compelled to retreat, leaving the dead and wounded in the hands of the enemy. After he had rejoined the main force, the whole expedition made its way back to Fort Washington on the banks of the Ohio.

Congress reassembled on the first Monday in December, at Philadelphia, now the seat of government. A house belonging to Robert Morris had been hired by Washington for his residence.

Congress, at its opening, was chiefly occupied in financial arrangements intended to establish the public credit and provide for the expenses of government. According to the statement of the Secretary of the Treasury, an additonal annual revenue of $826,000 would be required, principally to meet additional charges arising from the assumption of State debts. He proposed to raise it by an increase of the impost on foreign distilled spirits and a tax by way of excise on spirits distilled at home. An Impost and Excise bill was accordingly introduced into Congress and met with violent opposition, but the bill was finally carried through the House.

Mr. Hamilton, in his former report, had recommended the establishment of a National Bank. A bill, introduced in conformity with his views, was passed in the Senate but vehemently opposed in the House, partly on considerations of policy but chiefly on the ground of constitutionality. On one side it was denied that the constitution had given to Congress the power of incorporation; on the other side it was insisted that such power was incident to the power vested in Congresss for raising money.

The question was argued at length, and, after passing the House by a majority of 19 votes, came before the executive for approval. The cabinet was divided on it. Jefferson and Randolph denied its constitutionality; Hamilton and Knox maintained it. Washington required of each minister the reasons of his opinion in writing and, after weighing them, gave his sanction to the act and the bill was carried into effect.

The objection of Jefferson to a bank was not merely on constitutional grounds. In his subsequent writings he avows himself opposed to banks as introducing a paper instead of a cash system— raising up a moneyed aristocracy and abandoning the public to the discretion of avarice and swindlers. Paper money might have some advantages but its abuses were inevitable and, by breaking up the measure of value, it made a lottery of all private property. These objections he maintained to his dying day, but he had others which may have been more cogent with him in the present instance. He considered the bank a powerful engine intended by Hamilton to complete the machinery by which the whole action of the legislature was to be placed under the direction of the Treasury and shaped to further a monarchical system of government. Washington, he affirmed, was not aware of the drift or effect of Hamilton's schemes. The opposite policy of these rival statesmen brought them into incessant collision. "Hamilton and myself," writes Jefferson, "were daily pitted in the cabinet like two cocks." The warm-hearted Knox always sided with his old companion in arms. Randolph commonly adhered to Jefferson. Washington's calm and massive intellect over-ruled any occasional discord.

In the mean time two political parties were forming throughout the Union under the adverse standards of these statesmen. Both had the good of the country at heart but differed as to the policy by which it was to be secured. The Federalists, who followed Hamilton, were in favor of strengthening the general government so as to give it weight and dignity abroad and efficiency at home; to guard it against the encroachments of the individual States and a general tendency to anarchy. The other party, known as republicans or democrats, and taking Jefferson's view of affairs, saw in all the measures advo-cated by the Federalists an intention to convert the Federal into a central government, preparatory to a change from a republic to a monarchy.

The particulars of Harmer's expedition against the Indians, when reported to Congress, gave great dissatisfaction. The conduct of the troops, in suffering themselves to be surprised, was for some time stigmatized as disgraceful. Further troubles in that quarter were apprehended for the Miamis were said to be less disheartened by the ravage of their villages than exultant at the successful ambus-cades of Little Turtle.

Three Seneca chiefs, being at the seat of government on busi-ness of their own nation, offered to visit these belligerent tribes and persuade them to bury the hatchet. Washington encouraged them in the undertaking. "By this humane measure," said he, "you will render these mistaken people a great service and probably prevent their being swept off the face of the earth. The United States require only that these people should demean themselves peaceably."

Washington had always been earnest in his desire to civilize the savages; the true means, he thought, was to introduce the arts and habits of husbandry among them. In concluding his speech to the Seneca chiefs, he observed, "Tell your nation that it is my desire to promote their prosperity by teaching them the use of domestic animals and the manner that the white people plough and raise so much corn; and if, upon consideration, it would be agreeable to the nation at large to learn those arts, I will find some means of teaching them at some places within their country as shall be agreed upon."

As the Indians north-west of the Ohio still continued their hostilities, one of the last measures of Congress had been an act to augment the military establishment and to place in the hands of the executive more ample means for the protection of the frontiers. A new expedition against the belligerent tribes had, in consequence, been projected. General St. Clair, governor of the territory west of the Ohio, was appointed commander-in-chief of the forces to be employed.

In the course of the present session, Congress granted the applications of Kentucky and Vermont for admission into the Union, the former after August, 1792, the latter immediately.

On the 3d of March the term of Congress expired. Washington, after reciting the various important measures that had been effected, testified to the great harmony and cordiality which had prevailed. In some few instances, he admitted, especially on the subject of the bank, "the line between the southern and eastern interests had appeared more strongly marked than could be wished . . . but the debates," adds he, "were conducted with temper and candor."

Washington had been deeply chagrined by the disasters of Harmer's expedition resulting from Indian ambushes. In taking leave of his old military comrade, St. Clair, he wished him success and honor but gave him a solemn warning. "Beware of a surprise! You know how the Indians fight. I repeat it—Beware of a surprise!" With these warning words sounding in his ear, St. Clair departed.

In March Washington set out on a tour through the Southern States. The route projected was by Fredericksburg, Richmond, Wilmington (N.C.), and Charleston to Savannah; thence to Augusta, Columbia, and the interior towns of North Carolina and Virginia, comprising a journey of 1887 miles, all which he accomplished without any interruption from sickness, bad weather, or any untoward accident.

He returned to Philadelphia on the 6th of July, much pleased with his tour. It had enabled him, he said, to see with his own eyes the situation of the country and to learn more accurately the disposition of the people than he could have done from any verbal information.

"Every day's experience of the government of the United States," writes he to David Humphreys, "seems to confirm its establishment and to render it more popular. A ready acquiescence in the laws made under it shows, in a strong light, the confidence which the people have in their representatives and in the upright views of those who administer the government."

To his comrade in arms, Lafayette, he also writes exultingly of the flourishing state of the country and the attachment of all classes to the government: "While in Europe, wars or commotions seem to agitate almost every nation, peace and tranquillity prevail among us, except . . . where the Indians have been troublesome. . . . This contrast between the situation of the people of the United States and those of Europe . . . may, I believe, be considered as one great cause of leading the people here to reflect more attentively on their own prosperous state and to examine more minutely, and consequently approve more fully, of the government under which they live than they otherwise would have done. But we do not wish to be the only people who may taste the sweets of an equal and good government. We look with an anxious eye to the time when happiness and tranquillity shall prevail in your country and when all Europe shall be freed from commotion, tumults, and alarms."

Sympathy with the popular cause in France prevailed with part of Washington's cabinet. Jefferson was ardent in his wishes that the revolution might be established. He felt that the permanence of our own revolution leaned, in some degree, on that of France, that a failure there would be a powerful argument to prove there must be a failure here, and that the success of the French revolution was necessary to stay up our own and "prevent its falling back to that kind of half-way house, the English constitution."

Outside of the cabinet, the Vice President, John Adams, regarded the French revolution with strong distrust. His official position, however, was too negative in its nature to afford him an opportunity of exerting influence on public affairs. "My country," writes he, "has, in its wisdom, contrived for me the most insignificant office that ever the invention of man contrived or his imagination conceived."

While the public mind was thus agitated with conflicting opinions, news arrived in August of the flight of Louis XVI from Paris and his recapture at Varennes. Jefferson, who was the first to communicate the intelligence to Washington, observes, "I never saw him so much dejected by any event in my life." Washington, himself, declares that he remained for some time in painful suspense as to what would be the consequences of this event. Ultimately, when news arrived that the king had accepted the constitution from the hands of the National Assembly, he hailed the event as promising happy consequences to France and to mankind in general; what added to his joy was the noble part which Lafayette had acted in this great drama. "The prayers and wishes of the human race," writes he to the Marquis, "have attended the exertions of your nation and, when your affairs are settled under an energetic and equal government, the hearts of all good men will be satisfied."

(CHAPTER 63)

The second Congress assembled at Philadelphia on the 24th of October; on the 25th Washington delivered his opening speech. After remarking upon the prosperous situation of the country and the success which had attended its financial measures, he adverted to the operations against the Indians for the protection of the Western frontier. Some of these operations, he observed, had been successful, others were still depending.

To reconcile some of the people of the West to the appointment of St. Clair as commander-in-chief in that quarter, a local board of war had been formed for the Western country, empowered to act in conjunction with the commanding officer of the United States in calling out the militia, sending out expeditions against the Indians, and apportioning scouts through the exposed parts of Kentucky.

Under this arrangement two expeditions had been organized in Kentucky against the villages on the Wabash. Very little good was effected, or glory gained by either of these expeditions. Indian villages were burned and fields laid waste; some warriors were killed and prisoners taken and an immense expense incurred.

Of the events of a third enterprise, led by St. Clair himself, no tidings had been received at the time of Washington's opening speech. The troops for his expedition assembled early in September in the vicinity of Fort Washington (now Cincinnati). There were about 2000 regulars, and 1000 militia. The regulars included a corps of artillery and several squadrons of horse. An arduous task was before them. Roads were to be opened through a wilderness, bridges constructed for the conveyance of artillery and stores, and forts to be built so as to keep up a line of communication between the Wabash and the Ohio, the base of operations. The troops commenced their march directly North, on the 6th or 7th of September, cutting their way through the woods, and slowly constructing the line of forts.

After placing garrisons in the forts, the general continued his march. A number of the Virginia troops had already, on the 27th of October, insisted on their discharges; there was danger that the whole battalion would follow their example and the time of the other battalions was nearly up. The plan of the general was to push so far into the enemy's country that such detachments as might be entitled to their discharges would be afraid to return.

The army had proceeded six days after leaving Fort Jefferson and were drawing near where they were likely to meet with Indians when, on the 30th of October, 60 of the militia deserted in a body, intending to supply themselves by plundering the convoys of provisions which were coming forward in the rear. A regiment was detached to apprehend these deserters, if possible, and, at all events, prevent the provisions from being rifled. The force thus detached consisted of 300 of the best disciplined men in the service with experienced officers.

Thus reduced to 1400 effective rank and file, the army continued its march to a point 29 miles from Fort Jefferson and 15 miles south of the Miami villages, where it encamped, November

3d, on a rising ground with a stream 40 feet wide in front, running westerly.

The troops were encamped in two lines. The immediate spot of the encampment was very defensible against regular troops but it was surrounded by close woods, dense thickets, trunks of fallen trees, with here and there a ravine and a small swamp—all the best kind of cover for stealthy Indian warfare.

The militia were encamped beyond the stream about a quarter of a mile in the advance on a high flat, a much more favorable position than that occupied by the main body.

It was the intention of St. Clair to throw up a slight work on the following day and to move on to the attack of the Indian villages as soon as he should be rejoined by his previously detached regiment. About half an hour before sunrise on the next morning (Nov. 4th), a horrible sound burst forth from the woods around the militia camp. It was the direful Indian yell, followed by the sharp reports of the deadly rifle. The militia returned a feeble fire and took to flight, dashing helter-skelter into the other camp. The first line of the continental troops which was hastily forming was thrown into disorder. The Indians were close upon the heels of the flying militia and would have entered the camp with them, but the sight of troops drawn up with fixed bayonets checked their ardor and they threw themselves behind logs and bushes immediately commencing an attack upon the first line, which soon was extended to the second. The weight of the attack was upon the centre of each line where the artillery was placed. The artillerists were exposed to a murderous fire; every officer and more than two-thirds of the men were killed and wounded. Twice the Indians pushed into the camp, delivering their fire and then rushing on with the tomahawk, but each time they were driven back.

St. Clair preserved his coolness in the midst of the peril and disaster. Seeing to what disadvantage his troops fought with a concealed enemy, he ordered Colonel Darke, with his regiment of regulars, to rouse the Indians from their covert with the bayonet and turn their left flank. This was executed with great spirit: the enemy were driven about 400 yards but, for want of cavalry or riflemen, the pursuit slackened and the troops were forced to give back in turn.

The savages had now got into the camp by the left flank; several charges were made, but in vain. Great carnage was suffered from the enemy concealed in the woods; all the officers of the second regiment were picked off, excepting three. The spirits of the troops flagged under the loss of the officers; half the army was killed, and there appeared to be no alternative but a retreat.

At half-past nine, St. Clair ordered Darke to make another charge, as if to turn the right wing of the enemy, but, in fact, to regain the road from which the army was cut off. This object was effected. "Having collected in one body the greatest part of the troops," writes one of the officers, "and such of the wounded as could possibly hobble along with us, we pushed out from the left of the rear line, sacrificing our artillery and baggage." It was a disorderly flight. The troops threw away arms, ammunition, and accoutrements. Fortunately, the enemy did not pursue above a mile or two, returning, most probably, to plunder the camp.

By seven in the evening, the fugitives reached Fort Jefferson, a distance of 29 miles. The retreat was continued to Fort Washington, where the army arrived on the 8th at noon, shattered and broken-spirited. In this disastrous battle the loss amounted to 677 killed, including 30 women, and 271 wounded.

Poor St. Clair's defeat has been paralleled with that of Braddock. No doubt, when he realized the terrible havoc that had been made, he thought sadly of Washington's parting words, "Beware of a surprise!"

In the course of the present session of Congress a bill was introduced for apportioning representatives among the people of the several States according to the first enumeration.

The constitution had provided that the number of representatives should not exceed one for every 30,000 persons, and the House of Representatives passed a bill allotting to each State one member for this amount of population. This ratio would leave a fraction, greater or less, in each State. Its operation was unequal, as in some States a large surplus would be unrepresented, and hence, in one branch of the legislature, the relative power of the State be affected. That, too, was the popular branch, which those who feared a strong executive, desired to provide with the counterpoise of as full a representation as possible.

To obviate this difficulty the Senate adopted a new principle of apportionment. They assumed the total population of the United States, and not the population of each State, as the basis on which the whole number of representatives should be ascertained. This aggregate they divided by 30,000: the quotient gave 120 as the number of representatives; and this number they apportioned upon the States according to their population; allotting to each one member for every 30,000, and distributing the residuary members (to make up the 120) among the States having the largest fractions.

After an earnest debate, the House concurred and the bill came before the President for his decision. The sole question was as to its constitutionality. Washington took the opinion of his cabinet. Jefferson and Randolph considered the act at variance with the constitution. Knox was undecided. Hamilton thought the clause of the constitution somewhat vague and was in favor of the construction given to it by the legislature. After weighing the arguments on both sides, the President made up his mind that the act was unconstitutional. He accordingly returned the bill with his objections, the first exercise of veto power. A new bill was substituted and passed into a law, giving a representative for every 33,000 to each State.

Washington had observed with pain the political divisions which were growing up in the country and was deeply concerned at finding that they were pervading the halls of legislation. The press, too, was contributing its powerful aid to keep up and increase the irritation.

Heart-weary by the political disagreements which were disturbing the country and marring the harmony of his cabinet, the charge of government was becoming intolerably irksome to Washington; he longed to be released from it. But one more year of his presidential term remained to be endured; he was congratulating himself with the thought when Jefferson intimated that it was his intention to retire from office at the same time.

Washington was exceedingly discomposed by this determination. He observed to Jefferson that he really felt himself growing old, that his bodily health was less firm and his memory, always bad, was becoming worse. The other faculties of his mind, perhaps, might be evincing to others a decay of which he himself might be insensible. This apprehension, he said, particularly oppressed him. For these reasons he felt himself obliged to retire; yet he should consider it unfortunate if, in so doing, he should bring on the retirement of the great officers of government, which might produce a shock on the public mind of dangerous consequence.

Jefferson, in reply, stated the resolution he had formed, on accepting his station in the cabinet, to make the resignation of the President the epoch of his own retirement. He did not believe, however, that any of his brethren in the administration had any idea of retiring.

Subsequently, Washington had confidential conversations with Madison on his intended retirement from office at the end of the presidential term and asked him to think what would be the proper time and mode of announcing his intention to the public. Madison remonstrated in the most earnest manner against such a resolution, setting forth in urgent language the importance to the country of his continuing in the presidency. Washington listened to his reasoning with profound attention but still clung to his resolution.

In consequence of St. Clair's disastrous defeat and the increasing pressure of the Indian war, bills had been passed in Congress for increasing the army by adding three regiments of infantry and a squadron of cavalry (which additional force was to serve for three years, unless sooner discharged) and for establishing a uniform militia system.

St. Clair resigned his commission and was succeeded in his Western command by General Wayne, still in the vigor of his days, being forty-seven years of age. Washington's first thought was that a decisive expedition might retrieve the recent frontier disgrace and put an end to the persevering hostility of the Indians. In deference, however, to the clamors which had been raised against the war and its expenses and to meet what appeared to be the prevalent wish of the nation, he reluctantly relinquished his policy and gave in to that which advised negotiations for peace.

In regard to St. Clair, a committee of the House of Representatives ultimately inquired into the cause of the failure of his expedition and rendered a report in which he was explicitly exculpated. Public sentiment, however, remained adverse to him but Washington, satisfied with the explanations which had been given, continued to honor him with his confidence and friendship.

Congress adjourned on the 8th of May and soon afterward Washington set off on a short visit to Mount Vernon. The season was in all its beauty and never had this rallying place of his affections appeared to him more attractive. How could he give up the prospect of a speedy return to its genial pursuits and pleasures from the harassing cares and janglings of public life.

He now renewed the request he had made of Madison for advice as to the proper time and mode for announcing his intention of retiring and for assistance in preparing the announcement. "I would fain carry my request to you further," adds he. "As the recess [of Congress] may afford you leisure and, I flatter myself, you have dispositions to oblige me, I will, without apology, desire . . . that you would turn your thoughts to a valedictory address from me to the public." He then went on to suggest a number of the topics and ideas which the address was to contain, all to be expressed in "plain and modest terms."

Madison, in reply, advised that the notification and address should appear together and be promulgated through the press in time to pervade every part of the Union by the beginning of November. With the letter he sent a draft of the address. Before concluding his letter, Madison expressed a hope that Washington would reconsider his idea of retiring from office and that the country might not be deprived of the inestimable advantage of having him at the head of its councils.

On the 23d of May, Jefferson also addressed a long letter to Washington on the same subject. "When you first mentioned to me your purpose of retiring from the government, . . . I was in a considerable degree silent. I knew . . . that, before forming your decision, you had weighed all the reasons for and against the measure, had made up your mind in full view of them, and that there could be little hope of changing the result. . . . I knew we were some day to try to walk alone and, if the essay should be made while you should be alive and looking on, we should derive confidence from that circumstance, and resource if it failed. The public mind, too, was then calm and confident and therefore in a favorable state for making the experiment. But the public mind is no longer so confident and serene."

Jefferson now launched out against the public debt and all the evils which he apprehended from the funding system, the ultimate object of all which was, said he, "to prepare the way for a change from the present republican form of government to that of a monarchy, of which the English consititution is to be the model."

"The confidence of the whole Union," writes he, "is centred in you. Your being at the helm will be more than an answer to every argument which can be used to alarm and lead the people in any quarter into violence or secession. . . . I appeal from your former determination and urge a revisal of it, on the ground of change in the aspect of things. . . . I cannot but hope that you can resolve to add one or two more to the many years you have already sacrificed to the good of mankind."

The letter of Jefferson was not received by Washington until after his return to Philadelphia; the purport of it was so painful to him that he deferred from day to day having any conversation with that statesman on the subject. A letter written in the mean time by Jefferson to Lafayette shows the predominant belief which was shaping his course of action. "A sect," writes he, "has shown itself among us, who declare they espoused our constitution not as a good and sufficient thing in itself, but only as a step to an English constitution, the only thing good and sufficient in itself, in their eyes. It is happy for us that these are preachers without followers and that our people are firm and constant in their republican purity."

In regard to the suspicions which were haunting Jefferson's mind, Hamilton expressed himself roundly in one of his cabinet papers: "The idea of introducing a monarchy or aristocracy into this country by employing the influence and force of a government continually changing hands towards it is one of those visionary things that none but madmen could meditate and that no wise man will believe."

On the 10th of July, Washington had a conversation with Jefferson and endeavored to allay the suspicions which were disturbing the mind of that ardent politician. There might be desires, he said, among a few in the higher walks of life, particularly in the great cities, to change the form of government into a monarchy, but he did not believe there were any designs; and he believed the people in the Eastern States were as steadily for republicanism as in the Southern.

Hamilton was equally strenuous with Jefferson in urging upon Washington the policy of a re-election as it regarded the public good and wrote to him fully on the subject. It was the opinion of every one, he alleged, with whom he had conversed that the affairs of the national government were not yet firmly established; that the period of the next House of Representatives was likely to prove the crisis of its national character; that if Washington continued in office nothing materially mischievous was to be apprehended, but, if he should quit, much was to be dreaded; that the same motives which had induced him to accept originally ought to decide him to continue till matters had assumed a more determinate aspect; and that the clear path to be pursued by him would be again to obey the voice of his country.

Edmund Randolph also, after a long letter on the "jeopardy of the Union," which seemed to him "at the eve of a crisis," adds: "You suffered yourself to yield when the voice of your country summoned you to the administration. Should a civil war arise, you cannot stay at home. And how much easier will it be to disperse the factions which are rushing to this catastrophe than to subdue them after they shall appear in arms?"

Not the cabinet, merely, divided as it was in its political opinions, but all parties, however discordant in other points, concurred in a desire that Washington should continue in office—so truly was he regarded as the choice of the nation.

But though the cabinet was united in feeling on this one subject, in other respects its dissensions were increasing in virulence. Washington at length found it necessary to interfere and attempt a reconciliation between the warring parties. In the course of a letter to Jefferson (Aug. 23d), on the subject of Indian hostilities, "How unfortunate then," observes he, "and how much to be regretted that, while we are encompassed on all sides with armed enemies and insidious friends, internal dissensions should be harrowing and tearing our vitals. . . . My earnest wish and my fondest hope, therefore, is, that instead of wounding suspicions and irritating charges, there may be liberal allowances, mutual forbearances and temporizing yieldings on all sides. . . . Without them, . . . our enemies will triumph, and, by throwing their weight into the disaffected scale, may accomplish the ruin of the goodly fabric we have been erecting."

Admonitions to the same purport were addressed by him to Hamilton. "I would fain hope that liberal allowances will be made for the political opinions of each other and, instead of those wounding suspicions and irritating charges, . . . that there may be mutual forbearance and temporizing yielding on all sides. Without these I do not see how the reins of government are to be managed or how the Union of the States can be much longer preserved."

Hamilton was prompt and affectionate in his reply, expressing sincere regret at the circumstances which had given rise to the uneasy sensations experienced by Washington. "It is my most anxious wish," writes he, "as far as may depend upon me, to smooth the path of your administration and to render it prosperous and happy. And, if any prospect shall open of healing or terminating the differences which exist, I shall most cheerfully embrace it though I consider myself as the deeply injured party. . . . I know I have been an object of uniform opposition from Mr. Jefferson from the moment of his coming to the city of New York to enter upon his present office. I know, from the most authentic sources, that I have been the frequent subject of the most unkind whispers and insinuations from the same quarter. I have long seen a formed party in the legislature under his auspices bent upon my subversion. . . . Nevertheless, I pledge my hand to you, sir, that, if you shall hereafter form a plan to re-unite the members of your administration upon some steady principle of co-operation, I will faithfully concur in executing it during my continuance in office."

Jefferson, too, in a letter of the same date, assured Washington that to no one had the dissensions of the Cabinet given deeper concern than to himself—to no one equal mortification at being himself a part of them. His own grievances,which led to those dissensions, he traced back to the time when Hamilton, in the spring of 1790, procured his influence to effect a change in the vote on Assumption. "I was duped . . . by the Secretary of the Treasury and made a tool for forwarding his schemes, not then sufficiently understood by me; and of all the errors of my political life, this has occasioned me the deepest regret. . . . That I have utterly, in my private conversations, disapproved of the system of the Secretary of the Treasury, I acknowledge and avow; . . . this was not merely a speculative difference. His system flowed from principles adverse to liberty and was calculated to undermine and demolish the republic by creating an influence of his department over the members of the legislature."

Jefferson considered himself particularly aggrieved by charges against him in Fenno's Gazette, which he ascribed to the pen of Hamilton, and intimated the possibility that, after his retirement from office, he might make an appeal to the country. "I will not suffer my retirement to be clouded by the slanders of a man whose history, from the moment at which history can stoop to notice him, is a tissue of machinations against the liberty of the country which has not only received and given him bread but heaped its honors on his head."

On the 18th of October Washington made one more effort to allay the discord in his cabinet. Finding it impossible for the rival secretaries to concur in any system of politics, he urged them to accommodate their differences by mutual yieldings: "Why, then, when some of the best citizens of the United States—men of discernment—uniform and tried patriots—who have no sinister views to promote but are chaste in their ways of thinking and acting, are to be found, some on one side and some on the other of the questions which have caused these agitations—why should either of you be so tenacious of your opinions as to make no allowance for those of the other? . . . I have a great, a sincere esteem and regard for you both and ardently wish that some line could be marked out by which both of you could walk."

(CHAPTER 64)

It was after a long and painful conflict of feelings that Washington consented to be a candidate for a re-election. There was no opposition on the part of the public and the vote for him in the Electoral College was unanimous. George Clinton, of New York, was held up for the Vice-presidency in opposition to John Adams but the latter was re-elected by a majority of 27 electoral votes.

Though gratified to find that the hearts of his countrymen were still with him, it was with no emotion of pleasure that Washington looked forward to another term of public duty and a prolonged absence from the quiet retirement of Mount Vernon.

The session of Congress, which was to close his present term, opened on the fifth of November. The continuance of the Indian war formed a painful topic in the President's address. Efforts at pacification had been unsuccessful; preparations were therefore making for an active prosecution of hostilities, in which Wayne was to take the field. The factious and turbulent opposition which had been made in some parts of the country to the collection of duties on spirituous liquors distilled in the United States was likewise adverted to by the President and a determination expressed to assert and maintain the just authority of the laws. In a part of the speech addressed to the House of Representatives, he expressed a strong hope that the state of the national finances was now sufficiently matured to admit of an arrangement for the redemption and discharge of the public debt.

The address was well received by both houses and a disposition expressed to concur with the President's views and wishes. The discussion of the subjects to which he had called their attention soon produced vehement conflicts of opinion in the house, marking the growing virulence of parties. The Secretary of the Treasury, in reporting a plan for the annual reduction of so much of the national debt as the United States had a right to redeem, spoke of the expenses of the Indian war and the necessity of additional internal taxes. The consideration of the report was parried or evaded and a motion made to reduce the military establishment. This gave an opportunity for sternly criticizing the mode in which the Indian war had been conducted, for discussing the comparative merits and cost of regular and militia forces, and for inveighing against standing armies as dangerous to liberty. These discussions led to no result and gave way to an inquiry into the conduct of the Secretary of the Treasury in regard to certain loans which the President, in conformity to acts of Congress, had authorized him to make but concerning the management of which he had not furnished detailed reports to the legislature. A report of the Secretary gave all the information desired but the charges of official misconduct against him continued to be urged with great acrimony to the close of the session, when they were signally rejected.

Washington, though he never courted popularity, was attentive to the signs of public opinion. The time for entering upon his second term of Presidency was at hand. There had been much cavilling at the parade attending his first installation. To guide him on the coming occasion, Washington called the heads of departments together and desired they would consult with one another and agree on any changes they might consider for the better. As they were divided in opinion and gave no positive advice as to any change, no change was made. On the 4th of March, the oath was publicly administered to Washington by Justice Cushing in the Senate Chamber in presence of the heads of departments, foreign ministers, such members of the House of Representatives as were in town, and as many other spectators as could be accommodated.

It was under gloomy auspices, a divided cabinet, an increasing exasperation of parties, a suspicion of monarchical tendencies, and a threatened abatement of popularity that Washington entered upon his second term of presidency.

Early in April intelligence was received that France had declared war against England. Popular excitement was now wound up to the highest pitch. What, it was asked, were Americans to do in such a juncture? Could they remain unconcerned spectators of a conflict between their ancient enemy and republican France?

Washington was at Mount Vernon when he received news of the war. He forthwith despatched a letter to Jefferson. "War having actually commenced between France and Great Britain," writes he, "it behooves the government of this country to . . . maintain a strict neutrality."

Hastening back to Philadelphia, he held a cabinet council on the 19th of April to deliberate on the measures proper to be observed by the United States in the present crisis and to determine upon a general plan of conduct for the Executive. It was unanimously determined that a proclamation should be issued by the President, "forbidding the citizens of the United States to take part in any hostilities on the seas and warning them against carrying to the belligerents any articles deemed contraband according to the modern usages of nations and forbidding all acts and proceedings inconsistent with the duties of a friendly nation towards those at war." It was unanimously agreed also that, should the republic of France send a minister to the United States, he should be received.

Washington's proclamation of neutrality was at variance with the excited passions of a large portion of the citizens. They stigmatized it as a royal edict, a daring assumption of power, an open manifestation of partiality for England and hostility to France.

Washington saw that a deadly blow was aimed at his influence and his administration, but he was convinced that neutrality was the true national policy and he resolved to maintain it, whatever might be his immediate loss of popular favor. His resolution was soon put to the test.

The French republic had recently appointed Edmond Charles Genet, or "Citizen Genet" as he was styled, minister to the United States. He had served in various diplomatic situations until the overthrow of the monarchy, when he joined the popular party, became a political zealot, and was rewarded with the mission to America.

A letter from Gouverneur Morris, our minister to France at the time, apprised Jefferson that the Executive Council had furnished Genet with 300 blank commissions for privateers, to be given clandestinely to such persons as he might find in America inclined to take them.

Genet's conduct proved the correctness of this information. He had landed at Charleston on the 8th of April, a short time before the proclamation of neutrality, and was received with great rejoicing and demonstrations of respect. His landing at a port several hundred miles from the seat of government was a singular move for a diplomat but his object was soon evident. It is usual for a foreign minister to present his credentials to the government to which he comes before he enters upon the exercise of his functions. The contiguity of Charleston to the West Indies made it a favorable port for fitting out privateers against the trade of these islands; during Genet's short sojourn there he issued commissions for arming and equipping vessels of war for that purpose and manning them with Americans.

In the latter part of April, Genet set out for the north by land. As he proceeded on his journey, the newspapers teemed with accounts of the processions and addresses with which he was greeted. On the 16th of May, Genet arrived at Philadelphia. His operations at Charleston had already been made a subject of complaint to the government by the British minister but they produced no abatement in the public enthusiasm.

On the following day, various societies and a large body of citizens waited upon him with addresses, recalling with gratitude the aid given by France in the achievement of American independence and extolling and rejoicing in the success of the arms of the French republic.

This enthusiasm of the multitude was regarded with indulgence, if not favor, by Jefferson as being the effervescence of the true spirit of liberty, but it was deprecated by Hamilton as an infatuation that might "do us much harm and could do France no good."

Washington, from his elevated and responsible situation, endeavored to look beyond the popular excitement and regard the affairs of France with a dispassionate and impartial eye, but he confessed that he saw in the turn they had lately taken the probability of a terrible confusion, to which he could predict no certain issue.

On the 18th of May, Genet presented his letter of credence to the President, by whom, notwithstanding his unwarrantable proceedings at Charleston, he was well received, Washington taking the occasion to express his sincere regard for the French nation.

Genet's acts at Charleston had not been the sole ground of the complaint preferred by the British minister. The capture of a British vessel by the French frigate Ambuscade formed a graver one. Occurring within our waters, it was a clear violation of neutral rights. The British minister demanded a restitution of the prize and the cabinet were unanimously of opinion that restitution should be made. There was no difficulty with the French minister on this head, but restitution was likewise claimed of other vessels captured on the high seas and brought into port by the privateers authorized by Genet. In regard to these there was a difference of sentiment in the cabinet. Hamilton and Knox were of opinion that the government should interpose to restore the prizes. Jefferson and Randolph contended that the case should be left to the decision of the courts of justice.

Seeing this difference of opinion in the cabinet, Washington reserved the point for further deliberation, but directed the Secretary of State to communicate to the ministers of France and Britain the principles in which they concurred, these being considered as settled. Circular letters, also, were addressed to the Governors of several States requiring their co-operation, with force if necessary, to carry out the rules agreed upon.

Genet took umbrage at these decisions of the government and expressed his dissatisfaction in a letter, complaining of them as violations of natural right and subversive of the existing treaties between the two nations. His letter induced a review of the subject in the cabinet and he was informed that no reason appeared for changing the system adopted. He was further informed that in the opinion of the executive, the vessels which had been illegally equipped should depart from the ports of the United States.

Genet was not disposed to acquiesce in these decisions. He was aware of the grateful feelings of the nation to France; the people, he thought, were with him, if Washington was not, and he believed the latter would not dare to risk his popularity in thwarting their enthusiasm. He persisted, therefore, in disregarding the decisions of the government and spoke of them as a departure from the obligations it owed to France, a cowardly abandonment of friends when danger menaced.

Another event added to the irritation of Genet. Two American citizens, whom he had engaged at Charleston to cruise in the service of France were arrested on board of the privateer, conducted to prison, and prosecutions commenced against them. The indignant feelings of Genet were vented in an extraordinary letter to the Secretary of State. When speaking of their arrest, "The crime laid to their charge," writes he—"the crime which my mind cannot conceive and which my pen almost refuses to state—is the serving of France, and defending with her children, the common glorious cause of liberty."

The lofty and indignant tone of this letter had no effect in shaking the determination of government or obtaining the release of the prisoners. Washington was very much harried and perplexed by the "disputes, memorials, and what not" with which he was pestered by one or other of the powers at war. It was a sore trial of his equanimity, his impartiality, and his discrimination, and wore upon his spirits and his health. He was aware that, in withstanding the public infatuation in regard to France, he was putting an unparalleled popularity at hazard; and, in so doing, set a magnanimous example for his successors in office to endeavor to follow.

In the latter part of July, Washington was suddenly called to Mount Vernon by the death of the manager of his estates. During his brief absence from the seat of government occurred the case of the Little Sarah. This was a British merchant vessel which had been captured by a French privateer and brought into Philadelphia, where she had been armed and equipped for privateering, manned with 120 men, many of them Americans. This, of course, was in violation of Washington's decision, which had been communicated to Genet.

General Mifflin, now Governor of Pennsylvania, being informed on the 6th of July that the vessel was to sail the next day, sent his secretary to Genet to persuade him to detain the vessel until the President should arrive, intimating that otherwise force would be used to prevent her departure.

Genet flew into one of the transports of passion to which he was prone; declared that the President was not the sovereign of the country and had no right, without consulting Congress, to give such instructions as he had issued to the State Governors; he threatened to appeal from his decision to the people and to repel force by force should an attempt be made to seize the privateer.

Apprised of this menace, Governor Mifflin forthwith ordered out 120 of the militia to take possession of the privateer and communicated the circumstances of the case to the cabinet.

Jefferson now took the matter in hand and on the 7th of July in an interview with Genet, repeated the request that the privateer be detained until the arrival of the President. Genet instantly went into an immense field of declamation and complaint. Jefferson made a few efforts to be heard but, finding them ineffectual, suffered the torrent of vituperation to pour on. In the course of his complaints, Genet censured the executive for the measures it had taken without consulting Congress and declared that, on the President's return, he would certainly press him to convene that body.

He had by this time exhausted his passion and moderated his tone and Jefferson took occasion to say a word. "I stopped him," writes he, "at the subject of calling Congress; explained our constitution to him as having divided the functions of government among three different authorities, the executive, legislative, and judiciary, each of which were supreme on all questions belonging to their department and independent of the others; that all the questions which had arisen between him and us belonged to the executive department and, if Congress were sitting, could not be carried to them nor would they take notice of them."

Genet, taken aback at finding his own ignorance in the matter, subsided and, the subject of the Little Sarah being resumed, Jefferson pressed her detention until the President's return, intimating that her previous departure would be considered a very serious offence.

When Jefferson endeavored to extort an assurance that she would await the President's return, Genet evaded a direct committal, intimating, however, by look and gesture, that she would not be gone before that time. Jefferson was accordingly impressed with the belief that the privateer would remain in the river until the President should decide on her case, and, on communicating this conviction to the Governor, the latter ordered the militia to be dismissed.

Hamilton and Knox, on the other hand, were distrustful, and proposed the immediate erection of a battery on Mud Island with guns mounted to fire at the vessel, even to sink her if she attempted to pass. Jefferson, however, refusing to concur in the measure, it was not adopted.

Washington arrived at Philadelphia on the 11th of July when papers requiring "instant attention" were put into his hands. They related to the case of the Little Sarah and were from Jefferson who, being ill with fever, had retired to his seat in the country.

In a letter written to Jefferson, he puts these indignant queries: "What is to be done in the case of the Little Sarah? Is the minister of the French republic to set the acts of this government at defiance with impunity? And then threaten the executive with an appeal to the people!"

Jefferson, in a reply of the same date, informed the President of his having received assurance that day from Genet that the vessel would not be gone before the President's decision. In consequence of this assurance of the French minister, no immediate measures were taken with regard to the vessel, but, in a cabinet council the next day, it was determined to detain in port all privateers which had been equipped within the United States by any of the belligerent powers. No time was lost in communicating this determination to Genet; in defiance of it, the vessel sailed on her cruise.

It must have been a severe trial of Washington's spirit to see his authority thus braved and insulted and to find that the people, notwithstanding the indignity thus offered to their chief magistrate, sided with the aggressors and exulted in their open defiance of his neutral policy.

Washington had exercised great forbearance toward the French minister, but the official communications of Genet were becoming too offensive and insulting to be longer tolerated. Meetings of the heads of departments and the Attorney General were held at the President's on the 1st and 2d of August, in which the whole of the official correspondence and conduct of Genet was passed in review; it was agreed that his recall should be desired. Jefferson recommended that the desire should be expressed with great delicacy; the others were for peremptory terms. In the end it was agreed that a letter should be written to Gouverneur Morris, giving a statement of the case, with accompanying documents, that he might lay the whole before the executive council of France and explain the reason for desiring the recall of Genet.

It was proposed that a publication of the whole correspondence and a statement of the proceedings should be made by way of appeal to the people. This produced animated debates. Hamilton spoke with great warmth in favor of an appeal. Jefferson opposed it. "Genet," said he, "will appeal also; it will become a contest between the President and Genet."

Washington, already weary and impatient, was stung by the suggestion that he might be held up as in conflict with Genet and subjected, as he had been, to the ribaldry of the press. The President, writes Jefferson, now burst forth into one of those transports of passion beyond his control, inveighed against the personal abuse which had been bestowed upon him, and defied any man on earth to produce a single act of his since he had been in the government that had not been done on the purest motives. In the agony of his heart he declared that he had rather be on his farm than to be made emperor of the world—and yet, said he indignantly, they are charging me with wanting to be a king!

All were silent during this burst of feeling—a pause ensued—it was difficult to resume the question. Washington, however, who had recovered his equanimity, put an end to the difficulty. There was no necessity, he said, for deciding the matter at present; the propositions agreed to respecting the letter to Morris might be put into execution and events would show whether the appeal would be necessary or not.

Washington had hitherto been annoyed and perplexed by having to manage a divided cabinet; he was now threatened with that cabinet's dissolution. Hamilton had informed him by letter that private as well as public reasons had determined him to retire from office toward the close of the next session, probably with a view to give Congress an opportunity to examine into his conduct.

Now came a letter from Jefferson, dated July 31st, in which he recalled the circumstances which had induced him to postpone for a while his original intention of retiring from office at the close of the first four years of the republic. These circumstances, he observed, had now ceased to such a degree as to leave him free to think again of a day on which to withdraw; "at the close, therefore, of the ensuing month of September, I shall beg leave to retire to scenes of greater tranquillity from those for which I am every day more and more convinced that neither my talents, tone of mind, nor time of life fit me."

Washington was both grieved and embarrassed by this notification. Full of concern, he called upon Jefferson at his country residence near Philadelphia and pictured his deep distress at finding himself, in the present perplexing juncture of affairs, about to be deserted by those of his cabinet on whose counsel he had counted. The public mind, he went on to observe, was in an alarming state of ferment; political combinations of various kinds were forming; where all this would end he knew not. A new Congress was to assemble, more numerous than the last, perhaps of a different spirit; the first expressions of its sentiments would be important and it would relieve him considerably if Jefferson would remain in office, if it were only until the end of the session.

Repeatedly, we discern Washington's efforts to moderate the growing antipathies between the eminent men whom he had sought to assist him in conducting the government. He continued to have the highest opinion of Jefferson's abilities, his knowledge of foreign affairs, his thorough patriotism; it was his earnest desire to retain him in his cabinet through the whole of the ensuing session of Congress. A compromise was eventually made, according to which Jefferson was to be allowed a temporary absence in the autumn and on his return was to continue in office until January.

In the mean time Genet had proceeded to New York, which was just then in great agitation. The frigate Ambuscade, anchored in the harbor, had been challenged to single combat by the British frigate Boston, which was cruising off the Hook. The challenge was accepted, a severe action ensued, and the Boston, much damaged, was obliged to stand for Halifax. The Ambuscade returned triumphant to New York and entered the port amid the enthusiastic cheers of the populace. On the same day, a French fleet of 15 sail arrived from the Chesapeake and anchored in the Hudson river. The officers and crews were objects of unbounded favor with all who inclined to the French cause.

In the midst of this excitement, the ringing of bells and the firing of cannon announced that Citizen Genet was arrived at Powles Hook Ferry, directly opposite the city. Genet entered the city amid the almost frantic cheerings of the populace. Addresses were made to him, expressing devoted attachment to the French republic and abjuring all neutrality in regard to its heroic struggle.

In the midst of his self-gratulation and complacency, however, he received a letter from Jefferson (Sept. 15th) acquainting him with the measures taken to procure his recall and inclosing a copy of the letter written for that purpose to the American minister at Paris. It was added that, lest the interests of France might suffer, the Executive would, in the mean time, receive Genet's communications in writing and admit the continuance of his functions so long as they should be within the law as announced to him and should be of the tenor usually observed towards independent nations by the representative of a friendly power residing with them.

The letter threw Genet into a violent passion and produced a reply (Sept. 18) written while he was still in a great heat. "Whatever, Sir," writes Genet, "may be the result of the exploit of which you have rendered yourself the generous instrument after having made me believe that you were my friend, . . . there is an act of justice which the American people, which the French people, which all free people are interested in demanding; it is, that a particular inquiry should be made, in the approaching Congress, into the motives which have induced the chief of the executive power of the United States to take upon himself to demand the recall of a public minister whom the sovereign people of the United States had received fraternally."

Unfortunately for Genet's ephemeral popularity, a rumor got abroad that he had expressed a determination to appeal from the president to the people. The audacity thus manifested by a foreign minister shocked the national pride. Meetings were held in every part of the Union to express the public feeling in the matter. In these meetings the proclamation of neutrality and the measures flowing from it were sustained, partly from a conviction of their wisdom and justice but more from an undiminished affection for the person and character of Washington, for many who did not espouse his views were ready to support him in the exercise of his constitutional functions. The warm partisans of Genet, however, advocated his right to appeal from the president to the people. The president, they argued, was invested with no sanctity to make such an act criminal; in a republican country the people were the real sovereigns.

(CHAPTER 65)

While the neutrality of the United States, so jealously guarded by Washington, was endangered by the intrigues of the French minister, it was put to imminent hazard by ill-advised measures of the British cabinet.

There was such a scarcity in France in consequence of the failure of the crops that a famine was apprehended. England determined to increase the distress by cutting off all her supplies from abroad. In June, 1793, therefore, her cruisers were instructed to detain all vessels bound to France with corn, flour, or meal, take them into port, unload them, purchase the cargoes, make a proper allowance for the freight, and then release the vessels; or to allow the masters of them, on a stipulated security, to dispose of their cargoes in a port in amity with England. This measure brought out an earnest remonstrance from the United States as being a violation of the law of neutrals. Another grievance which helped to swell the tide of resentment against Great Britain was the frequent impressment of American seamen, a wrong to which they were particularly exposed from national similarity. To these may be added the persistence of Great Britain in holding the posts to the south of the lakes which, according to treaty stipulations, ought to have been given up.

The hostilities of the Indians north of the Ohio, by many attributed to British wiles, still continued. Attempts at an amicable negotiation having proved fruitless, Wayne formed a winter camp near the site of the present city of Cincinnati, whence he was to open his campaign in the ensuing spring.

Congress assembled on the 2d of December (1793), the intrigues of Genet and the aggressions of England tending to increase the partiality for France and render imminent the chance of a foreign war.

Washington, in his opening speech, after expressing his deep sense of the public approbation manifested in his re-election, proceeded to state the measures he had taken, in consequence of the war in Europe, to protect the rights and interests of the United States and maintain peaceful relations with the belligerent parties. Still he pressed upon Congress the necessity of placing the country in a condition of complete defence. In the spirit of these remarks, he urged measures to increase the arms and ammunition in the arsenals and to improve the militia establishment.

One part of his speech conveyed an impressive admonition to the House of Representatives: "No pecuniary consideration is more urgent than the regular redemption and discharge of the public debt; in none can delay be more injurious or an economy of time more valuable." The necessity of augmenting the public revenue in a degree commensurate with the objects suggested was likewise touched upon.

In concluding his speech, he endeavored to impress upon his hearers the magnitude of their task, the important interests confided to them, and the conscientiousness that should reign over their deliberations. "Without an unprejudiced coolness, the welfare of the government may be hazarded; without harmony, as far as consists with freedom of sentiment, its dignity may be lost. But, as the legislative proceedings of the United States will never, I trust, be reproached for the want of temper or of candor, so shall not the public happiness languish from the want of my strenuous and warmest co-operation."

The choice of speaker showed that there was a majority of ten against the administration in the House of Representatives; yet it was manifest, from the satisfaction expressed at his re-election, that Washington was not included in the opposition which appeared to await his political system.

Notwithstanding the popular ferment in favor of France, both Houses seem to have approved the course pursued by Washington in regard to that country; as to his proclamation of neutrality, while the House approved of it in guarded terms, the Senate pronounced it "a measure well timed and wise."

Early in the session, Jefferson, in compliance with a requisition which the House of Representatives had made, Feb. 23d, 1791, furnished a comprehensive report of the state of trade of the United States with different countries, the nature and extent of exports and imports, and the amount of tonnage of the American shipping, specifying, also, the various restrictions and prohibitions by which our commerce was embarrassed and, in some instances, almost ruined. "Two methods," he said, "presented themselves by which these impediments might be removed, modified, or counteracted: friendly arrangement or countervailing legislation. Friendly arrangements were preferable with all who would come into them. . . . But," adds he, "should any nation continue its system of prohibitive duties and regulations, it behooves us to protect our citizens, their commerce, and navigation, by counter prohibitions, duties, and regulations." With this able and elaborate report, Jefferson closed his labors as Secretary of State.

Washington had been especially sensible of the talents and integrity displayed by Jefferson during his secretaryship and had made a last attempt, but an unsuccessful one, to persuade him to remain in the cabinet. The place thus made vacant in the cabinet was filled by Edmund Randolph, whose office of Attorney General was conferred on William Bradford of Pennsylvania.

The report of Jefferson on commercial intercourse was soon taken up in the House in a committee of the whole. A series of resolutions based on it were introduced by Madison and became the subject of a warm and acrimonious debate. The report upheld the policy of turning the course of trade from England to France by discriminations in favor of the latter; the resolutions were to the same purport. Though the subject was, or might seem to be, of a purely commercial nature, it was inevitably mixed up with political considerations. The debate, commenced with warmth and bitterness on the 13th of January, 1794, was protracted to the 3d of February, when the question being taken on the first resolution, it was carried by a majority of only five, so nearly were parties divided. The further consideration of the remaining resolutions was postponed to March, when it was resumed but, in consequence of the new complexion of affairs, was suspended without a decision.

The next legislative movement was also productive of a warm debate. Algerine corsairs had captured 11 American merchant vessels and 100 prisoners and the regency manifested a disposition for further outrages. A bill was introduced into Congress proposing a force of 6 frigates to protect the commerce of the United States against the cruisers of this piratical power. The bill was passed by both Houses, but by a small majority. It received the hearty assent of the President.

In the course of this session, fresh instances had come before the government of the mischievous activity and audacity of Genet, showing that, not content with compromising the neutrality of the United States at sea, he was attempting to endanger it by land. From documents received, it appeared that he had sent emissaries to Kentucky to enrol American citizens in an expedition against New Orleans and the Spanish possessions. Another expedition was to proceed against the Floridas, men for the purpose to be enlisted at the South, to rendezvous in Georgia, and to be aided by a body of Indians and by a French fleet.

These schemes showed such determined purpose on the part of Genet to undermine the peace of the United States that Washington, without waiting a reply to the demand for his recall, resolved to keep no further terms with that headlong diplomat. In a cabinet council it was determined to supersede Genet's diplomatic functions, deprive him of the consequent privileges, and arrest his person; a message to Congress avowing such determination was prepared but, at this juncture, came despatches from Gouverneur Morris, announcing Genet's recall. The French minister of foreign affairs had, in fact, reprobated the conduct of Genet as unauthorized by his instructions and Fauchet, secretary of the executive council, was appointed to succeed him.

About this time vigilance was required to guard against wrongs from an opposite quarter. We have noticed the orders issued by Great Britain to her cruisers in June, 1793, and the resentment thereby excited in the United States. On the 6th of November, she had given them additional instructions to detain all vessels laden with the produce of any colony belonging to France or carrying supplies to any such colony and to bring them, with their cargoes, to British ports for adjudication in the British courts of admiralty.

Captures of American vessels were taking place in consequence of these orders and heightening public irritation. They were considered indicative of determined hostility on the part of Great Britain and an embargo was laid, prohibiting all trade from the United States to any foreign place for 30 days and vigorous preparations for defence were adopted with but little opposition.

On the 27th of March, resolutions were moved that all debts due to British subjects be sequestered and paid into the treasury as a fund to indemnify citizens of the United States for depredations sustained from British cruisers and that all intercourse with Great Britain be interdicted until she had made compensation for these injuries and until she should make surrender of the Western posts.

The popular excitement was intense. "Peace or war" was the absorbing question. While the public mind was in this inflammable state, Washington received advices from Pinckney, the American minister in London, informing him that the British ministry had issued instructions to the commanders of armed vessels revoking those of November, 1793. Washington laid Pinckney's letter before Congress on the 4th of April. It had its effect on both parties: federalists saw in it a chance of accommodating difficulties and therefore opposed all measures calculated to irritate; the other party did not press their belligerent propositions to any immediate decision but showed no solicitude to avoid a rupture.

The war cry, however, is too obvious a means of popular excitement to be readily given up. Busy partisans saw that the feeling of the populace was belligerent. To adhere to a neutral position would argue tameness—cowardice! Washington, however, was too morally brave to be clamored out of his wise moderation by such taunts. He resolved to prevent a war if possible, by an appeal to British justice, to be made through a special envoy, who should represent the injuries we had sustained and should urge indemnification.

The measure was decried by the party favorable to France as an undue advance to the British government; they were still more hostile to it when it was rumored that Hamilton was to be chosen for the mission. Hamilton, aware of the "collateral obstacles" which existed with respect to himself, advised Washington to drop him from consideration and recommended John Jay, the Chief Justice of the United States, as the man whom it would be advisable to send. Jay was the person ultimately chosen. Washington, in nominating an additional envoy to Great Britain, expressed undiminished confidence in the minister actually in London. "But a mission like this," observes he, " . . . will announce to the world a solicitude for a friendly adjustment of our complaints and a reluctance to hostility."

By this measure Washington sought to stay the precipitate impulses of public passion, to give time to put the country into a complete state of defence, and to provide such other measures as might be necessary if negotiation should prove unsuccessful.

The French government having so promptly complied with the wishes of the American government in recalling Genet, requested, as an act of reciprocity, the recall of Gouverneur Morris, whose political sympathies were considered highly aristocratical. The request was granted accordingly, but Washington, in a letter to Morris notifying him of his being superseded, assured him of his own undiminished confidence and friendship.

James Monroe, who was appointed in his place, arrived at Paris in a moment of great reaction. Robespierre had terminated his bloody career on the scaffold and the reign of terror was at an end. The sentiments expressed by Monroe on delivering his credentials were so completely in unison with the feelings of the moment that the President of the Convention embraced him with emotion and it was decreed that the American and French flags should be entwined and hung up in the hall of the Convention in sign of the union and friendship of the two republics.

The excise law on ardent spirits distilled within the United States had, from the time of its enactment in 1791, met with riotous opposition. Now an insurrection broke out in the western part of Pennsylvania. Bills of indictment had been found against some of the rioters. The marshal, on the way to serve the processes issued by the court, was fired upon and narrowly escaped with his life. The house of General Nevil, inspector of the revenue, was assailed but the assailants were repulsed. They assembled in greater numbers; the magistrates and militia officers shrank from interfering lest it provoke a general insurrection; a few regular soldiers were obtained from the garrison at Fort Pitt. There was a parley at which the insurgents demanded that the inspector and his papers be given up and that the soldiers march out of the house and ground their arms. The demand being refused, the house was attacked and the garrison compelled to surrender. The marshal and inspector finally escaped and, by a circuitous route, found their way to the seat of government.

Washington deprecated the result of these outrageous proceedings. "If the laws are to be so trampled upon with impunity," said he, "and a minority, a small one too, is to dictate to the majority, there is an end put, at one stroke, to republican government."

It was intimated that the insurgent district could bring 7000 men into the field. On the 7th of August Washington issued a proclamation warning the insurgents to disperse and declaring that, if tranquillity were not restored before the 1st of September, force would be employed to compel submission to the laws. To show that this was not an empty threat, he made a requisition on the governors of New Jersey, Pennsylvania, Maryland, and Virginia for militia to compose an army of 12,000 men; afterwards augmented to 15,000.

The insurgents manifesting a disposition to persevere in their rebellious conduct, the President issued a second proclamation on the 25th of September describing in forcible terms his fixed purpose to reduce the refractory to obedience. Shortly after this he left Philadelphia for Carlisle to join the army, then on its march to suppress the insurrection.

On the 10th, the Pennsylvania troops set out from Carlisle for their rendezvous at Bedford; Washington proceeded to Williamsport, thence to go on to Fort Cumberland, the rendezvous of the Virginia and Maryland troops. He arrived at the latter place on the 16th of October, found a respectable force assembled from those States and learnt that 1500 more from Virginia were at hand. All accounts agreed that the insurgents were greatly alarmed at the serious appearance of things.

At Bedford he settled a plan of military operations. The Governors of Virginia, Maryland, and Pennsylvania were at the head of the troops of their States, but Governor Lee was to have general command. This done, Washington prepared to shape his course for Philadelphia.

Governor Lee marched with the troops in two divisions, amounting to 15,000 men, into western Pennsylvania. At the approach of so overwhelming a force the insurgents laid down their arms, gave assurance of submission, and craved the clemency of government. It was extended to them. As some discontent was still manifest, Major-General Morgan was stationed with a detachment for the winter, in the disaffected region.

It must have been a proud satisfaction to Washington to have put down without an effusion of blood an insurrection which at one time threatened such serious consequences.

In his speech on the opening of Congress (November 19th), Washington, with great satisfaction, had been able to announce favorable intelligence of the campaign of Wayne against the hostile Indians west of the Ohio. Leaving his winter encampment on the Ohio in the spring of 1794, he had advanced cautiously into the wild country west of it, skirmishing with bands of lurking savages as he advanced, and establishing posts to keep up communication and secure the transmission of supplies. It was not until the 8th of August that he arrived at the junction of the rivers Au Glaize and Miami, where the Western Indians had their most important villages. Here he threw up some works, which he named Fort Defiance. Strengthened by 1100 mounted volunteers from Kentucky, his force exceeded that of the savage warriors who had collected to oppose him, which scarcely amounted to 2000 men. These, however, were strongly encamped in the vicinity of Fort Miami, a British post 30 miles distant and within the limits of the United States, and seemed prepared to give battle, expecting possibly to be aided by the British garrison.

On the 20th, being arrived near the enemy's position, his advanced guard was fired upon by the enemy concealed in a thicket and was compelled to retreat. The general ordered an attack of horse and foot upon the enemy's position; the Indians were roused from their lair with the bayonet, driven through thick woods and pursued with great slaughter. It was trusted that this decisive battle and the wide ravages of villages and fields of corn with which it was succeeded would bring the Indians to their senses and compel them to solicit the peace which they had so repeatedly rejected.

In his official address to Congress, Washington had urged the adoption of some definitive plan for the redemption of the public debt. A plan was reported by Hamilton on 20th January, 1795, which he had digested and prepared on the basis of the actual revenues for the further support of public credit. The report embraced a comprehensive view of the system which he had pursued and made some recommendations, which after much debate were adopted.

So closed Hamilton's labors as Secretary of the Treasury. He had long meditated a retirement from his post but had postponed it, first, on account of the accusations brought against him in the second Congress, and, secondly, in consequence of events which rendered the prospect of a continuance of peace precarious. But these reasons no longer operating, he gave notice, that on the last day of January he should give in his resignation.

Knox likewise had given in his resignation at the close of the month of December. "After having served my country nearly twenty years," writes he to Washington, "the greatest portion of which under your immediate auspices, it is with extreme reluctance that I find myself constrained to withdraw from so honorable a station. But the natural and powerful claims of a numerous family will no longer permit me to neglect their essential interests. In whatever situation I shall be, I shall recollect your confidence and kindness with all the fervor and purity of affection of which a grateful heart is susceptible."

The session of Congress closed on the 3d of March, 1795.

(CHAPTER 66)

Washington had watched the progress of the mission of Jay to England with an anxious eye. He was aware that he had exposed his popularity to imminent hazard by making an advance toward a negotiation with that power, but he was aware that the peace and happiness of his country were at stake on the result of that mission.

At length, on the 7th of March, 1795, four days after the close of the session of Congress, a treaty arrived which had been negotiated by Jay and signed by the ministers of the two nations on the 19th of November, sent out for ratification.

Washington immediately made the treaty a close study; he considered it a matter, to use his own expression, of "give and take" and, believing the advantages to outweigh the objections, he made up his mind to ratify it should it be approved by the Senate.

As hostility to the treaty was already manifested, Washington kept its provisions secret so that the public mind might not be preoccupied on the subject. In the course of a few days, however, enough leaked out to be seized upon by the opposition press to excite public distrust. If it had been necessary to send a minister to England, said they, it should have been to demand reparation for wrongs inflicted on our commerce and the immediate surrender of the Western posts.

The Senate was convened by Washington on the 8th of June and the treaty was laid before it with accompanying documents. The

Session was with closed doors and the treaty underwent a scrutinizing examination.

The twelfth article met with especial objections. This article provided for direct trade between the United States and the British West India Islands in American vessels not exceeding 70 tons burden, conveying the produce of the States or of the Islands; but it prohibited the exportation of molasses, sugar, coffee, cocoa, or cotton in American vessels from either the United States or the Islands to any part of the world. Jay had not sufficiently adverted to the fact that, among the prohibited articles, cotton was also a product of the Southern States. Its cultivation had been but recently introduced there and at the time of signing the treaty very little, if any, had been exported. Still it was now becoming an important staple of the South, hence the objection of the Senate to this article of the treaty. On the 24th of June two-thirds of the Senate voted for ratification of the treaty, stipulating that an article be added suspending so much of the twelfth article as respected the West India trade and that the President be requested to open, without delay, further negotiation on this head.

In the mean time the popular discontent which had been excited concerning the treaty, was daily increasing. Such was the irritable condition of the public mind when, on the 29th of June, a senator of the United States (Mason of Virginia) sent an abstract of the treaty to be published in a leading opposition paper in Philadelphia.

The whole country was immediately in a blaze. Beside the opposition party, a portion of the Cabinet was against the ratification. Meetings to oppose the ratification were held in Boston, New York, Philadelphia, Baltimore, and Charleston. The smaller towns throughout the Union followed their example. The whole country seemed determined, by prompt and clamorous manifestations of dissatisfaction, to make Washington give way.

He saw their purpose; his own opinion was not particularly favorable to it, but he was convinced it was better to ratify it in the manner the Senate had advised, with the reservation already mentioned, than to suffer matters to remain in their unsettled and precarious state.

Before he could act a new difficulty rose to suspend his resolution. News came that the order of the British government of the 8th of June, 1793, for the seizure of provisions in vessels going to French ports was renewed. Washington instantly directed that a strong memorial be drawn up against this order as it seemed to favor a construction of the treaty which he was determined to resist. While this memorial was in course of preparation, he made a trip to Mount Vernon.

The opposition made to the treaty from meetings in different parts of the Union gave him the most serious uneasiness from the effect it might have on the relations with France and England. The violence of the opposition increased. Washington perceived that the prejudices against the treaty were more extensive than was generally imagined. Never, during his administration, had he seen a crisis, in his judgment, from which, whether viewed on one side or the other, more was to be apprehended. It was a crisis, he said, that most eminently called upon the administration to be wise and temperate as well as firm. The public clamor continued and induced a reiterated examination of the subject, but did not shake his purpose. "There is but one straight course," said he, "and that is to seek truth and pursue it steadily."

The difficult and intricate questions pressing upon the attention of government left Washington little mood to enjoy Mount Vernon, being constantly in doubt whether his presence in Philadelphia were not necessary.

Early in August came a mysterious letter, dated July 31, from Pickering, the new secretary of war. "On the subject of the treaty," writes Pickering, "I confess I feel extreme solicitude, and for a special reason, which can be communicated to you only in person. I entreat, therefore, that you will return with all convenient speed to the seat of government. In the meanwhile, for the reason above referred to, I pray you to decide on no important political measure in whatever form it may be presented to you. . . . This letter is for your own eye alone."

The receipt of this enigmatical letter induced Washington to cut short his sojourn at Mount Vernon and hasten to Philadelphia. He arrived there on the 11th of August and on the same day received a solution of the mystery. A despatch written by Fauchet, the

French minister, to his government in November was placed in Washington's hands with a translation made by Pickering. The despatch had been found on a French privateer captured by a British frigate and had been transmitted to the ministry. Lord Grenville, finding it contained passages relating to the intercourse of Randolph, the American secretary of state, with Fauchet, had sent it to Hammond, the British Minister in Philadelphia. He had put it into the hands of Wolcott, the new secretary of the treasury, who had shown it to the secretary of war and the attorney-general. The contents had been considered so extraordinary as to call forth the mysterious letter to Washington.

The following passages in Fauchet's intercepted despatch related to the Western insurrection and the proclamation of Washington:

"Two or three days before the proclamation was published, and of course before the cabinet had resolved on its measures, the secretary of state came to my house. . . . He requested of me a private conversation. It was all over, he said to me; a civil war is about to ravage our unhappy country. Four men, by their talents, their influence, and their energy, may save it. But, debtors of English merchants, they will be deprived of their liberty if they take the smallest step. Could you lend them instantaneously funds to shelter them from English prosecution? . . . It was impossible for me to make a satisfactory answer. You know my want of power and deficiency in pecuniary means. . . . Thus, with some thousands of dollars, the Republic could have decided on civil war or peace. Thus the consciences of the pretended patriots of America have already their price."

Washington revolved the matter in his mind in silence. The predominant object of his thoughts recently had been to stop public agitation on the treaty; he postponed any new question of difficulty until decided measures had laid the other at rest. On the next day, therefore, he brought before the cabinet the question of immediate ratification. It was agreed to ratify the treaty immediately but to accompany the ratification with a strong memorial against the provision order. The ratification was signed by Washington on the 18th of August.

His conduct towards Randolph, in the interim, had been as usual but, now that the despatch of public business no longer demanded the entire attention of the cabinet, he proceeded to clear up the doubts occasioned by the intercepted despatch. Accordingly, on the following day, as Randolph entered the cabinet, Washington handed him the letter of Fauchet, asking an explanation of the questionable parts.

Randolph appears to have been less agitated by the production of the letter than hurt that the inquiry concerning it had not first been made of him in private. He postponed making any specific reply until he should have time to examine the letter at his leisure.

In a letter to the President the same day he writes: "Your confidence in me, sir, has been unlimited and I can truly affirm unabused. My sensations, then, cannot be concealed when I find that confidence so suddenly withdrawn without a word or distant hint being previously dropped to me. This, sir, as I mentioned in your room, is a situation in which I cannot hold my present office, and therefore I hereby resign it. It will not, however, be concluded from hence that I mean to relinquish the inquiry. . . . To prepare for it, if I learn there is a chance of overtaking Mr. Fauchet before he sails, I will go to him immediately. . . . I here most solemnly deny that any overture came from me which was to produce money to me or any others for me; . . . nor was it ever contemplated by me that one shilling should be applied by Mr. Fauchet to any purpose relative to the insurrection."

Washington, in a reply on the following day, in which he accepted his resignation, observes: "Whilst you are in pursuit of means to remove the strong suspicions arising from this letter, no disclosure of its contents will be made by me and I will enjoin the same on the public officers who are acquainted with the purport of it."

Fauchet, in the mean time, having learnt previous to embarkation, that his despatch had been intercepted, wrote a declaration denying that Randolph had ever indicated a willingness to receive money for personal objects and affirming that he had had no intention to say any thing in his letter to his government, to the disadvantage of Mr. Randolph's character.

Randolph now set to work to prepare a pamphlet in explanation of his conduct. The vindication Randolph had been preparing appeared in December. In this, he gave a narrative of the events relating to the case, his correspondence with the President, and the whole of the French minister's letter. He endeavored to explain those parts of the letter which had brought the purity of his conduct in question but, as has been observed, "he had a difficult task to perform, as he was obliged to prove a negative and to explain vague expressions and insinuations connected with his name in Fauchet's letter." We are rather inclined to attribute to misconceptions and hasty inferences of the French minister the construction put by him in his letter on the conversation he had held with Randolph.

After the resignation of Randolph, Pickering was transferred to the Department of State, and James McHenry was appointed Secretary of War. The office of Attorney-General becoming vacant by the death of Bradford, was offered to Charles Lee of Virginia and accepted by him.

In his speech at the opening of the session of Congress in December, Washington presented a cheerful summary of the events of the year.

First he announced that a treaty had been concluded provisionally by General Wayne with the Indians northwest of the Ohio, by which the termination of the long and distressing war with those tribes was placed at the option of the United States.

A letter from the Emperor of Morocco, recognizing a treaty which had been made with his deceased father insured the continuance of peace with that power.

The terms of a treaty with the Dey and regency of Algiers had been adjusted in a manner to authorize the expectation of a speedy peace in that quarter and the liberation of a number of American citizens from a long and grievous captivity.

A speedy and satisfactory conclusion was anticipated of a negotiation with the court of Madrid, "which would lay the foundation of lasting harmony with a power whose friendship," said Washington, "we have uniformly and sincerely desired to cherish."

Adverting to the treaty with Great Britain and its conditional ratification, the result on the part of his Britannic Majesty was yet unknown but, when ascertained, would immediately be placed before Congress.

"In regard to internal affairs, every part of the Union gave indications of rapid and various improvement. With burthens so light as scarcely to be perceived; with resources fully adequate to present exigencies; with governments founded on the genuine principles of rational liberty; and with mild and wholesome laws, was it too much to say that our country exhibited a spectacle of national happiness never surpassed, if ever before equalled?"

There was, as usual, a cordial answer from the Senate but, in the House of Representatives, the opposition were in the majority. In the response reported by a committee, one clause expressing undiminished confidence in the chief magistrate was demurred to; the response was recommitted and the clause objected to modified.

In February the treaty with Great Britain, as modified by the advice of the Senate, came back ratified by the king of Great Britain, and on the last of the month a proclamation was issued by the President declaring it to be the supreme law of the land.

The opposition in the House of Representatives were offended that Washington should issue this proclamation before the sense of that body had been taken on the subject and denied the power of the President and Senate to complete a treaty without its sanction. They were bent on defeating it by refusing to pass the laws necessary to carry it into effect; as a preliminary, they passed a resolution requesting the President to lay before the House the instruction to Jay and the correspondence and other documents relative to the treaty. Washington, believing that these papers could not be constitutionally demanded, resolved to resist the principle, which was evidently intended to be established by the call of the House.

After mature deliberation and with the assistance of the heads of departments and the Attorney-General, he sent to the House an answer to their request. In this he dwelt upon the necessity of caution and secrecy in foreign negotiations as one cogent reason for vesting the power of making treaties in the President, with the advice and consent of the Senate, the principle on which that body was formed, confining it to a small number of members. To admit a right in the House of Representatives to demand and have all the papers respecting a foreign negotiation would, he observed, be to establish a dangerous precedent.

A resolution to make provision for carrying the treaty into effect gave rise to an animated and protracted debate. Meanwhile, the whole country became agitated on the subject; meetings were held throughout the United States and it soon became apparent that the popular feeling was with the minority in the House of Representatives who favored the making of the necessary appropriations. The public will prevailed and, on the last day of April, the resolution was passed, though by a close vote of 51 to 48. On the 1st of June this session of Congress terminated.

Shortly after the recess of Congress another change was made in the foreign diplomacy. Monroe, when sent envoy to France, had been instructed to explain the views of the United States in forming the treaty with England and had been furnished with documents for the purpose. From his own letters, however, it appeared that he had omitted to use them. Whether this rose from undue attachment to France, from mistaken notions of American interests, or from dislike to the treaty, the result was the very evil he had been instructed to prevent. The French government misconceived the views and conduct of the United States, suspected their policy in regard to Great Britain, and became bitter in their resentment. Under these circumstances it was deemed expedient to recall Monroe and appoint Charles Cotesworth Pinckney of South Carolina.

Meanwhile, in a letter to Monroe, dated August 25th, Washington had occasion to clarify his attitude toward France: "My conduct in public and private life, as it relates to the important struggle in which the latter nation [France] is engaged, has been uniform from the commencement of it and may be summed up in a few words. I have always wished well to the French revolution; . . . I have always given it as my decided opinion that no nation had a right to intermeddle in the internal concerns of another; that every one had a right to form and adopt whatever government they liked best to live under themselves; and that, if this country could consistently with its engagements, maintain a strict neutrality and thereby preserve peace, it was bound to do so by motives of policy, interest, and every other consideration that ought to actuate a people situated as we are, already deeply in debt and in a convalescent state from the struggle we have been engaged in ourselves."

Still the resentful policy of the French continued and, in October, they ordered the seizure of British property found on board of American vessels and of provisions bound for England—a direct violation of their treaty with the United States.

The period for the presidential election was drawing near. No one, it was agreed, had greater claim to the enjoyment of retirement, but it was thought affairs of the country would be in a very precarious condition should Washington retire before the wars of Europe were brought to a close.

Washington, however, had made up his mind irrevocably and resolved to announce, in a farewell address, his intention of retiring. Such an instrument had been prepared for him from his own notes by Madison when he had thought of retiring at the end of his first term. As he was no longer in confidential intimacy with Madison, he turned to Hamilton as his adviser and co-adjutor and appears to have consulted him on the subject early in the present year for, in a letter dated May 10th, Hamilton writes: "When last in Philadelphia, you mentioned to me your wish that I should re-dress a certain paper which you had prepared. . . . I submit a wish that, as soon as you have given it the body you mean it to have, it may be sent to me."

We forbear to go into how much of it is founded on Washington's original notes and topics, how much was elaborated by Madison, and how much is due to Hamilton's revision. The whole came under the supervision of Washington and the address certainly breathes his spirit throughout, is in perfect accordance with all his words and actions, and embodies the system of policy on which he had acted throughout his administration. It was published in September in a Philadelphia paper. On the 7th day of September Washington met the two Houses of Congress for the last time.

In his speech he recommended an institution for the improvement of agriculture, a military academy, a national university, and a gradual increase of the navy. The disputes with France were made the subject of the following remarks: "While in our external relations some serious inconveniences and embarrassments have been overcome and others lessened, it is with much pain and deep regret I mention that circumstances of a very unwelcome nature have lately occurred. Our trade . . . is suffering extensive injuries in the West Indies from the cruisers and agents of the French Republic; and communications have been received from its minister here, which indicate the danger of a further disturbance of our commerce by its authority. . . . It has been my constant, sincere and earnest wish, in conformity with that of our nation, to maintain cordial harmony . . . with that Republic. This wish remains unabated."

In concluding his address he observes, "I cannot omit the occasion to congratulate you and my country on the success of the experiment nor to repeat my fervent supplications to the Supreme Ruler of the universe . . . that the virtue and happiness of the people may be preserved, and that the government which they have instituted for the protection of their liberties may be perpetual."

The Senate, in their reply to the address, after concurring in its views of the national prosperity as resulting from the excellence of the constitutional system and the wisdom of the legislative provisions, attributed a great portion of these advantages to the virtue, firmness and talents of his administration, conspicuously displayed in the most trying times and on the most critical occasions.

The reply of the House expressed warm gratitude and admiration, inspired by the virtues and services of the President, by his wisdom, firmness, moderation, and magnanimity; and testifying to the deep regret with which they contemplated his intended retirement from office.

The reverence and affection expressed for him in both Houses of Congress and their regret at his intended retirement were in unison with testimonials from various State legislatures and other public bodies, which were continually arriving since the publication of his Farewell Address.

During the actual session of Congress, Washington endeavored to prevent the misunderstandings which were in danger of being augmented between the United States and the French Government. In the preceding month of November, Mr. Adet, the French Minister who had succeeded Fauchet, had addressed a letter to the

Secretary of State, recapitulating the complaints against the government of the United States made by his predecessors and himself, denouncing the insidious proclamation of neutrality and the wrongs growing out of it, and using language calculated to inflame the partisans of France. A copy of the letter had been sent to the press for publication. One of the objects Adet had in view in timing the publication was supposed by Washington to be to produce an effect on the presidential election; his ultimate object, to establish such an influence in the country as to sway the government and control its measures. Early in January, 1797, therefore, Washington requested the Secretary of State to address a letter to our minister to France stating all the complaints alleged by the French minister against the government, examining and reviewing the same, and accompanying the statement with a collection of letters and papers relating to the transactions therein adverted to.

In February the votes taken at the recent election were opened and counted in Congress. Adams, having the highest number, was declared President and Jefferson, having the next number, Vice President, their term of four years to commence on the 4th of March next ensuing.

Washington now began to count the days and hours that intervened between him and his retirement. On the 3d of March, he gave a farewell dinner to the foreign ministers and their wives, Mr. and Mrs. Adams, Mr. Jefferson, and other conspicuous personages of both sexes. When the cloth was removed, Washington filled his glass: "Ladies and gentlemen," said he, "this is the last time I shall drink your health as a public man; I do it with sincerity, wishing you all possible happiness." The gaiety of the company was checked in an instant; all felt the importance of this leave-taking.

On the 4th of March, an immense crowd gathered about Congress Hall. At eleven o'clock, Jefferson took the oath as Vice President in the presence of the Senate and proceeded with that body to the Chamber of the House of Representatives, which was densely crowded.

After a time, Washington entered amidst enthusiastic cheers and acclamations. Adams soon followed and was likewise well received but not with like enthusiasm. Having taken the oath of office,

Adams, in his inaugural address, spoke of his predecessor as one "who, by a long course of great actions, regulated by prudence, justice, temperance, and fortitude, had merited the gratitude of his fellow-citizens, commanded the highest praises of foreign nations, and secured immortal glory with posterity."

At the close of the ceremony, as Washington moved toward the door to retire, there was a rush from the gallery to the corridor, so eager were the throng to catch a last look of one who had so long been the object of public veneration. When Washington was in the street he waved his hat in return for the cheers of the multitude, his countenance radiant with benignity, his gray hairs streaming in the wind. The crowd followed him to his door. There, turning round, his countenance assumed a grave and almost melancholy expression, his eyes bathed in tears, his emotions too great for utterance, only by gestures could he indicate his thanks and convey his farewell blessing.

PART XIII

CHAPTER 67

The Last Years
[1795–1799]

————··◅∝▻··————

His official career being terminated, Washington set off for Mount Vernon accompanied by Mrs. Washington, her grand-daughter Miss Nelly Custis, and George Washington Lafayette, with his preceptors. Young Lafayette, the son of Washington's wartime associate, had been, since 1795, a student here, under the care and protection of Washington.

He is at length at Mount Vernon, that haven of repose to which he had so often turned a wishful eye throughout his agitated and anxious life and where he trusted to pass quietly and serenely the remainder of his days. "In a word," writes he, however, "I am already surrounded by joiners, masons, and painters, and such is my anxiety to be out of their hands, that I have scarcely a room to put a friend into, or to sit in myself, without the music of hammers and the odoriferous scent of paint."

Still he is at Mount Vernon, and as the spring opens the rural beauties of the country exert their sweetening influence. In a letter to a friend, he writes, "To make and sell a little flour annually, to repair houses going fast to ruin, to build one for the security of my papers of a public nature, and to amuse myself in agricultural and rural pursuits, will constitute employment for the few years I have to remain on this terrestrial globe. If, also, I could now and then meet the friends I esteem, it would fill the measure and add zest to my enjoyments."

The influx of strange faces—"come, as they say, out of respect to me"—soon became overwhelming and Washington felt the necessity of having some one to relieve him from part of the duties of Virginia hospitality. He bethought him of his nephew, Lawrence Lewis, who, in consequence of this invitation, thence-forward became an occasional resident at Mount Vernon. The place possessed attractions for gay as well as grave and was often enlivened by young company. One great attraction was Nelly Custis who, with her brother, had been adopted by the General at their father's death and brought up by him with the most affectionate care. She was a great favorite with the General whom she delighted with her gay whims and sprightly sallies, often overcoming his habitual gravity and surprising him into a hearty laugh.

She was now maturing into a lovely and attractive woman and the attention she received began to awaken some solicitude in the General's mind. This is evinced in a half-sportive letter of advice written to her during a temporary absence from Mount Vernon. "Love is said to be an involuntary passion and it is, therefore, contended that it cannot be resisted. This is true in part only for, like all things else, when nourished and supplied plentifully with aliment, it is rapid in its progress; but let these be withdrawn, and it may be stifled in its birth or much stinted in its growth. . . . When the fire is beginning to kindle and your heart growing warm, propound these questions to it. Who is this invader? Have I a competent knowledge of him? Is he a man of good character? A man of sense? . . . What has been his walk in life? . . . Is his fortune sufficient to maintain me in the manner I have been accustomed to live, and as my sisters do live? And is he one to whom my friends can have no reasonable objection? If all these interrogatories can be satisfactorily answered, there will remain but one more to be asked; that, however, is an important one. Have I sufficient ground to conclude that his affections are engaged by me? Without this the heart of sensibility will struggle against a passion that is not reciprocated."

The counsels of Washington and the feelings of Miss Nelly were soon brought to the test by the residence of Lawrence Lewis at Mount Vernon. A strong attachment for her grew up on his part, or perhaps already existed, and was favorably viewed by his uncle. Whether it was fully reciprocated was uncertain. A formidable rival to Lewis appeared in the person of young Carroll of Carrollton, who had just returned from Europe, adorned with the graces of foreign travel, and whose suit was countenanced by Mrs. Washington. These were among the poetic days of Mount Vernon, when its halls echoed to the tread of lovers.

Early in the autumn, Washington had been relieved from his constant solicitude about the fortunes of Lafayette. Letters received by Lafayette's son informed the youth that his father and family had been liberated and were on their way to Paris with the intention of embarking for America. Young Lafayette, eager to embrace his parents and sisters in the first moments of their release, and his tutor sailed from New York on the 26th of October. The account received of the liberation was premature. It did not take place until the 19th of September nor was it until February that the happy meeting took place between young Lafayette and his family, whom he found residing in the chateau of a relative in Holstein.

Washington had been but a few months at Mount Vernon, when he received intelligence that his successor in office had issued a proclamation for a special session of Congress. The French government had declared, on the recall of Monroe, that it would not receive any new minister plenipotentiary from the United States until that power should have redressed the grievances of which the republic had complained.

A few days afterwards, when Pinckney presented himself as successor to Monroe, the Directory refused to receive him. Its next step was to declare applicable to American ships the rules in regard to neutrals contained in the treaty which Washington had signed with England.

It was in view of these facts and of the captures of American vessels by French cruisers that President Adams had issued a proclamation to convene Congress on the 15th of May. In his opening speech, he announced his intention to institute a fresh attempt by negotiation to effect an amicable adjustment of differences on terms compatible with the rights, duties, interests, and honor of the nation, but in the mean time he recommended to Congress to provide effectual measures of defence.

In pursuance of the policy announced by Adams, three envoys extraordinary were appointed to the French republic, Charles Cotesworth Pinckney, John Marshall, and Elbridge Gerry—the two former federalists, the latter a democrat. The three ministers met in Paris on the 4th of October, (1797) but were approached by Talleyrand and his agents in a manner which demonstrated that the avenue to justice could only be opened by gold. With that view some of the most offensive passages in the speech of President Adams (in May 1797) must be expunged, a douceur of $250,000 put at the disposal of Talleyrand for the use of the Directory, and a loan of $6,400,000 made by America to France.

"We," replied the American envoys, "will not give you one farthing; before coming here, such an offer as you now propose would have been regarded as a mortal insult."

On this indignant reply, the wily agent intimated that if they would only pay, by way of fees, just as they would to a lawyer who should plead their cause, the sum required for the private use of the Directory, they might remain at Paris until they should receive further orders from America as to the loan required for government.

Being inaccessible to any such disgraceful and degrading propositions, the envoys remained several months in Paris unaccredited and finally returned at separate times without an official discussion of the object of their mission.

During this residence of the envoys in Paris, the Directory, believing the people of the United States would not sustain their government in a war against France, proceeded to enact a law subjecting to capture and condemnation neutral vessels and their cargoes if any portion of the latter was of British fabric or produce, although the entire property might belong to neutrals. As the United States were at this time the great neutral carriers of the world, this iniquitous decree struck at a vital point in their maritime power. When this act and the degrading treatment of the American envoys became known, the spirit of the nation was aroused and war with France seemed inevitable. Congress, on the 28th of May, authorized Adams to enlist 10,000 men as a provisional army, to be called by him into actual service in case of hostilities.

Washington was nominated to the Senate (July 3d) as commander-in-chief of all armies raised or to be raised. His nomination was unanimously confirmed on the following day and it was determined that the Secretary of War should be the bearer of the commission to Mount Vernon, accompanied by a letter from the President.

It was with a heavy heart that Washington found his dream of repose once more interrupted but his strong fidelity to duty would not permit him to hesitate. He accepted the commission, however, with the condition that he should not be called into the field until the army was in a situation to require his presence or it should become indispensable by the urgency of circumstances.

As to the question which had perplexed Adams whether, in forming the army, to call on all the old generals, Washington's idea was that no officer of the old army could expect, much less claim, an appointment on any other ground than superior experience and merit.

It was with such views that, in the arrangements made by him with the Secretary of War, the three Major-Generals were to be Hamilton, Charles Cotesworth Pinckney, and Knox, in which order he wished their commissions to be dated. By this arrangement Hamilton and Pinckney took precedence of Knox, an officer whom Washington declared he loved and esteemed, but he trusted the exigencies of the case would reconcile the latter to the position assigned to him.

Knox declined to serve under Hamilton and Pinckney on the principle that "no officer can consent to his own degradation by serving in an inferior station." Pinckney, on the contrary, cheerfully accepted his appointment, although placed under Hamilton, who had been of inferior rank to him in the last war. He regretted that

Knox had declined his appointment and that his feelings should be hurt by being out-ranked. "If the authority," adds he, "which appointed me to the rank of second major in the army, will review the arrangement and place General Knox before me, I will neither quit the service nor be dissatisfied."

Early in November (1798) Washington left his retirement and repaired to Philadelphia, at the request of the Secretary of War, to make arrangements respecting the forces about to be raised. The Secretary had prepared a series of questions for their consideration and others were suggested by Washington, all bearing upon the organization of the provisional army. Upon these Washington and the two Major-Generals were closely engaged for nearly five weeks. The result of their deliberations was reduced to form and communicated to the Secretary in two letters drafted by Hamilton and signed by the Commander-in-chief.

As it was a part of the plan on which he had accepted command of the army to decline the occupations of the office until circumstances should require his presence in the field and as the season and weather rendered him impatient to leave Philadelphia, Washington gave the Secretary of War his views and plans and then set out once more for Mount Vernon.

We have spoken earlier of a love affair growing up at Mount Vernon between Lawrence Lewis and Nelly Custis. The parties had since become engaged, to the General's great satisfaction, and their nuptials were celebrated at Mount Vernon on his birthday, the 22d of February, 1799. Lawrence had recently received the commission of Major of cavalry in the new army which was forming and Washington made arrangements for settling the newly married couple on a part of the Mount Vernon lands which he had designated in his will to be bequeathed to Nelly.

As the year opened, Washington continued to correspond with the Secretary of War and General Hamilton on the affairs of the provisional army. The recruiting business went on slowly, with interruptions, and Washington, who was not in the secrets of the cabinet, was at a loss to account for this apparent torpor.

The fact was, that the military measures taken in America had produced an effect on French policy. Talleyrand had written to the

French Secretary of Legation at the Hague, Pichon, intimating that whatever plenipotentiary the United States might send to France to put an end to the existing differences between the two countries would be undoubtedly received with the respect due to the representative of a free, independent, and powerful nation. Pichon communicated a copy of this letter to the American minister in Holland, who forthwith transmitted it to his government. Adams laid this letter before the Senate on the 18th of February, at the same time nominating William Murray to be minister plenipotentiary to the French Republic. Before the Senate decided on the nomination of Murray, two other persons were associated with him in the mission, Oliver Ellsworth and William Richardson Davie.

Throughout succeeding months, Washington continued to superintend from a distance the concerns of the army and he was at the same time endeavoring to bring the affairs of his rural domain into order. A sixteen years' absence from home, with short intervals, had, he said, deranged them considerably, so that it required all the time he could spare from the usual avocations of life to bring them into tune again. It was a period of incessant activity and toil, therefore, both mental and bodily. He was for hours in his study occupied with his pen and for hours on horseback, riding the rounds of his extensive estate, visiting the various farms and superintending and directing the works in operation. All this he did with unfailing vigor though now in his sixty-seventh year.

Winter had now set in, with occasional wind and rain and frost, yet Washington still kept up his active round of in-door and out-door avocations. He was in full health and vigor, dined out occasionally, had frequent guests at Mount Vernon, and, as usual, was part of every day in the saddle, going the rounds of his estates.

The morning of the 12th was overcast. That morning he wrote a letter to Hamilton heartily approving of a plan for a military academy, which the latter had submitted to the Secretary of War. "I sincerely hope that the subject will meet with due attention and that the reasons for its establishment which you have clearly pointed out in your letter to the secretary will prevail upon the legislature to place it upon a permanent and respectable footing."

About ten o'clock he mounted his horse and rode out as usual to make the rounds of the estate. "About one o'clock," he notes, "it began to snow, soon after to hail, and then turned to a settled cold rain." Having on an over-coat, he continued his ride without regarding the weather and did not return to the house until after three.

His secretary, Lear, approached him with letters to be franked, that they might be taken to the post-office in the evening. Washington franked the letters, but observed that the weather was too bad to send a servant out with them. Lear perceived snow hanging from his hair and expressed fears that he had got wet but, as dinner had been waiting for him, he sat down to table without changing his dress.

On the following morning the snow was three inches deep and still falling, which prevented him from taking his usual ride. He complained of a sore throat and had evidently taken cold the day before. In the afternoon the weather cleared up and he went out on the grounds between the house and the river to mark some trees which were to be cut down. A hoarseness which had hung about him through the day grew worse towards night but he made light of it.

In the night he was taken extremely ill with ague and difficulty of breathing. Between two and three o'clock in the morning he awoke Mrs. Washington, who would have risen to call a servant but he would not permit her lest she should take cold. At daybreak, when the servant woman entered to make a fire she was sent to call Lear. He found the general breathing with difficulty and hardly able to utter a word intelligibly. Washington desired that Dr. Craik, who lived in Alexandria, should be sent for and that in the mean time Rawlins, one of the overseers, be summoned to bleed him before the doctor could arrive.

A gargle was prepared for his throat but whenever he attempted to swallow any of it he was convulsed and almost suffocated. Rawlins made his appearance soon after sunrise and made an incision. The blood ran freely and Mrs. Washington, uncertain whether the treatment was proper and fearful that too much blood might be taken, begged to stop it. Mrs. Washington's doubts prevailed and the bleeding was stopped after about half a pint of blood had been taken. External applications were now made to the throat and his feet were bathed in warm water but without affording any relief.

His old friend, Dr. Craik, arrived between eight and nine, and two other physicians were called in. Various remedies were tried, and additional bleeding, but of no avail.

"About half-past four o'clock," writes Lear, "he desired me to call Mrs. Washington to his bedside, when he requested her to go down into his room and take from his desk two wills which she would find there and bring them to him, which she did. Upon looking at them, he gave her one, which he observed was useless as being superseded by the other and desired her to burn it, which she did, and took the other and put it into her closet."

In the course of the afternoon he appeared to be in great pain and distress from the difficulty of breathing. About five o'clock, Dr. Craik came again into the room and approached the bedside. "Doctor," said the general, "I die hard but I am not afraid to go. I believed, from my first attack, that I should not survive it—my breath cannot last long." The doctor pressed his hand in silence, retired from the bedside, and sat by the fire absorbed in grief.

Between five and six the other physicians came in and he was assisted to sit up in his bed. "I feel I am going," said he. "I thank you for your attentions but I pray you to take no more trouble about me; let me go off quietly; I cannot last long." He lay down again; all retired excepting Dr. Craik. Further remedies were tried without avail in the evening.

"About ten minutes before he expired (which was between ten and eleven o'clock)." writes Lear, "his breathing became easier. He lay quietly; he withdrew his hand from mine and felt his own pulse. I saw his countenance change. I spoke to Dr. Craik, who sat by the fire. He came to the bedside. The general's hand fell from his wrist. I took it in mine and pressed it to my bosom. Dr. Craik put his hands over his eyes and he expired without a struggle or a sigh. While we were fixed in silent grief, Mrs. Washington, who was seated at the foot of the bed, asked with a firm and collected voice, 'Is he gone?' I could not speak, but held up my hand as a signal that he was no more. ' 'Tis well,' said she in the same voice. 'All is now over; I shall soon follow him; I have no more trials to pass through.' "

The funeral took place on the 18th of December. About eleven o'clock the people of the neighborhood began to assemble. The corporation of Alexandria, with the militia and Free Masons of the place and eleven pieces of cannon arrived at a later hour. A schooner was stationed off Mount Vernon to fire minute guns.

About three o'clock the procession began to move, passing out through the gate at the left wing of the house, proceeding round in front of the lawn and down to the vault, on the right wing of the house, minute guns being fired at the time. The troops, horse and foot, formed the escort; then came four of the clergy. Then the general's horse, with his saddle, holsters, and pistols, led by two grooms in black. The body was borne by the Free Masons and officers. Several members of the family and old friends followed as chief mourners. The corporation of Alexandria and numerous private persons closed the procession. The Rev. Mr. Davis read the funeral service at the vault, and pronounced a short address, after which the Masons performed their ceremonies and the body was deposited in the vault.

Such were the obsequies of Washington, simple and modest, according to his own wishes—all confined to the grounds of Mount Vernon which, after forming the poetical dream of his life, had now become his final resting-place.

On opening the will which he had handed to Mrs. Washington shortly before his death, it was found to have been carefully drawn up by himself in the preceding July. By an act in conformity with his whole career, one of its first provisions directed the emancipation of his slaves on the decease of his wife. He also made provision in his will for such as were to receive their freedom under this devise but who, from age, infirmities, or infancy might be unable to support themselves.

A deep sorrow spread over the nation on hearing that Washington was no more. Congress, which was in session, immediately adjourned for the day. The next morning it was resolved that the Speaker's chair be shrouded with black, that the members and officers of the House wear black during the session, and that a joint committee of both Houses be appointed to consider the most suitable manner of doing honor to the memory of the man, "first in war, first in peace, and first in the hearts of his fellow-citizens."

Public testimonials of grief and reverence were displayed in every part of the Union. Nor were these sentiments confined to the United States. When the news of Washington's death reached England, Lord Bridport, who had command of a British fleet of nearly 60 sail of the line, lowered his flag half-mast, every ship following the example. Bonaparte, First Consul of France, on announcing Washington's death to the army, ordered that black crape be suspended from all standards and flags throughout the public service for ten days.

We have traced the career of Washington from early boyhood to his elevation to the presidential chair. It was an elevation he had neither sought nor wished, for, when the independence of his country was achieved, the modest and cherished desire of his heart had been "to live and die a private citizen on his own farm." But power sought him in his retirement. The weight and influence of his name and character were deemed all essential to complete his work, to set the new government in motion, and conduct it through its first perils and trials. With unfeigned reluctance he complied with the imperative claims of his country and accepted the power thus urged upon him, advancing to its exercise with diffidence and aiming to surround himself with men of the highest talent and information but firm in the resolve to act as his conscience told him was "right as it respected his God, his country, and himself." He knew no divided fidelity, no separate obligation; his most sacred duty to himself was his highest duty to his country and his God.

The character of Washington may want some of those poetical elements which dazzle and delight the multitude, but it possessed fewer inequalities and a rarer union of virtues than perhaps ever fell to the lot of one man: Prudence, firmness, sagacity, moderation, an overruling judgment, an immovable justice, courage that never faltered, patience that never wearied, truth that disdained all artifice, magnanimity without alloy. It seems as if Providence had endowed him in a preëminent degree with the qualities requisite to fit him for the high destiny he was called upon to fulfil—to conduct a momentous revolution which was to form an era in the history of the world and to inaugurate a new and untried government, which, to use his own words, was to lay the foundation "for the enjoyment of much purer civil liberty, and greater public happiness, than have hitherto been the portion of mankind."

The fame of Washington stands apart from every other in history, shining with a truer lustre and a more benignant glory. His memory remains a national property where all sympathies throughout our widely-extended and diversified empire meet in unison. Under all dissensions and amid all the storms of party, his precepts and example speak to us from the grave with a paternal appeal; his name—by all revered—forms a universal tie of brotherhood, a watchword of our Union.

Chronology

(BY THE EDITOR)

———∞———

1732	February 22*	George Washington born near Bridges (Pope's) Creek, Westmoreland County, Virginia.
1748	March–April	Washington joins surveying group going to South Branch of Potomac River, taking him into Shenandoah Valley.
1749	May	King George II charters the Ohio Company with a vast grant of land along the upper Ohio River, an area also claimed by the French.
1751	September	Washington accompanies dying half-brother, Lawrence, to Barbados, remaining with him until late December.
1752	November	Washington commissioned major in Virginia militia.

*(February 11, old style calendar)

1753	October– December	Washington leads party sent by Governor Robert Dinwiddie of Virginia to demand French cease encroachment upon Ohio country. Demand delivered (December 12) at Fort Le Boeuf, but rejected.
1754		Outbreak of French and Indian War, which later became the American phase of the Seven Years' War.
	March	Washington receives commission as lieutenant colonel in Virginia militia.
	May 27	Washington, leading small force to confront French at Fort Duquesne, defeats French troops in skirmish near Great Meadows, where he erects Fort Necessity.
		Washington promoted to colonel.
	July 3	Washington, attacked by superior French force, surrenders Fort Necessity.
1755	February–July	Major General Edward Braddock arrives in Virginia to command forces in America. With Washington as aide, Braddock intends attack on Fort Duquesne but is defeated (July 9) at Monongahela by French and Indians and fatally wounded. Washington leads survivors in retreat to Fort Cumberland.
1756	May 17	France and England formally declare war (Seven Years' War) against each other after years of undeclared conflict.

1758	July	Washington elected by Frederick County to House of Burgesses; re-elected 1761.
	July 26	British take Louisburg from French.
	August 27	British capture Fort Frontenac from French.
	November 25	British take Fort Duquesne from French, renaming it Fort Pitt (later became Pittsburgh).
	December	Washington resigns commission as colonel in Virginia militia.
1759	January 6	Washington marries Martha Dandridge Custis, widowed mother of two children.
	July 26	British take Fort Ticonderoga from French.
	Late Spring	Washington moves family to Mount Vernon from Williamsburg and becomes planter.
	September 17	British defeat French at Quebec.
1760	September 8	British defeat French at Montreal.
	October	Reign of George III begins.
1763	February	Treaty of Paris signed, ending Seven Years' War. One provision required France to cede Canada to Great Britain as well as all territory east of the Mississippi (except New Orleans).
1765		Washington elected by Fairfax County to House of Burgesses; re-elected 1768, 1769, 1771, 1774.

	March	Stamp Act passed by Parliament as a tax measure, requiring revenue stamps on newspapers, pamphlets, legal documents, etc. Strong colonial protests led to its repeal later (March 17, 1766).
1767	June	Townshend Revenue Act passed by Parliament establishing an import duty in the colonies on tea, glass, paper, lead, etc. It met with increasingly angry colonial resistance and was repealed (April 12, 1770) with the exception of the duty on tea.
1772	November	Boston re-establishes its Committee of Correspondence to carry on reciprocal communication with other towns, mostly in Massachusetts. The system spreads during the next two years throughout most of the colonies.
1773	May 10	Tea Act provides East India Company with right to monopolize tea trade with colonies.
	December 16	Angry colonists, dressed as Indians, board British ships in Boston harbor and throw their cargoes of tea overboard. This leads, in 1774, to a series of reprisals ("Intolerable Acts"), including a restriction on public gatherings and an act requiring Massachusetts colonists to provide quarters and supplies for British troops in the colony.

Chronology

1774	May	Reign of Louis XVI of France begins.
	September–October	Washington attends First Continental Congress, held at Philadelphia, as delegate from Virginia.
1775	April 19	Battles of Lexington and Concord.
	May–June	Washington attends Second Continental Congress.
	May 10	Fort Ticonderoga captured by Ethan Allen.
	June 16	Washington chosen by Congress to be Commander-in-Chief of Continental Army.
	June 17	British take Bunker Hill and Breed's Hill.
	July 3	Washington assumes command of Continental Army at Cambridge.
	November 13	Richard Montgomery takes Montreal but attack (with Benedict Arnold) on Quebec fails.
	December 31	American expedition against Quebec, led by Arnold, fails.
1776	January	Paine's *Common Sense* is published, calling for full American independence.
	March 17	British evacuate Boston; Americans occupy it.
	April 13	Washington arrives with troops at New York City.

Chronology

	July 4	Declaration of Independence adopted by Congress.
	August 22–29	Battle of Long Island (British victory).
	September 15	Washington evacuates New York City; British occupy it.
	October 28–29	Battle of White Plains.
	November	Fort Washington and Fort Lee taken by British.
	December	Fearing British attack, Congress moves from Philadelphia to Baltimore.
	December 26	Washington's surprise crossing of Delaware River results in defeat of Hessians at Trenton.
1777	January 3	Battle of Princeton (American victory), followed by establishment of winter quarters at Morristown.
	July 5	Ticonderoga evacuated by Americans.
	July	Marquis de Lafayette and Baron Johann de Kalb arrive as volunteer officers to aid American cause.
	August 6	Battle of Oriskany (American victory).
	August 6–16	Battle of Bennington (American victory).
	September 11	Battle of Brandywine (British victory).

Chronology

	September 26	British occupy Philadelphia under General Howe.
	October 4	Battle of Germantown (British victory).
	October 7	Burgoyne defeated at Bemis Heights.
	October 17	Burgoyne surrenders at Saratoga to Americans.
	December	Winter quarters established at Valley Forge.
1778	February 6	Alliance between France and United States signed in Paris.
	February	Baron von Steuben, Prussian officer, arrives to aid Washington.
	May 4	American Continental Congress ratifies treaty of alliance with France.
	June 18	British evacuate Philadelphia.
	June 28	Battle of Monmouth Court House.
	December	Winter headquarters established at Middlebrook.
	December 29	British take Savannah.
1779	July 16	Anthony Wayne captures Stony Point.
	December	Washington establishes winter quarters at Morristown.
1780	May 12	British take Charleston.

	May 25	Mutiny of Connecticut troops at Washington's camp at Morristown put down.
	July 10	French troops (under Rochambeau) arrive at Newport with strong naval escort.
	August 3	Arnold placed in command of West Point.
	August 16	Battle of Camden, South Carolina (British victory).
	September 23	Major John André captured near Tarrytown after rendezvous with Arnold. Arnold, learning of André's arrest, flees (September 25) to British vessel after miscarriage of his plan to betray West Point; André executed (September 28).
	October 7	Battle of King's Mountain (American victory).
1781	January 1–10	Mutiny of Pennsylvania troops.
	January 17	Battle at the Cowpens (American victory).
	March 15	Battle at Guilford Court House (American victory).
	September 5	French fleet (under De Grasse) defeats British fleet at Chesapeake Bay.
	September 8	Battle at Eutaw Springs (American victory).
	September	French squadron (under De Barras) reinforces De Grasse's fleet.

	September 28	Americans and French begin siege of Cornwallis at Yorktown.
	October 19	Cornwallis surrenders at Yorktown.
1782	July 11	British evacuate Savannah.
	November 30	Preliminary peace treaty signed in Paris.
	December 14	British evacuate Charleston.
1783	April 19	Congress proclaims end of hostilities.
	April	About 7000 Loyalists depart United States, last of about 100,000 to move to Canada or Europe.
	September 3	Final peace treaty with Great Britain signed in Paris.
	November 3	Congress issues order disbanding most of army.
	November 25	British evacuate New York City.
	December 4	Washington bids farewell to officers at Fraunces' Tavern in New York City.
	December 23	Washington resigns commission and returns to Mount Vernon.
1784	January 14	Congress ratifies final peace treaty with Great Britain.
1786	August	Outbreak of armed rebellion in Massachusetts, led by Daniel Shays, asking for relief of debt-laden farmers against foreclosures. Rebellion put down by state militia by February, 1787.

Chronology

1787	May 25	Washington (chosen as one of Virginia's delegates) elected president of Federal Constitutional Convention.
	July 13	Congress passes Northwest Ordinance, barring slavery from the Northwest Territory.
	September 17	Constitution approved and signed by delegates to Federal Convention; Congress submits Constitution to states for ratification.
1789		Federalist Party formed with considerable public support for its advocacy of a stronger central government; led mainly by Hamilton.
	February 4	Washington elected President of United States by unanimous vote, with John Adams as Vice President.
	April 30	Washington inaugurated as first President of United States (in New York City).
	July 14	Outbreak of French Revolution.
	October–November	Washington tours New England states.
1790	September	Washington arrives at Philadelphia, new temporary capital (for 10 years) of nation, pending move to site on Potomac River (to be determined by President).
1791	April–June	Washington tours Southern states.

1792

Republican Party (which with many transformations emerged as the Democratic Party in 1828) created in opposition to Federalist Party (especially its alleged preference for trade over agricultural interests); led mainly by Jefferson.

December 5

Washington re-elected President of United States by unanimous vote, with John Adams as Vice-President.

1793   March 4

Washington inaugurated as President for second term at Philadelphia.

April 22

Washington proclaims national neutrality toward European "belligerents."

December 31

Jefferson's resignation as Secretary of State becomes effective.

1794   July

"Whiskey Rebellion" in western Pennsylvania (to protest excise tax) begins and is forcefully suppressed by November through the use of Federal forces.

1795   January 31

Hamilton resigns as Secretary of Treasury.

1796   September 19

Washington's Farewell Address (dated September 17), announcing retirement from presidency, published in Philadelphia newspaper.

Chronology

1797	March 4	Washington retires from public office and returns to Mount Vernon. John Adams becomes President, with Thomas Jefferson as Vice-President.
1798	July 4	In view of mounting tension with France, Washington appointed Lieutenant General and Commander-in-chief of Armies of United States.
1799	December 14	Washington dies at Mount Vernon and is buried (December 18) in family tomb.

Index

Index

Anthony's Nose, 185, 201, 210, 306, 366, 369
Appomattox River, 550
Arbuthnot, Admiral, 451, 453, 461, 463, 468, 469, 479, 546, 547, 548
Armstrong, Captain, 443, 563, 627
Armstrong, Major-general, 348, 351, 355, 378, 413
Arnold, Benedict, 106–107, 130–132, 136–137, 140, 146–149, 154–156, 159, 162–166, 179–180, 184, 188, 202, 248–251, 299–302, 306–309, 323, 324, 340, 344–346, 360–362, 364–365, 371–372, 382, 404, 418, 457–461, 467, 479–480, 506–507, 520–521, 525–526, 533, 534, 545, 546–547, 549, 550, 551, 567; treason of, 488–506
Arnold, Mrs. Benedict (Margaret), 459, 498, 500, 501, 506
Articles of Confederation, 525
Ashley River, 462
Ashley's Gap, 7
Assunpink, 280
Atlee, Colonel, 217, 219
Augusta (ship), 384
Augusta, 440, 472, 513, 561
Augusta County, Virginia, 263
Aylett, Anne, see Washington, Mrs. Augustine (Anne)

Baird, Sir James, 439
Balcarras, Lord, 371, 372
Ball, Colonel, 405
Ball, Mary, see Washington, Mrs. Mary Ball
Baltimore, Maryland, 569
Bancroft, George, x
Bank, National, 628, 630
Barbados, 13
Barbary states, 613
Barras, Count de, 553, 566, 570–571
Barren Hill, 414
Barton, Lieutenant-colonel, 322

Baskingridge, 267
Basset, Colonel, 582
Batt's Hill, 433
Baum, Lieutenant-colonel, 340–343
Baxter, 253, 254
Baylor, Lieutenant-colonel, 437
Beall, 243, 244
Bear Hill, 367, 368
Beattie's ford, 535
Bedel, Colonel, 184
Bell's Mills, 541
Belvoir (estate), 5, 6, 17, 95
Bemis's Heights, 360
Bennington, 335, 340–344
Benson, Egbert, 589
Bergen Point, 213
Bermuda, 13
Bernard, Sir Francis, 79
Bethel, 301
Beverley, 489
Beville, 555
Bienville, Celeron de, 10
Biggins Bridge, 470
Billingsport, 376, 377, 382
Bird, Colonel, 294
Black Stock Hill, 518
Blair, John, 619
Bland, Colonel, 352, 469
Bland, Richard, 91
Blue Ridge mountains, 7
Bonaparte, xxi, 685
Boone, Colonel, 513
Bordentown, 274, 277, 278, 410
Boscawen, Admiral, 58, 63
Boston (British ship), 652
Boston, Massachusetts, American Revolution and, 108–119, 122–128, 135–136, 140–144, 152–154, 157, 159, 160, 170–176, 325, 335, 436, 438, 449, 553; rumor of British cannonading of, 93, 96
"Boston massacre," 84, 173
Boston Port Bill, 89, 90, 94, 192
Boston Tea Party, 89

Index

Botetourt, Lord, 81, 82, 83, 84, 86
Bouquet, Colonel, 61, 62, 63, 64
Bourdett's Ferry, 241
Bourlamarque, 67
Bowdoin, James, 259
Bowling Green, 570
Braddock, Edward, xiv, 29–44, 45, 46, 48, 63, 64, 86
Bradford, William, Attorney General, 656, 668; death, 668
Brandywine River, 351–352
Brannan, Colonel, 517
Brandt, Joseph, 121, 185, 316, 336, 337, 434–435, 442, 508
Breach, the, 204, 205
Breed's Hill, 113, 114
Breyman, 342, 343, 361, 362
Bridges Creek, 2, 3, 4
Bridges' regiment, 112
Bridport, Lord, 685
Bristol, 269, 270, 271, 276
Broad River, 530, 531, 532
Brodhead, Colonel, 442
Bromfield, Major, 567
Bronx, 239, 241, 242
Brooklyn, 177, 186, 212–220, 222, 223, 451
Brooks, Major, 112, 372
Brown, John, 133, 137–139, 145, 146, 163, 164
Brunswick, 252, 260, 261, 262, 264, 265, 267, 268, 277, 278, 281, 283–285, 288, 308, 309, 310, 424, 425, 426
Brunswick, Duke of, 179
Bryant, 237
Bryon, Admiral, 430, 434, 438, 439
Buffalo Ford, 483
Buford, Colonel, 472
Bull Hill, 306
Bunker's Hill, 112–115, 117, 118, 120, 122, 123, 136, 142, 143, 144, 172, 175
Burdett's Ferry, 211
Burgoyne, John, 110, 124, 143, 188, 310, 312, 313–314, 316, 317, 318,

320, 321, 322, 324, 325, 326, 329, 330, 331, 332–335, 339, 340, 342, 343–347, 358–361, 363–365, 369–375, 385–388, 391, 399, 412, 413
Burlington, 277, 281
Burr, Aaron, 136, 209, 425
Burton, Lieutenant-colonel, 41, 43
Bush River, 561
Butler, Jane, see Washington, Mrs. Jane
Butler, John, 434, 435, 442
Butler, Richard, 438
Butler, Zebulon, 435, 442
Butterfield, Major, 184
Byrd, Colonel, 58

Cadwalader, John, 269, 271, 275–278, 280, 412, 418
Cadwalader, Lambert, 239, 253, 254, 255
Caldwell, James, 456
Callbeck, Mr., 151
Calvert, Benedict, 88
Camden, 481–484, 486–487, 507, 508, 511, 512, 525, 527, 529, 545, 560
Campbell, Colonel, 164, 165, 291, 367, 368, 439
Campbell, William, 513, 514, 515, 534, 542, 575
Canada, American Revolution and, 131–140, 145–149, 154–156, 159, 162–167, 171, 176, 178–182, 184–189, 201, 202, 207, 232, 251, 293, 294, 295–310, 312, 313, 327, 333, 334, 335, 360, 364, 401–404, 508, 510, 551; French and Indian War and, 66–70
Canepo Hill, 300, 302
Cape Breton, 58, 63
Cape Diamond, 155, 163, 164
Cape Fear River, 533, 544, 545
Caramhe, Lieutenant-governor, 154
Carleton, Guy, 132, 134, 135, 145, 146, 148, 152, 155–156, 162, 166, 179,

Index

Huntington, Colonel, 302, 391, 397, 417

Impressment of American seamen, 654
Independence, American, birth of, 76
Inflexible (ship), 249
Indians, 2, 7, 9, 10–12, 14–15, 18–19, 20, 22, 25, 26, 30, 31, 33, 35, 37, 38, 40, 41, 42, 43, 44, 47, 48, 50, 52, 56, 60, 61, 62, 64, 65, 66, 69, 70, 84, 85, 598; American Revolution and, 121, 130, 131, 133–135, 137, 138, 139, 146, 147, 154, 167, 184, 185, 249–251, 304, 313, 314–315, 316, 318, 321, 324, 330, 333–334, 336, 337–338, 340, 341, 344–347, 359, 361, 362, 363, 370, 374, 414, 434–435, 441–442, 508, 513, 551; depredations by, 626–630, 631, 655; expeditions against, 626–627, 629, 632–635, 637–638, 651–662; Pontiac's War, 73–74; treaties with, 625, 668
Innes, Colonel, 27
Iredell, James, 619
Irvine, Colonel, 188
Irvine, James, 394
Irving, Washington, ix–xxi
Isle la Motte, 135, 188
Isle aux Noix, 67, 68, 135, 137, 138, 375
Isle of Orleans, 67, 180

Jack, Captain, 33, 37
Jackson, 237
James Island, 204
James River, 525, 550, 556, 557, 559, 570, 571, 598, 599
Jameson, Lieutenant-colonel, 496, 500
Jamestown, 559, 560
Jamieson, Colonel, 471
Jay, John, 189, 602, 613, 614, 623, 663–664; Chief Justice, 619, 659
Jay Treaty, 663, 666, 669–670
Jefferson, Thomas, xix, 525–526, 546,

557; attitude toward French Revolution, 631; attitude toward retirement of Washington, 639–640; Genet affair and, 646, 647, 649, 651, 653; retirement plans, 636–637, 652, 656; rivalry between Hamilton and, 625–626, 628, 639, 641–642; Secretary of State, 619–629, 636, 638–639, 645, 650, 651, 656; Vice President, 673
Jeffrey's Point, 186
Jerseys, 252–287, 307–311, 313, 377, 391, 392, 393, 399, 410, 417–425, 436–437, 440, 457, 473–477, 524, 554, 555, 567, 581
Johnson, Lieutenant-colonel, 434, 435, 442, 446
Johnson, LJohnson, Guy, 121, 132, 133, 185
Johnson, Sir John, 121, 167, 185, 310, 313, 315, 336, 337, 338, 508
Johnson, William, 32, 46–48, 66, 121
Johnson family, 121, 130, 185
Johnstone, George, 416
Joncaire, Captain, 11–12

Kelly, Major, 283, 285
Kennebec River, 49, 134, 136, 140
Kennet Square, 351
Kentucky, admission into the Union, 630
Keppel, Commodore, 30, 32
Kiashuta, 85
Kichline's riflemen, 217
King's Bridge, 186, 189, 196, 210, 212, 221, 227, 229, 236–238, 246, 253–254, 286, 438, 456, 479, 490, 510, 554–556, 593
King's Creek, 532
King's Ferry, 247, 259, 429, 443, 493, 500, 501, 566, 584
King's Mountain, 514–516, 532, 534
Kingston, 284, 285, 370

Index

Index

Index

Index

Shirley, Governor (Massachusetts), 32, 46, 48, 49

Shoreham, 105, 106

Short Hills, 474–476

Shreve, Colonel, 422, 476

Shuldham, Admiral, 174

Silliman, General, 300–301

Simcoe, Colonel, 520, 526, 551, 558, 573

Sinepuxent Inlet, 329

Skene, Colonel, 332, 335, 340

Skenesborough, 107, 202, 315, 319, 320, 322, 332, 334, 359

Skinners, 493

Sleepy Hollow, 494

Slough, the, 113, 115

Smallwood, 209, 217, 219, 222, 243, 307, 348, 356, 357, 372, 378, 380

Smith, Colonel, 100, 101, 102

Smith, Joshua Hett, 490–495, 501, 505

Smith, Samuel, 382, 388

Smith, William, 589

Smith's Clove, 445

Smuggling, 76, 84

"Society of the Cincinnati," 590

Somerset court-house, 309

Sorel River, 135, 137, 145, 146, 148, 186, 187, 188, 248

Sourland Hills, 309

South Carolina, American Revolution and, 453, 461–464, 471–473, 478, 481, 511, 516, 519, 529, 544, 545, 560, 564, 581

Spanktown, 311

Sparks, Jared, x, xi

Specht, 370

Speedwell's Iron Works, 543

Spencer, Joseph, 109, 125, 127, 136, 227, 229

Springfield (New Jersey), 474–477, 567

Stamp Act, 76–78, 94; repeal of, 79

Stark, 273, 274

Staten Island, 177, 178, 191, 193, 197, 207, 208, 210, 212, 213, 215, 225, 226, 233, 236, 310, 312, 313, 349, 425, 455, 473–475, 477, 523, 524, 528

Stark, John, 103, 111, 114, 115, 116, 118, 330, 339, 341–344, 402, 404, 475, 476, 502, 506, 510

Steele, Elizabeth, 536

Stephen, 262, 272, 299, 307, 348, 351, 353, 378, 380, 394

Stephens, Adam, 19, 23, 46

Steuben, Baron, 408, 413, 463, 464, 502, 508, 519, 525, 526, 534, 547, 548, 549, 558, 577, 588, 595, 611

Stevens, 483–485, 533, 539, 542

Stewart, 35, 43, 44, 422, 423, 447, 522, 523, 542–543

Stickney, Colonel, 342

Stillwater, 316, 334, 339–340, 341, 344

Stirling, Lord, 160, 177, 182, 185, 215, 217–219, 232, 247, 252, 254, 262, 264, 265, 272, 299, 307, 310, 311, 325, 349, 351, 353, 378, 401, 404, 413, 423, 426, 450, 451, 455, 473–474, 502

Stobo, Major, 26

Stockwell, Lieutenant, 339

Stoddart, Captain, 405

Stony Brook, 282, 283, 285

Stony Point, 367–368, 443–449, 452, 566

Stuart, Colonel, 561, 564, 574–576

Sugar act, 94

Sugar Hill, 318

Sulgrave, 2

Sullivan, John, 109, 127, 136, 142, 172, 177, 178, 187, 188, 202, 203, 213, 218, 220, 225, 239, 267, 268, 269, 272–274, 288, 307, 309, 312, 317, 325, 326, 348–349, 351–353, 378–381, 429–434, 442, 508, 527

Sullivan's Island, 204, 205

Sumner, 574–575

Sumter, Thomas, 482, 484–486, 511, 517–518, 544, 560–564, 574

Index

Sunbury, 440
Supreme Court, U.S., 618–619
Susquehanna River, 436, 442, 569
Sutherland, Major, 450–451
"Swamp Fox," *see* Marion, Francis
Swan Point, 331
Swedes' Ford, 414
Symonds, Colonel, 342

Talbot, Captain, 388, 389
Talleyrand, 678, 680
Tallmadge, Major, 496, 501, 510
Tanacharisson (Indian chief), 10–11
Tappan, 480, 500, 501
Tappan Sea, 199, 200, 201, 235, 252, 294, 305, 366, 444, 554
Tarleton, Banastre, 462, 469–472, 485, 486, 517–518, 529–533, 535–537, 539–541, 543, 557–559, 573
Tarrytown, 200
Tartar (ship), 234, 238, 252
Tash, Colonel, 235
Tate, Captain, 519
Taxation, 76–82, 83, 88–89, 91, 412, 454, 602, 628
Taylorsville, 271
Tea, tax on, 83–84, 88
Teller's Point, 554
Ten Broeck, General, 372
Ternay, Chevalier de, 466, 478, 487
Thacher, James, xi
Thames River, 567
Thayer, Major, 388, 389
Thicketty Run, 38
Thomas, John, 109, 111, 125, 127, 136, 172, 173, 176, 178, 180, 181, 186
Thompson, Colonel, 205
Thompson, General, 178, 187, 188
Three Islands, 435
Three Mile Point, 316, 318
Three Mile Run, 394
Three Rivers, 187, 188
Throg's Neck, 237–238, 446, 448, 479
Throg's Point, 237, 239

Thunderer (ship), 249, 315
Ticonderoga, 47, 48, 54, 58, 59, 66, 67, 68, 69, 248, 293, 294, 363, 364, 375; *See also* Fort Ticonderoga
Tilghman, 245, 288, 527; death of, 601
Tilly, M. de, 546, 547
Tinicum, 266
Treason, 82; Arnold and, 488–506
Trembly's Point, 455
Trent, William, 14, 18, 20
Trenton, 262, 264, 265, 270–278, 279, 280, 281, 282, 284, 287, 325, 523, 524
Trial by jury, 77, 82, 94
Triplet, Captain, 519
Triumph (ship), 588
Troublesome Creek, 541, 543
Trumbull, Governor (Connecticut), 126, 127, 203, 326, 358
Trumbull, Joseph, 126, 127, 202, 328, 394
Trydraffin, 356
Tryon, Governor (New York), 121, 159, 167–170, 171, 178, 189, 190, 191, 300–301, 412, 445, 481
Turkey Creek, 530, 532
Turtle Bay, 223, 227
Tybee Bay, 462
Tyger River, 517–518

Valcour Island, 249
Valentine's Hill, 239, 554, 555
Valley Forge, 396–398, 404, 405, 406–407, 409, 413–415, 454, 460
Valley of Wyoming, 434–436
Van Braam, Jacob, 12–13, 15, 16, 17, 19, 26, 27
Van Cortlandt, Pierre, 161, 200, 330, 361
Van Schaick, Colonel, 442
Van Schaick's mill, 343
Van Wart, Isaac, 494
Varick, Colonel, 297
Varnum, 312, 381, 382, 387, 388, 391, 397, 417, 420, 429

Index

American independence, 95; quoted on national policy ideas, 602; recreational activities of, 72–73; re-election as President, 643; retirement plans, 636–640, 643, 671–674, 675; small-pox attack, 13; Society of the Cincinnati and, 590; Stamp Act and, 77–79; statesman, 604; stepchildren, 70–71, 73, 87, 582, 600; surveying expedition (1748), 7–8; testimonials to 685; West and, xiv; wife's estate and, 70–71; will, 683, 684

Washington, Mrs. Jane, 2

Washington, John (ancestor), 2

Washington, Mrs. John (Anne), 2

Washington, John Augustine (brother), 2, 99, 128, 153

Washington, Laurence (ancestor), 2

Washington, Lawrence (step-brother), xiii, 2, 3–4, 5, 8, 9, 12, 13, 71; death of, 13

Washington, Mrs. Lawrence (Anne), 4, 13–14

Washington, Lund, 551

Washington, Martha, 66, 72, 87, 88, 95, 99, 210, 582, 597, 675, 677, 682, 683, 684; as First Lady, 615–616, 617, 622; children, 70–71, 73; correspondence with George, 109–110, 153; estate of, 70–71; joins George at Cambridge, 153–154; See also Custis, Martha

Washington, Mrs. Mary Ball (mother), xiii, 2, 4, 31–32, 45; death of, 617

Washington, Mildred (sister), 2

Washington, Samuel (brother), 2

Washington, William, 273, 274, 469–472, 519, 531–532, 537, 542, 543, 574–576

Wasshington family, 2

Wassington family, 2

Waterbury, General, 250, 251

Wateree River, 483, 485–486, 561

Watertown, Massachusetts, 122

Wayne, Anthony, 293, 306, 307, 331, 351, 353, 356–357, 376, 378, 379, 380, 418, 419, 421, 423, 437, 446–448, 522–524, 545, 557–559, 570, 637, 643, 653, 661–662, 668

Weathersfield, 553

Webb, Major-general, 54

Webster, Lieutenant-colonel, 470–471, 535, 542–543

Weedon, 230, 307, 351, 354, 573

Weems, Maxon, x

Wentworth, General, 4

Wessyngton, 1, 2

West Point, 410, 436, 444–445, 447, 448, 451, 453, 467, 475, 477, 479, 480, 489–506, 510, 523, 566

Westchester County, 456–457, 510, 552, 566

Westfield, 311

Westham, 526

Westover, 526, 557

Wetzell's Mill, 540

Whippany, 567

Whipple, Commodore, 463, 469

Whipple, William, 341

Whiskey, Rebellion, xix–xx, 660–661

White, Colonel, 471

White Clay Creek, 350

White Marsh, 381, 394, 414

White Plains, 196, 197, 239, 241, 245, 429, 436, 438

Whitehall, 319

Wilkinson, 267–268, 364, 370–371, 375 401, 402, 404–405

Willett, Colonel, 336, 338, 339, 442

Williams, Colonel, 47, 214, 216, 218, 483

Williams, David, 494

Williams, James, 513–515

Williams, Otho, 537, 538, 540, 541, 542

Williamsburg, 558, 569–573, 581

Willis's Creek, 152

Wills' Creek, 20, 21, 23, 24, 27, 34, 35

Willys, Major, 627

Index

Wilmington, 332, 347, 348, 355, 533, 534, 540, 544, 545

Wilson, James, 183, 619

Winchester, Virginia, 50–53, 55, 56, 61, 62, 581

Wingate, Mr., 616

Winnsborough, 516, 529

Winter Hill, 124, 127

Wintermoot's Fort, 435

Wisner, Henry, 186, 247

Wolcott, 666

Wolfe, James, 58–59, 66, 67–69, 154

Wolfe's Cove, 154, 164

Wood Creek, 323, 333, 336

Woodford, 307, 424, 469

Woolford, Colonel, 484

Wooster, David, 109, 166, 180, 187, 300–302

Writs of assistance, 76

Yadkin River, 536

Yagers, 456

Yellow Springs, 355

York, 548

York River, 568, 569, 570, 571, 572

Yorktown, 355, 402, 405, 568, 572–574, 577–582

Youghiogeny River, 21, 30, 38

Young's house, 456, 494

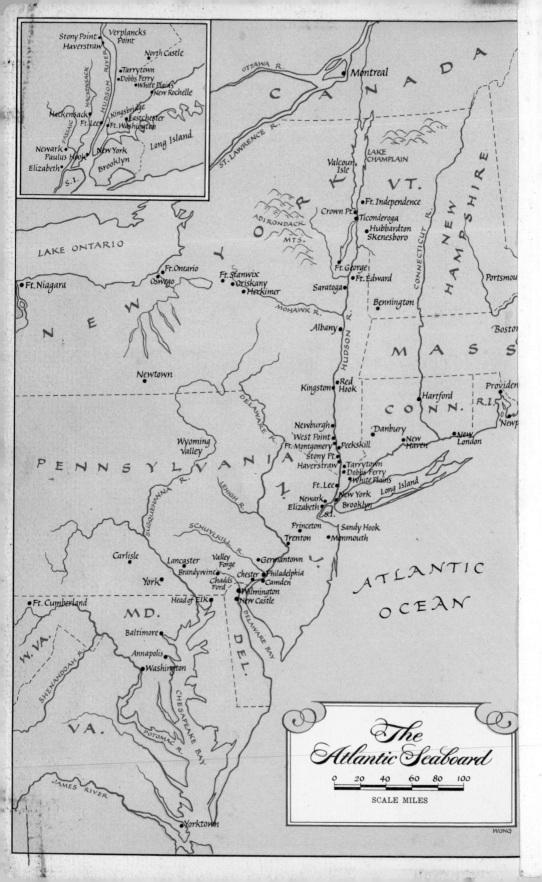

The Atlantic Seaboard

SCALE MILES
0   20   40   60   80   100

WONG